RIGHT TURN

RIGHT TURN

CHALLENGES, OPPORTUNITIES AND
AN URGENT CALL TOWARD ROAD SAFETY IN GHANA

PAULINA AGYEKUM, PhD

Library of Congress Cataloguing-in-Publication Data

Right turn: Challenges, opportunities, and an urgent call toward road safety in Ghana, by Paulina Agyekum, PhD

ISBN:
978-1-7358852-3-0 Hardback
978-1-7358852-4-7 Paperback
978-1-7358852-5-4 E-Book

Includes references and index
1. Road Safety   2. Leadership   3. Government, Public Policy   I. Title

In order to maintain anonymity, in some instances the author has changed the names of some individuals, some identifying characteristics and details such as physical properties, occupations and places of residence.

First Edition

Rights for publishing this work or in non-English languages are administered by the publisher or the author.

Dr Paulina Agyekum is, without a doubt, a citadel of knowledge in road safety. She is a seasoned researcher of international repute and an accomplished transport specialist. She has demonstrated excellence in several research works and evaluations of various road safety programmes in Ghana and beyond. Her works are acclaimed by the National Road Safety Authority of Ghana and donor agencies such as the World Bank and ECOWAS. With such a well-written book birthed on sound knowledge, experience, and years of research in road safety by Dr Paulina Agyekum, a read will surely light your candle at it.

Martin Owusu Afram
Director for Research, Monitoring, and Evaluation
National Road Safety Authority, Ghana.

I have known the author of this book, Dr Paulina Agyekum for over 20 years as someone well vested in road transport planning and road traffic safety issues. She has been involved in solving so many road safety issues including the development of national road safety strategies and their related action plans and the conduct of needs assessment towards strengthening capacity for road safety management. Her knowledge in road safety especially her ability to prescribe road safety remedial measures, has been a great asset in writing this book.

Dr William Agyemang
Deputy Director / Principal Research Scientific
Traffic Engineering, Building and Road Research Institute (BRRI of CRSIR)

I had the pleasure of conducting joint undergraduate studies with Paulina on driver and pedestrian behaviour, and her thorough understanding of the subject matter and general contribution to the study design is worthy of note. Again, Paulina's knowledge and appreciation of road safety issues make this book a must read and I highly recommend it.

Dr D. A. Obeng
Regional Transport Research and Education Centre, Kumasi
Kwame Nkrumah University of Science and Technology, Kumasi

Dr. Paulina Agyekum's research, fieldwork, and advocacy towards road safety and transportation in Ghana and, for that matter, in Africa will have a lasting impact on the lives of many on the African continent. As a visionary who understands the importance of building a solid infrastructural foundation with practical knowledge and information for the development of the 21st-century citizenry, Dr. Agyekum prolifically displays her vast wisdom, knowledge, and understanding of the pertinent issues related to the improvement and development of the road safety industry.

Professor Nana K. Asare
Texas Southern University, Houston, Texas

Road Safety is a global concern which needs to be addressed locally. The author contextualises road safety issues in Ghana drawing from her local and international experience manoeuvring through the academic sphere to the practical issues. This is a book meant for everyone passionate about achieving "Vision Zero". I highly recommend it to students, transportation professionals, road safety experts, policy makers and any person who is desirous of ensuring the menace on Ghanaian roads become a thing of the past.

Ing. Dr Patrick Amoah Bekoe
Chief Engineer, Department of Feeder Roads
West and Southern Africa Regional Manager, International Roads Federation

I have known Dr Paulina Agyekum since September 2008 and I can attest with no doubt that she is an epitome of in-depth knowledge and experience in regard to transport related issues pertaining to Ghana and West Africa as a whole, especially in road safety. Her enormous experience in road safety coupled with her impeccable writing skills, present in this book a great deal of knowledge worth harnessing, which I highly recommend.

Ing. Evans Tutu Akosah
Senior Engineer, Ablin Consult Engineers & Planners Ltd., Accra

CONTENTS

Preface..XV

Acknowledgement XVII

Foreword..XIX

Chapter 1: Situational Analysis Of Road Safety..................1

1.1 Introduction..1

1.2 Ghana – A Country Profile.......................................3

1.3 Road Trafic Crash - A Modern Epidemic...............7

1.4 Road Safety 17

1.3 Institutional Arrangements For Road Safety Management 31

1.4. Way Forward On Ghana's Road Safety Agenda...................35

Chapter 2: Trends And Progress In Road Traffic Crashes...................37

2.1 Introduction..37

2.2 Overview Of Road Safety Performance Measurement 38

2.3 Global Road Safety Performance Indicators...................49

2.4 Trends In Global Road Safety Performance By Set SPIs 52

2.5 Performance Asssessment Of Road Safety Trends In Ghana.............55

2.6 Impact Of Road Traffic Crashes On The National Economy 70

2.7 Conclusion...71

Chapter 3: Road Safety Management In Ghana 85

3.1 Introduction..85

3.2 The Road Safety Management System (RSM)...................86

3.3 Standards For Road Safety Management 90

3.4 RSM In Ghana...91

3.5. RSM By The Institutional Management Functions 102

3.6 Road Safety Strategies And Action Plans 133

3.7 Conclusion...138

CHAPTER 4: INFRASTRUCTURE 151

    4.1 CONCEPTS AND PRINCIPLES ON INFRASTRUCTURE SAFETY 151

    4.2. GUIDELINES AND POLICIES ON ROAD INFRASTRUCTURE SAFETY 153

    4.3 ROAD INFRASTRUCTURE SAFETY PLANNING 156

    4.4 SAFE ROAD DESIGN 166

    4.5 ROAD CONSTRUCTION STAGE 209

    4.6 ROAD INFRASTRUCTURE SAFETY AT ROAD OPERATION STAGE 212

    4.7 CHALLENGES TO SAFE INFRASTRUCTURE MANAGEMENT IN GHANA 215

    4.7 CONCLUSION 216

CHAPTER 5: VEHICULAR SAFETY 219

    5.1 INTRODUCTION 219

    5.2 VEHICLE SAFETY POLICIES, STANDARDS AND REGULATIONS 222

    5.3 SAFE VEHICLE OPERATION 239

    5.4 VEHICLE CRASH FATALITY RECORDS IN GHANA 248

    5.5. VEHICLE SAFETY INTERVENTIONS IMPLEMENTED IN GHANA 252

    5.6 SAFE VEHICLE TECHNOLOGIES AND OPERATIONS 253

    5.7 CONCLUSION 257

CHAPTER 6: SAFE ROAD USER 263

    6.1 INTRODUCTION 263

    6.2 THEORIES AND PRINCIPLES ON THE HUMAN FACTOR IN ROAD SAFETY 264

    6.3 DRIVER SAFETY 270

    6.4 MOTORCYCLE SAFETY 308

    6.5 PASSENGER SAFETY PROFILE 329

    6.6 CHARACTERISTICS OF PEDESTRIAN SAFETY 342

CHAPTER 7: POST CRASH CARE IN ROAD SAFETY 365

    7.1 INTRODUCTION 365

    7.2 THEORIES CONTEXTS AND PRNCIPLES IN POST CRASH CARE 366

    7.3 EMERGENCY MANAGEMENT FRAMEWORK 373

    7.6 THE PRE-HOSPITAL CARE FOR POST-CRASH VICTIMS 381

7.7 Post Crash Care At The Fixed Medical Facility Level......417

7.8 Post-Crash Rehabilitation And Integration......430

7.9 Conclusion......442

Chapter 8: Road Safety Education (RSE)......445

8.1 Introduction......445

8.2 Policies And Regulations On RSE......452

8.3 Road Safety Education Process......454

8.4 RSE By Professional Development And Skills Training......458

8.5 Road Safety Educational Campaigns......472

8.6 Conclusion......492

Chapter 9: Road Traffic Law Enforcement......493

9.1 Introduction......493

9.2 Road Traffic Laws And Traffic Offences......499

9.3 Functions Of Traffic Enforcement Agencies......507

9.4 Police Enforcement Planning......513

9.5 Road Safety Enforcement Implementation Methods......515

9.6 Police Enforcement Tools......538

9. 7 Road Traffic Crash Handling By The Police......546

9.8 Conclusion......551

Chapter 10: The Future Of Road Safety Development......555

10.1 Introduction......555

10.2. Summary Review Of DOA (2021-2020)......557

10.3 The Next Steps To Road Safety In Ghana......561

10.4 The Essentials For Road Safety In Ghana On The Way Forward....584

10.5 Conclusion......586

Acronyms......589

References......595

About The Author......613

PREFACE

This book has attempted to provide a good insight into Ghana's road safety management by way of a comprehensive information point for better understanding and appreciation of the national road safety profile. The theoretical background of different aspects of road traffic crash (RTC) and road safety by international standards and best practices are presented for comparative analysis of the state of road safety in Ghana.

An attempt has also been made to elaborate on different perspectives of the multiple aspects of road safety in terms of what has been done, what is being done and what needs to be done. These are applied as benchmark information for exploring the state of Ghana's road safety work with regards to existing road safety programmes, policies, legislation, institutions, contextual factors relating to politics, environment, economics, capacity and the related impact on road traffic fatalities and injuries in Ghana.

The book draws on and gratefully acknowledges the many listed sources from which information was obtained, including road safety publications by road safety affiliated agencies of the United Nations especially the World Health Organisation (WHO) and the United Nations Committee of Experts (UNCE). Others are the World Bank, diverse academic and non-academic publications, books of similar nature, published and unpublished journals in addition to many other sources not captured.

ACKNOWLEDGEMENT

The writing of this book has been done with motivation and the passion to contribute towards life-saving from road traffic crashes. I am first and foremost grateful to God almighty as the prime mover for inspiring me with the idea and for providing the intellectual guidance for the writing of the book. I am also grateful for the theoretical support from the various authors whose work have been cited as benchmark information for comparison with Ghana's road safety performance for providing the best examples that could be emulated in the country.

I thank my able assistant Ing. Evans Tutu Akosah for being my mentor and technical assistant in the writing of the book especially with regards to the aspect on road infrastructure safety. I cannot thank him enough for the diverse contributions, suggestions, advice, comments, discussions and assessments of each stage of the book. My immense gratitude also goes to the National Road Safety Authority (NRSA) of Ghana for access to data, access to research outputs and interactive communications which contributed to enrich the book and to reflect the actual road safety situation on the ground.

Specifically, I thank Ing. Mrs May Obiri Yeboah the immediate past Director General of the NRSA for assisting with critical review and editing of some of the chapters in the book and for providing related information including unpublished data. I thank Ing. David Adonteng the current Director General of NRSA for proving critical inputs for the initial start-up of the project by reviewing the first chapter of the book.

To Lawyer Martin Afram, Director for Research, Monitoring, and Evaluation of the NRSA, I am grateful for believing in my ability to write the book and the related encouragement. I thank Mr John Kwatia for clerical support and proof reading of some chapters. I am grateful to my family members especially Nana Asare for the moral support to finish this work.

Finally to my brother and my friend Professor Kwame Dapaah-Afriyie, MBchB, MBA.FACP.SFHM.FGCPS, I cannot thank you enough for being there for me all the time because amongst the many things that you do for me, this one too you made time to edit the chapter on post-crash care.

To all who have assisted in diverse forms to make the writing of the book a reality I just want to say *"Esie ne kegya ni aseda"*.

FOREWORD

The National Road Safety Authority (NRSA) of Ghana is the statutory lead agency for road safety management in Ghana. The Authority's responsibility is to develop and promote road safety in the country, coordinate and regulate activities, procedures and standards related to road safety and provide for related matters to reduce the incidence of road traffic crashes, fatalities and injuries.

The institution, since its establishment as a Commission in 1999 through its transformation from 2019 as an Authority, has made very significant achievements in road safety performance through Policy and Development, Development and Implementation of Strategies and Action Plans, Establishment and Maintenance of Database, Awareness Creation, Advocacy, Research, Monitoring and Evaluation and Human Capacity Building, among others.

Ghana is recognized as one of the leading frontline states in road safety management. A report produced by the UN-Economic Commission for Africa in 2015 positioned Ghana ahead of fifteen (15) countries in Africa road safety related systems and practices in relation to policies, laws and regulations, strategies and action plans to engender safe road use practices for the good of public safety on the roads.

The NRSA owes many individuals and organizations, both public and private a lot of gratitude for their support, technical and financial towards the above achievements.

A special portion of the Authority's gratitude is dedicated to Dr Paulina Agyekum, the Managing Consultant of M/s Ablin Consult, Engineers and Planners Ltd. Dr Agyekum has since the establishment of the NRSA been and remain connected to the institution, individually and through her corporate entity, providing expert technical consultancy and advisory services to the Authority in Research, Evaluation and related studies to inform road safety policy and capacity development and strategic interventions to enhance road safety management in Ghana.

To me, as Transport Specialist, and haven risen through the ranks of Deputy Director, Director and now the Acting Director General of the National Road Safety Authority, I have known Dr Paulina Agyekum all these while and I can say without doubt or malice that, Dr Paulina Agyekum's general knowledge in road transport and special interest and attention for road safety coupled with her thorough analytical assessment of issues, her calm attitude as a person, very easy to work with and her willingness to take, discuss and respond to feedbacks and questions, has aided the NRSA to keeping Ghana's road safety management in focus and on track.

The NRSA, as an institution is currently undergoing a process of transformation and restructuring from a Commission into a full-fledged Authority. The foundation laid by Dr Paulina Agyekum is highly in play and contributing significantly to the transition processes.

Ing. David Osafo Adonteng
Ag. Director General
National Road Safety Authority, Ghana

CHAPTER 1

SITUATIONAL ANALYSIS OF ROAD SAFETY

Writing under the topic Road accidents, a GhanaWeb columnist: Wisdom Bonuedi on Thursday, 23 April 2020 described the road traffic crash situation in Ghana as a carnage to behold with the following story: "He picked phone, called the father from another region, informed his younger siblings to stay home and not to engage in what society abhors; finally bid his mother farewell and sat on his motor bike to buy foodstuff for the family only never to return to life.

That is the tragic story of a brother and our breadwinner who was crushed down by a speeding Government of Ghana (GV) registered Land Cruiser at Otwereso, near Akim Oda in the Eastern Region. He lost his life through motor accident on the crucifixion day (Good Friday)? That bloody Friday. He did not even whisper a cry."

He was of the opinion that, for so long, road accidents have been swallowing a sizable majority of citizens of Ghana daily and the number keeps surging and multiplying. To him, it was closing up and drawing nearer and nearer but it seems little attention is given to these 'killers' of the land. To him there was no need to hush the issue up because there is much to do and to do well. He called for intensified sensitization of the citizenry on measures to deter other road users from committing similar blunders. This background information summarises the objective of this book.

1.1 INTRODUCTION

In Ghana, road transport has been and still is the most important mode of transport accounting for 95% and 90% of passenger and freight carriage respectively (National Transport Policy - NTP, 2020). This is estimated to translate into the movement of about 22 million people and 122 million tons of goods annually (MoT, 2017). Thus, the road transport system contributes significantly to the socio-economic development of the country. With an average road traffic crash (RTC) statistic of about 2,000 fatalities and 14,000 injuries per annum in Ghana (NRSSIII, 2011 – 2020), coupled with increasing motorization levels, the issue of road traffic safety becomes even more important requiring due attention.

Guided by global statutory regulations and plans for road safety, Ghana has over the past two decades sought to address its RTC related challenges through the implementation of diverse country-specific programmes and activities. Examples include the implementation of the Presidential Special Initiative (PSI) for Road Safety in 2019, the Arrive Alive Campaign of 2020 and the Stay Alive Campaign of 2022. Though such interventions have achieved some successes, there have also been some challenges with respect to limited funding for road safety activities, limited safety features on road and in vehicles, deficient trauma care systems and ineffective enforcement measures with limited public engagement on road safety issues.

Coupled with the challenges, information on the different aspects of road safety is scattered and knowledge of the different perspectives of road safety is fragmented. This does not lend to a holistic understanding and appreciation of the state of road safety performance in Ghana. The object of this book is first and foremost to posit Ghana's road safety performance in comparison with well acknowledged and recommended best practices in road safety management at the global level. Secondly, the book is also aimed to as much as possible bring together available evidence, information, data, studies etc. on the state of Ghana's road safety issues on a common platform that will provide insight into the current scenario and provide good inputs for the way forward.

In this regard, the book has attempted to map out a complete overview of Ghana's road safety trajectory across all components of the requirements of the United Nations Decade for Road Safety Action (UN DOA) implemented from 2011-2020. Attention has been drawn to key missing gaps in Ghana's road safety work in order to correct the current practice of extensive focus on highly visible but limited aspects of road safety needs. The book is specifically designed to serve as both a guideline and a working tool for increased knowledge and skills amongst road safety professionals and non-professionals as well as new comers in the field of road safety. Practical examples, various graphic illustrations and pictures where possible have been employed to enhance ease of understanding and better appreciation of the road safety issues in Ghana.

The book has also been analysed within both technical and non-technical contexts. It is therefore not targeted at any conclusion but rather expected results are to be those which will be obtained by the reader who will use it for a specific purpose as needed. As such it is expected that the book will be resourceful to both senior policy makers in road safety such as politicians, transport experts, road engineers, legal entities, public health officials, law enforcement officers, financing entities, academic researchers. Others are road safety partner entities such as, the private sector, Community Based Organisations (CBO's), Non-Governmental Organisations (NGOs), Media personnel, road transport service providers and road users at all levels with interest in road safety.

It is hoped that the book has managed to attain the objective of assessing the causal evidence on implemented road safety priorities in Ghana and the feasibility and prospects for advancing Ghana's road safety work beyond 2020 towards the attainment of the country's safety targets anticipated in the Sustainable Development Goals (SDGs) by 2030.

1.2 GHANA – A COUNTRY PROFILE

1.2.1 Socio Economic Characteristics of Ghana

A. Physical Characteristics: *Ghana is located in the West African Region and it is bounded on the north by Burkina Faso, on the east by Togo, on the south by Atlantic Ocean and on the west by Cote d'Ivoire. It has a total land area of 238,540 km2 with a north-south extent of about 670 km and a maximum east-west extent of about 560 km. The relief is undulating with half of the country lying above sea level and with a highest point of 883meters.*

The climate is of the warm, humid type with mean annual temperatures ranging from 26.1 °C near the coast to 28.9 °C in the extreme north. The mean rainfall is at an average of 1,209.75 mm per annum with a bimodal distribution in the southern part of the country, giving rise to major and minor farming seasons and a unimodal distribution in the northern part of the country giving rise to only one farming season.

The vegetation is of six agro-ecological zones defined as the strand and mangrove vegetation found along the coast; the moist semi deciduous forest in the southern part; the savannah vegetation with scattered trees mainly found near river course; the tropical rain forest with high trees mostly found in the south western corner and the coastal shrub and grassland found in the south eastern part of the country with dense shrub without grass.

B. Demographic Characteristics: *The population of the country is estimated at about 30.8 million people (2020), with an annual growth rate of about 2.1% (Population and Housing Census General Report, 2021).*

C. Economy: *The Gross Domestic Product (GDP) was US$72.35 billion as at 2020 with transport contributing US$ 2.47 billion and rated as the 8th contributor to GDP (trading-economics.com/Ghana/gdp).*

D. Governance System: *The Governance system is constitutional republic with two spheres of government; national and local with the later divided into sixteen administrative units* *or regions (see Figure 1.1) with three (3) types of assemblies at the higher levels of local government: Metropolitan, Municipal and District Assembly (MMDAs) level of governance.*

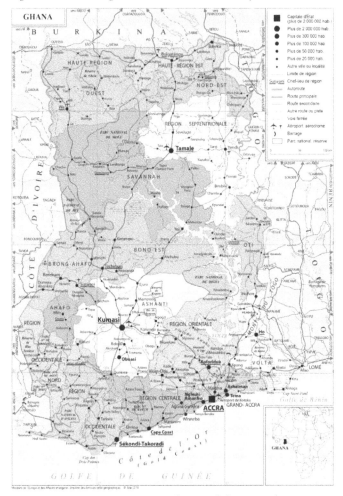

Figure 1.1: Regions in Ghana and their capitals

1.2.2 Overview of the Road Transport Service Sector in Ghana

The sector is guided by government policies and various strategies defined within sector medium term development framework (MTDF) aimed at providing efficient and effective transport infrastructure and services to facilitate economic growth and poverty reduction.

A. Institutional framework for road transport system in Ghana:

i. The Ministry of Transport (MoT): MoT in Ghana is the sector ministry responsible for transport and its related safety aspects. The sector draws guidance from the National Transport Policy (NTP) of 2020, the Integrated Transport Plan and various National MTDFs rolled out by the Government every four (4) years towards the achievement of Ghana's Development Agenda.

ii. The Ministry of Roads and Highways (MRH): The MRH is overseeing ministry responsible for the administration, planning, control development, maintenance and operation of the country's road network. The road network is further classified into three main categories as trunk, urban and feeder roads. The trunk roads run through the country connecting the regions and linking Ghana to its neighbouring countries. The urban roads are the roads within the cities and urban areas, while the feeder roads connect farm gates, villages and towns to the main trunk roads. Thus, there are three (3) sub road sector agencies namely the Ghana Highway Authority (GHA), the Department of Urban Roads (DUR) and the Department of Feeder Roads (DFR) responsible for the administration, planning, control, development, maintenance and operation of the trunk, urban and feeder roads and their related facilities respectively in the country. The Ghana Road Fund Secretariat (GRFS) which finances the routine and periodic maintenance of road and related facilities; road safety activities and other relevant matters as may be determined by the Board is also under the MRH.

B. The Road Network and Vehicle Fleet in Ghana:

i. Length of Ghana's Road Network: As of 2016, Ghana had a total of 78,401.20km of roads made up of 14,582.62 km of trunk roads, 15,461.77km of urban roads and 48,356.81km of feeder roads (MRH, Presentation May 2021).

ii. The Vehicle Fleet in Ghana: Ghana had an estimated vehicle fleet of 2,344,541 vehicles as of 2017. About 65.9% of these are in the two major cities of Ghana which are 52.2% in Accra and 13.7 % in Kumasi, (DVLA Vehicle Registration Records, 2017). The MoT reports that the vehicle-to-population ratio grew from 50 vehicles per 1000 people in 2010 to 70 in 2015.

C. Road Passenger Transport Regulation: *Before the 1980's road passenger transport was regulated under the Omnibus Services Authority (OSA) Decree (NLCD 337) of 1969. The decree nationalised all City, Municipal, Urban and Local Council bus undertakings within one unitary body responsible for both the planning and the provision of public transport services with regards to licensing of vehicles, traffic signage, police traffic control, overcrowding front seat among others. This was repealed in 1972 with the functions being split into two by the creation of a separate Licensing Authority to license and regulate the bus transport sector while OSA continued to provide bus service.*

The provision of transport services was further deregulated to enable private sector participation resulting in taxis and "Tro-tro" (a shell of vehicle, usually a minivan or a medium bus) becoming the most dominant modes of public transport in the mid-1980s but with the expected benefits from competitiveness not being achieved. Further to this, Government of Ghana (GoG) operated passenger transport undertakings including the State Transport Corporation (STC) and the City Express Services Ltd. were privatised in 1990s causing urban public transport services to continue to be largely dominated by the private sector especially by para-transit operations referred as "Tro-tro's". Overtime private bus service with high occupancy mostly used for both intercity and intracity bus operation including the VIP Jeoun Transport Company Ltd, O.A. Travel and Tours Ltd. etc. have also been introduced. Potential operators in the private sector begin operation after procurement of vehicles, registration and satisfaction of the standard procedures of vehicle roadworthiness.

Government owned public transport operation was reintroduced in 2002 with the establishment of the Metro Mass Transit (MMT), as a high vehicle occupancy service in response to public concerns with increasing traffic congestion and transport fares. In addition, the Ayalolo intra city bus services were also established to provide non subsidised rapid bus services to ease traffic congestion in the cities.

Currently passenger bus transport operation is done by both the public (5%) and private (95%) (CUTs International, 2014), sector for both intercity and intra-city service. Also, about 85% of road transport passenger services are predominantly provided by commercial transport service operators including intra and intercity transport services made up of large, medium and mini bus services, shared taxies, cargo trucks and the recently introduced online taxi platforms e.g., Uber, Yango, Bolt, etc. as well as commercial motorcycle services deemed illegal by law.

The category of buses used for these operations include, mini buses, medium buses and large buses. The mini-buses in Ghana typically have a seating capacity ranging from twelve (12) to sixteen (16) passenger occupancy rates, medium buses have eighteen (18) to twenty- four (24) seating capacity whilst the large buses have capacity of up to about eighty (80) passengers. Larger or higher occupancy bus service operates on longer inter-city routes while minibuses and saloon cabs mostly operate on the intra-city and village routes. The use of bus transport services is about 46% by all road transport passengers compared to other options such as the use of private vehicle at 19% and hired taxi services at 35%. This is because bus transport service is affordable compared to the other two modes (CUTs International, 2014).

The commercial passenger bus transport service is also categorised by formal and informal operations. The formal includes transport services run by operators under structured management such as Intercity STC Coaches Ltd, MMT, Ayalolo Bus Service, VIP Jeoun Transport Company Ltd, O.A. Travel and Tours Ltd etc. The service provision is dominated by medium and large buses which mostly operate on major inter-city and intra city bus routes. This also includes school transport and transport for carting workers under special arrangements.

The informal commercial bus passenger transport operations are mostly by adaptive services characterized by ease of market entry and exit, reliance on indigenous resources, small scale operations and extended family ownership of capital. This is largely due to an absence of any kind of normative policy framework with minimal government intervention and regulation. Thus, the norms and codes of operation are usually developed by unions such as the Ghana Private Road Transport Union (GRPTU), Progressive Transport Owners' Association (PROTOA), etc. or individual owners. In 2019, a bill was drafted to incorporate the regulation of informal bus transport services by the National Road Safety Authority (NRSA).

Generally, the formal public commercial bus transport service has the best balance of safety, expense, speed and comfort, especially when travelling between major towns for intercity service compared to the informal transport operations. This is because the informal operations especially the "Tro-tro's" are not run on any formal operational schedules but will depart for their destination once the bus is full at a loading point. It is normally dominated by single bus ownership at 63% with about (95%) of the buses bought in second hand state contributing to about 27.1% of bus fatalities in the country (BRRI, 2020).

With the given mandate of the NRSA to regulate the services of commercial transport operation in the country, it is expected that the level and quality of service will be improved with regards to comfort, neatness and safety. They will also be regulated appropriately to observe effective maintenance procedures and controls for ensuring safe vehicle roadworthiness. This will address the current practice of reactive maintenance procedures instead of preventive maintenance which causes vehicles to experience frequent breakdowns and ultimately fail to live up to the recommended technical lifespan. It is anticipated that good regulation will ensure improved service delivery and reliability without compromising on safety.

1.3 ROAD TRAFIC CRASH - A MODERN EPIDEMIC

Injury and fatality occurring through RTCs is recognized as an important public health problem at the global level by the World Health Organisation (WHO) and it is proposed for it to be recognized as such at regional and national levels. This is because it is estimated that, globally about 1.35 million people die from RTCs annually making it the 8th leading cause of death in the world. In addition to this, it is also estimated that about 20 to 50 million more people sustain non-fatal injuries from RTCs and these injuries are an important cause of disability worldwide with such people suffering life-altering injuries with long-lasting effects (WHO, 2009).

Predictions on RTC fatalities by World Health Statistics (2008) indicated that it could also become the 5th leading cause of global deaths at an estimated fatality rate of 2.4million deaths per annum by 2030 in the world, unless immediate and effective action is taken due to the proliferation of motor vehicles and related inherent unsafe conditions in road traffic.

According to Bliss and Breen (2011), the turn of the twentieth century marked an awakening of international organizations to the effects of increasing motorization and the related impacts of RTCs on global economies. In regard of this, the UN defined some directives to guide national strategies towards mitigating increasing RTC challenges for the global community at large. An important milestone from this, was the launching of the DOA (2011 to 2020). With the programme having ended, the UN has proclaimed an extended DOA from 2021-2030. The main goal is also to reduce road traffic deaths and injuries by at least 50% from 2021 to 2030.

Notwithstanding these global guidelines and plans on road safety, the risks posed by RTCs and the corresponding policy responses vary by region and country. Therefore, understanding these specificities help in developing appropriate context-specific strategies to respond to the unique situation of a given region or country. This requires each country to act according to its road safety situation and need. Also, it is said that the findings from the evaluation of global road safety performance cannot be generalized for all countries, especially between developed and developing countries due to inherent socio-economic differences which does not allow for comparisons to follow similar trends. So, it is important for countries to know their performance level according to their situation.

Thus, the WHO's Save LIVES Technical Package (2017) recommended that it is necessary for countries to first assess their ongoing implementation of road safety measures to determine what works and what needs to be improved. Specifically, each country is advised to i) know where it is with its road safety efforts; ii) establish where it wants to be in the future, iii) establish how it will get to where it wants to be; iv) define the practical steps needed to get there as well as define the modalities for sustaining gains and for mitigating challenges along the way. Also, the WHO's Road Traffic Injury Report (2011), recommended that country level road safety initiatives need to be inclusive and aligned to global innovations, be based on available evidence and be innovative.

In Ghana, such international standards have provided insights into opportunities available for maximizing the value of what is being done to improve road safety in the country and the necessary institutional capacities for meeting such demand. Specifically, such standards have guided inferential reasoning on;

i.   *the scale of the road safety problem and the level of its recognition in the country;*

ii.   *the complexity of the specific road safety peculiarities in the country;*

iii.   *the level of understanding and appreciation of the road safety issues, what is being done*

iv.   *and the effectiveness of its outcomes;*

v.   *the gaps between national and required international standards, set and achieved road safety targets, related causes and the key aspects for future consideration;*

vi.   *the good achievements made especially with regards to best practices and how they can effectively be sustained;*

vii. the level of knowledge on new potentials to mitigate crash risk factors and the means for attaining them.

In Ghana, the approach to road safety management has also been structured to be consistent with tenets the UN DOA. This has served as a good reference and also provided in-depth and expanded knowledge especially with regards to the growing body of evidence on sustainable road safety interventions. It has also provided critical benchmarks for comparison with Ghana's quest for better performance in road safety.

1.3.1 Road Traffic Crashes (RTC)

A. Definition of a Road Traffic Crash (RTC): *An RTC as depicted in Figure 1.2 is defined as a human tragedy associated with serious health problems, negative socio-economic growth and poverty, (Mavoori, 2020). It may be technically defined or metaphysically defined.*

Figure 2.1: Examples of road traffic crashes (Source NRSA)

i. Technical Definition of RTC: In technical terms, RTCs are said to result from the simultaneous integration of human, physical and mechanical factors in a traffic system which causes injuries and death because the human body is "frail" when dealing with the magnified forces of kinetic energy from a vehicle in a crash (UNCE, 2015). RTC is also contextualized as any incidence involving at least one road vehicle, occurring on a road open to public circulation and in which at least one person is injured or killed, with intentional acts of murder, suicide and natural disasters excluded (Insee, 2009). It can also be an event on the road that involves the collision of either two or more vehicles, or a vehicle and a vulnerable road user (cyclists or pedestrian), or a vehicle and a fixed object, e.g. bridge a (RTMC, 2008).

The above technical definition of RTC presents it as an outcome of one or more faults in a complex traffic system involving, a road, vehicle and a road user. This definition makes RTC a quality measure of the road transport system as well as a man-made tragedy of high price to mobility with existing and proven measures that can be put in place to salvage and save lives (WHO, 2004). It is on the basis of this that global, regional and local agenda for improving road safety are recognized and promoted. However, even within the technical context, there are still some recognized road safety myths and a compilation of some of the common ones by the WHO (2018) are presented in Table 1.1.

Table 1.1: Nine Common Road Safety Myths

Myth	Fact
1. Road safety statistics and facts are not needed for news reporting on crashes, because crashes are just isolated episodes caused by human error.	Fatal crashes are not simply the result of wrong behaviour. More commonly, they result from gaps and faults in road traffic systems that fail to take into account and minimize the possibility of human error.
2. Increased numbers of traffic road deaths are the price that low- and middle-income countries must pay in order to develop, just as high-income countries did	Rising numbers of fatalities on the roads in low- and middle-income countries are linked to development and motorization but occur in large part because road safety concerns are not being adequately addressed as the transport systems develop. While road transport is vital to a county's development, maximizing the efficiency of road transport systems without adequate attention to safety leads to loss of life, health and wealth.
3. In countries with more road traffic deaths, people have a greater risk of dying in a crash	Not necessarily. For comparisons between countries, use of the total number of road traffic deaths alone may be misleading because it can result in comparisons of populations of unequal size. Apart from countries with small populations, death rates per 100,000 population more accurately reflect the risk for dying in a crash than absolute numbers.
4. High-income countries have managed to achieve safer roads in a short time.	Australia, North America and several countries in Europe where a comprehensive approach to road safety (the "safe system approach") is used have indeed seen marked decreases in road traffic deaths and serious injuries. These results were achieved, however, only after decades of "holistic action". Low- and middle-income countries, where road safety management is generally weaker, should expect to invest similar amounts of time and effort to obtain similar results. This doesn't mean that injuries and fatalities cannot be reduced in the short term: in fact, the lessons learnt from high-income countries show that many cost-effective interventions can and have had a positive impact in the short term.
5. More cars on the road means more deaths on the road	Not always. It is true that when low- and middle- income countries motorize quickly, a lag in the introduction of safety measures can result in more road traffic deaths, including deaths of pedestrians and other vulnerable road users. When countries invest adequately in road safety, however, there is no simple correlation between the number of vehicles and the number of fatalities
6. One country, one set of road traffic data	Unfortunately not. In any given country, road traffic data can come from a number of sources (e.g. the health sector, police, nongovernmental organizations, academia, etc.) Ideally, data systems should be linked and provide the same numbers but in practice, good coordination is difficult to achieve.
7. Dangerous drivers are the main problem; educating them is the main solution	There are multiple, often complex reasons for crashes. Countries that do best in terms of road safety have recognized this and focus on improving the safety of all parts of the system (the road environment, vehicles and road users) to minimize the impact of human error, as opposed to focusing predominantly on educating drivers.
8. There's no need to clutter a story on creative road safety measures with a lot of facts	WHO urges reporters to check all road safety stories against known facts and evidence by researching studies or interviewing experts. While we support innovative approaches to road safety, solutions must be based on evidence. Fortunately, in road safety, there is a lot of scientific evidence about what works and what doesn't.
9. Speed cameras are just money-making machines for the police and the state	Actually, speed cameras are an efficient, cost– effective speed management tool. They can make enforcement consistent, help to deter offenders and reduce the need for individual police intervention. As they don't require the collection of penalties at physical interception points, they can also help to reduce potential corruption in enforcement. In addition, countries where speed cameras are used most effectively, the proceeds are earmarked and reinvested into making the country's roads safer.

Source: WHO 2018 – Nine Common Road Safety Myths Factsheet

ii. Socio Cultural/ Metaphysical Definition of RTC: RTCs in some belief domains and values are seen as spiritually motivated. This metaphysical view defines RTC as a sign of some supernatural spirit such as witchcraft seeking to destroy humankind through the spillage of blood for which some transcendental and heavenly interventions are required (Gur-Ze'ev, 2003). Some explanations given to this include RTCs being a sign of sacrificial demand from a god or deity of some sort owning a specific road location for which regular pacification rituals are required to stop such occurrences.

Commenting on the issue Leplat (1983), wrote that modern mentality is still impregnated with a fatalistic conception of RTCs. Thus, authors like Kouabenan (1998), also caution that it will be erroneous to think that beliefs and practices concerning road safety are outmoded or that they only concern outmoded people since they continue to guide road user behaviour. Rubin Z. and Peplau L. A (1975) adds that if a belief in a fair world may be useful for purposes of increasing the personal efficiency of people, further studies would be necessary in order to determine its exact role. This means that road safety must be produced in the form of goods and services not only based on technical solutions but with due consideration for broader socio-cultural and ethical/community values.

A report by the OECD (1984) intimated that RTCs are the result of a critical combination of circumstances and cannot be attributed to a single cause. Accordingly, Kouabenan (1998), called for strategies towards preventing RTCs to be based on both technical and social considerations. Therefore, whilst in the past, the cause of RTCs was limited to the dangerous driver, this has been changed to a critical combination of circumstances. A World Bank report by Carlsson and Hedman (1990), followed this line of reasoning by calling for a systematic approach to road safety with consideration for a wider scope of elements guided by the necessary preventive actions as determined by the causes. In this regard, some literature suggests for analysis of RTCs not to differ between experts and laymen and also to link to certain characteristics inherent in the social values to which he/she belongs in addition to technical considerations.

In Ghana, both technical and metaphysical definitions (Typical examples of such beliefs in Ghana are as exhibited below), of RTC are upheld by different sections of society with the latter being the case for even some technical personnel and safety specialist. Typical examples include the conduct of purification rites at RTC locations, the use of talisman and charms by some drivers for protection against RTCs etc.

However, the NRSA is emphatic on its definition of RTCs being traffic crashes resulting in injury, death or property damage involving at least one vehicle on a public road. (A typical example is the redesign of the Suhum Junction which halted excessive fatalities irrespective of perceived need for a deity pacification at the time against the backdrop of existing evidence and examples indicating that the implementation of appropriate safety measures can result in the mitigation of RTC risk factors for good outcomes, the view of the author in writing this book is in support of the NRSA's definition of an RTC.

B. Key Elements of RTCs

i. Causes of RTCs: Traditionally, the word accident is often used to describe RTCs based on the occurrence of an incident by chance which cannot be prevented. However, experts define road accidents on the basis of a combination of unsafe events that leads to a negative outcome. By this, road accident is said to emanate from an interaction of human, infrastructure and vehicular factors. The World Road Association (2006) estimates the margin of contribution of each of these factors in an RTC as presented in Figure 1.3.

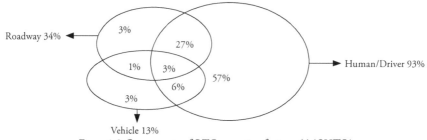

Figure1.3 Components of RTC causative factors, (AASHTO)

Within each of these elements, there are also many sub elements which also contribute to RTCs as elaborated in Figure 1.4. Due to this, the traditional word "road accident" which connotes the occurrence of an incident by chance used to describe RTCs is disputed because it has been established that RTCs have causative factors which can be prevented to avert the injuries and fatalities resulting from them. Thus, though the terms "road crash" and "road accident" are often used interchangeably in literature, it is recommended for the word "road traffic crash" to be used instead and the term RTC has also been adopted for this book.

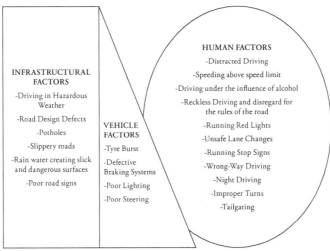

Figure 1.4: Examples of causes of RTCs by components

ii. Theories on Causes of RTCs: Due to the fact that it is not simple to establish which combination of factors are exactly responsible for the occurrence of RTCs accident theories are used to provide a logical and rational explanation as to why certain events, people, equipment come together to generate such an outcome. These are systematically organized knowledge applicable in a variety of circumstantial scenarios within set assumptions, accepted principles and rules of procedures to explain the causes of accidents. Each theory provides an explanation on why accidents occurs and they include the following:

a). The Domino Theory by Heinrich's H. W (1950): It uses the analogy of a chain of connected events described as dominos which interlink to cause accidents (in this case RTCs). These events could include (i) the social environment and ancestry which encompasses anything that may lead to producing undesirable traits in people; (ii) faults of a person which refers to personal characteristics that are conducive to accidents; (iii) unsafe act or condition which is often the identifiable beginning of a specific incident; (iv) accident when something occurs that is undesirable and not intended; and (v) injury which is the unfortunate outcome of same. The view is that if just a single domino is removed, the entire process ceases and no injury will occur. Therefore, what is needed is to identify intervention points that if acted on will prevent the outcome of an accident. However, the theory is discounted for being simplistic.

b). The Energy Release Theory by Haddon (1970): The theory relates to the rate of energy release to prevent severity of injuries and it requires for the prevention of energy store up in an uncontrolled way. It requires a vent release mechanisms and control measures to modify energy release rate. Examples in road traffic includes the provision of segregated lanes to address the safety challenges of mixed traffic. The theory is criticized for only focusing on a small part of a wider challenge.

c). Multiple Causation Theory by Petersen 1971: This theory purports that multiple factors combine in random fashion (without any given order) to produce an accident. It is one of the first that recognizes the critical role that management and leadership play in road safety with the following as critical elements i) Authorization to identify and eliminate hazardous conditions; and ii) Appropriation - where adequate resources are provided to fulfil the safety mission.

An example is the multiple causation model based on the 4 M's of Man, Media, Machine and Management used to help identify which combinations are most likely to provide the catalyst to bring conditions together for injuries to manifest. Another Multiple Causation Theory places emphasis on the prevention of the negative event based on the '3 E's' of road safety as Engineering, Education and Enforcement. Though accepted to be multi component as required by road safety management, the theory has been further advanced.

d). Ferrell's Human Factor Model Theory by Heinrich et al (1980): It also defines multiple causes of RTCs based on human errors such as (i) Overload action that exceeds the ability of component to handle the amount; (ii) Inappropriate response that is knowing about the hazard but not doing anything about it; and (iii) Inappropriate activities that is not trained to do the job that is being done based on a person underestimating the level of risk associated with the situation.

e). Petersen's Accident/Incident Model: It is also an extension of the human factors theory with a few changes, refinements and additions such as considerations for Ergonomic traps or environmental aspect of incompatibility e.g. management failure; personal failure, financial shortfalls, psychological failings that is perceived low probability of an accident occurring, systems failure; the inability of the organization to correct errors and lack of training and poor policy.

f). Epidemiology Theory by Gordon and James Gibson 1949: This theory studies relationship between environmental factors and accidents or disease. It is of two key components as predisposition characteristics where a worker may be predisposed to certain actions and situational characteristics such as poor attitude to risk taking. The notion is that these characteristics can cause or prevent accidents given certain situations or conditions.

g). *Systems Theory: The theory is of the view that rather than the environment being full of hazards and a person being error prone, a systematic model of a harmony between man, machine, and environment can prevent accidents. The assumption is that under normal circumstances, the chances of an accident occurring is very low except when someone or something disrupts this harmony by changing one of the components or the relationships between the three, then the probability of an accident occurring increases substantially.*

Another aspect of the theory focuses on risk-taking being associated with choice of action with the premise that the decision to move forward with a task is only taken when it is decided the potential benefits outweigh the potential loss (Firenze, 1978). In other words, a common task previously taken has well known risks and benefits, while a new task often has more unknown factors.

h). *Behaviour Theory: This theory, which is also referred to as behaviour-based safety (BBS) by Geller E. Scott (2001) is based on seven principles by which an accident can occur or be prevented which include intervention, external factors, motivation to behave in the desired manner, focus on the positive consequences of appropriate behaviour, application of scientific methods, integration of information and planned interventions.*

i). *Combination Theory: The common disadvantage of all the above theories is that there is extensive variability of the factors that cause accidents which makes it difficult to exactly predict the future trends of accidents by using any particular model or theory. Thus, the combined theory is of the view that a single theory may not suit all circumstances so a combination of theories must be considered for optimal solutions*

This must be done through hazard identification, risk assessment and mitigation, training and education, resource management, safety communication, continuous monitoring of safety performance, emergency response planning and continuous improvement in safety performance. Other aspects include the setting of safety goals for safety management, revision of organizational structure, ensuring management commitment and responsibilities with safety accountabilities (Fu G et al 2019).

This is reflected in the concept of the application of road safety pillars as adopted by the UN and elaborated in Section 1.4.2 item d (i) of this chapter. It presents a systematised approach to road safety management by a combination of RTC causative factors and solutions determined to be either directly or collectively at the root of the challenge within the road safety environment and are equally deemed the source of the solutions to mitigate the challenges.

Ghana has aligned with the UN approach of a combination of different RTC causative factors with respect to the use of road safety pillars so the benefits and dis-benefits of the other theories are not accorded much premium or relevance in the determination of the cause of RTCs and related interventions.

C. Effects of Road Traffic Crashes: Generally, RTCs not only cause immeasurable loss and trauma for the victims, their families and friends, they also result in enormous economic loss to the country. This is because they impose a huge burden on already re-source constrained health service due to the demands of emergency care from the health facilities, the police, the fire services and other rescue services. They also drain limited family resources by imposing huge burdens of care on the family of the RTC victim especially where long-term care of the victim is required towards recovery. In a situation where the RTC victim is the bread winner of the family, the future of dependents could even be jeopardized.

Typical effects of RTCs in Ghana are presented in the immediate sub-sections (see Figure 1.5).

Fatality due to RTCs (Source: NRSA)

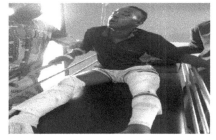
Injury and hospitalisation due to RTCs (Source NRSA)

Economic loss due to RTCs

Vehicle (property) damage due to RTCs (Source NRSA)

Loss of State Properties (Source NRSA)

Increased Police workload due to RTCs (Source: NRSA)

Figure 1.5: Examples of typical effects of RTCs in Ghana

1.4 ROAD SAFETY

1.4.1 Definition of Road Safety

Road safety can be defined in simple terms as the application of countermeasures (policies and strategies) to mitigate RTC risk factors.

A. Approaches to Road Safety: According to the OECD/ITF (2016), the approach to road safety has evolved over the years through the following stages and continues to do so.

i. The Individual Road User Approach: Traditionally, in the 1960s, road safety focused on the correction human errors with much emphasis on the individual road user through educational measures (OECD/ITF, 2016). However, approach was characterized by dispersed, uncoordinated and insufficiently resourced institutional units who performed isolated single functions, (Koomstra et al 2002).

ii. The Matrix Approach: In the 1970s, Haddon (1970) proposed a shift away from the individual road user approach to an injury-prevention matrix that encouraged joint evaluation of all the factors that contribute to road injury using a defined methodology for assessing the effectiveness of a full range of potential countermeasures. By this, many more aspects of road safety were recognized including roads, vehicles, people, pre-crash, in-crash, and post-crash. However, there was no consideration for institutional management functions.

iii. The Systems Approach: The systems approach introduced in the 2000s uses an approach based on road safety as a complete whole rather than as isolated parts which must be addressed from all dimensions. This must include targeted results, institutional leadership, action plans with numerical outcomes in the form of a broad packages of system-wide measures. The institutional management functions must also be characterised by multi-sectoral coordination, effective resource allocation and monitoring and evaluation (WHO, 2004; Bliss, 2004) and it is currently accepted as the global best-practice.

iv. Complex System Approach: The systems approach has further been enhanced towards a broader context of decisions relating to potential issues that governments are likely to face in trying to understand what road safety means and where it is heading. Contextualizing this, a recent report from the 3rd Global Ministerial Conference on Road Safety held from 19th-20th February 2020 recommended the comprehensive integration of road safety activities into the daily operations of governments, businesses and corporations through their entire value chains as the way to promote road safety in the future. It argues for further engagement of the public and private sectors and civil society in road safety activities.

In Ghana, at the beginning of the governorship of Sir Frederick Gordon Guggisberg of the Gold Coast, from 1919 to 1927, a ten-year development programme prescribed priority for improvements in various sectors of the economy including improvement in transportation and other service, (DVLA, 2012). With this, the initial construction of road suitable for use mostly by light Ford trucks was done at the end of World War I for transporting cocoa from the hinterlands to the market with some sealed sections (DVLA, 2012).

However, there was little considerations for road safety activities at this stage. Road safety remained uncoordinated under the management of a road safety committee headed by the Motor Transport Unit of the Ghana Police until 1998 when road safety management was placed under a restructured management framework as a part of the implementation of a Ghana Road Safety Project (GRSP) launched under the Transport Rehabilitation Project (TRP) of 1991 to 1993 funded by the World Bank.

The objective was to increase the knowledge, skills and capabilities of key Ghanaian organizations and professionals to tackle the country's road safety problems more effectively. The GRSP was designed around five (5) mini-projects that bordered on strengthening the National Road Safety Committee, the Vehicle Examination and Licensing Division (VELD), the Ghana Highway Authority (GHA), the Department of Urban Roads (DUR) and the Motor Traffic and Transportation Unit (MTTU) of the Ghana Police Service (GPS).

The project was complemented with the establishment of an improved data system on RTCs and a key recommendation to transform the National Road Safety Committee into the National Road Safety Commission (NRSC). This was with the requisite legal mandate, staffing and funding to enable the Commission promote and coordinate road safety activities in Ghana. From 1993 to 1994, the second phase of the TRP was implemented with the principal objective of further development of the road safety component by focusing on the continued assistance to consolidate the achievements of the road safety programme under the first phase of the TRP. It provided support in the form of training, equipment, materials and budgetary support to the National Road Safety Committee, the Building and Road Research Institute (BRRI), GHA, DUR, MTTU and VELD.

In 1997, the merger of the then MRH and the Ministry of Transport and Communications (MOTC) into the Ministry of Road Transport (MRT) brought the principal road safety stakeholder agencies namely the GHA, DUR, VELD and the NRSC under a single Ministry. The merger presented the greatest opportunity for the coordination of road safety activities in the country and in 1999, Act 567 established the NRSA which has now been transformed into the NRSA with impending changes in its operational functions. After the TRP 2 ended in 1994, two phases of an Urban Transport Project (UTP) were implemented from 2007 to 2017 and funded by the World Bank. This project also had support for road safety components with the objective to upgrade the performance of the NRSC. The activities related mostly to the development of safety standards, development of road safety materials, dissemination of information and internal capacity development on safety especially with regards to urban transportation issues.

With Ghana's transportation system still dominated by road transport which has the highest proportion of all journeys and a continuously growing vehicular population at an annual average rate of 10%, the country has and is still experiencing its related share of road safety challenges. As such diverse road safety interventions have been implemented overtime including the application of integrated road safety strategies and action plans to suit its purpose. On the way forward the country is working to integrate different transport policies towards mobility, safety and environment in line with the next steps for the extended DOA (2020-2030).

B. General Principles of Road Safety: The key principles developed from the outcome of the 3rd Global Ministerial Conference on Road Safety held from 19th-20th February 2020 for the way forward on road safety beyond 2020 include the following:

i. Recognition of trauma prevention as a shared responsibility including individuals, families, schools, workplaces, industrial groups, communities and governments guided by proactive measures.

Ghana is yet to attain the status of preventing road trauma as a shared responsibility of all and this should be key on Ghana's road safety agenda for the extended DOA from 2021 to 2030.

ii. Need for people to learn to engage in safe behaviours on roads to protect themselves guided by user understanding of the implications of their actions and what their limitations are in the road traffic system and what they need to do to be safe.

The aspect of safe road environment by road user understanding of the implications of their actions, what their limitations are in the road traffic system and what they need to do to be safe is of limited achievement in Ghana.

iii. Promotion of active forms of transport such as walking and riding complemented with information dissemination to road users about crash risks associated with mixed road use.

Some education on active forms of transport especially cycling has been promoted in the past by the Centre for Cycling Expertise (CCE, Ghana – A Ghanaian NGO which supports and promotes sustainable non-motorised transport) but the impact has been minimal. Also, effective joint education on safe mixed road use particularly by different categories of road users in mixed traffic environments must be well promoted.

iv. Implementation of safe infrastructure and speed limit measures over time to provide environments that are forgiving of human error.

Safe infrastructure and speed limit measures such as the installation of speed calming measures and speed enforcement measures are undertaken in Ghana but without the application of advanced technologies such as the development of forgiving roads for human.

v. Implementation of programmes and policies on road safety based on evidence-based backed by consistent evaluation of new programmes to ensure that road safety practices are continuously improved.

Programmes and policies on road safety are guided by RTC statistics and new programmes are fairly evaluated to ensure that road safety practices are continuously improved in Ghana.

vi. New road safety measures implemented nationally and internationally should be reviewed on an ongoing basis and those that are shown to be effective in reducing trauma should be considered for their application.

New road safety measures implemented nationally are reviewed on an ongoing basis but the extent to which those that are shown to be effective in reducing trauma are considered for their application is not known in Ghana.

C. Effects of road safety: Effective road safety management produces the following results:

i. Saves lives and prevents injuries.

ii. Enables people to live healthy and full lives.

iii. Prevents emotional and psychological trauma.

iv. Saves an immense amount of public money.

v. Saves families from loss of funding and other resources.

vi. Reduces the burden on over-stretched public services, such as health and social care.

vii. Supports other public policies, such as improving health by helping and encouraging people to walk and cycle in a safe and attractive environment.

viii. Helps to tackle health inequalities.

ix. Improves community cohesion and quality of life.

1.4.2 Road Safety Conventions, Regulations and Partnerships

Across the world, experience and knowledge in road safety have influenced the development of a myriad of road safety conventions and regulations at the global, regional and local levels to guide effective implementation of road safety actions. These are in the form of agreements, guidelines, recommended actions etc. by international entities such as the UN. They serve as legal foundations binding for countries that accede to them to guide effective management of road safety. They provide relevant foundations from which regional and country specific road safety policy goals, traffic rules and regulations can be developed.

A. Global Conventions and Regulations on Road Safety: These were systematically developed through UN agencies such as the Inland Transport Committee of United Nations Economic Commission for Europe (UNECE). They provide standard frameworks for both basic and complex road safety practices globally. They are administered by relevant working parties (WP's) or administrative committees who are also in charge of updating and amending them. They are backed by performance-based monitoring review so as to provide lessons for amending existing agreements and conventions as well as for the creation of new ones. There are fifty-eight (58) UN legal instruments in the area of inland transport out of which five (5) road safety instruments are considered to be priorities for accession (UNECE, 2015). An overview is provided as follows:

i. United Nations Convention 1949: The UN road safety conventions are traced to as far back as 1947 with the setting up of the UN convention 1949. The convention paved the way for international interventions in road safety practices with the objective of promoting the safety of road traffic. It established uniform rules on road signs and signals, made provisions for motor vehicles and trailers in international traffic as well as drivers of motor vehicles and cyclists also in international traffic.

ii. United Nations Convention 1968 on Traffic Safety: The 1968 Convention on Road Traffic Safety, commonly known as the Vienna Convention, is a follow up international treaty on the Convention 1949. It was also designed to facilitate international traffic and to increase road safety with standard traffic rules among Contracting Parties (CPs). The Convention was agreed upon in Venice on 8th November 1968 but came into force on 21st May 1977. It provides rules on all aspects of international road traffic and safety and also serves as a reference for national legislation. It follows the 1949 Convention on Road Traffic and its Protocol on Road Signs and Signals, with two Conventions on consolidated Resolution on Road Traffic (R.E.1) and on Road Signs and Signals (R.E.2). These entail final provisions and rules of road, signs and signals and provisions applicable to motor vehicles, trailers motor vehicles and cycles in international a). Conventions on Road Signs and Signals (1968): Specifically, the conventions on road signs and signals provides uniform road signs, signals, symbols and markings to facilitate international road traffic and increase safety. They include three categories of road signs as danger warning, regulatory and informative which are provided with norms on shapes, dimensions, colours, visibility, norms on traffic light signals, road markings and road works and level crossing signs with over 200 reference signs.

b). Conventions on Vehicle Regulations (1958, 1997 and 1998: These are

- The 1958 Agreement concerns the adoption of uniform technical prescriptions for all manufactured parts for wheeled vehicles, equipment including headlamps, braking, tyres, safety belts etc. With over 130 regulations it seeks to remove technical barriers to international trade and also promote safe and environmentally friendly vehicles.

- The 1997 is on the adoption of uniform conditions for periodical technical inspections of wheeled and the issuance of inspection certificates for cross-border use of road vehicles.

- The 1998 Agreement also concerns the establishment of global technical regulations for wheeled vehicles, with regards to electronic stability control, pole side impact and emission tests among others. New regulations are being added as needed to keep up with progress on safety and technology. Also, countries with established regulatory agencies are required to apply a self-certification regime, conduct market surveillance and enforce production compliance.

c). Transport of Dangerous Goods (1957): This is based on the European Agreement for the international carriage of dangerous goods by road. The provisions are aimed to prevent RTCs and property damage during the loading, transport and unloading of dangerous goods. They also provide internationally recognized classification and identification of dangerous goods as well as prescribe the construction of vehicles and tanks transporting dangerous goods.

d). Professional Driver Fatigue (1970) European Agreement: This prescribes the number of maximum driving hours by professional drivers and crews with prescribed rest periods for reducing fatigue related RTCs, especially for those engaged in international road transport with the following benefits:

- Admission to international traffic.
- A set of agreed road traffic rules.
- Reference for national legislation.
- Mutual recognition of vehicle certificates and driving permits.

- Facilitation of international traffic, trade and tourism.
- Enhanced road safety.

The 1968 convention also established the Working party (WP) on Road Traffic Safety (WP.1), as an intergovernmental body in 1988 which changed its name to the Global Forum for Road Traffic Safety in 2017. Till date it remains the only permanent body in the UN system that focuses on improving road safety. The provisions become legally binding for governments that accede to them through the submission of an instrument of ratification or accession to the UN Secretary-General. However, it can only be signed by the Head of State, Head of Government or the Minister of Foreign Affairs of a country without any financial obligation or fee. Once a treaty enters into force, it is not possible to invoke national law as grounds for non-implementation and internal constitutional procedures must be followed to advice.

iii. The UN General Assembly Resolutions on Road Safety: Since they were first published, the resolutions have been updated on several occasions to take into account innovations, new developments, successive amendments and consolidated revisions as sampled in Table 1.2. This is to assist countries to develop voluntary global performance targets on key risk factors and service delivery mechanisms to reduce road traffic fatalities and injuries. While the resolutions do not have the binding force of the Conventions, they go into more detail and provide a catalogue of measures and practices that countries are called on to implement on voluntary basis. However, whilst diverse global and international principles/facilities are available to support country effort at RTC mitigations, simply adopting and adapting these knowledge resources does not ensure effective road safety implementation by itself.

Table 1.2: Amended resolutions by the UN General Assembly

UN General Assembly Resolutions	World Health Assembly Resolutions	UN Secretary General's Reports
• Improving global road safety, A/72/271 (2018)	• Time for Results, WHA 69.7 (2016)	• Improving global road safety, A/74/304 (2019)
• Improving global road safety, A/70/260 (2016)	• Road safety and health, WHA57.10 (2004)	• Improving global road safety, A/72/359 (2017)
• Improving global road safety, A/68/269 (2014)	• Prevention of road traffic accidents, EB57.R30 (1976)	• Improving global road safety, A/70/386 (2015)
• Improving global road safety, A/66/260 (2012)	• Prevention of road traffic accidents, WHA27.59 (1974)	• Improving global road safety, A/68/368 (2013)
• Improving global road safety, A/RES/64/255 (2010)	• Prevention of traffic accidents, EB43.R22 (1969)	• Improving global road safety, A/66/389 (2011)
• Improving global road safety, A/RES/62/244 (2008)	• Prevention of traffic accidents, WHA19.36 (1966	• Improving global road safety, A/RES/64/266 (2009)
• Improving global road safety, A/60/5 (2005)		• Improving global road safety, A/RES/A/62/257 (2007)
• Improving global road safety, A/RES/58/289 (2004)		

Source: UNECE consolidated resolution of road traffic (2010)

Having signed on to the UN Convention 68 on road traffic, road signs and signals on 22nd August 1969, the Government of Ghana (GoG) agreed to comply with uniformed UN regulations. These served as a foundation for member states to build national legal frameworks. However, the challenges that Ghana's accession to these conventions and treaties present to the country is yet to be studied. There is need therefore to assess how Ghana's adoption of international road safety principles have translated into road safety benefits towards the achievement of the country's road safety objectives.

iv. UN-DOA (2011-2020): The DOA (2011-2020) was a plan of action by the UN General Assembly developed in 2010 to stabilize unacceptable trends in global RTC fatalities and injuries by 2015 and thereafter reduce the later by 50% by the end of 2020. Each UN member country was expected to implement the DOA by first acknowledging their state of RTC situation as basis for safety targets within the next five (5) years and beyond. They were to develop plans and strategies to get them to where they want to be as well as monitor and evaluate implementation. The road safety interventions were defined within five set pillars to reflect the different characteristics of road safety components as guide to effective implementation of set interventions as depicted in Figure1.6.

Figure 1.6: Road safety pillars of the UN-DOA 2011-2020

Country obligations the DOA included the following:

• Adherence to and full implementation of major UN road safety related regulations.

• Development and implementation of sustainable road safety strategies and programmes.

• Strengthening the management of infrastructure and capacity for technical implementation of road safety activities.

- Improvement of the quality of data collection.

- Monitoring of progress and performance on a number of predefined indicators.

- Encouragement of increased funding to road safety and better use of existing resources.

- Building capacities at national, regional and international level to address road safety.

Ghana acceded to and aligned with the goals of the DOA (2011-2020) through the adaption of its various principles and guidelines to augment already existing initiatives on road safety. Accordingly, the country also adopted the themes of the road safety pillars with the only difference being with the isolation of improved enforcement as a sixth pillar. This was in recognition of the importance of road safety enforcement to Ghana's situation since enforcement was diffused within the road user theme in the DOA guidelines as presented in Figure 1.7.

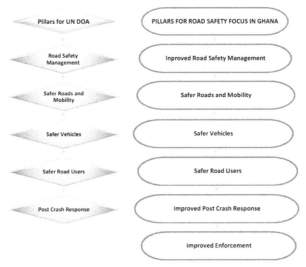

Figure 1.7: Comparison of UN-DOA and Ghana's road safety pillars

v. Road Safety and the SDGs: In September 2015, the UN adopted the 2030 Agenda for sustainable development to replace and build on the achievements of the Millennium Development Goals (MDGs). The 17 SDGs and their 169 targets are intended to balance the economic, social and environmental dimensions of development and stimulate action over the next 15 years in these critical areas. With the omission of road safety from the MDGs, the theme was duly integrated into the SDGs. They include two targets that relate to road safety, one in Goal 3 (on health) and the other in Goal 11 (on sustainable transport in cities and human settlements).

These are target 3.6 which states that by 2020, the number of global deaths and injuries from RTCs should be halved and target 11.2 which states that by 2030 access to safe, affordable, accessible and sustainable transport systems should be provided for all and thereby improve road safety. Though Goal 3.6 is very specific about halving road deaths and injuries by 2030, it does not specify a reference value by which the halving is compared with.

vi. Global Road Safety Partnership Profile: A broad range of UN agencies and other global partners have joined forces to reduce road traffic fatalities and injuries worldwide. The roles and contributions of such key agencies are as summarised in Table 1.3.

Table 1.3: Road Safety Partners Profile

Road Safety Partner Institution	Functions
World Health Organization (WHO)	WHO aims to integrate road safety into public health programmes around the world in order to reduce the unacceptably high levels of road traffic injuries.
United Nations Economic Commission for Europe (UNECE)	UNECE pursues the objective of road safety through the elaboration and whenever necessary, updating of internationally agreed safety rules and regulations on the various components of road traffic. In addition, UNECE carries out advocacy activities, collects and disseminates information and statistics on road crashes and their causes as well as on the national measures to prevent them by organizing meetings of intergovernmental bodies specialized in the various areas of road safety.
United Nations Economic Commission for Africa (UNECA)	UNECA aims to provide policy assistance towards the development of an efficient, safe, affordable and well-managed regional transport system that would facilitate regional integration in Africa. UNECA's mandate on road safety and security is to: organize seminars on African road safety initiatives; collect and disseminate data on safety and security issues related to all modes of transport.
Organization for Economic Cooperation and Development European Conference of Ministers of Transport (OECD/ECMT)	The European Conference of Ministers of Transport (ECMT) is an intergovernmental organization established by a protocol signed in Brussels on 17th October 1953. It comprises the Ministers of Transport of 43 member countries who meet to cooperate on policy.
World Bank	The World Bank promotes the improvement of road safety outcomes in low- and middle-income countries as a global development priority. Its mission is to assist countries to accelerate their implementation of the recommendations of the *World report on road traffic injury prevention*, with an emphasis on building their capacity to invest in road safety and mobilizing global partnerships in support of this.
World Road Association (PIARC)	For many years, the Road Safety Committee of the World Road Association (PIARC) has been working on collision prevention in the areas of: road safety engineering; road safety politics; and road users' behaviour. Important issues that have recently been addressed are: development of road safety audits to eliminate design faults; evaluation of road safety measures and programmes; framework for the development of road safety politics and its testing in different countries; road design standards related to safety and user behaviour analysis, i.e. human factors in road design (Source the PIARC *Road safety manual*).
African Road Safety Observatory (ARSO)	ARSO was established by the AU in collaboration with UNECA, SSATP of the World Bank and the FIA under the Department of Infrastructure and Energy of the African Union (AU). The objectives of the Observatory are to facilitate the exchange of knowledge between road safety experts and governments in Africa; and to coordinate road safety strategies, initiatives and information at the continental level
Global Road Safety Partnership (GRSP)	GRSP is a global partnership between business, civil society and government dedicated to the sustainable reduction of death and injury on the roads in developing and transition countries. By creating and strengthening links between partners, GRSP aims to increase awareness of road safety as an issue affecting all sectors of society.
FIA Foundation for the Automobile and Society	The Foundation's objectives are the promotion of public safety and public health, the protection and preservation of human life and the conservation, protection and improvement of the physical and natural environment. In the area of road safety this is achieved through road safety advocacy to raise the global profile of road safety. It promotes research and the dissemination of results.

Road Safety Partner Institution	Functions
Association for Safe International Road Travel (ASIRT)	ASIRT is a non-profit organization based in the United States that promotes road safety through education and advocacy with the aim to improve global road safety and reduce deaths and injuries resulting from road crashes by: informing travellers of potential road risks; training and support of road safety on governmental organizations abroad; and facilitation of the exchange of road safety expertise.
International Road Federation (IRF)	The IRF mission consists of the promotion of the concept of the "forgiving road" and safe mobility in general, with active participation in the work of UNECE Working Party 1 and other UN bodies.
World Health Organization (WHO)	WHO aims to integrate road safety into public health programmes around the world in order to reduce the unacceptably high levels of road traffic injuries. A public health approach is used, combining epidemiology, prevention and advocacy. Special emphasis is given to low- and middle- income countries. WHO's objectives for road safety are: to incorporate road traffic injury prevention and control into public health agendas around the world; to build capacity at national and local level to monitor the magnitude, severity and burden of road traffic injuries; to promote action-oriented strategies and advocate for prevention and control of road traffic injuries.
United Nations Economic Commission for Europe (UNECE)	UNECE pursues the objective of road safety through the elaboration and whenever necessary, updating of internationally agreed safety rules and regulations on the various components of road traffic, to be implemented by its Member States and all other interested States with a view to ensuring a high level of road traffic safety in their countries. In addition, UNECE carries out advocacy activities, collects and disseminates information and statistics on road crashes and their causes as well as on the national measures to prevent them, and organizes meetings of intergovernmental bodies specialized in the various areas of road safety.
United Nations Economic Commission for Africa (UNECA)	UNECA aims to provide policy assistance towards the development of an efficient, safe, affordable and well-managed regional transport system that would facilitate regional integration in Africa. Accordingly, UNECA played a key role in the implementation of the 2002 Plan of Action of the Conference of African Ministers of Transport and Communication. In this regard, UNECA's mandate on road safety and security is to: organize seminars on African road safety initiatives; collect and disseminate data on safety and security issues related to all modes of transport. They are also to collected information on communication, infrastructure and service development as well as provide assistance to United Nations Member States and Regional Economic Communities to improve safety and security in infrastructure and services development, including the establishment of national and regional bodies to coordinate road safety.
Organization for Economic Cooperation and Development European Conference of Ministers of Transport (OECD/ECMT)	The European Conference of Ministers of Transport (ECMT) is an intergovernmental organization established by a protocol signed in Brussels on 17th October 1953. It comprises the Ministers of Transport of 43 member countries. ECMT is a forum in which Ministers responsible for transport, and more specifically the inland transport sector can cooperate on policy.
World Bank	The World Bank promotes the improvement of road safety outcomes in low- and middle-income countries as a global development priority. Its mission is to assist countries accelerate their implementation of the recommendations of the *World report on road traffic injury prevention*, with an emphasis on building their capacity to invest in road safety and mobilizing global partnerships in support of this, to achieve measurable results
World Road Association (PIARC)	For many years, the Road Safety Committee of the World Road Association (PIARC) has been working on collision prevention in the areas of: road safety engineering; road safety politics; and road users' behaviour. Important issues that have recently been addressed are: development of road safety audits to eliminate design faults; evaluation of road safety measures and programmes; framework for the development of road safety politics and its testing in different countries; road design standards related to safety and user behaviour analysis, i.e. human factors in road design (Source the PIARC *Road safety manual*).
African Road Safety Observatory (ARSO)	ARSO was established by the AU in collaboration with UNECA, SSATP of the World Bank and the FIA. The Observatory is under the Department of Infrastructure and Energy of the AUC. The objectives of the Observatory are to facilitate the exchange of knowledge between road safety experts and governments in Africa; and to coordinate road safety strategies, initiatives and information at the continental level

Road Safety Partner Institution	Functions
Global Road Safety Partnership (GRSP)	GRSP is a global partnership between business, civil society and government dedicated to the sustainable reduction of death and injury on the roads in developing and transition countries. By creating and strengthening links between partners, GRSP aims to increase awareness of road safety as an issue affecting all sectors of society. GRSP seeks to establish sustainable partnerships and to deliver road safety interventions through increased resources, better coordination, management, greater innovation, and knowledge sharing both globally and locally.
FIA Foundation for the Automobile and Society	The FIA Foundation objectives are the promotion of public safety and public health, the protection and preservation of human life and the conservation, protection and improvement of the physical and natural environment. In the area of road safety this is achieved through; road safety advocacy to reduce the tragic toll; of deaths and injuries on the road and raise the global profile of road safety; promoting research, disseminating the results of research and providing information in any matters of public interest; promoting the safety of drivers, passengers, pedestrians and other road users; conducting research and educational activities and offering financial support to third party projects through a grants programme.
Association for Safe International Road Travel (ASIRT)	ASIRT is a non-profit organization based in the United States that promotes road safety through education and advocacy. ASIRT aims to improve global road safety and reduce deaths and injuries resulting from road crashes by: informing travellers of potential road risks; assisting in the formation, training and support of road safety on governmental organizations abroad; facilitating in the exchange of road safety expertise; engaging government leaders and agencies, corporations and the medical and tourist communities in addressing global road safety
International Road Federation (IRF)	The IRF mission consists of the promotion of the concept of the "forgiving road" and safe mobility in general, with active participation in the work of UNECE Working Party 1 and other United Nations bodies. IRF in Geneva, Brussels and Washington DC, benefits from the wide experience of its members all over the world to promote safe roads, namely through efficient road planning and construction, as well as maintenance operations to upgrade road quality, safety and technical requirements for the implementation of recognized measures that lead to the use of high-quality materials, high-performance road safety equipment, road signs and markings.

Source: United Nations road safety collaboration: a handbook of partner profiles, Version I, March 2005

Ghana affiliates with most of the mentioned entities either directly or indirectly towards the implementation of road safety activities. However, the extent of association and related benefits from each entity has not been determined.

B. African Conventions and Regulations on Road Safety: These included the following

i. The African Decade of Action for Road Safety: In response to the UN DOA (2011-2020), this was developed and adopted by African Ministers of Transport in November 2011 and at an African Union Summit in January 2012 with the following supporting frameworks:

a. Intergovernmental Agreement on Road Standards and Norms for Trans-African Highways (adopted June 2014).

b. African Road Safety Charter (adopted January 2016).

c. Dissemination (Transport Sector Support Programme): West and Central Africa-June 2016, North Africa (Arab Maghreb)-December 2016 and Eastern and Southern Africa- April 2017.

As a subsidiary guideline to the DOA, it provided a practical tool to fast track and support African governments in the development of their national and local road safety action plans. With the same objective as the DOA, the plan aimed to stabilize and reduce RTCs by 50% by the year 2020. The plan also articulated the need for country response to the global road safety agenda.

ii. The African Road Safety Charter: The charter contains policy guidelines to promote road safety in Africa through knowledge sharing, technical assistance, peer reviews and harmonization of road safety programmes, activities and data. Its objectives include:

a. Speed-up implementation of national, regional and continental road safety programmes.

b. Contribute to the coordination of road safety in the continent.

c. Facilitate the formulation of comprehensive road safety policies at country level.

d. Enhance private sector and civil society organization participation in road safety issues.

e. Promote the harmonization of the collection, treatment and dissemination of road safety data.

As a Charter, it is a constituent treaty and all members are bounded by its articles with violating governments being censured by the AU respectfully. Typically, countries that have acceded are required to do the following:

• Consult with industry representatives and civil society to ensure full transparency and legal certainty for everyone affected by the new rules.

• Conduct and provide a cost-benefit analysis, outlining the resources required for implementation e.g. road safety capacity building and knowledge transfer.

• Determine a list of any required national legal reforms.

• Modify road traffic rules and road safety activities to conform to the charter.

Ghana signed unto the African Road Safety Charter on the 4th of July 2017 as an expression of the willingness of the government to comply. It aimed to apply the strategic policy frame-work for delivering on Africa's goal for all-inclusive and sustainable road safety development. This has also enabled effective road safety collaboration with other countries across Africa.

iii. African Road Safety Observatory (ARSO): The ARSO was established by the AU in collaboration with UNECA, SSATP and FIA. It is under the Department of Infrastructure and Energy of the AU. Its objectives are to facilitate the exchange of knowledge between road safety experts and governments in Africa; and to coordinate road safety strategies, initiatives and information at the continental level (www.afric-aroadsafetyobservatory.org).

It is an online portal available for any device with free and accessible knowledge resources and tools such as statistics, maps, reports and factsheets. It combines traditional functions of analysing and sharing road safety performance data and provide knowledge and information as a Dialogue Platform and a crowd sourcing tool. It is hoped to produce knowledge to inspire safety funding, policies and interventions in Africa and also provide recommendations to update the African Road Safety Action Plan and the African Road Safety Charter. Key among the resolutions made at the General Assembly were:

a. Member states of the AU should accede to the UN Road Safety Conventions.

b. All member states should also sign and ratify the African Road Safety Charter.

c. All member states should actualize these resolutions/recommendations before the Global Ministerial Road Safety Conference scheduled for February 2020 in Sweden.

Ghana has participated in a range of training programmes targeting different local stakeholders, policymakers, NGO's and journalists with regards to the implementation of the ARSO. The country has subsequently posted its road safety data on the online platform of the observatory.

Generally, Ghana's participation in these global/African conventions has translated into road safety gains evidenced by country visits from sister nations to understudy Ghana's road safety management systems.

iv. United Nations Economic Commission for Africa (UNECA): The UNECA was established in 1958 as one of the UN's five (5) regional commissions with the mandate to promote the economic and social development of its member states to foster intra-regional integration and promote international cooperation for Africa's development. It is made up of fifty-four (54) member states and it plays the dual role as a regional arm of the UN and as a key component of the African institutional landscape, making it well positioned to make unique contributions to address the Continent's development challenges.

a). The Economic Commission for Africa (ECA): The ECA harnesses resources and brings them to bear on Africa's priorities in the following thematic areas; (i) Macroeconomic Policy; (ii) Regional Integration/Trade and Social Development; (iii) Natural Resources; (iv)Innovation and Technology; (v) Gender and Governance. ECA also provides technical advisory services to African governments, intergovernmental organizations and institutions. In addition, it formulates and promotes development assistance programmes and acts as the executing agency for relevant operational projects including road safety.

It collaborates with African countries to raise the status of road safety on the continent by identifying road safety priorities, providing platform for performance review as well as technical assistance and advocacy for road safety. It specifically helped with the preparation of the African Road Safety Action Plan – 2011-2020 as well as its monitoring and evaluation. The Commission collaborated with the AU for the drafting of the African Road Safety Charter in 2016.

1.3 INSTITUTIONAL ARRANGEMENTS FOR ROAD SAFETY MANAGEMENT

1.3.1 The West African Road Safety Organization (WARSO)

A. Objective of WARSO: The West Africa Road Safety Organization (WARSO) was established on 8th May, 2008 under the auspices of the Economic Community of West African States (ECOWAS) to promote road safety in West Africa. WARSO aims to;

i.   promote road safety in the West African sub region by supporting international policies, resolutions, plan of actions and declarations relating to road safety;

ii.   promote exchange of information/ideas and experiences among member countries;

iii. organise joint programmes and activities through conferences and workshops to discuss best practices and;

iv.   encourage and support innovation in road safety management.

B. Achievements of WARSO: WARSO has aligned itself with the 5 pillars of the DOA. WARSO has been applauded and adopted by the AU as a best practice for other regions in Africa to emulate in establishing a similar body. Some of the activities undertaken include the following:

i. Harmonisation of the use of standard retro-reflective tapes by vehicles in West Africa to aid in vehicle conspicuity.

ii. Development of a standard format for RTC data collection and the initiation of the development of a Regional Vehicle Administration and Information System (RVAIS) to ensure a uniformed vehicle registration system in the sub-region.

iii. Introduction of Passenger Manifest to collect information on both drivers and passengers at bus terminals before the start of a journey and a school road safety programme incorporating road safety education into basic education curriculum.

iv. Development of a template to monitor and evaluate the performance of member countries to help WARSO identify member countries that have shortfalls and come out with solutions to assist them.

v. Challenges of WARSO: The key challenge is that the position of WARSO as a sub-regional agency within the ECOWAS set up is not well defined. It is hosted and funded by dues paid by the member states and has a small secretariat hosted by Nigeria. However, there is a lack of full human resource capacity and the expertise required as well as limited funding. Thus, there is need for ECOWAS to streamline the role of WARSO within its structure to enable a sub-regional ownership. WARSO is also not able to effectively facilitate technical support to countries needing such assistance and should be developed to enable it offer the necessary assistance to non-performing countries.

Ghana is a member of WARSO and has played a key role in the facilitation of WARSO by hosting the annual general meeting of WARSO on two occasions that is 2012 and 2019. Ghana has held different executive positions in WARSO and this includes Deputy General Secretary (2008-2016) and 1st Vice President (2016-date).

1.3.2 Road Safety Insitutional Management in Ghana

The NRSA is the lead agency responsible for the management functions of road safety in Ghana with the mandate coordinate all road safety activities in the country and to exert compliance by road users through rigorous regulations and inspections. This has become possible through the passage of the NRSA Act 993 of 2019 which has repealed the NRSC Act 567 of 1999. The Authority is represented in every region of Ghana and it works with thirteen (13) key stakeholder entities to drive the national vision of making Ghana a country with the safest road transportation system in Africa. The NRSA is also a goal-oriented organization with a committed and dedicated staff who work with passion and a sense of duty.

The key driving factors include common or shared vision, mission and strategic goals which are accomplished through various activities or tasks performed towards the achievement of set targets. It is also a research-based institution inspired by the need for accurate and reliable data for promoting road safety work in the country.

1.3.3 A. Road Safety Strategy Development in Ghana

A. Summary of Road Safety Interventions Implemented in Ghana: *The DOA recommends for the development of proactive, integrated multi-sectoral and data led national road safety policies, strategies and action plans to reduce and prevent RTCs and related casualties. The NRSA fulfilled this mandate through the development of a national road safety policy in*

2008 with the collaboration of key road safety stakeholders. It has also been designing and coordinating the implementation of data-led road safety programmes and activities since its establishment in 1999.

The first strategic framework was the National Road Safety Strategy 1 (NRSS 1) covered the period 2001-2006. The second road safety strategy of NRSS II was for the period 2006 to 2010. The third NRSS III was implemented between 2011 and 2020 in response to the launching of the DOA and a fourth NRSSS IV has also been developed to correspond to the extended DA from 2021 -2030.

B. Summary of Achievements on Ghana's Road Safety Work: *The NRSA applies time tested education modules, engineering measures, effective enforcement strategies and emergency response services to demand a favourable road user attitude and protect lives and properties as well. This is attested by the fact that the World Bank in 2004 recognised Ghana's efforts at managing road safety and identified Ghana as a model for road safety management in developing economies. The result of this recognition has been the several study visits from countries like; Lesotho, Gambia, Namibia, Uganda and Liberia to under study Ghana's road safety management system.*

However, Ghana's performance on road safety gains has been of mixed outcomes. This is so because RTC fatalities which recorded lower figures in the early years after the start of the DOA in 2011, had a changed trend from 2017 when, casualties from RTCs started rising after the decreases in the early stages of the NRSS III and thus eroding the gains made in the early years. Specifically, though by the year 2015 for example, the number of people killed had reduced by 18.0% it increased by 15% in 2020 relative to the base year of the strategy (2011), (BRRI 2020). This is mainly attributed to increasing use of motorcycles for commercial transport and the related safety challenges. Irrespective of this, the highly motivated and committed staff of the NRSA is poised to promote best road safety practices for all categories of road users with a target to reduce Ghana's RTC fatality rate to a single digit by 2030.

C. Opportunities for Road Safety Promotion in Ghana: *Over the last few decades, Ghana's knowledge of the causes of crashes and potential remedies for eliminating crashes, reducing crash risks and limiting their (negative) consequences has increased considerably which provides opportunities for good progress to be made on the way forward. Currently, Ghana has also fulfilled the majority of the requirements for best road safety practices as bedrock for advancing the course of road safety activities into the future with regards to the following:*

i.   *Establishment of clear institutional and organizational roles and responsibilities for road safety work.*

ii.   *Creation of a vision for road safety achievements in the future.*

iii. *Application of an integrated approach to meet the multi sectoral needs of road safety work with defined coordination systems.*

iv. *Development of road safety policy framework and formulation of road safety legislations and regulations to streamline legal requirements.*

v. *Identification of road safety problem areas by means of crash statistics.*

vi. *Development of counter measures to mitigate identified problems as closely as possible.*

vii. *Creation and implementation of multi sectoral road safety strategies and at national levels with regional plans.*

viii. *Education of decision-makers and the public on matters of road safety and the marketing of countermeasures to put pressure on decision makers and authorities.*

ix. *Creation of effective enforcement systems to ensure compliance to road traffic safety regulations.*

x. *Establishment of process monitoring systems with continuous measurements of safety performance indicators to ensure road safety result matches with specified targets for each problem area.*

xi. *Use of independent body to follow-up and evaluate the results of the road safety efforts in comparison with road safety plans.*

D. Threats to the Future Progress of Road Safety Management in Ghana: *In spite of the achievements made in Ghana with regards to the road safety work in the country, it cannot be established that ultimate performance in road safety management has been attained. The future of road safety work remains uncertain due to challenges such as the following:*

i. *The ever-increasing vehicular fleet in the country coupled with the enormous increase of travelled (motorized) kilometres on the roads.*

ii. *Uncertainties around the vision of the transport system in the future due to unforeseen challenges such as increase in the use of commercial motorcycle transport which is not currently legalised or regulated but is impacting negatively on road crash trends and related causalities but still not formally managed.*

iii. *The yet to be achieved full explanation of crash developments at an aggregated level and the related important explanatory factors causing limited understanding of how or why Ghana is at its state of road safety progress. This does not ensure sustained efforts nor creates the opportunity for added value.*

iv. *The challenge of research gaps which has not enabled all factors causing road safety challenges to be well understood for appropriate mitigation.*

v.   *The difficulty of proving the effectiveness of implemented countermeasures in the phase of the multifaceted nature of the road safety concept which does not ensure cost effective comparison between countermeasures and road safety impact statistics nor the linkages between road safety budgets/crash costs and safety benefits.*

vi. *The difficulty of predicting potential safety impact of future incremental changes and the difficulty of knowing how to respond to emerging new technologies.*

vii. *Uncertainties around political, private sector and civil society engagements for accomplishing good road safety results due to the lack of institutionalization of such partnerships.*

viii. *The challenge of limited funding levels and limited expertise for effective road safety work.*

ix. *The yet to be established road safety problem as a public health problem as recommended by the WHO in (1999).*

x.   *The challenge of not simply copying from the international community rather ensuring that their standards are adapted to local conditions.*

1.4. WAY FORWARD ON GHANA'S ROAD SAFETY AGENDA

In the past two decades, Ghana has implemented diverse RTC counter interventions guided by both international road safety best practices and to some extent country specific needs. The country is now looking beyond 2020 for the possible attainment of the objectives of the road safety component of the SDGs up to the period 2030. This implies that, Ghana's road safety work must move unto higher performance levels over and above what is currently being done. To attain this, the achievements and failures, the contributory factors, the lessons and the critical issues to direct the future of Ghana's road safety work beyond 2020 must be wholly contextualised. This requires, a comprehensive and balanced view of Ghana's road safety performance to direct the way forward.

To this effect, there must be a paradigm shift in the way road safety is viewed towards shared responsibilities for road safety management by the entire citizenry especially through awareness creation so as to create an effective road safety community for the country. In order to achieve this, there must be a comprehensive and reflective review of the various polices, objectives, strategies and plans of action as well as the account of factors that influence and promote best practice road safety to provide good insight into the state of road safety in the country. This must be done by the building of evidence on the results of the current approach to road safety management to avoid repeating previous mistakes.

More importantly, road safety work must be supported with the right and adequate resources for effective outcomes. It is hoped that, the comparative performance of Ghana's road safety work with global guidelines on the technical, legal, political, economic, and socio-cultural factors needed for best practice road safety efforts will advance and sustain Ghana's momentum in its road safety management. It is expected that the discussions on Ghana's achievements made and failures encountered in implementing its road safety management will inform and direct Ghana's effort to achieve the level of global road safety target projected for the year 2030.

CHAPTER 2

TRENDS AND PROGRESS IN ROAD TRAFFIC CRASHES

It is said that "if you can't measure it, you can't manage it". If you don't measure, then how do you know how you are doing, (Drucker P. 2014).

2.1 INTRODUCTION

Road safety performance outcomes must be measured to know how well or how poorly a road safety management system is doing. This is necessary to reflect the state of various functional areas of the road safety management systems. Therefore, it is considered to be the core of any successful effort to improve road safety for any country and for determining how to prevent RTCs most effectively and efficiently (WHO, 2011).

Specifically, the outcome of a road safety performance measurement can be used to (i) monitor the progress of ongoing activities for necessary correction; (ii) evaluate the impacts of implemented actions; (iii) conduct comparisons between two or more jurisdictions; (iv) make decisions in investment priorities; (v) identify most effective methods; (vi) determine the factors contributing to good and bad road safety results; (vii) determine critical risk factors mitigating against the achievement of good road safety results and (viii) establish what needs to be done to ensure better performance.

Essentially, road safety performance measurement is required to be done through the identification of some elements that defines performance dimensions of the road safety outcomes. This is referred to as road safety performance indicators (SPIs). These are established through collation and analysis of information on RTC records or from surveys over specific time periods. They are usually presented in meaningful formats in unbiased, precise and non-subjective ways amenable to verification and comparisons.

This chapter of the book examines trends in the measured state of Ghana's road safety performance by the contextualisation of what constitutes road safety performance measurement and the relevant indicators for such measurement. The information is used as backdrop for assessing the end results of Ghana's road safety interventions implemented from 1991 to 2020 as basis for determining the successes and failures of Ghana's road safety efforts so far.

2.2 OVERVIEW OF ROAD SAFETY PERFORMANCE MEASUREMENT

2.2.1 Features of Road Safety Performance Measurement

Performance measurement is defined as the process of evaluating the results on products, services and works of a system or structure using set indicators. Indicators are management tools that provide easily accessible and concise information for measurement. According to CIDA (1996), an indicator can be a number, a fact, an opinion or a perception that points to a specific condition or situation which can be measured to establish changes over time. These can be used on their individual merit or can be combined into composite indices which range from relatively simple to highly complex models depending on the number of variables involved.

A. Road Safety Performance Indicators (SPIs): SPIs are levels are based on targeted effects of road safety interventions undertaken. They are therefore used to measure the outcomes/performance of implemented road safety interventions. They cover essential elements associated with all road safety disciplines including organisational policy and regulatory frameworks, highway planning, road design, operation and maintenance; safe vehicle standards, transport services; law enforcement activities for road safety; road safety educational programmes, RTC emergency preparedness and response activities as well as public health care needs for RTC victims towards improvement in road safety measures.

B. Purpose of (SPIs): SPIs can be used for the following purposes:

i.   To diagnose the factors causing RTCs and what can be done.

ii.   To show the state of road safety performance and related effectiveness of interventions implemented.

iii. To compare road safety performance between different groups and set targets.

iv.   To monitor road safety progress over time in order to analyse trends in road traffic crash fatalities and injuries.

v.   To assess the effects of road safety actions and relevance of implemented road safety activities.

vi. To show how coordination channels between different bodies involved in road safety functions.

vii. To predict further evolution on road safety.

In Ghana, SPIs are also used to assess RTC outcomes at different levels but the extent to which SPIs provide actionable information on road safety is yet to be studied. The extent to which they are adjusted to suit specific needs as and when required is also not known. They are also not used for outcome impacts on different groups, they do not reflect coordination channels the contributions of the different entities involved in road safety functions.

This is because, when SPIs are presented in a composite form to measure the end result of diverse and integrated road safety interventions undertaken, it becomes complex and impossible to determine the exact and magnitude of contribution of each intervention on the end result. Finally, they are not used to predict further evolution on road safety for the future and it is recommended for these aspects to be addressed.

C. Attributes of SPI's: According to Wouter Van den Berghe and Heike Martensen (2017), SPIs can have

i. Geographical scope (i.e. organisation, city, region, country, world etc.);

ii. Time span (i.e. month, quarter, mid-term, year, decade etc.);

iii. Numerical Format (i.e. percentage, proportion, ratio etc.)

iv. Representation/Visualisation e.g. (i.e. maps graph and tables). It is further suggested for SPIs

v. Linked to a data source, be reliable, accurate and representative

D. Categories of SPIs: SPIs can be categorised as follows:

i. Qualitative and Quantitative SPIs: SPIs can be qualitative and quantitative. Qualitative SPIs are non-numerical indicators used to measure subjective opinion, judgment, perception etc. on a subject and the quality of change. They provide information in a textual or written form, (Davies, 2000). Quantitative SPIs are however, numerical and maybe expressed as units, proportions, rates of change and ratios and are normally analysed through statistical data methods.

ii. Direct and Indirect SPIs: SPIs can be classified as direct indicators when they possess sufficient degree of validity, reliability and availability to describe local, national or international RTC situations and 'indirect' when they have latent relationship to the RTC situation (ECMT, 2002).

iii. SPIs by Time Dimensions: SPIs can be time-related as 'before', 'during' and 'after' whereby 'before' indicators are drawn from road safety preparatory factors such as policies, legislation, strategies; 'during' indicators are drawn from the implementation phase of safety activities such as traffic law enforcement; and 'after' indicators are drawn from post RTC situations such as care of RTC victims.

iv. SPIs by Counter Effects: SPIs can be problem-related on the basis of the negative impacts of RTCs or intervention-related with reference to policies, strategies and action interventions, (OECD, 2003).

v. Global and Local SPIs: SPIs can be defined at global, national and regional. They can also be based on locational or thematic RTC causative and impact factors relating to in-country situation.

Ghana's SPIs are used for setting targets and for benchmarking against future expectations. They are measurable and includes both direct and indirect variables. They are also broadly classified as fixed and variable SPIs. They are based on crash related statistics with defined geographical scope by region and district. They also define statistical impacts of crash types by crash frequency and severity with regards to crash locations, collision types, crash types by day, month, time, weather conditions, light conditions etc. In addition, they are also classified by performance on other aspects of road safety such as crash types, frequency and severity by road type, vehicle types, road user categories etc.

These are mainly used to assess overall outcome performance of road safety interventions and the relevance of implemented activities to set priorities. The indicators are also duly linked to a data source with information derived data collated by the BRRI from police records on RTCs.

Typically, the main sources of crash data must be from the police, births and deaths (B&D) registry and hospitals. However, data from the other sources aside the police are not well coordinated and a study by the BRRI (2021) has established discrepancies in the road safety data in from the different sources which must be corrected.

Ghana also has variable SPI's used to monitor progress and performance of specific road safety interventions to determine the effectiveness of the processes applied. Such SPIs are not fixed and information on such SPIs are obtained from the conduct of periodic and specialised studies during or after implementation. Examples are SPI's on impaired driving, speeding, fatigue driving, use of vehicle restraint etc. as presented in Table 2.1.

The key constraints are limited indicators for emergency response and care with the exception of the indicator on emergency response time, lack of SPIs to measure performance on road safety management, policy issues, organizational systems, socio economic factors etc. In addition, most of the SPIs are more generic than problem focused with much emphasis on the end results rather than the causative factors.

The same variables have also been used for a period of time. Since, the variables must match current need, there is should be periodic reviews to meet this requirement. This should be done by the setting of an SPI management regime for periodic revision of the defined variables. Also, there should be strict adherence to the scheduled data to mitigate the current practice whereby the activity is skipped in some years due to funding limitations.

E. Proposed Structure for SPIs: Koornstra et al. (2002) and LTSA (2000) puts SPIs into a five-staged pyramid shaped target in a hierarchical order drawn from the concept of the project cycle. The structure presents road safety as a system with interdependencies whereby the size (width) of a level indicates the quantity of factors influencing that level with the higher level having the least number of influencing factors (see Figure 2.1).

Figure 2.1: Five-staged pyramid shaped target hierarchical structure (Koornstra et al., 2002; LTSA, 2000)

i. Impacts of RTCs by Social Costs: The end result of every RTC is the socio-economic consequences reflected in costs and this is at the apex of the pyramid. Such costs are expressed in terms of the cost of lost life, medical costs for the treatment of the victim, public cost incurred from the use of the services of emergency response personnel, loss of household production from taking care of the victim, professional rehabilitation costs, legal costs, hospital visiting costs, funeral costs, property damage and administrative costs of insurance companies (Ra-MoW, 2008).

However, these costs do not include the physical pain, loss of body function, disfiguration, emotional stress, the pain of loss of quality of life and other suffering from casualties as well as stress and pain suffered by immediate families (Evans, 2003).

Another aspect of challenge is the estimation of the monetary value of life. Examples include the use of what the population would be willing to pay for safety improvements that result in the avoidance of one premature death. However, this method has been discounted by authors like Burrows and Brown (2008) for producing varying values. The Quality-Adjusted Life-Years (QALY) and the Disability-Adjusted Life Years (DALY) methods from the WHO's Global Burden of Disease Concept are recommended instead.

The QALY combines the length of life (mortality) and quality of life (morbidity) into a single number to measure the value and benefits of health outcomes referred as years lived in perfect health gained. The DALY measures the gap between an ideal health status and an ideal health situation where an entire population lives to an advanced age free from disease and disability referred as years in perfect health Lost.

However, both methods are criticised for not capturing emotional and mental health impacts, impact on carers and family members as well as non-health effects such as economic and social consequences, (Sassi F, 2006). It is also said that QALY's can lack sensitivity and may be difficult to apply to chronic diseases and preventive treatments whilst the derivation of health utilities or the specific state of health can also be subjective (Philip et al, 2009). Also, the life expectancy figure for the DALY may also be over-estimated when actual local life expectancy is shorter.

Irrespective of these limitations the methods provide a single measure of mortality and morbidity for assessing the cost of life and their application in public health to enable policy makers make informed decisions. However, it is not the author's intention to give a detailed description of these methods and it is suggested that interested readers may conduct further research on the topic if deemed necessary.

The key components for impacts of RTCs by social costs in Ghana from a study by the BRRI (2021) included casualty related costs such as lost output, medical costs and human costs defined as grief and emotional stress estimated to be 25% of total social costs for fatal RTC, 50 % for serious RTCs and 20% for non-serious RTCs based on studies adopted from other developing countries. Others are crash related costs such as property damage and administration costs. However, this approach is simplistic and its true representation of the monetary value of life in Ghana is not proven.

ii. Final RTC Outcomes by Number Killed and Injured: The second level SPIs from the top of the pyramid is based on the number of people killed and injured from RTCs. In this regard, RTC injury is defined as physical damage to the human body resulting in a reduction in the functional health status (Bhalla et al. 2009) and RTC fatality is defined as the related death caused either at a crash scene, on the way to a health facility, hospital, home, etc. Whilst an injury can be classified to be minor, moderate or severe depending on the level of impairment, fatality is based on the time duration between the crash and the occurrence of death which can be within a day, a week, a month or a year as defined by a country (WHO, 2018).

In Ghana, final outcomes of RTCs are defined by the number killed and injured with the later further identified as serious and slight injuries. Those killed are identified to be those who die at the RTC, on the way to a health facility and within thirty (30) days at the health facility. The key challenge is limitation in the police follow up to record such information.

iii. Intermediate Outcome Safety Performance Indicators: The third level of SPIs within the structure are referred to as intermediate outcomes which link final outcomes to policy output to show how well road safety interventions are working. They include the safety qualities of the traffic system such as safety quality of roads e.g., safe design standards, vehicles e.g., crashworthiness, human behaviour e.g., alcohol limit compliance and trauma management domain e.g., the medical system.

Intermediate outcome safety performance indicators in Ghana are also defined by the alignment of crash and casualty statistics with road type, vehicle type, demographic characteristics such as age and sex and environmental factors such as day and night.

iv. Safety Output Measures and Programmes: The fourth level SPIs from the structure includes indicators on road safety countermeasures relating to quality of road safety policies/legislations, strategies and action plans, monitoring and evaluation, research etc. (Morsink et al., 2005). However little knowledge is readily available on valid indicators for the output indicators since operational definitions are lacking as well as data on the typical occurrence of these conditions.

Where safety output measures and programmes are concerned, there are hardly any such SPIs used in Ghana.

v. Road Safety Input from Structure and Culture: The fifth, or base level, of the model consists of factors that inform road safety decisions including statics on physical factors such as climate and dynamic factors such as demography, cultural factors including values, norms, ideological and aesthetic attitudes that vary across countries and people. Both structural and cultural indicators are said to be able to influence road safety but are themselves not influenced by road safety policies.

In Ghana, indicators from the structure and culture aspects includes crash and casualty characteristics by age group as well as for climate and dynamic factors such as weather conditions. The summary of SPIs by the set components in Ghana are as presented in Table 2.1.

Table 2.1: Summary of Indicators for Road Safety Crash Statistic Reporting in Ghana

Pillar	Level of Indicator	Description	Attributes
Road Safety Management	Final Indicators	Traffic Fatality Indices	Direct, After, Local
Road Safety Management	Final Indicators	Traffic Crashes and Casualties	Direct, After, Global
Trends in Fatalities			
Pillar 2 Road Infrastructure	Intermediate Outcome Indicator	Annual Distribution of Fatalities by Road Environment	Direct, After, Local
Pillar 4 Road User	Intermediate Outcome Indicator	Annual Distribution of Fatalities by Road User Class	Direct, After, Global
Pillar 4 Road User	Intermediate Outcome Indicator	Annual Distribution of Urban Fatalities by Road User Class	Direct, After, Local
Pillar 4 Road User	Intermediate Outcome Indicator	Annual Distribution of Non-Urban Fatalities by Road User Class	Direct, After, Local
Pillar 4 Road User	Structure and Culture	Annual Distribution of Fatalities by Age Group	Direct, After, Global
Pillar 4 Road User	Structure and Culture	Annual Distribution of Fatalities by Sex	Direct, After, Global
Trends in Casualties			
Pillar 4 Road User	Intermediate Outcome Indicator	Annual Distribution of Casualties by Road User Class	Direct, After, Global
Pillar 4 Road User	Intermediate Outcome Indicator	Annual Distribution of Urban Casualties by Road User Class	Direct, After, Local
Pillar 4 Road User	Pillar 4 Road User	Annual Distribution of Non-Urban Casualties by Road User Class	Direct, After, Local
Pillar 4 Road User	Structure and Culture	Annual Distribution of Casualties by Age Group	Direct, After, Global
Pillar 4 Road User	Structure and Culture	Annual Distribution of Casualties by Road Environment	Direct, After, Local
Pillar 4 Road User	Structure and Culture	Annual Distribution of Casualties by Sex	Direct, After, Global
Pillar 3 Vehicle safety	Intermediate Outcome Indicator	Vehicle Type Involved in Accidents	Indirect, During, Local
National Road Traffic Casualty Characteristics (2018, 2017, 2011, 2001)			
Pillar 2 Road Infrastructure	Final Indicators	Collision Type Resulting in Deaths and Injuries	Direct, During, Local
Pillar Road Safety Management	Intermediate Outcome Indicator	Road User Class Involved in Deaths and Injuries	Indirect, During, Local
Pillar 3 Road user	Intermediate Outcome Indicator	Action of Pedestrian Associated with Deaths and Injuries	Indirect, During. Local
Pillar 4 Road User	Structure and Culture	Age of Persons Killed or Injured in Crashes	Direct, After, Global
Pillar 3 vehicle Safety	Intermediate Outcome Indicator	Types of Vehicle Involved in Fatal and Non-Fatal Crashes	Indirect, During, Local
Pillar 1 Road Safety Management	Structure and Culture	Month During Which Persons Were Killed or Injured in Crashes	Indirect, During, Local
Pillar 1 Road Safety Management	Structure and Culture	Day of Occurrence of Crashes	Indirect, During, Local
Pillar 1 Road Safety Management	Structure and Culture	Hour of Occurrence of Crashes	Indirect, During, Local
Pillar 4 Road User	Intermediate Outcome Indicator	Driver Error Associated with Deaths and Injuries	Indirect, During, Local
Pillar 2 Infrastructure	Intermediate Outcome Indicator	Road Description Prevailing in Crashes	Indirect, During, Local
Pillar 1 Road Safety Management	Structure and Culture	Weather Conditions Prevailing During Crashes	Indirect, During, Local
Pillar 1 Road Safety Management	Structure and Culture	Light Conditions Prevailing During Crashes	Indirect, During, Local

E. Selection of SPIs: The guidelines for the selection of SPIs and the steps involved as recommended by authors like Etika A (2018), are as follows:

i.   SPIs must be related to important aspects of road safety (impact, results, causes, etc.).

ii.   They must afford a balanced assessment of the road safety system.

iii. They must have direct relationships with set targets.

iv.   They must be used on directly available data.

v.   There must be a level of accuracy subject to verification and scientific validation.

vi.   They must be easily understood, address the needs of all road users and also be cost effective.

vii. They must be measurable in a reliable and systematic way.

Since there are a large number of causal factors contributing to RTCs, picking one factor over the other is not easily achieved and according to Al Haji (2005) the procedure for the development of SPIs in each area must be by the following steps:

Step 1 - Definition of unsafe operational conditions of the Traffic system.

Step 2 - Development of a relationship between problem areas and opportunities for intervention.

Step 3 - Establishment of a scale of programme for road safety improvements.

Step 4 - Analysis and categorization of safety interventions into divisions and sub divisions of factors.

Step 5 - Definition of characteristics of the factors that are known to reduce the risk of fatal and serious injury.

Step 6 - Selection of performance attributes of the factors which can be quantified and on which data can be readily available.

Step 7 - Expression of the selected indicators with values in a meaningful way by associating numbers with physical quantities in the form of units of measurement which are of standardized values.

In Ghana, there are no records of set procedures for the selection of the SPIs that have been in use for years and their applicability have also never been verified. It is anticipated that the final indicators used for reporting on road crashes, casualties, fatalities and injuries might have originated from the replication of some international best practice which has never been reviewed or configured to suit country specific needs.

F. Limitations of SPIs Applications: Generally, SPIs vary in scope and its use is criticised by ETSC (2001) as being prone to random fluctuations, with short-term changes in the recorded number which does not necessarily reflect a change in the underlying long-term expected number. Also, the combined effect of all road safety measures into a single indicator is discounted for the fact that they are produced from incomplete statistics. Besides, the count of crashes does not reflect crash causative factors which needs to be understood for effective mitigations.

In Ghana, explanatory variables are also not assigned to the recorded statistics on the SPIs for better understanding of the RTC causative factors to effectively guide RTC interventions. Thus, there is need for good quality data with assured continuity and added value to current practices.

G. Combination of SPIs into Road Safety Indices (RSIs): SPIs can also be combined into composite multi-dimensional indices for ease of interpretation rather than trying to find a trend in many separate indicators. Such combined multivariable road safety indicators are put together with a view towards an acceptable level of safety. According to the WHO (2010), in recent time the use of indices to analyse or measure road safety has been growing rapidly in view of the complex and multidimensional character of RTC occurrence.

i. Characteristics of RSIs: The RSIs is the sum of many dimensions where each dimension is a sum of combined indicators. The balance of indicators within each dimension must be subject to available data. Both indicators and dimensions will give a broad picture of road safety and not focus on one particular aspect.

However, successful multidimensional indices are said to be contingent on a number of conditions such as not being be too complex or too simple. This is because a simple index may not be accepted at the researcher and policy maker level and a complex index may be too difficult to explain to a wider audience.

ii. Examples of Road Safety Indices: Some examples of RSIs include the following:

a. Road Safety Performance Index (RSPI): It measures several areas of road safety, among which are road user behaviour, infrastructure and vehicles.

b. Traffic Management Indicator (TMI): These reflect the degree or level of performance by various road safety functional areas such as traffic legislation; traffic safety in schools e.g., number of students reached; road safety communication i.e. the number of TV and radio advertisement conducted; enforcement e.g., number of roadblocks per location per time period and number of traffic prosecutions; and Infrastructure e.g., length of road in good condition.

c. Law Compliance Indicator (LCI)/Traffic Performance Index (TPI): Reflects level of lawlessness of road users and vehicles e.g., traffic offences committed, traffic offence rates i.e. number of road users committing offences.

d. Road Crash Indicator (RCI): RCI takes into account related issues in the TPI. They are developed from national fatal crash information elements including elements such as fatal crashes per crash type, and fatalities per user group.

e. Road Safety Index (RSI): This is obtained from a combination of the TPI and RCI. It is used to reflect the overall road traffic environment including elements within the road traffic management scene thus indicating the overall improvement in the traffic safety system.

iii. Development of Road Safety Indices: The process for the development of RSIs involves the selection of indicators, data preparation e.g., weighting, aggregating and development of a value score from the combination of the values of weighted indices using mathematical models. This is followed by robustness testing and evaluating the final scores. Also, most composite indices follow the linear functional form. The typical (standard) composite index of RSDI will take the following forms presented in Box 2.1:

Box 2.1: Sampled formulas for estimating RSDI

Equ. 1

$$RSI = \frac{\sum_{i=1}^{n} w_i V_{ei}}{\sum_{i=1}^{n} w_i V_{si}}$$

Where 'n' is number of groups that define the overall factors to contribute accident.

'W_i' is the relative weightage allocated with i^{th} service characteristics.

'V_{ei}' is the value score for i^{th} service characteristics of the existing situation

'V_{si}' is the value scores for i^{th} service characteristics.

-the value of $\sum (W_i * V_{si})$ is computed to be 100

- the value score is for safe road condition by local operating conditions

-the numerator is computed on the basis of observations made for each factor for a given road.

-the value scored for each factor is assessed after measuring each sub-element for V_{ei}.

Source: Kushnappa B K et. JRTIR April 2020, Volume 7, Issue 4

Equ. 2

$$SAFETY = \left(\sum_{i=1}^{n} W_i R_i \right) * km$$

Expressed as: SAFETY $= (w_1.R_1 + w_2.R_2 + ... + w_n.R_n) *$ kilometres

Where

R is the risk of particular factor kilometres is the exposure in traffic, and

w is the weight of the risk factor in a particular country

Source: Koornstra, (1996)

Equ. 3

$$RSDI = \frac{\sum_{i=1}^{n} w_i X}{\sum_{i=1}^{n} w_i}$$

Expressed as : $RSDI = \frac{W_1 X_1 + W_2 X_2 + W_3 X_3 + \cdots W_n X_n}{W_1 + W_2 + W_3 + \cdots W_n}$

Where: w_i: the weights of the Xi

X_i: normalised indicators

In most approaches $\sum_{i=1}^{n} w_i = 1$ and ranged from 0 to 1

Source: Al Haji, G 2005

In Ghana, some of the SPIs are also expressed as composite indices (RSIs). These include the estimation of fatalities per 10,000 vehicles, fatalities per 100,000 population, fatalities per 100 casualties and fatalities per 100 crashes. Specifically, the injury severity score which standardizes the severity of injuries sustained during trauma is also used in Ghana. This is especially used for patients with multiple injuries and it is calculated as indicated in Box 2. 2.

Box 2.2: Estimation of the injury severity score in Ghana

1. Determination of injury in six regions of the human body as (i) head, neck and spine, (ii) face that is mouth, nose eyes and ears; (iii) chest that is the thoracic spine and diaphragm; (iv) abdomen including abdominal organs and lumbar spine including pelvic contents; (v) externalities or pelvic girdle, pelvic skeletons and (vi) External.

2. Scoring by severity score of the worst injury as (i) No injury -0; (ii) Minor Injury -1; (iii) Moderate injury – 2; Serious – 3; (iv) severe – 4; (v) Critical -5; and Unsurvivable - 6.

3. Choose the three most severely injured body systems

4. Perform injury Severity Core calculation by adding the three highest squared scores as: ISS = highest 1^2+highest 2^2+ highest 3^2

Where a body system has a score of 6, ISS is automatically set to have the highest value of 75 points since the ISS takes values from 0 to 75 points.

Where the ISS score >15 with major trauma

Also

Bolorunduro et al. defines ISS severity as

Less than 9 = minor; 9-15 = moderate; 25 and more very severe /profound

The regions with the highest score are i. Abdomen – 3points; 2. Chest – 2points and 3 Face -1point.

Source: Omni Calculator

iv. Application of RSIs: Some applications of road safety indices for measuring performance include:

a). The OECD four mainstream Modelling Approaches classified as:

•   Descriptive models which source for information from RTC data to describe why it happens.

•   Predictive/Analytical models based on how changes in independent variables are expected to influence dependent variables.

- Risk models which aim to identify and quantify risk factors that explain and predict individual road-user behaviour.

- RTC Consequence Models which are aimed to reduce the consequences of RTCs by identifying influential factors such as those related to the roadway environment, vehicle safety and emergency services; etc.

b). Benchmarking Models: Al-Haji & Asp, (2006) proposes a four type models for benchmarking RSIs between countries which are:

- Product Benchmarking used to compare RTC death rates.

- Practices Benchmarking used to compare activities related to human, vehicle and road performance (e.g. seat belts use, crash helmets use, motorways level, etc.).

- Strategic Benchmarking used to compare National Road Safety Programme (NRSP) e.g., road safety management, enforcement and organisational framework.

- Integrated Benchmarking used to compare countries in terms of the three previous types of benchmarking altogether.

v. Constraints to the Use of RSIs: Some constraints to the use of RSIs are as follows:

- The indices highlight the differences between countries but fail to explain such differences;

- They do not predict the future of road safety due to limited data and the lack of operational definitions.

- Many of such models suffer from a lack of sound theoretical foundation and flexibility so are restrictive to predictability and the possibilities for generalization, Hakim et al., (1991) and Stewart (1998).

- A composite index is considered to be successful only if it is accepted by the (majority of the) road safety community, including decision makers, policy formulators and researchers.

2.3 GLOBAL ROAD SAFETY PERFORMANCE INDICATORS

2.3.1 Categories of Global SPIS and RSIS Commonly Applied

A. Categories of Global SPIs: The types of global SPIs defined by the World Report on Traffic Injury Prevention (2018) are as follows:

i. SPIs based on Exposure to Traffic Crash Risk: These include SPIs derived from exposure of road users to RTCs by factors such as socioeconomic deprivations, demographic factors, urban population density, land use planning and practices, rapid motorization, traffic characteristics, etc.

ii. SPIs based on Factors Influencing Crash Involvement: These include SPIs based on risk factors such as excessive speed, impaired driving from alcohol or drug use, bad user eyesight, defective vehicles, etc.

iii. SPIs based on RTC Severity: These include SPIs defined by RTC causative factors with severe impacts such as excessive speed, impaired driving, non-use of vehicle restraints, lack of protective roadside objects such as guardrails, barriers, etc.

iv. SPIs based on Factors influencing Severity of Post-Crash Injuries: These include post-crash injuries such as the state of a person's injury leading to death in some instances e.g. delayed crash detection, crashes involving fire outbreaks, leakage of hazardous materials, delayed post-crash response, difficulties in extrication of victims from damaged vehicles, inappropriate pre-hospital care, poor care at medical facilities, etc.

B. Categories of Global Road RSIs: These include SPIs expressed in relation to other variables such as the following:

i. Traffic risk: SPIs based on the risk of a person being killed in road crash per vehicle or per vehicle-km.

ii. Personal risk: SPIs based on the risk of a person being killed in road crash per number of inhabitants.

iii. Changing trend of road crash rates: SPIs based on the percentage change of death trend over time.

iv. Safer vehicles: SPIs based on the assessment of safety characteristics of vehicles that affect the number of vehicle-related crashes (e.g. type of vehicle, new cars in a city, inspection of vehicles, index of national crashworthiness, vehicle inspection, etc.).

v. Safer roads: SPIs based on different aspects of the quality and conditions of roads (e.g. state of road condition, surface type and national expenditure on roads).

vi. Safer people (road user behaviour): SPIs based on the assessment of human behaviour and traffic safety with respect to speeding, drink-driving, helmet use, seat-belt use, driver training, etc.

vii. Socioeconomic factors: SPIs based on investments in relation to health and rescue level, education level per capita, urban population, income level, etc.

viii. Traffic police and enforcement: SPIs that measure traffic police and enforcement effectiveness.

ix.   Road safety organisational structure: SPIs that measure the efficiency of the overall road safety programme, action plans, data system, research, legislations and the level of cooperation between key stakeholder entities.

C. Examples of Global SPIs: The fragmentation of disciplines associated with road safety does not lend to easy identification of performance indicators and various approaches are used. The situation becomes more challenging when comparing the performance of one country with the other due to different road safety managements systems with local specific content in different countries.

From Literature, some of the diverse sets of SPIs recommended by different authors at the global level include the SPI master list by Ghazwan Al-Haji (2007) for global use and road safety performance indicators proposed for member European States by Herman et al (2009). Each category of SPI places different levels of emphasis on different aspects of road safety based on what is considered to influence road safety management as defined through research. Though not all of them are based on critical road safety components.

Al-Haji's global master list considers all aspects of the road safety pillars with the exception of post-crash related SPIs. These include SPIs related to traffic safety, economic factors, socio-cultural factors, enforcement and other SPIs for organisational systems. The master list also includes some road safety composite indices.

Herman et al.'s (2009) SPIs proposed for member European States have no SPI's on road safety management, socio economics and organisational systems. The list however, provides detail emphasis on road design attributes as well as some of the omitted characteristics by Al Haji such as SPIs on headway and use of headlights during the day. Others are child restraint use, helmet use by cyclists/moped riders and SPIs on drug impairments. Others are composite index SPIs such as speed by road type and road design characteristics, alcohol use by road type, use of vehicle restraints e.g. seatbelt use by vehicle seating position.

A comparison of the set of recommended SPIs with attributes corresponding to the five staged SPI structure including its direct or indirect impact on RTCs, the time of application and the level of its global or local relevance to the Ghanaian situation is as presented in Appendix 2.1.

From Appendix 2.1, Ghana has to some extent followed the common rules and good practices in the choice of SPIs in comparison to the global examples. However, indirect indicators are not used. Those that are not used are not accorded much premium in the Ghanaian context or are difficult to obtain data on and measured. However, on the way forward there should be research to determine those relevant for reducing the RTC problem in Ghana

2.3.2 Key Road Safety Performance Indicators (KPIs):

SPIs are required to be as low as possible for ease of data collection and management. Thus, according to Etika (2018), key SPIs must be prioritised as key performance indicators (KPIs). KPIs are recommended to have the following attributes:

- Have representation in each field of road safety study that is within each of the road safety pillars of intervention.
- Correspond to selected interventions and to the stages in the road safety process.
- Have representations for each of the layers of the pyramid.
- Correspond with ability to collect reliable data on the indicators.

Good examples of KPIs and the reasons for their selection is as presented in Appendix 2 .2.

The key challenge associated with the selected KPIs in Ghana, the lack of measuring protocols for selection within each category of road safety pillar.

2.4 TRENDS IN GLOBAL ROAD SAFETY PERFORMANCE BY SET SPIs

2.4.1 Predictions on Road Safety Before, During and After the DOA

A. Global Predictions on road safety performance before the DOA: Examples of global projections on road Safety ahead of the DOA (2011-2020) include the following:

i.　Vehicle Growth: In 2011, the approximate total of 1 billion vehicles in the World was projected to double by 2020, (UNCE 2012).

ii.　Road Traffic Crashes: Kopits and Cropper (2003) projected that the global road fatality rate from RTC's will grow by approximately 66% between 2000 and 2020.

iii.　Mathers & Loncar (2005), projected that RTC fatalities will increase on average by over 80% in low-income and middle-income countries (LMICs) and decline by almost 30% in high-income countries (HICs).

iv.　It was also predicted that by 2015, road injuries will be the leading cause of healthy life years lost by children (5-14 years).

B. Global Road Safety Performance during the DOA Implementation (2011-2020): The state of implementation of the DOA (2011-2020) by the WHO (2018) indicated a decline in safety fatalities relative to population and vehicular growth. However, the pace was regarded not to be fast enough to compensate for rapid population and increasing motorization worldwide. Therefore deaths, in global RTC was still described as remaining unacceptably high.

RTC fatalities were also estimated to be three times higher in LMICs than in HICs. This was affirmed by a survey by the African Development Bank Group (AfDB) in 2013 that despite the implementation of the DoA, RTC is still a growing problem in Africa. This is anticipated to have resulted from rapid increases in urbanization and motorization without sufficient improvement in road safety strategies.

Thus, Africa is deemed to take the highest share of the RTC burden relative to its low level of motorization at 200 per 1,000 population compared to 600 in West Europe, and over 800 in USA (WHO, 2018). Similarly, the road network density is also considered to be very low in Africa estimated at 8km/100 square km compared with USA at 67km/100 square km and West Europe at 163 km/100 square km (WHO, 2018). Other examples of trends in road safety performance at the Global level are as presented in Figures 2.2 and 2.3.

i. Road Safety performance by Population from 2008-2017: From Figure 2.2 while the Global population change was a 9% increase between 2008 to 2017, that of Africa was about 28% while that of Ghana was about 24% increase within the same period.

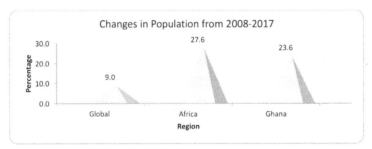

Figure 2.2: Percentage change in population between 2008 and 2017 in selected geographical regions

ii. Changes in Vehicle Registration Count for 2008 and 2017: Between 2008 and 2017, the percentage change in vehicle registration was lower at 37.4% for Ghana compared to the continental value of 43% and the global value of 54% (See Figure 2.3 for details).

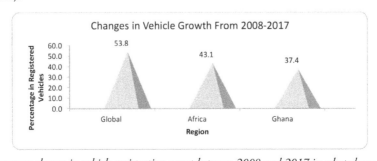

Figure 2.3: Percentage change in vehicle registration count between 2008 and 2017 in selected geographical regions

iii. Changes in Fatalities for 2008 and 2017: In terms of fatalities, the percentage change recorded at the global level at 9.8% between 2008 and 2017 was not too different from that of Ghana at 9.4% but significantly different for Africa as a whole (see Figure 2.4 for details).

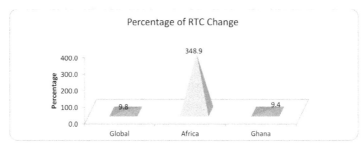

Figure 2.4: Percentage change in fatality count between 2008 and 2017 in selected geographical regions

iv. Comparison of RTC Rates: Performance on RTC rates at the global level, in Africa and in Ghana is as summarised in Table 2.4.

Table 2.4: Road safety casualty rates in selected geographical regions

Region	Global	Africa	Ghana
Fatalities/ 100,000 Population in 2010	18.5 (IHME-WHO,2013)	31 (IHME-WHO,2013)	
Fatalities/100,000 Population in 2019	16.7 (data.worldbank.org)	29 (data.worldbank.org)	26 (data.worldbank.org)
Fatalities/ 10,000 Vehicles in 2010	135	106.1 (IHME-WHO,2013)	
Fatalities/10,000 Vehicles in 2019			
Crash Cost/GDP 2010	3% (2013)	3.7% (IHME-WHO,2013)	
Crash Cost/ GDP 2019			

* Uncompleted table spaces is attributed to lack of data availability

C. Predictions on Road Safety Performance for the Future (up to 2030): Some predictions on global road safety performance up to 2030 are as summarised below:

i.   Without sustained action RTCs are predicted to become the 7th leading cause of death by 2030 (WHO Key Factsheet).

ii. Population growth is forecasted for developing countries accompanied by a rise in vehicle numbers.

iii. By 2030, RTC fatalities and injuries will be the second largest cause of healthy life years lost by men.

iv. Road fatalities in Sub-Saharan Africa is projected by the WHO to increase by 112%, from approximately 243,000 in 2015 to 514,000 in 2030. However, it is said that the correct number is unknown due to poor RTC data recording and management system in the region (Baluja R, 2009).

Thus, it is deemed that a lack of understanding of the actual road safety situation in Africa due to poor performance measurement is one of the major barriers to improving the road safety situation in Africa.

2.5 PERFORMANCE ASSSESSMENT OF ROAD SAFETY TRENDS IN GHANA

2.5.1. Ghana's Road Safety Performance Ranking by UNECA

Though Ghana did not meet the DOA (2011-2020) target of halving road traffic fatalities, it can be said that the road safety situation has improved by some margin as detailed below.

A. Ghana's Road Safety Performance by Comparison with Sixteen African Countries:

An assessment by UNECA of the performance of sixteen (16) African countries with regards to the implementation of the African Road Safety Action Plan reported in Mid-year July 2015, ranked Ghana first in good performance as presented in Figure 2.5.

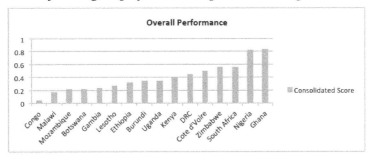

Source: ECA calculation based on survey data

Figure 2.5: Ranking of road safety performance of selected African countries

B. Summary of Trends in Road Traffic Crash Outcome in Ghana (1991-2020): *In Ghana, though the general outcomes from the RTC records indicated recognisable reduction between 2014 and 2017, it started increasing beyond that period with 2020 recording the highest crashes with a totally reversing the trend. This is mostly attributed to a number of factors captured in the body of this book.*

i. All-Crashes, Fatalities, Population and Registered Vehicles in Ghana (1991-2020): The relationship between trends in All-crashes, fatalities, injuries, population and the number of vehicle registrations indicated an increase in all the variables. However, the rate of change in the variables except for population were not constant with variations determined by year specific activities and conditions which cannot be explained by chance alone. The annual increase in population appeared to be at a faster rate compared to the annual increase in fatalities.

However, the population growth rate was comparable to that of the registered vehicles until a drop in 2011 in the latter which started increasing again up to 2020. Casualties were generally higher than fatalities and All-crashes but both casualties and All-crashes had weak upward trends. The rate of change also varied with time (see Figure 2.6).

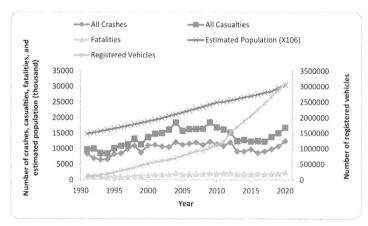

Figure 2.6: Count of crashes, casualties, fatalities, population and registered vehicles from 1990 to 2020

ii. Rate of Change in All-Crashes, Fatalities, Population and Registered Vehicles (1991-2020): From the results presented in Table 2.5, the rate of population growth and the rate of vehicle growth in the country could be contributing to the increasing rate of casualties in the country. Thus, there is need to put in measures to ensure that the rate of vehicular growth is commensurate with safe traffic systems as required. Also, the percentage change in the above variables had All-crashes recording the lowest value at 49% increment. This was followed by All-casualties at 73.5%. Population increased by 105.2% whilst fatalities recorded 174.8% with vehicle growth recording the highest of 2249.6%.

From the results, it can be inferred that though crashes increased at a relatively lower rate there were higher records of fatalities which implies that crashes are becoming more fatal. This could be partly be attributed to poor post-crash response and poor medical care which reduces survival rates.

Table 2.5: Rate of change in crashes and casualties

	All Crashes		All Casualties		Fatalities		Estimated Population (X106)		Registered Vehicles	
Year	Freq.	Annual % change	Freq.	Annual % change	Freq.	Annual % change	Freq.	Annual % change	Freq.	Annual % change
1991	8370		9693		920		14821		132051	
1992	6922	-17.3	10030	3.5	914	-0.7	15222	2.7	137966	4.5
1993	6467	-6.6	8578	-14.5	901	-1.4	15634	2.7	157782	14.4
1994	6584	1.8	8488	-1.0	824	-8.5	16056	2.7	193198	22.4
1995	8313	26.3	10132	19.4	1026	24.5	16491	2.7	234962	21.6
1996	8488	2.1	10952	8.1	1049	2.2	16937	2.7	297475	26.6
1997	9918	16.8	11448	4.5	1015	-3.2	17395	2.7	340913	14.6
1998	10996	10.9	13205	15.3	1419	39.8	17865	2.7	393255	15.4
1999	8763	-20.3	11439	-13.4	1237	-12.8	18349	2.7	458182	16.5
2000	11087	26.5	13747	20.2	1437	16.2	18845	2.7	511063	11.5
2001	11293	1.9	14838	7.9	1660	15.5	19328	2.6	567780	11.1
2002	10715	-5.1	15077	1.6	1665	0.3	19811	2.5	613153	8.0
2003	10542	-1.6	16185	7.3	1716	3.1	20508	3.5	643824	5.0
2004	12175	15.5	18445	14.0	2186	27.4	21093	2.9	703372	9.2

	All Crashes		All Casualties		Fatalities		Estimated Population (X106)		Registered Vehicles	
Year	Freq.	Annual % change	Freq.	Annual % change	Freq.	Annual % change	Freq.	Annual % change	Freq.	Annual % change
2005	11320	-7.0	15813	-14.3	1779	-18.6	21694	2.8	767067	9.1
2006	11668	3.1	16348	3.4	1856	4.3	22294	2.8	841314	9.7
2007	12038	3.2	16416	0.4	2043	10.1	22911	2.8	922748	9.7
2008	11214	-6.8	16455	0.2	1938	-5.1	23544	2.8	942000	2.1
2009	12299	9.7	18496	12.4	2237	15.4	24196	2.8	1030000	9.3
2010	11506	-6.4	16904	-8.6	1986	-11.2	24865	2.8	1122722	9.0
2011	10887	-5.4	16219	-4.1	2199	10.7	25099	0.9	1225754	9.2
2012	12083	11.0	15241	-6.0	2240	1.9	25510	1.6	1532080	25.0
2013	9200	-23.9	12509	-17.9	1898	-15.3	26004	1.9	1708958	11.5
2014	9152	-0.5	12863	2.8	1836	-3.3	26505	1.9	1885836	10.4
2015	9796	7.0	12367	-3.9	1802	-1.9	26942	1.6	2062714	9.4
2016	8651	-11.7	12522	1.3	2084	15.6	27424	1.8	2256180	9.4
2017	9133	5.6	12339	-1.5	1823	-12.5	28027	2.2	2467787	9.4
2018	9840	7.7	13837	12.1	2020	10.8	28413	1.4	2679394	8.6
2019	10808	9.8	15094	9.1	2073	2.6	29600	4.2	2891001	7.9
2020	12484	15.5	16820	11.4	2528	21.9	30419	2.8	3102608	7.3
Average		2.1		2.4		4.4		2.5		11.6
1991-2020		49.2		73.5		174.8		105.2		2249.6

iii. Who Dies in Ghana: In Ghana, road traffic crashes affect cross cutting population groups and an overview of a compilation of news headlines on reported casualties and fatalities are as presented Figure 2.7.

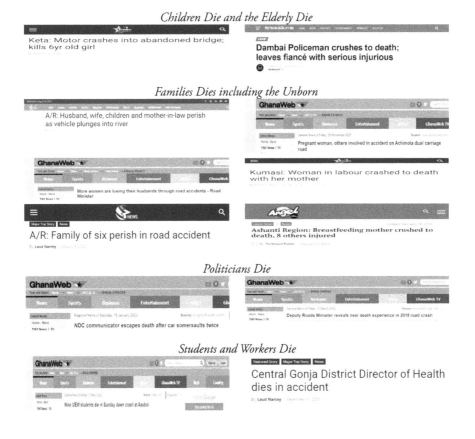

Children Die and the Elderly Die

Keta: Motor crashes into abandoned bridge; kills 6yr old girl

Dambai Policeman crushes to death; leaves fiancé with serious injurious

Families Dies including the Unborn

A/R: Husband, wife, children and mother-in-law perish as vehicle plunges into river

Pregnant woman, others involved in accident on Achimota dual carriage road

More women are losing their husbands through road accidents - Roads Minister

Kumasi: Woman in labour crashed to death with her mother

A/R: Family of six perish in road accident

Ashanti Region: Breastfeeding mother crushed to death, 8 others injured

Politicians Die

NDC communicator escapes death after car somersaults twice

Deputy Roads Minister reveals near death experience in 2018 road crash

Students and Workers Die

Nine UEW students die in Sunday dawn crash at Asuboi

Central Gonja District Director of Health dies in accident

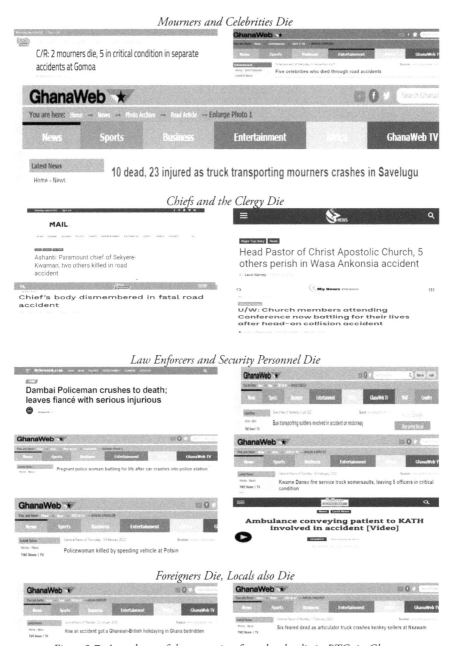

Figure 2.7: A catalogue of the categories of people who die in RTCs in Ghana

C. Trends in All-Crashes in Ghana

i. Relationship between crashes and years of incidence (1990-2020): The number of All-Crashes recorded in 2020 appears to be the highest ever with a substantial deviation from the expected value.

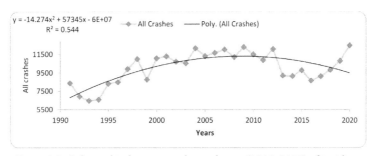

Figure 2.8: Relationship between crashes and years (1990-2020) of incidence

D. Trends in Road Traffic Crash Fatalities in Ghana

i. Relationship between Fatalities and Years of Incidence (1990-2020): The rate of change in fatalities from 1993 to 2010 was about 70% with a decline in percentage change from 2013 to 2015 but with 2020 recording the highest fatalities ever.

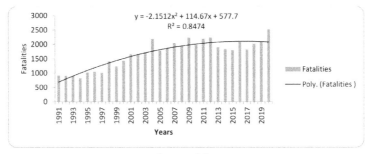

Figure 2.9: Fatality trend from 1991 to 2020

ii. Fatality trend from 2010 to 2020: Fatality trend, between 2010 and 2020 (the period for the implementation of the DOA) appeared to have reduced at a rate of about 24 fatalities per annum (see Figure 2.10).

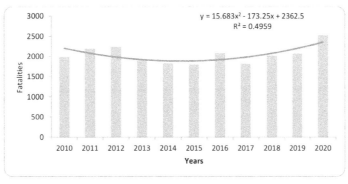

Figure 2.10: Fatality Trend from 2010 to 2020

iii. Fatalities per 100,000 Population: The rate of increase in fatalities per 100,000 population was about 21% from 1991 to 2020 compared to that of the population was about 53%

(see Figure 2.11). This implies that on the average, fatalities per population (in 100,000) will likely drop in subsequent years if safety interventions are sustained.

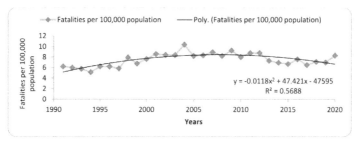

Figure 2.11: Trend in fatalities per 100,000 population (1990 -2020)

iv. Fatalities per 100 Crashes: Fatalities per 100 crashes followed a linear relationship in years (see Figure 2.12). It also increased at a rate of about 2.2% in every 10 years as well as at about 0.35% for the whole period.

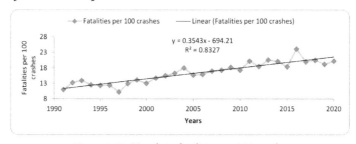

Figure 2.12: Trends in fatalities per 100 crashes

E. Trends in Road Traffic Crash Casualties in Ghana

i. Distribution of RTC Victims by Injury Type 2001-2017: In Ghana, between the years 2001 and 2017 out of those who suffered casualties from RTCs, more people sustained injuries at about 51%. About 37% suffered injuries that involved hospitalisation. This requires health facilities for the treatment of minor injuries to be made available on all RTC prone roads.

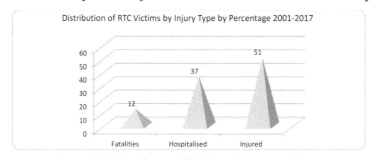

Figure 2.13: Distribution of RTC by injury type in Ghana

ii. Relationship between casualties and years of incidence (1990-2020): The rate of change in casualties per year was not constant especially from 1993 to 2010 and it was also very high at an average of about 423% (see Figure 2.14). The percentage change had a downward trend from 2010 and 2017 before starting to increase again up to 2020. The number of casualties recorded in 2020 was the highest since 2011 and this calls for increased and sustained efforts in road safety interventions for good outcomes.

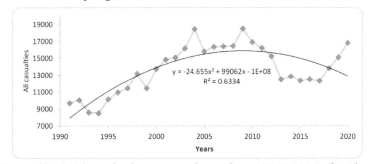

Figure of 2.14: Relationship between casualties and years (1990-2020) of incidence

iii. Trends in Fatalities per 100 Casualties: The trend in fatalities per 100 casualties was linear (see Figure 2.15) and it increased at an average of about 2.2% in every 10 years with an average the rate of change increasing by about 22% from 1990 to 2020.

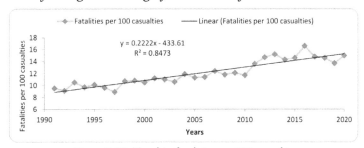

Figure 2.15: Trend in fatalities per 100 casualties

iv. Percentage change in casualty injury for 2011 to 2020 relative to 2010 records: Using 2010 values as reference to all values recorded after 2010, there was a consistent decrease in the incidences of all casualties and slightly injured (see Figure 2.16). Percentage change in the seriously injured was virtually negative until 2018 where it began to recorded positive change over the 2010 value. The percentage changes in fatalities exhibited a cyclical pattern until 2017 after which there was a sustained increase. Within the period, crashes became more fatal and also recorded much more serious casualties compared to minor ones.

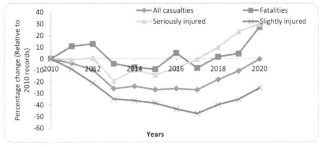

Figure 2.16: Percentage change in casualty injury for 2011 to 2020 relative to 2010 records

v. Trends of estimated population from 1991 to 2020: There was a constant increase of 53% (in millions) in estimated population every year since 1991 (see Figure 2.17).

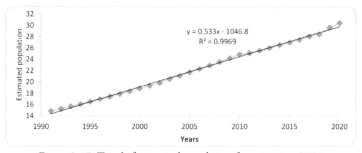

Figure 2.17: Trend of estimated population from 1991 to 2020

F. Trends in RTC by Vehicular Attributes in Ghana

i. Relationship between Registered Vehicles and Years (1990 -2020): There was a consistent growth in annual registered vehicles (see Figure 2.18) and this is expected to continue at a rapid pace.

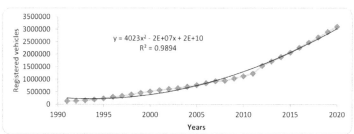

Figure 2.18: Relationship between registered vehicles and years (1990-2020) of incidence

ii. Distribution of types of vehicles involved in crashes: Cars have the highest frequency in crashes, compared to the other vehicle types. Buses and HGV were the next most important source of crashes, following cars. It is interesting to note that Motor cycle and tricycle crashes which used to be among the least in the 1990s was about the same as that of HGV in 2020 (see Figure 2.19).

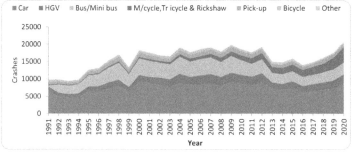

Figure 2.19: Distribution of types of vehicles involved in crashes

iii. Trend in Fatalities per 10,000 Vehicles: The rate of change in fatalities per 10,000 vehicles was about 2.3% (see Figure 2.20). Per the trend line, it is also expected to increase at a very small rate in subsequent years.

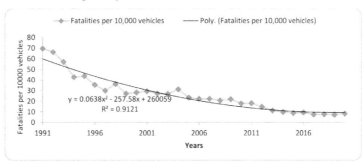

Figure 2.20: Trend in fatalities per 10,000 vehicles

G. Trends in RTC by Road User Class in Ghana

i. Annual Distribution of Fatalities by Road User Class: Major sources of fatalities includes buses, followed by pedestrians and then cars (see Figure 2.21). Bus fatalities were much higher between 2001 and 2009. Two and three wheelers which used to have much lower fatalities started increasing substantially after 2004. As at 2020, fatalities due to two and three wheelers exceeded all the other sources. This signifies a need to focus on interventions that will reduce increasing fatalities from three and two wheelers.

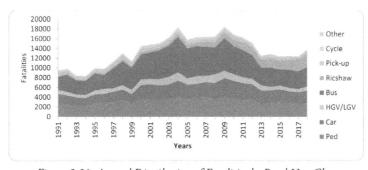

Figure 2.21: Annual Distribution of Fatalities by Road User Class

ii. Fatality Trends by Road User Class: Fatality records, expressed as a percentage of the 1991 values for all the road user types were stable and comparable until 1999 after which some changes emerged. For Pedestrian, Car, HGV/LGV and bus, there was a little steep change in pattern over their respective patterns prior to 2000. The most striking case had to do with two and three wheelers which exhibited a dramatic increase with years (see Figure 2.22).

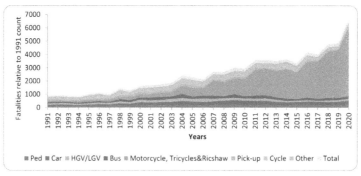

Figure 2.22: Fatality trend (1991-2020) by road user class

iii. Trends in Pedestrian fatalities 1990-2018: Trends in pedestrian fatalities was quadratic with the model explaining about 84% of the variation in pedestrian fatalities (see Figure 2.23). The percentage in pedestrian fatality incidence peaked in 2009 and 2012 before decreasing between the years 2013 to 2018. However, it started increasing again from 2019 to 2020. The rate of change in pedestrian fatality from 1993 to 2020 was 28%. See Figure 2.24 for examples of marked and unmarked pedestrian crossing road sections in Ghana.

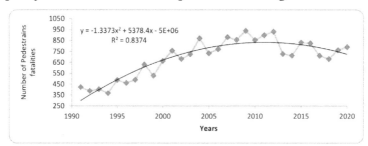

Figure 2.23: Pedestrian fatalities trend (1991-2020)

Figure 2.24: Examples of pedestrian crossing sections in Ghana (Source NRSA)

iv. Trends in Car Fatalities 1990-2020: The trend in car fatalities has been undulating with an increase from 1990 up to 2009 before a decrease in 2015 and a rise again in 2019 peaking in 2020 with the rate of change from 1993 to 2020 being 9.5% (see Figure 2.25).

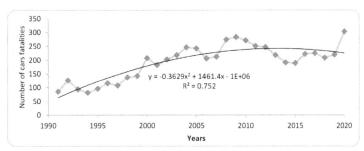

Figure 2.25: Car fatalities trend (1990-2020)

v. Trend in Fatalities by Buses and Minibuses 1990-2020: The trend exhibited in the data was quadratic showing an expected further drop in numbers in subsequent years. From 1990 there was a rise in bus fatalities which started decreasing up to 2015 before rising again up to 2020 with the rate of change from 1993 to 2020 being 12.7% as indicated in see Figure 2.26. See Figure 2.28 for examples of buses in Ghana involved in RTCs.

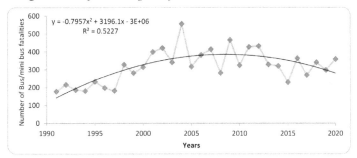

Figure 2.26: Bus fatalities trend (1990-2020)

vi. Trends in Fatalities by Heavy Goods Vehicle (HGV)/ Light Goods Vehicles (LGV) 1990-2020: The trend exhibited in the data was quadratic showing an expected further drop in numbers in subsequent years. The recent numbers in HGV/LGV fatalities which is slightly lower than the previous one is also about 52% reduction in the highest numbers ever attained in 2006 with the highest of 270 being recorded in 2005 before decreasing to a lowest of 85 in 2017 which started increasing again from 2018 to 2020. The rate of change from 1993 to 2020 was about 6.2% (see Figure 2.27). See examples of HGVs in Ghana involved in RTCs in Figure 2.28.

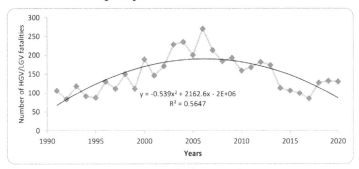

Figure 2.27: HGV/LGV fatalities trend (1990-2020)

Figure 2.28: Examples of HGVs in Ghana involved in RTCs (Source NRSA)

vii. Trend in Fatalities by Motorcycles and Tricycles 1990-2020: The trend equation explains about 96% of the variation in fatalities. Fatalities due to two and three wheelers in 2020 was the highest ever with about 43% increase over the previous value and a consistent increase peaking in 2020 at 829. The rate of change from 1993 to 2020 was 3.8%. Based on the trend line, which is quadratic, Motorcycle and tricycle and two and three wheelers fatalities are expected to increase in subsequent years as indicated in Figure 2.29. See Figure 2.32 for examples of motorcycles in Ghana involved in RTCs.

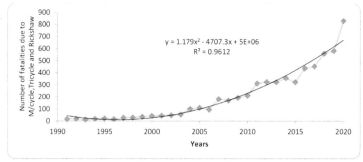

Figure 2.29: Motor cycle and tricycle and two and three wheelers fatalities trend (1991-2020)

Figure 2.30: Examples of motorcycles in Ghana involved in RTCs (Source: NRSA)

viii. Trend in Fatalities by Pick-ups 1990-2020: The trend in pick-up fatalities follows a second order polynomial. In respect to fatalities from pick-ups, the numbers recorded in 2020 is the highest since 2010 and about 125% increase over the previous value but the nature of the trend line suggest possible reduction in fatalities in subsequent years. The rate of change from 1993 to 2020 was 0.45% (see Figure 2.31).

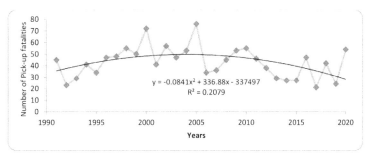

Figure 2.31: Pick-up fatalities trend (1991-2020)

ix. Trend in Fatalities by Cycles (1990-2020): Fatalities due to cycles in 2020 was a slight reduction over that of the previous year but it is expected that cycle fatality incidence will continue to reduce further in subsequent years. The rate of change from 1993 to 2020 was 3.8% (see Figure 2.32).

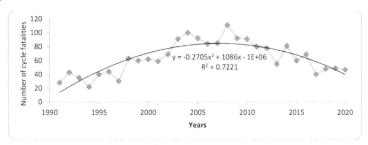

Figure 2.32: Cycle fatalities trend (1991-2020)

x. Percentage Change in Other Road User Fatalities, 2020 Compared to 2010: There was no clear trend in fatalities due to other road user crashes. The rate of change from 1993 to 2020 was 0.15%. The fatalities recorded in 2020 was about 113% increase over that of the previous year. (See Figure 2.33).

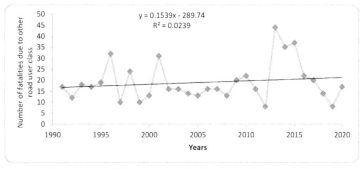

Figure 2.33: Other road user fatalities trend (1990-2018)

xi. Percentage Change in Road User Fatalities-1991 Compared to 2018: There was a percentage decrease in road user fatalities between 1991 and 2018 by a margin ranging between 18% and 44% for all road user classes with the exception of two/three wheelers which increased by about 124%. (See Figure 2.34).

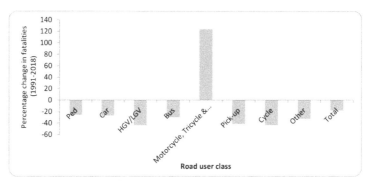

Figure 2.34: Percentage Change in Road User Fatalities, 2018 Compared to 1991

xii. Percentage Change in Road User Fatalities, 2020 Compared to 2010: The percentage change, from 2010 to 2020, in road user fatalities was positive but small for car and bus on one hand and large (166%) for two and three wheelers. Each of the remaining road user classes had decreased fatalities by a margin between 7.5% and 48%. (See Figure 2.35).

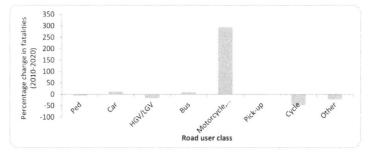

Figure 2.35: Percentage change in Road User Fatalities, 2020 Compared to 2010

2.5.2 Distribution of RTC by Cultural and Structural Indicators

A. Environmental Factors

i. Trends in fatalities by Road Environment: The percentage fatalities, relative to 1991 values, was consistently higher in the urban environments than the non-urban environments (See Figure 2.36). The gap between the two environments started widening after 2011.

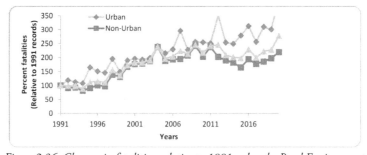

Figure 2.36: Changes in fatalities, relative to 1991 values by Road Environment

ii. Distribution of Fatalities by Sex for all Road User Groups: Gender played a very important role in the fatality incidences from 1991 to 2020. The trend for males and females' groups quadratic. Males appeared to be high risk group compared to females. The 2020 incidence among the males was the highest ever whilst that of the females was only a small percentage (1%) increase over the previous year's record and constituted about 75% of the highest ever recorded among the females. (See Figure 2.37).

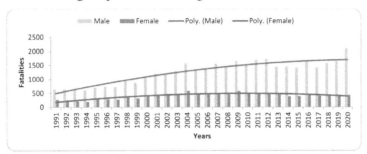

Figure 2.37: Annual Distribution of Fatalities by Sex

iii. Percentage Change in Annual Distribution of Fatalities by Sex: The percentage change of fatalities relative to 1991 values for females was consistently lower than that of males. Though the percentage change in fatalities with respect to gender was almost always positive after 1997, the gap between that of the males and females started widening from 2004. (See Figure 2.38).

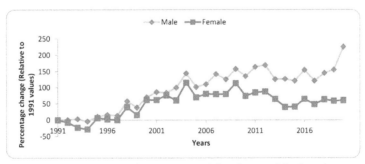

Figure 2.38: Percentage change in annual distribution of fatalities by sex

iv. Annual Distribution of Fatalities by Road User Age Group: Fatalities were generally higher for ages 26 to 35 years. Two age groups (16-25, 36-45) had similar distribution patterns. The lowest incidence occurred among the oldest age group (over 65 years), followed by less than five-year-olds and 56- to 65-year-olds. The fatalities in the age group 6-15 were similar in pattern with that of 16-25 until the year 2005 after which it started to drop to be among the lowest in 2020. Fatalities among the age group 46-55 was between that of 0-5 and 16-25. (See Figure 2.39).

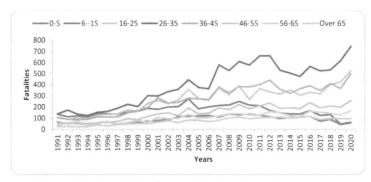

Figure 2.39: Annual distribution of fatalities by road user age group

v. Percentage Change in Road User Age Groups, 2010 Compared to 2020: The percentage change in road user fatalities between 2010 and 2020 by age was positive for the ages between 16 and 65, with the highest of 95% change occurring in the 16-25 age group. The change in that of the over 65-year-olds though negative, was very small. The two age groups, 0-5 and 6-15, respectively had a reduced incidence of 57% and 71% respectively (See Figure 2.40).

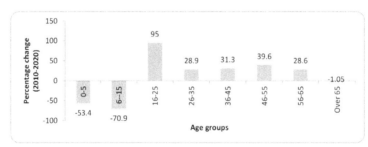

Figure 2.40: Percentage change in road user age groups, 2020 Compared to 2010

2.6 IMPACT OF ROAD TRAFFIC CRASHES ON THE NATIONAL ECONOMY

Road traffic cost components constitute a significant percentage of national GDP. This is incurred from the breakdown of cost on damaged property; workplace productivity loss; household productivity cost; medical cost, traffic congestion and other costs. Thus, if good investments are made to improve road safety, the benefits will spread throughout the economy. It is estimated that fatal and nonfatal crash injuries will cost the world economy approximately $1.8 trillion from 2015 –2030. That is equivalent to a yearly tax of 0.12% on global gross domestic product (GDP), (WHO, 2009).

In Ghana, macro-economic studies have revealed that the country spends up to US$230 million every year treating injuries and traffic fatalities. The study established that the cost of RTC to the Ghanaian economy is estimated at about 1.6 % of the GDP. About 68% of the

RTC cost components relates to loss of quality of life whilst (32%) relates to economic costs (BRRI, 2004). The same study further defined RTC cost components as property damage (16%); Administration (8%); Lost Output (43%); Medical Cost (5%); and Human cost made up of pain, grief and suffering (28%). (See Figure 2.41) for some other estimates. The cost of RTCs on the economy thus in turn affect society at large, thus the statement in Figure: 2.42 cannot be overemphasised.

Figure 2.41: Cost of RTCs in Ghana

Ghana News Agency   Home   Social   Business   Education   Entertainment   Science   Health   Politics

Road safety promotes national development- President Akufo-Addo

Figure 2.42: Impact of RTC on Development

2.7 CONCLUSION

The analysis on vital safety performance indicators for Ghana provides enough evidence to establish the fact that there has been consistent variability by yearly trends and patterns in the country's road safety performance. The trends indicate that some years recorded better performance than others. Thus, the subsequent chapters of this book, has discusses the essential factors influencing road safety performance for better outcomes. The discussions draw on theoretical and conceptual background issues, recommended international standards and regulations, country background, country policies and regulation, implemented strategies, resultant effects, challenges and counter interventions. These factors are used to determine Ghana's road safety performance so far in comparison with what is required and what can be done towards improved performance for the way forward.

Appendix 2.1: Recommended Master list of macro road safety indicators and dimensions in Literature and Availability in Ghana

Core Dimensions and Indicators	Type	Availability in Ghana
Road User Behaviour:		
% of seat belt use	Intermediate Outcome	This is done by special commissioned studies on periodic basis without a set schedule
% of crash helmet use	Intermediate Outcome	Ditto
% of children <12 years (correctly) sitting in a child's seat in the front or rear seat of a car	Intermediate Outcome	Not Available
% of all drivers exceeding speed limits	Intermediate Outcome	Speed limit is checked by the police but records on number of defaulting drivers is not available
% of surveyed (car) drivers exceeding the speed limit on various road types	Intermediate Outcome	This is done by special commissioned studies on periodic basis without a set schedule
Minimum age for driving	Intermediate Outcome	Available
% of drivers with valid driver's license	Intermediate Outcome	Available
% of motorcyclists with valid rider's license	Intermediate Outcome	Available
Consumption of alcohol per capita (litres)	Intermediate Outcome	Not Available
% of drivers with alcohol	Intermediate Outcome	This is done by special commissioned studies on periodic basis without a set schedule
% of drivers above the legal BAC limit in police checks	Intermediate Outcome	This is done by special commissioned studies on periodic basis without a set schedule
% of surveyed (car) drivers disrespecting the alcohol limit	Intermediate Outcome	This is done by special commissioned studies on periodic basis without a set schedule
% of fatal RTCs in which someone was drinking and driving	Final Outcome	Not available
% of fatalities resulting from RTCs with ≥1 driver impaired by alcohol	Final Outcome	Not available
% of drivers with drugs concentration > legal limit	Final Outcome	Not available
% of fatalities resulting from RTCs with ≥1 driver impaired by drugs	Final Outcome	Not available
Average (free flow) daytime speed per road type and vehicle type	Intermediate Outcome	This is done by special commissioned studies on periodic basis without a set schedule
Average (free flow) speed per road type and vehicle type at night	Intermediate Outcome	This is done by special commissioned studies on periodic basis without a set schedule
Variation in speed per road type and vehicle type	Intermediate Outcome	This is done by special commissioned studies on periodic basis without a set schedule
Median (or other percentile) of the set of observed speeds divided by the speed limit of the road class	Intermediate Outcome	This is done by special commissioned studies on periodic basis without a set schedule
Median of the set of absolute differences between each of the observed speeds in the road class and the median of all observed speeds divided by the median of the set of observed speeds	Intermediate Outcome	Not available
Existence of a law – fully or partially – obligating the use of daytime running lights	Intermediate Outcome	Not available
Total usage rate of daytime running lights	Intermediate Outcome	Not available
Usage rate of daytime running lights per road type and vehicle type	Intermediate Outcome	Not available
% of drivers with an inappropriate headway on various road types	Intermediate Outcome	Not available
% of motorists exceeding allowable driving hours	Intermediate Outcome	This is done by special commissioned studies on periodic basis without a set schedule

Core Dimensions and Indicators	Type	Availability in Ghana
Number of pedestrian deaths by frequent locations	Final Outcome	This is done by special commissioned studies on periodic basis without a set schedule
Vehicle Safety:		
Index of national crashworthiness (vehicle crash performance)	Intermediate Outcome	Not Available but possible to estimate
Distribution of vehicles by age: % of new cars	Intermediate Outcome	Not Available but possible to estimate
Mass classes of car fleet (%)	Intermediate Outcome	Available
Composition of the vehicle fleet: % of cars, vans, buses, trucks and motorcycles in total # of registered vehicles	Intermediate Outcome	Available
Registration of vehicles by vehicle type	Intermediate Outcome	Available
% of new cars obtaining 1, 2, 3, 4 or 5 stars respectively in the total # of new passenger cars	Intermediate Outcome	Not available
% of vehicles with certified road worthiness per annum	Intermediate Outcome	Not Available but possible to estimate
% of vehicles with insurance cover per annum	Intermediate Outcome	Not Available but possible to estimate
% of motorcycles with certified road worthiness per annum	Intermediate Outcome	Not Available
% of motorcycles with insurance cover per annum	Intermediate Outcome	Not Available
Road Safety:		
% of roads paved	Intermediate Outcome	The statistics is available at the road agency level and with the MRH
Total paved roads (km) per capita/vehicles	Intermediate Outcome	Total paved roads available but not per capital vehicles
Total motorways/freeways (km) per capita/vehicles	Intermediate Outcome	Not Available but possible to estimate
Km of motorway per km of paved road	Intermediate Outcome	The statistics is available at the road agency level and with the MRH
Road (network / intersection) density (km/1000 km2)	Intermediate Outcome	Not available
Share of network length per road type	Intermediate Outcome	Available
Share of intersections per road type	Intermediate Outcome	Not available
% of road network not fulfilling safety design standards	Intermediate Outcome	Not available
% of roads with audited designs	Intermediate Outcome	Not Available but possible to estimate
% of roads ranked using iRAP ratings or inventoried for road safety features	Intermediate Outcome	Not Available
% of road length with which road safety feature	Intermediate Outcome	Not available
% of road length with road shoulders	Intermediate Outcome	Not available
% of road length with signalised intersections	Intermediate Outcome	Not available
% of road length with a wide median or median barrier	Intermediate Outcome	Not available
% of road length with a wide obstacle-free zone or roadside barrier	Intermediate Outcome	Not available
% of road length with facilities for separation of slow vulnerable traffic and other motorized traffic	Intermediate Outcome	Not available

Core Dimensions and Indicators	Type	Availability in Ghana
% of high-risk and critical road length dualised	Intermediate Outcome	Not Available but possible to estimate
Number and type of RTC caused by road condition by road category	Outcome	Available by road type and not by road condition
National expenditure on roads (engineering/maintenance) % of GDP	Social Costs	Expenditure on road development and maintenance available but by % of GDP will have to be estimated
National expenditure on roads (safety measures) % of GDP	Social Costs	Not Available but possible to estimate
National expenditure on roads per total vehicles	Social Costs	Not Available but possible to estimate
% of road network satisfying the safety design standard expenditure on roads as GDP share	Intermediate Outcome	Not available
Socioeconomic Indicators:		
% of urban population	Safety Input Measures	Available (GLSS)
% of 15-24 years old in the total population	Safety Input Measures	Available (GLSS)
Population density (people per km2)	Safety Input Measures	Available (GLSS)
Life expectancy (years)	Safety Input Measures	Available (GLSS)
Illiteracy: % of persons over 15 years unable to read	Safety Input Measures	Available (GLSS)
% of people in unemployment	Social Costs	Available (GLSS)
Number of lost work- days	Social Costs	Not available
Gross National Product (GNP) per capita	Social Costs	Available
Expenditure on health care as GDP share	Social Costs	Available
Post-Crash Response and Care:		
Population per physician	Intermediate Outcome	Available (GLSS)
Number of EMS staff in service (according to categories)	Intermediate Outcome	Not Available but possible to estimate
% of physicians and paramedics out of the total EMS medical staff	Intermediate Outcome	Not available
Population per EMS staff	Intermediate Outcome	Not available
Number of EMS stations	Intermediate Outcome	Not Available but possible to estimate
Number of EMS transportation units in service (according to categories)	Intermediate Outcome	Not available
EMS transportation units per 10,000 citizens	Intermediate Outcome	Not available
% of BLSU, MICU and helicopters / planes out of the total EMS units	Intermediate Outcome	Not available
EMS stations per 10,000 citizens	Intermediate Outcome	Not available
EMS vehicles per 100 km road length of total public roads	Intermediate Outcome	Not available
EMS stations per 100 km length of rural public roads	Intermediate Outcome	Not available
Total number of beds in permanent medical facilities (according to categories)	Intermediate Outcome	Not Available but possible to estimate
% of beds in certified trauma centres and trauma departments of hospitals out of the total	Intermediate Outcome	Not available
Population per hospital beds	Intermediate Outcome	Available

Core Dimensions and Indicators	Type	Availability in Ghana
Population per trauma care beds	Intermediate Outcome	Not available
Number of the total trauma care beds per 10,000 citizens	Intermediate Outcome	Not available
% of calls to emergency medical services due to a RTC	Intermediate Outcome	Not Available but possible to estimate
Average arrival time of emergency medical services at the RTC scene	Intermediate Outcome	Variable by emergency agency
% of EMS responses which meet the demand for response time; to be accompanied by a data item "The demand for a response time, min".	Intermediate Outcome	Not available
Share of road casualties treated in intensive care units	Intermediate Outcome	Not available
Average acute care days related to RTCs in hospital	Intermediate Outcome	Not available
Average length of stay in the hospital after a RTC	Intermediate Outcome	Not available but possible to estimate
Share of road casualties who died during hospitalization	Final Outcome	Estimated by the Police/BRRI
% of fatalities at RTC sites and % at hospitals	Final Outcome	Estimated by the Police/BRRI
Traffic Risk:		
Number of road crashes	Final Outcome	Available in the road traffic crash statistics data base in Ghana compiled by the BRRI
Number of road crashes resulting in deaths	Final Outcome	Available in the road traffic crash statistics data base in Ghana compiled by the BRRI
Number of road crashes resulting in serious and minor injuries	Final Outcome	Available in the road traffic crash statistics data base in Ghana compiled by the BRRI
Fatality rate (per vehicles-km)	Final Outcome	Not Available but possible to estimate
Fatality rate (per person-km)	Final Outcome	Not Available but possible to estimate
Fatalities per vehicles	Final Outcome	Available in the road traffic crash statistics data base in Ghana compiled by the BRRI
Fatalities per paved road	Final Outcome	Not available
Severity index (number of fatalities per total casualties)	Final Outcome	Not available
% of fatalities trend (increase or reduction) over time	Final Outcome	Information is available from 1999 to 2020 by BRRI
% of serious injuries trend (increase or reduction) over time	Final Outcome	Information is available from 1999 to 2020 by BRRI
Personal Risk:		
Fatality rate per population	Final Outcome	Not Available but possible to estimate
Fatality rate per population age	Final Outcome	Available in the road traffic crash statistics data base in Ghana compiled by the BRRI
Traffic Police and Enforcement:		
The annual number of random breath tests (per vehicles)	Intermediate Outcome	This is done by special commissioned studies on periodic basis without a set schedule
% of drivers failing random breath tests	Intermediate Outcome	This is done by special commissioned studies on periodic basis without a set schedule
The annual number of speed-violation notices (per vehicles)	Intermediate Outcome	Not available
% of all drivers exceeding speed limits in police checks	Intermediate Outcome	This is done by special commissioned studies on periodic basis without a set schedule
The annual number of seat belt violation notices (per vehicles)	Intermediate Outcome	This is done by special commissioned studies on periodic basis without a set schedule
% of drivers violating seat belt use in police checks	Intermediate Outcome	This is done by special commissioned studies on periodic basis without a set schedule
The technical means/equipment available to the traffic police	Intermediate Outcome	Not available

Core Dimensions and Indicators	Type	Availability in Ghana
% change in coverage of automated enforcement	Intermediate Outcome	Not available
% of prosecutions, convictions, fines as against arrests	Intermediate Outcome	Not Available but possible to estimate

Organisational Structure:

How far the cooperation between the key bodies is	Safety Output Measures	In place but not measured
The development of the 'National Road Safety Council' and NGO's	Safety Output Measures	Established
The cooperation between the key stakeholders and NGO's	Safety Output Measures	In place but not measured
The funds level spent on road safety measures	Safety Output Measures	Available for NRSA but not that of other stakeholder entities is not known
Legislations level, data collection level and statistics	Safety Output Measures	Established
Inspection of vehicles	Safety Output Measures	Compiled by DVLA
Number of driving licenses delivered per total vehicles fleet	Safety Output Measures	Not Available but possible to estimate
Number of national campaigns in the last three years	Safety Output Measures	Not Available but possible to estimate

Appendix 2.2: Summary of good examples of global KPIs

1. Unit of Measurement	Description	Details	Advantages	Disadvantages	EU Example	Applicability in Ghana
Road Safety Management						
Economic Development (GDP)	-Measures the economic and social costs of RTCs the economy	-RTC cost as % of country GDP	-Measures cost of RTC on economy and the Losses caused by RTCs	Cost of Human Life is difficult to measure with accuracy	-Not used as KPI in Europe	There has been a one-off estimation but it is not considered as KPI
Total cost of crashes for society;	-Measures cost of fatalities and serious injuries -Measures loss of life, productive working hours, pain/grief, damage to property, health costs, etc. associated with RTCs	-Medical cost per injured person; Costs of crashes for employers (absence, replacement, …); Average financial compensation for traffic victims % of traffic victims who stopped working	Measures cost of RTC on economy	-Cost of Human Life is difficult to measure with accuracy	Number lost work days, Insurance Claims, Value of Property	There has been a one-off estimation but it is not considered as KPI
Country Population	-Relative figure showing ratio of fatalities to population to determine the level of road safety risk per population threshold	Fatalities per 100,000 population	-Shows the impact of road traffic crashes on human population. -Useful for international comparisons	-Road safety intervention capacity and capability differ by country so it does not provide common platform for comparison -Some population estimates might not be accurate	Number of deaths per 100,000 population	Applied in Ghana for Global comparisons

1. Unit of Measurement	Description	Details	Advantages	Disadvantages	EU Example	Applicability in Ghana
-Crash Related KPIs	Absolute figures indicating the number of people injured in road traffic crashes to determine frequency of occurrence of road safety crashes. -To determine the number of deaths from such crashes. Trends in RTC records usually expressed in terms of severity : minor, serious, permanent disability, fatality	Crash ID, date, impact type, crash data, crash type, impact type, Location, crash severity eg. Number of road crashes, Number of road crashes resulting in deaths, Number of road crashes resulting in injuries	-Report on Crash Data and Road Safety Elements are used to check the effectiveness of practices taken in response to each practice objective -Useful for planning for RTC interventions and for comparison with best practices where they have been achieved relevance of implemented activities to the priorities	Not very useful for making comparisons across different contexts due to differences in definitions. Road safety intervention capacity and capability differ by country so it does not provide equal platform for comparison -There is also a challenge of under reporting	Number of road crashes, Number of road crashes resulting in deaths -Number of road crashes resulting in injuries, Number of road crashes resulting in injuries	-Number of Crashes -Number of Casualties -Fatality Rate -Number of injuries -Severity Index
7. Policy and Organisational Performance	-Vision, Target, National RS plan, Lead agency, dedicated budget, monitoring attitudes & behaviour	-For assessing basics of road safety management Policy & plans as well as programme evaluations	-Determines level of compliance with Global standards.	Facilitates the implementation and updating of the plan or programme based on monitoring	Not used as KPI in Europe	Not used as KPI in Ghana

Safer Roads:

1. Unit of Measurement	Description	Details	Advantages	Disadvantages	EU Example	Applicability in Ghana
-Number of accidents caused by road defects	-Number of RTC prone roads with unprotected road-user risk	-Major roads with appropriate safety ratings -Percentage of roads with appropriate iRAP safety ratings	-Requires accurate records causative factors by road defects	-Achieve safer roads because safer roads includes general improvements, maintenance and targeted investments in road infrastructure.	-Number of accidents caused by road defects	-Percentage of high risk roads

1. Unit of Measurement	Description	Details	Advantages	Disadvantages	EU Example	Applicability in Ghana
Safety Features on Roads	-Functional class, type, condition, surface type, junction, junction controls, road curve, road segment grade, speed limit, obstacles, facilities for vulnerable road users, roadside built environment, Shoulder sealing	Percentage of roads in good condition -Percentage of high speed roads with a median barrier -Total length of cycle network (separated from main road) -Proportion of urban roads with sidewalks	-To create safer roads and more forgiving roadsides to minimise the impact of human error on road trauma	-High costs of road assessment measures makes it difficult to measure	-Type and number of road safety installations, on RTC prone corridors, -Percentage of roads with pedestrian facilities by type, -Percentage of road network not fulfilling safety design standards	% of roads with road shoulders % of roads with signalised intersections % of road length with a wide obstacle-free zone or roadside barrier % of road length with facilities for separation of slow vulnerable traffic and other motorized traffic % of high-risk and critical roads dualised % of roads with which road safety feature (matched against crash records)
-Road Safety Audits	-Assess the level of safety on a road		% of roads with audited designs			
Black spot treatments	Enables correction of road defects	Number of road safety audits conducted -Number of Black spot treated	Enables the state of road condition to be kept safe	Requires funding and expert inputs which might not be adequate	-Number and type of RTC caused by road condition by road category	-Not used as KPI
Environmental Effects	-Provides information on locational conditions at RTC scene	-Time, weather conditions, light conditions	-Guides the implementation of defensive driving measures	-All factors are not captured at the Driver Training stage	-Not used as KPI in Europe	Not used as KPI in Ghana

Safe Vehicles:

1. Unit of Measurement	Description	Details	Advantages	Disadvantages	EU Example	Applicability in Ghana
Casualties per vehicle-km	-To determine the level of risk per km travel	-Fatalities per vehicle-km travelled -Number of road deaths per billion kilometres travelled.	-Determine the level of risk per km travel	-Does not take into account non-motorized travel	-Not used as KPI in Europe	-Not used as KPI in Ghana
Vehicle Registration	-It is used to correlate number of vehicles with the number of traffic crashes and casualties	-Number of Registered Vehicles and licensing	This is important for measuring vehicle ownership	Does not factor in quality of vehicle	-Not used as KPI in Europe	-Not used as KPI in Ghana % of vehicles with insurance cover per annum -Percentage roadworthy vehicles % of vehicles with certified road worthiness per annum

1. Unit of Measurement

	Description	Details	Advantages	Disadvantages	EU Example	Applicability in Ghana
Vehicle Characteristics	-Establish the impact of vehicular age on RTC -Provides information on the possible contribution of vehicle factors to RTC	-Average age of vehicles -Vehicle Type; model, year of manufacture, engine size, inspection, special functions -% of new vehicles sold with star rating, -Passenger cars with highest safety rating -Percentage of cars with worn out tyres; -Percentage of cars with technical defects	Improve the crash worthiness of the vehicle fleet -Gives good basis for the development of safe vehicle policies	-Requires good records on vehicle registration and assessments	-Average age of vehicles involved in RTC -Percentage of RTC caused by vehicular defects by type of defect	Composition of the vehicle fleet: % of cars, vans, buses, trucks and motorcycles in total # of registered vehicles
Casualties by Vehicle Characteristics	-Relative figure showing ratio of fatalities to motor vehicles.	-Fatalities per10,000 vehicles -Fatalities per 100,000 vehicles	-Shows the relationship between fatalities and motor vehicles. -Useful for international comparisons.	-A limited measure of travel exposure because it omits non-motorized transport and other indicators of exposure	-Number of deaths per 100 million vehicle- -Fatalities per10,000 vehicles	-Number of deaths per 10,000 registered vehicles
Motorcycle Characteristics	Provides a basis for assessing the level of RTC risk by number of motorcycles in the traffic stream	-Proportion of motorcycles amongst the motorized vehicles	-Minimises the risk of motorcycle crashes, -Can lead to policies to reduce the severity of injury when a crash occurs by motorcycle	-The indicator in itself does not provide a good basis for assessing motorcycle safety		-% of motorcycles with insurance cover per annum -% of motorcycle with certified road worthiness per annum
Overloading	-Increase the safety of motorcycling -Highlights safety risks of overloaded trucks	-% of overloaded trucks	-Highlights safety risks of overloaded trucks	-Overloading of trucks are not easily measured	-Not used as KPI in Europe	-Not used as a KPI in Ghana

Safe Road Users:

1. Unit of Measurement

	Description	Details	Advantages	Disadvantages	EU Example	Applicability in Ghana
Driver Registration						% of drivers with valid driver's license % of motorcyclists with valid rider's license

1. Unit of Measurement	Description	Details	Advantages	Disadvantages	EU Example	Applicability in Ghana
1. Speeding	-Levels of mean traffic speeds so as to lower traffic speeds for the benefit and protection of all road users -Road accidents caused by speeding and violation of road traffic rules -Traffic complying with speed limits on national roads -Traffic complying with speed limits on local roads	-Average traffic speed in urban areas (km/h) Average traffic speed in rural areas (km/h)	Measures safety behaviours of all road users in order to improve the key safety behaviours of all road users	-In some countries these are not easily measured when RTC's do occur		Percentage exceeding posted speed limits -Average travel speeds in settlement areas -Average travel speeds on highways -% of surveyed (car) drivers exceeding the speed limit on various road types -The annual number of speed-violation notices (per vehicles) (E) -% of all drivers exceeding speed limits in police checks (E)
2. Drunk Driving	-Accidents, fatalities and injuries caused by drink driving Reduce alcohol/drug impaired driving	Levels of drink driving; -Number of drivers or riders killed with BAC above the legal limit -Drivers who do not drive after consuming alcohol or drugs	-Measures safety behaviours of all road users in order to improve the key safety behaviours of all road users	-In some countries these are not easily measured when RTC's do occur	Percentage of motorists exceeding 0.08 mg/ml -BAC on accident prone roads	-Percentage of motorists exceeding 0.08 mg/ml BAC -% of drivers above the legal BAC limit at police checks -Annual number of random breath tests (per vehicles) (E) -% of drivers failing random breath tests (E) -% of drivers with drugs concentration > legal limit (E)
Occupant Restraint	-Occupant Restraint, Non wearing of seatbelts	Car occupants using a seat belt or child seat -Level of helmet use by powered two-wheeler users and cyclists	-Measures safety behaviours of all road users in order to improve the key safety behaviours of all road users	-In some countries these are not easily measured when RTC's do occur	-Percentage of seatbelt usage -Percentage of crash helmet usage	-% of seat belt use% of children <12 years (correctly) sitting in a child's seat in the front or rear seat of a car -% of crash helmet use -The annual number of seat belt violation notices (per vehicles) -% of drivers violating seat belt use in police checks
4 Fatigue Driving	-It is normally by number of hours of driving without rest	Number of accidents involving fatigue driving	-Measures safety behaviours of all road users in order to improve the key safety behaviours of all road users	--In some countries these are not easily measured when RTC's do occur		-Percentage of motorists exceeding allowable driving hours
Use of Mobile Devices	-Good indicator for checking distractive driving	-Drivers not using mobile devices whilst driving	-Measures safety behaviours of all road users in order to improve the key safety behaviours of all road users	-In some countries accurate records are not kept	-Not used as KPI in Europe	-Not used as KPI in Ghana

1. Unit of Measurement	Description	Details	Advantages	Disadvantages	EU Example	Applicability in Ghana
Pedestrian Safety	-To achieve safer walking	-Number of pedestrian deaths by frequent locations	Ensures pedestrian safety in the traffic stream	Pedestrian needs are not priortised	Pedestrian fatality	-Pedestrian fatality
Driver Training	Developing knowledge, skill and behaviour of all road users	-Percentage of certified trained drivers		This will first require a knowledge of driver population, before the certified ones could be identified and this is not feasible		
Traffic Offences	-Reduce the impact of high risk drivers	-Number of Traffic Offences recorded	-Provides insight into the extent of public awareness of RTC issues	-Requires good documentation on traffic offences	Number of Traffic Offences recorded	The technical means/equipment available to the traffic police Number of driving licenses delivered per total vehicles fleet % change in coverage of TRAFFITECH % of prosecutions, convictions, fines against arrests

Post-Crash: 1. Unit of Measurement	Description	Details	Advantages	Disadvantages	EU Example	Applicability in Ghana
Emergency Response Time	-Measures post- crash preparedness and response capacity	Average time for emergency services to arrive at the crash site -Average intervention time at the crash site -Emergency medical services arriving at priority accident scenes within 18 minutes	-Enables the mitigation of post-crash deaths resulting from poor post - crash response	Most countries in the developing world do not rate it as important	-Average response time from alarm to treatment	-% of calls to emergency medical services due to RTC -Average arrival time of emergency medical services at the crash scene
Ambulance Service	-Enables assessment of efficiency of the transport of an RTC victim to the hospital -Level of availability of effective transport for RTC Victims	-Number of ambulances per 10, 000 people	-Enables assessment of efficiency of the transport of an RTC victim to the hospital	-It mostly inadequate in developing countries	Number of ambulances per 10, 000 people	Not used as KPI in Ghana

1. Unit of Measurement	Description	Details	Advantages	Disadvantages	EU Example	Applicability in Ghana
3. Medical Treatment of RTC cases	Determines the number of treated RTC cases	-Average length of stay in the hospital / -% of severely injured people of whose life was saved	Share of road casualties who died during hospitalisation	-Records are not well kept in developing countries	-National Patient Register with RTC	-Not used as KPI in Ghana Average length of stay in the hospital after a RTC / -% of calls to emergency medical services due to RTC / -% of fatalities at RTC sites and % at hospitals / -Share of road casualties who died during hospitalization
Number of EMS	-Availability of first aid care for RTC	EMS stations per 10,000 citizens / Number of medical staff available per 10,000 people / -Number of total trauma care beds per 10,000 citizens	EMS stations per 10,000 citizens and per 100 km length of rural public roads		EMS stations per 10,000 citizens and per 100 km length of rural public roads	-% of fatalities at RTC sites and % at hospitals
Emergency Treatment	Share of road casualties who died during hospitalisation	Average intervention time at the crash site / -Emergency medical services arriving at priority accident scenes within 18 minutes	-Enables the mitigation of post-crash deaths resulting from poor post-crash response	Most countries in the developing world do not rate it as important	Average response time from alarm to treatment	-Share of road casualties who died during hospitalization
Hospital beds	-Share of road casualties who died during hospitalisation	Number of medical staff available per 10,000 people / -Number of total trauma care beds per 10,000 citizens / -Average length of stay in the hospital / -% of severely injured people of whom the live was saved				
Post-Crash Rehabilitation		-% of injured traffic victims with a permanent disability % of traffic victims with psychological problems; -% of traffic victims requiring adaptation of the home				

CHAPTER 3

ROAD SAFETY MANAGEMENT IN GHANA

"True Public safety requires a collaboration between law enforcement and the community" Betsy Hodges.

3.1 INTRODUCTION

Road Safety Management (RSM) is defined as "a systematic process aimed at reducing the number and severity of road-related traffic crashes (OECD, 2002). Because road safety is multi-disciplinary and multi-sectoral, it is a complex process to manage. As such, a systems-based approach with a common lead guided by the principle of a holistic framework by the linking of essential RSM functions from different sectors is recommended.

In Ghana, RSM has evolved through different stages overtime with necessary adjustments applied as and when needed for improved performance. The country has to a large extent responded to recommended best practices and global standards on RSM whilst also ensuring that local specific RSM needs are addressed. Currently, a lead government road safety agency is in place with responsibility for policy formulation, facilitation of the development of legislative tools for traffic safety, establishment of road safety strategic framework and action plans, conduct of research and coordination of road safety activities and accountability.

The agency also works with a continuously transforming safety agenda in order to address emerging challenges. It ensures that the key elements and operational processes of conventional RSM practices recommended by international road safety organisations such as under the DOA 2011 – 2020 are applied. The lead agency is also backed by responsible road safety stakeholder entities from other sectors with defined roles and responsibilities. Irrespective of this, RSM in Ghana is characterized by constraints such as limited resource capacity, poor coordination etc.

This section of the book discusses Ghana's RSM system as a critical aspect of the road safety work in the country, especially with regards to what it represents, its importance, what is being done, how it is being done, related challenges, the proactive ways by which safety problems can be identified before they arise and how they can be mitigated when they do occur.

3.2 THE ROAD SAFETY MANAGEMENT SYSTEM (RSM)

3.2.1 Key Elements of an RSM System

A. Definition of RSM: According to Bliss and Breen (2008), effective RSM is focused on institutional management functions. It draws on the principle that road safety is produced just like any goods with the production process defined by three interrelated elements namely (i) institutional management functions; (ii) interventions and; (iii) results with each component linked to the other in the form of a pyramid as depicted in Figure 3.1 with Figure 3.2 elaborating on the road safety institutional management functions in Ghana.

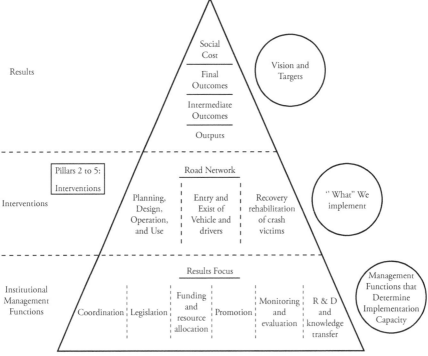

Figure 3.1: RSM production process

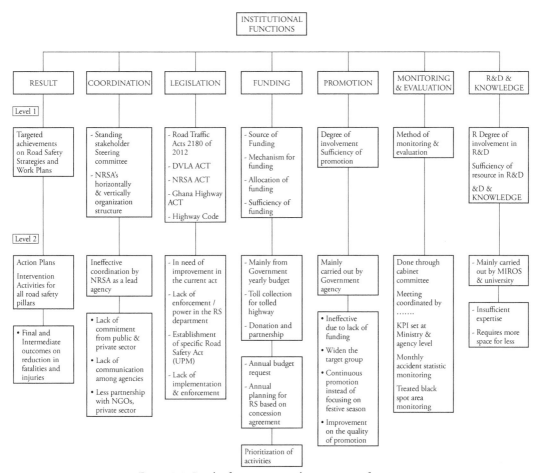

Figure 3.2: Road safety institutional management functions

B. RSM's Institutional Management Functions: This consists of seven functions as listed below:

i.   Results-focus as the overarching function.

ii.   Coordination.

iii. Legislation and supporting systems.

iv.   Funding and resource allocation.

v.   Promotion and advocacy.

vi.   Monitoring and evaluation.

vii. Research and knowledge transfer.

C. Implementation of Defined RSM Interventions: The RSM interventions expected to be implemented within the institutional management functions also include the following aspects;

i.   planning, designing, operating and using road infrastructure with reference to the DOA road safety pillar 2 on safe roads and pillar 3 on safe vehicles;

ii. entry and exit of vehicles and road users to and from road network with reference to the DOA road safety Pillar 3 on safe vehicles and pillar 4 on safe road use;

iii. recovery and rehabilitation of road crash victims from the road network with reference to the DOA road safety pillar 5 complemented with enforcement and public education.

D. Expected Results, Outputs and Outcomes: The third stage of the RSM framework is results-focused expressed in terms of final outcomes, intermediate outcomes, or outputs which form the metrics of road safety measurement as discussed in detail in Section 2.2.1, Item D of Chapter 2 of this book.

Though the above framework is presented as a guide for effective RSM, Papadimitriou & Yannis (2013) describe the process as being too complex and difficult to describe in a standardised way. Therefore, Bliss & Breen (2009), recommends for countries to set their own limits because RSM is to identify innovative solutions and a compendium of RSM Functions by Varhelyi (2016) showing the different ways of RSM implementation is as summarized in Table 3.1.

Table 3.1: Compendium of Road Safety Management Practices

Elements for Best Road Safety Management Practice

DOA	SUPREME handbook 2007
1) Establish a lead agency ;	1) Institutional organisation of road safety and specifically road safety visions;
2) Develop a national strategy ;	
3) Set realistic targets for road safety activities ;	2) Road safety programmes and targets;
4) Ensure sufficient funding;	3) Efficiency analysis;
5) Establish and support data systems	4) Resource allocation processes.
OECD Report Paris 2002	OECD report Paris, 2008
1) Identify a lead agency to guide the national road safety effort;	1) Improved data collection;
2) Assess the problem, policies and institutional settings relating to road traffic injury and the capacity for road traffic injury prevention in the country;	2) Setting robust interim targets;
	3) Ambitious long term vision;
	4) Adopting a Safe System approach;
3) Prepare a national road safety strategy and plan of action;	5) Improving key institutional management functions;
4) Allocate financial and human resources to address the problem;	6) Supporting research and development through knowledge transfer;
5) Implement specific actions to prevent road crashes, minimize their consequences and evaluate the impact of these actions;	7) Establishing adequate funding for effective safety programmes;
	8) Meeting management challenges, especially building political support;
6) Support the development of national capacity and international co-operation	9) Adopt the "Safe System" approach

Elements for Best Road Safety Management Practice

ETSC report 2006
1) Political support and commitment;
2) Public and private sector awareness and involvement in road safety;
3) Legislation;
4) Traffic safety vision or philosophy;
5) Strategy;
6) Performance targets;
7) Public health approach;
8) Systemic perspective;
9) Road safety action plan;
10) Scientific choice of measures;
11) Institutional roles and responsibilities;
12) Allocation of responsibility for countermeasures;
13) Funding;
14) Monitoring and evaluation;
15) Accident data;
16) Safety performance indicators and exposure data;
17) Research;
18) Best practice exchange;
19) Training;
20) Enforcement;
21) Emergency response;
22) Holistic approach

Muhlrad (2015)
1) A long-term vision - preferably to be decided by the parliament so that it becomes law;
2) A medium-term strategy which creates the framework in which successive road safety intervention pprogrammers will be designed and implemented;
3) Short-to-medium term (four to five year) quantitative targets of injury reduction to be used for calibrating further efforts;
4) A road safety programme coordinating all interventions planned to meet the targets;
5) A funding mechanism ensuring annual financing of the action programme and support activities;
6) Setting up implementation conditions to ensure that human, technical and financial resources are available when needed.

The Road Safety Manual issued by PIARC (2016)
1) The road safety management system focusing on results and the importance of governmental and top management leadership and management capacity;
2) The Safe System approach;
3) Effective management and use of safety data;
4) Road safety targets, investment strategies, plans and projects;
5) Roles, responsibilities, policy development and programmes;
6) Intervention selection and prioritisation;
7) Monitoring and evaluation of road safety interventions.

Bliss & Breen (2009)
1) A country's safety management capacity that sets the limits to improvements in road safety;
2) Institutional management functions, and more specifically the role of the lead agency promote the Safe System approach, and put forward seven institutional management functions providing the foundation for an effective national RSM system;
3) Results focus – a strategic orientation that links all actual and potential interventions with results;
4) Coordination;
5) Legislation;
6) Funding and resource allocation;
7) Promotion;
8) Monitoring and evaluation;
9) Research, development and knowledge transfer

Global Status Report [2009]
1) The responsible institutions for road safety actions must have the necessary human and financial resources to act effectively;
2) Develop and endorse a national strategy with realistic targets and earmarked funding for implementation;
3) Promote multi-sectoral collaboration in road safety work;
4) Promote collaboration between the different sectors involved in collecting data on road traffic injuries.

The Global Status Report on Road Safety (2013)
1) Officially endorsed targets and indicators;
2) Improving the quality of data on fatalities, injuries and interim indicators;
3) Coordination of efforts by a well-resourced lead agency;
4) A multi-sectoral national strategy that includes specific targets;
5) Monitoring and evaluation of outputs and outcomes.

The Safety Net (2009)
Institutional management functions which produce;
-Interventions, which in turn produce;
-Results
-Results focus, which is the overarching function;
-Coordination;
-Legislation;
-Funding and resource allocation;
-Promotion;
-Monitoring and evaluation;
-Research, development and knowledge transfer.

Johnston (2010)
1) Constituency – unless the public demands action, appropriate resources will not be applied;
2) Commitment – without political will from the top, success will be limited;
3) Cooperation – RSM demands actions from a large number of stake holders;
4) "Coordination is vital to integration and synergy across institutional efforts"

Elements for Best Road Safety Management Practice
_____

African Decade for Road Safety action

1) Establish/strengthen national road safety lead agency with legal, financial and human backing;
2) Prepare and approve a road safety policy/strategy and set realistic and attainable road safety targets;
3) Advocate road safety to become one of the focus areas for development plans;
4) Promote and assist road safety research and studies and use good practices from other countries;
5) Develop and implement a sustainable and accurate national database on road crashes;
6) Harmonise vehicle and driver registration data systems;
7) Commit to an appropriate road safety component in all relevant international partner funded interventions;
8) Promote private sector and civil society organisations' involvement in road safety.

Source: Road Safety Management - the need for a systematic approach, Varhelyi (2016)

Ghana's approach to RSM started over a decade ago (16 years) ahead of the DOA (2011-2020) and the highlights of Ghana's RSM is as discussed in detail in the subsequent subsections of the chapter.

3.3 STANDARDS FOR ROAD SAFETY MANAGEMENT

3.3.1 Global Standards for Road Safety

A. International Organisation for Standardization's (ISO 39001): Published in the ISO/TC 241 in October 2012, it aims for RSM to facilitate the implementation of preventive and corrective actions by guiding organizations through a process of continual improvement in road safety performance. It specifies that an RSM system must define the (i) Scope and context of activities; (ii) Leadership; (iii) Planning; (iv) Implementation; (v) Monitoring and Evaluation; and (vi) Continual improvement Small M. and Breen J. (2017).

The guideline is also focused on corporate responsibility for road safety by internal mechanisms such as the integration of RTC management into overall business strategy to demonstrate commitment to both safety and social responsibility. The benefits include prevention of avoidable deaths, contributing to faster planning, design and operation and use of road traffic system, cutting organisational RTC and incident costs, reducing the number of work days lost to injury and reducing insurance premiums and repair cost.

B. RSM by the UN DOA (2011-2020): RSM is the first prioritised road safety pillar under the (DOA). It focuses on the key principles of ownership, authority and accountability to bring road safety performance under control. Table 3.2 presents the elements of RSM defined in the DOA.

Table 3.2: Elements of RSM defined in the DOA

Expected Accomplishment	Activities
Established/strengthened Lead Agencies	• Establish/strengthen national road safety lead agency with legal, financial and human backing.
	• Prepare & approve a Road Safety (RS) Policy/Strategy
	• Set realistic and attainable RS targets
	• Advocate RS to become one of the focus areas for development plans
	• Promote and assist road safety research and studies and use good practices from other countries
	• Create knowledge management portals on road safety issues in Africa
	• Establish self-standing RS Financing
	• Allocate at least 10% of road infrastructure Investment to Road Safety
	• Allocate sufficient financial and human resources to improve RS
	• Allocate 5% of road maintenance resources to road safety
Improved Management of Data	• Develop and implement a sustainable and accurate national database on RTCs
	• Enforce mandatory reporting, standardized data in conformity with
	• International definitions, and provision of sustainable funding
	• Develop a National Crash Analysis and Reporting System
	• Harmonize data format in road crash reporting in line with international standards;
	• Harmonize vehicle and driver registration data system.
	• Build capacity for data management on road safety
	• Engage local and regional research centres on road safety data Management
	• Establish/strengthen and harmonize injury data system to be recorded by Health Facilities
	• Establish a baseline data on road safety
Develop/Strength Partnership and collaboration	• Commit appropriate Road Safety component in all relevant international partner funded interventions.
	• Transport corridors to put in place appropriate road safety programmes and carryout related activities
	• Establish national associations of road accident victims and survivors
	• Promote Private Sector and Civil Society Organizations involvement in RS development effort/ programme

Source: Decade for Road Safety Action – UN General Resolution 74/299

3.4 RSM IN GHANA

3.4.1 RSM Policy in Ghana

A national road safety policy is identified to be a critical initiative in the effort to elevate road safety issues to a position of high priority on the national agenda. It guides the coordination of the rules and actions of relevant stakeholder agencies, the private sector and non-Governmental organizations (NGOs) towards a joint effort to RSM. In October 2009, the WHO requested all countries worldwide to formulate road safety policies and develop strategies that would address road safety issues in their respective countries. The DOA 2011-2020 stipulated that such road safety policies and strategies should be of long-term vision, have quantitative objectives and action plans with sustainable funding and full political support.

Ghana's National Road Safety Policy (NRSP) of 2008 was established a year ahead of the call by the UN for countries to establish road safety policies. It was formulated to provide clear strategic directions for road safety programmes and activities for the NRSC now NRSA. It aimed to co-ordinate, underpin and validate road safety interventions introduced in the country and it is characterized by relevant content relating to sixteen (16) key road safety issues and challenges with sixteen (16) policy statements and recommended strategies and activities as listed in Box 3.1

Box 3.1: Road Safety Policy Issues in Ghana

1. Policy on Road Transport Industry
2. Policy on the Driver
3. Policy on the Vehicle
4. Policy on Road Infrastructure
5. Policy on Intermediate Means of Transport (IMTs)
6. Policy on Pedestrians and Vulnerable Road User (VRUs) Safety
7. Policy on Road Safety Legislation
8. Policy on Enforcement
9. Policy on Post Road Traffic Crash Care
10. Policy on Road Safety Database
11. Policy on Funding for Road Safety Programmes
12. Policy on Research into Road Safety Issues
13. Policy on Inter-Agency Collaboration and Coordination
14. Policy on Human Resource Development for Road Safety Activities
15. Policy on Monitoring and Evaluation of Road Safety Activities
16. Policy on Road Safety Awareness

Source: National road Safety Policy

Though, the NRSP has been complied with to a large extent since 2009, it is of the view that after ten (10) years of implementation within which numerous road safety interventions and activities have been implemented including the DOA 2011-2020 and lessons learnt, there is need for the NRSP to be reviewed. This is because various change scenarios have emerged from the road transport industry in general and the road safety conditions in the country specifically. Moreover, NTP of 2008 which is the umbrella policy for the management of the transport industry developed alongside the NRSP in the same year has been reviewed and there is need for a corresponding review of the NRSP to reflect the new mandate of NRSA.

3.4.2 The National Road Safety Commissin (NRSC)

The NRSC provided leadership for promoting road safety initiatives in the country from 1999 to 2018. It also coordinated road safety activities among state and private agencies at national, local and community levels for effective implementation of traffic safety programmes.

A. Objectives and Philosophies of NRSC

i. Strategic Objective of the NRSC: The main objective of the NRSC was to plan, develop, promote and coordinate policies related to road safety.

ii. Corporate Philosophies: The NRSA's organizational philosophies included:

a). National Vision: "Ghana, a country with the safest road transport system in Africa".

b). Corporate Vision: "A reputable organisation with a highly motivated staff committed to reducing the fatality rate per 10,000 vehicles to a single digit".

c). Corporate Mission: 'To promote best road safety practices for all categories of road users through the conceptualization, design, implementation and monitoring of data-led road safety interventions.

B. Functions of NRSC: *The key functions of the NRSC under Act 567 of 1999 are as presented in Table 3.3.*

Table 3.3: Functions of NRSC

Theme	Function
Coordination	-Co-ordinate, monitor and evaluate road safety activities, programmes and strategies.
	-Act in liaison and co-operation with government agencies, the Driver and Vehicle Licensing Authority and other such bodies as it may determine to promote road safety.
Policy	Advise the Minister on the formulation of road safety policies and action programmes.
Standards	-Establish with the road authorities, procedures for safety audit of projects for road construction, reconstruction or improvement.
	-Set standards for road safety equipment in consultation with the Building and Road Research Institute (BRRI), the Ghana Standards Board and other bodies with relevant knowledge and expertise on road safety and ensure compliance with the standards.
Promotion- Sensitization/Education	Undertake nationwide road safety education.
	Encourage the development of road safety education as part of the curriculum and the training of teachers in road safety.
Partnerships - Collaboration	Collaborate with such foreign and international bodies as the Commission considers necessary for the purpose of this Act.
Research	Promote road safety research
Strategies/Action plans	-Carry out special projects for the improvement of road safety.
	-Develop a long-term road safety plan.
Enforcement	Recommend to the Minister and such bodies as it may determine measures calculated to prevent accidents involving the use of vehicles on roads.
	Conduct investigations into road safety issues and advise the Minister on them.
Database Management	-Develop and maintain a comprehensive database on road safety for the information of the public.
	-Gather and publish reports and information relating to road safety.

Source: NRSC ACT 567 of 1999

C. Challenges faced by the NRSC: *Though the NRSC worked diligently to attain its set objectives and functions, it did not have the mandate and the legal right to demand compliance and accountability from the other road safety stakeholder entities whose activities it coordinated. This is because each stakeholder entity worked on the basis of their own internal rules and regulations and this necessitated for the NRSC to be upgraded to the status of an authority equipped with the mandate to effectively regulate the activities of the other road safety stakeholder entities.*

3.4.3 The National Road Safety Authority (NRSA)

A new Act, Act 993 of 2019 was enacted to upgrade the NRSC to the status of the National Road Safety Authority (NRSA) with the following objectives and functions:

A. Objectives and Philosophies of NRSA: *The object of the Authority is to reduce the incidence of RTCs, fatalities and injuries through the i) promotion of road safety; ii) development and co-ordination of policies in relation to road safety and; iii) implementation and enforcement of standards for road safety. The philosophies remain the same as that of the NRSC.*

B. Functions of the NRSA: *The key functions of the NRSA are as stated in Table 3.4. The regulatory requirements and modalities to support the NRSA have also been developed as summarised in Box 3.2. The corresponding institutional changes that will facilitate the operation and achievements of its functions were still in progress as at the time of writing this book. A summary of comparison of the similarities and deviations in the two road safety management Acts of Parliament is as presented in Table 3.4.*

Table 3.4: Functions of the NRSA

Theme	Function
General Management	Perform any other relevant function for the attainment of the object of the Authority.
Development of standards	-Collaborate with the Building and Road Research Institute, the Standards Authority and other bodies with relevant knowledge and expertise in road safety to develop standards for road safety equipment and ensure compliance with the standards. -Recommend to the Minister the minimum standards and guidelines for the delivery of quality road transport services by all categories of road users that the Authority may consider necessary; -Establish the procedure and standards for road safety audit with the road authorities and collaborate with the road agencies to ensure implementation of findings of road safety audits in accordance with existing design, construction and maintenance procedures and standards for the provision of road infrastructure;
Development of Regulations	Issue notices in the form of directives, procedures or cautions to persons to provide for or correct irregularity in procedures, standards, practices and operations in order to prevent or minimize road traffic crashes, fatalities and injuries; -Ensure institutional compliance with procedures and standards related to road safety; and
Collaboration	-Collaborate with the Ghana Education Service and other relevant bodies to develop road safety education as part of the curriculum for pre-tertiary level schools and colleges of education; -Collaborate with other relevant agencies to co-ordinate, monitor and evaluate road safety activities, programmes and strategies -Collaborate with relevant foreign and international bodies to achieve the object of this Act;
Promotion-Education and sensitization	Undertake nationwide road safety education, campaigns and publicity

Theme	Function
Monitoring	Monitor the importation and sale of road safety equipment or devices for the safe use of roads;
Conduct of Research	Collaborate with other relevant agencies to promote studies, research, surveys and analysis for road safety improvement and publish reports and information relating to road safety;
Development of Road Safety Strategies and action plans	Develop a long-term plan for the promotion of road safety and the reduction of road traffic crashes, fatalities and injuries and collaborate with the Driver and Vehicle Licensing Authority, road agencies, enforcement agencies, crash response agencies and road transport service providers to implement the plan.
Database Management	Develop and maintain a comprehensive database on road safety for the information of the public;
Enforcement	-Ensure compliance with laid down road safety standards and procedures for the development, use and provision of road safety related infrastructure, services or undertaking; -Collaborate with the Driver and Vehicle Licensing Authority, road agencies, enforcement agencies, District Assemblies and other public or private bodies that the Authority may determine to ensure compliance with existing procedures and standards to reduce the risk of road traffic crashes, fatalities and injuries in the design, construction and use of public roads; -Receive complaints and investigate violations of road safety standards, Regulations and best practices and advise the Minister on the measures required to prevent or minimise the road safety risks;

Source: NRSA Act 993 of 2019

Box 3.2: National Road Safety Authority Regulations, 2021

- Preliminary Provisions

- Road Safety Initiatives, Advertisements, Programmes and Campaigns

- Road Traffic Crash and Road Transport System Investigation

- Management of Funds

- Road Safety Audit Certification and Approvals

- Inspections and Compliance Notices

- Development of Road Safety Standards

- Licensing and Registration of Transport Operations

- Provisions on Specific Licences

- Obligations of Specific Operators

- Safety Audit and Operator Safety Ratings

- Operational Managers, Road Safety Officers, Transport Units, Transport Departments and Related

- Service Providers

- Miscellaneous Provisions

C. Current Governance Structure and Lines of Authority for RSM in Ghana: *The structure for the governance of RSM in Ghana is both horizontally and vertically linked from the National to the regional level for both political and administrative level of management. The internal hierarchical decision structure is from the MoT, a Board, a Director General, Departmental heads and regional offices by geographical distribution as depicted in Figure 3.3.*

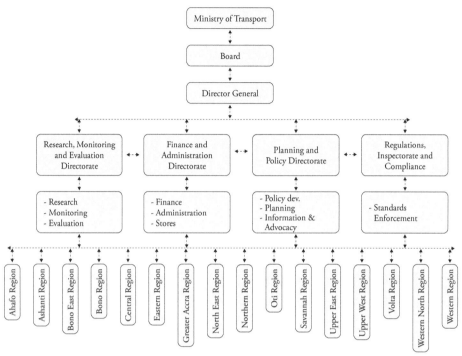

Figure 3.3: Governance Arrangement

i. The MoT: The NRSA falls directly under the MoT which is the public sector entity with the overall responsibility to govern, direct, control and hold the NRSA accountable to its responsibilities. The provision of road transport infrastructure and transport services is separated in Ghana so the MoT is responsible for only transport services.

ii. NRSA's Governing Board: The NRSA is governed by a thirteen (13) member Board made up of representatives from the institutions listed in Table 3.5 including a Chairman and the Director General with the latter having a three-year tenure. There is also a secretary to the board elected from the NRSA. The board ensures that the mission and vision of the NRSA are achieved through good counsel and facilitation of the provision of resource to carry out their functions.

Table 3.5: Institutions Comprising the NRSA Board

Sector	Institution
Transport	Ministry of Transport
	Driver and Vehicle licensing Authority
Infrastructure	Ministry of Roads and Highway
Justice	Ministry of Justice and Attorney General
Security	Motor Transport and Traffic Department (Ghana Police Service)
Insurance	National Insurance Commission
	Ghana Insurers Association
Media	Broadcasting Industry
	Ghana Journalist Association
Local Governance	Ministry of Local Government & Rural Development
	Ghana Standards Authority

iii. Director General: The day-to-day management and administration of the Authority lies with the Director General. She/he is assisted by four-front-line Directors with responsibilities for Planning / Programmes; Research, Monitoring / Evaluation; Finance / Administration and Regulation, Inspectorate and compliance.

iv. Departments/Divisions: The organogram of the NRSA is further divided into departments or work units with each headed by a Divisional Director. These are the planning / programming / management directorate; research / monitoring /evaluation directorate; Regulation, Inspectorate/ compliance and the financial / administration directorate.

a.   The planning and programming directorate undertake the organization's corporate planning, including annual action plan development; budgeting activities and work implementation.

b.   The research, monitoring and evaluation conducts research into road safety interventions such as the development of standards / rules and reviews performance.

c.   The regulation, Inspectorate and compliance directorate enforces compliance with standards and rules.

d.   The financial and administration division is the corporate services division which provides information services, human resources, financial contract and facilities management.

v. Regional Offices: The NRSA has sixteen (16) Regional Offices each of which is headed by a Regional Director who is responsible to the Director General. Their main role is to implement NRSA's designated role and coordinate the road safety activities of safety stakeholder entities at the regional, metropolitan municipal and district (MMDA) level.

vi. (MMDA's): Though there are no established road safety operational offices at the MMDA level of administration, the local Governance Act assigns the following road safety responsibilities to the MMDA's.

a.   Land use planning and control of new development with unsafe effects of roadside activities such as citing of billboards and control of encroachment on pedestrian walkways.

b.   Issuance of permit for traffic Impact Assessment.

c.   Licensing for commercial transport operation.

d.   Posting of Traffic Wardens at pedestrian crossing points.

There are some activities going on at the metropolitan and municipal levels in collaboration with the Transport Departments (DoTs) for those who have them. The DoT's are funded by the assemblies. District road safety committees, represented by various stakeholders are being used in those without DoTs. However, they are not seen as part of the Assemblies committees and so are not funded by them. Overtime, it is envisaged that the NRSA will be represented at all districts by committees which will take the responsibility from the DoTs with direct funding from the NRSA.

D. Limitations of NRSA's Organisational Structure: *The key constraints to the current governance structure for road safety is that RSM is not effectively functional at the lower level of Ghana's administrative governance structure. This means that national and regional targets for road safety improvements are not effectively generated, adapted and applied to local situations and there is a lack of fitness of purpose and commitment to implement road safety interventions. Though a district level guideline for RSM was developed by the NRSA to mainstream road safety their development agenda's it has not been effectively applied. (See Figure 3.4).*

Figure 3.4: The Crest of the NRSA

The only exception is that the Accra Metropolitan Assembly (AMA) has with the assistance of the Bloomberg foundation developed its own action plan for road safety drawing on existing action frameworks by the NRSA. There are also plans to extend the assistance to the Kumasi Metropolitan Assembly (KMA). Others have only been engaging in a few road safety campaigns and enforcement activities with the NRSA's regional offices. Also, the NRSA has posted representatives at all MMDA's to collaborate with them as a part of its new mandate to regulate commercial transport services in the country. The major activity in this regard is to participate in the vehicle certification process and to check safety compliance at that level before the issuance of operational permits. Aside this, not much is also done with regards to road safety coordination amongst the respective road safety stakeholder entities at that level.

It is therefore recommended to streamline local governance of road safety activities with effective engagements through a bottom-up safety planning and implementation approach to ensure commitment to road safety delivery at that level. It is also recommended for the NRSA to raise the RSM profile at the MMDA level by:

i.   *Mapping out crash data at the level of MMDA's for better appreciation of local situations.*

ii.   *Engaging and motivating MMDA's to prioritise road safety by assisting them to adapt national road safety action plans to local level needs and developing their own road safety plans.*

iii. *Encouraging MMDA's to commit part of their budgets and other resources to road safety interventions such as minor infrastructure works, safety campaigns, enforcement etc.*

iv.   *Encouraging MMDA's to implement by-laws on encroachment on walkways, citing of billboards etc.*

v.   *Conducting extensive training in road safety at the MMDA level for effective implementation and monitoring of road safety programmes.*

E. Organisational Capacity and Capability of the NRSA: *The organisational capacity and capability of the NRSA is as discussed below:*

i. NRSA's Organisational Capacity: Road safety is multi-disciplinary involving expertise from sectors such as listed in the immediate sub-section:

a.   *Road Safety Management: Transport Planners/Managers, Financial Experts, Sociologists, Statisticians, Economists, Business/ Public Administrators.*

b.   *Safe Roads: Highway engineering by Civil Engineers.*

c.   *Vehicle Safety: Mechanical and transportation engineers and transport experts.*

d.   *Safe Road User: Law enforcement entities e.g. Police and experts from the judiciary.*

e.   *Educational sector: Educationists, Media Personnel and Civil Society Advocates.*

f.   *Post-crash care: Medical Doctors, Nurses, Paramedics, Public Health Experts, First Aid Experts, and Fire Officers.*

It is recommended for any designated RSM set up to have the full complement of the experts in the various disciplines as core professional staff. These should work as professional liaison officers who will coordinate, facilitate and provide professional perspectives to the aspects of road safety activities relevant to their specific areas of expertise.

Also, the degree of professional engagement in road safety is classified to be of either direct or indirect significance, depending on the extent to which the professional activity has a bearing on road safety. To this effect a Transport Research Board's (TRB) special Report in (2007) classified professionals with a direct bearing on road safety as those who work full time in road safety establishments. These have professional skills that use scientific methods and statistical techniques to identify current and potential safety problems, develop countermeasures, evaluate their effects, and present the results of complex analyses in ways that can be understood and used by decision makers. Those of indirect bearing are those in other agencies whose activities impact on some aspects of road safety.

In Ghana, the NRSP aimed to give special attention for the development of the requisite human resource for the road safety sub-sector. The key challenges identified in relation to this and the suggested mitigations are as presented in Table 3.6.

Table 3.6: Ghana's Policy Content on Human Resource for Road Safety

Key challenges	Strategies	Remarks
• There are no specialized courses that have been structured to provide training for road safety. • There is no structured road safety education for teachers from the basic level through to the tertiary level. • Inability of the road safety sub-sector to retain the few professionals who are trained for road safety work.	• Government will ensure that adequate human resource capacity is available at all levels of road safety institutions for research, management, enforcement etc. • Ensure adequate road safety capacity development at all levels of society for effective promotion and implementation of road safety activities. • Institute a system that would encourage specialization in the various disciplines in road safety. • Train enough personnel in safety issues for targeted stakeholders.	In Ghana, there are a small number of professionals who have specialized in road safety within the key stakeholder organisations.

An institutional needs assessment conducted by the NRSA in 2019 established that the NRSA lacks the full capacity the required professional work force. A comparison of the existing professionals and what is actually needed is as presented in Table 3.7. Subsequent to the findings of the study the NRSA is working to develop a technically linked human resource outlay that will produce goodness of fit between operations and required expertise.

Table: 3.7: Required Road Safety Expertise Compared to that Existing at the NRSA

Pillar	Core competencies for Road Safety Professionals	Roles and Responsibilities	Existing skills of road safety professionals at the NRSA
Road Safety managers	Policy experts Transport Experts Project Managers Directors and staff of governors' Experts in statistics Information technologists Human capital Managers Financial experts	-Leadership role in promoting safety initiatives by developing, implementing, and managing road safety programmes	With the exception of financial experts and Data Analysts, the other competencies are lacking

Pillar	Core competencies for Road Safety Professionals	Roles and Responsibilities	Existing skills of road safety professionals at the NRSA
Road User Safety	Transport Expertise Planners Sociologists Highway safety officers Educationists Training managers	Describe major trends that are ongoing and emerging and explain their potential effects on safety	-Planners -Researchers -Educationists -Communication Experts
Vehicle Safety	Mechanical Engineers Biomechanics, Transportation industry specialist Safety inspectors	Motor carrier safety, and automobile inspection crash-testing vehicles Monitoring graduated licensing programmes, establishing driver licensing standards, setting requirements for driver education	Safety inspectors
Road Infrastructure Safety	Civil Engineering Experts	-Construction and maintenance of roads -Management of traffic safety problems -Installing guardrails, medians, signals, -Improving dangerous sections -Road inspections and assessment of RTC situations	-Civil Engineers within the NRSA function as safety managers but core civil activities are undertaken by the road sector agencies
Enforcement	Safety regulators Traffic Enforcement Expertise (Security Personnel) Legal Experts	Enforce motor vehicle laws and regulations patrol officers dedicated to traffic safety	-Enforcement Expert -Legal Expert (Communication)
Post-Crash Response	Health Professionals Medical Doctors Epidemiologists Psychologists Paramedics	-Emergency medical services -Administer state injury prevention programmes	None

ii. NRSA'S Organisational Capability: In addition to the above the NRSA is also limited by the number of personnel needed and as at the time of the study, there was an estimated number of about 6 NRSA personnel including both technical and non-technical staff per region with each one of them responsible for an average of 3 to 4 districts. Also, only 29% of the staff of the NRSA had professional skills of some sort. The agency is in the process of populated with the requisite number of personnel needed for effective and efficient work deliver as part of an ongoing organisational restructuring process to match its status as an authority. The estimation of the scale and scope of the projected road safety workforce based on predictions of its future dimensions under the NRSA are as summarised in Appendix 3.2.

3.4.4 Similarities and Differences of NRSA and NRSC

Though there are similarities between the road safety functions listed in the NRSA and NRSC that of the NRSA is more focused on the development of standards due to its mandate to ensure compliance. The details of the functional comparisons between the two RSM Acts are as listed in Table 3.8.

Table 3.8: Similarities and Differences in Functions of the NRSC and the NRSA

Theme	Similarities and Discrepancies
Coordination	-Both the NRSC and the NRSA have the function to coordinate road safety activities, programmes and strategies
Policy	The NRSC had a defined function for the formulation of road safety policies and action programmes along with advisory policy services to the respective Minister of Transport. Though not categorically mentioned in the NRSA, it remains a part of its functions
Regulation and Development of standards	-Both the NRSC and NRSA have the function to collaborate with the BRRI, the Standards Authority and other relevant bodies to develop standards for road safety equipment and ensure compliance of use -Both have the function to establish procedures for road safety audits with road authorities -Both have a function to make recommendations to the Minister of Transport and such bodies as it may determine on measures calculated to prevent RTCs involving the use of vehicles on roads. -Only the NRSA has a defined function to ensure institutional compliance with procedures and standards related to road safety -Only the NRSA has a defined function to issue notices or cautions to persons to provide for or correct irregularities to prevent or minimize road traffic crashes -The NRSA additionally has to establish standards and ensure the implementation of safety audit findings -Only the NRSA has a defined function to recommend to the Minister the minimum standards and guidelines for the delivery of quality road transport services by all categories of road users
Promotion (Education)	-Both have the function to undertake other relevant functions to promote road safety However, NRSA's function is more general in scope than NRSC's which is limited to special projects -Both have the function to collaborate with foreign and international bodies on road safety education -Both have the function to undertake nationwide road safety education -Both have the function to develop road safety education as part of curriculum and the training of teachers. The NRSA seeks to partner with GES and other relevant bodies to develop road safety education for pre-tertiary level schools and colleges of education whiles the NRSC's function was not specific about it. -Both are required to act in liaison in co-operation with government agencies, the Driver and Vehicle Licensing Authority (DVLA) and other such bodies as it may determine to promote road safety. -Only the NRSA has a defined function to ensure compliance with laid down road safety standards and procedures for the development, use and provision of road safety related infrastructure, services or undertaking -Only the NRSA has a defined function to collaborate with the DVLA, road agencies, enforcement agencies, MMDAs and other public or private bodies to ensure compliance with existing procedures and standards to reduce the risk of road traffic crashes
Road safety strategy	-Both have the function to develop long term road safety plans -The NRSA functions further details out key road safety stakeholders and their involvement in the implementation of road safety plan
Monitoring	Only the NRSA has a defined function to monitor the importation and sale of road safety equipment or devices for the safe use on the roads
Database management	Both have the function to develop and maintain a comprehensive database on road safety for the information of the public
Research	-Both have the function to promote road safety research and studies and the publication of related reports -The NRSA further highlights engagement with other relevant agencies to achieve this function whilst the NRSC function does not
Enforcement	-Both have the function to investigate road safety issues and advise the Minister accordingly to minimize road safety risks
Post-Crash	NRSA has the right to launch investigations into road traffic crashes

3.5. RSM BY THE INSTITUTIONAL MANAGEMENT FUNCTIONS

3.5.1 Road Safety Coordination

Road safety coordination is often between a lead road safety agency, road safety stakeholder agencies, the private sector, community representatives etc. The partnership is based on an action-related agenda to address operational and strategic issues. Each entity identifies their component of road safety actions within their own operations for necessary interventions.

In Ghana, many government departments share responsibility for road safety at the national, regional and local levels. A framework of road safety coordination for the various stakeholder entities in Ghana is as presented in Figure 3.5.

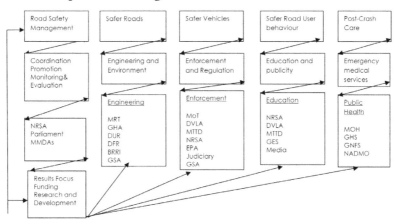

Figure 3.5: A Framework of Road Safety Management Function in Ghana

A. Responsibilities of Road Safety Stakeholder Entities in Ghana: *The road safety stakeholder entities develop road safety strategies and action plans within their jurisdictions coordinated by the NRSA. Each entity is then given the responsibility to implement their part of the action interventions within a set time frame using internally generated resources. The process is then supported by regular joint monitoring sessions coordinated by the NRSA on quarterly basis. An evaluation is also conducted by an independent consultant at the completion of each action phase. The statutory responsibility for road safety by each such agency is as follows:*

Stakeholder entity	Responsibilities
 Ghana Highway Authority (GHA) Department of Urban Roads (DUR) Department of Feeder Roads (DFR)	i. Road Agencies: There are the three road agencies with responsibility for the safe planning, design, development, construction, maintenance and operation of highways by the Ghana Highway Authority (GHA), urban roads by the Department of Urban Roads (DUR) and feeder roads by the Department of Feeder Roads (DFR) under the jurisdiction of the Ministry of Roads and Highways (MRH).
 Driver and Vehicle Licensing Authority (DVLA)	ii. DVLA: is responsible for the administration of state programmes for driver licensing, vehicle safety, inspection and registration.
 Motor Traffic and Transport Department (MTTD) of the Ghana Police Service	iii. The Motor Traffic and Transport Department (MTTD) of the Ghana Police Service is responsible for the enforcement of motor vehicle laws and regulations as well as security control at the scene of crashes as part of emergency response and the conduct of crash investigations.

Stakeholder entity	Responsibilities
 Ghana National Fire Service (GNFS)	iv. The Ghana National Fire Service (GNFS) is responsible for the rescue and evacuation of persons trapped in vehicles involved in RTCs as well as fire control in situations of fire outbreaks as part of RTCs. They for managing RTCs involving hazardous materials
 Ghana National Ambulance Service (NAS)	v. The Ghana National Ambulance Service (NAS) provides timely pre-hospital emergency medical care to the injured at the RTC scene as well as transport RTC victims to facility-based medical centres.
 Ghana Red Cross Society (GRCS)	vi. The Ghana Red Cross Society (GRCS): administers life-saving first-aid treatments to RTC victims as well as train community first aid respondents in the management of RTC injured victims at crash scenes.
 Saint John Ambulance (SJA)	vii. The Saint John Ambulance (SJA): provides first aid to RTC victims as well as train first respondents.
 National Disaster Management Organization (NADMO)	viii. The National Disaster Management Organization (NADMO): provides first aid and rescue support services at crash scenes as well as relief support to victims.
 Ghana Health Service (GHS)	ix. Ghana Health Service (GHS): oversees the operations of state health facilities, administer state injury prevention interventions and maintain trauma and injury databases.
 Ghana Education Service (GES)	x. Ghana Education Service (GES): though not recognised as a statutory road safety stakeholder entity, the GES coordinates with the NRSA for the development of road safety educational materials and school curricula for pupils and students as well as for the conduct of educational campaigns amongst school children.
 Local Government Service Secretariat (LGSS)	xi. Local Government Service Secretariat (LGSS): it establishes traffic laws in their jurisdictions and apply sanctions for non-compliance. They also serve as focal points for state safety programmes involving MMDAs.
National Development Planning Commission (NDPC)	xii. National Development Planning Commission (NDPC): includes road safety as a planning goal with performance criteria as well as integration of road safety strategies into national development plans to ensure effective funding of road safety projects.

Figure 3.6: Road Safety Stakeholder Crests

A major advantage of Ghana's stakeholder coordinating measures involving the road safety stakeholder entities is that it provides a common platform for work integration, sharing of ideas and knowledge etc. towards the achievement of common goals.

B. Challenges with road safety coordination: *The NRSP of 2008 states that Government will spell out the institutional responsibilities of the various stakeholders of road safety and take appropriate measures to ensure that the required legal, institutional and financial arrangements for road safety is put in place. However, the following remains a challenge to the achievement of the set objective for stakeholder collaboration.*

i. Missing Stakeholder Entities: Currently there are missing stakeholder entities which should be represented on the NRSA's road safety stakeholder committees but which are not. These include the Judiciary which is responsible for criminal procedures with respect to road safety enforcement, the Ministry of Education, the Ministry of Finance which is responsible for funding allocation to infrastructure development, health care etc. Others are representatives of Non-Governmental Organisations (NGOs); Civil Society Groups (CSOs) for whom road safety is of much concern and the private business sector.

ii. Disjointed Action Plans: Each stakeholder agency independently prepares its own road safety actions and budgets with no regard for an integrated approach. This results in wide variations in the type, range and quality of the activities implemented. This creates overlaps without the maximisation of limited resources. Typical examples are the road sector agencies, post-crash response teams etc. There is therefore a need to encourage road safety stakeholder entities to engage with each other especially with regards to common activities to address this. This must be done through stakeholder education for better understanding of road safety system as a whole, the importance of their contributions and the need for interaction between its elements so as to contribute to strong relationship and support systems for road safety work in Ghana

iii. Unbalanced Performance Levels: Also, whilst one entity performs well on an aspect, another can underperform to offset the gains made by the other. Thus, plans must be developed to complement each other's efforts.

iv. Treatment of Road Safety as a Non-Core Function: Some of the stakeholder entities who do not have road safety as their core agency function do not accord it the necessary premium within their operations and may allocate limited funding for the purpose. A typical example is road construction whereby some major road projects after construction record higher RTC's before speed calming or other safety installations are introduced compelling some community members to self-construct substandard road safety facilities such as speed humps.

In some cases, road safety activities are diffused with other agency programmes without separate budgets making it difficult to identify and evaluate achievements on outputs and outcomes such as the integration of road safety into maintenance budgets. It is therefore recommended that the road safety be clearly defined within agency strategic frameworks with estimated budget line items for approval by the NDPC and funding allocation by the Ministry of Finance supported by activity implementation flow charts.

v. Limitation of Coordination to National Level Operation: Currently, collaboration between the NRSA and its stakeholder entities are mostly limited to the head-office level. Regional engagements are very limited and that of the MMDA level is virtually non-existent. There is therefore a need to strengthen stakeholder activities and engagements at the regional and MMDA levels. (See Figure 3.7). Stakeholder entities should be categorized by ability so appropriate support can also be accorded as needed. Currently a platform has been developed for effective interaction with NGOs at the national level and this has to be disseminated to the regional and district level, albeit that very few NGOs are currently involved in road safety work.

Figure 3.7: Systems Approach to Road Safety Management

3.5.2 Road Safety Legislation

According to the WHO (2013), a comprehensive road safety legislation which incorporates evidence-based measures as well as strict and appropriate penalties, backed by consistent and sustained enforcement and public education has been proven to reduce traffic injuries and fatalities. It specifically identifies five (5) key risk factors for mandatory inclusion in road safety legislation as speeding, drink-driving, non-use of motorcycle helmets, seatbelts, and child restraint. It also calls for the enactment of new laws and the amendment of existing ones to support road safety strategies.

In Ghana, the road transport industry has been duly guided by road traffic laws and regulations. And this commenced ahead of the launching of the DOA 2011-2020. Such regulatory instruments have had successive repeals and amendments over the years to correct anomalies, upgrade existing laws and include omissions and the process continues as and when needed. Examples are as follows:

A. Ghana's Road Traffic Acts and Amendments: *Road Traffic Enactments in Ghana are summarised below and detailed in Appendix 3.3:*

i.   *Road Traffic Ordinance, 1952 (No. 55).*

ii. *Road Traffic (Amendment) Ordinance, 1957 (No. 18).*

iii. *Road Traffic Act 1959 (No. 21).*

*iv.	Road Traffic (Amendment) Act, 1971 (Act. 381).*

*v.	Road Traffic (Amendment) Law 1983 (P.N.D.C.L. 43).*

*vi.	Road Traffic Offences (Powers of Arrest) Law, 1992 (P.N.D.C.L. 304).*

*vii.	Road Traffic (Amendment) Act 1998 (Act 553).*

*viii.	Road Traffic Act 2004, Act 683.*

*ix.	Road Traffic (Amendment) Act 2008, (Act 761).*

*x.	Road Traffic Regulations, 2012 (L.I.2180.*

*xi.	Road Traffic (Amendment) Act 2020.*

B. Other Legislative Instruments on Road Transport and Safety: *Other legislative instruments on safety aside the traffic laws include the following:*

i. The PNDC Law 330 (CEPS Management Law) 1933: The law strengthened customs preventive functions to include duties for the erstwhile border Guards in addition to the revenue collection role. Though the main purposes of the law are not related to road safety, it retains aspects impacting standards of vehicle importation and training of drivers of motor vehicles and their examiners.

ii. The Ghana Police Act 1974: The Police Act gives the Ghana Police Service (GPS) the mandate to establish the MTTD to enforce Road Traffic Laws and Regulations.

iii. The GHA ACT 540 of 1997: This Act gives GHA the mandate to ensure effective, efficient and safe management of trunk roads in Ghana.

iv. The Road (Vehicle Use) Fee Act 556, 1998: The Act was enacted to provide for the imposition of fees for the use of vehicles on roads to generate funds for routine and periodic maintenance of the roads and to provide for related problems such as road safety.

v. The DVLA Act 1999, Act 569: Driver licensing and motor vehicle registration in the country dates back to the 1950's. The functions were then carried out by the Commissioner of Police (CoP), under the Ministry of Interior, in accordance with the provisions of the Road Traffic Ordinance No.55 of 1952. The geographical spread of the CoP's functions, in this regard, started with cities and towns such as Accra, Ho, Koforidua and Wa.

In1993, it was decided to transfer the functions of driver licensing and motor vehicle registration to a new organization which operated as a division of the Ministry of Transport and Communications. The organization was designated the VELD with the mandate to carry out the functions of driver licensing and motor vehicle registration throughout the entire country. VELD was later transformed and renamed as DVLA with an enabling Act of Parliament, Act 569 of 1999.

A key objective of the DVLA is "to promote good driving standards in the country, and ensure the use of roadworthy vehicles on the roads and in other public places". However, by the DVLA Act, it does not have authority to harmonize vehicle standards, importation of spare parts, etc. That responsibility is rather reflected in section 89 of the PNDC Law 330 (CEPS Management Act 1993).

vi. National Road Safety Commission Act 1999 (Act 567): Refer to section 1.2.2 Item A of Chapter One.

vii. The Ghana Highway Code of 1974: The Ghana Highway Code is the official state recognised traffic teaching and learning material widely used in traffic by motorists and driving schools in Ghana. It is the standard for acceptable road user behaviour by teaching road users how to drive, ride or walk on the roads in order to avoid RTCs. This is to attain road safety by strict compliance of its provisions by motorists and pedestrians.

viii. The National Road Safety Authority Act 993 2019: This is an amendment of NRSC ACT 567 of 1999 to transform the Commission to "Authority" status without conflicting existing ACTS especially DVLA ACT 569, Police ACT and GHA ACT 540.

C. Effective application of road safety regulations: *It is recommended for road safety regulatory applications to be subject to consistent upgrades and amendments as the need arises by participatory process through public engagements for ownership and effective implementations.*

In Ghana both the amendment of the road traffic law 2008 to the LI 2180 and the LI 2180 to LI 2020 were subject to public consultative processes as indicated below but the margin by which it can be said that the public are well informed on road traffic regulations cannot be established. (See Figure 3.8).

Figure 3.8: Stakeholder Consultations on Traffic Regulations

D. Constraints to road traffic laws and regulations: *Some of the constraints to effective road traffic regulations in Ghana are as follows:*

i. Lack of adherence to most of the existing Acts, regulations and by-laws and the absence of a regulatory authority to enforce compliance. Guidelines should be developed for prosecutors and law enforcement agencies to use in prosecuting road traffic safety offences.

ii. The legislative instruments on road traffic safety have Laws and regulations spread out in multiple legislations. For example, Act 683 makes overarching provisions on vehicle construction and use and LI 2180 also makes further provisions on construction and use. It is proposed for such multiple laws and regulations on road traffic safety scattered in multiple legislations be harmonized into a comprehensive instrument for ease of appreciation, reference and application.

iii. Some aspects of road traffic safety e.g. post-crash response and the handling of RTC victims have not been captured by existing laws and regulations on road safety as is in the case of other countries such as prohibition of the handling of RTC victims by lay persons as in Burkina Faso. It is proposed for the enactment of subsidiary legislations to address omitted issues.

3.5.3 Road Safety Financing and Resourcing

It is said that a good RSM should have access to sufficient and sustainable funding and some of the elements of a good road safety financing system includes the following;

- Use of a business approach to justify road safety funding allocation.
- Introduction of investment schemes to generate additional funding.
- Application of cost-effective measures in funding allocation to maximise resource utilisation.
- Application of good accounting systems with routine monitoring and auditing.
- Conduct of research to back effective utilisation of road safety funds.
- Establishment of dedicated road safety funds.

A. Funding Sources for Road Safety Activities: Various options for having a secured and appropriate road safety funding include proposed as best practice includes the following

i. Application of cost recovery systems through commercialisation

ii. Commitment of revenue from fines paid for traffic offences to road safety work especially for enforcement;

iii. Increased funding allocations from government treasury.

iv. Allocation of part of insurance premium to road safety management with.

v. Promotion of funding support from development partners, the private sector and Charitable Organisations etc.

Most of the funding for road safety activities in Ghana is provided by government especially with regards as provided in Table 3.9. However, with the exception of a contribution of a part of the revenue generated by the DVLA, Ghana does not pluck fines back into road safety work.

Table 3.9: Road Safety Funding Sources in Ghana

Road Safety Funding Source	Ministries	Sector Agencies	Road Safety Component
Government of Ghana's Consolidated Fund	Ministry of Finance	National Development Planning Commission	National Development Planning Agenda
	Ministry of Transport	-National Road Safety Authority -Driver and Vehicle License Authority	Transport services and operations
	Ministry of Roads and Highways	-Ghana Highway Authority -Department of Urban Road -Department of Feeder Roads	Road Development, maintenance and operation
	Ministry of Health	-Ghana Health Service -National Ambulance Service	Medical Care
	Ministry of Interior	-Ghana Police Service -Ghana National Fire Service -National Disaster Management Organisation	Enforcement and emergency response
	Ministry of Local Government and Rural development	Transport Departments	Safety at local government level
Road Fund	Ministry of Roads and Highways	-Ghana Highway Authority -Department of Urban Road -Department of Feeder Roads	Road maintenance
	Ministry of Transport	National Road Safety Authority	Road Safety Management
Internally Generated Revenue	Ministry of Transport	Driver and Vehicle License Authority	Driver and Vehicle Safety
Donor Sources	All Ministries	All Affiliated Agencies	All Components
Charitable donations	Non-Governmental Organisations'	Ghana Red Cross Society St John Ambulance	Emergency response as well as education and training
Insurance Premium	Ministry of Finance Ghana Insurers Association Insurance Commission	National Road Safety Authority	Road Safety Management

i. Consolidated Fund: The consolidated fund is the central government budget allocated from government treasury. This invariably applies to all components of road safety activities within each of the government's development agenda. However, it is of a general view that this source of funding falls short of the required threshold.

ii. The Road Fund: The Road Fund is generated from user fees from fuel tariffs, road tolls, driver and vehicle licensing fees, vehicle registration, road worthy charges and transit fees etc. It is mostly used to finance road maintenance with some allocation for road safety. In Ghana, it is estimated that the fund allocates an average of about US\$2million (2%) for road safety activities per annum and this is also considered to be inadequate.

iii. Development Loans and Grants: Funding from donor partners including multilateral and bilateral lending institutions also contribute to road safety through loans, grants, and technical assistance for infrastructure development and in some cases equipment supply. Ghana has benefited from such sources for work activities in diverse road safety components as sampled in Table 3.10.

Table 3.10: Road safety projects implemented with donor funding

SN	ACTIVITY	AMOUNT
Ghana Urban Transport Project – Agence Francaise de Development (AFD), International Development Association (IDA), World Bank		
Institutional Development	• Capacity Building for NRSA Staff • Procurement of Logistics for the NRSA	
Transport Sector Project – International Development Association (IDA), World Bank		
Improvement of Post-Crash on Ghana's roads	• Provision of 8No. First Aid Posts on the N1 and the N6	
Transport Sector Improvement Programme – World Bank, European Union		
Institutional Development	• Consultancy services for capacity needs assessment study for the National Road Safety Commission	• US$135,918.25
	• Consultancy services for Technical Assistance for the establishment of the National Road Safety Authority	• US$390,000.00
Awareness Creation	• Consultancy services for production of road safety education Audio-Visuals	• US$127,000.00
	• Procurement of Vehicles for Road Safety Education in communities	• US$511,713.11
Child Safety in Schools	• Consultancy Services for Identification of Basic School Locations for Installation of Road Crossing Aids ("Lollipop Stands") to Improve Child Safety in Ghana	• US$170,000.00
	• Production and erection of Lollipop Stands	• US$100,000.00
Road Accident Database Management	• Consultancy Services for Review and Design of a comprehensive plan for implementing iMAAP as the Nationwide Road Accident Database Management System (RADMS) for Ghana	• US$1,050,000.00
Research	• Consultancy Services for a Study to Determine the Scale and Magnitude of Safety among the Three (3) High Risk Road-User Groups in Ghana (Pedestrian, Passenger and Motorcyclists)	• US$148,083.50
	• Consultancy Services for a Study to determine the level of Travel Speeds in Ghana to serve as a baseline for Monitoring and Evaluation of Speed Management Programmes	• US$132,640.40

iv. Internally Generated Funds (IGF): According to Kazentet (2015), an IGF consists of funds collected from within own resources to supplement government funds.

In Ghana some of the road safety stakeholder entities including the NAS, GNFS and the GRCS are able to generate IGF from private corporate entities who engage their services such as staff training, event standby services etc. The DVLA also maintains a proportion its revenue from vehicle and driver registration etc. whilst the Police are earmarked to keep a proportion of fines from defaulting road users as IGF as soon as the proposed spot fine programme becomes effective.

v. Insurance Premium: Part of the insurance premium paid by vehicle owners on their vehicles are also used as proxy for road user safety fee in some countries. In Ghana the National Insurance Commission is by law required to allocate funds to the NRSA on annual basis but without a defined threshold. This creates uncertainty about how much would be allocated by year for effective planning.

vi. Proposed Fines and penalties: In some countries fines and penalties charged for road user offenses are also used for funding road safety activities.

In Ghana, though this has been discussed extensively, concrete measures are yet to be put on the ground for it to be effective.

vii. Charitable Donations and Corporate Support: Private firms and corporate entities also contribute to road safety by donations in cash and kind to both government-led programmes and that of non-government organizations. Examples in Ghana are as listed in Table 3.11.

Table 3.11: Charitable Organizations and Corporate Entities

SN	ORGANISATION / CORPORATE ENTITY	YEAR OF SUPPORT
I	Ghacem Limited	2016
II	Vivo Ghana (Shell Ghana)	2012 – date
III	Rana Motors	2021
IV	Ghana Insurers Association	2021
V	Coca Cola Bottling Company	2021
VI	Coalition of Journalist for Road Safety	2021

B. Percentage Allocation by Funding Sources for the NRSA: *In Ghana the road fund is the major source of funding for road safety followed by allocations from the National Insurance Commission. Table 3.12 provides the details of funding sources by percentage allocation to the NRSA.*

Table 3:12: Proportion of Funding Allocation by Funding Source to the NRSA

Funding Source	Percentage Contribution to NRSA Budget
Road Fund (by Law)	70
National Insurance Commission/ Ghana Insurers Association	20
Government of Ghana's Consolidated Fund	<5
Corporate Sponsorship	<1
Donor Sources	Intermittent

Source: NRSA, 2021

C. Constraints to Sustainable Road Safety Funding in Ghana: *The country is yet to achieve the DOA requirement for a self-standing dedicated road safety funding. Therefore, road safety activities are severely challenged with funding constraints. Figure 3.9 provides trends in NRSA actual funding releases by year compared to budget and that for actual road fund releases against budget presented in Figure 3.10. Similar trends pervade with the other road safety stakeholder entities.*

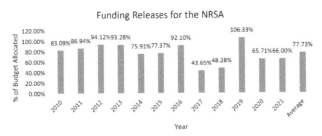

Figure 3.9: Funding releases for the NRSA

Figure 3.10: Percentage of Road Fund Received by Year

Currently the new NRSA Act 993 section 19 and 20 proposes the following percentage allocation of funding from the following sources as listed in Table 3.13.

Table 3.13: Proposed proportional allocation from funding sources

Funding Source	Proposed Percentage Allocation to Road Fund
Road Fund Annual Budget	3%
Vehicle Registration and Inspection Fees	2%
Insurance Premium	2%

Further to this, the Act states that the National Insurance Commission (NIC) and the Ghana Insurance Association (GIA) shall meet annually for the review of;

i.   *insurance stickers determined for motor insurance; and*

ii. *assessment of the beneficiaries of the moneys accruing to the NIC in respect of insurance stickers for motor insurance;*

iii. *also, subject to article 181of the Constitution and section 76 of the Public Financial Management Act, 2016 (Act 921), the authority may obtain a loan or other credit facility from a bank or any other financial institution which may be guaranteed by the Government.*

D. Suggestions for Improved Road Safety Funding: According to Navarro-Moreno J. et al. (2020), there is an established correlation between the amount of investment in road safety and its positive impact.

Therefore, there is the need for the provision of adequate funding for road safety activities in Ghana to ensure that road safety plans are delivered successfully. Currently the NRSA is normally is sometimes forced to cut down their road safety actions because of limited funding. Aside, the concept of a dedicated road fund recommended in literature for best practice to ensure sufficient and sustainable road safety funding, the following can also be considered to improve Ghana's road safety funding situation:

i.   *The dedication of revenue generated from traffic related activities such as fines from traffic offenses as well as fees for vehicle registration and licensing etc. solely to road safety activities.*

ii. *The dedication of user charges from specific sectors to related safety needs in those sectors such as;*

 a. *institution of a safety levy on driving license to fund national professional driver training centres to ensure that all professional drivers are of equal driver qualification;*

 b. *dedication of a proportion of fees from vehicle registration, road worthiness certificates and the transit fees to enforcement activities and education of vehicle safety;*

 c. *dedication of a proportion of the road fund allocation for road maintenance to the correction of safety related road defects within the maintenance activities of the road agencies;*

 d. *commitment of part of the statutory 17% of the Ghana National Health Insurance Scheme to the funding of RTC emergency response care at designated RTC prone centres in the country;*

 e. *mandatory integration of road safety into all road related donor-funded projects with clearly defined budget line items and cost stations solely for the road safety activities;*

 f. *there should be policy commitment to post-crash care as an emergency public health care component as was done with Covid-19. (See Figure 3.11).*

Figure: 3.11: Perceptions on the Impacts of RTCs

iii. *Optimization of the use of limited resources for road safety activities through;*

 a. *shared resources by stakeholders engaged in similar road safety activities;*

 b. *conduct of joint public private sector road safety schemes such as engagement with transport unions to commit a proportion of membership due for driver refresher training;*

 c. *application of cost-effective measures to maximise the use of limited funding through the prioritisation of options to convince politicians about the economic benefits of committing funds to road safety;*

 d. *Corporate support to road safety work should also be institutionalised for continuity and sustainability;*

E. Funding for Road Safety Equipment: The use of specialised equipment is an essential component of the road safety work spanning from simple to sophisticated equipment for training, traffic control, enforcement and treatment of the injured.

In Ghana such equipment are also applied albeit on a limited scale compared to that of the advanced countries and examples are as follows

i.   *Provision of speed guns and alcometers to the MTTD to enhance performance in enforcement activities.*

ii. *Supply of ambulance units to the NAS.*

iii. *Procurement of a simulator for professional driver training through private sector collaboration in the form of a Public Private Partnership (PPP) arrangement with the Ghana Technical Training Centre (GTTC).*

iv. *Procurement of tow trucks for the removal of disabled vehicles from the road by PPP arrangements.*

v.   *Provision of information and communication technology (ICT) infrastructure and communication equipment to facilitate road safety activities through the introduction of surveillance cameras for enhanced enforcement*

vi. *Development of various computer various softwares for the development and analysis of road safety data to enhance road safety work. (See Figure 3.12).*

Figure 3.12: Examples of Emerging Road Safety technologies in Ghana

However, the extent to which theses have facilitated road safety work is not yet researched but it is of general view that these are woefully inadequate for the scope of road safety works needed. Also, there is no formal schedule on equipment application to support effective road safety work in the country.

3.5.4 Road Safety Promotion

Road safety partnerships are formed in RSM to bring together different organizations who can contribute to advance the course of road safety.

Key partnerships in Ghana's RSM system are as discussed in the immediate sub-sections.

A. Political Support for Road Safety:

i. Parliamentary Affiliations in RSM: Political support is very important for achieving road safety targets. Thus, road safety managers are required to provide sound advice to government on road safety policies while also accommodating political decision making (International Transport Forum, 2008).

In Ghana, road safety has been promoted to a high-profile political recognition. Typically, the NRSA submits annual reports to parliament as well as conducts continuous engagement with the presidency through invitation of the President and Vice to its functions. (See Figure 3.13).

Figure 3.13: Examples of the Political Involvement in Road Safety

In 2019, a presidential initiative on road safety implemented under a special programme of action to reduce RTCs dubbed Presidential Special Initiative for Road Safety (PSI) with the following components:

a. *Release of an amount of GHS 6.50 million by the Ghana Road Fund to the NRSC for public education and sensitization in road safety.*

b. *Release of an amount of GHS 330.00 million by the MRH for the provision road furniture such as signs and markings, speed calming and pedestrian safety facilities on existing roads.*

c. *Release of funding to the Ghana Police Service (GPS) for the implementation of automated traffic enforcement operations under a PPP arrangement.*

However, initiated was not institutionalised for sustainability, unlike the Nigerian example whereby there is an instituted private sector honours from the office of the president for those who contribute resources to road safety. In Ghana, the Kofi Annan road safety awards could be extended to have such an extended component to encourage private sector contributions to road safety work in the country.

ii. Formation of Inter-Ministerial Road Safety Committee: An inter-ministerial road safety committee headed by the Ministry of Interior (MoI) and made up of MRH, MoT, Ministry of Communication (MoC) to coordinate road safety activities of the constituent ministries has also been set up to promote road safety work at the political level. However, the extent to which this initiative has translate into increased resource allocation for road safety is not known.

B. Private Sector Engagement in Road Safety Activities in Ghana: Private sector partnership in road safety is recognized as one of the key institutional functions in the systems approach to RSM.

Examples of private sector engagements in road safety in Ghana include the following and examples and some of the specific private entities engaged with are as listed in Table 3.14.

i. *The joint sale of reflective tapes.*

ii. *Joint partnership for the establishment of a driver's academy.*

iii. *The installation of surveillance cameras on major roads to check safety errors.*

iv. *The DVLA's engagement with Private Vehicle Testing Stations (PVTS) for vehicle road worthy certification.*

v. *Private corporate entities who provide sponsorship for road safety activities although mostly done on ad hoc basis without sustained reliability.*

vi. *Private sector collaboration for road safety research*

Table 3.14: Corporate Entities supporting road safety activities in Ghana

SN	Organisation / Corporate Entity	Year of Support
I	Ghacem Limited	2016
II	Vivo Ghana (Shell Ghana)	2012 – date
III	Rana Motors	2021
IV	Ghana Insurers Association	2021
V	Coca Cola Bottling Company	2021
VI	Coalition of Journalist for Road Safety	2021

Generally, private sector engagement for road safety delivery has not been developed to the levels whereby their contributions will make significant changes to road safety sustainability in Ghana.

On the way forward it is therefore suggested for the following to be considered:

a. *A substantive study must be conducted to position private sector inputs in road safety development in the country and to identify potential opportunities yet to be fully utilized.*

b. *Strategic partners for additional and special private sector engagements in road safety work should also be identified by the collation of information on what activities the private sector is willing to promote, to voice and to achieve to support road safety.*

c. *A policy on private sector support to road safety work should be clearly defined to cover, leveraging private sector funding for road safety projects, private sector engagements in road safety educational campaigns etc.*

d. *A framework for private sector support integrations, knowledge share and synergy creation in road safety work should be developed.*

e. *Industries such as alcoholic beverage producers should be mandated by law to commit to responsible marketing and best practice initiatives for safe road use.*

f. *Fleet operating companies should be encouraged to invest in safer vehicles, safe driving by self-funded driver refresher training programmes with specific content in defensive driving development of driver operational schedules, control of dangerous driving behaviour such as speeding, keeping within driving hours, avoiding overloading and ensuring that vehicles are well maintained.*

g. *Commercial transport owners should be encouraged not to make unreasonable demands that will instigate unsafe driving.*

h. *Standardised and documented guidelines should be developed for safe commercial transport service operation in Ghana for driver union compliance and for passenger care*

i. *Transport related business entities such as motor companies and spare parts dealers should be encouraged to support research in new technologies and share knowledge on best practices etc.*

C. Role of International Agencies in RSM: In recognition of the importance of the role of international agencies in road safety, the UN General Assembly in April 2016 adopted resolution 70/260 to consider the possibility of establishing, from voluntary contributions, a road safety trust fund to support the implementation of road safety-related SDGs. Pursuant to this resolution, with the support of the Secretary-General, the United Nations Road Safety Fund (UNRSF) was established in 2018 as a UN Multi-Partner Trust Fund for member States.

Ghana has benefited from this fund through the activities of the global road safety facility (GRSF). In addition to this the country has also received diverse donor support for diverse road safety activities including the provision of road infrastructure, equipment for enforcement activities and capacity development as listed in Table 3.14 above.

The key constraint is the ad hoc and intermittent nature of such support which does not ensure reliability and consistency on what to expect for planning purposes. They usually are project-based with a start and an end. Thus, international support road safety work must be reviewed for sustainability especially with regards to technical knowledge and skills not locally available.

D. Role of Non-Governmental Organisations (NGOs) in Road Safety: These include international, national and locally based NGOs, community-based organisations (CBOs), faith-based organizations etc. who provide additional support to government effort on road safety work. Leif A. E. (1994) recommends for engagements with such entities to include:

i. Having appropriate NGO partnerships by formal arrangements.

ii. Addressing time issues.

iii. Addressing flexibility issues.

iv. Addressing Funding issues.

v. Addressing Procurement and disbursement issues.

vi. Definition of roles and responsibilities.

vii. Addressing of contractual/legal issues.

viii. Addressing of capacity-building issues

In Ghana, NGO activities in road safety are mostly in the areas of road safety education and sensitization, training of first respondents for post-crash response and care, road safety advocacy etc. Currently there are two categories of NGO activity in Ghana.

a. Local NGOs: NGO activities in road safety by Ghanaian entities include 'Ghanalert' which engages in passenger education and welfare, 'the Safe drive initiative', the 'Street Sense' etc.

b. International NGOs: Some international agencies involved in road safety work in Ghana include the Bloomberg foundation, Amend, Transaid etc. These include two (2) NGOs with representations on the standing road safety stakeholder committee and these are the Ghana Red Cross Society (GRSC) and the St John Ambulance (SJA) who mostly engage in the training of first respondents at community and corporate levels. Examples of the areas of support by some of the NGOs are presented in Table 3. 15.

Table 3.15: NGOs and CSOs engaged in road safety in Ghana

SN	NAME	AREA OF SUPPORT
I	Amend Ghana	Child Safety
II	Street Sense Organisation	Driver and Motorcycle Safety
III	AMA Bloomberg Initiative for Global Road Safety	General Road Safety Improvement in Cities
IV	Ghana Driver and Road Safety Awards Foundation	Rewarding Driver Excellence
V	Goshen Bliss Entertainment (Face of Road Safety, Africa)	Road Safety Advocacy

Some of the key challenges associated with NGO activities in Ghana include the following:

* *There are very few NGO involvement in road safety work in Ghana so there should be campaign to encourage more NGOs to join road safety work in Ghana.*

* *The activities of fake NGOs who use road safety as a means for making illegal monies by soliciting for funds from well-meaning people for their private gains. This should be addressed by the adaption of good recommendations as suggested by Leif A. E. (1994) above. They should be duly registered, licensed and trained to operate with effective monitoring to ensure compliance*

E. Community Participation in Road Safety: This generates effective impacts because communities develop a sense of ownership and applies local knowledge. This helps to ensure that correct problems are identified with appropriate solutions as they are closer to road users. It also puts pressure on road managers to act on local priorities.

In Ghana, the NRSA also engages with local communities for road safety work by formal and informal means. The formal activities include engagement with religious bodies, traditional entities, NGOs, CBOs, national service personnel etc. in the implementation of some road safety educational activities as indicated in Figure 3.14.

Figure 3.14: Sample Publications on NRSA Engagement with Religious Entities

The informal activities include voluntary road safety advocates, voluntary community support such as self-assigned traffic wardens who volunteer their services for free at crossing points to assist child pedestrians; volunteers who provide intermediary traffic control services during blackouts and faulty traffic signal operations; volunteer pothole maintenance services; volunteer alertness of an RTC when they occur; humanitarian response to RTC situations such as voluntary transfer of RTC victims to health facilities by available drivers with vehicles; and among others. Constraints to community engagements in road safety mainly have to do with lack of leadership, skill and resources.

An SSATP study on community participation in traffic safety recommends for the involvement of road users in stakeholder committees; coordination with road safety professionals; participation in programme implementation; funding and training through the establishment of community funds and foundations. Additionally, it recommends the creation of awareness about the barriers and knowledge of community solutions to ensure that appropriate steps are taken to maximise the likelihood of community participation in road safety (sstp.org.)

3.5.5 Monitoring and Evaluation (M&E) of Road Safety Strategies

M&E of road safety programmes and projects is a part of the RSM functions. Monitoring refers to systematic performance review of a programme or project before, during or after implementation for comparison of outputs, achievement on set targets, outcomes and impacts with set objectives using set performance indicators. Evaluation involves assessment to determine the level of achievement on project objectives and activities for the attainment of expected results and desired change. The types of monitoring activities can be categorised as follows:

A. Process monitoring: Road safety process monitoring is performed continuously in the life of an intervention to establish what is going well or not going well for appropriate corrections toward the achievement of set objectives and targets.

B. Impact Monitoring: Road safety impact monitoring is focused using data to determine the effect of the treatment or programmes/projects.

The process involves the selection of indicators, identification of data types needed by source, definition of data collection methods, data collection, processing, analysis, reporting and knowledge sharing. This is essential to drive improvements and also help to ensure that targets are met.

In Ghana the M&E of road safety interventions is a critical component of RSM. It is conducted by the NRSA in joint collaboration with the statutory road safety stakeholder entities. Process monitoring is conducted through performance review of ongoing road safety actions plans by the standing stakeholder committee at quarterly, mid-term and yearly interval. Impact monitoring is undertaken after completion of project action plans at bi-annual intervals by independent consultants engaged by the NRSA.

Another aspect of impact monitoring involves the evaluation of specific project interventions such as focused campaigns on drink driving, seatbelt use, fatigue driving, etc. Some of the key issues that are addressed include:

i.   *Establishment of the differences between scheduled and achieved activities.*

ii. *Determination of milestones achieved and identification of tasks that are behind schedule and the causative factors.*

iii. *Matching of budget scope and scheduled activities.*

iv. *Identification of new targets and timelines and where possible new budget levels which should be set.*

v.   *Identification of follow-up activities to ensure that corrective factors from monitoring results are effected*

C. Constraints to Effective Road Safety Monitoring: *Some of the key constraints to the realisation of the benefits of the NRSA's M&E processes includes the followings:*

i. Project progress challenges identified are not always addressed and the same issues keep reoccurring especially with regards to funding shortfalls. In this regard, a scheduled framework for addressing project implementation challenges identified from monitoring activities should be developed after monitoring process to guide the implementation of mitigation factors. Also, where budget shortfalls are identified, project rescaling and prioritisation should be prepared to enable the implementation of critical activities within the available budgets for maximum benefits.

ii. The lack of assessment of technical capacity and capability for the achievement of set project targets as a part of the M&E process. This is due to assumed capacity availability for effective implementation of works. Capacity needs assessment for the implementation of set action plans should therefore be conducted as a part of the activity planning process to determine what capacity development activities will be needed to complement set programmes.

3.5.6 Road Safety Data Management

Effective RSM is data-driven and evidence-based since RTC data provides information on crash level, patterns and risk factors necessary for policy direction, basis for prioritising investments and the countermeasures needed.

A. Principles of road safety data collection and management: The factors causing RTC's are complex and the following principles from literature are key to RTC data collection and analysis

i.   RTC databases should be comprehensive and accurate to accurate decision making.

ii.   The data should include all dimensions and causes of RTCs for appropriate road safety strategies.

iii. The information must be from appropriate sources backed by authentic data collection and analysis methods with adequate coverage well-presented.

iv.   The data must be of good quality and be presented in an integrated from the relevant sources such as data from the police on crash records, health records of RTC victims, death registration, vehicle and road data.

v.   The frequency of the data collection must be commiserated with data utilisation regimes and must incorporate relevant and essential components for required purposes.

vi.   Raw data should be available for ease of analysis in whichever format required.

vii. The databases should have crash narratives and diagrams typically found in original crash reports for ease of interpretation and analysis

B. Road Safety Data Variables: This often include road data, traffic data, vehicle data, crash records, health records on RTC victims, death records on RTC victims, Insurance data etc. Table 3.16 provides examples of the content of RTC data variable collated from literature.

Examples of the RTC data types in Ghana are also as summarized in Table 3.17.

Table 3.16: Summary of road safety data variables

Rational for Road Safety Data	Road Safety Data Elements
Magnitude, trends and patterns of road traffic fatalities and injuries	Number of crashes involving all road users.
	Number of all road users killed in road traffic crashes.
How big is the problem?	Number of all road users injured in road traffic crashes.
	Total number of road traffic fatalities and injuries, preferably disaggregated by road user types.
What types of traffic conflict lead to crashes?	Involvement of cars, trucks, heavy goods vehicles, public transport vehicles, motorcycles, bicycles and animal-drawn carts, etc. Vehicle manoeuvres (e.g. turning).
On what day of the week and at what time do road traffic crashes occur?	Date and time of injuries.
How serious are the injuries?	Severity of road traffic crashes
What types of crash lead to disability or life-threatening outcomes?	Outcome following collisions.
Who is involved in road traffic collisions?	Age and sex of those killed or injured in road traffic crashes.
How many people live in the country being assessed?	Population
Where do road traffic crashes occur?	Place of crash (specific location such as urban, rural and type of road). Dangerous road locations
Complementary Information	Total number of persons in the population under study (including disaggregation by urban and non-urban, by age and income).
How and why do people typically travel around the country?	Transport modes used. Trip distances. Trip purposes. Origins and destinations of trips
What is the socioeconomic condition of the country under assessment?	Gross domestic product. Proportion of adults employed. Household income.

Table 3.17: Characteristics of Other Data Types

Category of Data Type	Description of Data Type	Constraints
Traffic Data	Fatalities by vehicle types Data on Traffic Flow patterns	Not compiled as part of road safety data
Vehicle and Driver Data	Vehicle population by category Vehicle Registration data Vehicle Licensing data Vehicle Roadworthiness data Driver licensing data	Missing data include vehicle road worthiness data.
Health Data	-Data on transfer time, -Data on health care needs such as number of medical facilities with accident centres, number of hospital beds, number of paramedics, RTC medical care givers, number of doctors, number of ambulances, -Data on RTC injury type -Data on death certificates -Data on classification of cause of death -Data on types of injuries treated by severity	-Data not collated as part of RTC database -Misclassification of cause of death
Insurance Data	Data on types of Damages including injuries and deaths -Data on vehicle damages	Not compiled as part of road safety data
RTC Data Elements	-Number of crashes involving all road users. Number of all road users killed in road traffic crashes. Number of all road users injured in road traffic crashes. Total number of road traffic fatalities and injuries, preferably disaggregated by road user types -Distribution across the time of the day -Distribution across the week -Distribution across the year -Distribution across the regions	Missing data include the causes of crashes by the use of cause codes

Category of Data Type	Description of Data Type	Constraints
Road Characteristics Road layout, design and environment	-Road Length by category -RTC by road location -RTC by collision type Value addition to this require a study on Intelligent Transport Systems (ITS) which will pick traffic information in real-time for immediate response	Data on hazardous road sections is missing
Road User Type Data	-Fatalities by road user type -Fatalities by age and sex -Distribution across age groups -Data by Driver License by four, three and two wheelers Category -Road service licensees for public transport	
Demography Demographics of the county from Ghana Statistical Services,	Country population Population distribution by region/districts	
Enforcement	Statistics on traffic violations	Records of violations are not made by the Police
Transport Characteristics	Transport modes used. Trip distances. Trip purposes. Origins and destinations of trips	Data is available in piecemeal There is no information on transport service characteristics

C. RTC Data Collection Methods: Around the world, RTC statistics are collected by the police who register information on crashes since they are usually among the first to reach the scene. The information is often recorded using paper / electronic forms that are very condensed and contain all the necessary details. The forms are filled at the scene of the RTC and are usually supplemented with other information, in the form of attachments such as statements from drivers, pedestrians and witnesses (ADB, 2000).

In Ghana first hand RTC data is collected by the MTTD with a standard form at RTC sites. (See Appendix 3.4) for sample RTC scene data collection form used by the police. The second stage is a follow up to health facilities for records on victim survival after 30 days of RTC occurrence (which is the standard for ascertaining RTC fatality that occur outside the RTC scene in Ghana). These visits are also made by the MTTD officers though this cannot be certified to be done as required. The RTC location is also coded accurately as a part of the RTC report to be used for evaluation of road safety strategy and policy.

D. RTC data quality: This relates to the definitions used for road traffic death and injury; the level of completeness of reporting on road traffic injuries; the extent of omissions; the type of errors existing in the data measurement, mode of data recording, coding and entry as well as data analysis and reporting.

In some cases, the MTTD does not complete the filling of the form at the RTC scene but rather at the office and this results in loss of some of the RTC memory in Ghana. Others are difficulties in determining age and sex of victims especially in fatal crashes with mangled human bodies as well as burns from fires. There is need therefore to enforce passenger data records by Transport operators before journey take offs especially for commercial transport operations to address this challenge.

E. Data storage and management: This refers to information systems used to process, analyse and store data and for keeping recorded data be it electronic or manual.

In Ghana police RTC data is collated in raw state and analysed by the BRRI on contract basis for the NRSA. An electronic-based road safety information system is used for the data processing, analysis, storage and reporting on annual basis. The data outputs generated are as listed in Table 3.17 above. This is required to be updated on annual basis except for a few instances where the data collation is delayed for one reason or the other mostly due to limited funding.

E. Data harmonisation and integration: It is recommended to develop a comprehensive single source of Road Safety Information System (RSIS) which links all the data elements frequently used along with crash data such as health, insurance, road and vehicle data etc. By integrating road safety data, safety professionals are able to identify all elements that may lead to higher frequency or injury severity and as such develop a systemic approach to reduce those risk elements.

The process for achieving this is in progress in Ghana. The key achievement on data integration so far relates to the integration of vehicle registration and insurance databases enabling the Police by the click of a given code to check the state of validity of a vehicle's insurance through a simple process as;

i. *dial *920*57#;*

ii. *enter the vehicle number in the pop-up;*

iii. *press send*

iv. *receive a notification with the vehicle insurance particulars, if it is genuine.*

F. RTC information dissemination: RTC information is required to be disseminated widely within the road safety community to help to increase awareness of road safety activities and related challenges (Hills and Baguley, 1994). These are done on diverse online information-sharing platforms such as the GLOBESAFE, a platform for information sharing among road safety organizations (www.globesafe.org) and the ARSO for Africa on which Ghana is signed.

However, Ghana has not graduated to the stage of developing a national road safety portal open to the public.

G. Utilisation of RTC data systems: Road safety data is used by different actors in the road safety fraternity for different purposes and they include the following:

i. Identification of high-risk groups.

ii. For objective planning and resource management.

iii. For effective monitoring and evaluation of achievements on set targets.

iv. For international comparisons to inspire better performance.

H. Constraints on road traffic crash data management: According to Bhalla et al (2014), most official government statistics especially in developing countries underreport road traffic injuries or are characterised by biased reporting. This is o perceived to vary by injury severity, with comparatively less underreporting of deaths. The under reporting is said to be often caused by limited police capacity and refusal to report RTC's by the parties involved in some instances.

According to the WHO, on average official data in LICs do not record 84% of the deaths and in 51% in MICs. This is because most countries conduct relatively few studies to validate the quality of police data by cross checking with other data sources such as RTC death records at hospitals, mortuaries, death registers and funeral records. The WHO therefore uses several formula-based methods to adjust for underreporting (WHO, 2010), but these are not discussed in this book.

The sources of RTC data in Ghana as well as their respective strengths and weaknesses are presented in Table 3.18 and the related challenges are as discussed in the immediate sub sections.

Table 3.18: Strengths and weaknesses of RTC data sources in Ghana

Data Sources	Strengths	Weaknesses
Ghana Police Service (MTTD)	• It is national in terms of coverage • Collect most of the important data elements • Available on daily basis • Raw data can be analysed in whichever format you want	• Most of the information derived from this data source is fatal injuries • There are no electronic linkages with the other data sources • The data is provided in raw absolute formats and not in tabulated or other customized specifications • Demonstrates a weak link to other systems for follow up of injuries • Definitions on the severity of injury by the police is not standardized as per international requirement. • The Police aren't trained to differentiate the same.
Ghana Health Service (Various Health Institutions)	-Information about RTC related health data picks on the burden and severity of RTCs. -It is required for determining the types of health services required for managing injuries and the cost of treating patients.	• People with minor injuries not seeking formal medical care are not captured; • There is poor access to health facilities; • Injuries treated at private hospitals remain unrecorded • There is problem with collecting data death data within 30 days of the occurrence of an RTC as stipulated by the WHO. • Lack of training, expertise, interest or time on the part of health workers, who may do not record all relevant details of the injury; • Incorrectly data coded by health workers or persons responsible for data extraction or data entry.
Ghana Statistical Service	Provides information on transport characteristics and general population data	The data collection regime for transport information is erratic and the last was in 2017
Birth and Death Registration Department	Provides records on deaths caused by RTC	Data is not currently well defined for ease of extraction of RTC related deaths

Data Sources	Strengths	Weaknesses
The Ghana Insurance Commission and Insurance companies	The insurance sector offers financial security against the costs of damages and medical treatment incurred either by or levied against clients involved in road crashes	Absence of a common database for all insurance companies including both private and public insurance companies
Records of the National Ambulance Service	Provides information on number of ambulances, distribution, number of paramedics, availability and frequency of service	Data records do not segregate RTC related cases from other emergency cases. Information is not well disseminated and utilisation is considered to be low
The National Road Safety Authority (NRSA) and the Building and Road Research Institute (BRRI)	Provides all data on essential RTC elements including injuries, fatalities etc. Common data elements for crash data include information on date, location, injury severity, types of vehicles, and characteristics of persons involved.	Data does not provide details on causes of RTCs
Private Road Transport Companies	Records on membership by type of service	Data not available
National Road Agencies	Data on road network characteristics and traffic	Traffic data is erratic
The Driver and Vehicle Licensing Authority	Provides data on vehicle and driver characteristics	Details of vehicle composition is based on engine capacity and not by vehicle type. Data on road worthy vehicles is not readily available Data on vehicle removed from the traffic system is not accurately data Driver registration by vehicle class is also not available

i. Limited coverage Road Safety Data Coverage: In Ghana, whereas the current data management system provides readily available data on final outcomes of RTCs (crashes, casualties, fatalities, injuries etc.), it has limited information on intermediate outcomes such as seat belt usage rates, road user attitudes and beliefs, speeding behaviour, etc. This data is only available in occasional research reports for specific geographic locations rather than from a consistent data collection regime countrywide and this must be corrected.

ii. Underreporting: There are unreported RTC cases especially in remote places as well poor hospital follow ups by the police on the 30 days survival rate. A report prepared for the WHO, by the NRSA, on the level of discrepancies in road safety databases in Ghana indicated that that the level of discrepancies between the police database and the sample from the hospital is about 16%. Data obtained from the births and deaths registry lacked the prerequisite variables (date and location of crash) to be used to conduct a meaningful linkage and the absolute deaths compared abysmally to the police records. For example, over the study period, 454 road deaths were registered by the births and deaths registry while 4,601 fatalities were recorded by the police. (WHO/NRSA, 2021).

iii. Raw RTC Data Reporting Format: The police data is provided in raw absolute formats without customized specifications until the application of further processing and analysis by the BRRI. It is also characterised by information processing formats mostly suited only for the preparation of case dockets for prosecution. Others are delayed crash data records, incomplete crash forms, over reliance on incorrect eye witness accounts on causes of crashes due to delays in data collection, wrongly assigned faults and wrong choice of crash type usually based on eye witness accounts and physical simulation of RTC crash patterns by the police resulting in related subjective influences on the data. Adequate training is recommended to be provided to the Police to address this challenge.

iv. Failure to Define some RTC Causative Factors: There are also difficulties in determining some vehicle and driver RTC causative factors especially with regards to impaired driving, fatigue driving, poor driver health situations and none visible vehicle defects due to the inability to provide proof for such causes by the Police. There is need therefore to train and equip the MTTD with modern equipment for the purpose.for the conduct of further investigations such as blood alcohol test, urine test for drugs, speed level assessment levels etc.

v. Classifications on Injury Severity: These are not easily determined by the Police since they are not medical personnel and have also not been trained to differentiate same. There is need for close collaboration between the police and the health sector to establish accurate information on this.

vi. Data Aggregation: Some data components are only presented as national statistics with no details for sub administrative levels such as the MMDA level though the procedure of data collation is bottom up. This does not encourage a bottom-up approach to road safety planning to meet local specific challenges and the reverse should be applied.

vii. Lack of RTC Data Integration: The current road safety database on the essential RTC elements is not linked to the other databases defined in Table 3.21a, though it is globally recommended for integrated databases to be developed for effective road safety analysis. Ghana has currently used the Microcomputer Accidents Analysis Package (MAAP) system for road safety data analysis, to link its road safety data base with police records, health records, mortuary records, death registration records, road and vehicle records etc. under the Road Accident and Data Management System (RADMS) pilot project. The outcome is expected to be expanded to cover the rest of the country.

viii. Lack of Provision for Unique RTC Records Demands: This includes situations such as RTC fatalities involving Moslems who need to be buried within the shortest possible time by the demands of the faith. The best practice is the Nigerian situation based on the use of a special template as a crash form dubbed the D10 data template and information system. This is used to capture crash details for Moslems throughout the country even at the local level to facilitate the processing of a Moslem victim from an RTC fatality for quick release of the body for burial.

3.5.7 Technologies in Road Safety Data Management

These include RTC data systems for storage, reporting and retrieval. The data once captured are processed, refined and analysed for required outputs (AfDB, 2000). Currently they are tailor made computer-based software developed and designed for road safety information management. Such systems are designed for predefined user requirements (Heinrich and Mikulik, 2005).

A. Features of Road Safety Management Information Systems: The GRSP, (2003), reported and recorded the following as key features required for such systems are as presented in Box 3.3:

Box 3.3: Features of RTC database management systems by GRSP

- Where did the accident occur? (Location data)
- When did the accident occur? (Attribute data)
- Who was involved? (Deaths, injuries, etc.)
- What were the consequences of the collision? (Costs)
- What were the environmental conditions? (Descriptive)
- How did the collision happen? (Descriptive)
- Development of valuable assets management system such as digital assets management facilities and infrastructure. Eg. Black spot data management system and accident data management.
- Decision support information tools designed to improve strategy, decisions and problem solving.
- Data Quality improvements that reduce operational errors.

B. Examples of Road Safety Data Management Systems: Some examples of international RTC database systems are as follows:

i. The Microcomputer Accidents Analysis Package (MAAP): The MAAP is the most recognized international computer software for RTC data management system developed by the Transport Research Laboratory, (TRL1994). It consists of two basic parts. The first allows accident investigators to record accident data. The second part of the package includes the accident analysis data application within which different types of analyses can be made. The analysis engine provides extensive reporting facilities in different formats that lead to better understanding of the situation and of the causes of RTCs. It uses both graphical and tabular data presentation methods as well as presentation of location information on maps.

ii. The Swedish Traffic Accidents Data Acquisition (STRADA): This is configured along the lines of the MAAP systems.

iii. The Community Road Accident Database (CARE) by the European Commission on Transport.

iv. The International Road Traffic and Accident Database (IRTAD) developed and operated by the members of the Organization for Economic Cooperation and Development (OECD).

v. The SfingeNETSafety Manager Systems: It is a web application for collection and analysis of accidents data developed by Centro di ricerca per ilTrasporto e la Logistica (CTL) – "Sapienza" Università di Roma; and

vi. The Driver Road Safety Information Management System by the World Bank for Developing Countries.

In Ghana, the NRSA through its work with the TRL and BRRI have conducted a pilot trial for the establishment of a digitised crash data collection, processing and storage system dubbed as the Road Accident data Management System (RADMS). The system has a digitised application for the collection of crash data using simple applications like the mobile phone which is directly transported to the BRRI by the police after completion of the digitised crash form. This is in turn downloaded into the Internet Based Microcomputer Accident Analysis Package (iMAAP- Cloud, a web-based Accident Analysis Software System) which is an upgrade of the MAAP system by TRL.

The system has the advantage of providing real time crash data as an upgrade of the current manual system which had some years of data backlog. Preparations are also underway to roll out the application of the system following the successful pilot phase of the project. The key challenge is that over the years, the NRSA has not as yet developed its internal capacity for independent management of the road safety management systems. It has mostly depended the BRRI a third-party service provider for the operation of the system. This does not ensure absolute ownership and control by the NRSA and should be corrected.

3.5.8 Road Safety Research and Development in Ghana

RSM research provides critical understanding of barriers towards the achievement of good road safety results and it is required to cover all the aspects of road safety needs including road engineering, vehicle factors, education, health, legislation, enforcement and emergency care.

A. Road Safety Policy on Research in Ghana: *It required in RSM for road safety policy on research to be in place and the policy content on research in Ghana as indicated in Box 3.5.*

Box 3.5: Road Safety Policy Content on Research

Policy Strategies

- Promote holistic and integrated road safety research initiatives to guide policy formulation and interventions.

- Encourage own-account or sponsored research into relevant or critical road safety issues.

- Develop mechanisms for consolidating and disseminating road safety research findings.

- Identify sustainable funding sources to finance research projects

NRSP 2008

B. Examples of Road Safety Research Studies in Ghana: *Some research studies covering the defined pillars conducted by, the NRSA and other entities including private consultants; international institutions and partners; the academia especially higher educational institutions at bachelor, master and doctorate levels and affiliated research entities such as the BRRI. Typical studies by the NRSA are as listed below in Box 3.6:*

Box 3.6: Examples of road safety research conducted in Ghana

- The Socio-Economic Cost of Road Traffic Accidents in Ghana (BRRI, 2006)

- Evaluation of Fatigue Campaign for Road Safety for the National Road Safety Commission (Ablin, 2007)

- Consultancy Services for the Evaluation of Road Safety Education and Publicity Programmes of the NRSC in Five Regions (Ablin, 2008)

- A study on "Used Tyres" in Ghana and its Impact on Road Safety in Ghana (Grid-Goal-Besuma Associate, 2008)

- Validation of Vehicle Fleet in Ghana (BRRI, 2008)

- A study into the Conditions of Service of Commercial Vehicle Drivers and their impact on Road Safety (Ablin, 2008)

- A study to determine the Social and Psychological Influences on Driver Behaviour and Its Impact on Road Safety (NRSA In-house, 2009)

- Study of the Emergence and Use of Motorcycles for Commercial Transport Services in Ghana (Ablin, 2010)

- Needs Assessment Study towards Strengthening the Capacity for Emergency Response Services for Road Crash Victims (Ablin, 2012)

- A study to assess the Scale and Magnitude of Pedestrian safety in Ghana's Road Traffic System and Recommendations for the Cost-Effective measures by which the problem can be addressed (BRRI, 2014)

- A study to determine the Level of Compliance of Seatbelts and Crash Helmet Usage in Ghana (BRRI, 2015)

- A study to determine the Scale Magnitude of Driving under the influence of alcohol and its impact on Road Safety in Ghana (BRRI, 2015)

- Preparation of Region-Specific Analysis of Critical Road Traffic Crash Statistics and Recommendations for Improvement (Ablin, 2016)

- Evaluation of the Effectiveness of Pedestrian and Passenger Safety Campaigns in Ghana (Ablin, 2016)

- A Study to Determine the Scale and Magnitude of Safety among the Three (3) High Risked Road-User Groups In Ghana (Pedestrians, Passengers And Motorcyclists) (Ablin, 2019)

- Consultancy Services for a Study to Determine the Level of Travel Speeds in Ghana as a Baseline for Monitoring and Evaluation of Speed Management Programmes (Vision/IRTI, 2019)

Some research outcomes in Ghana have also been used to influence legislation and as well changed industrial practices in these areas:

i.　*Legislation on Helmet use and seatbelt use.*

ii.　*Development of effective road safety campaign methods.*

iii.　*Provision of traffic safety around school zones.*

C. Constraints to Road Safety Research: Some of the key challenges to road safety research in Ghana include:

i. The absence of a national road safety research agenda: There is no prioritised road safety research themes in Ghana by the road safety stakeholder entities and research is mostly conducted by the NRSA on ad hoc basis. There is a need for a strategic research framework on the six pillars of road safety to ensure adequate coverage of the road safety research needs.

ii. Limited funding support for research: The NRSA is saddled with the imbalance of committing some of its limited funding for most of the road safety research studies. Individual stakeholder entities could source for budget line items for their internal research needs. There could also be joint research with industries, stakeholders and other collaborators such as the ECOWAS where feasible to reduce cost.

iii. Lack of research repository: Various research studies have been and are undertaken by different entities including the academia, the NRSA itself, some NGOs such as the street sense etc. However, there is no research repository to host previous research outputs for ease of access. Thus, it is not uncommon for the NRSA to repeatedly request for research reports from service provides long after the completion of such studies. The NRSA should therefore facilitate the development of a repository on previous research findings both internal and external so that recommended solutions can be available to facilitate effective utilisation, avoid repetitions of previous studies and a waste of limited resources.

iv. Poor Dissemination of Research Outcomes: There is also a lack of set mechanism for dissemination of research information to respective entities for application. Appropriate platforms should be established for road safety research knowledge share.

iv. Road safety engineering interventions not informed by research findings. This is because the entities do not apply consistent monitoring to standards adopted from international specifications to ascertain their efficacy to mitigating identified constraints in Ghana. It is hoped that the array of knowledge gaps and suggested strategic actions proposed in the book can serve as a key reference point to advance road safety research in Ghana.

3.6 ROAD SAFETY STRATEGIES AND ACTION PLANS

Road safety involves the implementation of a number of countermeasures identified by need and different stakeholder entities to achieve set objectives. These are essential to positively impact on road traffic deaths and injuries in the short and long term. Since road safety is multi-sectoral and multidisciplinary such plans must cover all aspects. These must be backed by appropriate regulatory frameworks, effective institutional structures and effective data management systems with key focus on desirable change in road safety trends. They are to be within realistic targets for at least five (5) to ten (10) years and backed by scheduled action timelines and allocation of specific resources, (WHO, 2018).

In Ghana, the NRSA has since its establishment under the NRSC in 1999, with the collaboration of its stakeholder agencies been designing and implementing data-led road safety activities within a set strategic framework. They are mostly composed of strategies defined for different components of road safety covering all the pillars.

3.6.1 Development of Road Safety Strategies and Action Plans

The development of road safety strategies and action plans involves the preparation of well justified, prioritized and coordinated activities of action to mitigate such problems for implementation guided by set goals. Other aspects include the setting of activity timelines, targeted outputs, budgets and assigned responsibilities for activity implementation by components with monitoring schedules.

Such strategic action plans are to be informed by RTC statistical records as well as through consultations and coordination with all stakeholders so that stakeholder components will be duly reflected. In Ghana, the process is conducted through the following steps:

- *Formulation of stakeholder working committee.*
- *Conduct of stakeholder consultations.*
- *Road safety policy statement and element analysis.*
- *Road safety statistical assessment.*
- *Problem analysis and opportunities by the application of problem and objective tree assessment, SWOT analysis etc.*
- *Development of strategies for key challenges, constraint and weaknesses.*
- *Enumeration of action plans / programmes for each strategy with targets, timelines, roles and responsibilities etc.*
- *Conduct of validation workshops to finalise outcomes*

3.6.2 Road Safety Strategies and Action Plans Developed for Ghana

Ghana has since the year 2000 implemented three national road safety strategies complemented with action plans. The strategies are developed for long to medium (5-10years) term implementation from which two-year short term action plans are extracted and implemented until the completion phase of a particular strategic framework. This approach provides a list of concrete actions able to be managed within available budgets at specific time periods. It also allows lessons learnt from the assessments of past performance to inform the implementation of new actions plans for good results.

A. National Road Safety Strategy I (NRSS I): *The first National Road Safety Strategy (NRSS I) implemented by the NRSC was from 2001-2005. It was implemented six years ahead of the launching of the DOA and was initiated in line with resolutions from the African Ministerial Conference on Road Safety in 2000. The NRSS I focused mostly on developing the foundations for a good road safety management system. This included the establishment of relevant institutional frameworks for RSM in Ghana, road safety human resource capacity mobilization, definition of work modalities, collation of relevant working tools such as the development of road safety policies and legislation etc. It also provided a broad road safety activity framework by components and sub components on the road safety pillars though the pillars were not specifically defined at the time.*

B. National Road Safety Strategy II (NRSS II): *The NRSS I was followed by the NRSS II 2006-2010 to consolidate the gains made in NRSS I. Thus, the key issues that emerged from the evaluation of NRSS I as well as newly identified challenges formed the basis for the development of the NRSS II. Its focus was mainly on resource development especially with regards to training and capacity development for effective implementation of different aspects of road safety programmes, conduct of research for evidence-based road safety interventions, the development of manuals and guidelines to streamline road safety actions as well as the implementation of targeted road safety countermeasures of high priority.*

C. National Road Safety Strategy III (NRSS III): *The NRSS III covered a ten-year period, 2011 – 2020. Its development took into specific consideration of the demands of the DoA 2011-2020 as it applied to Ghana's situation. The Broad objective was to halt unacceptable levels of road traffic fatalities and injuries by 2015, and thereafter, reduce it by 50% by end of 2020. It was sub divided into three action plans covering a two-year period each spanning 2011-2013, 2015-2017 and 2018 -2020.*

The key reference point in the implementation of the NRSSIII has been the need to empower the NRSC to ensure compliance to implementing approved road safety programmes and activities by key stakeholder Agencies and the enhancement of the capacity of the NRSC to facilitate effective coordination and collaboration among stakeholders. It also focused on seeking sustainable funding and the introduction of innovative measures for effective road safety implementation in Ghana. Although almost all the three strategies have addressed aspects of the road safety pillars defined in the DoA, the third strategy placed more emphasis and also highlighted on important issues such as the wearing of seat belts, use of mobile phones, etc.

D. National Road Safety Strategy IV (NRSS IV): *This has been prepared for the period 2021 to 2030 to correspond to the extended DOA for the next steps in the global road safety agenda. The key aspects involved correction of past errors, decentralisation of road safety planning and implementation to the district level with an implementation strategy to suit the role of NRSA as an authority. It is also aimed to achieve the set SDGs.*

All the national road safety strategies of Ghana are implemented through coordinated and collaborative efforts of the NRSA and the key stakeholder agencies involved in road safety work. Each stakeholder entity is made responsible for the implementation of their component of the action plans. All activities in the strategies were monitored and appraised at regular intervals to assess status based on set indicators and identification of challenges for redress. A summary of the main action points within each of the implemented road safety strategic frameworks in Ghana is as presented in Appendix 3.5.

E. Constraints to the development and implementation of NRSS's in Ghana: *Some challenges associated with the implementation of the road safety strategies and action plans in Ghana include:*

i. Limited funding: This results in the inability to achieve set targets and objectives for reduced injuries and fatalities in RTCs. Due to this, over the years, most activities have repeatedly been rolled over year after year. The selection of road safety activities should also be prioritised to ensure maximum utilization of limited resources. Stakeholder institutions should identify opportunities for soliciting and generating increased internal funding to support project implementation.

ii. Complexity of the Road Safety Problem: The complex interaction between human behaviour, the social, physical environment and the different circumstances within which RTCs occur makes it difficult to determine the level and adequacy of interventions for each of the multiple elements required to address road safety challenges. It is thus proposed for the use of results already proven from research and experience especially in regard of solutions to simple and common RTC problems.

iii. Limited Road Safety Expert Capacity: There is an imbalance between set action thresholds and available road safety capacity. In setting targets within individual action plans, there should be careful assessment of stakeholder internal capacity. Risk factors associated with the activities in relation to resource availability should be analysed so that set activities can be balanced with personnel and resource availability to ensure full completion of activities.

iv. Implementation of disjointed road safety countermeasures: Road safety interventions earmarked for implementation should be analysed for inconsistencies, areas for multiple linkages and interdependencies. This should be done by the categorisation of related components for full coverage on all aspects of road safety needs in an orderly manner.

v. Requirements for the integration of corrections: old challenges must be addressed before the implementation of completely new actions and efforts should be made to introduce relevant innovations.

vi. Lack of Adequate Local Capacity: There should be back up technical support for the implementation of road safety activities at the local level by the following measures:

a. Development of a local management structure for organized collaborative network.

b. Identification of perceived strengths and weaknesses.

c. Division of competences along technical and resource availability.

d. Balancing of work schedules so that the implementation of road safety projects does not interfere or delay with other work functions of stakeholder agencies.

e. Establishment of a strong communication system.

vii. Implementation Gaps: Successful response to some road safety domains is still missing. Currently, post-crash response and user behavioural change are considered to be some of the critical missing performance gaps in Ghana's road safety achievement. Besides, new ideas on some aspects of road safety such as extended partnerships with vehicle fleet operators for the establishment of internal road safety systems are yet to be achieved.

viii. Lack of Adequate Preparations for Emergency Road Safety Challenges: An example is the unexpected occurrences such as the sudden increase in the use of motorcycles for commercial operations in Ghana and the related consequence on increased RTCs for which solutions are yet to be effected. Contingency provisions should be made for activity diversification in set action plans to reflect current need. Change of governments with new agenda may also introduce emergency changes into road safety action plans with related continuity challenges. Intensive orientations should be provided for newly instituted political leadership to address this.

3.6.3 National Development Planning Agenda and Road Safety

It is required that due recognition be given to road safety in a country's development agenda. This is important to enable adequate funding provisions to be made for road safety.

In Ghana, road safety components are captured as separate themes within some sectoral development frameworks of the different road safety affiliated sectors which feed into the national development agenda. Appendix 3.6 provides a comparison between The National Medium-Term Development Policy Framework (MTNDPF)-2022-2025 and the sector development frameworks of the MoT and the MRH as they correspond with set road safety pillars. However, it impacts of resource allocation for road safety work is not known. Some constraints associated with road safety and the National Development Agenda includes the following:

i. Lack of Coordination: Sectoral road safety components defined in sector medium term development frameworks are not coordinated and do not complement each other with regards to similarities, the level of interventions and the respective geographical location. This creates inconsistent and disjointed road safety programmes. It is recommended for the NRSA to map out all sector road safety plans for a holistic appreciation and to correct errors.

ii. Lack of Road Safety Budgets Line Items in Local Development Plans: There has been the omission of road safety activities and budgets in local government medium term development plans. Therefore, sector development plans should define a hierarchy of sub elements for different administrative levels for budgeting.

3.6.4 Road Safety Results

Within national domains, road safety outputs and outcomes are important for determining and understanding project effects and the level of achievement of set objectives. However, an output from a road safety project does not necessarily determine its effects, outcomes and the changes resulting from the implementation such projects. Currently, key outcome indicator to monitor the success of road safety interventions is by comparison of the number of fatalities and serious injuries before and after project interventions. This is because according to a report by ROSPA, (2014), it is not easy to link a particular road safety interventions RTC casualty reductions.

It is, therefore, not advised to try to measure the effectiveness of a project/ intervention through causality reduction rates because it cannot be pinpointed with certainty how much of an intervention that affected the results and how this was achieved. To link a particular intervention to changes in casualty reduction would need a road safety project to be conducted on a large scale over a long period of time under conditions of a scientific trial. This will require a great deal of resources which are not easily available. Other constraints associated with the definition of road safety results includes the following:

i. Difficulty in Isolating the Other Factors Influencing Road Safety Results: This is because of the complexity of the range of road safety interventions often vary by content and processes. This is the situation even when there is good evidence that shows there is increased risk or a risky issue has been addressed. Since it is not easy to separate the effects of road safety interventions from the influence of other factors and the results may only be inferred. Causative factors must be studied differently such that proxy outcome measures categorized as direct and indirect, short and long term etc. provide adequate basis for justifying outcomes.

3.7 CONCLUSION

In Ghana, the RSM has evolved significantly guided by global recommended best practices. The most outstanding issues relate to addressing current limitations and increasing the application of technology where feasible. This must be systematically done towards the achievement of set targets for RTC reductions on the way forward. The subsequent chapters of this book discuss how the other road safety pillars are being managed in Ghana and the aspects to be improved.

Appendix 3.1 NRSC Staffing Positions

Positions	Professional Competency for Road Safety	Total
Executive Director	Professional	1
Directors	Professional	2
Deputy Director (Regional Manager)	Non Professional	8
Internal Auditor	Non Professional	1
Assistant internal Auditor	Non Professional	1
Communications Manager	Non Professional	1
Principal Administration Manager (Head of Admin. and HR)	Non Professional	1
Administration Officer	Non Professional	1
Assistant Administration Officer	Non Professional	1
Procurement Officer	Non Professional	1
Senior Planning Officer	Professional	1
Planning Officers	Professional	9
Assistant planning Officers	Professional	5
Principal Accountant	Non Professional	1
Senior Accounts officer/ Senior Accountant	Non Professional	2
Accounts Officer/ Accountant	Non Professional	9
Secretaries	Non Professional	6
Stenographer secretary	Non Professional	9
Transport officer	Non Professional	1
Senior drivers	Non Professional	8
Driver	Non Professional	7
Stores office	Non Professional	1
Planning Assistant	Non Professional	1
Receptionist	Non Professional	1
Advocates	Professional	10
Total		89

Appendix 3.2: NRSA's proposed positions in the scheme of service

Position	Requirement in SoS				
OFFICE OF THE DIRECTOR-GENERAL DIRECTORATE	1. DIRECTOR-GENERAL				
RESEARCH, MONITORING AND EVALUATION (RM&E)	2.Director, Research, Monitoring & Evaluation	3.Deputy Director - Research Unit	5.Principal Manager - Research Unit	7. Senior Manager – Research Unit	9.Manager – Research Unit
		4.Deputy Director - Monitoring & Evaluation Unit	6.Principal Manager – M&E Unit	8.Senior Manager – M&E Unit	10.Manager – M&E Unit
	11. Assistant Manager – RM&E Unit	12.Chief Assistant – RM&E Unit	13.Principal Assistant – RM&E Unit	14.Senior Assistant - RM&E Unit	
PLANNING AND PROGRAMMES (P&P)	15.Director	16.Deputy Director - Planning	17.Principal Manager – Planning	18.Senior Manager – Planning	19.Manager – Planning
	20.Assistant Manager – Planning	21.Deputy Director – Programmes	22.Principal Manager - Programmes	23.Senior Manager – Programmes	24.Manager – Programmes
	25.Assistant Manager - Programmes				
REGULATORY, INSPECTORATE AND COMPLIANCE (RI&C)	26.Director – RI&C	27.Deputy Director – RI&C	28.Principal Manager – RI&C	29.Senior Manager – RI&C	30.Manager – RI&C
	31.Assistant Manager – RI&C	32.Chief Assistant – RI&C	33.Principal Assistant – RI&C	34.Senior Assistant – RI&C	
FINANCE AND ADMINISTRATION DIRECTORATE	35.Director	36.Deputy Director – Finance	37.Principal Finance Manager - Finance	38.Senior Finance Manager – Finance	39.Manager – Finance
	40.Assistant Finance Manager	41.Chief Finance Assistant	42.Principal Finance Assistant	43.Senior Finance Assistant	44.Deputy Director – Human Resource
	45.Deputy Director – Human Resource	46.Principal Manager – HR Operations	47.Senior Manager - Training and Staff Development	48.Manager – HR Operations	49.Assistant Manager - HR
	50.Deputy Director - Administration	51.Principal Manager – Administration	52.Senior Manager – Administration	53.Manager - Administration	54.Assistant Manager – Administration
	55.Chief Assistant – HR/Administration	56.Principal Assistant – HR/Administration	57.Senior Assistant HR/Administration	58.Principal Manager – Procurement	59.Senior Manager – Procurement
	60.Manager – Procurement	61.Assistant Manager – Procurement	62.Chief Assistant – Procurement	63.Principal Assistant – Procurement	64.Senior Assistant – Procurement
	65.Senior Manager – Estates	66.Manager - Estates	67.Chief Assistant – Estates	68.Principal Assistant – Estates	69.Senior Assistant – Estates
	70.Senior Manager – Transport	71.Manager – Transport	72.Assistant Manager – Transport	73.Chief Assistant – Transport	74.Principal Assistant – Transport

Position	Requirement in SoS				
	75.Senior Assistant – Transport	76.Chief Driver – Transport	77.Senior Driver – Transport	78.Driver Grade I - Transport	79.Driver Grade II - Transport
	80.Senior Private Secretary – Secretarial	81.Private Secretary - Secretarial	82.Stenographer Secretary/ Receptionist – Secretarial	83.Secretary – Secretarial	84.Senior Manager – Records
	85.Manager – Records	86.Assistant Manager – Records	87.Chief Records Assistant	88.Principal Assistant – Records	89.Senior Records Assistant
	90.Chief Assistant – Library	91.Principal Assistant – Library	92.Senior Assistant – Library	93.Principal Manager – MIS	94.Senior Manager - MIS
	95.Manager – MIS	96.Assistant Manager – MIS	97.Chief Assistant – Assistant	98.Principal Assistant – MIS	99.Senior Assistant – MIS
	100.Deputy Director – Internal Auditor	101.Principal – Internal Auditor	102.Senior Internal Auditor	103.Internal Auditor	104.Assistant Internal Auditor
	105.Chief Internal Audit Assistant	106.Principal Internal Audit Assistant	107.Senior Internal Audit Assistant	108.Deputy Director – Corporate Affairs	109.Principal Manager – Corporate Affairs
	110.Senior Manager – Corporate Affairs	111.Manager – Corporate Affairs	112.Assistant Manager – Corporate Affairs	113.Chief Assistant – Corporate Affairs	114.Principal Assistant – Corporate Affairs
	115.Senior Assistant – Corporate Affairs	116.Principal Manager – Legal	117.Senior Manager – Legal	118.Manager – Legal	119.Assistant Manager – Legal
REGIONAL OFFICE					
Regional Director	135. Regional Directors (16 Number)				

Appendix 3.3: Details of Ghana's Road Traffic Acts and Amendments

a. *Road Traffic Ordinance, 1952 (No. 55): Road Traffic Ordinance 1952 gives regulations on (i) licensing including driving license, taxi and passenger lorry license, roadworthiness certificate, number plates, marks on commercial vehicles; (ii) Vehicles, opening doors, alighting, reversing, obstruction, parking and stopping, traffic signs, police traffic control, overcrowding front seat; construction of vehicles, vehicles in dangerous condition; (iii) commercial vehicles overcharging, table of fares, excess passengers, seats etc.*

f. *Road Traffic Offences (Powers of Arrest) Law, 1992 (P.N.D.C.L. 304): The Purpose was to confer the Powers of Arrest to a member of the Ghana Private Road Transport Union (GPRTU) in an authorized uniform to arrest any person who drives a commercial vehicle e.g., recklessly or dangerously, carelessly; or while under the influence of drink or drug*

h. *Road Traffic Act 2004, Act 683: This Act was enacted in December 2004 to consolidate and revise the Road Traffic Ordinance 1952 (No.55). It provides a more comprehensive regulation of road traffic and road use, to ensure safety on roads and to provide for related matters. The Act ensures safety on the roads under seven (7) separate parts as follows:*

- *Principal Road Safety provisions (e.g. major driving offences)*
- *Restrictions on road use in the interest of road safety*
- *Registration and Licensing of Motor vehicles and Trailers*
- *Licensing of Drivers of Motor vehicles*
- *Tests of Vehicles and Issue of Road use Certificate*
- *Licensing of Drivers of Commercial vehicles*
- *Miscellaneous Offences and General Provisions*

Section 135(1) of the law repealed the following:

- Road Traffic Ordinance, 1952 (No. 55);
- Road Traffic (Amendment) Ordinance, 1957 (No. 18);
- Road Traffic Act 1959 (No. 21);
- Road Traffic (Amendment) Act, 1971 (Act. 381);
- Road Traffic Offences (Powers of Arrest) Law, 1992 (P.N.D.C.L. 304);
- Road Traffic (Amendment) Act 1998 (Act 553);
- Road (Vehicle Use) Fee Act, 1998 (Act 556; and Road Traffic (Amendment) Law 1983 (P.N.D.C.L. 43).

i. *Road Traffic (Amendment) Act 2008, (Act 761): This law was enacted in 2008 to amend the Road Traffic Act 683 of 2004 to reduce the penalties for motor traffic offences and for related matters. Essentially this law amends Act 683 by substitution of the penalties for offences specified in that Act.*

j. *Road Traffic Regulations, 2012 (L.I.2180): The Regulations closely mirrors the provisions of Section 133 (a) to (z) of Act 683. It has a set of Regulations made by the Minister in May 2012 pursuant to section 133 of Act 683 for the effective implementation of the said Act. In particular, its provisions regulate the following broad areas:*

- *Vehicle Registration*
- *Licensing*
- *Vehicle Construction and Use*
- *Commercial Vehicles*
- *International Convention provision*
- *Traffic other than Motor traffic*
- *General provisions*

The purpose of this legislative instrument among others is to provide for the processes and procedures for complying with the provisions in Act 683. For example, Section 38 of Act 683 prohibits the driving of a vehicle without having registered it and Section 2 of LI 2180 provides for the process and procedure to be adopted to affect the registration.

h. *Road Traffic (Amendment) Act 2020: This act repeals the following sections and regulations of the LI 2180, 2012*

- *Section 4(2) on driving under influence of alcohol or drugs*
- *Section 13 on seat belt / child restraint system*
- *section 14 on carrying of children in motor vehicles*
- *section 40(1) on registration numbers*
- *section 52(1) on interpretation of trade licenses*
- *section 92(3) on test of condition of motor vehicle*
- *section 99(1) on test of condition of motor vehicle on roads,*
- *regulation 3(1) on verification of weights*
- *regulation 5(2) on Tests of Condition of Motor Vehicle*
- *regulation 8(1) on Issue of Road Use Sticker*
- *regulation 9 on Exemption from requirements for road use certificate*
- *aspects of regulation 10 on Vehicle registration number plate*
- *aspects of regulation 16(1) on Re-registration of existing registered motor vehicle*
- *aspects of regulation 17(1) on Change of Ownership*
- *aspects of licensing regulation 23 – 29, 37, 195*
- *regulation 30(2) on Driving with uncorrected defective eyesight*
- *regulation 31 on Upgrading of Class*
- *aspects on number plates in regulation 34 - 35*
- *regulation 43 on Driver re-training and re-testing*
- *regulation 45(2) on Change of Name*
- *regulation 46 on Armed Forces and Police driving permit*
- *regulation 47(4) on Production of Driver's License*
- *regulation 48 on Vehicles not conforming to Regulations*
- *aspects on vehicle characteristics in regulation 50, 52, 62, 65, 74, 80*
- *aspects on axle load and driving of vehicles in regulation 96 / 101*
- *aspects on broken down vehicle or trailer in regulation 102*
- *aspects on registration of commercial vehicles in regulation 102, 124, 126, 127, 129, 130, 131, 134*
- *aspects on speed limiters, logbooks and tachographs in regulation 135, 163*
- *aspects on vehicle inspection in regulation 158*
- *aspects on prohibition of use of certain roads in regulation 160*
- *aspects on disobedience to police and fire service officials in regulation 168, 169, 173*
- *aspects on road signs and markings in regulation 174, 176*
- *aspects on automated road traffic law enforcement*

Appendix 3.4: RTC scene data collection form used by the police

GHANA POLICE SERVICE / BRRI			**ROAD ACCIDENT REPORT**	
1 REPORT NUMBER / **YEAR**	**2 Region** Road Name		**3 Police Station**	

4 No of vehs involved	5 Day	6 Month	7 Year	8 Day of Week 1 Mon 2 Tue 3 Wed 4 Thu 5 Fri 6 Sat 7 Sun	Time(24hrs)	9 hour	minutes

| 10 No. Casualties KILLED
 11 No. Casualties INJURED | **12 Accident Severity**
 1. Fatal   2. Hospitalised
 3. Injured Not-Hospitalised   4. Damage Only | **13 Weather**
 1. Clear
 2. Fog/mist
 3. Rain
 4. Dust/smoke
 5. Dazzle
 6. Other | **14 Light Conditions**
 1. Day
 2. Night- No Lights
 3. Night- Lights OFF
 4. Night- Lights ON |

15 Road Description
1. Straight and flat
2. Curve only
3. Incline only
4. Curve & Incline
5. Bridge (name river)
----
6. Crest

16 Road Surface Type
1. Tar Good
2. Tar few Potholes
3. Tar many Potholes
4. Gravel
5. Earth few Potholes
6. Earth many Potholes

17 Shoulder Type
1. Tarred
2. Untarred
3 No Shoulder

18 Shoulder Condition
1. Good   2. Poor
3. Overgrown   4. No Shoulder

19 Road Separation
1. Median
2. No Median

20 Road Width (m)

21 Surface Condition
1. Dry
2. Wet
3. Muddy

22 Surface Repair
1. Good
2. Potholes
3. Rough

23 Location Type
1 Not at junction   6
2   7. Railway Crossing
3   8. Other
4
5

24 Traffic Control
1. None
2. Pedestrian -X
3. Signals
4. Stop sign
5. Give Way
6. Other

25 Collision Type
1. Head on
2. Rear end
3. Right Angle
4. Side Swipe
5. Ran off road
6. Hit Object on road
7. Hit Object off road
8. Hit parked vehicle
9. Hit Pedestrian
10. Hit Animal
11. Other

26 Hit and Run
1. Not Hit & Run
2. Hit & Run

27 Roadworks
1. Not At Roadworks
2. At Roadworks

28 Collision Code

VEHICLE 1		**VEHICLE 2**	

29 Vehicle Type
1. Car   6. Motor Cycle
2. HGV   7. Pickup
3. Tractor   8. Bicycle
4. Bus   9. Other
5. Minibus   10. Unknown

30 Registration No.

31 Ownership / Usage
1. Govt.   6. Police/ Military
2. Company   7. Emergency
3. Private   8. Other
4. Taxi   9. Unknown
5. Bus

32 Vehicle Manoeuvre
1. Right Turn   6. Diverging   11. Sudden Stop
2. Left Turn   7. Overtaking   12. Parked Off Road
3. U Turn   8. Going Ahead   13. Stopped On Road
4. Cross Traffic   9. Reversing   14. Other
5. Merging   10. Sudden Start

33 Vehicle Damage
1. None   3. Extensive
2. Minor   4. Unknown

34 Defects
1. None   6. Lights
2. Brakes   7. Multiple
3. Steering   8. Other
4. Tyres
5. Suspension

35 Vehicle Direction
1. North   3. South
2. East   4. West

36 Driver Name	37 Sex	38 Age	39 Nationality

40 Driver Injury
1. Fatal
2. Hospitalised
3. Not- Hospitalised
4. Uninjured
5. Unknown

41 Licence No.
Restriction

42 Lic. Status
1. Full
2. Provisional
3. Learner
4. Unlicensed

43 Place of Issue   Expiry Date   Issue Date

44 Drink/Drugged Driving
1. Not Suspected
2. Suspected
3. Tested and Positive
4. Tested and Negative
5. Unknown

45 Driver Error
1. None   7. Improper Overtaking
2. Inexperience   8. Improper Turning
3. Inattentive   9. Fatigued/Asleep
4. Too Fast   10. Other
5. Too Close
6. No Signal

(VEHICLE 2 repeats the same fields 29–45 as VEHICLE 1)

PASSENGER CASUALTIES

	VEH NO 46	SEX 47	AGE 48	SEVERITY 49	POSITION 50	ACTION 51
1.						
2.						
3.						
4.						
5.						
6.						
7.						
8.						
9.						
10.						

49 & 55 Injury Severity

1. Fatal
2. Hospitalised
3. Injured Not-Hospitalised

50 Passenger Position

1. Front Seat
2. Rear Seat
3. Motorcycle Passenger
4. Bus Passenger
5. Inside
6. Outside sitting
7. Outside standing
8. Other

58 Drink / Drugs

1. Not Suspected
2. Suspected
3. Unknown

PEDESTRIAN CASUALTIES

	VEH NO 52	SEX 53	AGE 54	SEV 55	ACTION 56	LOCATION 57	DRINK 58
1.							
2.							
3.							
4.							

57 Pedestrian Location

1. Pedestrian Crossing
2. Within 50m of Crossing
3. On Central Refuge
4. In Road Centre
5. On Footpath / Verge
6. Unknown
7. Other

51 Passenger Action
1. Boarding
2. Alighting/jumping
3. Falling from vehicle
4. Other

56 Pedestrian Action
1. No Action
2. Crossing Road
3. Walking Along Road
4. Walking along Edge
5. Playing On Road
6. On Footpath
7. Other

59 TYPE	60 TOWN/VILLAGE CODE	61 Km	62 100 m	63 ROUTE NUMBER
☐	☐☐☐☐	☐☐☐	☐	☐☐☐☐☐

64 EASTERNS	65 NORTHERNS	66 NODE 1	67 NODE 2	68 DIRECTION
☐☐☐☐☐☐	☐☐☐☐☐☐	☐☐☐☐	☐☐☐☐	☐

Sketch of the Accident Scene:
Mark road names, vehicle position, vehicle direction, and manoeuvre, etc

69 Police Description of Accident

Site Location Sketch:
Mark road names, junctions, prominent buildings, landmarks etc. Indicate distance from crash site to these points.

Appendix 3.5: Summary of Road Safety Actions

Theme	NRSS I: 2001-2005	NRSS II: 2006-2010	NRSS III: 2011-2020
Improve Road Safety Management	• Preparation of new Road Traffic Regulation • Setting up of NRSC regional offices • Creation of dedicated MTTUs in the regions • Development of a national accident database • Revision of accident report format • Upgrade of data management system with adoption of MAAP • Development of systems for prioritisation of road safety activities • Development of accident research capacity • Streamlining of activities of driving schools • Recruitment and training of staff of NRSC • Institute mechanism for road safety coordination • Establish Regional Road Safety Committees • Institute monitoring and evaluation of road safety activities by stakeholders • Development and promotion of NRSS I • Development of MIS network for NRSC headquarters and regional safety committees	• Conduct a study to computerize accident data management • Training of NRSC, GHA-RSED, DUR personnel on MAAP • Annual compilation and analysis of RTC data from the MTTU • Establishment of a twice-a-year progress review regime on implementation of action plans • Development of a proposal for establishing a National Drivers Academy	• NRSC upgraded to 'Authority' status • National Advocate for Road Safety identified and established • Increase road safety awareness among key decision makers • Institution of Monitoring and Evaluation procedures for road safety interventions • Intersectoral collaboration/communication on Road Safety issues established • Road Safety Capacity Needs Assessment conducted • Improved Road Safety capacity among Stakeholders • Established national road transport regulatory body • Development of a comprehensive Road Safety Information Database • Improved storage and accessibility of all RTC data • Advocacy for a fixed percentage of annual funds from traditional funding sources (Road Fund Board, NIC/GIA) • Encouraged corporate support and innovations for funding Road Safety activities • Promotion of Road Safety Research • Identification of sustainable funding sources for Research Projects • Promotion of stakeholder priority accord for Road Safety issues

Theme	NRSS I: 2001-2005	NRSS II: 2006-2010	NRSS III: 2011-2020
Safer Roads and Mobility	• Establishment of road safety units among the road safety agencies • Assignment of one safety engineer by region within the road agencies • Introduction of the conduct of road safety audit • Review of safety components of Highways Design Standards • Promotion of axle load control • Training of engineers in road safety • Construction of single lane bridges in rural areas • Evaluation of accident black spots • Introduction of a 2 accident spots treatment regime per city • Installation of crash barriers, line markings, traffic signs and weighbridge stations • Introduction of the use of mobile weigh pads for axle load control • Safe route to school project implemented in all cities	• Introduction of Road safety audit and certification programme and training of road safety engineers • Introduction of safe road section treatment as evaluation line item in tender procedures for trunk road projects • Evaluation of treated road sections for safety purposes • Conduct of road safety audits on selected roads • Development of manuals and guidelines for safe road maintenance activities • Safety training for contractors • Institutionalisation of road safety audits in road management • Development of safe crossing points on selected roads • Construction of traffic calming measures • Treatment and evaluation of black spots • Institutionalisation of safe walk to school project	• Capacity development for Planning, Design, Construction, Maintenance and Operation of Road Infrastructure • Establishment of dedicated line budgets for safety in road projects • Conduct of treatment of hazardous road sections • Incorporation of Road Safety into Land-use and Transportation Planning • Construction of segregated lanes for two and three-wheelers • Incorporation of Pedestrian Safety Facilities in Road Construction • Training of two and three-wheeler riders on the safe use of the road • Enhancement of instituted road safety audit measures • Capacity development for road safety management
Safer Vehicles	• Capacity and infrastructure development for DVLA • Institution of monitoring and evaluation team • Development of vehicle testing methods	• Studies into the impact of over aged vehicles on road safety • Research into causes of RTCs by haulage trucks • Research into the conditions of service of commercial vehicle drivers • Research into the impact of "home used tyres" on road safety • Validation of quantity of vehicular traffic fleet • Research into eye related problems among commercial drivers • Evaluation of promotion of increased use of seatbelts and crash helmets • Establishment of the age profile and safety of commercial vehicle drivers • Establishment of safe procedures for vehicle conversion and maintenance for commercial operations • Establishment of appraisal procedures for driver testing • Licensing of private garages for vehicle inspection and certification • Development of driver and vehicle data management system	• Development of standards and Specifications for vehicle importation and assembly in Ghana • Revision of legislation on Vehicle Modification • Enforcement and intensification of laws on the use of unauthorised vehicles for commercial purposes • Capacity improvement for enforcement on vehicle testing regulations • Capacity development for effective monitoring of PVTS • Enforcement of laws on driver qualification index

Theme	NRSS I: 2001-2005	NRSS II: 2006-2010	NRSS III: 2011-2020
Safer Road Users	• Institution of road safety education programme for children • Conduct of road safety awareness campaigns • Introduction of machine-readable licenses • Public campaigns on access to GcNet system	• Development of road safety education curriculum • Conduct of road safety education for teachers • Manual for road safety education in schools developed • Development of road safety campaign materials • Training of students and teachers in colleges in road safety • Institutionalisation of the conduct of safety workshops in first cycle institutions • Development of Monitoring and evaluation systems for safety education in schools • Conduct of driver skills development training • Conduct of speed, fatigue, alcohol campaigns • Conduct of training for commercial drivers • Training and certification of driving schools	• Upgrade of driver training and testing methods e.g., introduction of the use of Simulators for driver training • Introduction of driver refresher training courses • Conduct of road safety education for pedestrians and VRUs • Improvement in documentation on RTCs • Institutionalisation of Road Safety Education in the Educational System • Training of MMDAs and Union Executives on Road Safety related Issues • Establishment of Driver Academy Model Schools • Training of Instructors for Driving Schools • Training of teachers on Road Safety issues • Enhancement of National Capacity for driver testing and licensing • Awareness raising of the socio-economic and health implications of RTCs at all levels of society • Enlightenment of various Road User Groups on their roles and responsibilities for minimizing RTCs
Improved Post-Crash Response	• Identification and equipment of National Secretariat for NAS in collaboration with GNFS • Appointment of Interim Board for the NAS • Acquisition of Ambulances and distribution to selected Fire Stations. • Creation of public awareness of the role of the NAS • Launching of the Ghana Ambulance Service	• Development of a campaign on awareness and accessibility for RTC emergency services • Establishment and equipment of Ambulance stations in all regional capitals and district capitals. • Training of Emergency Medical Technicians (EMTs) for all regional and district ambulance stations • Development of a Proposal for the establishment of a National EMT training centre. • Establishment of a common emergency number for land line as well as mobile telephones in Ghana • Training of volunteers along highways in first aid skills. • Establishment of Manned emergency posts with basic medical equipment along accident-prone highways	• Training of targeted groups in Pre-hospital Injury Care and First-Aid administration • Establishment of National Trauma Management System for Pre-hospital, and Post hospital-based care to provide quick and effective treatment to RTC victims • Promotion of Community participation in provision of Emergency Services • Improvement, encouragement, co-ordination and cooperation among Health Care Centres, e.g., NAS, MTTU, GRCS, NGOs and other Emergency Service Organisations (ESOs) for quick response to Road Traffic Crash situations • Incorporation of Basic principles of First Aid in the syllabi of Driving Schools, Police Training Courses and Basic Schools

Theme	NRSS I: 2001-2005	NRSS II: 2006-2010	NRSS III: 2011-2020
Improved Enforcement	• Promotion of Free-flow traffic • Control of over-speeding, drunk driving and fatigue driving • Establishment of mechanisms for red light jumping, clamping and towing of vehicles. • Enforcement of Laws on licensing • Collaboration with DVLA to check fake identification number plates and institution of spot fines	• Supply of modern speed radar guns and modern alcometers and other materials distributed to all the regional MTTUs • Training of personnel of the GPS/MTTU in enforcement of the Traffic Act 683 and Regulations • Training and organisation of personnel into dedicated Traffic Enforcement Teams	• Elevation of road safety violations to a high priority Law Enforcement by the MTTD, Prosecutors and Judges, MMDAs, Transport Operators instituted • Enforcement of Laws and Regulations on the Non-use of Motorcycles for Commercial Transport Operations • Application of Modern Technology to facilitate the processes for Road Safety Enforcement • Establishment of Education and Training Programmes in the use of Applied Technology for Law Enforcement • Development of a mechanisms for apportioning fines from road traffic violations for funding Road Safety activities of the NRSC

Appendix 3.6: Analysis of Road Safety in Ghana's National Medium-Term Development Policy Framework (MTNDPF)-2022-2025

Road Safety Pillars	National Shared Growth Development Agenda	The Medium-Term Development Framework For MRH	The Medium-Term Development Framework for MoT	Remarks
Road Safety Management	Strengthen health and safety standards in planning, design, construction, operations and maintenance for road transport -Implement a Ghana Road Safety Support (GRoSS) Initiative	-Mainstream road safety into all road development and maintenance projects -Work closely with the NRSC in implementing the new strategy III -Ensure financing of road safety aspects of road development and maintenance. -Budgetary allocation of funds for road safety under BP4 of sector expenditure	-Advocacy and collaboration -Development of road safety database -Research and monitoring -Engage PPP arrangements for Road Safety Financing	They all point out the need to improve road safety management
Safe Roads	-Incorporate pedestrian safety facilities in planning, design, construction and maintenance of road infrastructure (SDG Targets 3.6, 9.1, 11.2) -Promote dedicated safe, reliable and appropriate facilities for Non-Motorised Transport (NMT) users -Maintain and free-up all existing NMT facilities from encroachment -Improve road furniture (street lighting, road markings and road signage -Ensure the provision of Intelligent traffic management systems	-Provision of NMT facilities in urban areas across the country -Conduct road safety audit at the feasibility stage of projects	Facilitate efficient and safe use of Non-Motorised Transport facilities such as bicycle lanes and pedestrian walkways in congested central business districts	The frameworks highlight the need for the design of an all-inclusive and safe road transport system
Safe Vehicles			-Driver training, testing and licensing and vehicle inspection and registration	Only the MoT framework defined strategies to promote safe vehicles
Safe Road Users		-Adoption of the safe system approach to the development of a road transport system that is better able to accommodate human error. -Development of guidelines for accessibility for PLWDs and other vulnerable groups in the road traffic regulations to guide road designers in their work	Road safety education and sensitization	They acknowledge the role of education in ensuring the safety of road users

Road Safety Pillars	National Shared Growth Development Agenda	The Medium-Term Development Framework For MRH	The Medium-Term Development Framework for MoT	Remarks
Post-Crash Response	-Passage of the Health bill which includes the emergency preparedness and response plan into law Establish emergency facilities for accident victims along major transport corridors -Strengthen acute emergency care services involving pre-hospital (e.g., ambulance services) and hospital emergency services -Enhance capacity for prompt removal of accident and broken-down vehicles -Establish a well-resourced emergency centre in each district -Passage of the Health bill which includes the emergency preparedness and response plan into law -Promote equal opportunities for Persons with Disabilities in social and economic development -Strengthen institutions and systems that ensure the protection, inclusion and capacity building of Persons with Disabilities		Enhance the capacity for road crashes response including the accelerated establishment of trauma centres	The national agenda and MoT framework are consistent in their focus
Enforcement	Enforce national road traffic laws and regulations			The sectoral frameworks do not highlight enforcement as part of their strategies

CHAPTER 4

INFRASTRUCTURE

"Bleeding roads; The Major Highways Killing Ghanaians" - Ghana web, 25th January 2019.

Poor road infrastructure also contributes to the occurrence of road traffic crashes (RTC) and the UNESCAP, (2017) intimated that there is a strong correlation between road infrastructure design and road safety. Thus, road infrastructure, must ensure that appropriate safety systems are in place and according to Kapila K. et al (2013), safe road infrastructure must be prioritised in road traffic safety interventions and rather than simply building roads on the basis of mobility and accessibility.

Currently, it is said that different countries are at different levels in the application of safety in road infrastructure development, maintenance and operation with most developing countries characterized by obsolete road engineering designs with limited safety. Also, such countries are struggling to match up to the demands of the rapid changes with new vehicle technologies and the related infrastructure safety needs.

This is because safety considerations must be integrated into new roads and be retrofitted into existing ones as a matter of importance in road infrastructure management (Koornstra et al., 1992) but with funding challenges. This chapter discusses the integration of safety into the various stages of road infrastructure development, the related safety impacts and challenges as well as some initiatives required in Ghana to improve road infrastructure safety on the way forward.

4.1 CONCEPTS AND PRINCIPLES ON INFRASTRUCTURE SAFETY

4.1.1 Concepts on Road Infrastructure Safety

The United States Department of Transportation of the Federal Highway Administration (FHWA) has proposed the concepts of nominal and substantive safety as fundamental concepts for considerations to guide the application of safety in road design as follows:

A. Nominal Safety: The concept of nominal safety is based on all road design elements meeting the minimum design criteria with the provision of design features with the interventions not aligned with actual or expected safety performance on a particular road or a particular road section.

B. Substantive Safety: Substantive safety is based on the provision of crash location specific road safety interventions normally derived from existing crash data. However, this does not always directly correspond to its level of nominal safety.

In line with this, it is recommended for good understanding of both nominal and substantive safety design in each specific situation so as to apply design standards and criteria to their full extent since there maybe variations by road type.

In Ghana, some new roads might be influenced by the nominal safety concept based on existing design standards whilst interventions such as the correction of hazardous road sections be applied at specific locations. However, in some instances, safety challenges can emerge after a new road has been opened to traffic due road user errors such as over speeding on new roads with food ride quality. However, road safety installations are also sometimes omitted in new road designs causing after thought corrections after serious RTCs have been recorded.

4.1.2 Principles of for Safe Road Infrastructure Development

Meng L. et al. (2006), defines a set of five basic traffic safety principles to be considered as follows:

A. Adaptation of Safety Policy into Safe Road Infrastructure Provision: *In Ghana, the policy guidelines on safe infrastructure development are defined in the NSRP of 2008.*

B. Application of Road Infrastructure Safety by Road Functions: This principle aligns road infrastructure safety to road network functionality by hierarchy to ensure that safety features provided in a particular road class conforms to its unique requirements. However, according to a report by the TRL (1991), uniquely defined road function by road use type have never been specifically conformed to or realized for the design of an entire network in any country.

In Ghana, the entire road network has been classified by trunk, urban and feeder roads as well as by other sub-divisional categories as discussed in chapter one section 1.2.2 item A(i) of this book. However, the functional class of the roads are not effectively related to safety per say but rather more focused on mobility and access functions.

C. Road Infrastructure Safety by Environmental Factors: This is in relation to environmental adaptability of road designs to the limitations of road use. This is because safe road infrastructure also depends on environmental conditions such as rain, floods, humidity, temperature, ground conditions etc. which can occur permanently or temporarily.

In Ghana, such environmental considerations are integrated into road designs to some extent. However, it is not uncommon to observe some environmental challenges with road design outcomes such as flooded road sections immediately after some new road constructions.

D. Road Infrastructure Safety by Expected Road User Behaviour: This principle requires adequate information about expected road user behaviour to be embedded in road infrastructure safety management to meet the needs of all road users in the traffic stream.

In Ghana, some considerations for road user behaviour are made in the development of roads such as the bounding of medians and islands with crash barriers and barbwires to protect pedestrians from crossing at wrongful road.

E. The Safe System Approach to Road Infrastructure Safety Development and Management:

This applies to the simplification of the driving task through the provision of "Error Forgiving Roads" and "Self-Explaining Roads" which are based on the concept that human behaviour is difficult to change on permanent basis so the road environment should be adapted to the limitations of the road user in order to simplify their task within a "safe system approach" (Evans, 2004). However, in practice, these developments have not progressed with logical consistency and there are differences in the extent and stage of development of these factors from one country to the other.

In Ghana, the state of knowledge and application of these concepts both for new road development and on existing roads is not clear.

4.2. GUIDELINES AND POLICIES ON ROAD INFRASTRUCTURE SAFETY

4.2.1 Global Guidelines on Road Infrastructure Safety

A summary of selected global policies and guidelines on road infrastructure safety and applicability in Ghana is as presented in Table 4.1.

Table 4.1: Selected global policies and guidelines on road infrastructure safety and Applicability in Ghana

Source	Applicability in Ghana
Road Infrastructure Management evolved as follows: a) Provision of mobility in the pre-1950's b) Focus on congestion management- 1950's c) Increased interest of administrators - 1960's d) Recognition of problems with existing knowledge -1980's; e) Introduction of congestion management, and road safety auditing in design- mid-1980's to mid-1990's; and f) Science based road safety management with emphasis on the development of safety in road design guides and manuals - 1990's e.g. AASHTO Strategic Highway Safety Plan -2000; Highway Safety Manual and the PIARC Road Safety Manual.	There has been increasing awareness of the importance of road infrastructure safety with increasing importance of concepts such as conduct of road safety audits and black spot analysis.
UN Conventions 1968 - No.2: Development of protocol/ convention on Road Signs and Signals of 1949/ 1968 to ensure safe infrastructure.	Ghana has adopted the provisions on road signs and signals by the 1968 convention
DOA- Pillar 2: Safer roads and mobility with prioritised consideration for road infrastructure development in road safety such as provision of appropriate facilities for pedestrians and other vulnerable road users -Introduction of corrective upgrade programmes to mitigation measures as part of day-to-day network management; -Conduct of road safety audits on infrastructure for each type of road user especially vulnerable users.	-Road construction in Ghana has to some extent made provisions for pedestrian and other vulnerable road users eg. provision of foot bridges with wheel chair access. -Safety audits are also conducted on some scale and training for the development of audit capacity has been organised in the past.
World Bank: There should be: a) Decreased demand for car use through urban design; b) Speed restriction zones; c) Separation of vulnerable road users and vehicles; d) Allocation of at least 10% of road infrastructure Investment to Road Safety and e) Allocation of 5% maintenance funding for the maintenance of road safety installations.	-provisions have been made for the use of high occupancy commercial transport. -Some segregated road lanes have been provided b -specified funding allocation thresholds are yet to be attained.
Save Lives: a) Infrastructure provision for all road users e.g. bicycle and motorcycle lanes; Roads side safety; design of safer intersections; Separation of service roads from through roads; prioritizing people by putting in place vehicle-free zones; restricting traffic and speed in residential, commercial and school zones and providing better, safer routes for public transport UNRSC (2020) a) Development of a National Safer Road Infrastructure Action Plan; b) Update of National Design Standards and Specifications to align with the established UN guidelines; c) Convention on Road Traffic and Road Signs and Signals defined and adopted; d) Global Road Safety Performance Targets adopted; e) National Road Assessment Programme established / enhanced with relevant local content; f) Policy Targets for new and existing roads to conform to inter-national best practices for road infrastructure safety established; g) Training, accreditation and certification scheme in place for Road Assessment Programme established; h) Road safety audits on new roads and road safety inspections on new and existing roads in place; i) Immediate safety impact on roads currently under construction or due to be built and financing partnership identified for the upgrade of existing roads; j) Road Safety data analysis, performance tracking, monitoring and evaluation in place.	a) Infrastructure safety interventions are captured in National Road Safety Strategies b) The National Road Design Standards and Specifications is yet to be updated to align with established UN guidelines. E.g. the GHA design manual of 1991 does not make specific provision for road safety. However, the Low volume road design manual of 2019 makes provision for road safety; c) Ghana has ratified the UN Convention 68 on Road Traffic and Road Signs and Signals; d) Global Road Safety Performance Targets are yet to be adopted in Ghana so RISM in Ghana are not guided by these targets though some aspects are reflected. e) A national Road Assessment Programme is emerging. f) Policy Targets for new and existing roads to conform to international best practices for road infrastructure safety is in the process of being established in Ghana; g) Some training in road safety audit have been provided for some road engineers in the country with certificates of participation but the level of accreditation by interna-tional standards does not exist. h) Road safety audits on new roads and road safety inspections on new and existing roads are undertaken for some road projects; i) The extent of application is not known; j) Data analysis is mainly done by the NRSA but its impacts on the safety performance of the respective road agencies is not clear.

4.2.2. Road Infrastructure Safety Policy in Ghana:

The policy statement on road infrastructure safety in Ghana stipulates that the Government will undertake steps to promote best safety practices on trunk, urban and feeder roads. Such safety practices will be applied through planning, design, construction, operation and maintenance of roads and related devices (NRSP, 2008). The key challenges and related strategies associated with this are as listed in Table 4.2.

Table 4.2: Road infrastructure safety policy challenges and strategies

Challenges	Strategies	Status of Application
Safety for road users has often been overlooked in land-use and transportation planning and highway development resulting in excessive conflicts especially in settlements along the roadway.	Improve the capacity and awareness of all stakeholders in the planning, design, construction, operation and maintenance of road infrastructure through training on the safety implications inherent in road planning, design and construction as well as the dissemination of appropriate road safety knowledge.	-Training in some aspects such as safety audits and sensitization on safe infrastructure installations have been effected but on a limited scale.
Limited safety considerations in road design and construction result in road designs that are not sufficiently 'forgiving' of driver error.	Review design standards, codes, guidelines, recommended practices, access control and development control procedures to ensure best global practices for road safety are incorporated wherever appropriate.	-A Low Volume Road Design Manual - 2019 have been developed with safety considerations but the level of application and effectiveness is not known. -However, safety standards are yet to be fully incorporated in the GHA road Design Guide 1991
Existing road networks have safety defects that become critical when traffic density increases	Promote the installation or posting of appropriate markings and signage including realistic speed limits at requisite locations on the road.	-Strategy does not directly align with challenge -Retrofitting on existing roads with road signs, markings, speed humps etc. have been ongoing but with limited maintenance due to limited funding
Lack of effective road maintenance leading to hazardous surface conditions	Adopt accident reduction strategies for existing roads through hazardous spot improvement programmes	-Effective road maintenance to match the magnitude of safety considerations required is difficult to attain due to limited funding
Delays in upgrading road infrastructure to match the rate of traffic growth in both urban and rural areas contribute to road traffic accidents.	Institute measures to require all new and rehabilitation road schemes to undergo safety audits at all stages of road development.	-Strategy does not directly align with challenge -The upgrade of roads is in place but with limited level of application
Poor traffic management in towns and cities resulting in congestion and traffic accidents. Sections at which there is mixed traffic of pedestrians, cyclists and vehicle generates excessive conflicts.	Incorporate road safety considerations into land use and transportation planning to minimize road user conflicts especially in settlements along the road.	-There have been discussions on the road agencies working in tandem with district assemblies for effective land use mechanisms in road infrastructure management but level of achievement of the set strategy is unknown.
Speed limits are usually not posted on trunk roads leading to excessive speeding and very serious accidents.	Some speed limits are available on some roads	-In the first-place mere posting od speed limits on roads does not guarantee speed control -Secondly the measure is vague on the expectation that the availability of some posted speed limits will address the problem. -Coupled with this, there is limited compliance from different studies conducted by the NRSA but mitigation measures have not been applied except for some level of enforcement and education measures.
Some posted speed limits in towns and cities are not compatible with the design of the facility and the environment	Progressive correction of signage measures to correspond to changes in road use	The margin of application is not known

Source: NRSP, (2008)

4.2.3 Procedures for Implementing Safe Road Infrastructure

The procedures for implementing safe road infrastructure follow the infrastructure life cycle and categorized into six main stages by Elvik, R. (2010) as:

a. Planning and Design.

b. Construction and Pre-opening.

c. Normal operation.

d. Maintenance and Renewal.

e. Error correction and Hazard elimination.

f. Major upgrading and Renewal.

However, for purposes of this book, these are classified as:

a. Planning.

b. Engineering design.

c. Construction.

d. Operation/Traffic Regulation.

e. Maintenance.

See Figure 4.1 for the Illustrated Framework and detailed discussions in the immediate subsections.

Figure 4.1: Infrastructure life cycle

4.3 ROAD INFRASTRUCTURE SAFETY PLANNING

A road infrastructure safety plan is a framework of activities and the measures to be undertaken in order to ensure that road safety components are incorporated within road infrastructure projects. Such plans relate the safety specifications of a road section to an appropriate level of safety and how they are to be managed.

4.3.1 Elements of Road Infrastructure Safety Planning

A. Types of Road Planning Methods, Applications and Uses: Elvik R. (2010), defines the methods for road infrastructure planning as the analytic tools that helps to detect emerging safety problems on the road network, the most important factors contributing to RTC fatalities and injuries from such problems and the related measures required for corrections.

i. Methods of Road Infrastructure Safety Planning: These include:

a) Road assessment procedures includes the conduct of road inspections, in depth investigation and ranking of high-risk sections for sequential and prioritised application of mitigation measures.

b) Application of efficiency assessment tools through the conduct of safety audits on road designs/ operational activities and assurance of safe network operations after interventions.

c) Conduct of impact assessment by the use of performance indicators to determine how well safety interventions are performing with mitigation measures applied where there is need for such. An overview of the methods is as summarised in Table 4.3.

Table 4.3: Methods for Road Infrastructure Safety Planning

Type of Method	Description
1. Road Assessment Programmes	These methods involve the collection of road characteristics data which are then used to identify safety deficits or determine how well the road environment protects the user from death or disabling injury when a crash occurs.
1.1. Road safety inspection	A preventive tool consisting of a regular, systematic, on-site inspection of existing roads, covering the whole road network carried out by trained safety expert teams, resulting in a formal report on detected road hazards and safety issues, requiring a formal response by the relevant road authority.
1.2. High Risk Sites	A method to identifying, analysing and ranking sections of the road network which have been in operation for more than three years and upon which a large number of fatal RTCs in proportion to the traffic flow have occurred.
1.3. In-depth Investigation	In-depth Investigation is the acquisition of all relevant information and the identification of one or several of the following: a. causes of RTCs b. injuries, injury mechanisms and injury outcomes c. how the RTCs and injuries could have been prevented
1.4. Network Safety Ranking	A method for identifying, analysing and classifying parts of the existing road network according to their potential for safety development and RTCs cost savings.
2. Efficiency assessment tools	Efficiency assessment tools (e.g. cost-benefits analysis) determine the effects for society of a given investment, for instance in road safety, in order to prioritize investment alternatives.
2.1. Road Safety Audit	An independent detailed systematic and technical safety check relating to the design characteristics of a road infrastructure project and covering all stages, from planning to early operation characterized by the identification of unsafe features of a road infrastructure project for planning purposes.
2.2. Safe Network Operation	It relates to daily management of the road infrastructure by the maintenance of roads for good serviceability and safety.
3. Road Safety Impact Assessment.	The purpose is to demonstrate, on a strategic level, the implications on road safety of different planning alternatives of an infrastructure project. This is used as basis to guide the selection of road corridors to be considered for inclusion in road safety plans for improvement
3.1 Road Infrastructure Safety Performance Indicators	Road Infrastructure Safety Performance Indicators aim to assess the safety hazards by infrastructure layout and design (e.g. percentage of road network not satisfying safety design standards).

Source: Luca Persia et al. (2016)

ii. Mode of Application of Road Infrastructure Management Methods: These methods are applied on the basis of existing policies and systems such as:

a) The use of reactive approach with emphasis on the correction of defects on existing roads.

b) The use of a proactive approach for new roads and (c) by considerations for an entire road network or a part by focusing on road network peculiarities at specific road sections.

iii. Use of Infrastructure Management Tools: The methods must also consider the use of recommended conventional infrastructure management tools and processes as sampled in Figure 4.2 by Persia L. et al, (2016).

Figure 4.2: Road safety procedures in each stage of road development Source: Luca Persia et al. (2016)

B. Road Infrastructure Planning Process: The road infrastructure planning process must be applied at both national and local levels with scheduled programmes, assigned technical teams and dedicated funding guided by the following steps:

Step 1: Determination of the state of road infrastructure safety in the country: This must be done by:

i. Policy Review: This is done to identify the main policy barriers to the implementation of safe road infrastructure and the extent to which road safety assessment is built into existing policies by benchmarked global best practices to identify gaps and required changes to be effected.

In Ghana, the MRH as an overarching agency for road management in Ghana does not have a substantive safe infrastructure policy as yet. This implies that there are no policy standards on infrastructure safety legally binding on the road sector agencies. There are only some internal policy guidelines used by the different road agencies without legal compulsions. It is therefore recommended for the MRH to establish policy guidelines and legislation in order to ensure the integration of safety into safe infrastructure planning procedures in the country.

ii) Definition of the Methods and procedures for Road Infrastructure Planning: This must be done to streamline the activities involved in for consistency and ease of implementation as well as for effective monitoring.

In Ghana, the implementation of road infrastructure safety does not have any set procedures but rather most interventions are done on ad hoc basis as and when needed and this must be streamlined.

iii. Establishment of financing arrangements: The planning process must specify the required financial arrangements for the conduct of road assessment activities

In Ghana, there is no dedicated budget line item for road infrastructure safety planning by the MRH. This is because, there is no substantive policy on how much of the respective road agency's funds should be committed to safety action plans. In the absence of such policy controls, expenditures are informed by internal agency objectives and priorities. Consequently, the level of commitment of funding to the implementation of such plans and its effect is variable. Therefore, considerations should be made to provide dedicated and adequate funding for safe infrastructure works. Ways of sourcing for additional funds must also be explored so that safe roads can be provided.

Step 2: Functional Classification of Road Network for Appropriate Design characteristics: Functional classification of roads and the corresponding safety standards suited to each road class must be defined for an entire road network. This is to ensure consistent safety messaging for particular road service level in order to inform the road user on what to expect and how to behave to keep safe.

In Ghana, there are clear engineering properties characterising the service level of each road class. However, there is no consistency of safety installations by road type except for the fact that most sealed roads are provided with more safety measures compared to unsealed roads irrespective of whether the road is a trunk, urban or feeder road.

Step 3:

i. Network Screening or Road Safety Inspection (RSI): This involves a systematic inspection of roads both in part or as whole in order to determine safety deficiencies of high risk often through risk focused visual assessment of road infrastructure features using crash data where available and reliable.

The could be done by road condition surveys with drones or vehicles equipped with GPS, video cameras, distance measurement devices etc. to identify safety hazards on the road such as intersection type and design, markings, pavement condition, roadside hazards, walkways, facilities for vulnerable road users etc. that are known to influence the likelihood and severity of a crash on selected segments of the road. Engage with key members of affected communities and other interested parties by engineers and planners are also recommended for shared solutions to challenges.

The output includes a database with road location and required safety attributes for further analysis. This could be done with the use of Safety Management Systems (SMSs) where available, to draw attention to locations that need more detailed investigations or immediate interventions or to guide the preparation and programming of pending works on high-risk road sections.

In Ghana, an institutionalized process for screening the entire road network is yet to be established though at the road agency level, sectional road inventories are conducted for the development of databases on some engineering features such as road surface type, condition type, width, length, traffic volume etc. to feed into performance budgeting systems for strategic investment analysis.

The outcome is used to prepare generic cost estimates per road improvement activity type for funding within the road sector investment component for the national development plan. The data is also used for monitoring sector performance progress especially with regards to changes in the lengths of roads improved, surface type and condition mix.

There is currently no record of a comprehensive review of all the safety aspects of the entire road infrastructure in the country though there is good awareness for such an initiative to be undertaken on some high-risk roads. Thus, safety inspections as a proactive or a preventive measure should be given a higher premium in Ghana with regular inspections.

ii. In Depth Investigations: In addition to the network screening process, detailed investigation of defective road sections must also be done. This may be in the form of analysis of hazardous road sections (Accident Black spot Analysis) to help understand the specific causes and factors contributing to the occurrence of particular type of RTCs repetitively on such spots. They may also be in the form of follow up RTC investigations to take more detailed information for defining location specific problems. This is often integrated with national road safety post-crash investigations and crash monitoring systems to expand evidence-based on effective infrastructure treatments in the country that reflects local conditions.

In Ghana, both Accident Black Spot Analysis and the road Accident Investigations (RAI) are done but on very limited scale guided by RTC fatality and injury records at specific road sections. Besides, the limited interventions that are undertaken are not usually supported with impact evaluations to establish the actual benefits gained to motivate replications and extended applications.

Step 4:

i. Crash Risk Assessment and Estimation: After road inspections and detailed analysis of RTC locations, risk metrics are developed to help determine the measure of safety performance of the road network based on both actual and predicted fatality estimations. In doing this, some crash risk assessment models are used for the purpose of obtaining estimated cost values of crashes as inputs for the development of infrastructure investment plans.

This includes the use of star rating models and risk mapping frameworks. These are objective measures of assessing the likelihood of an RTC occurring and its severity at a road section by road user category. It provides guidance for the determination of an appropriate treatment strategy for identified road deficiencies based on the potential impact on a particular road user category per defined road section. Within the model, road sections are classified into categories and ranked according to safety risk related factors, such as RTC concentration, traffic volume and traffic typology for motor vehicles, motorcycle, pedestrians and bicycles.

The International Road Assessment Programme (iRAP) tool is the most resourceful star rating model developed by a registered charity organisation dedicated to saving lives. The severity of RTC for each road user category is rated based on Star Rating Scores (SRS) set on a 5-star scale with the safest roads scoring the maximum of 5-star rating and the least safe road scoring the lowest of 1-star rating.

The key protocols of the iRAP model includes the following but it is not the intention of the author to provide the details of the iRAP methodology but rather an indicative overview for the readers further research if interested which is available at http://toolkit.irap.org/.

a). Development of a Policy Criteria for the Implementation of iRAP with the following as best global standards:

- Setting of a target to eliminate high risk whereby it is globally recommended for (1-and 2-star) rated roads to be eliminated by the end of the action decade for road safety.

- Setting of minimum star rating for all new road designs to ensure no more killer roads are built.

- Ensuring that all new roads have a higher rating than existing roads.

- Conducting a road safety assessment (iRAP Star Rating and Investment Plans) on the highest risk roads or roads with high traffic volumes in the country/region.

b) Implementation approach of the iRAP: The approach to the implementation of the iRAP must include:

- Risk Mapping of Injuries and deaths by road type and section.

- Conduct of physical road inspections to identify road defects with likelihood for causing injuries and deaths by road sections at 100m interval for vehicle occupants, motorcyclists, pedestrians and cyclists.

- Data Analysis and processing by coding of attributes using the road database by the development of Star Rating Scores (SRS) developed by combining relative risk factors using a multiplicative model).

- Star rating of high-risk attributes important for road safety for vehicle occupants, Motorcyclist, Pedestrian and Cyclists based on SRS scores for each 100m of road.

- Production of reporting options which allows for the display of results by length (in kilometers) and percentages for each of the four road user groups where available.

c) Application Sotwares for iRAP: Currently there are some general iRAP application softwares including the ViDA available for free online use at http://vida.irap.org. The application has in-built star rating demonstrator tools that enables star rating for designs (SR4D) for individual road locations. This can be sourced from the iRAP Road Attribute Risk Factor factsheets in the Documents section of the iRAP website at: http://irap.org/about-irap-3/methodology. It also incorporates procedural components developed to guide the selection and implementation of various corrective measures for identified defects on the road based on in-built matrices that define the risk of a particular route under consideration.

d) Examples of Applied iRAP: The iRAP charity group works in partnership with government and non-government organizations such as the FIA Foundation, Global Road Safety Facility (GRSF) and FedEx governed by the Global Technical Committee (GTC) to implement the iRAP. It is now active in more than 70 countries throughout Europe, Africa, Asia Pacific, North, Central and South America and examples of adapted models by some countries are as summarised in Table 4.5.

Table 4.4: Examples of adopted iRAP models by countries

Type of iRAP Model	Description
EuroRAP RPS 1.0	-Based on homogeneous sections and a limited set of road attributes that provide protection to car occupants. The use of regularly updated Road Assessment Program (RAP) data to track the overall performance of national road networks between 1999 and 2004 has shown reductions of about half in the length of roads in the highest risk band in Spain, Britain and Sweden (Lynam et al, 2007).

Austroads Stereotypes	-Star Rating for Schools (SR4S): An evidence-based tool for measuring, managing and communicating the risk children are exposed to as pedestrians -ANRAM: Uses iRAP Star Ratings and crash data to provide enhanced fatality and serious injury estimates for Australian roads -AusRAP, KiwiRAP: Illustrate Star Ratings for a range of typical cross-section and operating speed scenarios on the Australian road network
ThaiRAP Light Star Ratings	-Developed and used in Thailand with a subset of the Star Rating methodology and linked to a road asset database.
ChinaRAP	With technical and funding support from GRSF, ChinaRap became the first country-owned Road Assessment Programme (RAP) in any low- or middle-income country. A primary outcome is the integration of local research into Road Assessment models
India iRAP	As part of efforts to curb road deaths and serious injuries, the World Bank Global Road Safety Facility (GRSF) invited the International Road Assessment Programme (iRAP) to work with the Ministry of Road Transport and Highways (MoRTH), public works departments, research institutes, local engineering firms and motoring clubs to assess the safety of Indian roads. Most of the roads were rated just 1- or 2-stars for safety and it was estimated that 76,000 deaths and serious injuries occur on the roads each year at a cost of INR 182.2 billion (USD 2.8 billion). However, iRAP Safer Roads Investment Plans made a good economic case for the solutions. (iRAP India Project Summary, 2015).
BrazilRAP	The National Department of Transport Infrastructure DNIT applied IRAP to assess approximately 3400km of roads. The objective is to prevent road deaths with the introduction of safer road infrastructure to Brazil. It tackled problems on the highest risk roads around the country.
Nigeria iRAP Rating	It aims to assess road infrastructure with a view to improve the safety of roads. In addition, the main focus of is placed on improvement of roads for vulnerable road users such as pedestrians and three-wheel vehicles.

ii. Crash Risk Mapping: Crash risk maps are used to graphically where the crash risks is greatest for all categories of road users by vehicle type. It also highlights the road characteristics to provide an indication of the overall safety performance of a particular road. It shows the number of fatal and serious collisions per km travelled and the risk arising from the interaction of road users, vehicles and the road environment also displayed.

iii. Combination of Crash Risk Maps and Star Ratings: These are often used together as part of a strategic approach to managing risk and investment.

In Ghana, a pilot application of the iRAP model has been effected on sampled roads with recommendations for corrective interventions yet to be applied. It is anticipated that the outcome of the interventions if applied will guide further expansion of the iRAP model to other eligible roads in the country. In the long term a substantive policy for the application of such scientific models should for effective safe road planning and investment in the country.

Step 5: Definition of Countermeasures for identified Crash Risks: Following the identification and rating of crash defects, countermeasure options are tested for their potential to reduce deaths and injuries using a series of triggers. This is done by the matching of countermeasures with the identified engineering defects on the road. The countermeasures are then designed and implemented using corresponding treatment strategies either by the grouping of intervention categories for mass action treatment options or by the likely source of funding.

In Ghana, countermeasures are applied for the correction of road defects after identification, though implementation is often subject to funding availability. It is recommended for best practice to focus on short term measures within a period of incubation to allow for long term preparations and in some cases funding sourcing before substantive interventions are applied.

Step 6: Justification of Expenditure through Economic Analysis: Application of economic tests by cost benefit analysis is done for each counter measure to determine its economic benefit in terms of prevented deaths and injuries. This is applied especially where there are budget constraints in order to ensure cost-effectiveness within a limited budget.

In Ghana, the prioritisation of safe road countermeasures is not undertaken as separate investment analysis. Rather, options for countermeasures for the correction of known road defects may be considered as an integral part of a general road investment analysis process. This is usually done for major trunk and urban road projects and in a few cases feeder roads projects using relevant road investment analytical tools such as the HDM-4.

In such instances in-built accident cost savings (based on RTC Statistics) are estimated based on the willingness to pay concept as a part of the benefits to be gained over the cost of investment to establish the viability of the rate of the investment return for decision making. However, the process does not specifically focus on the margin by which safety countermeasures are prioritised over another.

Step 7: Development of Infrastructure safety investment plan (ISIP). The ISIP provides a set of prioritised tasks or solutions identified for solving specific road infrastructure safety problems with allocated costs. These can be presented in baseline form or after application of corrective measures in the form of Safer Roads Investment Plans (SRIP).

In Ghana, there is no substantive policy for the preparation of dedicated ISIP to support road infrastructure safety management. So far there are only the infrastructure safety strategies defined in the NRSS by the road sector agencies. Even with this, the extent to which the quantity of interventions listed are informed by knowledge of the existing road conditions is not known. Also, individual road agencies define their components of road infrastructure safety activities with related costs as a part of their general infrastructure MTDF plans

Due to this, there is limited focus on road infrastructure safety and they are usually not adequately budgeted for but rather random interventions may be effected when funds are available to do so. Thus, there is need to develop resilient and quality infrastructure safety investment plans. Also, since the cost of RTCs caused by a road defect significantly outweighs the investment in improving the road facility, deliberate considerations should be made to mainstream infrastructure safety planning in the road infrastructure investment planning process. Specific actions defined within the NRSS plans must correspond to what is within the MTDF.

The two plans must feed into each other and the extent to which funding commitments are made for such purposes should be very clear. In some instances, budgets for addressing infrastructure safety needs are combined as a part of road maintenance budget costs or traffic management budgets which may not be adequate for the safety components. At the programming or project level budgeting, however, sections of the road network or individual road networks may be screened in detail in order to identify defects for direct costing on a limited scale. Though the investment components prepared by each road agency into the MTDF are also dovetailed into the national development plan with estimated budgets for road infrastructure safety, the interface between such plans and the budgets components defined in the NRSS is not clear.

Step 8: Performance tracking of how inbuilt safety interventions contributes to the reduction of RTC deaths and injuries: This must be done by monitoring and evaluation of the effects of road safety upgrades after the star rated interventions have been implemented. Detailed crash data can be used to analyse a comparison between the before and after situation of the crash characteristics to help provide evidence that road user risk has reduced.

In Ghana, impact assessment of infrastructure safety interventions are not well defined with the exception of a few isolated cases. A typical example is the study on speed control measures by Afukaar, K.F. (2003) which indicated that the installation of rumble strips on the main Accra – Kumasi Highway reduced crashes by 35% and fatalities by 55%. Otherwise, it is generally assumed that the benefits of road safety interventions should reflect in the general crash statistics of safety performance involving all aspects of safety interventions not only limited to infrastructure interventions.

C. Resource Inputs for Road Infrastructure Safety Planning: These involve data availability, technical capacity/knowhow and funding availability.

i. Data Availability: Good quality data is essential for road infrastructure safety assessments since such data could be compromised by random accident counts, lack of road assessment tools, wrongful identification of defective road sites etc. for which well-defined structures must be established to address. Another challenge is with the challenge of the translation of infrastructure safety plans into implementable projects.

In Ghana, this is attributed to the fact that dedicated ISIPs are not purposely developed through the above discussed processes.

ii. Funding: The challenge of limited funding and other resource availability affects effective application of scientific models in road infrastructure safety planning.

In Ghana, there is no dedicated funding to support the preparation of ISIP's in Ghana. The earmarked proportion of the road fund for road safety activities are allocated partly to the NRSA and also to the road agencies not as stand-alone budget line items for road infrastructure safety development but rather as part of the budget for road maintenance or improvement activities. Thus, there is need to setup road infrastructure safety investment plan with dedicated funding.

iii. Capacity Development for Road Infrastructure Safety Planning: Though, there is need for technical capacity and expertise for managing ISIP processes because they are complex there is a lack of opportunity for education and training in their use within most countries.

It is therefore recommended for countries to solicit technical assistance to in the development of adequate capacity through training especially by the iRAP foundation. The recommended training content includes the following:

a. Introduction to iRAP

b. Planning and procuring an iRAP project

c. Crash rate risk mapping

d. Star Rating for Designs

e. Star Rating for Schools

f. Introduction to iRAP Methodology

g. Road survey

h. Road attribute coding

i. Accessing and Understanding Star Ratings and Safer Road

j. Investment Plans

k. Creating your own Star Ratings and Safer Road Investment Plans

In Ghana, the level of technical capacity for effective road infrastructure safety planning must be assessed for appropriate training measures to be provided. This will enable the key staff to appreciate the importance and mode of application of the method.

4.4 SAFE ROAD DESIGN

The safety of a road infrastructure is defined by the geometric and structural design of the roadway in order to optimise operational safety and transport efficiency within constraints of limited budgets, environmental concerns and other social outcomes.

4.4.1 Road Infrastructure Defects Causing RTCs

Road characteristics must be designed to minimise bottlenecks in order to encourage sensible and attentive driving and to reduce the possibility of an RTC occurring. This is because bad road characteristics can trigger wrong perception and wrong driving reactions (Dewar, 2008). Thus, improvements in the design, construction and maintenance of road infrastructure can significantly improve road safety.

A. Roadway Defects that can cause RTC's: Examples of poor road features are as summarized in Table 4.6.

Table 4.6: Examples of poor road features

Poor Road Designs	Application in Ghana
a) Lack of proper guardrails	In Ghana all of the features are
b) Existence of blind Curves	applicable in addition others such as
c) Overly narrow lanes	-Poor street lighting
d) No shoulder or dangerous shoulder or not providing adequate shoulder area for vehicles to stop if necessary	-Inadequate pedestrian crossing points
e) Excessive grades	
f) Lack of proper signage regarding safe speed, approaching curves, or approaching hazards	
g) Visual impediments such as bushes or trees that were not adequately cleared during construction	
h) Inadequate road drainage	
i) Merging lanes that aren't long enough, congested roads, frequent curves, narrow bridges, short sight distances, and in general situations that increase uncertainty increase workload	
j) Unclear traffic signs, poor lane markings, poor road surfaces	
Poor Road Maintenance	-Silted drains
a) Failure to trim overgrown vegetation that may be blocking the view of the road or a sign	-Lack of maintenance of street lighting systems
b) Failure to maintain missing or damaged traffic signals and other traffic signs	-Poor shoulder maintenance
c) Uncorrected potholes, guardrail or median damage	-Reduced effective road width especially on rural roads
d) Excessive oil or gravel due to resurfacing or road maintenance procedures	
e) Faded paint markings, like the center line or road edge markings	
Effects of Bad roadway Features on Safety	All these are applicable in Ghana
a) Poor ride quality such as potholes can result in loss of vehicle control and slippery surface can result skidding of vehicle	
b) Poor marking and signage especially in the night can result in vehicular run-off	
c) Traffic congestion can result in driver impatience and irritation causing wrongful decisions	
d) Lack of understanding of road design by road users of the benefits of compliance can result in inappropriate use of roadway	
e) Lack of parking space: This can cause wrongful parking causing obstruction and traffic congestion resulting in driver impatience	
f) Hazard such as stockpiled material on carriageway can cause confusion which in turn leads to impulse decisions behind the wheel.	

B. Road Characteristics Contributing to Specific Crashes: Specific road characteristics that contributes to RTC types from literature are as summarized in Appendix 4.1.

C. Principles of Safe Road Design: Generally, roads must be designed with safety considerations to minimise or avoid RTCs caused by road defects.

In Ghana major highways are mostly designed to higher standards than feeder roads due to higher traffic levels. However, such roads can have counter benefits on safety when drivers over speed due to good ride quality and adequate sight distance. Some recommended guidelines for the preparation of safe road designs include the following in Table 4.8.

Table 4.8: Principles of safe road design

Themes	Application in Ghana
Policy a) Policy guideline should be by the concept of the Safe System approach and other technological developments b) Policy must be continuously updated c) Codes and manuals for prevailing road use must be reviewed d) Provision of adequate financing for safe infrastructure development	a) Typically, road safety policies, standards and guidelines are directly copied from other countries without due consideration of local conditions. b) Policy is not continuous updated c) Codes and manuals have not been reviewed except the manual for the low volume roads d) Funding for road development is characterized by consistent shortfalls
Objective a) Minimisation of bottlenecks on the roadway which can be dangerous to the road user	Road design is not solely guided by bottlenecks on roadway
Approach a) Design approach must target specific road traffic crash types e.g., head-on crashes; b) Obsolete design standards must be reformed guided by the application of low-cost options but standards must not be compromised on the basis of budget cuts. c) Design must address environmental factors e.g., wet road surfaces d) Access Management must complement geometric design to avoid conflicts e) The design must inform road user about expected behaviour to avoid confusion, (Pasanen, 1992). f) Design ambiguities should be avoided g) There should be demonstration projects for new designs on trial basis h) Innovative approaches should also be considered i) Design standards must maintain the balance between safety, economic cost and efficiency. j) Design must meet the mobility and access needs of all users especially vulnerable road users eg. Lane segregation k) Design standards must be subjected to safety audits. l) Safety engineering departments must be established m) Design must provide information on traffic operation eg: signage and road markings n) Important information should be repeated where relevant, to enhance driver awareness. o) Design must be consistent by avoiding the provision of varied roadway safety features p) Design must control unsafe user activity at conflict locations e.g. intersections q) Design must guide road users where the road direction is obscured with adequate warning r) Safety engineering capacity must be developed	a) This is not done consistently b) Design polices are compromised due to limited budgets. There may even be reluctance to change established practice c) Environmental considerations are taken into account in road design in Ghana d) Access management is done for some roads e) Not done in all cases f) Compliance is intermittent g) This is not done h) The pace of adoption of new knowledge and innovations is slow and the frequency of updates is also slow. i) The magnitude of application is not known j) This sis considered in some situations k) Some road designs are subjected to safety audits l) All road agencies have safety engineering departments m) This is sometimes done n) This is done sometimes o) It is not known the extent to which this is applied p) This is considered in road engineering in Ghana q) This is applied in some instances r) This is done sometimes

D. Priorities for Safe Road Infrastructure Design: The typical engineering technologies required to be applied in safe road design in the AASHTO (2010) are as follows:

- Description
- Purpose of the Road
- Principles of the Element
- Features of the Element
- Types of the Element

- Safety Related Criteria of the element
- Effects of the Safety Criteria on Safety

4.4.2. Design of Road Geometry

Geometric design of a roadway is the determination of the layout of the physical elements of the roadway to the requirements of the driver and vehicle for, safety, comfort and efficiency. It ensures that the design of the road fits the topography of a particular site. The main features of a geometric design of a roadway are; (i) Road Alignment (i.e. Horizontal and Vertical alignments); (ii) Cross section components (i.e. Lateral and vertical clearances) and (iii) the intersection (i.e. Access control).

A. Key Criteria for Geometric Design: The design of the main features mentioned above are determined by the following safety-oriented design controls and criteria.

- Design Speed
- Topography
- Traffic Factors
- Environmental and other Factors

i. The Design Speed: Speeding refers to driving faster than the sign-posted speed limit that is unsafe for the condition, (Speed Management Policy 2018). The design speed is the main factor on which geometric design elements depends and it is determined by the (i) road class; (ii) road terrain (i.e. Plain or flat, rolling or mountainous and Steep) as well as the road user. The design speed in turn influences the grades or tangents, horizontal and vertical curves, lane widths and sight distance of the roadway. According to Fitzpatrick et al. (2003), there should be more harmonious relationship between the desired operating speed, the actual operating speed and the posted speed limit."

Policy standards for speed control and management includes the introduction of variable speed limits for appropriate road sections and land use type. Speeding must be controlled by physical elements such as traffic calming measures eg. rumble strips combined with conspicuously marked speed control bumps, or better, speed tables combined with zebra pedestrian crossings, roundabouts etc. since they are more efficient than road signage limiting speeds.

In Ghana, variable speed limits are applied such that within settlements the speed limit 50km, on trunk roads it is 80 and on high-speed roads it is 100km, (See Figure 4.5). Also, posted speed limits within settlements are sometimes combined with speed humps and tables.

Figure 4.5: Samples of Posted Speed Limits in Ghana

a). Speed Control by Crash Type: Critical speed levels in traffic crashes differ depending upon the type of crash being considered and it is said that the human factor cannot survive uncushioned speed impact of more than 40km/hr. Thus, it is concluded that speed control cannot work unless vehicle and road system work together if more than 70km/hr is to be survived, www.irap.net.

In Ghana, according to Afukaar K F, (2003), after examining the effectiveness of various speed control measures established loss of control from speeding as the most contributory factor to crashes.

b). Creation of Speed Zone by Road User and by Landuse Type: This involves relating speed control to the type of road user needs. An example is the creation of low-speed zones for vulnerable road users such as in School Zones. Another example is the provision of segregated road lanes for non-motorised transport (NMT's) such as cycle lanes as well as designing for walking with assigned speed target of 20-30km/hr. for residential roads.

In Ghana 30kph is recommended within Schools zones, Playgrounds, Health Facilities, Church and Mosque environments, Market Centres, Shopping Centres, or where human activity is predominant. There are also some provisions for segregated roadways by required road user category known. This may sometimes be supported with speed humps and pedestrian crossing facilities.

ii. Topography and Environmental Features: The topography, physical features and land use of an area affects the safety of traffic flow and operational performance on a roadway. Specifically, steep grades and restrictive sight distance affect the capacity of 2-lane highways and land use has a significant effect on highway geometry.

In Ghana, plain terrain on highway has 100km/hr as the permissible design speed whereas the same speed on rolling terrain is permitted to 80km/h and on mountain terrain is 50km/h.

iii. The Traffic Factor: The aspects of the traffic factor that influence the geometric design of a road include both the physical characteristics and turning capability of vehicles such as traffic volume, composition and speed as detailed below:

a). Traffic Volume: Traffic volume affects the road capacity in terms of the number of lanes required. Average daily traffic (ADT) is the general unit of measure for traffic volume and it is defined as the total traffic volume during a given time period (>1day, and <1year), divided by the number of days in that time period. For design purposes the Average Annual Daily Traffic (AADT) is considered since it caters for seasonal changes of variations in traffic over the year. It is defined as the average twenty-four-hour traffic count collected over a period of one year which is estimated as (AADT = Total traffic volume in one year / 365).

b). Design Hourly Volume and Capacity: Since the traffic volume fluctuates by time in a day with a combination of peak and off-peak periods where congestion might be created in the first and there will be free flow in the later, it is deemed uneconomical to design for congestion free conditions. Therefore, as good practice, the design of the road must consider the Design Hourly Volume.

c). Design vehicle: In practice a mix of different vehicle types use a road and in geometric design the physical characteristics and proportions of vehicles of various sizes using the road is a key control factor. Thus, a representative vehicle is identified in the traffic stream as the design vehicle. Its physical characteristics which affect the roadway geometry such as the width of the traffic lane, the length affecting the roadway capacity, turning radius at junctions, the height affecting vertical clearance of structures and the weight affecting the structural or pavement design of the roadway is used as the standard.

By this, design vehicles are normally in four groups as passenger Cars, Buses, Trucks, and Recreational Vehicles and the design vehicle is typically the largest vehicle that normally uses the road. After determining the appropriate design vehicle, a decision is made as to the level of design space provision is to be made.

In Ghana three (3) design vehicles are identified in the road design guide as small vehicle, large vehicle and trailer.

d). Environmental and Other Factors: Factors such as road functional classification, aesthetics, landscaping, noise pollution and other local conditions are also given due consideration in the design of road geometry to ensure mobility and ability to move goods and passengers to their destination in a reasonable time. Thus, the key elements considered are

- Accessibility- the ability to reach desired destination.
- Physical Characteristics and performance of Drivers and Pedestrians.
- Design Level of Service (LOS) etc.

iv. Criteria for Safe Geometric Design: The Criteria for safe geometric design includes the following:

a) Criterion I: Consistency between Successive Design Elements: In connection to this, the 1984 AASHTO Policy on the Geometric Design of Highways recommended the following to be in place:

- Ensuring consistent alignment.
- Avoidance of the introduction of sharp curves.
- Avoidance of sudden changes from areas of flat curvature to areas of sharp curvature.

In Ghana the road design incorporates consistency in road geometric design to ensure consistent alignment.

b). Criterion 2: Harmonizing Design Speed and Operating Speed: Harmonizing design speed and operating speed is another important safety criterion that should be considered in the design, redesign, or rehabilitation processes especially for two-lane highways and networks. To achieve this goal, the 85th-percentile speed of every independent tangent or curve must be in tune with the existing or selected design speed according to the recommended design speed ranges.

c). Criterion 3: Providing Adequate Dynamic Safety of Driving: Glennon et al. (1987), indicated that the probability of a highway curve becoming an RTC black spot increases with decreasing pavement skid resistance, (side friction factor). Thus, Lamm, R., (1984), intimates that sufficient friction supply should be a main safety consideration in designing, redesigning, or resurfacing roadways especially for curve design.

d). Combination of Criteria: Each of the discussed safety criteria does represent a separate safety aspect in highway geometric design thus the ideal conditions is recommended to have;

- at least 2-lanes for each direction;
- all vehicles moving at approximately the same speed;
- adequacy in the width of traffic lane, shoulders, and clearances to vertical obstructions beyond the edge of the traffic lane; and
- avoidance of restrictive sight distances, grades, and improper superelevation curves.

Road design standard in Ghana, meets this criterion.

B. Road Alignments

i. Horizontal Alignment: The horizontal alignment consists of straight sections of the road known as tangents connected by horizontal curves. Its design is important for facilitating smooth transition from one of the mentioned elements to the other. Its key components considered are the horizontal curve, superelevation, type and length of transition curves; widening of carriageways on curves and set-back distance. The safe design factors include the following:

a). Straight/Tangent Sections: Monotonous straight sections of a roadway pose safety problems for the road user as drivers tend to over speed and also lose concentration because their task become too easy. Appropriate curves are required to be introduced in the design of such sections to reduce speeds and improve driver alertness which in turn reduces road traffic crashes (RTCs) and casualties.

In Ghana, RTCs occurring on straight sections of roads contribute significantly at about 71% and 90% of passenger and pedestrian casualties, respectively, (NRSA, 2019) which should be of concern in road design considerations.

b). Horizontal curves: The design of a horizontal curvature of a road is important because a road with a horizontal curve without adequate radius, superelevation and sight distance to satisfy the design speed pose serious safety threats to the driver. This is because a curve with radius lower than that required for the design speed and without superelevation compromise the safety of road users as it results in vehicles skidding off the road due to the high resultant effect of centrifugal (outward) forces.

Crash risks are also higher for isolated curves (where the driver might not be expecting it) and lower for curves in a sequence of similar-standard curves. The risk of crash victims suffering serious injuries is relatively high for horizontal curve radius below 150m. If the travel speed of a vehicle exceeds the suitable limit or design limit of the curve, then the vehicle loses control and a serious "out of control' crash may take place.

Curve sections contribute about 13% and 15% of passenger and pedestrian casualties, respectively, in Ghana (NRSA, 2019).

c). Curve Widening: Curve widening refers to the extra width of carriageway that is required on a curved section of a road over and above that required on a tangent section. Usually on sharp curves (with radii less than 150m for Ghana).

As a heavy goods vehicle or articulated trailer turns, the rear wheels follow the front wheels on a shorter radius. This has the practical effect of increasing the effective carriageway width required if the same clearance is to be maintained between opposing goods vehicles on curved sections as on tangent sections of single carriageway roads, or between adjacent vehicles travelling in the same direction on dual-carriageway roads. Moreover, there is the natural tendency for drivers to shy away from the edges of the carriageway as they carry out turning manoeuvres. This further reduces the clearance between vehicles and increases the crash potential at these locations.

According to a study by NRSA (2019), sharp curves (without adequate widening) was ranked 2nd 69.8% amongst other unsuitable roadway layout which constitutes the core safety risk factors in Ghana. In order to avert the effects of the aforementioned reasons to improve the safety of road users, the need for curve widening is imperative.

d) Sight Distance on Horizontal Curves: Sight distance is the length of highway visible ahead to the driver of a vehicle. Adequate sight distance especially on curves ensures that drivers have sufficient distance of clear vision ahead that enables them to avoid hitting unexpected obstacles. Obstructions from natural road side features such as trees and bushes can reduce the sight distance on horizontal curves hampering the safety of road users.

Others are shops, long boundary walls along the roadside, sign posts, bill boards, shops, kiosks etc. Safety can be ensured by clearing all obstructions along horizontal curves to improve sight distance. Roadside obstructions should not be allowed without sufficient setback or offset to ensure clear vision of roadside (at least 1.5 m from the edge of carriageway) in road design. If roadside obstructions cannot possibly be removed, then they should be shielded with proper markings, (See Figure 4.6 for examples of obstructed horizontal alignments. A safety focused horizontal alignment design should therefore be the one that ensures the following safety design considerations with illustrations provided in Table 4.9.

Roadside obstructions contribute about 6% of passenger RTC fatalities in Ghana (NRSA, 2019).

Table 4.9: Safety Considerations for Horizontal Alignment Design of Road

Design element	Undesirable	Desirable	Safety consideration
Horizontal alignment			Avoiding monotonous straight sections and introducing large radius horizontal curves to engage the attention of drivers
Horizontal alignment			Ensuring consistency in alignment by avoiding abrupt change in speed
Horizontal alignment			Providing adequate superelevation on horizontal curves
Horizontal alignment			Widening of horizontal curve sections to improve clearance between opposing traffic
Horizontal alignment			Provision of adequate off-set distance from road side features to improve sight distance

Source: Kapila et al, 2013

C. Vertical Alignment: The vertical alignment is the elevation or profile of the centre line of the road. It consists of straight sections known as grades connected by vertical curves which influence vehicle speed, acceleration and deceleration, sight distance, vehicle operation cost and comfort while travelling at high speeds. Therefore, the design of the vertical alignment involves the selection of suitable grades (slopes/gradients) for tangent sections and the design of the vertical curves (crests and sags) with adequate radii and lengths.

This is because vertical grades and curves have significant influence on the safety of traffic operations on the roadway though Sag curves are not known to have any significant effect on safety. The most crucial effect crests have on safety is through sight distance. There is a small relationship between crash risk and vertical grade and the crash risk also increases more rapidly for grades beyond 6% as vehicle speeds becomes more difficult to manage. The key elements of vertical alignment include the following:

a) Stopping sight distance: This is the distance required for a driver to recognise a need to stop and brake to a stop from a particular speed. Horizontal and vertical curves limit a driver's sight distance, particularly crests. There is the suggestion of a small increase in crash risk as sight distance over a crest decrease especially in situations of overtaking. This risk increases more rapidly for sight distances below 100m. Road widening (either as wider shoulders or an overtaking lane) over a crest with less than adequate sight distance can be an effective countermeasure rather than flattening the crest. Improving limited sight distance at locations where other vehicles may be slowing or stopping (in particular intersection sight distance) can also be extremely important for safety purposes.

b) Gradients: Gradients need to be considered from the standpoint of both steepness and length when the safety of road users comes into play. Steep gradients above 10% and of length above 200m significantly compromise the safety of users especially where overloaded heavy vehicles form a significant proportion of the traffic flow and must therefore be avoided. Steep uphill / ascending gradients can result in RTC (head-on collision) between vehicles in opposing traffic streams on 2-lane roads, as faster vehicles try to overtake slower heavy trucks where they should not, (See Figure 4.7).

Safety can be compromised on downhill gradients due to the possibility of increased speed combined with inadequate skid resistance, inclement weather, worn out tyres and longer braking distance, making it more difficult for a vehicle to be controlled. This is also a more significant problem for heavier vehicles like trucks. According to Elvik et al (2009), a two-lane highway located in steep terrain can have 15% more road crashes than a similar road located in a level terrain condition.

Also, RTC's are more predominant on steeper gradients and that reducing the gradient from over 7% to a range of 5-7%, significantly reduces RTCs by about 20%. In a situation where there are restrictions in meeting gradient requirements due to a challenging terrain, a climbing lane can be provided for heavier vehicles which can reduce probability of crashes by 25% on a two-lane roadway section.

Typical examples of climbing lanes for heavy vehicles in Ghana are located on the Konongo Kumasi section of the Accra Kumasi Highway. In Ghana, RTC passenger and pedestrian casualties resulting from Steep (inclined) roadway sections constitute about 8% and 4%, respectively (NRSA, 2019).

Figure 4.7: Sample Publication on Overloading in Ghana

c) **Vertical Curves:** Safety on vertical curves (crest and sag) has to do with the adequacy of curve lengths and curve radii which are influenced by sight distance. Two concepts of sight distance are considered to the design of vertical curves; the stopping sight distance (SSD) and passing or overtaking sight distance (PSD). The third concept which is the

meeting sight distance (MSD) is usually desirable for entire length of narrow single carriageways of width less than 5.0 meters. Crest curves with inadequate (shorter) lengths
and (smaller or sharper) radii than required for the specified design speed, have limited
Stopping Sight Distance (SSD) which affects the ability of a vehicle to stop safely when
it encounters an obstacle in its way which could be a slow-moving vehicle, broken down
vehicle, pedestrians crossing, etc., before hitting it.

In the case of sag curves, stopping sight distance is not a problem in the day but rather
in the night since how far the driver can see is dictated by the distance of travel by the
headlight. Passing or Overtaking Sight Distance (PSD) is applicable to two-lane roads
to enable drivers to use the opposing traffic lane for passing (overtaking) other vehicles
without interfering with oncoming vehicles. Inadequate PSD aggravates the risk of involvement in RTC on vertical curves and according to Caliendo (2001), the number of
crashes reduces with increasing sight distance.

Also, a study by Olson et al. (1984) as cited by Glennon (1987) indicated that crest
curves with limited SSD exhibited 50% higher crash rate than curves with adequate
SSD. Safety on vertical curves can therefore be improved by the provision of adequate
sight distance through the specification of vertical curve lengths and radii that meet the
requirement of the specified design speed. A safety focused vertical alignment should
therefore be the one that ensures the following safety design considerations with illustrations provided in Table: 4.10.

*In Ghana, for a typical speed of 80km/hr on a two-lane highway, the minimum SSD and
PSD required are 110 meters and 500 meters, respectively, with corresponding minimum
crest/sag curve length of 70 meters, crest curve radius of 3000 meters and sag curve radius
of 2000 meters (Source, Ghana Highway Authority Road Design Guide). However, the
contribution of crest curves to RTC casualties is minimal at 0.2% for passenger casualties
and 0.1% for pedestrian casualties (NRSA, 2019). Irrespective of how minimal it is, there is
still the need to eliminate RTC casualties as every individual life matters.*

Table 4.10: Safety Considerations for Vertical Alignment Design of Road

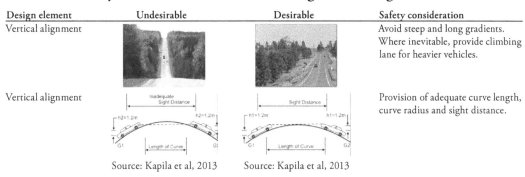

Design element	Undesirable	Desirable	Safety consideration
Vertical alignment			Avoid steep and long gradients. Where inevitable, provide climbing lane for heavier vehicles.
Vertical alignment	Source: Kapila et al, 2013	Source: Kapila et al, 2013	Provision of adequate curve length, curve radius and sight distance.

4.4.3 Cross Section of a Roadway

The cross section of a roadway basically consists of elements that form the effective width of the roadway, which in turn affect vehicular movement including Pavement Surface characteristics; Width of Carriageway; Cross Slope or Camber Median or Traffic Separator; Kerbs and Road Margins. Others are road shoulders, roadside barriers, drains/gutters, street lights, sidewalks and side slope of cuttings or embankments.

The elements of the roadway cross section may differ depending on whether it is located in an urban or rural setting. The design and characteristics of the aforementioned elements greatly affect the safety of the road facility. Inconsistent road cross-section without transition zones influences driver errors by creating surprise situations for drivers and other road users especially during sudden change in number of lanes and this can cause vehicle run off. The detail design elements include the following:

A. Pavement surface characteristics: The important surface characteristics of the pavement are: Friction, Roughness, Light reflecting characteristics and Drainage of surface water. Defective road pavement surface such as potholes contributes to RTCs by resulting in loss of vehicle control and tyre bursts. Unsealed roads, although not likely to be considered a high-risk can have potholes and corrugations result in vehicle run offs, (See Figure 4.8).

Figure 4.8: Examples of Poor Road Surface Conditions in Ghana (Source MRH)

In Ghana, unknown presence of potholes requiring slow-downs and causing sudden speed brakes often results in RTCs. Likewise unexpected change in road surface condition where drivers are not able to adapt their speed to appropriate level causes RTCs. The statistics on RTC by road surface type is as presented in Figure 4.9. Significantly, it is on paved roads surfaces at without much potholes that most of the RTC's occur at 81.57% whilst earth road with few or many earth roads records the least at 2% each. This is because paved roads in good condition have the advantage of good ride quality whose benefit is offset by the practice of high speed by drivers on such roads

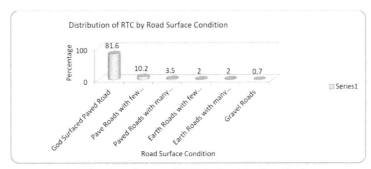

Figure 4.9: Distribution of RTC by Road Surface Condition

B. Proper Drainage Facility: Drainage and disposal of water from the road pavement is considered important because of the following reasons;

i.   to maintain stability, good surface condition and increased life of the pavement.

ii.   to maintain adequate drainage facility integration between roadway and adjacent land use.

The functionality of the drain can be maintained through repairing and proper cleaning. Thus, adequate attention must be given to the safety considerations of drainage facilities when designing and upgrading roadways as follows:

a.   Road side drains should be designed to have adequate capacity to avoid ponding on road surfaces which can contribute to RTC by drivers veering off into open drains.

b.   Deep, steep-sided drainage channels can result in more damage in the case of vehicles going off the road so must be avoided to minimize damage to vehicles running off the road.

c.   Saucer drains should be considered over open channel U or V drain.

d.   Existing open channel drains should be covered where possible or provision should be made for some physical barrier to separate them from the carriageways.

In Ghana, such incidence sometimes occurs during the flooding of road surfaces from heavy downpours causing some drivers to lose their lives. Also, both open and covered drains are provided as presented in Figure 4.10. Covered drains are usually provided in urban areas alongside the provision of sidewalks to provide safety for the pedestrian.

Poor drainage facilities and structures also result in safety hazards for drivers in Ghana. This is especially in relation to open drains at the edge of the road which increases the likelihood of vehicles falling into them and also prevents pedestrian safety. Such open channel drains also increase the difficulty in vehicle manoeuvring that may lead to an RTC. Other practices such as the removal of sewerage covers causing gap holes in the middle of the road contributes to RTCs. Of key significance is the silting of roads with debris from uncovered open spaces and wrongful environmental habits by the citizenry. This includes the dumping of refuse into open drains with some people even pushing rubbish into the small openings for covered drains.

Figure 4.10: Examples of Covered and open drains in Ghana

C. Width of Carriageway: It is the total width of road on which vehicles are allowed to move determined based on the width of the design vehicle expected to use the roadway. The width of carriageway also varies for various classes of roads e.g. single lane road, two lanes without raised kerbs, two lanes with raised kerbs, Intermediate Carriageway and Multi-lane roads.

i. Traffic Lanes: The traffic lane is basically the portion of the carriageway allocated to a single line of vehicles usually delineated by longitudinal markings. The number of traffic lanes required is determined based on traffic demand (projected volumes) and the typical capacity of an ideal single lane. The traffic lane width on the other hand is selected based on traffic operation efficiency and safety, construction and maintenance costs considerations. The width of the traffic lane does not only influence the comfort of driving and operational characteristics of a roadway, but it is also an important parameter affecting road RTC Frequency and crash severity.

For any functional classification of a roadway, when the lane width reduces, the probability of crashes increasing drastically is high. This is due to limited room to escape from an unforeseen on-coming vehicle from the opposite direction because the lateral clearance between opposing traffic reduces causing difficulties for vehicles to stay within the designated lane as their speeds increase.

For example, a study by Zegeer et al. (1988) which looked at safety risks on a two-lane undivided highway, found that when the lane width was increased from 2.75 meters to 3.65 meters, the probability for head-on or other related crashes was reduced by 50%. Therefore, the provision of adequate wider lanes suitable for a specified design speed and anticipated traffic flow characteristics is essential in enhancing the safety of the road facility.

In Ghana, the GHA Road Design Guide specifies the lane width based on design speed as well as functional and terrain classification. Traffic lane width varies from 2.75 meters to 3.65 meters according to the GHA standards.

ii. Road Shoulders: A shoulder is that portion of the roadway adjacent to the traffic lanes that is used primarily as refuge parking area for distress vehicles. It serves as a safe recovery zone for out-of-control vehicles especially when it is a hard shoulder and also prevents pedestrians from sharing the roadway with motorists. A narrow shoulder however compels pedestrians and non-motorised traffic to share the traffic lane with motorised traffic due to limited space. A study by Zegeer et al. (1988), revealed that the percentage reduction in RTC for hard shoulder widths of between zero and 3.65 meters, is about 16% for 0.6 meters of widening, 29% for 1.2 meters of widening, and 40% for 1.8 meters of widening.

The importance of wider shoulders is more critical on two-lane two-way roads whereby a two-lane two-way road ADT greater than 2,000, the probability of crashes for a very narrow width or no shoulder increases drastically, and if no shoulder is present the chance of a crash increases by 50%. Edge of carriageway markings may be very cost-effective in reducing shoulder damage and maintenance costs.

It is recommended that where hard (paved) shoulders cannot be provided, at least soft (unpaved) shoulder should be ensured on the both sides of the road. Also, if it is not possible to provide sufficient shoulder along the road, the verge of the road should be maintained with the use of reflective edge marking on the road. Proper edge marking should also be provided to help distinguish the shoulder from the main carriageway. Excessively large shoulder drops off either from resurfacing or erosion discourages use of the shoulder. Ideally there should be no shoulder drop off but small drop off up to 50mm can be tolerated.

In Ghana, shoulder width varies from 1.5 meters to 3.0 meters depending on the functional classification of the road in accordance to the GHA design standards. Nonetheless, there are places where no shoulder can be accommodated such as on minor access roads or mountainous roads. It is also not uncommon to see some residential/commercial roads without shoulders with edges located close to entrances of people's rooms with people stepping straight unto the road from their rooms (See Figure 4.11).

Others such as the parking of vehicles on road shoulders causes obstructions to drivers with related RTC challenges. This is because oftentimes the onus is on the driver to adjust to the road environment because all are not built to the required standards. In a study conducted by NRSA (2019), the "absence of stopping lanes / shoulders" was ranked 9th amongst the key infrastructure related safety risk factors in Ghana.

Figure 4.11: Examples of Road Shoulder Types in Ghana

iii. The Road Median: A median is a section of a divided highway that separates the lanes in opposing directions to provide a recovery area for out-of-control vehicles;

provide stopping areas during emergencies; reduces the effect of glare of headlight; and provide refuge for pedestrians to cross the road.

The median may be in form of pavement markings, physical dividers or area separators. According to Harkey et al. (1998), the wider the median, the better the safety situation of road users with a study revealing that a multilane divided highway with a 3.0 meter-wide median has a 4% greater probability of crashes than a highway with a 9.0 meter wide median. Also, another study found that even for urban arterial roads, a conversion from an undivided urban arterial to one with of a raised-curb median could result, in an average of 10% reduction in road crashes (Sayed and Sawalha, 2001). Therefore, median barriers must be highly priortised in multi-lane highways for safety and operational efficiencies.

In Ghana, the median width ranges from 2 meters to 4 meters for urban areas and above 10 meters for rural areas in accordance to the GHA Design standards. Though in Ghana some median facilities are provided on some roads (see), it is not uncommon to see medians with gaps in them See Figure 4.12. Currently, majority of pedestrian RTC fatalities (83.1%) occur at non-junction road sections typically referred to as unsignalised midblock road segments (NRSA, 2019). This is mostly attributed to the non-availability and inadequate pedestrian refuge and median widths.

Figure 4.12: Examples of Median Types in Ghana

iv. Kerbs: Kerbs indicates the boundary between the pavement and median or foot path or a road shoulder. Kerbs may be mainly divided into three groups based on their functions as Low kerb; Semi-barrier type kerb and Barrier type kerb. They can also be mountable and non-mountable based on the heights. For safety considerations mountable kerbs are preferred in between the median and the carriageway to help out of control vehicles take refuge on the median. On the other hand, non mountable kerbs with higher heights are preferred for purpose of pedestrian protection.

In Ghana, all the mentioned types of kerbs are applied but on a limited scale but the criteria for the provision of each type of kerb is not clear, (See Figure 4.13). Studies have not also been conducted to prove the effectiveness of each type of kerb in protecting road users.

Figure 4.13: Examples of Road Kerbs in Ghana

Passing or Overtaking Lane: Restricted overtaking opportunities due to inadequate sight distances and lack of gaps in opposing traffic flow can result in high RTC rates typically head-on collisions through unsafe overtaking. Therefore, an additional lane is usually provided on two-lane, two-way highways in one direction covering a short distance, (usually, between 1 – 2 km) to assist faster traffic in overtaking slower vehicles in the traffic stream safely. Also, Long stretches of single carriageway roads with inadequate or no opportunities for overtaking also creates safety problems.

Studies by Austroads (2019) indicated that the reductions in injury crashes as a result of passing lane installation ranged from 20 to 40%. Therefore, in order to enhance safety and efficient operation on busy two-lane highways where dualisation is not envisaged in the interim, it is recommended to provide passing lanes at specific sections where required.

Head-on collision which mostly result from wrongful overtaking accounts for 27% of passenger fatalities in Ghana and these are more predominant on trunk roads at 46% (NRSA, 2019), (See Figure 4.14).

Figure 4.14: A signpost on overtaking lane

vi. Sidewalks: A sidewalk is a footpath along the side of a road, designed for use by pedestrians by separating them and minimizing their interaction with motorized traffic. Reviews by Mead et al. (2014) indicated that having sidewalks along streets and highways is associated with a substantial reduction in pedestrian crashes. A road with a sidewalk or wide shoulder can reduce pedestrian crash by 88.2% compared to a road without a sidewalk (McMahon et al. 2002).

In Ghana, 23% of pedestrians are exposed to RTC due to inadequate walkways (NRSA, 2019). This is attributed to limited funding for the construction of sidewalks on required roads. In addition, street widening is often made at the expense of sidewalks, squeezing the pedestrians into the remaining space and generating large distances to be traversed. Others are occupation of sidewalks by traders and thereby creating dangers for pedestrians. (See Figure 4.15).

Figure 4.15: Types of Walkways in Ghana

vii. Cross Slope or Camber: Cross slope or camber is the slope provided to the road surface in the transverse direction to drain off rain water from the road surface. It contributes to the durability of the road by the draining of surface water and also that of safety of road users by avoiding slippery road surface due to stagnant water.

In Ghana road design standards require the formation of camber.

viii. Side slopes or Embankments: Side slopes are provided on embankments and fills to provide stability for earthworks of the road. Non-recoverable roadside slopes contribute significantly to rollover crashes and this serves as a safety feature by providing a recovery area for out-of-control vehicles. Therefore, roadside slopes should be as flat as practical to make them recoverable.

Some side slopes are provided on some roadways in Ghana.

viii. Roadside Clearance: Also known as horizontal clearance or lateral offset, roadside clearance is the distance between the edge of the roadway or shoulder to a vertical roadside obstruction, and the type of obstruction a vehicle might hit. It is estimated in literature that crash risk can potentially be reduced by 35 to 45% when all roadside hazards are removed (e.g. trees, poles, fences, etc.).

Roadside obstruction is also a safety problem in Ghana especially regarding the installation of advertising billboards along urban streets.

4.4.4. Road Intersections

A road intersection is defined as a place where two or more roads meet at a grade (same level). They are high risk locations because different road users (trucks, buses, cars, pedestrians, motorcycles etc.) are required to use the same space and the movement of vehicle in different directions which can cause conflicts. Therefore, it required to design for an orderly traffic movement with adequate capacity to avoid queues and delays in order to avoid RTC's at such locations.

This is because a good intersection design slows down traffic to allow drivers more reaction time to change their direction and as well decrease severity when collisions do occur. They are also designed to promote pedestrian safety and comfort.

A. Principles for a good Intersections Design: Examples of good principles for good junction designs from literature includes the following:

i.   The number of junctions along a road section should be kept at a minimum.

ii. The geometric layout should eliminate hazardous movements by drivers by separating diverging and merging traffic movements.

iii. The layout of the junction should be easily understandable and the inter-green time should be extended to incorporate adequate all red period for drivers in a 'dilemma' zone.

iv. Speed change lanes (acceleration/deceleration lanes) must be used on high-speed, high-volume roads.

v.   For right turn from the main road, offside diverging lanes or exclusive right turn lanes should be used either by providing raised medians or ghost islands.

vi. A corner radius of intersections must be large enough to allow easy turning of long vehicles and must be delineated by pavement markings for easy.

vii. An appropriate design vehicle should be chosen (e.g. a 15.5m long articulated vehicle) and its track width on different turning radii and lock (steering angle) determined.

B. Sources and Types of Conflicts at Junctions: They are high risk locations for crashes because road users on conflicting paths are required to use the same space and a collision can occur if they are not separated in time. The major sources of detrimental impact at junctions can be identified as crashes, congestion and delay. The conflicts occurring at a junction can be categorised into three types as;

i.   diverging Traffic streams from a common direction dividing themselves into two or more streams going in different directions;

ii.   merging traffic streams from two or more different directions joining together into a single stream going in one common direction; and

iii. crossing traffic with the intersection of two traffic streams each entering from a different direction and leaving by a different exit.

C. Types of Road Junctions: Road junctions are of different shapes as described in Table 4.12.

Table 4.12: Types of road junctions

Junction type	Description
T-junction	T-junction: A T-junction has three arms of which one arm is a main road whereas the other one is usually a minor road connecting the main road. The roads of a T-junction meet at right angles and are preferably used for convenience.
Y-Junction:	Y-Junction: A Y-junction has three arms of which all the three roads are of equal sizes. It is generally seen at places of heavy traffic. It is pretty useful in the distribution of traffic.
Acute Angle Junction	Acute Angle Junction: Acute Angle Junctions can be used at places with very low density and very less space for a Junction. They are generally not preferably used because, they create lot of chaos in heavy traffic especially with the turning for heavy and bigger vehicles which becomes a problem.
Cross Junctions	Cross Junctions: Three roads meet at the same road junction. Priority here is given to the major road which the two side roads joining. Caution needs to be taken as cars will be coming from the opposite side road and, in this case, some form of priority must be adhered to.
Staggered Junction:	Staggered Junction: A staggered junction is a place where several roads meet a main road at a slight distance apart thus they do not all come together at the same point.
Multiple Junction	Multiple Junction: When multiple roads meet at a same point, the junction is termed as "Multiple Junction".
Grade Separated (Interchange)	Grade Separator: When two roads cross each other at separate grades, they can be separated by allowing one Passover by means of a bridge or flyover

D. Road safety Criteria for Safe Intersection Design: Key elements of consideration for safe junction design includes the following: (Safety Net 2007).

i.   Coordination of the vertical and horizontal alignment to prevent poor integration to minimise discomfort from these two elements as challenges to the driver.

ii.   Prioritisation of major traffic with the provision of a clear "right-of-way" and sep-arated conflicts (in space and time) to minimise conflict areas from differences in relative speeds between vehicles.

iii. Provision of vehicle paths for all vehicular and non-vehicular traffic with "simple" and consistent designs.

iv.   Provision of safe intersection sight distance by maximising sight lines; reducing speeds; altering the traffic control, making geometric changes, cutting trees/grass, and provision of roundabouts or signals

E. Junction control Measures: They include measures such as junction type conver-sions and junction alignment improvements as follows:

i. At-Grade-separated Junctions: At-grade separated junctions have all the legs of the intersection joining or crossing at the same level for basic traffic manoeuvers such as merging, diverging, crossing and weaving. They are classified as channelized intersec-tions where vehicles are confined to a specific space and unchannelized intersection with rotary intersections being of special type. They are normally used for roads in rural or urban areas where the traffic volume and speed are low and they can be classified as follows:

a). Priority junctions: Priority junctions are provided where the traffic flows on minor roads and the overall numbers of turning manoeuvres are relatively low provided with visibility to enable drivers approaching from the minor to see the vehicles on the major road in good time. Priority junctions can be major/minor priority controlled by a 'yield' or 'Stop' sign.

b). Roundabouts: They are junctions with counter-clockwise circulatory traffic used to improve traffic flow by a reduction of traffic speeds, elimination or reduction of specific types of conflict points that typically occur at angular intersections. The configuration of a roundabout allows all traffic to come from one direction, with uniform yielding rules (e.g. give way to users already in the roundabout). Crashes occurring at round-abouts are mostly side swipes that are less severe than right angle crashes occurring at cross junctions.

c). Traffic signal-controlled Junctions; Signalised junctions are applied on roads with higher traffic volume on both the major and minor roads especially for crossroads. The disadvantage of traffic-signal control is that it can increase delays and operating costs in uncongested conditions. This can however be averted by using demand-actuated traffic signals.

Traffic management centres are also used to facilitate traffic movement on congested lanes at intersection. Others are altering the sequence of signal colour indication for movement (e.g. flashing amber at night) and signal pre-emption for emergency vehicles. However, some studies in literature have revealed that flashing amber at night has increased the number of crashes in some situation.

In Ghana, signalised traffic signals are mainly used in cities and a few major towns but not in rural areas. There is also currently a pilot traffic management centre in operation the capital city but the outcome benefits on safety is yet to be established.

ii. Grade: These are junctions are relatively safe even for higher driving speeds and for higher proportion of vehicles coming from the secondary road. The grade separated junctions have roads constructed at different elevations including over-bridge and under-bridge. They can be with or without interchanges. These are used:

a. Where high-capacity main roads demand a good traffic performance.

b. Where at-grade junctions have reached the maximum capacity or there are records of high crash history.

c. Where the traffic volume at the junction is heavy and delays must be avoided.

d. Where junctions may involve considerable earthwork or acquisition of land.

e. In situations where high travel speeds are necessary and when there are short distances between the junctions.

The disadvantages of grade-separated junctions are high construction costs and large area requirements. They can also influence drivers to increase speed, which may in turn increase crash rate at adjacent road sections.

In Ghana, the use of both at Grade and grade separated junctions are popular. However, the key challenge is that because they are not considered in terms of area wide interventions, traffic challenges are carried from grade separated intersections to at-grade intersections. Plans are underway to coordinate traffic movement at connected intersections to reduce congestion on the way forward.

Safety Effects of Geometric Design Elements: A compendium of before and after studies of the safety impacts of some geometric design interventions is as presented in Table 4.13.

Table 4.13: Examples of Safety impacts of some geometric design interventions from Research

Geometric Design Element	Description
Road Curves Radii	Zhang (2009), supported some previous studies which found and stated that the curve sharpness has a significant impact on the crash rates.
Road Gradients.	Glennon et al. (1987 and Glennon, J. (1985), investigated the results obtained for several studies performed in the US and concluded that roads which were designed with grade sections have a higher road crash rates compared to roads which were designed with level sections.
Super elevation	A study conducted by Ali Aram (...). on two-lane highways concluded that sharper horizontal curves drastically increase the rate of crash occurrence, which is explained furthermore by the fact that sudden changes in horizontal alignments along the road, declines drivers' expectancy which, therefore, accordingly, raises the probability of crash occurrences
Lane Number.	A considerable number of investigations indicate that lane number is associated with road crashes, Deo Chimba. (2004). In a study of road geometrics, velocity and volume relationships with road crashes; lane volume was found to affect crash occurrences positively.
Lane Width.	Jerry et al., (2009) - Jerry, Pigman, John, S., Wendel, R., & Dominique, L. (2009) intimates that while it might be rationally presumed that wider lanes reduce the effect of incidents generating from driver mistakes, it can be argued that high operating speeds can oppose this effect.
Sight Distance	The possibility of crashes occurring is higher in some road sections with a poor visual distance due to a small radius of horizontal and vertical curves and also with road sections where the sight distance of overtaking is not adequate to the drivers (Zhang Yingxue, 2009).
Crest Curves	The minimum number of crest curves to be provided on a road section rely on the stopping sight distances provision at all points. TRB (1987) in their report No. SR concluded that the geometrical design of vertical crest has not been proven to significantly affect the frequency and severity of crashes on roadways.
Number and Density of Access	Mouskos et al. (1999), found out that about 30 % of crash rates on multilane highways occur in the mid-block sections and that can explain the main reason which is the existence of access points. Another study performed by Karlarftis et al. (2000) on rural multilane highways showed that presence of access points and medians have the most significant impact on road crashes followed by the effect of pavement conditions.
Shoulder Width	Several studies agreed on shoulder width impact on crash rates on roadways. Particularly, lane width is linked together with shoulder width with respect to road conditions (Deo Chimba, 2004).
Median Width and Type	A study conducted by Hadi Et al. (1995), found that raised curb, crossover resistance and stripped medians are attributed to decline of road safety.
Median Barriers	Studies examining barriers had different views regarding the impact of barriers on crash rates (Nikiforos et al., 20 et al (...) and Hauer, E. (2004), stated that the use of median may have a potential influence on road safety. TRB Annual Meeting - have concluded that safety is increased with the existence of median barriers. On the contrary, another group of researchers indicated a general increase of crash rates with barriers presence, however a decline of the severity was observed by Elvik, R. (1995).
Roundabouts	Roundabouts reduce the types of crashes where people are seriously hurt or killed by 78-82% when compared to conventional stop-controlled and signalized intersections, per the AASHTO Highway Safety Manual. The overall improvement in mobility depends on the distribution of vehicles arrivals and the daily variations in traffic conditions; it is therefore difficult to establish a general rule. It has been found, though, that waiting times at signalised junctions are reduced heavily by the construction of a roundabout, Hydén C., Várhelyi A. (2000).
Staggered Junctions:	The effect of staggered junctions appears to strongly depend on the proportion of traffic of the secondary (minor) road at the crossroads before the staggering. Only when traffic of the secondary (minor) road is important can the number of crashes be significantly reduced. Staggered junctions may result in 33% reduction of crashes when the traffic on the minor road is normal or heavy traffic volume roads
Traffic Control Junctions	Traffic control at junctions was found as one of the most promising investments for the improvement of road safety. These include the implementation of 'yield' signs, 'stop' signs or traffic signals and the upgrade of traffic signals (Yannis G., Evgenikos P., Papadimitriou E., 2008).

Source: Md Hasibul Islam et al (2019)

4.4.5 Traffic Control Devices

A traffic control device is the medium used for communicating between the traffic engineer and road users and they include traffic signs, road markings, traffic signals and parking control.

A. Principles of traffic control devices: The control device should fulfil the following needs:

i.   Each device must have a specific purpose for the safe and efficient operation of traffic flow.

ii. It should command attention from the road user by being visible and being placed in such a way that no extra effort is required to see it.

iii. It should convey a clear message with simple meaning to enable the driver to properly understand the meaning in a short time by the use of colour, symbols and legend as codes.

iv. Road users must respect the signs since some drivers tends to ignore overuse, misuse and confusing messages of devices.

B. Features of Traffic Control Devices: These include the following:

i. Symbols and Colours: Traffic control devices come in a variety of shapes and colours with each having a specific meaning for easy identification.

a). Colours: The most used colours are red, green, yellow, black, blue and brown. The colour red indicates that a driver should stop or yield, while the colour yellow indicates caution. Consistent use of colours also helps the drivers to identify the presence of a sign ahead.

b). Shapes: The second element to the colour of the device is the shape. The categories of shapes normally used are circular, triangular, rectangular, and diamond shape with two exceptional shapes being octagonal shape for STOP sign and inverted triangle for GIVE WAY/YIELD sign. Diamond shape signs are not generally used.

c). Images: Rather than relying on words, images are usually used as traffic signs such as an animal crossing or children at play, to convey a message. This is significant because it aids anyone who does not speak a country's language in to comprehend its meaning.

d). Legend: It is an important aspect in of traffic signage for ease of understanding by the driver. It is required to be short, simple and specific so that it does not divert the attention of the driver. Symbols are normally used as legends to enable person unable to read the language understand.

e). Pattern/Marking: It is normally used in the application of road markings, complementing traffic signs. Generally solid, double solid and dotted lines are used. Each pattern conveys different type of meaning. The frequent and consistent use of pattern to convey information is recommended so that the drivers get accustomed to the different types of markings and can instantly recognize them.

C. Road Signs: Signs are mounted on the side of the road or overhead to inform, warn and guide drivers as to direct what actions are required for road users to make correct decisions quickly.

i. Key Elements of Road Signs: The key elements include the following:

a.   Safety: Traffic signs are an essential element of a modern and safe road infrastructure.

b.   Cost Effectiveness: They represent simple and cost-effective interventions that can generate impressive rate of return in terms of road safety.

c.   Information: Road signs can regulate road use; warn of a hazard at sharp bends; junctions; crossings; blind corners; steep gradients; on-going road works; inform and help the road user on how to navigate the road in good time.

d.   Visibility: It helps regulate traffic, provide crucial visual guidance, and can alert drivers on potential hazards on the road.

e.   Drivers: Traffic signs make the rules clear and keep drivers safe.

f.   Pedestrians and Cyclists: Traffic signs also protect pedestrians and cyclists who use the road. Signs let people know when and where they can cross a road and alert drivers to their presence.

g.   Traffic Flow: Traffic signs help traffic to flow easily and to control potential crashes.

h.   Hazard: They are also effective substitutes for physically preventing a wrongful road user action from occurring.

ii. Criteria for the Setting of Road Signs: Road signs must meet the following requirements:

a). Road signs must conform with the Vienna Convention for purposes of harmonization to minimize divergences between countries. However, Currently, there is a no traffic sign for 'black spots' in the Vienna Convention which has meant that Member States have had to develop their own vision of what such a sign could look like.

Ghana has ratified the Vienna convention on road signs and also has its peculiar signage for indicating RTC blackspots with the number of fatalities recorded at such locations.

b) Road signs must be credible (believed), compliant with standards and correct.

c). Innovation Traffic Signs: Traffic signs have evolved over the years and are still evolving e.g., different types of LEDs, solar power, and more dynamic designs.

d). Overloading of road signs: A road section must not be loaded with too many signs to confuse a road user.

Ghana has a standard for the placement of signs determined by site specific need.

e) Positivity: Signs must be kept "positive" and tell drivers what they can or must do when possible.

f). Simplicity and Consistency: The message conveyed must always be simple and presented in a consistent manner.

g). Placement: Signs must be correctively placed where needed and the presence and message must be according to specific circumstances.

In Ghana, there have been instances where billboards have been erected to cover road signs which poses a danger to road users.

h). Functionality: The functionality of traffic signs depends on their visibility and recognisability during daytime and night-time. During the day this requires that the sign face and symbol colours are not faded in such a way that it becomes impossible to recognise the message. Ad¬ditionally, during night-time, the sign should be able to reflect the light from the headlights of an approaching vehicle back to the driver of that vehicle.

iii. Road Sign Inventory: It is very important to develop a sign inventory on the type, size, location, age etc. to know what signs are missing or where maintenance efforts can be best applied.

In Ghana, the level to which such inventories are undertaken and its uses is not known.

iv). Maintenance: Traffic signs should be maintained on a regular basis and replaced either once their visual performance begins to fall below the de¬sired level or in case of damage to the signs.

In Ghana, the key challenge is consistency of maintenance and functionality during black-outs. It is not uncommon to observe long duration of non-functional traffic signals at very critical junctions causing RTC's in some cases. The police are forced to in and of duty in such situations as traffic managers. The situation is often attributed to limited funding. It is therefore critical for effective maintenance regimes to be set for the maintenance of such signals by the respective road agencies.

The efficiency of road sign maintenance in Ghana is not studied and its adequacy is also unknown. Replacement of missing and vandalized signs should also be a part of sign maintenance programmes. These includes missing signs which might be because of theft, signs blown down by a storm, crumple from crushes etc. which are difficult to read, particularly at night. Vandalization of road signs for use as scrap to be recycled into steel products for financial gains is a common practice in the country.

v. Monitoring: This involves inspection of traffic signs to assess the degree of compliance with required standards.

The level of monitoring for traffic sign defects is also unknown in Ghana.

vi. Installation Information: The guideline for the efficient installation the signs are as summarized in Table 4.14.

Table 4.14: Guidelines for efficient installation of road signs

Location	Height
-Roads signs are to be placed at where they are needed -They are to be placed as advance warning signs before the hazard or action point -Must be of good horizontal and lateral alignment to the road with the later defined by Lateral Placement near the edge of road with minimum clearance which does not obstruct sight distance and obstruction to pedestrians and cyclists. List of items that can obstruction road signs include the following: -Vegetation -Trees with canopies -Other infrastructure/buildings -Distracting background (advertising, signs, shop fronts) -Street lighting, other poles -Bus stops -Public utility services -Side streets, driveways -Not close to a potential hazard	-Measured to bottom of sign
	Orientation -All signs should face the road user for whom the message is intended -KEEP RIGHT – angled to face left turners -Road signs facing traffic must rotate 5° away from traffic to reduce headlight reflection
	Overhead mounting: These are to be done on the following: -On urban arterial roads -high volume of large trucks -narrow footpath, verandas, vegetation -multilane carriageways -On urban motorways -On arterial roads -access points to motorways -At important rural interchanges

vii. Types of Road Signs: These are classified into three main groups as:

a). Regulatory Signs: They are compulsory and inform road users of traffic laws and regulations. They are usually round in shape with red sign and white bars.

b). Warning signs: These are used to warn the driver about hazards ahead. They can also be temporary for example signs giving instructions when a portion of road is under construction. They are usually triangular.

c). Guide (information): Guide signs generally provide the driver with navigational information to enable them get to their destination safely. Examples of road signs by type are as provided in Table 4.15.

Table 4.15: Examples of road signs

Category	Description	Example
Regulatory: control	To give you very specific instructions	A round red sign with a white bar across it means no entry
Regulatory: command	To tell you to drive in a certain way	A blue sign with a taxi on it means that only taxis may use that lane or area
Regulatory: prohibition	To prohibit you from driving in a certain way	A round prohibition sign with a red line through an arrow pointing right means that there is no right turn allowed
Regulatory: reservation	To inform you that a particular lane or area may only be used by a certain type of vehicle	A vertical rectangular sign with a bus on it means only buses may use that lane or area
Warning: road layout	To warn you of changes in the layout of the road	A triangular warning sign with a "T" on it is informing you that there is a T-junction up ahead
Warning: direction of movement	To warn you to anticipate something up ahead	A triangular sign with a bicycle on it is telling you to anticipate cyclists
Guidance: location	To let you know where you are	A white sign with a name and the highway symbol lets you know what highway you are travelling on
Guidance: route markers	To give you information about the route you are travelling on	A green sign with the names of nearby towns and numbers lets you know how far you are away from these places in kilometres.
Chevron Alignment Markers (CAMs)	They are used to provide advance warning of abrupt changes in horizontal road alignments	Rectangular shape with yellow background and black arrows

viii. Effectiveness of Signs on Road Safety: Traffic signs help to regulate traffic operations. Some examples of certified effects of road signs through research are as summarized in Table 4.16

Table 4.16: Impacts of road signs

Type of sign	Effectiveness
Stop signs	Stop signs are used to control movements at intersections where it has been determined that a full stop on an approach to an intersection (FHWA 2012). This is to reduce crash rate and improve safety performance by the provision of some level of control on the road
Yield signs	Control movements at intersection approaches where drivers must prepare to stop if necessary to yield to the right-of-way (FHWA 2012). It is most suitable on the approaches to a through street where conditions are such that a full stop is not always required. The level of safety performance is minimal because there is room for driver discretion there which could be subject to error. One study found that yield signs produced travel time savings greater than stop control or no control
Speed Limit Signs	The purpose of a speed limit sign is to provide drivers with information about the speed limit established by law, ordinance, or regulation or as adopted by an authorized agency based on an engineering study (FHWA 2012). It further states that speed limit signs shall be posted at points of change from one speed limit to another; speed limit signs, is one of the treatments with unknown crash effects (AASHTO 2010). From an operational and human behaviour point of view, it can be assumed that drivers need regular postings of the speed limit and/or may not know the statutory speed limit along a particular roadway
Warning Signs	Additional factors to consider in the installation of these signs include traffic volume, functional classification, 85th percentile speeds, and engineering judgment (FHWA 2012). It is to control movements at intersections and for specific purposes and situations along the road as needed and prevent RTCs caused by impending hazards through the provision consistent caution

D. Road Markings: Painted marks on the roadway delineate road lanes to guide and control traffic to promote the correct use of the roadway. They also provide pedestrian safety marking, improves night time visibility and parking space allocation as well as the following:

i. Attributes of Road Markings

a. They mark the lanes and define the two directions of traffic.

b. They help to utilise the whole road.

c. They warn and help drivers with information about the road.

d. They manage traffic and complement other signs.

e. They establish areas of the road reserved for traffic and those that are free of vehicles.

f. Road markings regulate basic traffic and in terms of priority they are the last behind law enforcement officers.

ii. Principles of Road Line Markings

a. There is need to use retro-reflective markings that are visible under all weather conditions because their effectiveness depends on their luminance.

b. There is need to harmonise the colour and dimensions of lane and carriageway edge markings. *This is done in Ghana.*

c. There is need to install continuous lines to delineate the edge of the carriageway. *This is also done in Ghana.*

d. Effective road markings must be clearly visible to the driver, day, and night, and in all weathers. *Line markings in Ghana are visible but the extent of reflection may fade overtime due to sand and dust deposits on the road surface overtime.*

e. In the case of missing or totally worn markings, improvements will be extremely beneficial. *In Ghana, worn out markings are predominant.*

f. The national codes of practice must be simple and with positive approach. *Ghana has a national code of practice.*

g. If there is any conflict between signs, the most restrictive one is imposed. *The same applies in Ghana.*

h. The markings should be consistent along a route and across a region. *In Ghana, the same markings are used everywhere.*

i. Markings must be present where needed. *This cannot be said for all roads in Ghana. (See Figure 4.16).*

Figure 4.16: Example of faded line marking on an old road (a) and road line marking on a new road (b)

iii. Types of Pavement Markings: These includes the following:

a. Dividing lines (centre lines)

b. Lane lines

c. Edge lines

d. Pavement arrows

e. Stripes and chevron markings

f. Words

g. Symbols

The meanings of the most common line markings are as listed in Table 4.17.

iv. Types of Materials for Road Line Markings: Materials used for Road Line Marking are paint (the lowest in quality), thermoplastic and also tactile (the best quality and retro-reflective glass beads

v. Guideposts and Delineators: Delineation of the carriageway can be by markings and physical barriers such as cones, studs (Cat – eye) and bollards. They can be extremely cost effective in maintenance, traffic operations and safety. *In Ghana, road studs are provided on some roads but on a limited scale.*

v. Width Markers: These are installed on culverts, Bridge piers, ridge end posts and Railway level crossings guardrails and other structures where there are width restrictions. *(See Figure 4.18).*

Figure: 4.18: Sample Width Makers

vi. Parking Lines: The provision of sufficient, safe and secure parking areas should form an integral part of road infrastructure design.

C. Street Lighting: In road Infrastructure good lighting systems for safety are required. The effect of lighting on night time travel and on safety is very critical especially for raining and foggy weather conditions.

In Ghana, poor street lighting including inadequate and defunct street lights and this also hampers visibility and expose road user to RTCs. A study by the NRSA (2019) attributed poor street lighting to 65% of the occurrence of motorcycle RTCs. This is followed by poor lighting at 26% and inadequate traffic control devices at 9% as depicted in Figures 4.19

Figure 4.19: Motor rider RTC exposure by road furniture (2019)

D. Roadway Defects Created by Bad Community Behaviour: *In Ghana, this maybe from digging of trenches and removal of sewerage covers etc. which create danger spots along the road especially during the night. It is also not uncommon to see such spots marked with* *a stick with a tied red handkerchief by some good Samaritans to warn motorists about the danger instead of immediate correction of the problem*

Others are the spillage of vehicle oils on roads causing bitumen to be dissolved with the related creation of soft spots leading to quicker road deterioration. Defect vehicle axles especially that of Heavy goods vehicles also creates longitudinal lines on long stretches of new roads causing often causing openings on sealed road surface for water to seep in and cause the road to deteriorate quicker. Stationary overloaded heavy goods vehicles over long time durations also causes quicker deterioration of road surfaces. Such practices result in higher demands on limited maintenance funding resulting in negligence with RTC risks overtime. A concerted effort should be mad by the road authorities to monitor and correct such

4.4.6 Design for Vulnerable Road Users

The safety of vulnerable road users such as pedestrians, disabled and children is also required by international conventions to be sufficiently addressed in safe road design to ensure that they are not unnecessarily exposed to high-risk safety situations, (See Figure 4.21).

Figure 4.21: Sample Publication on Road Infrastructure and the needs of the Vulnerability

Infrastructure needs for the vulnerable includes.

a. The provision of a predictable road environment to reduce conflicts between vehicles.

b. The removal of conflict points such as separation of traffic flow directions through the provision of median barriers, segregated lanes as well as with speed control measures. Others are widening and repair of footpaths and improving pedestrian crossings.

c. Land use control by the removal of obstructions in walkways such as utility poles, trees as well as hawking activities which deters them from having access to the use of the facility and to improve surface friction for wheelchair users etc.

d. Provision of barriers to protect them such as erection of guardrails to separate walking areas from motorized traffic influencing land use planning alongside major roads by removing barriers and street furniture on footpaths.

A. Road Design for Pedestrian Safety: This includes control of vehicular speeds, minimization of pedestrian-vehicle conflicts, ensuring adequate walkway separation, provision of speed humps etc.

In Ghana, over the past decade various efforts have been made through strategic interventions to provide several speed calming measures on high-risk roads. Pelican crossings have been installed for safe pedestrian crossing; overhead foot bridges have also been installed on critical roads. The results of a study on the level of utilisation of these installation in 2019 is as summarised in Table 4.18.

Table 4.18: Utilization of pedestrian crossing safety infrastructure

Type of Pedestrian Crossing Facility Used	Average
Zebra Crossing	46.4%
Islands and medians	4.6%
Traffic Warden Post	8.9%
Over/Under pass	11.8%
Pelican Crossing	28.3%
Others	0%
Total	100%

i. Elements of Poor Pedestrian Infrastructure Safety: Poor Pedestrian safety: This includes:

a). Pedestrians walking on the roadway because sidewalks are used by hawkers or illegal vehicle parking or by property owners.

b). Pedestrians crossing multi-lane streets at unspecified locations or with minimal pedestrian crossing facilities.

c). Inadequate provision for pedestrian facilities in road design. See Figure 4.22).

Figure 4.22: Sample of publications on pedestrian infrastructure needs.

d). Provision of zebra crossing on high-speed roads instead of pedestrian footbridges or underpasses.

In Ghana, examples can mostly be found in built areas on highways e.g., Osino Junction on the Accra – Kumasi Trunk Road

e). Provision of limited pedestrian crossing with traffic lights, pedestrian foot bridges, etc. *There are some examples of this in Ghana, but with limited adequacy.*

f). Construction of kerb extensions to slow drivers making turns, increase of pedestrian visibility and shortening of the total distances needed to cross the street to make it easier for slower pedestrians like small children, disabled and the elderly to cross the street safely. *There are some examples of this in Ghana, but with limited adequacy.*

g). Protection of intersections and provision of medians, such as the provision of raised islands or medians at intersections or between opposing lanes of traffic to allow pedestrians a safe place to wait or cross. *There are some examples of this in Ghana, but with limited adequacy.*

h). Absence of pedestrian footbridges on critical highways creating conflicts between pedestrian and vehicular movements especially on high-speed roads.

In Ghana some critical highways such as the after the George Interchange end of the N1 do not have footbridges causing frequent pedestrian knock downs. Also, in situations where some provisions for pedestrian foot bridges have been there is the challenge of ineffective patronage on the part of some pedestrians, (see Figure 4.23). However, the use underpasses are not popular due to security reasons.

Figure 4.23: Example of pedestrian footbridges in Ghana

i). Lack of well-planned footpaths and walkways to provide continuous space for walking.

In Ghana, even in situations where walkways are provided, they are sometimes truncated at sections causing pedestrians to share those sections of the road with motorists and thus putting their lives in danger. Aside these challenges pedestrian walkways are often occupied by various activities forcing pedestrians to share the road with motorists.

j). The major road furniture identified by pedestrians themselves for exposing them to RTCs risks include inadequate crossing installations like pelican and zebra crossings at 44%, inadequate road signs and markings at (20%); absence of guard rails and inadequate walkways at (25%) and limited visibility (poor street lighting) at 12%. The high percentage of pedestrians exposed to RTCs due to inadequate crossing installations explains the fact that 68% of pedestrian fatalities in Ghana in 2019 occurred while pedestrians were crossing the road. Besides the number and adequacy of pedestrian road safety facilities in Ghana are not known because they are not comprehensively inventoried.

k). Other Factors Associated with Pedestrian Infrastructure Safety in Ghana includes pedestrian are exposure to high fatality possibilities from walking along the road or at the edge in the absence of walkways. Also, in some cases guard rails are either vandalised or are poorly maintained making them ineffective. Studies, indicates that key infrastructure factors causing pedestrian RTC's especially with regards to the absence of pedestrian safety installations contributes to 39% of pedestrian fatalities.

Also, sometime the provision of pedestrian installations is sometimes deemed secondary to main road design features and maybe considered as add-ons when a need is realised from recurring RTC situations at specific road locations. Thus, it is not uncommon in Ghana to see affected communities taking the law into their hands by digging through newly constructed highways for safety purposes or constructing makeshift speed rumps below standards specifications and without warning signs which can in turn create additional problems.

The next factor causing pedestrian safety problems non-functional safety installations due such as broken-down pelican crossings and eroded pedestrian crossing markings from poor maintenance practices. Careless use of pedestrian facilities also contributes to pedestrian RTC fatalities at 35%. This is because such situation creates more challenges for the physically challenged, children, pregnant women etc. Wrongfully sitting and non-safety installation contributes to 24% of the RTC fatalities followed by poor Drainage systems at 2%. (See Figure 4. 24)

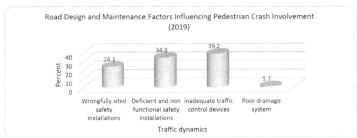

Figure 4.24: Road Design and Maintenance Factors Influencing Pedestrian Crashes

B. Road Infrastructure Design for Child Safety: Highlights of safe road design facilities for children includes provision of good visual, physical and regulatory cues such as traffic signs, high visibility, raised crossings, kerb extensions and detectable road markings that alert drivers of the presence of children so speeds can be reduced. Others are avoidance of obscuring a child's vision with parked vehicles as well as ensuring parking restrictions near zebra crossings.

In Ghana, some clustered school zones are specifically provided with pedestrian crossing facilities as well as lollipop stands to guide safe road crossing by the children.

C. Road Infrastructure Design for the Safety of the Aged and Disabled: Disabled pedestrians are sensitive to stairs, kerbs, rough road surface etc. and provision must be made for them in road designs. This should be done by the removal of obstacles where feasible on pedestrian walkways to allow barrier free access for the wheelchair bound; provision of reflective sheeting's of higher reflectivity (at shorter viewing distance) for traffic signs, provision of street name signs and temporary traffic control signs to meet their needs. Others are provision of ramps connecting bus interchanges, provision of climbing lane for wheelchairs to access overhead foot bridges and ensuring smooth walking surfaces for wheelchairs and white canes.

In Ghana, special provisions are made for wheelchair users in the construction of some overhead footbridges. Aside this most of the best practice examples are not applied.

D. Road Infrastructure Design for Intermediate Means of Transport (IMTs): This includes addressing traffic conflict created by two wheelers such as bicycles/motorcycles and three wheelers such tricycles.

The safety requirements for IMTs include provision of segregated lanes to prevent mixed traffic, maintaining good road surface conditions, installation of warning signs, ensuring that skid resistant materials are used on road surfaces, provision of adequate road shoulders as recovery areas with sealing, installation of mountable kerbs, provision of good visibility with, signs in their rightful place, fitness of supereelevation to road designs with delineations in place to help in the reading of the road.

Others are provision of opening sign lines around curves, control of intersections with signals, removal of hazards around the roadside and provision of safety barriers to prevent the use of motorcycle lanes by another motorist etc.

In Ghana both two wheelers that is motorcycles and cycles and three wheelers referred as Motor king or "Aboboyaa" and rickshaws also referred as "Pragia" present unique challenges to road design. The key challenge has to do with limited provision of segregated roads for such recommended as best practice, (See Figure 4.25. Other challenges have to do with when they are stopping, turning, or slowing down. This is because some of them fail to maintain good balance especially during U-turns etc. Poor road condition on gravel roads and road with potholes also prevents smooth ride quality.

Figure 4.25: Examples of Modal Share between NMT's and Vehicles

4.4.7 Other Road Infrastructure Safety Designs Required:

A. Road Safety on Rural Roads: The DOA (2011-2020) recommended for the safety of rural road infrastructure to be given adequate attention by member states.

In Ghana, rural roads are of two categories that is major highways sections traversing rural communities and feeder roads linking rural communities. Whilst the policy of the MRH is to ensure safety on all road types, pedestrian facilities such as footbridges etc. are not often provided at the rural sections of major highways causing pedestrian safety risks. Most feeder roads are not provided with markings because most of them are gravel and earth surfaced.

B. Other Specific Safety Design Considerations: These include those summarized in Table 4.19.

Table Figure 4.19: Other Safety Design Features for Road Infrastructure

Design Element	Description	Applicability in Ghana
Design for Existing Roads:	Retrofitting of safety installations on existing roads by both reactive approaches and proactive approaches through routine redesign and upgrade to improve the safety and efficiency of road performance, eg. Installation of rumble strips on road shoulders and centreline's that warns motorists of lane departure, Installation of median Barriers, Redesign of roads with safety recoverable edges, Installation of roundabouts Improvement of turning lanes Properly setting of traffic control device to extend the duration of the inter-green time Installation of pedestrian refuge areas in crosswalks away from the sidewalk and along with raised medians Re-design of roads with better walkways The design of a new intersection or the replacement of an existing intersection	In Ghana all these are applicable with the exception of installation of rumble stripes on road shoulders
Design for Wet and dark crashes:	Wet weather crashes and those occurring in dark conditions are high risk roads and requires -Ensuring adequate surface texture -Provision of street lighting -The creation of more speed zones on high-risk rural roads to help make roads more self-explaining, and to establish criteria for what roads with different speed limits should look like' -The provision of sufficient safe and secure parking areas as an integral part of road infrastructure safety management.	In Ghana, the creation of speed zones is not considered for high-risk rural roads, there is also poor provision of street lighting systems with most major highways not having any street lights at all. The provision of safe parking spaces is also not a standard design practice

Design Element	Description	Applicability in Ghana
b) Location of Utilities:	-Road construction may make it necessary to relocate some ground utilities e.g., pipelines, telephone lines, electricity lines, fire hydrants or utility poles. -Certain designs could also necessitate the relocation of many underground utilities such as storm water drainage systems; sanitary sewer manholes, lines and laterals and under- ground traffic signal system hardware.	In Ghana this is applicable
Safety Fence and Barrier:	-Many different types of barriers provide an effective means for channeling pedestrian flows e.g. -Guardrails and safety fences placed sufficiently far from the edge of the carriageway so as not to cause a hazard to vehicles through the use of bollards instead of continuous concrete barrier is not encouraged -Provision of any form of safety barrier, and proper designed speed reducing devices	This is applicable in Ghana though in some instances bollards are used rather than concrete barriers which are sometimes vandalized by road users for their specific interests
Vehicle Traffic Management:	Vehicle traffic management measures include -Management of mixed vehicle types in the traffic stream since slow- and fast-moving vehicles in the traffic stream creates safety challenges. -Reduction of number of access points to major highways for example full access control -Protection against certain animals	In Ghana key examples of access management include -provision of service lanes for local traffic whilst access to the main road for through traffic is minimised -Provision of longer acceleration and deceleration lanes at AT-grade junctions on high-speed roads Design for the protection of animals is not applicable in Ghana
f) Congestion at Bus Spot:	The location of bus stops must be considered when contemplating the design of the intersection. The objective is not to place the boarding or alighting passenger at risk because of the design to address traffic congestion of buses near bus stops. Safety Bus Stop Facilities for Passengers including the implementation of a bus priority system, improvement of bus facilities, appropriate bus shelters and provision of bus bay are key examples for the reduction of congestion at bus stops	In Ghana, though bus bays are incorporated into road designs the storage length is mostly inadequate causing congestions at such points. This is because in some instances they are use d for the parking of vehicles or as bus terminal by commercial vehicles
i. Loading Zones:	For areas with businesses, another item that must be considered is the location of loading zones. Certain designs could cause problems for delivery truck operators, who unload shipments for nearby businesses or the pedestrians, who must weave their way through the parked vehicles. In many areas, these vehicles can range from simple mini vans to full-length tractors and semi-trailers.	In Ghana, this turns to be a major problem for city centres due to the lack of consideration of loading zones for heavy goods vehicles. Though some few interventions such the creation of loading and offloading zones for heavy vehicles have been made for some products at the outskirts of cities for some products eg onion market in Accra

4.4.8. Infrastructure Defects By and Best Value Treatment

Some effective design strategies that can address some key crash types are as presented in Table 4.20.

Table 4.20: Summary of key crash types by Infrastructure Defects and best value treatment

Key crash type	Recommended Safe System treatments.	
Head-on	-Median barriers (solid/semi-rigid and flexible) -Safe System speeds -Marked median treatments eg ATP markings Improved delineation (signs and markings) Active signs	Harm reduction speeds -Increased intervention levels -Skid resistance -Hazard removal
Run-off-road	-Roadside barriers -Clear zones -Safe System speeds -Wider shoulders -ATP markings	-Improved delineation -Harm reduction speeds -Increased intervention levels -Skid resistance -Planting policies -Hazard removal
Intersections	-Grade-separated interchanges or overpasses -Roundabouts -Safe System speeds -Wider shoulders and separated Turning facilities	-Improved delineation and active signs -Harm reduction speeds -Improved Intervention levels eg. Skid resistance, Improved sight -Visibility through Various treatment -Improved sight visibility

4.4.9 Modern Approach to Safe Road Design

Modern roads are designed to reduce the chance of harm to drivers and pedestrians so instead of focusing on people's actions, the designs make it easier for people to use the road safely. This is driven by the philosophy that people make mistakes, so roads need to be predictable and forgiving of mistakes.

A. Safe Systems Approach to Road Design: The safe system approach to road design requires that no road user is killed or seriously injured from the road characteristics in its use. This is because, according to Dewar (2008), road design determines driver workload so should consider the abilities and limitations of all road users.

i. Benefits of the Safe System Approach: Some of Benefits of the safe system approach to road designs includes:

a. Provision of self-explanatory roads which beneficiary drivers understand and easily comply with.

b. Provision of road designs that enables the driver to navigate the road system safely and comfortably.

ii. Recommended Safe Road Design Measures: These include the following:

a). Self-organizing roads: This enables a driver to "automatically" select appropriate speed due to configured geometric features provided without relying on road signs.

b). Self-explaining roads/Forgiving Roads: These are road designs aimed to reduce RTC risk by correcting human error.

iii. Key Elements of the Safe Systems Road Design Approach: The approach creates a simple road environment that limits the range of behavioural choices for users. While safety performance associated with these methods is not well understood yet, an implied outcome is that of less severe crashes. However, the safe system approach cannot be used to address personality traits like aggression, the will to violate traffic rules consciously or mistakenly, driving under the influence of medication or age, where concerned.

The level of applicability of the safe system approach in road infrastructure design in Ghana is as presented in Table 4.21.

Table 4.21: Application of safe design systems in Ghana

Type / Examples of Safe System	Application in Ghana
I. Anticipating Human Error:	
Reduction of the opportunity for error by a road user	Not Applicable
Separating Users in Space by segregating the physical space to provide travellers with a dedicated part of the right-of-way eg Cycle lanes, pedestrian walkways etc.	Applicable on a limited scale
Separating Users in time and reducing vehicle interactions with vulnerable road users. Eg footbridges	Applicable on a limited scale
Increasing Attentiveness and Awareness by alerting users to potential hazards and/or the presence of other users. Eg rumble strips	Applicable on a moderate scale
Increasing visibility to allow greater visibility between drivers and pedestrians. Eg - Avoidance of parking at the corners -Street lighting that increases night-time visibility that allows users to be visible to one another	Applicable on a limited scale
Increasing Attentiveness eg -Rumble strips; -In-vehicle lane departure systems -Rapid flashing Beacons that warn drivers of the presence of crossing pedestrians.	Applicable on a limited scale
2. Accommodating Human Injury Tolerance	
Design roads so that they are forgiving of errors eg. Provision of a gentle road embankment slope to allow run-off vehicle to recover	Applicable in Ghana
Reduce Speeds by keeping speeds to a level where any mistake is not punished by serious injury eg Traffic calming treatments that induce slower speeds, Traffic signal timing that minimizes high speed flow,	Not Applicable in Ghana
Physical roadway designs (eg width, horizontal alignment) to limit free flow speeds eg narrow lanes, introduction of horizontal curves	Applicable on a limited scale
Reduce Impact Forces: eg alternative intersections, such as roundabouts to reduce the angle and speeds of entering vehicles to limit impact forces. Designs which limit right-angle conflicts.	Applicable on a limited scale
Roadside crashworthiness recovery eg embankments, Clear zones, breakaway supports, etc.	Applicable in Ghana

B. Technological Applications in Road Infrastructure Design: These are integrated into road infrastructure designs based on the provision of automated systems to substitute human efforts for performance.

A key deployment challenge with infrastructure-based information technology systems (ITS) is the need to accommodate the interface of older vehicles with existing infrastructure in Ghana.

4.4.10 Supporting Tools for Safe Road Infrastructure Management

The types of tools available for road safety infrastructure management includes the following.

A. Conduct of Road Safety Audit (RSA) by Country: Road safety audit is a systematic examination of roadway elements to establish safety concerns for recommended desirable changes or modifications to meet the required safety needs at all the stages of the road infrastructure development cycle. This allows road safety hazards to be identified and corrected.

i. Criteria for the Implementation of Road Safety Audits: Road safety audit;

a. must be performed by an independent audit engineer not involved in the project at the planning and design stages of the road infrastructure;

b. must be performed by a multi-disciplinary team at the operational phase when the road is opened to traffic;

c. must assesses all the safety factors accounting for road user capabilities and limitations in the road project and its use;

d. must have standard guidelines in the form of manuals to be developed but there is no substantive standard or guideline for road safety auditing by the road agencies in Ghana;

e. must make legal provisions for the conduct of road safety audits.

In Ghana, the legal status for the conduct of road safety audits by the respective road agencies is not clear. Though the GHA has an internal policy to do so, the extent of application, quality control and the legal implications of non- compliance remains fuzzy.

A summary of the criteria for the conduct of road safety audits are as outlined in Table 4.23.

Table 4.23: Criteria for Road Safety Audits for Infrastructure Projects

Criteria at the draft design stage	Criteria for the detailed design stage
-Geographical location (e.g. exposure to landslides, flooding, seasonal and climatic conditions and seismic activity); -Types and distance between junctions; -Number and type of lanes; -Kinds of traffic admissible to the new road; -Functionality of the road in the network; -Meteorological conditions; -Driving speeds; -Cross-sections (e.g. width of carriageway, cycle tracks, foot paths); -Horizontal and vertical alignments; visibility; junctions layout; -Public transport and infrastructures; -Road/rail level crossings	-Layout -Coherent road signs and markings; -Lighting of roads and intersections; -Roadside equipment; -Roadside environment including vegetation; -Fixed obstacles at the roadside; -Provision of safe parking areas; -Considerations and facilities for vulnerable road users (e.g. pedestrians, cyclists, motorcyclists); -User-friendly adaptation of road restraint systems (central reservations and crash barriers to prevent hazards to vulnerable users).
Criteria for the pre-opening stage	**Criteria for early operation**
-Safety of road users and visibility under different conditions such as darkness and under normal weather conditions; -Readability of road signs and markings; -Condition of pavements.	-Assessment of road safety in the light of actual behaviour of users.

B. Capacity for Road Safety Audit: Road safety auditors are basically required to have sufficient knowledge, skill and experience in crash investigation and analysis, road safety engineering, crash prevention work, traffic engineering and road planning.

In Ghana, both experts from the road sector agencies and the private sector have benefited from training in the application of road safety audits but it cannot be said that there are certified auditors of the above criteria. Also, the margin of capacity adequate for the conduct of road safety audits in the industry is not known. At the pre-operation stage, ad hoc committees are constituted to assess the road condition to establish the safety of use. Therefore, it can be concluded that there is limited auditor training programmes and the level of institutionalization of these programmes are not known.

C. Funding Availability for Road Safety Audit: Adequate budgetary provisions are required to be made for the conduct of road safety audits.

In Ghana, there are no specific budgetary provisions for the conduct of road safety audit in road projects since audits on road designs are done by in-house personnel of the road agencies and ad hoc committees are set up for the audit at the pre-opening phase of the road operation.

D. Approach to the Implementation of Road Safety Audits: This includes the following:

i.   Selection of the Audit Team
ii.   Provision of Project background Information
iii. Commencement Meeting
iv.   Safety Analysis
v.   Probability Estimation and Rating
vi.   Risk Management
vii. Safety reporting
viii. Presentation of Report
ix.   Response Report

However, in Ghana, the procedures for the conduct of road safety audits are not well streamlined.

4.5 ROAD CONSTRUCTION STAGE

4.5.1. Policy and Legal Requirements for Safe Road Construction

Road safety is critical during the construction phase of a roadway. It involves the observation of a safe work zone for the construction workers and affected communities.

In Ghana, the MRH has an environmental management policy with components on safe road construction especially on the need for the development of traffic management plans (Environmental Assessment Guidelines for the Transport Sector (EPA, 2010).

A. Causes of Unsafe Road User Conditions at Construction Sites: These include the following:

i.   Presence of dangerous equipment, the risk of collision and traffic congestion causing safety risks for both motorists and road workers alike.

ii. Potential falls from improperly constructed road surfaces and unprotected edges causing vehicle strikes or falling/flying objects from rotating equipment or unguarded parts.

iii. Possible electrocutions from contact with utility lines or live circuits.

iv. Speeding traffic in road construction work zones.

v.   Inadequate signposting and lighting and drivers failing to notice ongoing road work.

vi. Driving stress from long stretches of highway under construction caused by obstructions such as garbage, construction materials, etc. occupying the road space.

vii. Speeding by motorists who may not notice road works, those who may disregard signs for them to slow down as well as those who may fail to pay attention to work zone signs or flaggers indicating they should slow down or come to a stop etc.

viii. Activities at the roadside that are not merging properly with the construction environment.

ix. Drivers who enter prohibited areas of the construction work zones and endanger the lives of workers.

B. Road Construction Work Zone Safety Measures: These include:

i. Safe Construction Traffic Management: This is done by keeping vehicles and pedestrians separated, minimizing vehicle movements, avoiding access obstructions to residential/commercial areas, providing parking facilities, signs and markings, defining loading and offloading zones, and providing diversion and detour routes for road obstructions to prevent RTCs.

In Ghana, some of the traffic management challenges with safety implications confronted during the road construction stage include improper posting of road signs, lack of provision of detour roads for road closures, poor road surface maintenance and provision of inadequate signage etc.

ii. Development of Traffic control plan: This specifically includes the provision of clear demarcation for the movement of vehicles by the provision of measures to guide drivers and their movements through lane closures and traffic diversions. It could also be done through the installation of advance warning by traffic signs and clearly marked lanes for guiding users mostly with delineator such as Safety Cones, Traffic Cylinders, Tapes, Drums, Painted lines, guide Posts, and Post-mounted Reflectors etc. to control and guide the flow of traffic.

Others are barricades from excavation, material storage area etc. and the establishment of transition sub-zone which is an area for steering and guiding traffic in and out of the diverted path around the work sub-zone and turning movements. It also includes the establishment of work sub-zones with clearly delineated areas for actual works and maintenance works to avoid intrusion of vehicles moving into the work area.

iii. Road Safety for drivers/motorists at construction zones: These include the:

a). Use of Flagmen to direct traffic at the construction site.

b). Use of driver and operator safety measures through training in equipment operation, application of brakes to equipment, stopping construction vehicles or equipment and parking with the use of appropriate block behind or in front of the tyres as an extra layer of precaution.

c). Training of drivers in the wearing of a seatbelt, buckling up, exercise of caution around worksite vehicles, proper signalling by vehicle operator to shut down the equipment.

d). Placement of speed-monitoring devices to alert motorists of their speed before entering the work zone.

In Ghana some challenges for drivers and road users at construction sites includes failure to develop and effectively implement traffic management plans for construction projects resulting in congestion when vehicles enter and exit the workplace, absence of special vehicles like large vehicles and mobile cranes, loading from the side of road onto the site, poor traffic control by flags men, Lack of separation of heavy vehicles and light vehicles, poor parking arrangements, lack of transmission of emergency messages etc. This is mainly attributed to poor monitoring and supervision by responsible authorities for ensuring that the right thing is done.

Stockpiling of construction materials on the road also reduces road lane width. Together with lack of provision of road detours or provision of road detours without directional signs RTCs can occur. Others are dusty road surfaces not regularly watered, disrupted traffic, lane blockade, difficulty in movement of heavy vehicles, poor signage etc. which also causes safety problems.

iv. Safety Training at construction Zones: Some of the initiatives to avoid work zone crashes at the construction site include the following:

a. Training of drivers, machine operators and construction workers in the identification of potential hazards through stringent observations, alertness on site, checking for blind spots and taking of appropriate precaution for safety precautions.

b. Training in awareness and management of worksite equipment usage, proper control of vehicles entering and exiting in the work site and understanding of the channel lanes where walking is prohibited.

c. Training in the use of spotters when loading and unloading equipment from vehicles such as the safe place to stand, the gestures to use to communicate with vehicle operators etc.

d. Training in understanding and use of communication signals for activities such as equipment or vehicle entering or exiting the worksite to ensure everyone's mutual safety.

e. Training in the application of parking brakes to equipment and the use of appropriate blocks behind or in front of tyres when parking on an incline as an extra layer of precaution.

f. Training in the importance of seatbelt wear even for short rides and the necessary precautions required for approaching a piece of machinery with the highest degree of caution as well as signalling vehicle operator to shut down the equipment with acknowledgment from the driver before approaching or crossing the path.

4.6 ROAD INFRASTRUCTURE SAFETY AT ROAD OPERATION STAGE

The safety of road use at the operation stage involves ensuring that the roadway is safe for use by the user after construction. The key safety interventions at this stage include the following:

4.6.1. Road Infrastructrure Safety at the Pre-Operation Stage

This is done to determine potential safety integrity of the completed road and to identify unsafe features for corrections often through road safety audits.

In Ghana, this is also done on some major road projects though it is not uncommon to witness roads being open to full traffic whilst construction is still ongoing without the necessary safety precautions.

4.6.2. Road Infrastructrure Safety at the Full Operation Stage

A. Safe Traffic Management Systems: A key infrastructure safety concern at this stage of the infrastructure management cycle is the control and operation of vehicles by day/ and night. These are provided to ensure safe and responsible behaviour by all road users. A key measure required include the creation of speed management and traffic calming, provision of public transport facilities, parking and free flow management at road work zones.

In, Ghana such activities are undertaken but the extent of application and the benefits are yet to be established.

B. Monitoring and Evaluation of Road Infrastructure Safety: Monitoring involves an assessment of the road to determine the results and effectiveness of the types of treatments provided and used. Road inspections are conducted systematically to attain this. The key monitoring activities include:

i. Roadside Landuse Management: Negative land use activities after the road is opened for operation may cause obstructions to effective road use such as occupation of pedestrian walkways by hawkers, establishment of unapproved structures, installation of billboards etc.

In Ghana, the key challenge has to do with adherence to land use policies concerning roadside use involving unapproved activities on the road reserve with difficulty of enforcement and control. An example is the conversion of a service lanes into a market e.g. at the Madina Zongo Junction. Another example is the establishment of a local restaurant under the Pokuase Interchange right after it was opened to traffic in Accra.

Presence of roadway obstacles such as fixed objects, light poles, trees, concrete barriers, fences, billboards, roadside, electric poles, trees, vegetation, buildings, shops and other human activities, long boundary walls at junctions, exposed rocks, steep high embankment slopes and manhole covers prevents the driver from knowing what is ahead which in turn can result in RTCs. This is often due to driver encounter with unprepared surprise situations.

Though by law collaborative efforts must be made between the road agencies and the respective MMDAs responsible for land use management to prevent such encroachments, there still remains a lot of challenges especially with securing the right of ways ahead of the roadway and this needs to be addressed.

ii. Road Maintenance: All roads in use require maintenance therefore continual monitoring for changes on the roadway is essential for checking road defects and deteriorations for maintenance and continued use. The activity is most effective when there is an existence of a rapid maintenance response system well- resourced and able to mobilize as needed on short notice. The key maintenance activities include:

a). Maintenance of Drainage Systems: This is done by keeping drainage structures free of debris and obstructions through frequent cleaning as well as the management of storm water drainage systems especially for emergency storm response.

b). Road Surface Maintenance: Correction of road surface deformities to ensure consistent good road quality for the road user especially with regards to the development of potholes, cracks etc.

Typical examples in Ghana are as provided in Figure 4.26

Figure 4.26: Examples of the surface of sampled roads in Ghana

c). Routine grass cutting to minimize poor visibility especially on rural roads

C. Identification and Treatment of Hazardous Road Section: This involves the identification and correction of road sections recording high RTCs. Treatment of hazardous road sections allows for timely corrections of safety interventions to avoid higher risk to routes. Typical safety measures and treatments effected are as summarized in Table 4.24.

Table 4.24: Treatment of Hazardous Road Section

-Removing or protecting fixed roadside obstacles; -Improving road shoulders, -Providing pedestrian facilities (eg. segregated footways, crossings), -Junction improvements, treatment of hazards, -Introduction of speed control devices, -Creation of median barriers, -Installation of access control measures and channelization -Construction of traffic islands, -Skid resistance treatment eg. improving grip/roughness of pavements -Improvement of delineation devices -Creation of safety zones, -Improving visibility under different weather and light conditions;	-Improving safety condition of roadside equipment such as road restraint systems; -Improving coherence, visibility, readability and position of road markings (incl. application of rumble strips), signs and signals; -Protection against rocks falling, landslips -Changing an overtaking layout; -Improving of road/rail level crossings; -Changing a road alignment; -Changing width of road eg. adding hard shoulders; -Upgrading the road to current design standards; -Restoring or replacing pavements; -Improving intelligent transport systems and telematics services for interoperability, emergency and signage purposes eg. using intelligent road signs;

Ghana embarks on high-risk road location treatment projects which are based on solid evidence of crash recurrent crashes at specific road locations but this is of a limited scope.

Aside this, follow up evaluations of interventions to correct hazardous sections are often not undertaken to determine the impacts of the effected changes and this needs to be corrected.

4.7 CHALLENGES TO SAFE INFRASTRUCTURE MANAGEMENT IN GHANA

A. Limited Emphasis on Safety in Road Design: *In Ghana, oftentimes roads are designed firstly for mobility purposes with marginal considerations for safety.*

B. Application of External Designs: *To a large extent external safe road designs are applied with little local specific content and it is recommended for the identification of country specific safety design challenges so appropriate mitigation measures can be effected.*

C. Use of Inconsistent Safety Standards in Relation to Some Safety Design Elements: *Typical example is the varied standards used for the design of speed humps on roads.*

D. Delayed Installation of Safety Elements on Roads: *Provision of safety installations is sometimes considered as an afterthought after a road is opened to traffic when RTC have been recorded. A typical example is as presented in Figures 4.27.*

Figure 4.27: Examples of Delayed Installation of Safety Elements on the Road

E. Limited funding availability for the execution of safe road design schemes: *Safety installations in road designs is the first cost item to be sacrificed in situations of budget cuts for road projects. It is recommended for road authorities to adhere to the World Bank standard of dedicating a minimum of 10% of road budgets and 5% of maintenance budgets to safer road infrastructure programmes to be applied. Due to the absence of data the adequacy of such systems for the needs of the vulnerable are also not met. Optimal utilisation of limited resources is also not ensured.*

F. Training and Capacity Development: *There is no training curricula and tools for the training of road safety engineers locally to validate and certified competent entities. Therefore, the level of knowledge to deliver on their responsibility to the optimum l is not known.*

G. Institutional Management: Currently there is very little institutional commitment and accountability to safe road infrastructure provision. Therefore, it is recommended to promote road safety accountability among road authorities, road engineers and urban planners.

H. Research: There is very little research on the benefits of cost-effective safe infrastructure interventions and the related effects. It is therefore recommended for pilot interventions to be tested to encourage wider application of good and cost-effective road infrastructure safety interventions countrywide.

4.7 CONCLUSION

Engineering safety on roads is clearly a priority issue which needs to be pursued seriously by road authorities and stakeholders. Much as there are promising actions of road infrastructure safety improvements there are also significant serious road safety engineering and design deficiencies still prevalent in many road locations in Ghana. There must be clear understanding of the relationships between RTC occurrence and various roadway and traffic engineering design features. In addition, both reactive (treatment of hazardous locations) and proactive (road safety audit, inspections and assessment) approaches must be considered as a matter of urgency for rapid and sustained improvements of infrastructure safety in the country.

Appendix 4.1: Summary of Road Characteristics Contributing to Road Traffic Crashes

Policy Issues

Poor knowledge of crash causative factors

Right angle crashes (intersection)

Restricted sight distance

High approach speeds

'See through' effect on a minor approach

Obscured control sign, control lines or signal lanterns

Presence of intersection not obvious (at time of day)

Traffic volumes too high for Give Way or Stop controls (insufficient gaps)

Run-off-road crashes

Narrow lanes or narrow seal

Severity of curve

Edge of the road is not evident

Shoulders/roadside do not allow recovery of control

Alignment of road is deceptive

Poor road surface condition

Motorcyclist crashes

Poor delineation, especially at curves

Poor road surface (roughness, potholes, debris)

Obstacles at the roadside

Insufficient number of gaps in oncoming traffic

Restricted sight distance

Pedestrian crashes

Inadequate crossing facilities

Too much traffic for adequate crossing gaps

Too many lanes of traffic to cross

High-speed, multi-lane and two-way traffic

Complex or unexpected traffic movements

Traffic hidden by parked cars, other objects or Excessive landscaping

A marked crossing which is not evident to drivers

Long signal cycles which encourage pedestrians to disobey signals

Inappropriate device or lack of devices for mix of pedestrians (e.g. for disabled users)

Inadequate lighting

Hit-fixed-object crashes

Islands not visible

Complex layout

Reasons as for run-off-road crashes

Crashes involving a parked vehicle

Unexpected parked vehicle in traffic lane

Edge line not visible

Lanes too narrow

Lane changing and manoeuvring

Lanes too narrow (for traffic mix, speed, curvature of road, angle of lanes)

Lane lines or edge lines not visible

'Edge drop' between road and shoulder/roadside

Presence of parked cars or other obstruction

Unexpected lane drop or merge area

Inadequate direction information

Roadside activity

Turning crashes with oncoming vehicles

Restricted visibility/sight distance

High approach speeds

Queued oncoming turning vehicles block visibility

Insufficient number of gaps in oncoming traffic

Too many lanes of oncoming traffic to cross

Complex intersection layout

Head-on crashes

Lanes too narrow (for traffic mix, speed, curvature of road, angle of lanes)

Centreline not visible

Poor delineation

Severity of curve cannot be judged

A hidden dip or crest

Insufficient overtaking opportunities

Inadequate skid resistance or pavement drainage

'Edge drop' between road and shoulder/roadside leading to driver overcorrection

Cyclist crashes

Speed environment too high

Inadequate separation of traffic

Interaction with vehicles

Poor road surface (roughness, potholes, debris)

Unexpected parked vehicle in traffic lane

Unexpected lane drops or merge area

Straight ahead rear-end crashes

Queued turning vehicles ahead

Traffic signals around curve or over crest

Other unexpected cause of delay ahead

Inadequate skid resistance or pavement drainage

Wrong offset timing of linked signals

'See through' effect of consecutive traffic signals

Inadequate inter-green phase on signals

Presence of parked cars

Unstable flow on high-speed road

Traffic 'friction' due to frequent pedestrian or parking movements

Turning vehicles where they are not expected (e.g. just before or just after signals)

Railway level crossing crashes

Location of crossing is not evident

Impending presence of train is not evident

Form of control is not accurately identified (or is not consistent)

Driver's attention distracted by intersection or other feature

Obscured control devices

Crashes involving U-turning vehicles

Inadequate turning facilities

Insufficient number of gaps in oncoming traffic

Poor sight distance

CHAPTER 5

————————

VEHICULAR SAFETY

5.1 INTRODUCTION

Vehicle factors contribute to road traffic crashes (RTCs) so improving vehicle safety is a key strategy used in addressing international and national road traffic casualty reduction goals and targets, (DaCoTa, 2012). This is because the safety of a vehicle can have a large impact on the survivability of the vehicle occupant as well as those that the vehicle may hit in the event of a crash, (toolkit.irap.org). Thus, increasingly at the global level, there is a drive to ensure better understanding of safe vehicle systems.

Ghana has experienced rapid growth in vehicle population in the past decade with related safety challenges. The country is specifically confronted with the challenge of implementing vehicle safety reforms as a user country with a mass of imported vehicles which mostly lack requisite safety systems. The country has mainly applied legislation, standards, regulations and enforcement for achieving vehicle safety in the country. This chapter of the book discusses vehicle safety management in Ghana to ascertain the extent to which vehicle safety can be optimized in the country for effective contribution towards the reduction of vehicle related RTCs and consequent fatalities and injuries.

5.1.1 Causes of RTC by Vehicle Factors

RTC's caused by vehicle related factors are mostly attributed the following factors:

A. Over Aged Vehicles: An over aged vehicle in poor condition is bound to cause a more fatal RTC since its parts can easily disintegrate.

In Ghana, over dependence on the use of over aged vehicles (which constitutes about 87% of the total vehicle fleet in the country) is deemed as the most highly ranked challenge factor causing vehicle related RTC's. This is because they are mostly defective and are of low quality.

B. Vehicles without Safety Technologies: Unsafe vehicles not fitted with vehicle safety features such as vehicle restraints eg. Seatbelts can result in higher RTC fatalities.

There is a huge backlog of old vehicle fleet without modern safety installations in use in Ghana

C. Vehicles with Severe Mechanical Defects: Vehicle defects causes vehicles to be in poor running condition with RTCs risks. These include severe mechanical and/or cosmetic defects. This is because a vehicle in poor condition can affect a driver's ability to maintain control of the vehicle. Some vehicular and motorcycle defects that cause Passenger RTC Severity/Fatalities are as listed in Tables 5.1 and Table 5.2 respectively.

Table 5.1: Types of Vehicular Defects

Vehicle Part	Description of Defects
Manufacturing Defects	This could be due to design/ manufacturing mistake on a vehicle or a vehicle part with failure of the manufacturer to provide adequate warning or instructions
Brakes	Faulty braking systems and brake failure can lead to very severe RTC's -Defective brakes refers to any brake component or device which is excessively worn; insecure; corroded; fractured; reduced in diameter; reduced number of strands; damaged; knotted and or displaced which can cause RTC. -Others are faulty brake tubes causing leakage of brake fluid resulting in partial replacement of brake pad and not the brake system can also cause RTCs.
Tyres	Defective tyres can lead to driver loss of control of a vehicle which can result in a severe RTC. -Defective tyres may be due to insufficient tyre pressure from lack of maintenance; load weights exceeding the tyre specifications; bad installation or bad fabrication of tyres. -It can also be due to the size and type of tyres, ply rating, load index, and speed rating being below the appropriate level for the vehicle. -The purchasing of non-tropical tyres which can causes overheating and tyre bursts. -Overloading on heavy trucks, expired tyres not replaced as required and the use of cheap second tyres which are not tropically built also contribute to RTCs.
Lighting	Vehicles with one headlight or both not functioning using the road at night can be of RTC risk. -Over aged lighting framework with poor reflectivity and infrequent replacement but with only the changing of bulbs can contribute to RTCs
Airbags	Airbags failing to deploy or deploying when they should not or with too much force can result in a victim receiving too much injuries, cause obstruction that leads to crashes or worsen the impact of a crash respectively.
Seatbelt	Seatbelts that unbuckle during RTC ejects victims and offers less protection. Absence of seatbelts in vehicles also contribute to RTC risk
Electrical System	These can cause fires during RTC situations Electronic malfunctions such as seizure of control functions during RTCs are also of high risk
Wheels/Steering Components	This can cause RTCs when they crack or break and cause driver loss of control. -It can be caused by infrequent Hydraulic oil replacement causing difficulty of vehicle control. -Steering pots not frequently serviced also contribute to RTC risk
Driver's Mirrors	-Broken mirrors or missing mirror components can impair a drivers vision and cause RTC's
Warning Systems	-Where the warning system is not working and hand gestures are used to alert the oncoming or rear vehicle can cause an RTC to occur
Fuel System	-This can cause fires from leakage and explosion of tanks as a result of lack of servicing from blockade, rusting of tanks, keeping of low fuel level especially for heavy vehicles and leaks from pipes connecting to the tanks.
Windshield wiper	-Can blind the driver during heavy rains to cause RTCs
Coupling and uncoupling	-Incorrect coupling and uncoupling of trailers of heavy vehicles can also cause RTCs.
Condition of Body	-Weakness in the vehicle body frame can cause breaks and tears during crashes which will expose victims to more severe effects
Water System	-This can cause overheating due to none functional fans, from defective thermostat, leaking water tanks
Security of Containers	Container fastening device missing; insecure; incomplete; seized; not fitted with a secondary locking device; not capable of adequately securing a container can result in RTCs

Source: (Institutfür Unfallanalysen, 2008); (BerufsgenossenschaftfürFahrzeughaltungen (BGF), 2003).

Table 5.2: Motorcycle Defects

Motorcycle Part	Type of Defect
Fuel Leakage	Fuel leakage from the fuel lines can cause RTCs
Tyres	-Foreign material lodged in the tyres; tyre tread below the depth of at least 2mm and tyres' air pressure below what is recommended in the vehicle manual can cause RTCs.
Wheels	Axle nuts not in place and not properly secured with the cotter pin not in place can cause RTCs.
Cables and Controls	Throttle cable without play of 3-4mm and not fully functional as well as gearshift and pedal can cause RTCs.
Lights & Mirrors (Incl. turning signals)	Not in good working condition and not positioned correctly can cause RTCs.
Engine oil	Engine leakages and general condition can cause RTCs.
Suspension	Suspension not functional with leaks can cause RTCs.
Stands	Insecure stand retracts with cut-outs witch not operating and spring not intact can cause RTCs.
Brakes	Wheel movement when the brake lever is fully pulled in or depressed can cause RTCs. Shortage of brake fluid level and brake pedal below15-20mm can also cause RTCs.
Drive Chain	Drive chain not slack (25-30mm) and not well lubricated can cause RTCs.
Battery	Dirty terminals with loose cables and battery not secure with vent tube blocked can cause RTCs.
Clutch	Clutch lever plays below 2-3mm, and clutch fluids level not adequate can cause RTCs
Steering	Steering not fully functional and aligned correctly can cause RTCs.

Source: (Institutfür Unfallanalysen, 2008).

Examples of Rickety Vehicles in Ghana are as presented in Figure 5.1.

Figure 5.1: Examples of rickety vehicles in Ghana

D. Unsuitable vehicle modifications: This includes mechanical changes to vehicles by third parties aside the manufacturer which in some cases might comprise the safety features resulting in RTCs. *This is a common practice in Ghana*

E. Poor Vehicle Maintenance: Poor vehicle maintenance culture in addition to the use of old vehicles contributes significantly to the cause of vehicle related RTC's. *In Ghana, this is made worse by the predominance of unskilled fitting mechanics and limited access to good vehicle parts.*

F. Poor Vehicle stability from Overloading: Poor vehicle performance from overloading also causes RTC's due to instability on the road. *This is also a common practice in Ghana*

5.2 VEHICLE SAFETY POLICIES, STANDARDS AND REGULATIONS

5.2.1 Global Vehicle Safety Standards, Regulations and Policies

Globally, safety in the automotive industry is highly regulated and automobiles, motorcycles etc. must comply with set norms and regulations, whether local or international to be accepted into the traffic stream. Vehicle manufacturers must also meet set safety standards and specifications before putting their vehicles on the market for sales in a harmonised manner. Examples of such standards are as discussed in the immediate subsection.

A. World Forum for Harmonization of Vehicle Regulations (WP.29): Before 1952, vehicle regulations and production standards were set by vehicle manufacturing companies at country or regional levels. With the creation of the UN WP.29 now the World Forum for Harmonization of Vehicle Regulations, globally harmonized regulations on vehicles in road safety, environmental protection and trade were set. It also works as a global forum for open discussions on motor vehicle regulations and it operates through the administration of three Multilateral UN Agreements as:

i. The UN Regulations annexed to the 1958 Agreement: This contains regulations for vehicles, their systems, parts and equipment related to safety and environmental aspects. They include performance-oriented test requirements and administrative procedures for approving vehicle systems, parts and equipment. It specifies conformity of production and as of 2015, there were 135 UN Regulations appended to the 1958 Agreement; on the approval and certification of vehicles. Most regulations cover a single vehicle component or technology. A partial list of current regulations applying to passenger cars as summarized below. However, different regulations may apply to heavy vehicles, motorcycles.

a. General Lighting

b. Headlamps

c. Instrumentation/controls

d. Crashworthiness

e. Tyres and wheels

f. Environmental compatibility

g. Automated/autonomous and connected vehicle regulations

h. Brake

ii. 1998 Agreement: This is on Global Technical Regulations (GTR's). They contain globally harmonized performance related requirements and test procedures for Periodical Technical Inspections (PTI's) of wheeled vehicles, equipment and parts which can be fitted and/or be used on wheeled vehicle. They provide predictable regulatory frameworks for the global automotive industry, consumers, and their associations. However, they do not contain administrative provisions for type approvals and their mutual recognition. *(See Table 5.3 for comparison with the standards in Ghana).*

Table 5.3: The Global Technical Regulations

Global Technical Regulations	UN	Application in Ghana
GTR 01:	Door Locks and retention components	Door Locks and Door Retention Components
GTR 02	MMTC- Measurement procedure for two wheels motorcycles equipped with positive or compression ignition engine with regard to emission of gaseous pollutants, CO_2 emissions and fuel consumption	MMTC
GTR 03	Motorcycle Brakes- Development of GTR concerning motorcycle brake systems	
GTR 04:	WHDC - Test procedure for compression ignition (C.I.) engines and positive ignition (P.I.) engines fuelled with natural gas (NG) or liquefied petroleum gas (LPG) with regard to the emission of pollution	Test procedure for compression ignition (C.I.) engines and positive ignition (P.I.) engines fuelled with natural gas (NG) or liquefied petroleum gas (LPG) with regard to the emission of pollution
GTR 05:	WWH –OBD- Board Diagnostic system for heavy duty vehicles and engines	Technical requirements for on-board diagnostic systems (OBD) for road vehicles
GTR 06	Safety Glazing- Regulation concerning safety glazing materials for motor vehicle equipment.	
GTR 07:	Head Restraints	Head Restraints
GTR 08	Electronic Stability Control Systems- Regulations on electronic stability control	Electronic Stability Control Systems
GTR 09	Pedestrian Safety	
GTR 10:	(OCE)- Regulations on heavy duty off cycle emission vehicles	Off-Cycle Emissions (OCE)
GTR 11:	Engines: Regulations on compression ignition engines for agricultural and forestry tractors and non-mobile machines	Test procedure for compression-ignition engines to be installed in agricultural and forestry tractors and in non-road mobile machinery
GTR 12:	Regulation concerning the location, identification and operation of motorcycle controls, tell-tales and indicators	Global technical regulation concerning the location, identification and operation of motorcycle controls, tell-tales and indicators
GTR 13:	Regulation on Hydrogen and fuel (ECE)	Global technical regulation on hydrogen and fuel cell vehicles
GTR 14	Pole side impact	Pole side impact
GHT 15	Harmonization of Worldwide harmonized Light Vehicles test procedure	
GTR 16	Tyres- UN Global regulations on Tyres	

Global Technical Regulations	UN	Application in Ghana
GTR 17	Crankcase and Evaporative Emissions of L(category vehicles	Measurement procedure for two- or three-wheeled motor vehicles equipped with a combustion engine with regard to the crankcase and evaporative emissions
GTR 18	On board Diagnostic (OBD) Systems for L category vehicles	Measurement procedure for two- or three-wheeled motor vehicles with regard to on-board diagnostics
GTR 19	Evaporative emission test procedure for Worldwide harmonized Light Vehicle Test	
GTR 20	Electronic Vehicle Safety (EVS)	Global Technical Regulation on Electric Vehicle Safety (EVS)
GTR 21	Determination of Electrified Vehicle Power-	

iii. UN Rules annexed to the 1997 Agreement: They concern PTIs of vehicles in use based on the adoption of uniform conditions for PTI's of wheeled vehicles and the reciprocal recognition of such inspection. Participation is open to States, Governmental Organizations (GOs) and NGOs, but decisions are taken by Governments.

B. The International Organization for Standardization (ISO): ISO is an independent, non-governmental organization global network of national standards bodies with one member per country. It establishes international standards and generates revenue in the development of a neutral environment by selling, maintaining and making new standards. Table 5.4 provides a summary of key ISO elements.

Table 5.4: Work of ISO

Safety Factors	Details	Application in Ghana
Coverage	They cover all road vehicles from motorcycles to cars, to articulated goods vehicles.	This applies in Ghana
Electric vehicles	A range of standards for road vehicles specifically for electric, hybrid and fuel-cell road vehicles.	Electric vehicles are yet to be introduced in Ghana
Intelligent transport systems	Intelligent transport systems which focus mainly on more than 220 standards*.	This is not applicable in Ghana
Tyres and other components	ISO/TC 31, Tyres, rims and valves - 78 standards for tyres and rims including that of motorcycles	Applied to some extent in Ghana
Vehicle safety	Provision of automotive safety lifecycle management, development, production, operation service, decommissioning and supports tailoring the necessary activities during these lifecycle phases	Not applied in Ghana
Looking forward	Cyber security connected vehicles eg GPS to other gauges and sensors telling you when your tyre pressure is low, there is constant interaction between in-vehicle embedded systems that communicate wirelessly. Hydrogen vehicle stations - If fuel-cell, electric and alternative-fuel vehicles are the future, there need to be adequate stations for refuelling them. A new technical specification,	Applicable to some extent in Ghana
ISO Traffic Safety Legislation and Regulation	Globally, road traffic safety-related standards include: Road traffic safety (RTS) - management systems, good practices for implementing commuting safety management,	Applied to some extent

Source: (ISO Vehicles, Sept 2018)

C. Global Plan for Road Safety Action (2011-2020) on Vehicle Safety: Pillar 3 of the DOA road safety action plan is on Safer Vehicles with defined activities as presented in Table 5.5.

Table 5.5: Global Plan for Road Safety Action (2011-2020) on Safer Vehicle

Activity	Description	Applied to some extent in Ghana
Activity 1:	Encourage Member States to apply and promulgate motor vehicle safety regulations as developed by the United Nation's World Forum for the Harmonization of Vehicle Regulations (WP 29).	Applied in Ghana
Activity 2:	Encourage implementation of new car assessment programmes in all regions of the world in order to increase the availability of consumer information about the safety performance of motor vehicles.	Applied in Ghana
Activity 3:	Encourage agreement to ensure that all new motor vehicles are equipped with seat-belts and anchorages that meet regulatory requirements and pass applicable crash test standards (as minimum safety features).	Applied in Ghana
Activity 4:	Encourage universal deployment of crash avoidance technologies with proven effectiveness such as Electronic Stability Control and Anti-Lock Braking Systems in motorcycles.	Not applied in Ghana
Activity 5:	Encourage the use of fiscal and other incentives for motor vehicles that provide high levels of road user protection and discourage import and export of new or used cars that have reduced safety standards.	This is done through tax variations in Ghana
Activity 6:	Encourage application of pedestrian protection regulations and increased research into safety technologies designed to reduce risks to vulnerable road users.	Not applied in Ghana
Activity 7:	Encourage managers of governments and private sector fleets to purchase, operate and maintain vehicles that offer advanced safety technologies and high levels of occupant protection.	Not applied in Ghana

5.2.2 Vehicle Safety Policies, Standards and Regulations in Ghana

Over the years, Ghana has developed relevant policies and regulations that are applicable in the country with periodic amendments and an outcome which largely reflects international standards. These address topics such as licensing and vehicle registration, motor vehicle manufacturing/assembling standards etc. An overview is as presented in the immediate subsections.

A. National Vehicle Safety Policies in Ghana:

i. The National Road Safety Policy on Vehicles: The key policy statement on vehicle safety in Ghana stipulates that the Government will take steps to strengthen the system to ensure that safety aspects are incorporated in all stages of vehicle assembly, modification, usage, operation and maintenance in line with prevailing international standards to minimize adverse safety and environmental effects of vehicle operation on road users and infrastructure. The details of the challenges and policy strategies are as summarised in Table 5.6.

Table 5.6: Key challenges and policy strategies on vehicle safety in Ghana

Theme	Key Challenges	Strategies for Vehicle Safety	Status of Application in Ghana
Vehicle Importation	There are no standards and specifications to regulate the importation and use of vehicles.	a. Enforce laws and regulations on the use of unauthorized vehicles for commercial purposes. b. Enforce laws and regulations on the use of seatbelts c. Review existing legislation on vehicle modification and conversion to ensure safe operation of such vehicles.	a. This has not been effectively applied. Eg. Commercial motorcycle operation b. Some commercial vehicles do not have seatbelts c. This has been done to some extent

Theme	Key Challenges	Strategies for Vehicle Safety	Status of Application in Ghana
Road Worthiness	There are large numbers of old vehicles with components either missing, malfunctioning or not functioning at all.	Set standards and specifications for the importation and assembly of vehicles.	This is done in the country but level of effectiveness is not known
Vehicle Maintenance	Poorly serviced or maintained vehicles that result in frequent breakdowns.		The challenge still pervades but the magnitude of its impact is not known
Vehicle Modifications	Illegal and inappropriately converted vehicles and use of inappropriate materials cause RTCs leading to serious injuries and fatalities.	a. License entities that engage in the modification or conversion of vehicles b. Improve the capacity of the DVLA to enforce compliance with regulations on modification and conversion of vehicles	Currently this is done in Ghana with some identified challenges such as insecure coupling of trailers to heads of HGVs and the use of iron instead of steel for vehicle seats in commercial buses
Vehicle Parts	The use of sub-standard parts and tyres.	Regulate the management of tyres and spare parts stocks by Motor Trading Firms and other dealers.	The state of achievement is not known
Vehicle Inspection	Lack of equipment and qualified staff for effective vehicle inspection resulting in several poor vehicles operating on the road.	Strengthen the capacity of the DVLA to effectively inspect vehicles to ensure compliance with regulations, conditions and operation	This has been achieved by the establishment of private vehicle testing stations (PVTS)/ inspectors
Vehicle Financing	The relatively high cost of new vehicles in Ghana		Not achieved

Source: NRSP 2008

ii. The National Automotive Policy: This is hereafter referred to as "the Auto Policy". As part of measures to transform Ghana's vehicle fleet into a safe, modern and environmentally efficient vehicle fleet, compulsory vehicle standards are required to ensure all vehicle components and parts meet appropriate standards. Their proper assembly and testing are confirmed by the Ghana Standards Authority (GSA) which issues a Homologation Certificate, (homologation - the certification process for vehicles or vehicle parts) following approval of the vehicle standards. The policy, among other things, grants the GSA the responsibility for the homologation of all vehicles manufactured and assembled in Ghana. Its essential components are as presented in Table 5.7.

Table 5.7: Key components of the National Automotive Policy

Policy item	Description
Vision:	-The vision of the Ghana Automotive Development Policy (GADP) is to make Ghana a fully integrated and competitive industrial hub for the Automotive Industry in the West Africa sub-region.
Scope of the Policy:	-The Auto Policy is to provide the necessary framework for the establishment of assembly and manufacturing capacity in Ghana. The average of vehicles to be assembled includes new passenger cars, SUVs and light commercial vehicles which would include pickups, minibuses and cargo vans. Additional policy interventions will be introduced in the course of implementation for assembling medium and heavy-duty commercial vehicles, and for the assembly of buses. For the purpose of policy implementation and effective regulation of incentives, Ghana has categorized auto assembly into Semi-Knocked-Down (SKD), Enhanced SKD and Completely-Knocked-Down (CKD), based on the qualifying list of local or foreign assembly, and Fully-Built- Units (FBUs). Each category is defined according to place of assembly or manufacture.
Strategic Objectives:	The strategic objectives of the Policy are: -To establish a fully integrated and competitive industrial hub for automotive manufacturing in collaboration with the private sector – global, regional and domestic;

Policy item	Description
	-To generate highly skilled jobs in automotive assembly and the manufacture of components and parts, with spillover effects into other sectors of the economy;
	-To establish an asset-based vehicle financing scheme for locally manufactured vehicles to ensure affordability for vehicle buyers;
	-To improve balance of payments through competitive import substitution and export market development;
	-To improve vehicle safety and environmental standards; and
	-To transform the quality of the national road transport fleet and safeguard the natural environment.
Thematic Areas	-Incentive and Regulatory Framework
	-Market Development and Trade Facilitation
	-Environment, Standards and Safety
	-Access to Industrial Infrastructure
	-Automotive Skills and Technology Upgrading
	-Developing Local Component Supply Chain
	-Labour Relations and Productivity
	-Legislative Measures
	-Participation in the Auto Programme
	Institutional and Governance Structures

Source: Ghana Automotive Development Policy (GADP)

B. Vehicle Standards and Specifications in Ghana: *There are also vehicle safety standards and specifications to guide vehicle acquisition, manufacture and assembly. These were aimed to transform Ghana's vehicle fleet into a safe, modern and environmentally friendly vehicle fleet. The GSA as a member of ISO draws on the ISO standards for this. Also, the GSA has established and approved 26 new standards for the regulation of the automobile industry under the Automobile Industry Standards (GSA/TC 05, 2019). The standards comprise 22 standards for vehicle part systems and 4 draft compulsory vehicle specifications through adoption of the UNECE's international standards.*

These include M1 category of vehicles (passenger vehicles with not more than eight seats); M2 category (passenger vehicles with more than eight seats; and N1 category vehicles for carriage of goods that has satisfied the requirement set by various statutory bodies. This has been done through a combination of different standards to improve vehicles in use and those yet to be acquired, (See Appendix 5.1). This is to ensure that all vehicle components and parts (both new and old) meet appropriate standards tested and confirmed by GSA with the issuance of a homologation certificate as a confirmation.

Provision has also been made for regulating vehicle standards for the establishment of vehicle assembly plants in the country some of which are already in operation. Furthermore, proposals have been made to develop regulations for imported vehicles with standards for whole vehicle marking system based on the South African Standard as a benchmark. Since these are still in progress it is hoped that Ghana will be able to undertake universal deployment of improved vehicle safety technologies for both passive and active safety overtime.

C. Vehicle Safety Regulations in Ghana: These are defined in a wide scope of evidence as summarized in Table 5.8.

Table 5.8: Categorisation of Vehicle Themes

Import Regulations (buy, sell or scrap a vehicle)	Maintenance of Current State	Vehicle Inspections
144. Visitor's vehicle	136. Passenger vehicle carrying freight and persons	5. Tests of condition of motor vehicle
145. Exemption of visitor's vehicle	59. non-transfer of liquefied petroleum gas or com-	6. Person to conduct
146. Registration plate and nationality sign	pressed natural gas cylinder	examination of motor vehicle

Registration, number plates and types of permits	Vehicle standards	Loads and towing
1. Register	50 & 51. Width, Height and length requirements	3. Verification of weights
2. Application to register	62. Tyres	52. Carriage of loads
4. Registration of vehicle and trailer	63. Brakes	53. Carriage of
7. Road use certificate	64. Engines	hazardous goods
8. Issue of road use certificate	65. Lamps	54. Safety require-
9. Exemption from requirement for road use certificate	66. Mirror, windscreen and glass	ments for carriage of hazardous goods
10. Vehicle registration number plate	67. Materials for windscreen, windows and partitions	87. Devices for
11. Refusal to fix registration number plate	68. Windows and windscreen of a commercial vehicle	detection of overloaded
81. General requirements for retro-reflector	69. Fire extinguisher and first aid kit	motor vehicle
12. Renewal of registration number	70 & 71. Wheels, axles and Steering	88. Checking of
13. Withdrawal of registration number	72. Suspension	weights
14. Registration of number plate manufac-turer and embosser	73. Wings, fenders, mud guards, wheel or mud flaps	92. Application of motor vehicle weight
15. Vehicle Lay-Off Certificate	74. Horns and Sirens	control regulations
16. Re-registration of existing registered motor vehicle	76. Direction indicator and Position of indicator	103. Requirements for towing of motor
82. Warning chevron sign on rear of certain motor vehicles	78. Red reflector	vehicle
89. Grant of special permit	79. Fitting of retro-reflectors at the front and rear comers of a motor vehicle	104. Specifications of
90. Special permit form	80. Fitting of retro-reflectors on the body of certain	towing truck and other
127. Issuance of commercial vehicle license	motor vehicles	requirements
130. Use of taxi	120. Manner of fitting of seatbelt	
131. Use of passenger carrying vehicle	126. Standards and specifications for taxis and buses	
132. Private use of passenger carrying vehicles	134. Construction of passenger carrying vehicle	
164. Speed limits for particular class of vehicles	138. Particulars to be written on passenger carrying vehicle	
135. Speed limiter, logbook and tachygraphy	142. Documents for vehicle being taken out of Ghana	
162. Registration and licensing of motor vehicles and trailers	48. Vehicle not conforming to Regulations	
55. Registration of liquefied petroleum gas or compressed natural gas fitted motor vehicle	57. Use of motor vehicle run on liquefied petroleum gas or compressed natural gas	
	58. License for installation of liquefied petroleum gas or compressed natural gas cylinder in a motor vehicle	
56. Numbering of liquefied petroleum gas or compressed natural gas cylinder and issuance of sticker	60. Offences and penalties for liquefied petroleum gas or compressed natural gas fitted motor vehicle	
	61. Transitional provisions for the use of liquefied petro-leum gas or compressed natural gas by motor vehicles	
	102. Regulations on broken down motor vehicle and trailer	
	111. Discharge of oil and other substances on the road	
	167. Authorised emergency vehicles	

Source: LI 2180 of 2012

5.2.3 Vehicle Acquisition in Ghana

In Ghana, vehicle acquisition is from two main sources. That is those imported into the country and those assembled by automobile plants in the country. The first is made up of retailers of imported used vehicles and a few distributers who deal in the retailing of new vehicles.

A. Vehicle Assembling in Ghana: *A number of vehicle assembly plants such as Gharmot, National Investment Corporation (NIC) vehicle assembly plant/ workshop and the Neoplan assembly plant were established when Ghana gained independence in 1957. (www. Mongnabay.com). However, following over a decade of de-industrialization, most of these enterprises did not survive in the era of restrictive trade regimes. This led to scarcity of foreign exchange (Dinye and Nyaba, 2001) and most of these plants were subsequently privatized due to poor management and over dependence on state funds for survival (Kwakye E, 1998).*

Overtime new vehicle assembly plants have been and are being established and currently, as part of the Government's transformational agenda. This is because Vehicle Assembly and Automotive Components Manufacturing has been identified as a strategic anchor industry to be facilitated and supported. Examples of Vehicle Manufacturing plants in Ghana are as follows:

i. Neoplan Automobile Assembly Plant-Kumasi: The plant was the first bus manufacturing assembly plant in West Africa. It produced Neoplan tropical buses and coaches locally for Ghana and the West Africa market ((www.neoplan.de). It has been operating for the past forty years. It has an integrated service centre in Kumasi where buses such as Tata Marcopolo, DVL Neoplan Yaxing, DVL Jonckheere, Daf and Fiat Iris bus/Iveco model are built for the Metro Mass Transit Company Limited (MMT, the VIP buses and coaches and the Transport Comfort Voyageur (CVT) buses in Burkina Faso.

ii. JGC Vehicle Assembly Plant – Accra: The Jospong Group of Companies (JGC), a mother company under which Zoomlion Ghana has established a subsidiary Vehicle Assembly Plant in Accra. This plant imports engines and builds vehicle parts to locally assemble DONGFENG vehicles and trucks suitable for transportation of waste and other construction equipment in the country.

iii. Vehicle Assembling under the Transformational agenda: As a part of the efforts to change the overdependence on imported second hands vehicles the government of Ghana has signed a Memoranda of Understanding (MoU-2019) with six (6) global automobile manufacturing companies – Volkswagen, Sinotruk, Nissan, Suzuki, Toyota and Renault to establish assembly plants within the terms, conditions and incentives package defined in the Ghana Automotive Development Policy (GADP). The essence is to produce affordable new vehicles in the Ghanaian vehicle market. The Original Equipment Manufacturer (OEM) production in Ghana provides access to various tax incentives under the Customs Amendment Act 2020, Act 104.

It is anticipated that a regional and autos production chain including their own parts production, which may create machinery and toll and die export opportunities for the mother companies will be achieved for wider Africa. Producers in Ghana may also receive reduced or duty-free access to a wide range of other African countries via the new African Continental Free Trade Agreement (AfCFTA). Most importantly, the assembled vehicles are required to conform to corporate safety standards by the mother company and standards of the GSA especially.

iv. The Katanka Automobile Assembling Plant: The Katanka automobile company is a Ghanaian automobile assembling firm, which has been assembling its brand of vehicles for the local and international markets. Its operational components include design, foundry, machining, Chassis/body building and a spray booth. It assembles completely knocked down vehicles (CKD) kits form China. It mainly produces sedans and SUV's as well as some military vehicles. Technical and Safety compliance on the company's production is required to be certified by the GSA. The Government has procured some of these vehicles for its own use.

B. Vehicle Importation: *In Ghana, majority of the vehicle fleet are imported in second-hand state from advanced countries at about 90%. According to the Ghana-Country Commercial Guide published on trade.gov in 2022, Ghana imports about 100,000 vehicles per year with an estimated value of US $1.14 billion annually. These are mostly imported into the country by Ghanaian's resident abroad or by used second-hand vehicle dealers for profit. The over reliance on second hand vehicles is attributed to limited affordability for new vehicles. However, since many of these vehicles would have been scrapped in their country of origin, the safety state of most of them would have been compromised at the time of importation. Table 5.9 provides an overview of the types and source of vehicles imported into Ghana.*

Table 5.9: Type and Sources of Imported Vehicles

Type of vehicle	Passenger Capacity	Make	Source
Cars	5	Corolla, Honda, Elantra, Atos, Matis, Almera, Luxury Cars, etc.	Europe, North America, Korea, Canada
SUV's	7	Land Cruiser, Fortuner, Range Rover, Prado, Ford, Honda, Mitsubishi, Suzuki, Isuzu, etc.	Europe, North America, Korea, Canada
Pickups	5	Nissan, Toyota, Ford, Mazda, Mitsubishi, Isuzu, etc.	Europe, North America, Korea, Canada
Light buses	12-23	Toyota Hiace, Nissan Urvan, 207 Benz Bus, Benz Sprinter, Hyundai Grace, etc.	Europe, North America, Korea, Canada
Medium Buses	30 – 33	Ford Dodge, Ford Ram, Toyota Coaster, Nissan Civilian, etc.	Europe, North America, Korea, Canada
Large buses	40 – 80	DAF, Jonchere, Yutong, VDAL Tata, Hyundai, Kia, etc.	Europe, North America, Korea, Canada
Tipper Trucks		Sinotruck, Foton, etc.	China
Motorcycles	2	Honda, Yamaha, royal, Suzuki, etc.	China, India
Three wheelers	4	Motor King	China, India

Source: Author's Survey

Not only are most of the vehicles important into the country are used, an estimated 90% of them are crashed vehicles brought in for local repair and use. These are mostly vehicles which have been wrecked, destroyed, or physically damaged by collision, fire, water or other occurrences bought at cheap costs for sales at higher profit margins by dealers. Vendors source for such vehicles from insurance companies in the home countries online. On arrival into the country, these are then serviced by sub-standard fitting mechanics and artisans with only the road worthy certificate as the safety operational permit. The issue is aggravated when fake roadworthy certificates are issued to enable such vehicles to be in use.

Since, such vehicles are from varied manufacturers from different countries, it has resulted in Ghana's fleet of imported vehicles being dominated by varying standards difficult to assess. Thus, under the Customs Amendment Bill 2020- the Government of Ghana attempted to ban the importation of crash vehicles into the country. However, the policy implementation has been suspended due to resistance from such dealers and discussions on the issue are still ongoing.

Currently, auto importers periodically contact Commercial Service Ghana to seek suppliers of specific autos as well as OEM and aftermarket parts to service the used autos in the Country. On the way forward, considerations should be given to an evaluation of the safety performance of such vehicles in commercial use especially those with over-hauled engines for policy making. This is necessary because the importers of such vehicles are much focused on economic gains with little regard for the safety risk of such vehicles.

i. Laws Governing Importation of Vehicle in Ghana: The law governing the importation of vehicles into Ghana is the Ghana Customs, Excise and Preventive Service (CEPS) (Management Law) PNDCL 330 of 1993, Sections 46, 47, 48, 78-94, 123-192. This law is complemented by CEPS (Management) Act 1998, (Act 552), Act 565, Act 598 of 14th April, 2001 on Commissioner's Orders and other Service instructions on vehicles. Ghana's Parliament Customs (Amendment) Act, 2020, Act 1014 was also passed into law on 30 April 2020 and assented by the President on the same date.

ii. Taxes and Incentives: Vehicles imported into the country attract various surcharges in terms of levies, taxes etc. A selective import duty taxation scheme that varies with the age of vehicle imported (see Table 5.10) is used. All vehicles imported into the country unless specifically exempted under the PNDCL 330 or other enactment attract the following:

a. Import Duty - (0%, 5%, 10%, and 20%).

b. Import VAT - (0% or 12.5%).

c. National Health Insurance Levy - (0% or 2.5%).

d. ECOWAS Levy - (0.5%).

e. Export Development Fund (EDIF) – (0.5%).

f. Examination Fee - (1%)

Ghana uses a Used Vehicle Valuation Module to obtain a Customs Classification and Valuation Report (CCVR) in the importation of used vehicles into the country. The age of a vehicle is a crucial determinant in valuation for duty purposes and it is calculated with effect from the year in which the motor vehicle was first manufactured. Table 5.10 provides an overview of taxes imposed on vehicle importation.

Table 5.10: Taxes on Vehicle Importation in Ghana

	TYPE OF VEHICLE	Import Duty (%)	VAT (%)	NHIL (%)	ECOWAS LEVY (%)	EDIF (%)	EXAM (%)	Processing Fee (%)
i								
a)	Ambulance	0	0	0	0.5	0.5	1	-
b)	Hearse	0	12.5	2.5	0.5	0.5	1	1
ii	Motor Cars							
a)	Motor cars including Cross Country and Estate Cars:							
	Of a cylinder capacity not exceeding 1900 cc;	5	12.5	2.5	0.5	0.5	1	-
	Of a cylinder capacity exceeding 1900 cc but not exceeding 3000 cc;	10	12.5	2.5	0.5	0.5	1	-
	Of a cylinder capacity exceeding 3000 cc;	20	12.5	2.5	0.5	2.5	1	-
b)	Designed for travelling on snow; golf cars and similar vehicles	20	12.5	2.5	0.5	0.5	1	-
iii	Motor vehicles designed to carry ten (10) or more persons (for example buses and coaches)	5	12.5	2.5	0.5	0.5	1	-
iv	Motor vehicles designed to carry thirty (30) or more persons	0	12.5	2.5	0.5	0.5	1	1
v	Motor vehicle for the transport of goods such as trucks, tippers, and lorries	5	12.5	2.5	0.5	0.5	1	-
vi	Tractors of H.S. Code 8701							
a)	Pedestrian controlled tractors – 8701.10	0	0	0	0.5	0.5	1	-
b)	Road tractors for semi-trailers – 8701.20	5	12.5	2.5	0.5	0.5	1	-
c)	Track-laying tractors – 8701.30	0	0	0	0.5	0.5	1	-
d)	Others – 8701.90	0	0	0	0.5	0.5	1	-
vii	Special purpose vehicles of H.S. Code 87.05 (for examples workshop vans, breakdown vehicle and mobile showrooms)	0	12.5	2.5	0.5	0.5	1	1
viii	Motor bikes	0	12.5	2.5	0.5	0.5	1	1
ix	Bicycles	0	0	0	0.5	0.5	0	1

NOTE: The use of log sheets and seat belts alone to check or confirm the age of vehicles is not reliable. What is on log sheets are more often dates of first registration of such vehicles and not dates of manufacture

Source: http://ghana-net.com/duty-on-cars.html

iii. New Car Assessment Programmes (NCAP): The Global New Car Assessment Programme (GNCAP) strongly advocates for better vehicle safety at the point of manufacture, (Global NCAP, 2015). It requires all components of vehicle systems to be safety tested and assessed using dummies before going on the market. The safety systems of the new vehicles are rated from zero to five stars with a zero-rating indicating the possibility of fatal consequences of an RTC and five stars indicating limited chance of injury or fatality in a crash situation, (Welle B. et al 2018).

Also, the standards go beyond what is required to make a vehicle safe to drive by the inclusion of other elements such as level of roof and side impact resistance and the quality of safety of the glass. Further recommendation is to link this with operating restrictions such as type of roads, driver qualifications, speed, etc. to the capability of the vehicle and the extent to which performance will be degraded by wear and tear.

The approach is known to create positive safety completion amongst vehicle manufacturers. Many countries also have minimum standards of crashworthiness with a ban being placed on the use of a vehicle on a public road if not considered fit under a Prohibition Notice (PG9). It becomes and offence to drive or tow such a vehicle when a prohibition notice is issued unless an exemption notice has been granted under certain circumstances.

In Ghana, the ratification of the motor vehicle safety regulations developed by the UN's World Forum with set guidelines by the GSA as presented in Table 5.7 serves as the basis for the conduct of this activity. Since there are no vehicle manufacturing companies in the country, this is applied through mandatory vehicle inspection schemes at the point of registration or renewal of road worthiness of a vehicle.

iv. Challenges with the Use of Second-hand Vehicles: Generally, it is of the view that newer vehicles are less likely to be involved in fatal crashes, due to the relatively new state and possible availability of crash protection features. Wegman, F.C.M, (1992), adds that older vehicles are of crash potential especially vehicles which are 4 to 6 years of age since they get involved in crashes from defects at about one and a half times frequency, while vehicles of 7 years and above are involved in about three and a half times frequency, when compared to vehicles younger than 4 years. He also estimates that the risk of dying in a crash is (71%) higher in a vehicle that is 18 years old or more compared to a vehicle that is 3 years old or less. This is attributed to the fact that mechanical defects become more common as a vehicle ages. With the WHO (2015), intimating that 80% of second- hand vehicles sold to developing countries do not meet UN safety standards since they are more or less dumping grounds for discarded vehicles from the advanced countries and it is commended to ban the exportation of vehicles that are close to the end of their economic mileage.

In Ghana, most of the second-hand vehicles imported into the country are between 5 to 20 years old at an average of about 14.2 years (NRSC 2012), especially for vehicles used for public private commercial transport services. With over (90%) of vehicles imported into the country being old within varying age ranges, the safety risk of the commercial vehicle fleet in Ghana cannot be over emphasised.

The practice of the purchase of second-hand vehicles especially those that have been involved in crashes thrives because of cheap cost ranging between US$1,000.00 - US$ 1,500.00 for saloon cars, US$ 3,000 for SUV's and US$ 9,000 for large buses with shipping cost of between an average of US$1,200 - US$ 1, 500.00. Refer to Table 5.11 for vehicle cost comparisons.

Table 5.11: Cost of Vehicles

Types of Vehicle	Purchase Price of second-Hand Vehicle from source (US $)	Local Market Price of a Second Hand Vehicle (US $)	Local Market Price of a Brand-New Vehicle (US $)	Percentage Difference in Cost
Saloon Cars	1,000-2,000	11,000 – 15,000	15,000 – 30,000	
4 X4 Vehicles, Ford, Pickups	9,000	50,000-70,000	60,000 – 90,000	
Small Buses		10,000 – 15,000	$27,000 -35,000	
Hyundai Grace,				
Medium		12,000-18,000	30,000 – 40,000	
Sprinter, Ambulance, Cargo, Passenger				
Large Buses		22,000 - 34,000	US 120,000	
DAF,				
Tipper Trucks		100,000 -150,000	300,000	
Motorcycles				
Tricycles				

On arrival in the country, there is limited possibility that local repair can restore the level of the safety installations to its original state. Aside this, the availability of spare parts for servicing such vehicles remains a challenge especially due to the fact that they are of diversified models and old with the possibility of the manufacturer having stopped producing the required parts.

There is also the challenge of limited availability and affordability since the foreign exchange for the procurement of such vehicle parts is also limited. This therefore results in situations where old second-hand vehicle parts from cannibalised vehicles, or vehicle parts of different vehicle models are fitted into others causing safety risks. Some recommended actions to correct the challenges are as follows:

a). Conduct of Research into the Safety Impact of Second-Hand Vehicles: The discrepancy of performance levels of the mass of second-hand vehicles and uncertified safety performance of the repair works required to be undertaken by local fitting mechanics must be studied to situate the problem in its true safety context. Also, efforts should be made to transform the safety requirements of the fleet of vehicles entering the country. Where possible the safety performance of the fleet of vehicles already in the country should be improved with interventions such as the retrofitting with elements such as seatbelts.

b). Revision of Taxes and Duties on Over Aged Vehicles: The current regulation whereby the importation of over aged vehicles attracts a penalty of 5% to 100% of the total cost as a form of control should be reassessed to determine the margin to which this has been a deterrent to the influx of unsafe vehicles.

c). Introduction of Aftermarket Support: It is recommended in literature for automotive manufacturing companies to be made to bear the responsibility of long-term / life-time support and warranties of their products through the franchise dealer of the importing country that were granted upon first sale of the vehicle. This will be in the form of aftermarket support through the supply of serviceable parts by franchise dealers using digital/on-line vehicle maintenance and parts catalogues of all used vehicle models exported to other countries.

Parent vehicle manufacturing companies could also encourage franchise dealers to stock fast moving service components of used vehicle exported without supported franchise as well as make the parts easily available to enable the vehicle operate optimally. In addition, as an interim measure the following could be considered:

- *Compulsory vehicle safety standards must be enforced to ensure that all components and parts of vehicles are able to meet appropriate safety standards.*

- *Vehicles assembled in the country must also be properly safety tested before certification by the GSA and registration by the DVLA.*

- *Older vehicles that are not able to meet such requirements must be gradually phased out of the system or be retrofitted with the necessary equipment in order to meet required standards.*

- *Legal requirements for minimum vehicle safety standards should be met before a vehicle can be put on the road in Ghana.*

d) Vehicle Capitalisation: For purposes of acquiring new vehicles with good safety standards governments are also encouraged to apply affordable and flexible fiscal incentives to encourage the procurement of new vehicles by owner's especially high occupancy commercial transport operators. This must involve the use of financing support to incentivize the purchase of newer vehicles since limited affordability for new vehicles instigates overreliance on cheap second-hand vehicles with reduced safety standards.

In Ghana, some initiatives undertaken to provide vehicle capitalisation in the country as part of the introduction of vehicle reform initiative to strengthen private sector financing of the bus transport industry are as follows:

- *Introduction of equity shares for the acquisition of new buses for a Rapid Bus Transit System (BRT). The equity share component failed and government had to procure the buses for independent management. This is addition to other private owned formal transport operation systems with independent management.*

- *Provision of loans for vehicle acquisition. This involved the provision of loans by some insurance companies under special arrangements with some transport unions to replace dilapidated vehicle fleet with the unions standing as sureties for investment recovery and funding recycling. However, such schemes have failed in the past due to payment defaults by the beneficiaries.*

- *Supply of new buses directly to vehicle transport unions including the Ghana Private Road Transport Union (GPRTU), the Progressive Transport Union (PROTOA) and others for operation and cost recovery for fund recycling and expanded benefits. The scheme also failed due payment defaults by the unions.*

- *Provision of Leasing Facilities by some private leasing companies through vehicle asset replacement arrangements with transport owners. However, these are on limited scale and most of the vehicles involved are not new.*

As of now, only (6%) of intracity bus operators and (7%) of intercity bus operators have benefitted from such schemes. Out of these (20%) were arranged by government and 70% were arranged by private people and formal funding institutions whilst 10% were arranged with private funding institutions. Currently, most of the loan schemes have stopped due to high default rate attributed to higher interest rates. However major constraints to these arrangements include:

- *High commercial risks resulting in low demand.*

- *Limited knowledge and uncertainties about the approach.*

- *Lack of business experience of traditional entrepreneurs.*

- *Long bureaucratic procedures e.g., the acquisition of the government supported loans took about a year and the private arrangements even takes longer with demands for expensive collaterals.*

- *Constraints with cost recovery due to Government regulation of fares, matched with expensive fuel prices and operational cost which makes cost recovery and debt servicing difficult.*

- *Besides the benefits are yet to be evaluated to determine its impact.*

On the way forward additional interventions could also include:

- *Provisions on Tax Incentives: This will minimise the cost of the vehicle importation and subsequent sales.*

- *Provision of Access to Bank Loans with flexible terms and conditions by ensuring that loans issued for the purchase of new vehicles are granted over longer repayment periods like 7 years as compared to the current shorter repayment period granted for 3 years with reasonable collateral requirements.*

- *Intensive education to local entrepreneurs and the unions about the obligations to the terms and conditions of such loan facilities*

C. Vehicle Building by Automobile Servicing Centres: *In addition to vehicle assembling and importation, in Ghana, there are mechanical industrial clusters in Ghana located at Suame Magazine (A suburb in Kumasi) and (Kokompe a suburb in Accra). According to Amerdome S. K. et al, (2013), these services have become necessary due to limited availability* *of formal vehicle servicing centres, lack of special equipment to handle technical problems in vehicle servicing and lack of knowledge of new skills and techniques.*

The centres engage in vehicle body building, hydraulic mechanics, chassis building, provision of machine tool shop operating, welding and casting services. Other automotive activities engaged at the centres include vehicle electronic component dealership, scrap dealership, tools dealership, blacksmithing, vulcanizing, auto electrical services, vehicles and vehicle accessories sales. Building of articulated trailers, truck buckets (cargo trucks), Tipper truck buckets, Fuel tankers and the production of automobile parts such as gears, shafts and bushes as well as vehicle alterations and vehicle modifications among other things are also undertaken.

Due to weak foundation in formal engineering the artisans adopt rudimentary engineering methods and techniques. The process is further made worse by the lack of documentations on technical processes for referencing and reproduction, Akayeti A. (2015). Thus, the activities of the automobile servicing centres are characterized by poor technical know-how and knowledge since training is by apprenticeship with trainers who are also limited in technical knowledge causing one level of poor knowledge to be passed on to the next mechanic.

D. Vehicle Modifications: These are classified as minor and complex as follows:

i. Minor modifications include changing of vehicle handles, roof racks, glass winding mechanisms, tyre type and aspect ratio, alarm systems, windscreen and lamp shields, seatbelts, radio and stereo systems, blinds and other internal screening systems (Queensland Transport, 2008). They do not reduce the structural strength of the vehicles, affect vehicle control and stability; affect the braking systems, does not cause nuisance to other drivers and does not contravene road traffic laws or safety.

ii. Complex modifications include engine upgrades, gearbox and rear axle changes, vehicle body modifications, steering and brake replacement. Others are additional axle or axle chassis extension, wheelbase alterations, increase in gross weight or mass, weight break modifications, change of vehicle types, engine changes and changing of steering position from left to right or vice versa.

In Ghana, varying vehicle modifications are made to original vehicle designs to meet specific needs by local vehicle technicians and artisans for both light and heavy vehicles. These include the following as presented in Box 5.1.

Box 5.1: Vehicle modifications undertaken in Ghana

- Conversion of cargo vehicles into passenger vehicles by installing fabricated seats, creating vehicle windows and glass fixing for Mercedes 207 and Sprinter buses.

- Conversion of petrol or diesel engines into Liquefied Petroleum Gas (LPG) engines to reduce operational cost of some commercial vehicles.

- Conversion of a cargo truck into a tipper truck.

- Changing of Automatic Transmission to Manual Transmission.

- Suspension system Alteration to lift the height of different vehicle types.

- Chassis Frame Alteration.

- Conversion of right hand drive vehicles to left hand drive vehicles.

- Addition of rear axles for trailers and rigid trucks to increase load carrying capacity.

- Fabrication of buckets to increase the load carrying capacity of trailers.

By regulation, in Ghana, complex vehicle modification requires approval from the DVLA. This is done by the submission of a formal request to the DVLA with the details of the owner's name, vehicle registration and chassis number as well as a physical inspection of the vehicle after the modification for certification for safe use by the DVLA. The essential elements of vehicle modifications in Ghana are as presented in Appendix 5.1.

iii. Safety Effects of Modifications: In Ghana, the best that is done is the level of road-worthiness of the vehicle after being modified irrespective of the extensive effects of vehicle modification as presented in Table 5.12

Table 5.12: Effects of Vehicle Modification on Safety

Modification defects	Description
Material defects	These include cracks, deformation, and corrosion associated with most of the materials
Overloading Effect on Engine	Where the vehicle weight limit has been exceeded, the engine does more work so as to produce enough power to move the vehicle.
Effect on Lighting	Finding the exact cables for the lighting systems to join to the existing one in order to meet the desired length could be difficult and sometimes impossible
Effect on Braking systems	The situation of the lighting system also goes for the braking system. But the alternative brake hoses used may not be able to withstand the required braking pressure and therefore may break when in operation
Effect on Load support system	An area of great importance where these modifications show an adverse effect on vehicle safety is in the load support system (leaf springs).
Chassis alteration	Modifications such as lengthening and increasing cargo truck capacity involve altering of the vehicle chassis which is against the law of vehicle modifications (section 2.6.1, Ghana Heavy Vehicle Construction and Use Guidelines).
Vehicle Ground clearance	The increase of the ground clearance of the modified vehicles to about 2.5-3 feet (762-914 millimetres) leads to an increase in the centre of gravity of the vehicle. A high centre of gravity is a possible cause of vehicles overturning while in operation.
Vehicle length	For trailer lengthening, the finished length is between 40 to 46 feet which violates the 36 specified by the DVLA. This makes it difficult for the vehicles to negotiate bends or move safely at roundabouts.
Loaded height of Vehicles	Load heights above the 5.4m stated by the DVLA leads to the vehicle falling on its sides when negotiating bends or the extra load may cause it rolling backwards when going up hills because many of the alternative braking systems cannot support the load.

Source: Akayeti A. (2015)

5.3 SAFE VEHICLE OPERATION

5.3.1 Statutory Conditions for Safe Vehicle Operation

As a general principle, the Government of Ghana (GoG) accepts certification and documentation vehicles by approval certificates for registration, road worthiness, ownership and insurance. granted by relevant authorities or contracting Parties such as PVTS discussed as follows:

A. Vehicle Registration: After a vehicle has been acquired it is required to be registered and insured before being put on the road and the process involves the following:

i. Proof of Vehicle Roadworthiness: In Ghana, the owner is expected to present the vehicle for a first-time inspection at the premises of the DVLA together with two copies of the vehicle's customs documents, two coloured recent passport photographs of the owner and an identification card. Where the application is done by a third party, there must be a power of attorney together with the passport photographs of the representative.

The inspection is based on the identification of vehicle defects such as cracks on the windscreen, worn out blades and tyres, faulty lighting systems and shock absorbers. Following the successful inspection of the vehicle with the required attachments at the DVLA premises, a registration stamp is then released subject to the payment of base or prescribed fee which varies by vehicle type. An E-roadworthy certificate with a quick response (QR) code which helps the MTTD personnel to authenticate the information and road worthiness of the vehicle is then released to the owner.

ii. Assignment of Number Plate: A form 'A' and a Vehicle Registration Certificate (VRC) is then released for completion and submission for approval following which a registration number is assigned and a number plate issued. Commercial vehicles are required to then obtain retro-reflective tapes.

B. Routine Road Worthy Certification for Vehicle Operation: *Routine Roadworthiness is the ability for a vehicle to be in a suitable condition for use on the road based on set standards.*

In Ghana, this is obtained by presenting the vehicle and expired road worthy certificate for inspection using a prescribed checklist by a registered PVT (See Table 5.13. Following a successful inspection, the vehicle owner is required to pay a fee for the release of a certificate in the form of a sticker required to be pasted on the windscreen of the front right corner of the vehicle. This is done at six month / one year intervals for commercial and private vehicle owners respectively. Roadworthy certificates are then issued to confirm the right of road use by the vehicle. Enforcement activities on the process are undertaken by the MTTD and the DVLA anytime at random intervals. Defaulting vehicle owners are liable to the law.

Table 5.13: Vehicle Inspection Elements

Sample Vehicle Inspection Components	Vehicle Parts Inspected in Ghana as per Section in LI 2120
-controls	62.Tyres
-displays	63.Brakes
-rear view mirrors	64.Engines
-the order of gear shifting	65.Lamps
-brake systems	66.Mirror, windscreen and glass
-headlights, brake lights, blinkers (turning	67.Materials for windscreen, windows and partitions
signals), backing lights, tyre standard	68.Windows and windscreen of a commercial vehicle
-tyre rim standard	69.Fire extinguisher and first aid kit
-safety glass for windows	70.Wheels and axles
-seatbelts and anchoring them correctly	71.Steering
-vehicle noise	72.Suspension
-smoke/gas emissions	73.Wings, fenders, mud guards, wheel or mud flaps
	74.Horns and Sirens
	75.Trailer
	76.Direction indicator
	77.Position of indicator
	78.Red reflector
	79.Fitting of retro-reflectors at the front and rear corners of a motor vehicle
	80.Fitting of retro-reflectors on the body of certain motor vehicles
	81.General requirements for retro-reflector
	82.Warning chevron sign on rear of certain motor vehicles
	83.Advance warning device

Source: LI2180, 2012

C. Acquisition of a Vehicle Insurance: *In Ghana, vehicle owners are required by the third-party insurance Act 195, to insure their vehicles before being used on the road in order to protect their liability to others and these include the following which determines the benefits that can be gained:*

i. Comprehensive Insurance: This covers all risks in addition to damaged vehicles such as theft, injury and death caused by a third party and natural factors such as floods and earthquakes.

ii. Third Party Insurance: This is the minimum motor insurance cover for the vehicle owner or another person driving the vehicle against death, injury, damage to property exclusive of the damage to the vehicle.

iii. Third Party Fire and Theft Policy: This is an extension of the third-party insurance which provides indemnity for loss or damage to the vehicle through fire or theft but does not include damage caused to the vehicle from collision and other crash types.

5.3.2 Statistics on Unsafe Vehicle Features Causing RTCs in Ghana

A. RTC Fatalities by of Vehicle Defects in Ghana: *Available statistics shows that the contribution of vehicle defects to passenger RTC fatalities is relatively minimal in Ghana. From Figure 5.2 records from 2001 to 2011 showed that about (13%) of RTCs were caused by vehicle defects in Ghana. These were made up of RTC's caused by faulty brakes in the lead at (4%), followed by tyres and steering defects at (3%) and (2%) respectively. Non-classified factors that contribute to RTCs was about (4%). Where motorcycles were concerned, only (5%) of motorcycle*

RTCs were attributed to mechanical failure. Of much concern is the unknown vehicle factors which contributed significantly to 87% RTCs. This implies that this proportion of factors are not accounted for or addressed in the design of countermeasures for vehicle related RTCs.

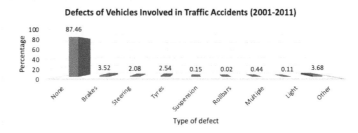

Figure 5.2: Defects of vehicles involved in traffic accidents (2001-2011)

i. RTC Fatalities by Types of Vehicle Defects in Ghana: An overview of the key risk factors for causing RTC that requires attention are as provided in the immediate sub-sections.

a). Poor Quality Vehicle Tyres: A study conducted in 2008 by the NRSA in Ghana established that (75%) of tyres imported into the country were in used condition with three out of every four tyres sold in Ghana being a used tyre and this increased the risk of RTC's by (30%). Fatal RTCs caused by faulty tyres was estimated at (3%) in 2017 and these were mostly attributed to tyre burst and blow outs from tyre pressure, overheating in the heat of the sun and worn-out tyres, (See Figure 5.3).

A policy on tyre standardization was therefore enacted under Regulation 62 of the Road Traffic Regulations of 2012, L.I 2180 followed by dealer engagements and sensitization as sampled below. The move sought to ban the use of substandard tyres in the country to ensure adherence as provided under the law.

Figure 5.3: Publications on Vehicle Tyres in Ghana

Another challenge has to do with the sale and use of expired tyres irrespective of existing legislation on it mostly due to enforcement challenges since it is impossible to record the year of manufacture of a high number of individual tyres at the port. Also, the importation of snow tyres into the country remains a challenge since tyre dealers are not able to differentiate between tyres suited to the weather conditions in the country and those that are not, (See Figure 5.4)

Figure 5.4: NRSA Engagements with Vulcanisers

b). Faulty Brakes: In Ghana, RTCs caused by a vehicle braking system is a challenge in the country and the examples presented in Figure 5.5 affirms the fact.

Figure 5.5: Examples of Publications on Vehicle Brakes

c) Poor Vehicle Lighting Systems: Challenges with poor vehicle lighting systems contributing to RTCs relates to aged bulbs with reduced illumination especially at night, missing light components with situations of a vehicle having only one headlight working. There are even situations where vehicles operate on the road with no light at all causing head-on collisions with other vehicles in some situations. Indeed, it is not even uncommon to see motorcycles without lights.

In recent times, the use of proscribed or additional lamps on vehicles is becoming popular though the use of such lamps contravenes Regulation 65 of the LI 2180 of 2012. It is required for two lamps to be used in front of a vehicle at a time though a maximum of four driving and sport or flood lamps are allowed on the vehicle. An example of the safety implications of this in Ghana is as presented in Figure 5.6.

Figure 5.6: Sample Publications on Vehicle Lighting

ii. Vehicle Factors Causing Pedestrian Crashes: It is intimated in literature that pedestrian crashes involving automatic vehicles with higher design speed levels has high possibility for deaths. Also, pedestrian crashes involving vehicles with bumpers (bulbar) have higher possibility for deaths. whilst vehicles with intelligent systems on the other hand are configured for better pedestrian detection and control mechanisms (T. S. Combs, 2019).

In Ghana, the use of bulbars is common because it is used as a protector against the destruction of the vehicle pumper in case of collision with another vehicle especially by those who use sub-urban vehicles (SUVs) and this has to be well investigated for appropriate laws to be effected.

iii. Other Vehicular Factors Contributing to RTCs in Ghana: Some of the diversified vehicle factors causing RTC's in Ghana as sampled in Figure 5.7.

Figure 5.7: A Sample publication on other Vehicle Factors

5.3.3 Vehicle Related RTCs by Vehicle Type

It has been revealed that some vehicle types are inherently riskier than others with regards to the possibility of death when an RTC occurs, (Padmanaban J. 2003), Studies conducted by the NRSA in Ghana in 2012 indicated that RTC fatalities caused by vehicle defects were most common amongst heavy goods vehicles at (59%). Mini buses follow at (22%) and large buses at (8%). Taxis and private cars were at equal proportion of (6%) each. This was mostly due to the fact that larger vehicles tend to be older due to higher cost of acquisition so majority of such vehicles in the system are old with high safety risk.

A. RTC Exposure by Defects on Heavy Goods Vehicles (HGVs): Heavy goods vehicles are defined as goods vehicles of over 3.5 tons maximum permissible gross weight.

They account for just a limited percentage of the vehicle fleet in the country. Their RTC involvement depends on a chain of complex interaction between the vehicle, the driver and the environment as a coordinated system.

In Ghana, generally RTC's involving heavy goods vehicles are mostly attributed to the following:

Overloading to reduce trip frequency. This is because an HGV in an overloaded state causes increased dimension and weight which in turn cause limited stability and deficient performance. They also cause overloading on the tyres and in situations of hot weather the tyres expand and easily burst under the weight of the load to cause RTCs.

Drivers with overloaded vehicles also often turn to occupy the centre of the road to ensure a stability and balance to prevent tipping to one side of the road when in motion. This displaces other vehicles which often results in RTC situations especially when an oncoming vehicle attempts to overtake such a vehicle with a high speed, (See Figure 5.8). The operational aspects involve the driver's limited ability to respond and change course in good time when overtaking another vehicle faced with an oncoming vehicle moving at a top speed.

Figure 5.8: Examples of Overloaded Vehicles in Ghana

i.   *Heavy goods vehicles are also known for the inability to effectively negotiate horizontal curves and other design features of roads which present safety hazards for drivers.*

ii. *Other vehicles overtaking by meandering between different HGVs moving in a file causes the need for emergency breaks by HGVs also causes RTC's especially in descends.*

iii. *HGV have high potential for fatalities when they hit someone or collide with a smaller vehicle. They also have bigger blind spots, so drivers are more likely to fail to see vulnerable road users, particularly children who are smaller and harder to spot.*

iv. *High operational and maintenance costs due to high costs of spare parts result in poor maintenance regimes or neglected maintenance which in turn causes serious mechanical failures resulting in RTC's. Examples of typical defects of truck parts are as presented in Table 5.14.*

Table 5.14: Typical defects of truck parts compiled from Diverse Literature Sources

Vehicle part	Defect
Wheels and Hubs	Fractured wheels, worn out wheel hubs, wheel stud holes elongated and damaged, wheel nuts missing, wheel seriously distorted or worn, incompatible wheels fitted etc. causing detachment
Tyre	Tyre retaining ring fractured or not fitted properly or tyres of different types and sizes fitted on an axle, tyres bulging or tread lifting, tyre fabric deep cut or damaged, tyre seriously under inflated, or worn out beyond legal limit, Expired tyres causing blowing out of tyres due to high temperatures and overloading
Vehicle to Trailer Coupling	Deformed, damaged or cracked pin, jaw, hook or ball, missing locking device or ill-fitting etc. causing adverse security of attached trailer with likely failure or detachment
Additional axle and wheel attachment	Insecure wheel attachment to chassis mostly due to modifications with weak security spring
Brake operation and performance	Parking brake not operating on some wheels; inability to set brake with trailers from the drawing vehicles; excessively worn-out brake mechanism causing inoperable or brake failures Insufficient reserve travel on brake lever Trailer Emergency Brake not working due to disconnected brake line
Insecure load,	Poor condition of securing equipment and unsuitable vehicle for load
Driving Mirrors	Drivers interior rear view and side mirrors missing, defective or insecure mirror
Poor Engine Performance	Excessive exhaust emission blinding other drivers
Clutch	Clutch slippage from overloading
Chassis	Rusted chassis causing truck derailment

B. RTC Exposure by Mini Bus Defects: *The mini bus industry is the most predominant of the public transport sector in Ghana because it is the most available mode used for different service types ranging from intracity buses (trotros), intercity buses, tourist coaches, hired buses, workers' buses, school buses, etc. Also, it is the most affordable to the public, making it highly patronised. Buses and mini buses are often significant contributors to RTC because of a number of factors including:*

i.   *Modification of goods vehicles into passenger vehicles using wrong materials such as hard iron instead of steel.*

ii. *Poor maintenance regimes causing poor lighting, worn out tyres, overheating from non-functional radiator fan, inadequate amount of coolant etc. Some of the key vehicle defects related to the buses which causes RTC's are as follows in Table 5.15.*

Table 5.15: Typical defects of bus parts compiled from Literature

Vehicle part	Defect
Tyres	Poor quality, worn out tyres with uneven treading and bulging; lost treading or overinflated second hand tyres which causes sudden bursting pressure and are easily punctured by debris on the road or easily gets blown outs or compromises tyre grips causing RTCs especially in severe temperature
Brakes	Worn brakes which causes slips and skidding with non-responsive or more braking distance
Lights	Non-functioning headlights, taillights and turning lights resulting in low visibility conditions such as night time, foggy roads or during stormy rains making it hard for other vehicles to see another and which directly influence the control over and safety aspects of vehicles and contribute to crashes.
Low Standard Repair shops	Patronage of substandard repair shops.
Shocks	Worn shock absorbers, defective
Wipers	Defective windshield and wipers which cause reduced visibility during rainy conditions and malfunctioning motors controlling wipers.
Engine Overheating	Problems with cooling system such as leakages, faulty radiator fan, and broken water pump etc.

**Ban Sprinter buses from embarking on long journeys —
Police Cdr.**

C. RTC Caused by Saloon Car Defects: *Whereas, private car owners have more emotional attachment and are maintenance conscious, commercial taxi operators with work and pay arrangements turn to be more cost conscious and this encourages them to take higher risks at higher speeds for increased trip frequencies as well as engagement in poor maintenance regimes as with the bus service which contributes to higher crash rates.*

D. Effects of RTCs by Motorcycles: It is estimated that users of motorcycles are 9 times more likely to crash and 17 times more likely to cause death in a crash, than users of other vehicles according to studies by (Hussain et al. 2005). He also intimated that most operational motorcycles in developing countries are small and medium-sized with engine sizes 150 c.c.

This creates challenges of stability and handling characteristics of the motorcycles since the control skills needed for them are more demanding than for vehicles especially in emergency situations. Another challenge with the size of the motorcycle has to do with limited visibility of motorcyclist to other drivers. Other motorcycle fatality causative factors include the following Table 5.16.

Table 5.16: Motorcycle fatality causative factors

Challenge	Description
Lack of Protection	-The lack of outer protection for motorcyclists unlike that of vehicles causes victims to get into direct contact with either the hard road surface or the crash objects due to impact absorption capacity.
Size	-Depending on an object, a fatality can result when a motorcyclist crashes into it. For example, when motorcycle riders get into head on collisions with another vehicle, they often result in fatalities because of the small size.
Power to weight Ratio	-Motorcycles also tend to have higher power-to-weight ratios than cars and an increasing number of motorcycles are capable of very high speeds and acceleration. -Being a single-track vehicle, a motorcycle can easily become unstable and capsize when braking, accelerating or on a slippery road surface because the wheel loses adhesion. This is critical when a motorcyclist is taking a bend.
Braking	-Braking can also cause a motorcycle to change its line on a bend. Such characteristics make motorcyclists particularly vulnerable if they take bends too fast to be able to stop in the distance, they see to be clear.
Wheel Locks	-The need to avoid wheel locks means that riders may find it difficult to use the brakes in an emergency situation (Elliott et al., 2003). -Some motorcycle crashes occur when a driver opens the door of their parked vehicle in the path of an oncoming motorcycle.

5.3.4 Vehicle Maintenance

Vehicle maintenance is an important component of safe vehicle performance and so it is a prerequisite to keep vehicles in safe operating condition. According to Ribbens H. et al, (1992), the most effective vehicle safety control is preventive maintenance. *Aspects of poor vehicular maintenance issues in Ghana are presented as follows:*

A. Poor Vehicle Maintenance Culture in Ghana: *There are no consistent scheduled vehicle maintenance regimes and reactive rather than proactive maintenance is practiced* with mechanical defects being ignored till they reach the state of almost grounding the vehicle. This applies even to simple routine maintenance activities such as oil/filter changes, lubrication, tightening belts and components, engine tune-ups, trace work, tyre rotation, brake checks, tyre checks, hose inspection/replacement and radiator maintenance are concerned.

B. Operational Economy: *Due to the high demand for profit making, commercial road transport operators in Ghana utilize their vehicles extensively with extensive wear and tear with little concern for safety.*

C. Use of Sub-Standard Garages: *The use of the services of sub-standard garages for vehicle maintenance also causes vehicles not to be well maintained for effective corrective measure with serious vehicle safety consequences.*

D. Use of Unsafe Vehicle Parts: *As mentioned earlier, due to the importation of aged vehicles of different types and models the use of cheap sub-standard vehicle spare parts such those locally manufactured by mechanical technicians at cheaper costs but with very little durability create high safety risk. Also, the practice of the use of different vehicle parts from different vehicle models on different vehicles e.g. using a Nissan part on a Toyota vehicle or a Toyota part of another model on another Toyota vehicle of a different design characteristics creates safety challenges.*

For example, on October 2, 2006, a letter was issued by Toyota Ghana Company Limited (TGCL) through "The Daily Graphic" to the general public to educate the public on the dangers and additional expenses that could be incurred when going for unauthorized parts not meant for their geographical location in carrying out these modifications.

E. Conversion of Vehicle for Different Use than Original Design: *The conversion of a vehicle into an unintended use such as the use of a cargo truck as a tipper truck for carting gravel in the construction business instead of buying a tipper truck also possess maintenance and safety challenges.*

F. Vehicle End-of-Life Recycling: It is said that vehicle importing countries have an opportunity to introduce small-scale end-of-life recycling technology and capability for used vehicles and their components.

Current, end of life process for vehicles in Ghana mostly involves resale of old dilapidated vehicles for use in rural areas. Another factor involves processing of unusable vehicle parts into scrap through the use of smelting plants. Records of vehicles whose life service have come to an end does not exist. There are no official mechanisms for taking out a vehicle that is no longer in use. Owners just abandon them at home or at mechanical shops without notification on the non-use of its number plate and this sometimes provides an avenue for theft and other criminal activities. There is need to set mechanisms for writing off vehicles that are no longer in use with effective enforcement.

5.4 VEHICLE CRASH FATALITY RECORDS IN GHANA

5.4.1 Contribution of Vehicular Factors to RTC Statistics in Ghana

Generally, the actual contribution of vehicular factors to RTC is difficult to establish because only visible mechanical failures causing RTCs are easily established. Others that are not visible are not easily determined. Thus, the perception that vehicle factors contribute less to RTCs in the country cannot be scientifically substantiated. On the way forward it is suggested that a study on the factors such as model, common defects, size, age etc. within the vehicle fleet in the country that could predisposed a vehicle to an RTC should be conducted and compared with those that actually result in RTCs so as to establish the risk level.

A. Frequency of Travel by Vehicle Type: *In Ghana, cars have the highest of daily travels at (9%) and this can be attributed to higher private car ownership compared with commercial vehicles due to affordability. Large buses are the most patronized modes by passengers with 4-6 times travel frequency in a week. This is because it is mostly used for both long and short distance travel as well as for both intercity and intra-city travel. Trucks have the highest of those with 1-3 times travel frequency in a week due to load carriage which is less frequent than passenger carriage (see Figure 5.9).*

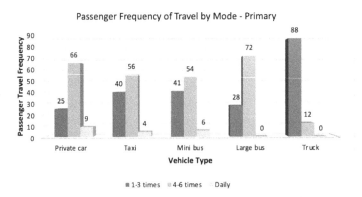

Figure 5.9: Passenger frequency of travel by mode – Primary

B. RTC Fatalities by Vehicle Type: *In 2012 the vehicle class with high exposure to RTCs were Buses and Minibuses at (38%), followed by cars at (28%) with Heavy goods vehicles* *being at (26%), (see Figure 5.10). This is because of the high passenger carriage capacity of buses compared the other vehicle types.*

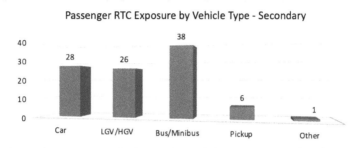

Figure 5.10: Passenger RTC exposure by vehicle type – secondary

C. RTC by Vehicle Type by Sex: *From a study in 2019 by the NRSA, more (61.0%) of females suffered from RTC fatalities from the use of buses compared to males. (Figure 5.11 presents the details). This is because buses are mostly used for commercial operations and more females are only able to afford such services compared to males who turns to higher levels of private vehicle ownership due to higher affordability levels.*

Also, females engage more in trading activities with higher travel frequencies for such purposes making them more susceptible to RTC's involving buses. However, males have more (25.5%) RTC fatalities from the use of Light/Heavy goods vehicles since these are vehicles used for the carriage of goods with the operations mostly done by males.

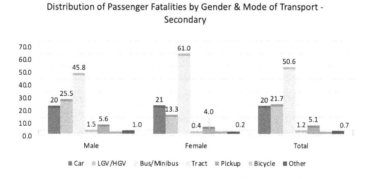

Figure 5.11: Passenger fatalities by gender and mode of transport – secondary

D. Location of RTC by Vehicle Type: *According to a study by BRRI in 2018, RTCs involving cars occurred mostly at crossroads at (35.5%); those involving buses occurred mostly at non – junctions (39.5%) and those involving Heavy goods vehicles mostly occurred at roundabouts (39.5%). The reasons are as summarized for each vehicle type in Table 5.17.*

Table 5.17: Reasons for Fatalities by Location Type & Vehicle Type

Fatalities by Location Type & Cars	Fatalities by Location Type & Buses	Fatalities by Location Type & HGV's
lack of understanding of shared space at junctions among road users if not signalized, stemming from the following factors contribute to the high involvement of cars in RTCs at junctions: -This is due to the difficulty of deciding who has the right-of-way at intersections especially when traffic signals are out of work and there is need to determine who needs to yield to whom. -Driver's blatantly ignoring traffic-control devices and putting both the driver and others at risk. -Not preparing to stop when approaching a light that's been green for a while, should the light change suddenly. -Lack of understanding that the yellow lights mean the driver must be preparing to stop unless it's unsafe to do so or the driver has already crossed the stop marking. -Failing to yield at intersections where a number of road users need to cross paths and share space. -Lack of alertness at intersections -Running through red lights -Assumption that the other driver will stop or slow down	-Not driving in the correct lane ahead of junctions on dual carriage ways e.g., a driver seeking to make a left turn or U-turn at a junction of a multi-lane dual carriage road while driving in the outer lane. This is typical to trotro drivers -A driver on the main road assuming he has the right of way and so not slowing down to the possibility of a crossing vehicle at unsignalised junctions e.g., trotros -Impatience and anxiety to do a quick turn therefore making reckless U-turns -Accelerating fast to merge with oncoming stream within a very limited gap which can result in the swerving by the other vehicle into another's lane -Misjudgement of the movement of other drivers especially abrupt stops by commercial vehicles within the driving lane to pick passengers -Disregard for traffic control devices especially jumping the red light	-Negotiating round-abouts with unstable overloaded heavy loads not adequately secured -Longer braking distance due to overloading especially when crossed by other vehicles on a descent. -Inefficient braking system due to vehicle modifications such as increased weight resulting from the addition of extra axles -Frequent tyre burst due to overloading and overheating

E. RTC by Collision Type by Vehicle Type: *A patient survey by the NRSA in 2019 indicated that the mode of vehicle with the highest exposure to passenger RTCs and consequent fatalities are buses at 72%. This is due to the fact that buses are relatively high occupancy vehicles with predominant use for both long and short distance travel including intercity and intra-city travel.*

Thus, in situations of RTCs, more people suffer casualties and fatalities at a go compared to low occupancy vehicles. This is followed by private cars at 18% and taxis at 10%. Minibuses have the highest fatalities resulting from sideswipe at (50%), Cars have the highest collision at right angle at (45.2%), heavy goods vehicle mostly have fatalities by different collision types at (44.5%). This implies that HGVs have higher levels of diverse collision types compared to other modes of road transport, (BRRI, 2018). Some good passenger crash protectors that vehicles are required to offer from literature include the summary in Table 5.18.

Table 5.18: Summary of Vehicle Crash Protection Features

Crash Protection Features	Crash protection features provide greater levels of injury protection to drivers and passengers in car crashes, they include
Crumple zones	Modern cars protect drivers and passengers in frontal, rear and offset crashes by using crumple zones to absorb crash energy. This means that the car absorbs the impact of the crash, not the driver or passengers.
Strong occupant compartment	The cabin of the car should keep its shape in frontal crashes to protect the driver and passenger's space. The steering column, dashboard, roof pillars, pedals and floor panels should not be pushed excessively inwards, where they are more likely to injure drivers and passengers. Doors should remain closed during a crash and should be able to be opened afterwards to assist in quick rescue, while strong roof pillars can provide extra protection in rollover crashes.

Crash Protection Features	Crash protection features provide greater levels of injury protection to drivers and passengers in car crashes, they include
Side impact protection	Increased side door strength, internal padding and better seats can improve protection in side impact crashes. Most new cars have side intrusion beams or other protection within the door structure. Some cars also have padding on the inside door panels. Increasingly, car manufacturers are installing side airbags that provide protection from severe injury. Head-protecting side airbags, such as curtain airbags, are highly effective in side impact and rollover crashes.
Seat belts	A properly worn seat belt provides good protection but does not always prevent injuries. Three-point lap/sash seat belts offer superior protection to two-point seat belts and should be installed in all seating positions. Recent improvements to seat belt effectiveness include: webbing clamps that stop more seat belt reeling out as it tightens on the spool pretensioners that pull the seat belt tight before the occupant starts to move load limiters that manage the forces applied to the body in a crash seat belt warning systems to remind you if seat belts have not been fastened
Airbags	Airbags are designed to supplement the protection provided by seat belts - they are not a substitute. The best protection in frontal crashes is achieved using a properly worn seat belt in combination with an airbag
Head rests	Head rests are important safety features and should be fitted to all seats - front and back. Head rest position is critical for preventing whiplash in rear impact crashes. Whiplash is caused by the head extending backward from the torso in the initial stage of rear impact, then being thrown forward. To prevent whiplash the head rest should be at least as high as the head's centre of gravity (eye level and higher) and as close to the back of the head as possible.

Source: http://www.howsafeisyourcar.com.au/Safety-Features/Crash-Protection-Features/

F. Vehicle Related RTC Crashes Statistics for Pedestrians: *The frequency of collision between pedestrians and cars are of a higher magnitude compared with other vehicle types at (47%), followed by bus and mini buses at (26%). Motorcycle and pedestrian crashes constitute the third highest pedestrian fatality rate by vehicle type at (10%) followed by light and heavy goods vehicles at (9%). Pick-ups, bicycles/tricycles as well as others are at (5%), (1.1%) and (2%) respectively (see Figure 5.12). The predominance of car involvement in pedestrian fatality is due to it being the vehicle class with the highest volume in the country.*

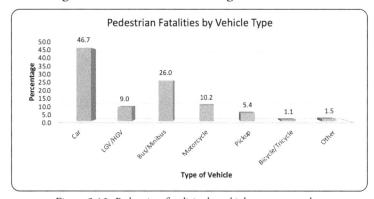

Figure 5.12: Pedestrian fatalities by vehicle type – secondary

5.4.2 Motorcycle Related RTC Crash Statistics

A. Age of Motorcycles: *Unlike automobiles, most 94% motorcycles are bought in brand new state. This is because of high affordability levels. A study in 2019 by the NRSA revealed* *that about 43%) of motorcycles studied were less than a year old and 43% were about a year with only about 4% being 2years old as presented in Figure 5.13.*

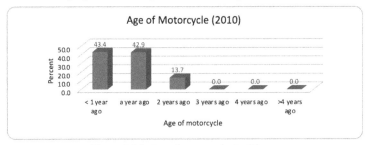

Figure 5.13: Age of motorcycles in Ghana

B. Types of Motorcycles Used in Ghana: *A sample of the range of motorcycles models mostly in use in Ghana especially those used for commercial operations include those presented in Figure 5.14 and the technical specifications as presented in Table 5.19.*

Table 5.19: Technical Specifications of Brands of Motor Cycles Used

Brands of Motor Cycles and their Basic Technical Specifications				
	Royal (150)	Royal (125)	Mitsuzu (125)	Honda (125)
Engine Capacity	150 cc	125cc	125cc	125cc
Engine Type	Petrol	Petrol	Petrol	Petrol
Tyre size (Front)	2.75x18	2.75x18	2.75x18	2.75x18
Tyre size (Rear)	3.00x18	3.00x18	3.00x18	3.00x18
Rated Seating Capacity	2	2	2	2

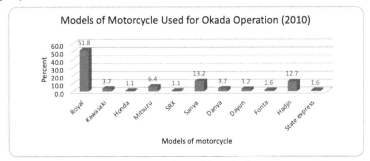

Figure 5.14: Models of motorcycles used for Okada operation in Ghana

C. RTC by Collision Type Involving Motorcycles: Generally, RTC by collision type involving motorcycles can be attributed to lack of conspicuity and motorcycle defects.

5.5. VEHICLE SAFETY INTERVENTIONS IMPLEMENTED IN GHANA

5.5.1 Vehicle Safety Activities Defined in Strategic Action Plans

Some key interventions on vehicle safety implemented in Ghana under the various road safety strategies include those listed in Table 5.20.

Table 5.20: Strategies for Vehicle Safety Investment

Theme	NRSS I	NRSS II	NRSS III
Safer Vehicles	• Vehicle testing methods improved by Oct. 2004	• A campaign on best practices in commercial vehicle conversion/ reconstruction, registration and maintenance developed and implemented in 2008 and an evaluation of the campaign carried out in 2009 • All DVLA technical staff across the country trained in refined procedures for testing commercial vehicle drivers by 2009 • Private garages licensed to undertake vehicle inspection and testing across the country	• Set and enforce Standards and Specifications for the importation and assembly of vehicles • Review existing legislation on Vehicle Modification and Conversion to ensure safe operation of such vehicles • Enforce laws and regulations on the use of unauthorized vehicles for commercial purposes • License Entities to engage in the modification of vehicles • Improve the capacity of the DVLA to enforce compliance with regulations on vehicle testing • Equip DVLA Staff for effective monitoring of performance of Private Garages

5.6 SAFE VEHICLE TECHNOLOGIES AND OPERATIONS

5.6.1 Emergence of Vehicle Safety Technologies

Over time, diverse safety related vehicle devices have emerged on the global vehicle market and its advancement is also still in progress. Such modern vehicle technologies are much safer and mostly ensure that vehicle occupants or other road users are much more protected compared with older vehicle models.

The Brasilia Declaration of the 2nd Global High-Level Conference on Road Safety recommends for all new motor vehicles to meet minimum occupant and other road users' protection, with regards to seat belts, air bags and other active safety systems such as anti-lock braking system (ABS) and electronic stability control (ESC) systems. This recommendation is a part of the Pre-Verification of Conformity (PVOC) that is a requirement before export in most countries.

It is also recommended that Vehicle identifiers (Chassis number and engine number) are not tampered with so as to ensure that lifetime and long-term warranty aspects of the vehicle will not be voided. Verification of the identifiers may also be included as part of the PVOC. This makes the importation of crash vehicle a key non- compliant issue in the world of vehicle safety.

A. Types of Intelligent Transport Safety Technology (ITST) for Cars and Motorcycles: From the (ssatp.org/ssatp/files/publications/Toolkits), ITS's are grouped as Automatic Vehicle Location, Drivers Console, Operations Control Centre, Driver Monitoring, Vehicle Systems Monitoring, In-vehicle Data Hub, and processor, Electronic Fare Collection, Travel Information Displays, Surveillance Equipment, Vehicle Identification and Communications.

For safety purposes these are also classified as (i) ITST which reduce the consequence of crashes, (ii) ITST which affect exposure to crash risk, (iii) ITST Technologies for High-Risk and vulnerable Road users eg, young novice drivers, pedestrians, older drivers, cyclists, motorcyclists and (iv), cultural minority groups such as children and the disabled. Examples of Minimum Global Vehicle Safety Devices are summarised in Table 5.21.

Table 5.21: Advance Vehicle Safety Technologies

Advanced Driver Assistance Systems: Advanced driver assistance systems (ADAS) are one of the emerging automotive markets, driven by a wide public and industrial interest in improved safety and comfort. Applications like lane departure warning, automatic cruise control, parking aids or night vision have already been introduced (Techmer, 2007).	**Monitoring Driver Vigilance; drowsiness, fatigue and inattention:** The detection of driver visual attention is very important for developing automatic systems that monitor the driver inattention, driver fatigue, and lack of sleep: a great number of fatalities occurring in motor vehicles could be avoided if these behaviours were detected and alarm signals were provided to the driver (D'Orazio et al, 2004). e.g; -in-vehicle driver impairment systems
Collision Warning and Avoidance System: Collision Warning System tries to detect any collision risk between two vehicles by means of radar and internal-vehicular sensor information. If the system detects collision risk, it will warn the driver so that a possible crash can be avoided (Ararat et al., 2006). E.g., -in-vehicle forward collision warning with headway feedback -incident management systems	**Visibility Enhancing System:** Advanced lighting systems serve the safety issue of conspicuity of motorcycles to other road users and provide better illumination of the road environment for motorcycle riders (Bayly et al., 2007). While, adaptive headlights ensure that the illumination from the headlight is projected on the intended path of the motorcycle when cornering. The position of the headlight is adjusted in accordance with the speed and position of the bike, so that it maintains a horizontal axis that is parallel with the road surface. E.g., -vision enhancement systems
Lane Detection and Lane-Change Warning System: Systems that monitor the vehicles position within the lane have been developed for cars and commercial vehicles. The position of the vehicle in the lane is monitored with laser, radar or video monitoring of the lane edge markings ahead and to the side of the vehicle. The system either provides warnings or actively supports the driver by altering the course of the vehicle if its position deviates from the lane. The relevance of these systems to motorcycles is debatable (Bayly et al., 2006). E.g., -lane departure warning systems -lane change collision warning systems,	**Seat Belt and Helmet Reminder System:** The intelligent seat belt reminder system is a device that detect occupants and their seat belt use in all seating positions, and then create a series of increasingly annoying visual and auditory alarms associated with vehicle speed or time to encourage seat belt use (Harrison and Senserrick, 2000).
Intelligent Speed Adaptation (ISA): Intelligent Speed Adaptation is a generic term for a class of ITS in which the driver is warned and/or vehicle speed is automatically limited when the driver is, intentionally or inadvertently, travelling over the posted speed limit for a given location. Specifically, ISA systems compare the current speed and position of the vehicle with the local posted speed limit and respond if the vehicle exceeds this posted limit (Young and Regan, 2002). Examples are; -in-vehicle speed alerting and limiting systems	**Partially automated driving systems:** This is where drivers can remove their hands from the steering wheel for periods of time. In addition, ICT companies, such as Waymo (currently worth 175 billion USD, are continuously improving the software of their automated vehicles.
crash data records	Anti-Locking Braking System (ABS) Pre-crash warning alerts & Autonomous emergency braking (AEB) Emergency breaks
Electronic Stability Control/Program (ESC/ESP)	Lane-keeping assist & cruise control
Crumple zones	Head restraints
Reverse camera	Automatic Parking Technology
Shatter-resistant glass	Continuous Variable Transmission (CVT) Technology
Indicators, mirrors & blind spot monitoring	517 Smart Car Gadget Technology
Lights & wipers	
Source: https://www.budgetdirect.com.au/blog/car-safety-features-in-modern-cars.html	

In Ghana in addition to the few new vehicles imported into the country with limited ITST's the DVLA plans for the retrofitting of seatbelts in the existing vehicle fleet as well as speed limiters and tachographs. (See Figure 5.15).

Figure 5.15: Publication on Installation of Speed Limiters in Vehicle

It is said that, the future outlook of vehicle safety technologies will advance to the level of significant reduction in crash statistics. This will be even more productive since, the potential value of developing an integrated approach to vehicle safety, linking preventive, crash protection and post-crash approaches into cooperative systems for drivers, passengers and vulnerable road users as well as vehicle and road network safety systems is being increasingly promoted, (DaCoTA, 2013). Also, there are monitoring mechanisms to encourage increasing development of new vehicle technologies with significant potential to further improve crash protection.

B. Dissemination and Uptake of New Technologies:

i. Dissemination of ITS: There is a call for a universal deployment of crash avoidance technologies with proven effectiveness in both the well-developed markets and emerging ones. Minimum vehicle safety standards are also encouraged to be set for all new vehicles sold in a territory based on occupant Injury classification (OIC) as set by the National Accident Sampling System (NASS), (www.oica.net/category/safety). This is also expected to be based on the exact needs of a population suitable to address the real problem in a given territory. In addition, it is to include the requirements of the safe system approach by reducing opportunity for human error with all vehicles being regulated in the same way everywhere in the world in order to see a benefit in road safety.

However, the feasibility of this being achieved in developing countries such as Ghana is not foreseen in the immediate future.

ii. Uptake of ITST: Generally, countries are encouraged to advance the use of these technologies through, consumer information schemes and incentives to accelerate the uptake of new technologies. It is also recommended to stimulate fleet owners to increase the demand for such vehicles. However, until recently, road safety had been an incidental by product of ITS development rather than the central issue guiding the design of systems due to technological motivation (monash.edu/muarc/archive/our-publications/other/rac0101).

Due to this, it is difficult to come to a definitive conclusion about whether a given ITS application will or will not enhance safety. Also, technologies have not been deployed on a large scale over a long enough time in traffic for the crash numbers to be a reliable indicator of a change in vehicle safety technology. Again, it is said that, they require further refinement and training before a more precise estimate of their potential to reduce crashes across the transport system can be certified.

It is also projected that it may take at least six decades before fully automated cars can drive safely on all public roads with the driver entirely removed from the control loop. There is a possibility that automated vehicles will share roads with road users as the uptake of automated vehicles will happen gradually. This will likely be characterised with potential safety consequences.

The situation in Ghana, presents a different challenge with regards to the use of in-vehicle ITS systems. This is because only a few vehicles bought in a brand-new state may have such technologies and it is not possible to retrofit all the huge fleet of old vehicles with all the essential safety technologies especially the new ones that are coming up. The level of availability of such vehicle safety in the current fleet of vehicles and the extent to which they contribute to the reduction of RTCs in the country is not known.

There is need, therefore for analytical studies into the type and level of distribution of in-vehicle ITS across the entire vehicle fleet in the country, in order to identify the limitations associated with their availability, the constraints posed by the mix of the different ITS technologies in some few vehicles and how best this challenge can be addressed. Specifically, options for some standard cost-effective measures which are compatible with the state of Ghana's development should be explored especially those that can be conveniently retrofitted into existing vehicles. Other aspects should be on how best the use of the existing ITS measures can be maximized in the country.

The feasibility of application of vehicle safety standardisation on the way forward will also have to be researched and regulatory requirements for ITS systems must be established in the form of in-vehicle safety guidelines for Ghana.

C. Benefits of Vehicle Technologies: These provide features such as better crash impact absorption, crash management capabilities, improved occupant protection systems and driver support and assistance systems. Further development expected to be advanced overtime include improvements in vehicle safety design and equipment for pedestrians and motorcyclists over the next decade. Research has also identified large scope for enhancing vehicle safety further although the increasing variety in the vehicle fleet is expected to bring new challenges over the next decade.

In line with this, all motor manufacturers are encouraged to apply these as much as possible to ensure the safety of their use. Some of the vehicle safety features that are said to have improved greatly include braking stability and lighting systems which have been improved by a mixture of technical evolution and advanced technologies that can significantly reduce the risk of crash occurrence, as well as offer greater protection from RTC injury situations.

5.7 CONCLUSION

Ghana challenge with vehicle technologies is the ability to keep pace of advancement. The reason is that Ghana is more of a user country and affordability is also limited by the predominant use of second-hand vehicles. The country lacks the ability to facilitate increased use of new vehicle fleets with assured safety installations. Mechanisms for retrofitting safety measures in old vehicles does not lend to easy implementation due to limited technical knowledge to do so at the local level. From this, it can be deduced that the country will continue to be populated with old vehicle fleets with limited or no safety installations. The new vehicle assembly plants must be encouraged meet safety compliance with training for their use especially for local mechanics.

Appendix 5.1: Vehicle Standards Specification in Ghana by Set Categories

Vehicle Categories	Relevant documents
Category M1 These are passenger vehicles that have at least for wheels and a seating capacity of not more than eight passengers in addition to the driver.	1. **GS 4003** Uniform provisions concerning the approval of retro-reflecting devices for power-driven vehicles and their trailers (UNECE 03R02 Rev. 3 – 31 May 2005, IDT) 2. **GS 4004** Uniform provisions concerning the approval of devices for the illumination of rear registration plates of power-driven vehicles and their trailers (UNECE 04R00 Rev. 3 – 19 August 2013, IDT) 3. **GS 4006** Uniform provisions concerning the approval of direction indicators for power-driven vehicles and their trailers (UNECE 06R01 Rev. 5 – 7 October 2011, IDT) 4. **GS 4007** Uniform provisions concerning the approval of front and rear position lamps, stop-lamps and end-outline marker lamps for motor vehicles (except motor cycles) and their trailers (UNECE 07R02 Rev. 5 – 30 June 2010, IDT) 5. **GS 4012** Uniform provisions concerning the approval of vehicles with regard to the protection of the driver against the steering mechanism in the event of impact (UNECE 12R04 Rev. 4 – 10 October 2012, IDT) 6. **GS 4013** Uniform provisions concerning the approval of vehicles of categories m, n and o with regard to braking (UNECE 13R08 Rev. 3 – 3 October 1996, IDT) 7. **GS 4013H** Uniform provisions concerning the approval of passenger cars with regard to braking (UNECE Regulation 13HR00 Rev. 1 – 17 January 2008, IDT) 8. **GS 4014** Uniform provisions concerning the approval of vehicles with regard to safety-belt anchorages, isofix anchorages systems and isofix top tether anchorages (UNECE 14R05 Rev. 3 – 23 May 2003, 9. **4017** Uniform provisions concerning the approval of vehicles with regard to the seats, their anchorages and any head restraints (UNECE 17R04 Rev. 3 – 20 March 1990, IDT) 10. **GS 4023** Uniform provisions concerning the approval of reversing lamps for power-driven vehicles and their trailers (UNECE 23R00 Rev. 3 – 19 September 2008, IDT) 11. **GS 4028** Uniform provisions concerning the approval of audible warning devices and of motor vehicles with regard to their audible signals (UNECE 28R00 Amend. 5 – 7 February 2018, IDT) 12. **GS 4030** Uniform provisions concerning the approval of pneumatic tyres for motor vehicles and their trailers (UNECE 30R02 Rev. 3 – 29 March 2007, IDT) 13. **GS 4039** Uniform provisions concerning the approval of vehicles with regard to the speedometer equipment including its installation (UNECE 39R00 Rev. 1 - 7 February 2003, IDT) 14. **GS 4043** Uniform provisions concerning the approval of safety glazing materials and their installation on vehicles (UNECE 43R00 Rev. 02 – 11 February 2004, IDT) 15. **GS 4046** Uniform provisions concerning the approval of devices for indirect vision and of motor vehicles with regard to the installation of these devices (UNECE 46R02 Rev. 2 – 29 November 2005, IDT) 16. **GS 4048** Uniform provisions concerning the approval of vehicles with regard to the installation of lighting and light-signalling devices (UNECE 48R04 Rev. 6 – 14 June 2010, IDT) 17. **GS 4051** Uniform provisions concerning the approval of motor vehicles having at least four wheels with regard to their noise emissions (UNECE 51R02 Rev. 2 -29 November 2011, IDT) 18. **GS 4054** Uniform provisions concerning the approval of pneumatic tyres for commercial vehicles and their trailers (UNECE 54R00 Rev. 2 – 16 April 2004, IDT) 19. **GS 4083** Uniform provisions concerning the approval of vehicles with regard to the emission of pollutants according to engine fuel requirements (UNECE 83R02 Rev. 1 -19 July 1995, IDT) 20. **GS 4090** Uniform provisions concerning the approval of replacement brake lining assemblies, drum brake linings and discs and drums for power-driven vehicles and their trailers (UNECE 90R02 Rev. 3 – 17 February 2012, IDT) 21. **GS 4112** Uniform provisions concerning the approval of motor vehicle headlamps emitting an asymmetrical passing beam or a driving beam or both and equipped with filament lamps and/or light-emitting diode (led) modules (UNECE 112R00 Rev. 2 – 22 September 2010, IDT) 22. **GS 4016** Uniform provisions concerning the approval of: I. Safety-belts, restraint systems, child restraint systems and ISOFIX child restraint systems for occupants of power-driven vehicles II. Vehicles equipped with safety-belts, safety-belt reminder, restraint systems, child restraint systems and ISOFIX child restraint systems (UNECE 16R04 Rev. 4 – 11 August 2000, IDT)

Vehicle Categories	Relevant documents
Category M2 These are vehicles with a seating capacity of more than eight passengers in addition to the driver and have a maximum mass not exceeding 3.5 tonnes	1. **GS 4048:2019**, *Uniform provisions concerning the approval of vehicles with regard to the installation of lighting and light-signalling devices.* 2. **GS 4046:2019**, *Uniform provisions concerning the approval of devices for indirect vision and of motor vehicles with regard to the installation of these devices.* 3. **GS 4043:2019**, *Uniform provisions concerning the approval of safety glazing materials and their installation on vehicles.* 4. **GS 4013:2019**, *Uniform provisions concerning the approval of vehicles of categories M, N and O with regard to braking* 5. **GS 4028:2019**, *Uniform provisions concerning the approval of audible warning devices and of motor vehicles with regard to their audible signals* 6. **GS 4017:2019**, *Uniform provisions concerning the approval of vehicles with regard to the seats, their anchorages and any head restraints* 7. **GS 4014:2019**, *Uniform provisions concerning the approval of vehicles with regard to safety belt anchorages, ISOFIX anchorages systems and ISOFIX top tether anchorages* 8. **GS 4016:2019**, *Uniform provisions concerning the approval of: I. Safety-belts, restraint systems, child restraint systems and ISOFIX child restraint systems for occupants of power- driven vehicles, II. Vehicles equipped with safety-belts, safety-belt reminder, restraint systems, child restraint systems and ISOFIX child restraint systems* 9. **GS 4083:2019**, *Uniform provisions concerning the approval of vehicles with regard to the emission of pollutants according to engine fuel requirements* 10. **GS 4051:2019**, *Uniform provisions concerning the approval of motor vehicles having at least four wheels with regard to their noise emissions* 11. **GS 4039:2019**, *Uniform provisions concerning the approval of vehicles with regard to the speedometer equipment including its installation* 12. **GS 4030:2019**, *Uniform provisions concerning the approval of pneumatic tyres for motor vehicles and their trailers* 13. **GS 4054:2019** *Uniform provisions concerning the approval of pneumatic tyres for commercial vehicles and their trailers* 14. **GS 4500:2019** Administrative Process for Homologation of Models of Motor Vehicles and its Variants
Category N1 This involves vehicles with a maximum mass not exceeding 3.5 tonnes with at least four wheels and used for the carriage of goods	1. **GS 4048:2019**, Uniform provisions concerning the approval of vehicles with regard to the installation of lighting and light-signalling devices 2. **GS 4046:2019**, Uniform provisions concerning the approval of devices for indirect vision and of motor vehicles with regard to the installation of these devices 3. **GS 4043:2019**, Uniform provisions concerning the approval of safety glazing materials and their installation on vehicles 4. **GS 4013:2019**, Uniform provisions concerning the approval of vehicles of categories M, N and O with regard to braking 5. **GS 4013H:2019**, Uniform provisions concerning the approval of vehicles of passenger cars with regard to braking 6. **GS 4028:2019** Uniform provisions concerning the approval of audible warning devices and of motor vehicles with regard to their audible signals 7. **GS 4017:2019**, Uniform provisions concerning the approval of vehicles with regard to the seats, their anchorages and any head restraints 8. **GS 4014:2019**, Uniform provisions concerning the approval of vehicles with regard to safety belt anchorages, ISOFIX anchorages systems and ISOFIX top tether anchorages 9. **GS 4016:2019**, Uniform provisions concerning the approval of: I. Safety-belts, restraint systems, child restraint systems and ISOFIX child restraint systems for occupants of power- driven vehicles, II. Vehicles equipped with safety-belts, safety-belt reminder, restraint systems, child restraint systems and ISOFIX child restraint systems. 10. **GS 4083:2019** Uniform provisions concerning the approval of vehicles with regard to the emission of pollutants according to engine fuel requirements 11. **GS 4051:2019**, Uniform provisions concerning the approval of motor vehicles having at least four wheels with regard to their noise emissions 12. **GS 4039:2019**, Uniform provisions concerning the approval of vehicles with regard to the speedometer equipment including its installation 13. **GS 4030:2019** Uniform provisions concerning the approval of pneumatic tyres for motor vehicles and their trailers 14. **GS 4054:2019** Uniform provisions concerning the approval of pneumatic tyres for commercial vehicles and their trailers 15. **GS 4500:2019** Administrative Process for Homologation of Model of Motor Vehicle and its Variants.

Vehicle Categories	Relevant documents
Homologation	-Establishment of a National Vehicle Homologation Programme for the Ghanaian automotive industry
	-The objective of the homologation is to ensure safety of road users and vehicle users and vehicle owners by protecting them against vehicles not suited for the climate and road conditions of Ghana
	-It is to increase the overall level of security and protection from vehicle theft and cloning
	-To ascertain clear and transparent procedures for homologation to encourage foreign direct investment in the sector

Source: GSA

Appendix 5.2: Essential Elements of Vehicle Modifications

Types of modifications	Extent of modification
-Wheel base alteration -Radiator change and thermostat removal -Conversion of cargo vehicle to commercial passenger vehicle -Conversion of petrol engine vehicles to gas (LPG) engine vehicles -Increase in vehicle capacity so as to carry more passengers or goods -Complete conversion of one vehicle type to another (e.g. cargo truck to tipper truck) -Various structural cosmetic changes such as coloured head lamps and tinted glass -Conversion of automatic transmission to manual transmission	-Slight change: this is when a part of the vehicle is modified in order to achieve desired performance. For example, lengthening trailer size to carry more loads or shortening it for easy manoeuvring in certain narrow areas. -Complete change: this is when the whole vehicle is converted from its present form to an entirely new form. Typical example of complete change is the conversion of a cargo truck to a tipper truck and a flatbed trailer to a cargo trailer.
Modifications that do not need approval	**Modifications that need approval**
-Reduction of vehicle strength structurally and its effects on vehicle control, vehicle safety, or nuisance to other road users. However, these modifications are still subject to compliance with the Road Traffic and Vehicle Safety standard rules. Other minor modifications include: -Door modification (changing of door handles, glass winding mechanism, etc.) -Tyre size and aspect ratio -Air conditioners -Alarm systems -Additional lighting -Roof racks -Windscreens and lamp shields -Seatbelts -Radio and stereo systems -Blinds and other internal screening systems subject to clear view	-Placement of engines which differ in capacity and/ or configuration from the original or replacing the radiator or thermostat which is also different in configuration from the original so as to achieve faster or lower cooling. -Steering system -Suspensions -Additional axle or axles -Chassis extension -Wheel base alterations -Increase in gross vehicle mass or gross vehicle weight rating -Brake modifications, including trailer brake connections -Change of vehicle type -Engine changes However, these are subject to continuous compliance with relevant road traffic and vehicle safety standards.
Modifications done to vehicles in Suame Magazine	**Alterations Done at Suame Magazine**
-Chassis extension or wheel base alteration -Conversion of petrol injection to carburettor system -Propeller shaft extension -Increase in vehicle capacity so as to carry more passengers or goods -Radiator change and thermostat removal -Complete conversion of one vehicle type to another (e.g., cargo truck to tipper truck) -Conversion of cargo van to passenger bus for commercial operations -Building or mounting of bodies on naked chassis (as it is done to get the Metro mass vehicle) -Conversion of automatic transmission to manual transmission -Changing of motor cycle to tricycle -Changing of left-hand drive vehicle to right hand drive vehicle -Conversion of transistorized ignition system to the coil ignition system. -Conversion of one door car to multiple door cars -Various structural cosmetic changes such as modifying of body styles, fixing of glasses, painting or spraying works, coloured head lamp and tinted glass -Conversion of petrol engine vehicle to gas (LPG) engine vehicle or vice versa	Suspension System (Leaf Spring) Alteration by giving more ground clearance beneath to the body and chassis for the vehicles to sustain more loads and to reduce shock and vibration due to too many irregularities on the road surface being transmitted to the occupants of the vehicle. Chassis Frame Alteration: by increasing occupancy chassis by extending in between wheels through the removal of the propeller shaft, rear brake pipes, cables for hand brake and other auxiliary components and parts and the removal and fixing of extension plate with power grinding and cutting machine. -Seat Production by converting some of the vehicle design and fixing bus seats for passengers eg. re-arrangement of 207 seats into five rows using galvanized pipe rather than solid steel because it can last longer, does not corrode easily and can withstand high pressure according to the artisan Fixing of Glass for example 207 buses where there are no portions for windows.

Modifications that are not allowed
-Leaf springs repairs or alterations
-Drive shaft repairs or alterations

Source: Ghana Heavy Vehicle Construction and Use Guidelines)

CHAPTER 6

SAFE ROAD USER

GhanaWeb ★

Latest News

Home - News

General News of Tuesday, 10 March 2020

Source: starrfm.com.gh

Accidents: Ghanaians are careless about their safety – Osei-Owusu

6.1 INTRODUCTION

It is a fact that every human being is a road user in one way or the other because each person in mobility takes the role as either a driver, passenger, pedestrian, motorcyclist, pillion rider and cyclist within different road traffic systems. The actions of road users on the road are influenced by personal elements such as their physical, mental and psychological abilities, their level of traffic risk awareness, ability to observe safe traffic practices, motivations to do so, ability to judge safe and unsafe traffic conditions, their lifestyles, life stages and experiences which determines their traffic safety practices.

Others factors are individual ability to take risk, level of understanding of road use, ability to apply road safety protocols, decision making abilities and ability to respond to emergency traffic safety needs which also determines how an individual behaves in the traffic system. Thus, each individual relates to and engages with different traffic conditions in their own unique way. Aside individual human factors, socio cultural norms and values also influence road user behaviour in the road traffic system.

Since the human factors that contribute to the of wide variation road user behaviour are also mostly intangible, they are deemed to be difficult to measure, standardise and regulate. This makes the actual means by which a desirable road user behaviour can be identified and corrected very complex. Due to this, road user safety management is perceived to be very problematic with the consequence that most of these factors are often ignored to some significant margins in making road safety decisions.

This makes human error the single most important cause of RTCs accounting for about 90% of them globally due mainly to wrongful behaviour and attitudes, (WHO, 2018). Thus, any effort to increase the level of road safety should primarily aim at the prevention of human errors in the road traffic system. A key proposal for tackling the complexity of road user safety is by a World Report on Road Traffic Injury Prevention, (2004), is to focus on common road user errors and to provide for equal protection for all road users.

This section of the book explores road user safety with regards to behavioural and attitudinal perspectives of safe road traffic use by the Ghanaian road user within the context of the barriers to the adoption of best practices as well as the incentives and opportunities for improvement in Ghana.

6.2 THEORIES AND PRINCIPLES ON THE HUMAN FACTOR IN ROAD SAFETY

6.2.1 Theories of the Human Factor in Road Safety

From literature different theories have been propounded about the role of the human factor in RTCs as a means of determining some standard protocols to guide effective road user management and these include the following:

A. Accident proneness theory: The theory considers certain individuals to be more likely than others to be involved in traffic crashes even with similar risk exposure. (Froggatt and Smiley 1964). Farmer and Chambers (1940) and Tillmann and Hobbs (1949) used it to examine many lifestyle variables that might affect driving and concluded that the physiological and psychological demand for mobility puts the driver who has limited capacity to manage the power and speed of a vehicle in difficult situation in a complex road traffic system be it either the driver's fault or not. Reason (1990), affirmed this on the basis of RTCs being caused by inappropriate driver response to the road traffic system. Elvik et al. (2009), argued against the driver focused theories on the basis of human error in traffic by attributing RTCs to the failure of the whole traffic system that is the interaction between the driver, vehicle, and road infrastructure rather than only the driver.

B. Cognitive/psychological theories: The theory states that an individual is able to regulate his or her level of preferred risk by choice, (Fuller, 2005) based on some motivating factors and the outcome of particular risky situations as well as the use of a particular mode of transport. Taylor (1964) and Näätänen and Summala, (1974) used the theory to deduce the first road user theory based on psychological approach with a suggestion of a zero-risk idea determined by increased experience, self-confidence with perceived risk diminished to the point of zero. Elvik (2004), considers the risk homeostasis and risk-compensation theories to be too vague in explaining specific factors underlying behavioural patterns because in his view behavioural adaptation is a wider term not easily adapted to the road-vehicle system.

C. The risk homeostasis theory: Wilde, (1982) formulated this theory on the basis that people do not always respond as expected to traditional safety initiatives, but rather adjust their response to more rules, administrative controls, new procedures and engineering technologies. Fuller and Santos, (2002) added that, the difficulty of the task homeostasis by which a driver manages a given level of task is affected by motivations, time constraints and the driver's own capability and ability to balance and handle the difficult task. However, if it is not well regulated it can cause a safety risk. Dulisse (1997), argued against the theory on the basis of people's reaction to a policy being counter-productive due to the possibility some traffic safety measures provoking negative consequences.

D. Economic theories of road user safety: The theory uses a risk-compensation theory which assumes that drivers are rational agents who choose between safety and driving intensity within a trade-off of expected benefits, (Michon,1989) and (Peltzman,1975). The theory compared to the psychological theories is considered to be more tractable and easier to develop hypothetical tests for.

E. Traffic Engineering Psychology for Road User Safety: It summarises the theories on human behaviour in road safety, with the view that every measure, adopted in an effort to contribute towards greater road safety involves a psychological aspect of the road user (Wien, Brno, Olomouc, 2015). Rothengatter, (1997), clarifies this on the basis that the momentary state of reflection in individual differences in the use of the traffic system which are unclear and difficult to standardise can be used to discount a single theory on road user behaviour. Dwelling on this, Elvik et al. (2009) used the idea that only the road user can influence their behaviour.

6.2.2 Principles on the Human Factor in Road Safety

A. Influence of Physical and Psychological Factors in Road Safety: From the theories, both physical and psychological characteristics influence road user behaviour. The physical characteristics of the road user are vision, hearing, strength and the reaction of the road user to an RTC situation. The psychological factors are the mental characteristics of the road user which influences their performance in traffic with regards to skill, intelligence, experience, knowledge and literacy, emotions such as anger, fear, superstition, impatience, anxiety, etc. These are as presented in Table 6.1.

Table 6.1: Key Psychological and Physical Elements of Causing Human Errors in RTCs in Traffic

1. Sub-Physical features of road user characteristics	Description
Vision	The field of vision includes acute or clear vision cone, fairly clear vision cone and peripheral vision cone and it decides some of the road user traffic practices such as the estimation of speed, with visual deficits having safety effects
Hearing	Hearing is an important characteristic to a driver's reaction to time for decision making, and response especially for pedestrians and cyclists compared to drivers
Strength	The lack of strength makes it difficult for drivers to respond to some traffic situations e.g., parking of heavy vehicles.

2. Sub – Psychological Features of road user characteristics	Description
Drunk/ speed Driving	Such a driver has very limited perception reaction time.
Road User Lost in thought syndrome	The road user in this state fails to recognize a dangerous situation on the road.
Risk unawareness	A risk unaware road user lacks understanding of a risky situation.
Overreaction in RTC situations	Such a driver engages in excessive crash-avoiding behaviour more likely to create higher fatalities
Inability to anticipate potential problems	Such a driver does not observe and look out for things that could end up causing an RTC
Fatigue	The driver lacks self-determined fatigue consciousness
Risky behaviours.	The driver wilfully engages in risky behaviours.
Panic in accident situations	Inability to stay calm in an accident situation so as to respond quickly but smoothly.
Wrongful action	Not choosing the correct course of action in the traffic stream
Getting away when needed	Not getting out of the way when necessary and when required to do so e.g., parking on the roadway.
Loose of control	Inability to recover and respond appropriately to an RTC situation.
Wrongful Response to RTC	Engaging in counter-productive acts in RTC situations

B. Road User Behaviour Influenced by Acts by other Road Users: Poor road user conduct in the traffic stream can also occur when different participants in specific situations act according to discrepant formal or informal traffic rules. According to Helmers and Aberg (1978), when formal traffic rules do not correspond with the road design, informal traffic rules, based on expectations about other road users' behaviour are developed through interactions between road users. Examples of concerns in road safety between the driver and other road users are as summarised in Table 6.2.

Table 6.2: Examples of Poor Road User Conduct

A. The Driver and the other driver	B. The Driver and the Passenger
-Using hand signals to communicate with other drivers and the risk of not being understood	-Drivers performing activities that may expose other passengers to the risk of damage, injury or discomfort e.g., smoking, making a call while driving, engagement in arguments with passengers etc.
-Wrong indication of turning signals by one driver to the other driver eg indicating left when turning right and the related risk	-Passenger distractions by conversation or misunderstanding e.g. drunk passenger
-Sudden stopping without signalling and the possible run in by the other diver	-An uncontrolled child activity in a moving vehicle
-Tailgating the other vehicle and possible run in at sudden brakes	-Distracted attention by female presence in the front seat
-Dangerous manoeuvring and sudden lane change	-Passenger critique of driver performance eg over speeding and under speeding
-Unpreparedness to react to other drivers needs in emergencies	-Fear of passenger reaction in difficult situations e.g., panicking passenger holding on to driver during near RTC situation

A. The Driver and the other driver	B. The Driver and the Passenger
-Counting on others to obey the rules of the road or to make allowances for you Driver inability to manage multiple risks effectively e.g. sudden braking in situation of tyreburst and skidding Unpreparedness to react to unforeseen situations such as unexpected sudden object fall e.g. a container falling off a moving truck	-Passenger ignorance and lack of knowledge on traffic regulations leaving the driver to engage in reckless driving without complaints
C. The Driver and the Pedestrian	**D. The Driver and the Motorcyclist**
-Driver application of different strategies (legal and illegal) to situations involving pedestrians crossing the road e.g., driver not yielding for pedestrians at both signalised and unsignalised pedestrian crossings like zebra crossing	-Driver inability to spot motorcycles because they are small e.g., Driver difficulty in spotting - motorcycles while merging or changing lanes
-Where the pedestrian disregards the speed of the driver by crossing the road leisurely at unauthorised locations	-Motorcyclists riding on the wrong side of the driver
-Competitive behaviour where the driver expects the pedestrian to stop and the later fails to do so.	-Turning high beams on, on approaching motorcycle,
-Where drivers are not able to lower their speeds sufficiently for adequate pedestrian crossing time	-Motorcyclists inappropriate movements e.g., meandering in between vehicles
-Where drivers are only willing to slow down or stop for crossing pedestrians when the speed of their vehicle is low.	-Driver difficulty at blind intersections
-Where the presence of pedestrians at a zebra crossing has little or no speed-reducing influence	-Driver failure to acknowledge that riders are more vulnerable than drivers and refusal to give away
	-Inability of drivers of larger vehicles to judge the speed of a motorcycle
-Lack of knowledge about the formal rules in specific situations	-Driver perception that there is a considerable amount of aggression and lack of courtesy on the part of motor riders -Opening of car doors in congested traffic conditions without checking for the presence of motorcyclists -Motorcyclists driving through 'red' lights at intersections

C. Environmental Features of Traffic System and Road User Safety:
Environmental factors that govern road user behaviour in the traffic streams include the elements listed in Table 6.3.

Table 6.3: Key Environmental Elements Causing Human Errors in RTCs in Traffic

Sub Environmental Features	Description
Poor Road Design Features	Intersections on curves hampering the visibility of approaching vehicles
Absence of Safety devices	The driver has limited commitment to the use of safety devices when such devices have not been provided/ installed
Poor weather conditions	Uncontrolled environmental factors such as rain, fog etc.
Poor land use design and practices	This includes occupation of walkways by hawkers

In Ghana, though not purposefully studied or applied, the theoretical context of the mentioned theories reflects significantly in road user behaviour. Vehicle safety systems, engineering of roadway systems, road safety education and enforcement directly influence the way road users and specifically drivers behave. For example, the presence of an MTTD official at an intersection is likely to deter drivers from crossing the red line. The issue of economic considerations in safety is also of very critical importance with regards to the operational economy of commercial driver behaviour in the country.

However, the magnitude of the impact of regulation on road user behaviour is difficult to establish since there are no records on what regulation is mostly complied with or not complied with. Also, though some studies on the psychological impacts of road user behaviour has been conducted by the NRSA its effectiveness and prescriptions for road user safety has not been established.

6.2.2 Standards, Regulations and Policies on Road User Safety

A. Global Standards on Road User Safety: At the global level key components on road user safety are set on risk perception, attitudes and driver training/driving skills. Others are availability of legal provisions on what is considered a violation of traffic laws and regulations and effective enforcement and rehabilitation. Key amongst the global standards are as follows:

i. The Convention on Road Traffic, 1968 on Road User Safety: Provisions for road user safety in the convention 68 are as summarized in Table 6.4.

Table 6.4: Aspects of UN Convention 68 on Road User Safety

UN Convention 68 on Road User Safety		Applicability in Ghana
Article 3	Contracting parties will take the necessary measures to ensure that road safety education is provided on a systematic and continuous basis, particularly in schools at all levels	This is mostly done in Ghana by the NRSA
Article 5	Road users shall comply with the instructions conveyed by road signs, traffic light signals and road markings	This is a requirement by statutory regulations in Ghana
Article 6	Road users shall promptly obey all instructions given by authorized officials directing traffic	Ditto
Article 7	-Road users shall avoid any behaviour likely to endanger or obstruct traffic, to endanger persons, or to cause damage to public or private property -Wearing of seatbelt is compulsory for drivers and passengers of motor vehicles, where available	Regulatory demands on user restraints are available in Ghana, however, road user's behaviours are very diversified and it cannot be said with certainty that all aspects are captured.
Article 9	Flocks and herds should be divided into sections for the convenience of traffic	Ditto
Article 19	-No road user shall enter a level crossing at which the gates or half-gates are across or in process of being placed across the road -Where gates or light signals are absent, no road-user shall enter a level crossing without making sure that no rail-borne vehicle is approaching -No road-user shall linger while traversing a level crossing	This is not applied in Ghana
Article 29	Every road user shall on the approach of a rail-borne vehicle clear the track as soon as possible to allow the rail-borne vehicle to pass	This is applied in Ghana
Article 34	Every road user shall leave room clear for a priority vehicle to pass on the carriageway and shall, if necessary, stop when warned by the vehicle's special luminous and audible warning devices	This is also a requirement in Ghana by law

ii. DOA Components on Safe Road User: Pillar 4 of the global road safety plan is on road user safety and a summary is as provided in Table 6.5.

Table 6.5: DOA components in safe road user

Objective	Activities		Applicability in Ghana
-Develop comprehensive programmes to improve road user behaviour. -Ensure sustained or increased enforcement of laws and standards, combined with public awareness/education.	Activity 1	Increase awareness of road safety risk factors and prevention measures and implement social marketing campaigns to help influence attitudes and opinions on the need for road traffic safety programmes.	This done to some extent
	Activity 6	Set and seek compliance with transport, occupational health and safety laws, standards and rules for safe operation of commercial freight and transport vehicles, passenger road transport services and other public and private vehicle fleets to reduce crash injuries.	There are rules and standards for commercial transport operation in Ghana
	Activity 7	Research, develop and promote comprehensive policies and practices to reduce work-related road traffic injuries in the public, private and informal sectors, in support of internationally recognized standards for road safety management systems and occupational health and safety.	This is done to some extent in Ghana

iii. Distribution of RTC Fatalities by Road User Category in Ghana: Ghana's average distribution of RTC fatalities by road user category for 2011, compared with some RTC statistics on fatalities by the WHO in 2018 indicated that for example pedestrian fatality at 40.6 % was close to that of the global estimate at 44.7 % and that of vehicle occupants including drivers at 34% was close to that of the global statistic of 33.7%. That of motorcyclists and pillion riders at about 14% was much lower than of the global statistic of 28%.

However as of 2020 the results indicated that motorcycles/tricycles and pillion rider fatality had risen to become the highest road user risk at 32.8% followed by pedestrian hits at 31%, passengers fatalities at 18.5% and driver fatalities at 13.5%. That of cyclists was at 1.85% with others at 0.67% as presented in Figure 6.1. This implies that Ghana has made good progress with reduction in RTC's for most user groups especially for pedestrian fatality and vehicle occupant fatality but the situation with motorcycles has worsened within a short spate of time.

This could be attributed to increased number of commercial motorcycle transport in the country though still an illegal activity by law. Others like tricycles and rickshaws previously unknown are also now making impact on Ghana's RTC statistics and this calls for the necessary attention.

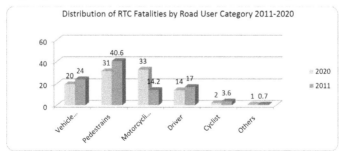

Figure 6.1: Distribution of RTC fatalities by road user category, 2011 - 2020

iv. Road User Counter Interventions Implemented in Ghana: There is increased concern for road user safety in the country (See, Figure 6.2). Also, in addition to the traffic regulations, road user safety strategic interventions implemented for the achievement of good road user safety results is as presented in Appendix 3.5.

Figure 6.2: Publications on concern for road user safety in Ghana

6.3 DRIVER SAFETY

6.3.1 Driver Safety Regulations by International Conventions

Driving is defined as the control of the movement of vehicle and when it stationary with the engine running, even for a short period of time.

A. Driver Safety Regulations by Conventions 68: The tenets of UN Convention 68 on driver safety and the level of compliance by Ghana's road safety regulations are as summarized in Table 6.6.

Table 6.6: UN Resolution on Road Traffic (R.E.1) compared with Ghana's LI 2180 on driver safety

Theme	Description	Application in Ghana
Article 8: Drivers	4. Every driver of a power-driven vehicle shall possess the knowledge and skill necessary for driving the vehicle;	Driver training is prerequisite backed by the f regulations in the LI2180
Article 41: Driving permits	b) Contracting Parties undertake to ensure that driving permits are issued only after verification by the competent authorities that the driver possesses the required knowledge and skills; the persons authorized to check if drivers have the necessary knowledge, skills and appropriate qualifications; the contents and procedure of both theoretical and practical exams are regulated by national legislation;	Driver testing is required for the issuance of license and it is undertaken by trained officials at the DVLA -Driver testing is regulated by National regulations
2.1.1.2 General principles of professional instruction	(a) Professional driving instruction should be based on some specific considerations	Ghana has a driver training manual
2.1.1.3 Instructors	Professional tuition should be given only by instructors approved by the competent national authority	Only driving schools can apply for licenses for their candidates
2.1.1.4 Vehicles used for tuition	Motor vehicles used for practical tuition should be so equipped	It is required by law for only vehicles with dual control systems to be used in driver training
2.1.1.5 Tuition	(a) The tuition provided should aim at promoting a correct attitude and behaviour in all kinds of traffic situations,	Basic training is provided with little emphasis on defensive driving
2.1.1.6 Instruction in the driving of heavy goods and passenger vehicles	(a) In addition to the instruction necessary to obtain a driving permit, it is recommended that drivers of heavy goods and passenger vehicles should be checked at regular intervals by the competent authorities	Training and certification have been established for drivers of heavy goods vehicles and there are police check points to regulate their activities
2.1.1.7 Supervision	The continued application of the provisions set out in points 2.1.1.2 to 2.1.1.6 above.	There is provision in the LI2180

Theme	Description	Application in Ghana
2.1.2 First aid training	(a) Appropriate measures shall be taken to ensure that candidates for driver's licenses receive proper training concerning […]	This is in place and a leaners license is issued ahead of substantive license
Annex III: Minimum requirements for professional driving instruction	-driving instructors; eligibility for recognition; disqualification; maintenance of standards	Whilst eligibility for driver training is established compliance is not effectively regulated.
Annex IV: Minimum requirements for professional driving instruction	-scope of tuition for theoretical and practical	This is in place
Annex V: Guidelines for methods of professional tuition, Principal guidelines	-Methods of theoretical tuition	Theoretical driver training is in place and some trainers use simulators
Annex VI: Additional recommendations for professional drivers	Annex VI: Additional recommendations for professional drivers of vehicles	Refresher training is being instituted

B. Driver Safety Regulations by the UN Decade for Road Safety Action (DOA):

The contents of the DOA regulations on road user safety and the level of application in Ghana is as summarised in Table 6.7.

Table 6.7: DOA Component for Road User Safety compared with Ghana's LI 2180 on driver safety

Theme	Description	Applicability in Ghana
Pillar 4	Safer road users Develop comprehensive programmes to improve road user behaviour. Sustained or increased enforcement of laws and standards, combined with public awareness/education to increase seat-belt and helmet wearing rates, and to reduce drink-driving, speed and other risk factors.	All these are in place in the country
Activity 1	Increase awareness of road safety risk factors and prevention measures and implement social marketing campaigns to help influence attitudes and opinions on the need for road traffic safety programmes.	These is undertaken by the NRSA
Activity 2	Set and seek compliance with speed limits and evidence-based standards and rules to reduce speed-related crashes and injuries.	Aside posted speeds limits along major roads, the are regulations on speed limits available in the LI2180;
Activity 3	Set and seek compliance with drink–driving laws and evidence-based standards and rules to reduce alcohol-related crashes and injuries.	It is available in LI 2180
Activity 4	Set and seek compliance with laws and evidence-based standards and rules for motorcycle helmets to reduce head-injuries.	It is available in LI 2180
Activity 5	Set and seek compliance with laws and evidence-based standards and rules for seat-belts and child restraints to reduce crash injuries.	It is available in LI 2180
Activity 6	Set and seek compliance with transport, occupational health and safety laws, standards and rules for safe operation of commercial freight and transport vehicles, passenger road transport services and other public and private vehicle fleets to reduce crash injuries.	Some provisions include the following 127. Issuance of commercial vehicle license 121. Registration of commercial vehicle operator 122. Issuance of commercial road transport operating permit 123. Issuance of commercial vehicle driving permit 128. Prohibition of use of motor cycle or tricycle for commercial purpose

Theme	Description	Applicability in Ghana
Activity 7	Research, develop and promote comprehensive policies and practices to reduce work-related road traffic injuries in the public, private and informal sectors, in support of internationally recognized standards for road safety management systems and occupational health and safety.	The following are available in the LI2180 (106. Rules of the road; 112. Placing injurious substances on the road; 113. Placing of construction materials and equipment on the road
Activity 9	Promote establishment of Graduated Driver Licensing systems for novice drivers	The following are provided for in the LI 2180 26. Learner's License 34. L - Plate 35. P - Plate

(Global Plan for the DECADE OF ACTION FOR ROAD SAFETY, 2011-2020, Version 3)

6.3.2 Driver Safety Policy and Regulations in Ghana

A. Driver Safety Policy in Ghana: Ghana established its road safety policy ahead of the DOA and the policy directions on drivers addressed essential critical components of the DOA requirement with respect to adequate training, speed limits, drunk driving, fatigue etc. as presented in Table 6.8.

Table 6.8: Ghana's Road Safety Policy for Driver's

Theme	Policy Challenge	Policy Objective/Strategy	Status of Application
Training	-Driver incompetent as a result of poor driver training.	-Strengthen system of driver training and licensing -Improve driver training and testing to include defensive driving and extended road tests/ hazard perception checks.	Ghana's system for Ghana training has been improved with the introduction of driver training manuals for driving schools, development of driver testing grounds, training of driver testing officers, introduction of practical and theoretical testing of prospective drivers, health screening with regard to eye sight.
	Inadequacy of driver training by either the Driving Schools or on the job training	Institute and legalise appropriate requirements for upgrading knowledge, skills and capability of drivers by continuous education and refresher courses.	Driver refresher courses introduced on a limited scale in the country.
	Drivers' difficulty in recognizing, understanding and interpreting road traffic laws, regulations and signs.	Establish model driving schools with adequate infrastructure and equipment in partnership with motor trading firms, private sector participants and NGOs.	Establishment of a prospective model drivers' academy has been proposed.
	Inability of commercial drivers to cope with emerging situations due to absence of specialized driver training,	Institute measures to enhance national capacity for driver testing and licensing by a system of accreditation to improve the quality of testing.	Driver testing and licensing systems improved as stated earlier.
	Non-existence ofProfessional education to upgrade the levels of expertise and competence and lack of periodic re-training or refresher courses for driver skills upgrade	Introduce the use of simulators for training drivers of high occupancy vehicles and hazardous goods vehicles.	Simulators acquired by the GTTC for the training of drivers.
Health	Poor health of some drivers (eyesight, epilepsy etc.)	Conduct of Eye test as part of driver licensing	Regulation for the conduct of eye test as part of the current driver licensing procedure established.

Theme	Policy Challenge	Policy Objective/Strategy	Status of Application
Licensing	Drivers with licenses and skills for smaller vehicles found driving heavy-duty vehicles without proper training or certification.		Though originally not addressed by the policy framework, currently driver training for heavy Goods Vehicle is being done
	Use of fake driving licenses		Biometric methods have currently been established to address the issue.
	Poor personnel, infrastructure, and equipment capacity by the (DVLA) for effective driver testing and licensing.		Driver testing grounds have been constructed at the head-office and a second one is being constructed in Kumasi.
Drunk Driving	Driving under the influence of alcohol, drugs and other related substance.		Establishment of Alcohol Limit
Fatigue Driving	Long driving hours by commercial drivers		Institute hourly limits for driving
Speeding	Speeding, and wrongful overtaking		Use of speed limiters and enforcement
	Overloading		Axle load weigh stations have been provided at vintage points in the country
Remuneration	Lack of motivation for driver (pay structure)		This is yet to be addressed

Source: NRSP 2008

B. Summary of Driver Safety Regulatory Standards in Ghana: *A summary of driver safety standards as defined in the LI 2180 and the under amended in November 2012 is as listed in Table 6.9.*

Table 6.9: Road Traffic regulations for the driver in LI2180 of 2012 and

LI 2180	Review of Road Traffic Regulations, 2012 (L.I. 2180 – Summary Issues
27. Application for Driver's License	Section -4(2) Alcohol concentration reduced from 0.08% to 0.05%.
38. Disqualification on revocation of license	Section 13 -: Seatbelt Conforms to the Standard approved by the DVLA.
39. Revoked or suspended license	-Section 14: (b) Child Restraint System approved by DVLA
40. Driving while license is suspended or revoked	-25 (4). Driver's License: for first-time applicant
41. Unlawful use of license	26 (4): Learner's License moved to regulation 27 as 27 (3)
44. Replacement of driver's license	26(5) (a)-(c) Composition of examination Moved to regulation 27
45. Change of name	26 (6). Learner's License: Will now become regulation 26(4)
46. Armed Forces and Police driving permit	26 (7) (a). Learner's License for learner's with the aid of glasses or other physical aid
47. Production of Driver's License	26 (14). Learner's License: A learner driving hours of 7.00p.m. and 5.00 a.m. edited to 10pm and 5am
101. Driving of motor vehicle	26 (18). Learner's License: Moved to Regulation 27. Amended
107. Prohibition on use of communication device while driving	27. Application for Driver's License and examination by an examiner.
108. Turning right on red	28 1(a): Conditions of grant of a license: moved to the learner license section (regulation 26)
109. Hand signals	29 (2). Eye Test: Addition for the renewal of driver's license
115. Molesting or obstructing a driver	29 (5). Eye Test: Edited
124. Registration of foreign commercial vehicle operator	30 (2). Driving with uncorrected defective eyesight
143. Documents for a person driving a vehicle outside Ghana	31. Upgrading of Class: Edit Heading to read:
147. Visitor's driving permit	37 (c): Age requirement for driving an agricultural tractor reviewed to 21years
	-Section 40(1): (d) Any other format that the Licensing Authority may prescribe with approval from the Minister responsible for Transport
	43. Driver re-training and re-testing amended
	45 (2). Change of Name to be gazetted

LI 2180	Review of Road Traffic Regulations, 2012 (L.I. 2180 – Summary Issues
148. Use of Foreign Driver's License	47 (4). Production of Driver's License should be immediate
168. Obedience to Police and Fire Service Officials	-Section 52 (1): Trade License Plate shall include plates, stickers, forms, certificates or any other format that the Licensing Authority may prescribe with approval from
169. Fleeing or attempting to elude Police Officer or authorized person	the Minister responsible for Transport
170. Obstructing intersection or pedestrian crossing	101. Driving of Vehicle: No driver shall leave a vehicle unattended.
171. Disregarding signs and barricades	102(2). Broken down Motor vehicle or trailer: An owner is responsible
173. Racing on streets or roads	121Registration of Commercial vehicle operators' addition of digital registration
174. Obedience to stop light, stop sign and yield right-of-way sign	-124(2)- Registration of Foreign commercial vehicle operator
175. Obedience to signals indicating approach of train	-168. Disobedience to Police and Fire Service Officials to be embedded in the spot fine
176. Passing stopped vehicle at pedestrian crossing	-169. Fleeing or attempting to elude a police officer or an authorized person to be embedded in the spot fine
177. Passing of school buses	-173. Racing on streets or roads to be embedded in the spot fine
178. Obedience to traffic control officers and devices	-174 (4) (c). Obedience to stop light, stop sign and yield right-of-way sign – correction where there is no yield
179. Restricted use of bus stop and taxi stand	-176. Passing a stopped vehicle at pedestrian crossing – recommendation
180. Parking in places reserved for persons with disability	-195. Interpretation of Accident edited
181. Driving in a procession	Others
182. Driving through a procession	-Regulation-Self-Driving Motor Vehicle Operator's License
183. Stopping and parking of buses and taxis regulated	-Regulation _ Self-Driving Motor Vehicle Operator's License Learner's license
187. Parking on highway and town road	-Application for Self-Driving Motor Vehicle Operator's License.
189.Use of television monitor on the dash board of motor vehicle	-Conditions for grant of Self-Driving Motor Vehicle Operator's License Regulation
190. Counterpart Driving License	-Upgrading of class
193. Penalties	-Renewal of Self-Driving Motor Vehicle Operator's License
Source: LI 2180	-Revocation, Suspension, Endorsement or Cancellation of Self-Driving Motor Vehicle Operator's License
	-Persons disqualified from holding a Self-Driving Motor Vehicle Operator's License
	-Disqualification on revocation of license
	-Revoked or suspended Self-Driving Motor Vehicle Operator's License
	-Driving while license is suspended or revoked
	-Prohibition of unlicensed person to operate motor vehicle
	-Replacement of Self-Driving Motor Vehicle Operator's License

6.3.3 Driver RTC Statistical Profile in Ghana

A. Driver RTC Demographic Statistic Profile in Ghana:

i. Driver Fatalities by Age in Ghana: Majority of drivers in Ghana are in the active age group of above 18 years to 58 years (See, Figure 6.3). The driver age cohort with the highest number of RTCs is between 26-33 at (32%) which does not deviate significantly from the global statistic 20-29 being those mostly killed, (Rospa, 2018). This is because younger drivers are easily distracted. Also of due concern is the small proportion of 0.3% of the driver population in Ghana who are below the legal age of 18 years (ref: Law LI 2180 section 26.(1)A person who is at least eighteen years old may apply for a learner's license). These categories of drivers also drive without licenses and are of high risk in the traffic stream.

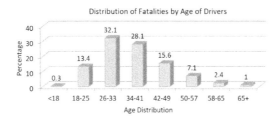

Figure 6.3: Distribution of fatalities by age of drivers

ii. Driver Fatalities by Sex in Ghana: More male drivers die from RTCs than females both at the global and national levels with Ghana's record being 65.5% males and 34.5% female. This is typically attributed to factors such as higher vehicular ownership amongst males than females; men driving for longer distances and engaging more in speeding, drunk driving as well as taking of higher risks than female drivers (see Figure 6.4).

However, it is argued in literature that the situation does not necessarily mean that women are perfect drivers since there is also a view point that women are less confident behind the wheels than men. Since no empirical studies have been conducted in Ghana to establish the reasons why more male drivers die in RTCs than females, such a study might be necessary to direct the right kind of driver training by sex.

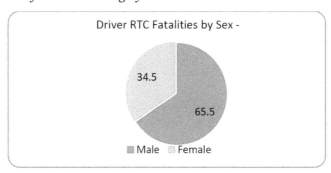

Figure 6.4: Driver RTC fatalities by sex

B. Driver Eligibility in Ghana

i. Educational Background of Drivers in Ghana: In Ghana, the legal requirement for driver certification is referenced as (ref: LI 2180 Clause (26 (3) should state that "An Applicant for a license shall be examined by a person authorised by the Licensing Authority for that purpose). The examination consists of - (a) an oral test; (b) a theoretical test; and(c) a practical driving test". Thus, it is mandatory for a driver to have some form of formal education to be able to successfully pass a theoretical driver test. Current records indicate that, most 66% of the drivers, meet the stipulated minimum requirement of a Basic Education Certificate Level (BECE) or Junior Secondary School Level (JHS) or a Middle School Leaving Certificate (MSLC).

From, Figure 6.5, the illiteracy rate of the driver population at 14% could imply that some drivers either do not have valid license to drive or did acquire their license before the regulation was passed.

Also of concern is the fact that some illiterate drivers in Ghana discount the importance of education in safe driving on the basis of having good RTC records. These are assumed to be mostly those drivers who started driving ahead of the passing of the LI2180. Such people are often with the notion that education does not impact on driver performance. This is especially typical of those who learnt driving by informal means or by apprenticeship and have also not acquired the license to drive but are driving anyway.

Others are those with fake licenses but are operating commercial transport. Research into driver educational status by driver RTC records will help to establish the actual effects of education on driver performance to dispute such a notion once and for all so prospective drivers will be motivated to do the right thing.

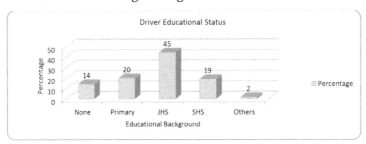

Figure 6.5: Driver educational status

ii. Driver Training in Ghana: The laws of Ghana, requires that prospective drivers are trained either by an experienced driver or by formal driving school but with a caveat that a driving license will be issued by a driver trained in a certified driving school-(Ref: LI 2180 Reg. 26, (5d) been certified by a recognised driver training institution as having undergone at least forty-eight hours of basic driver training).

Prior to this, a study by the NRSA in (2012), revealed that about 83% of drivers in Ghana learnt driving through various informal arrangements and only about 17% learnt driving through formal driving schools. Out of those who received informal driver training 12% were self-taught without the assistance of any instructor; 45% learnt driving through apprenticeship, i.e., by observation and 27% of them learnt driving through family or friends, (See Figure 6.6). In future studies matching driver RTC records with the mode of training should be conducted to establish the impact of informal modes of driver training on safety in the country.

Figure 6.6: Driver training mode

iii. Challenges Associated with Driver Training in Ghana: Some of the key challenges associated with driver training impacts on RTC in Ghana include the following:

a). Except for corporate entities such as logistics companies in formal operations and fuel distribution companies, for so many years there was no formal training for drivers of HGV's and the basis for which such drivers were licensed to operate was not known. It is only in recent times (2020) that formal and appropriate training for drivers of HGVs in Ghana has been established. However, this is a novice activity yet to be effectively implemented and with the modalities for sustained and continuous training yet to be established.

b). Another significant impact of poor driver training is the passing of bad driving habits from one driver to the other through informal training. This has resulted in a backlog of drivers with poor training background in the commercial road transport industry in Ghana where most drivers are trained through apprenticeship with consequent safety challenges. Such drivers do not also have the benefit of the use of the driver training manual developed for Ghana. Such drivers may be able to operate a vehicle but lack adequate knowledge in traffic regulations, signs and markings as well as requisite skills in defensive driving mechanisms etc. with implications for safety.

c). Though, there is a general perception that drivers trained informally learn more of practical driving mechanisms and less of theory whilst those who learn from training institutions gain more knowledge in theory than practical skills for driving, none of these are yet to be scientifically certified since driver error has never been defined on the basis of the training background. Currently there is a widespread illegal practice whereby applicants for driver license connive with driving schools for the acquisition of license at a reduced fee though not trained by them.

This is to circumvent the existing regulation whereby only driving schools can acquire a license for a prospective driver. This is mainly justified on the basis of lack of affordability of high cost of driver training by formal driver training schools. Irrespective of these challenges, Ghana has achieved significant strides with driver testing and licensing by the following interventions:

- *Standardisation of quality training for registered driving instructors.*
- *Certification of driver training schools.*
- *Development of driver training manuals for use by certified driving schools.*
- *Introduction of upgraded training and re-licensing of Instructors for Driving Schools by the DVLA with well-constructed testing grounds used for the purpose.*
- *Development of mandatory vehicle specifications for driver training by driving schools.*
- *Training of driver testing officers with new improved testing procedures*

Further to the above the author proposes for the following interventions to also be undertaken to advance driver training in Ghana.

- *There should be special focus for training 'Professional' road drivers for commercial transport operation as with the examples of some developed countries such as France and Germany where professional drivers undergo a two-to-three-year training in vocational driving before qualifying for commercial driving. This should also be complemented with refresher courses to improve and upgrade the quality of drivers in operation. To this effect the commencement of the ROSETA project for driver refresher training should be institutionalised by the NRSA.*
- *Existing vocational institutions such as the Government Technical Training Centre (GTTC), which engage in driver training programmes should be upgraded to train and re train professional drivers to feed the commercial road transport industry at affordable rate.*
- *There should be a legislation for mandatory commercial driver participation in refresher training and upgrade courses to enhance driver knowledge, skills and capability through continuous education.*
- *Consideration for widespread introduction of advanced driver training technologies such as the use of simulators which has been introduced into the country should be promoted.*
- *The proposal for the establishment of a National Driver Academy Model Schools which is still in the pipeline should be implemented through private partnership to address the challenge of funding shortfalls to facilitate the process.*

C. Driver Testing and Licensing: *A driving license enables a user to legally drive or operate a motor vehicle, (Talukdar A. 2011). The legal requirement for the acquisition of a license in Ghana is as specified (Ref: LI 2180 25, (1) A person may drive a motor vehicle if that person has (a) a learner's license, or (b) a driver's license. LI 2180, 28(1) The Licensing*

Authority shall, issue a driver's license, to an applicant if the applicant has passed as well as LI 2180 26, (5d) as quoted in section 5.2.3).

i. Classification of Driver License in Ghana: Due to differences in vehicle types used on the road which require different expertise for driving, driver's licensing is categorized by the type of vehicle for which a license can be used to drive as presented in Table 6.10. There are also diverse rules and stipulations for obtaining one license over the other listed in Ghana's road traffic Act LI2180. In some cases of an upgrade from a lower to a higher class, additional training might be required.

In addition to these a commercial driver's license is required for commercial transport operation in Ghana and international driving license is also required for drivers from other countries who decide to drive in the country. The key challenge with Ghana's license classification has to do with the fact that the basis for which a diver is upgraded without adequate training and testing is not known and this challenge would have to be addressed.

Table 6.10: Classification of Driver License in Ghana

License Class	Description
Category A	Drive Motorcycle with or without side car 1 up to 250cc
Category B	Drive Cars, cross country, minibuses, pick up vehicles Up to 3500 kg. (1-15 passengers)
Category C	Drive Buses and medium goods carrying vehicles Not exceeding 10,000 tons (1-45 passengers)
Category D	Drive Buses, coaches and heavy goods vehicles Not exceeding 35,000kgs (1-65 passengers)
Category E	Drive Agricultural, earth moving and industrial equipment 1. tractors 2. combine harvesters 3. graders 4. bulldozers 5. loaders 6. rollers 7. fork lifts
Category F	Drive Buses, coaches and heavy goods carrying vehicles Above 35,000kgs 1. rigid 2. articulators

https://www.ghanaroadtransport.com/2019/0 1/11/classification-of-ghana-driving-license/

ii. Current Status of Driver Licensing in Ghana: Some of the measures undertaken to improve driver licensing services by the DVLA in the post LI2180 period to facilitate the license acquisition and renewal process include the following:

a). Establishment of a variable express service at a relatively higher fee for those able to afford to reduce congestion on regular service activities. This is to encourage drivers to renew and acquire licenses with ease. Currently three (3) different express service level are offered by the DVLA and these include:

- *Provision of 'Same day' service for license renewal.*
- *Provision of a two-week service license renewal service.*
- *Provision of regular license renewal service.*

b). Digitisation with a new ICT system called Genesys for Driver Licensing activities which was launched in September 2017. Some of the online resources to facilitate the Driver Licensing process are as listed in Table 6.11. There has been an evaluation to determine its effectiveness and related challenges of these systems by the DVLA with a key recommendation for the integration of the systems which is yet to be implemented.

Table 6.11: Categorisation of Forms under First Schedule of L. I. 2180

1. Form A-regulation 2(1) and 17(1)(a)- Form of application to register a motor vehicle
2. Form A 1 - regulation 2(1) - Form of application to register a motor vehicle with personalized identification number
3. Form B - regulation 2(1) Form of application to register a trailer
4. Form C - regulation 4(7) - Form of vehicle registration particulars
5. Form D - regulation 7(5) - Form of road worthy certificate
6. Form E - regulation 17(1)(a) - Form of application to change ownership of a vehicle
7. Form F - regulation 23(4) - Form of a trade license
8. Form G - regulation 24(1) - Form of a trade license log book
9. Form H - regulation 25(2) - Driver's License
10. Form I - regulation 26(6) - Form of particulars on Learner Driver's License
11. Form J- regulation 26(18) - Form of application for physical assessment of an applicant for a Driver's License
12. Form K- regulation 27(1) - Form of application for Driver's License
13. Form L - regulation 28(5) - Form of Certificate of Competence
14 Form M -regulation 29(6) - Form of application for eye test for Driver's License and renewal of Driver's License
15. Form N- regulation 31(2) - Form of upgrade of class of driving license
16. Form 0- regulation 32(1) - Form of Driver's License (front)
17. Form 01 - regulation 32(1) - Form of Driver's License (back)
18. Form P - regulation 33(4) - Form of renewal of Driver's License
19. Form Q - regulation 44(2) - Form of application for replacement of Driver's License
20. Form R - Regulation 55(3) - Form of LPG vehicle permit application
21. Form R1 - Regulation 55(5) - Form of LPG Compliance Certificate
22. Form R 2- Regulation 58(4) - Form of application for auto LPG convertor
23. Form R 3 - Regulation 58(7) - Form of License to operate the business of auto LPG installations.
24. Form S - Regulation 122(3) - Form of application for commercial vehicle permit
25. Form SI - Regulation 122(5) - Form of commercial vehicle permit
26. Form TI - regulation 123 (1) - Form of Commercial Driver's Permit
27. Form T - regulation 123(2) - Form of application for Commercial Driving Permit
28. Form U - regulation 142 (1)(b) - Form of application for international certificate for motor vehicle
29. Form Ul - regulation 142 (l)(c) - Form of International Motor Vehicle Permit
30. Form V- regulation 143 (2) - Form of application for International Driving Permit
31. Form VI - regulation 143 (2) - Form of International Driving Permit

c). Introduction of driver licensing services on university campuses dubbed 'TERT DRIVE' to encourage tertiary students acquire authentic driver license in order to address part of the challenges associated with young driver.

d). Introduction of the Mobile Licensing Service whereby communities further from cities are visited by the DVLA licensing team for purposes of license renewal or issuance of new license for prospective drivers.

D. Driver Capacity in Ghana:

i. Number of Applications for Drivers License: Generally, the number of applicants for driver's license in Ghana shows a consistent growth especially from 2007 to 2011 after a dip between 2004 and 2006. Also, after a downward trend in 2013 to 2015 the trend switched to a rise again from 2016 onwards. The steep drop in the number of applicants in 2012 can be attributed to the changes introduced when the LI 2012 was effected and standards for driver certification were raise.

Out of the total of 1,733,943 tested driver license applicants from 1995 – 2018 78.3%
passed and 20.7% failed, (See Figure 6.7). Though the failure rate had initially been gen-
erally consistent with the rate of application for driver's license, the number started showing
a downward trend from 2017 indicating that the number of failures is reducing. Also, the
increasing trend from 2015 and the reducing failures indicates that the changes are yielding
good outcomes.

Figure 6.7: Summary of Drivers Who Applied for License, Passed and Failed

The before and after DOA implementation of the driver application scenario in Ghana also
indicated that the number of applicants increased with more drivers also passing the driver
testing procedure compared to the before situation. Thus, the failure rate also reduced, (See
Figure 6.8). This is a good indication of some good progress with respect to driver licensing
in the country.

Figure 6.8: Summary of Drivers Who Applied for License Before (2009) and After (2017) DOA on Road Safety

Irrespective of this, it is of critical importance for an extensive investigation to be conducted
into the current license validity status of the driving population in Ghana. This will guide
the conduct of authentic data led corrective measures through driver re-training and licens-
ing measures. Also, the margin of benefits from the reduction in delays in both acquisition
and renewal of licenses would have to be evaluated to validate the gains made.

ii. Number of Licensed Road Drivers in Ghana: Between the period January 1995 and
August 2018, a total of 1,357,083 valid driver license holders in Ghana were certified. Out
of this, 42.1% held license class A; 28.6% held license class B; and 29.3% held license class
C as presented in Figure 6.9. The statistics indicate that the percentage distribution of the
type of license holding is not commensurate with the distribution of vehicle by type. This

implies that some drivers are holding wrong types of licenses for driving wrong vehicles type. The magnitude of this challenge and its effects on driver performance would have to be further investigated for appropriate solutions.

Indeed, a study by the NRSA in 20212 indicated that some drivers are using licences owned by dead relatives whilst others have managed to drive for years with no licences at all.

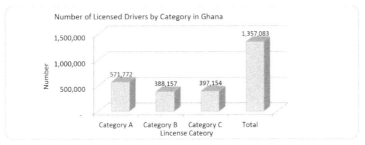

Figure 6.9: Number of Licensed Road Drivers in Ghana

E. Driver Skills, Capability and Experience in Ghana

i. Driver Experience: Records by a study conducted by (CREW, 2016), showed that about 85% of commercial drivers had over five (5) year's driving experience in the profession. This should have ideally given some positive indication for safety issues on the assumption that better skills and improved performance had been acquired from the years of experience. However, the years of driver experience did not reflect with the statistics on the percentage of RTC situations attributed to driver error. Another study of driver experience should be conducted to ascertain the merits in years of driving practice for informed decisions on driver re-training and upgrades in the country.

ii. Driver Knowledge on Traffic Regulations: Drivers are obligated to be knowledgeable in traffic rules to avoid negative attitudes and risky traffic safety practices. However, sometimes they do not comply with the formal rules out of poor knowledge of the traffic rules or total ignorance. Informal driver behaviour could also be due to vague or ambiguous traffic rules and regulations which are understood differently by different persons. Furthermore, some traffic rules are not congruent with road design, or the rules are not suited to human requirements or natural behaviour patterns.

In Ghana, drivers are expected to be knowledgeable in two key documentations on traffic regulations and these are the LI 2180, the amended version and Ghana's Highway Code. Though undocumented the extent to which knowledge from these documents are imparted during driver training can only be inferred to be effective to some extent for drivers trained by formal driving schools. This is because it is duly stipulated in the guiding syllabus for driver training schools. However, same cannot be said for drivers who are trained informally because they have to learn such rules by themselves to ensure they pass the theoretical component of the diving test.

A self-reported knowledge on driver aptitude test on traffic regulations from a study conducted by the NRSA in 2012, yielded the results presented in Figure 6.10. Using a scale of a below average score of (<50 points); an average score of (50 points) and an above average score of (>50 - 100 points) driver knowledge in rules and regulations was good at about (61%) and knowledge in signs and markings was also at (60%). However, this was self-reported so empirical studies should be conducted to assess driver test scores in rules and regulation to ascertain the actual state of driver knowledge in Traffic regulations since it is of serious consequence to driver performance in the traffic system.

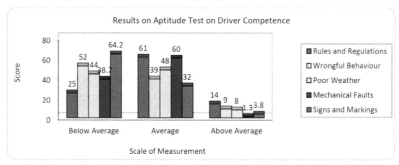

Figure 6.10: Results on Aptitude Test on Driver Competence

6.3.4 Driver Safety and Commercial Transport Operation in Ghana

A. Code of Commercial Transport Practice in Ghana: *In Ghana, vehicle operators are subjected to minimal regulation in terms of authority to operate as a commercial vehicle with regards to entry and exit, area of coverage, routing, standards of operation, maintenance of vehicles etc. Currently, there is no standard code of practice for informal commercial transport operation in the country, (Wilson T, 2006). Operators are licensed by respective, Metropolitan, Municipal and District Assemblies (MMDAs) and are supposed to be regulated by them to operate within their jurisdiction under the Local Governance Act, 2016 (Act 936) section 181 subsection 1 bye laws 2017.*

The bye laws require them to apply, pay fees, display license, comply with the number of passengers, keep records and define the duties of license holders as well as the records which are to be monitored and enforced, Thus, it is the duty of the driver to produce their license on request by law enforcers. Others are, restrictions, renewal, suspension, withdrawal, prohibitions, excess passengers and what to do when a license gets lost. Irrespective of this, most commercial transport operators operate with limited normative policy guidelines and minimal government intervention and regulation with diverse safety issues of concern.

Potential vehicle operators begin operation after procurement of vehicle and certification of standard procedures for roadworthiness. As such, most of the private informal operators who are in the majority have high numbers of unskilled drivers who accumulate skills outside formal education and training. About 95% of these are also informally employed i.e., without test, without formal contracts and with no checks on validity of license or experience. About 60% of these categories of drivers are managed and supervised by individual employers as suited to their requirements. 24% manage themselves and these constitute those who own their vehicles.

About 13% are managed and regulated by their respective unions and 4% are managed by different people e.g., family, etc. The predominance of individual ownership of vehicles coupled with the absence of a standardised regulatory system with mutual obligations of the parties involved has generated many inconsistencies. With this, the operational regulation by the different regulatory entities is varied and flexible with informal sanctions and punitive measures not effectively enforced and this creates safety concerns. There is therefore a need for formal guidelines under a simple code of practice agreed between road agencies, transport owners and operators, MMDAs, and the transport Unions for effective regulation of the industry.

B. Operational Characteristics of Commercial Transport Services: *The private informal road transport operators are mostly characterised by the use of old buses; damaged seats; delays in loading, ineffective communication between crew and passengers; drivers who do not observe caution; drivers not well trained; low occupancy vehicles taking higher traffic space; noisy trips; overloaded buses and frequent travel stops which is time consuming. The "trotros", also do not run any schedules but will depart for their destination once the bus is full at a loading point. The formal operations are normally characterised by adherence to general vehicle standards, driver training in defensive driving, control of fatigue driving, alcohol checks, speed control etc.*

C. Commercial Transport Driver Welfare Factors and Safety Impacts: *As of now there is no formalised system for addressing the needs of drivers in the commercial transport industry. The NRSA has been assigned the responsibility for regulating the commercial transport industry in the country but this is yet to be well effected and driver needs is not receiving the necessary attention. Some of the key issues for consideration include:*

i. Driver Engagement and Competition: In Ghana commercial driving is not considered as a specialized profession. It is open to all manner of people making it highly competitive. With an estimate of about three (3) drivers per every commercial vehicle, most drivers worry about job security. Besides there is no formalized code of practice in the engagement of a commercial driver with set criteria on qualification and experience.

Each vehicle owner in the informal sector sets his or her own terms for driver engagement making the driver susceptible to the requirements of the owner with only some marginal form of protection from the Unions who do not also operate with statutory rules. Therefore, there should be statutory conditions of employment to guide the informal commercial vehicle operator. This should include factors such as qualification, license type and grade, state of health certificate, employment and safety records endorsed by identified referees of good standing in society.

ii. Driver Welfare Factors: A number of commercial driver welfare issues affects their safety performance and some of these include the following:

a) Driver Remuneration: Most informal drivers are not paid salaries but rather receive commissions from vehicle owners based on performance. This instigates the need for drivers to maximize work performance for increased earnings resulting in situations of safety compromises such as delayed vehicle maintenance, extensive working hours, speeding etc. Driver unions must establish negotiated minimum wage rates for membership using the national minimum wage as a base rate with vehicle owners.

b). Insurance Cover: Even with motor insurance being a mandatory requirement for every vehicle in the country, a self-report estimate from a study be the NRSA in 2012 indicated that about 30% of commercial drivers in informal operations do not have insurance cover. Most drivers also complained about the complex and cumbersome processes involved in claiming for insurance (though unsubstantiated by statistics) after RTC situations. This discourages most of them from pursuing their legal claims making them worse off in the aftermath of RTCs. Those whose insurance cover would have expired within such periods do not receive anything at all.

To address these constraints a study by field observations of the state of commercial motor insurance should be conducted to ascertain the actual level of compliance and default with insurance cover. Also, police personnel could be assigned the responsibility to document the level of compliance and defaults from motor insurance as a part of their routine enforcement activities to guide appropriate mitigation measures. Drivers must also be educated and assisted to undertake private personal insurance schemes in addition to motor insurance to ensure adequate protection from RTC risks.

c). Union Welfare Schemes: The only welfare provision for most drivers is from membership dues paid by unionised drivers who operate from designated lorry stations or terminals. Drivers who do not have union membership do not have such opportunities. Even with this practice, about 56% of the funds are used to fund funerals for members with the rest going into service charges by union executives. Thus, in situations of injury from RTC or loss of employment the driver does not receive any support. Such schemes should be formally streamlined and managed well to provide security for the economic and health welfare needs of the members.

d). Driver Social Security: With only about 30% of drivers in formal employment having their Social Security being paid, the 70% remaining formal and informal commercial transport operators do not have any regularized funding support in case of RTCs or in retirement. About 31% of drivers in formal employment enjoy support for health care from their employers; 40% of them enjoy additional benefits such as accommodation, bonuses, commissions, payment of school fees, soft loans etc. However, the formal commercial transport industry controls only about 5% of the market share and this implies that the welfare of most commercial drivers in the country is woefully neglected and its implications on road safety cannot be overemphasised.

e). Driver Health Status: A study by the NRSC in 2008 involving about 700 commercial transport drivers in six (6) of the then 10 regions of Ghana which assessed driver working conditions revealed that about a third of the drivers interviewed acknowledged suffering from health-related problems such as; (hypertension, diabetes, asthma, ulcer, piles etc.) for which they were on permanent medication. 80% reported on frequent headaches due to long hours of driving in the heat of the sun and these reported fatigue as a major health challenge to effective performance. Thus, it is not uncommon to see commercial drivers buying refrigerated water and pouring on their heads to cool down the effect of the heat on the body, (See Figure 6.11).

About 27.6% of the drivers reported on stress resulting from traffic congestion, 14.9% from, inadequate sleep 11.8% bodily pains from the effects of poor road infrastructure, 11.7% from mental pressure to meet daily sales and 10.2% mental pressure from police harassment at 6%. Irrespective of the situations recounted, about 90% of the drivers claimed they did not have any challenges with their sight but this was based on self-reports without formal medical validation. The unions and employers should offer periodic health checks for the drivers using committed proportions of the contributions from drivers' dues.

Figure 6.11: Publication on Driver Eye Screening

f) Hours of Work: Since about 80% of the drivers do not own the vehicles they operate; they are mostly under pressure to meet this demand by increased number of trips and higher number of passengers transported. Thus, most drivers work for long hours with higher trip frequencies of which 43% is determined by the need to meet daily sales set by their employers; 30% is for personal gains after getting their daily sales; 20.7% is to make up for time lost in traffic congestions and 6.3% is for as long as there are passengers to be served even after official work hours, See Figure 6.12.

Figure 6.12: Publication on Driver Daily Sales

Thus, cumulatively, about 84% of the drivers work beyond the standard working hours of 8 hours per day. About 66% work beyond five working days in a week and about 70% of the drivers work all year without any form of leave. This causes driver fatigue which is recognised as significant contributory factor to RTCs. In addition, most drivers also travel at higher speeds beyond set speed limits in order to reduce travel time to secure more loads or passengers ahead of competitors especially with regards to floating drivers who do not belong to unions. The practice of hyper competition and the related excessive speeding usually result in fatal RTCs, (See Figure 6.13).

Figure 6.13: Driver Working Hours

Strategic campaigns were launched by the NRSC against fatigue in traffic targeting commercial vehicle in 2007 and nationwide and the evaluated results of the campaign of the programme in 2009 indicated that about (95%) of drivers still worked beyond the required 8 hours per day. The extent to which drivers comply with the statutory regulation for them not to drive continuously beyond 4 hours without break is not known and self-reports by drivers can also not be certified to be the truth and this must be investigated. The concept of a second or spare driver should be instituted over certain travel distances with remuneration aside what the substantive driver is paid. This will correct the current situation whereby a driver has to pay a second driver from their own resources which deters drivers from engaging second drivers on long journeys.

iii. Role of Government in Driver Welfare: Competent commercial drivers are a public commodity so government will have to take some responsibility in improving driver working conditions by taking the following actions:

a). Development of Standard Code of Practice for Driver Welfare: With the assignment of the NRSA as the commercial transport regulator in the country, the entity must develop a code of practice and core operational standards for commercial road transport in the country. Under the code individual vehicle ownership should be replaced by corporate business entities with professional and technical management systems from which vehicle owners could buy shares into and be paid fixed incomes and dividends.

This must be backed by law to enable autonomous operation under the corporate management system. It must ensure the payment of fixed monthly wages, driver insurance cover, and social security cover and the extension of union dues to driver welfare benefits including driver health care due to the high-risk nature of the industry from potential RTC situations.

iv. Facilitation of Implementation of Driver support Facilities and Services: The DVLA's agenda to introduce the installation and use of tachometers and speed limiters in vehicles to support safe driving must be facilitated.

v. Driver Safety Research: Further research in driver welfare needs should be conducted based on outreach programmes to solicit driver concerns so that appropriate measures can be applied.

vi. Driver Welfare at the Union Level: In addition to the formal transport regulatory agency, unions could be provided with the technical assistance on issues relating to safety commitment by vehicle owners and managers in the interim. Responsibility for some safety measures must be integrated into the functions of the unions including the following:

a). Safety Certification: There should be increased pre-trip inspections such as blood pressure checks, state of fatigue, alcohol intake, safety state of the vehicle by union executives ahead.

b). Driver Performance: Driver safety standards by the unions should be based on the principles of quality training; regulatory compliance and vehicle maintenance. A safety tally card should be kept on each driver for ensuring appropriate corrective measures.

c). Regulation of Driver Union: There should be driver code of conduct on speed limits, alcohol and substance intake etc. Good practices such as the tracking of the departure and arrival times of members should be sustained. Efforts should be made to enroll floating drivers who do not belong to unions in statutory driver unions. Also, competitions in good RTC records amongst union members could be instituted with rewards to motivate good driver behaviour. Drivers with RTC records should be assisted with safety training.

d). Driver Union Welfare schemes: Unions should also be team-based so they can create greater support network amongst its members. Complete and accurate records of driving performance should be kept by the Union on each individual to guide performance assessment. There should be standards for driver retention by vehicle owners to protect the interest of drivers. They should also negotiate with responsible agencies for the payment of social security by vehicle owners.

vii. Private Sector Contribution to Driver Welfare: Aside government and the driver union's private establishments can be set up to train and supply well trained professional drivers for the commercial transport industry.

viii. Employer Responsibilities to Driver The opinion of drivers should be solicited in operational decisions such as vehicle maintenance, general business decisions etc. e.g. mutual agreements on equity shares and attainability of daily sales. Vehicle owners should also insist on validity of license before entrusting vehicles to drivers supported with periodic rechecks.

ix. Responsibilities of Family Members to Driver Welfare: Driver, safety programmes should include the family members such as the spouses of the drivers and even children to sensitize them on the importance of safety as back up support for the drivers.

6.3.5 Driver Safety Errors

A. Causes of Driver Errors by Drivers: The factors which influence driver safety errors based on bad driver behaviour and attitudes of which the underlying cause is mostly attributed to the following:

i. Poor Driver Training: Some of the driver errors resulting from this are:

a.   Limited knowledge in traffic rules due to poor training.

b.   Poor management of unexpected traffic situations due to poor training.

c.   Lack of expertise in defensive driving due to poor training

ii. Driver Inexperience: Some of the driver errors resulting from this are.

a.   Driver, difficulty in managing complex manoeuvres or in wrong direction.

b.   Driver inability to avoid RTC due to the actions of other vehicles in given layouts.

c.   Premature action and late action such as wrongful application of emergency brakes.

d.   Prolonged action movement.

e.   Playing down other emergency situations.

f.   Driver counting on others to obey the rules of the road *iii. Self-Reported Causes of Driver Errors by Commercial Transport Operators: A self- reported study on causes of driver errors by drivers in Ghana showed that most drivers endorse wrongful conduct on the road as a major safety problem within their ranks. Most of these factors are interrelated and difficult to assess on merit. Interestingly low remuneration scored the second lowest in rank, which indicates that the problem of financial gain may not be of such a high level of significance as presented in Table 6.12.*

Table 6.12: Causes of Driver Error by Operators

Causes of Driver Error	Percentage	Rank
Lack of Understanding of Rules and Regulations	2.1	6
Pressure from Owner	8.4	3
Future Insecurity	3.2	5
Low Educational Level	2.1	6
Wrongful Conduct	67.4	1
Poor Training and Inexperience	9.4	2
Vehicle Operation, Maintenance	4.2	4
Low Remuneration	3.2	5
Total	100	

Source: Ablin Consult Survey, 2007

B. Types of Driver Errors

i. Reckless Driving: This involves a knowingly and openly disobeying traffic laws as follows:

a). Speeding: According to the WHO (2008), it remains a major risk for crashes with every 1 km/h decrease in speed decreasing crash risk by 2 - 3%. The UNCE, 92010) affirms to be true on the basis of enforcement of safe speed limits having been proven to be highly effective. Others are that:

- The time gained by driving faster is minimal and overestimated since on a journey of 100 km, only 6 minutes are gained by driving at 150 km/h instead of 130 km/h.

- Speed increases the risk of mistakes and fatigue sets in more quickly.

- Speed requires greater attention at night because the headlights' illumination is only up to 30m ahead and at a speed above 70 km/h an obstacle emerging into the lighted zone cannot be avoided;

- The faster the driving speed, the more visual perception is reduced since the field of vision is 100° at 40 km/h, but becomes 30° at130km/h;

- The higher the speed, the less the tyres adhere to the road.

Speed control in Ghana as a safety concern commenced ahead of the DOA with the launching of a speeding campaign implemented in 2008. Further on, other interventions have included the provision of seed guns to the police for highway speed checks on consistent basis which is ongoing as well as the introduction of log books on the start and end of commercial transport intercity journeys to control driver journey times. Others are the installation of speed calming measures and enforcement including a proposal to install speed limiters and tachometers in commercial vehicles yet to be effected,

However, the challenges with driver speeding in Ghana includes the following:

- *However, a study conducted by NRSA in 2019 showed that the proportion of vehicles exceeding the posted speed limit was still high on some highways especially on roads with good ride quality and on roads where commercial drivers compete excessively for more passengers as well as driver need to increase trip frequencies for more revenue. (See Figure 6.14).*

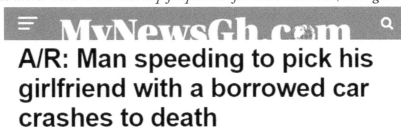

SPEEDING VEHICLE KILLS WOMAN, GRANDSON AT AMANFRO

Figure 6.14: Sample Publications on RTC Casualties caused by Speeding in Ghana

- *Speeding in Wrong Environment by ignoring obvious risks also causes higher possibility of RTC occurrence.*

- *Insufficient speed especially in mixed traffic situations with a combination of both fast and very slow-moving vehicles such causes driver impatience leading to wrongful overtaking. In Ghana slow moving vehicles such as motor tricycles used for transporting sachet water and refuse on city roads and a long convoy of slow-moving heavy goods vehicles on major highways causing driver impatience and leading to wrongful overtaking and related RTC consequences.*

b) Improper Overtaking: RTC from wrongful overtaking occurs when a driver fails to properly calculate the speed of an oncoming vehicle or overtakes another vehicle at a wrongful location such as a road section without a shoulder to escape or a shoulder with an obstructed n object.

In Ghana, RTCs caused by overtaking also happens, when another vehicle suddenly jumps in front of an overtaking vehicle without looking back, when an overtaking is done at a slow pace with other drivers closely following and when an on-coming vehicle with the right of way refuses to step onto the road shoulder to give way to the overtaking vehicle at close range. Others are when there are situations of multiple overtaking when an overtaking vehicle is also being overtaken by second and third vehicles.

c). Overloading: Overloading by goods vehicles especially HGVs on trunk roads.

In Ghana, RTC caused by overloading occurs when loads not well belted, when there is poor loading balance causing vehicles to topple to one side of the road and when an overloaded HGV drivers endanger the lives of other drivers by occupying the middle of a road for balance causing other drivers to swerve to other lanes or the bush. Falling loads from some moving and defaulting load heights colliding with overhead electric wires and gantries especially for loads above 4.5 to 5 meters also causes crashes.

Excess loads on vehicle axles above the set standards of 11 to 13tons per axle causes excessive tyre pressure leading to overheated tyres from friction with the road pavement during day time in the heat of the sun resulting in tyre bursts also causes RTCs. Unattended overloaded broken-down trucks left on the middle of the road which are not easily offloaded or moved causes obstructed clearance and vehicle run especially in situations of ineffective advance warning.

d). Wrongful Lane Change: Careless lane change done with little regard for interactions with same lane vehicles causes RTCs.

In Ghana, it is not uncommon to see drivers jumping in front of other vehicles with no advance warning for fear of being prevented to join the lane by other drivers. Others are the use of hand gestures to indicate lane change instead of the vehicle indicator system. Some drivers also give wrong lighting indicators by turning left whilst indicating a right turn. Of very critical importance is the unnecessary struggle for space by the vehicles involved creating an impression of the road being rolled away by the other vehicle and leaving no space for the other to use.

e) Other forms of Reckless Driving: In Ghana, These are of varied forms including forced swerving, jumping of red lights, load and offload of passengers on the road e for safe passenger embankment and dis-embankment. This due to the possibility of the passenger being knocked down straight from the vehicle or from rushing to cross the road. Tailgating also causes RTCs especially when there is an emergency brake by the vehicle in front.

ii. Distractive Driving: This involves situations where driver attention is diverted from the road unto other activities such as listed below with high potential for the occurrence of RTCs. In Ghana, these include:

a.   *Operation of electronic devices e.eg. radio, GPS devices, air conditioner, mobile devices, (including hands-free and texting on hand held mobile devices). Others are, windshield wipers and lights as well as eating, drinking and Smoking.*

b. *Disturbance from other passengers such as uncontrolled children, pets and other passengers.*

c. *Distractions outside the vehicle from outside person, objects or events. (See Figure 6.15).*

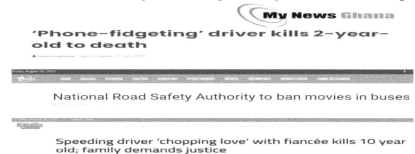

Figure 6.15: Publications on Driver Distractions Causing RTCs

iii. Impaired Driving: This is mostly attributed to factors such as follows:

a). Impaired driving from alcohol, substance and medications causing driver cognitive impairment.

In Ghana, some commercial drivers use alcohol as energy boosters to counteract fatigue with alcohol being sold at some lorry stations and terminals and the efforts to ban the practice has not been effective. It is also common to seek parked vehicles in front of drinking bars with the owners drinking openly. People behind the wheels also drink at funerals and other social functions with little concern for the fact that they are diving. This implies that little premium is attached to the seriousness of drunk driving by some drivers in the country and this must be addressed.

A campaign against driving under the influence of alcohol was launched and implemented in 2008 and 2010 and research into the magnitude of the problem was also conducted by the by the NRSA through the BRRI in 2012. The result showed that out of 2,736 drivers randomly stopped with their BrAC measured, 64% tested positive for alcohol and also exceeded the legal BAC limit of 0.08%; 19% had BrAC between 0.05 and 0.08% whilst the remaining 17% had ingested alcohol ranging between 0.001 to 0.05%. None of the 2% female drivers sampled had detectable alcohol indicating low female alcohol impairment whist driving in Ghana.

Driver use of drug related substances such as the ("asra") a powdered drug containing moringa and cocaine or weed) and "wee toffee" (acclaimed to be a potent drug but for which the enforcement agencies are not well equipped to detect. Such substances are also deemed to be energy for long distance driving and long hours of driving in the heat of the sun (See Figure 6.16).

Figure 6.16: Publications on Impaired Driving

Major interventions to address driver alcohol and substance abuse include driver educational campaigns and enforcement with alcometers tests by the MTTD. However, testing for drug intake is challenged by lack of equipment. The possibility of instant urine test for drugs for suspected drivers should be explored. Modern vehicular installations for detecting driver alcohol and substance abuse should also be explored. Drivers should be enlightened through education and effective punitive measures on which unsafe habits are of high risk to them (See Figure 6.17).

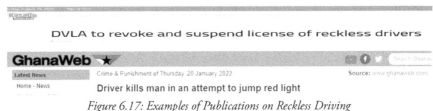

Figure 6.17: Examples of Publications on Reckless Driving

b). Fatigue Driving: Fatigue driving from long driving hours and lack of adequate rest and sleep by drivers often results in drowsiness, tiredness etc. which can cause RTCs to occur.

A study on fatigue driving in Ghana by the NRSA in 2008 reported that one (1) out of every five (5) drivers had reported on experiencing dangerous situations in traffic due to tiredness However, the key challenge was that they underestimated the dangers of driving when tired which posed a great danger to themselves and other road users, (See Figure 6.18).

Figure 6.18: Examples of Publication on Impacts of Fatigue Driving

Following the study, Ghana launched a fatigue campaign in 2009 and 2010 and an evaluation conducted in 2012 on its impacts revealed that the desire to make the required sales with additional commission accounted for mostly for fatigue driving amongst commercial drivers. Drivers should be tracked and monitored by their employers and union executives to ensure compliance. Adequate rest stops should also be provided along major roads for rest, meal breaks, naps and security. The adoption of the use of technical innovations such as mechanical tachometers as a recorder on hours of driving should be considered.

Most importantly, a complete overhaul of the operational economy of the commercial transport business is very critical to solving the remuneration problem. Drivers should be tracked, and scored on unsafe driving behaviours supported with real-time alerts and reminders to control the problem. The current log book system must be effectively enforced and alternative measures for reducing driver stress such as the use of spare drivers should be explored, though currently most drivers shy away from the use of spare drivers for economic reasons because they do not want to share their meagre commission.

c). Poor Visibility from Dazing Headlights: High beam from headlights at night blinds oncoming drivers from good visibility causing RTCs to occur.

iv. Lack of Occupancy Compliance: Limited compliance to the use of vehicle occupancy constraints such as seatbelts, helmets and child restraints results in high RTC fatality impacts etc. *This is also a challenge in Ghana.*

v. Other Factors: Other factors causing driver errors in traffic which are also typical to the Ghanaian situation include:

a). Negligent Parking: These include excessive on- street parking and haphazard parking on narrow busy roads which reduces road widths, increases unpredictability of the road environment and parked vehicles re-joining the traffic and vehicles looking for space to park.

In Ghana, in addition to the above the challenge of none compliance with required traffic impact assessment laws, wrongful siting of traffic generating land use systems and limited availability of parking spaces also contributes to this challenge

b). Limited Vehicular Volumes: This often leads to driver familiarity with the road and a sense of ownership with little driving caution resulting in driver errors.

In Ghana, this is very typical on rural roads and at night on highways when drivers assume they are alone on the road.

c). Events: In Ghana, seasonal influences such as destructive traffic behaviours during festive season, picnics and sudden road blocks for funerals also contributes to driver errors in traffic with consequences for the occurrence of RTC situations.

d). Inappropriate Warning of Hazards: This is especially bad where broken down vehicles or crashed vehicles are left on the road without proper warning signs by the use of reflective triangles as required by law. Due to concern for theft sometimes there is wrongful placement of the triangles e.g. on top of the vehicles or close to it instead of the stipulated 3.048 meters by law. In some instances drivers resort to the use of leaves and fuel containers which are not reflective at night.

C. Statistics on Fatalities by Driver Errors in Ghana: *A study on RTC records of trends in fatalities by driver behaviour showed that loss of control from undefined driver error is the highest at about 67% as presented in Figure 6.19. This is followed by inattentive driver error at 14% and speeding at 13%. Improper overtaking is at 3% with fatigue driving and driving close to each other following at an average of 1% each.*

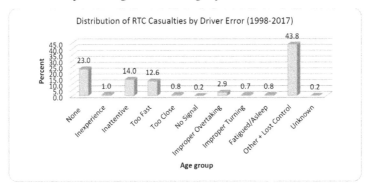

Figure 6.19: Distribution of RTC casualties by driver error (1998 – 2017)

The situation with driver RTC fatality by driver error at the beginning of the DOA and in 2018 shows that RTC fatalities from driver inattentiveness, improper overtaking and inexplicable factors are worsening, whilst very little has been achieved on driver loss of control and to some extent driver inexperience. However, some progress has been made with reduced fatalities from speeding which is encouraging since speed is deemed to be of very impact significance to RTC fatalities. (See Figure 6.20).

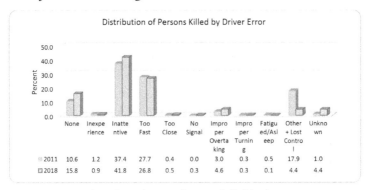

Figure 6.20: Distribution of persons killed by driver error

6.3.6 Road Infrastructure Features and Driver Safety Errors

Thus the, key challenge with infrastructure causing driver error is attributed to good sight distance, good ride quality, lack of identification and classification of roads by risk level for appropriate driver informed caution.

A. Driver Error and Road Geometry: Generally, roads must be designed with safety considerations.

In Ghana major highways mostly have higher design standards with good ride quality and adequate sight distance but may still be of high-risk safety threat due to the driver error of speeding and it can even be said that often times the higher the mobility standards the more RTCs are likely to occur.

Specifically, fatality records in Ghana shows that 78% of them occur at straight road sections followed by curved sections at almost 11% mostly due to poor visibility (see Figure 6.21). This implies that the role of driver error in the use of road infrastructure a significant contributory factor in causing RTCs rather than the state of the infrastructure itself and driver training in such issues must be priortised in addition to the provision of speed calming measures.

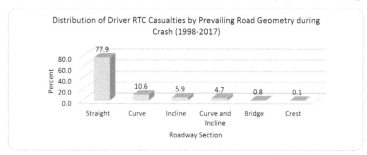

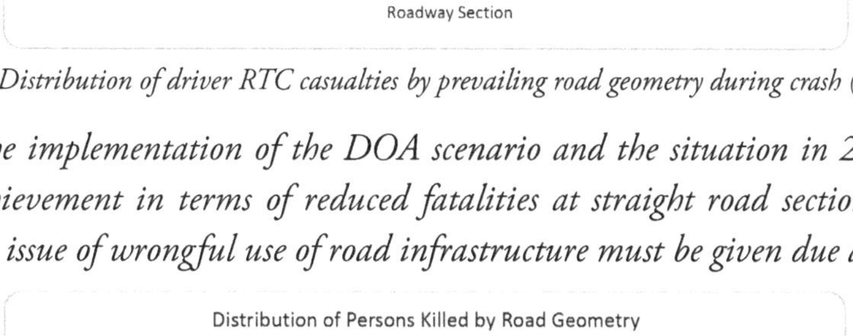

Figure 6.21: Distribution of driver RTC casualties by prevailing road geometry during crash (1998-2017)

The start of the implementation of the DOA scenario and the situation in 2018 indicates very little achievement in terms of reduced fatalities at straight road sections (see Figure 6.22) and the issue of wrongful use of road infrastructure must be given due attention.

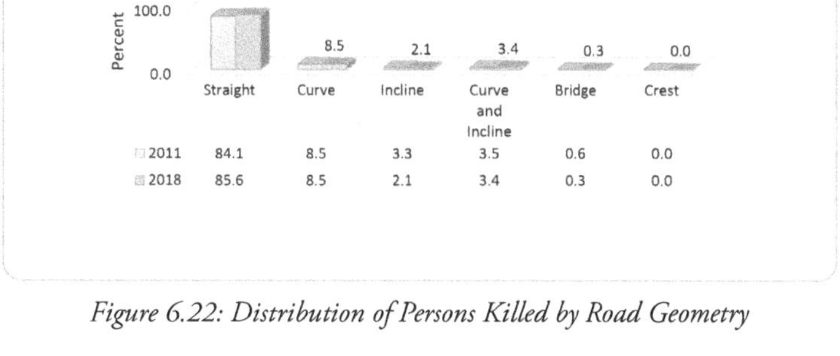

Distribution of Persons Killed by Road Geometry

	Straight	Curve	Incline	Curve and Incline	Bridge	Crest
2011	84.1	8.5	3.3	3.5	0.6	0.0
2018	85.6	8.5	2.1	3.4	0.3	0.0

Figure 6.22: Distribution of Persons Killed by Road Geometry

B. Driver Error and Speed Calming Measures: *In Ghana, though some speed calming measures such as speed calming measures are often provided for speed control driver failure to reduce speed and efforts to swerve the use of such facilities by the use of the road shoulder still causes RTCs. Also lack of uniformity in the provision of such facilities such as the combination of speed rumps and bumps on the same road length does not yield effective results. This is because some, drivers get confused between the use of speed tables, speed humps, rumble strips etc. In some cases also, long distance drivers complain of increased journeys times from the provision of excessive speed calming measures in sections of the road with human settlements since such facilities slow them down. Thus, driver behaviour with regard to the use of speed calming measures will have to be well investigated for effective results.*

C. Driver Error and Road intersections: *From recorded data, driver error remains the major cause of intersection related RTC's in Ghana. This is because 86% of RTCs in Ghana resulting in high-risk fatalities occur at road sections without junctions (see Figure 6.23). This is mostly attributed to excessive speeding at straight road sections in Ghana. Road traffic crashes at T-Junctions follow at 8.6%. This is normally due to poor observation and driver refusal to yield. RTC at cross roads follows at 5% with RTC at other locations being on a small scale.*

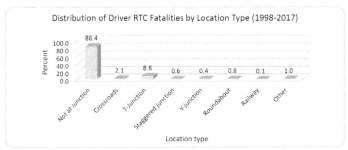

Figure 6.23: Distribution of RTC Fatalities by Location Type (1998-2017).

Fatalities by road location before the DOA (2011-2020) and 2018 showed little progress. This is because the challenge of RTC situations at straight road sections and cross sections worsened by small margins whilst efforts at dealing with fatalities at T-Junctions yielded some good results, (See Figure 6.24).

Figure 6.24: Distribution of Persons Killed by Location Type after DOA Implementation

D. Driver Error by Road Class: *Highways recorded the highest RTC severity at about (50%) between 1998 and 2017. This is because longer trip lengths are made on highways compared to the other road classes and this compels drivers to speed in order to reach their destinations within the shortest possible time. Also, though highways are often designed to high-speed levels but traverses built up areas where reduced speed levels are required but are not adhered to. Fatalities on urban roads is next at 34% and this is mostly attributed to reckless driving factors such as jumping of red light, poor intersection design, and distracted driving from the use of hand-held mobile devices. Rural roads have the least 16.3% of RTC fatalities as presented in Figure 6.25 and the reasons attributed are mainly to do with low traffic.*

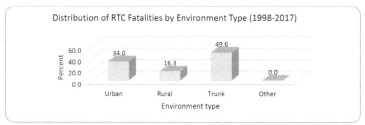

Figure 6.25: Distribution of RTC fatalities by environment type (1998-2017)

E. Driver Error on Multi Lane Roads: Two-way traffic roads increase the probability of higher RTC severity relative to one-way roads. Thus, ideally multi-lane roads should reduce the probability of higher RTC occurrence relative to single carriage roads.

However, the opposite happens in Ghana because drivers are more careful on single carriage-ways due to reduced lateral clearance with opposing traffic as compared to multi-lane roads which have enough space to encourage over speeding, overtaking and careless lane change etc. This is on assumption of little regard for interactions with same lane vehicles.

F. Service Roads: Service roads running parallel to the main road where traffic interfere with the movement of others also causes RTCs situations. This is because sometimes some drivers move in the opposite direction often causing pedestrian hits. Joining the main road with little care from the service roads also sometimes results in RTCs.

G. Wrongful Use of Road Furniture: *An example in Ghana is the use of laybys as parking and loading stations rather than for short-term stopping causing of the closure of lanes, congestion, driver impatience, stopping and joining of the road with little caution.*

H. Driver RTC Fatalities by Collision Type: Driver RTC fatalities by head on collisions accounts for (31%) and common causes include wrongful over taking, distracted driving, fatigue driving, bad weather conditions, disregard for traffic signs/signals and in some instances vehicle malfunction. These types of RTCs can be very serious and result in many different types of injuries especially when there is speeding. This is followed by vehicle run off road at 16% with these types of crashes often occurring on both curves and straights. This happens when drivers are distracted and swerve across the road to the wrong direction, when there is a vehicle defect or when there is a pothole and a driver attempts to avoid it.

Rear-end collisions and side swipe collision follow at about 15% and 10% respectively (See Figure 6.26). Rear end collisions occur when a vehicle strikes the rear of the vehicle in front of it as a result of sudden breaks mostly due to tailgating and sudden brakes, distracted driving and attempt to check a red light with the driver in front stopping for the amber light. These types of RTCs are rarely fatal but sometimes victims develop serious injuries resulting in fatalities. Side-swipe collisions or T-bone injuries occur when a driver fails to stop at an intersection, especially at traffic signals resulting in it striking another vehicle that has the right of way on the side. Side-impact collisions are particularly dangerous, since the sides of vehicles offer little protection against impact forces.

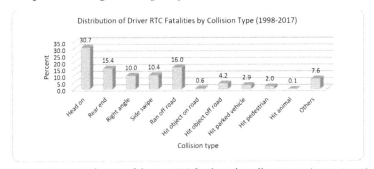

Figure 6.26: Distribution of driver RTC fatalities by collision type (1998-2017)

A comparison of RTC fatality by collision types at the start of the implementation of the DOA strategies compared to the situation as of 2018 indicates that there has been good progress with pedestrian RTCs as well as vehicle overturn. The pedestrian situation can be attributed to improved campaigns and increased provision of pedestrian safety installations. That of vehicle overturn can be attributed to improved curve design with provision of adequate curve radius and superelevation.

However, there has not been good progress with reductions in fatalities from other collision types such as head and rear end collision with run off being an emerging collision challenge. The limited improvement made for collision at 90 degree and side swipe could be attributed first to challenges at cross junctions due to none functional traffic signals at some intersections from poor maintenance. That of side swipe could be attributed to poor judgement of drivers entering roundabouts and in changing lanes on multi-lane roads. These factors have to be given more attention on the way forward. Refer to Figure 6.27 for details.

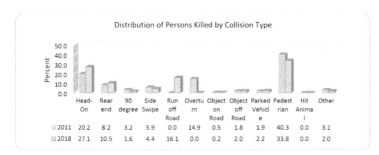

Figure 6.27: Distribution of persons killed by collision type

6.3.7 Driver Error by Vehicle Safety Factors

A. Effects of Vehicle Factors on Driver Errors: *This mostly include RTCs from tyre burst, engine overheat, brake failures and improper alertness of broken-down vehicles in Figure 6.28)*

Figure 6.28 Examples of abandoned broken down vehicles in Ghana

B. Driver Error by Environmental Conditions: These include the following:

i. Driver Error and Poor Lighting: In Ghana, most (67%) of fatalities by driver errors occur during day light compared to global records of higher fatalities by night. This implies that where there is good lighting, drivers take less safety precaution by being careless and reckless. This is followed by night driving on unlighted streets at night at 18.7% which can be attributed to poor visibility. Night street light on is about 11.8% whilst night street light off is about 3%. Figure 6.29 provides the details.

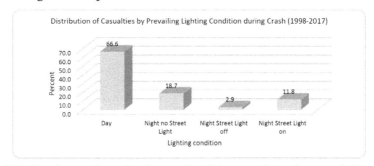

Figure 6.29: Distribution of casualties by prevailing lighting condition during crash (1998-2017)

The RTC fatality situation on lighting in 2018 compared to the start of the DOA shows that, fatality records in daylight and on streets with lights on is worsening, whilst that of street with no light has made little change (see Figure 6.30). This emphasises the fact that driver risk perception in good road environment is underestimated in Ghana.

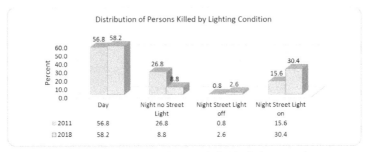

Figure 6.30: Distribution of persons killed by lighting condition

ii. Driver Error and Bad Weather Conditions: Adverse weather conditions such as rain and fog create poor visibility especially in hilly and forest areas and at night in unlighted road environments. The situation is made worse where there is poor surface condition which can cause a driver to lose vehicular control or lane runoff causing RTC.

This is especially on asphaltic pavements or slippery earth roads becoming slippery from rain worsened by worn out tyres since wet road surface reduces the friction of the road surface in contact with a vehicle's tyres as a thin film of water builds up between the road surface and the tyres reducing the stopping distances (OECD, 1976). The lack of adhesion may also be apparent around bends in the road or when attempting certain manoeuvres (Brodsky & Hakkert, 1988). Also splashes and spray from other vehicles can throw up surface water and dirt unto the windscreen causing momentarily blindness.

Flooded roads due to poor drainage reduces road lanes as well as in some instances cause vehicles to submerge in open drains Ghana, Foggy weather conditions which normally occurs during the dry harmattan season especially at dawn also results in fatal RTCs. This is especially true on highways, where drivers do not reduce their speed for fear of either losing sight of the vehicle in front or being struck by another vehicle from behind when the vehicle is stopped on the road. There is also a tendency to become isolated from the road environment whilst driving in fog.

Therefore, in foggy and rainy weather, drivers are often advised to use their headlights or park far away from the road in a safe location till the weather condition improves. In addition to this, there is need to provide for good lighting on the highways especially at sections with no settlements and on bends. Respective MMDAs and the road agencies should endeavour to make the provision of adequate lighting compulsory for most roads if not all. Knowledge and skills in defensive driving in such situations should also be provided in driver training programmes.

Statistically in Ghana, the vast majority 82% of RTC fatalities occur in fine non-hazardous weather conditions and this should be well investigated to determine the actual cause. RTC fatality in foggy weather is also estimated at 3.2% followed by RTC fatalities in rainy weather at 1.4%. Other weather related RTC fatalities in Ghana include windy, cloudy and smoky environment at 13.2% as depicted in Figure 6.31. Thus, it is important for the necessary skills to be imparted to drivers during training to enable them better manage extreme weather situations.

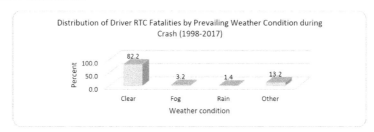

Figure 6.31: Distribution of driver RTC fatalities by prevailing weather condition during crash (1998-2017)

RTC fatality by driver error and weather condition did not change with regards to high records in clear weather conditions and in foggy conditions between the start of the DOA compared to the situation in 2018. However, some minor gains were made with regards to other weather conditions as depicted in Figure 6.32.

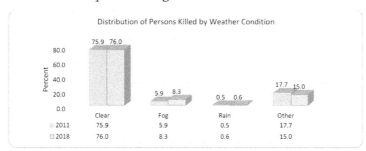

Figure 6.32: Distribution of persons killed by weather condition

C. Driver Error by Land Use Factors: *In Ghana, records of RTC fatalities by land use factors indicate that most 43% of the RTC locations occur on roads environments without built up facilities on major highways (see Figure 6.33). A speed study by (NRSA 2019) also revealed that the highest speed levels of beyond 120km/hr were recorded at such road sections. This implies limited driver caution at such road sections.*

Passenger RTC occurrence in commercial zones at 29% due to localised stressful conditions is next. Both RTC occurrence in residential and school zones are at the same level at 14% each indicating that there is some level of driver precaution for reduced speed at such sections. Since undeveloped highway sections turn to be distanced from built up settlements, there tends to be little enforcement making higher enforcement by the Police at such sections very critical.

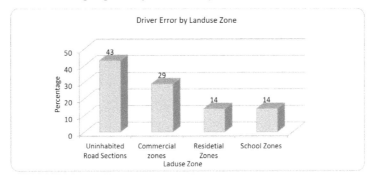

Figure 6.33: Driver error by land use zone

D. Driver Error and Post-Crash Effects: *In Ghana, wrongful driver actions after RTCs can result in serious consequence on post-crash effects and examples include the following:*

a. *Not switching off engine and smoking especially where one of the vehicles involved in the crash is carrying flammable and explosive goods or there is fuel spillage causing fires.*

b. *Standing at the wrong side of the road with possible hit by an oncoming vehicle.*

c. *Not moving a wrongfully positioned vehicle for purposes of not disturbing evidence.*

d. *Not providing adequate signals at RTC locations to prevent other vehicles from running into the crash vehicles and victims.*

e. *Transporting an RTC victim in a wrong vehicle with possibility for further injuries and death*

6.3.8 Overlapping Factors Causing Driver Errors

A lot of the major causes of RTC fatalities can overlap with each other. An example, is a drunk driver in bad weather, with high speed on poor road surface with many potholes or a road with very good ride quality. Such a situation can also cause RTCs with disastrous consequences. Thus, a notion that elements of the transport system, roads and vehicles, should be designed to accommodate the limitations and vulnerability of the human body in the form of a safe transport system is being promoted. This will make the mistakes of drivers to be corrected by the sustainable design of roads and vehicles.

However, until this becomes effective in Ghana, drivers must be taught and managed with expertise, so they can learn to drive safely since no vehicle is capable of keeping road users safe in any road traffic crash situation except their own skills that will provide them the best chance at survival.

6.3.9 Driver Safety Interventions Implemented

A. Driver Error Enforcement: *Driver safety enforcement issues include enforcing good driver behaviour and demanding vehicle safety and examples being implemented and could be implemented in Ghana are as follows:*

i. Driver Safety Enforcement by Various Government Agencies: Various road safety stakeholder entities including MTTD, DVLA, NRSA and MMDAs conduct enforcement activities

ii. Driver Safety Enforcement by Transport Operators: These must include internal driver monitoring and record keeping on license, road worthy and insurance validity for reminders on expiry dates by union executives. Others are conduct of weekly inspection of vehicles and review of passenger complaints about drivers for redress. Pre-departure vehicle inspections at lorry parks using well defined guidelines certified by the NRSA with punitive measures such as suspension or the payment of fines or in severe sacked from the unions must be instituted.

iii. Mitigation of Major Constrains to Driver Safety Enforcement: These includes the following:

a). Strict enforcement of regulations on speed limits, overloading and effective education on reckless and aggressive driving.

b). Modernisation of enforcement mechanisms and consistency with adequate resources eg funding, technical capacity and logistics to support enforcement activities.

c). Institution of effective punitive measures for drivers to feel the negative impact of their wrongful actions as deterrence for repeating same offences.

d). control of the activities of floating (roaming) drivers who do not belong to any unions for effective regulation.

e). The urgency in moving costs of non-compliance beyond bribery to potential commercial gains.

f). Introduction of self-financing measures for compulsory refresher driver training by unions

g). Restriction of drivers to specific travel speeds as implemented by the STC for long distance travels.

h). Implementation of continuous research backup for areas of need for effective interventions.

B. Driver Safety Campaigns: *The NRSA engages with national and local media as well as local to communicate driver safety messages to drivers. Some of the modes of driver campaigns and the campaign messages are as listed in (Table 6.13).*

Table 6.13: Driver Campaign Types and Messages

Description	Campaign	Safety Issues of Focus
Campiagn Modes	Occasional emphasis at Christmas and Easter	
	Campaign Activities	
	Advertorials on Road safety	
	Crash prone sites	
	Lorry stations	
	Community based Outreach programmes	
	Road Safety Advocates	
	Institutional Events e.g. Road Safety Week, Public Transport Days, Road Safety Awards	
	Social Gatherings e.g. Churches, Mosques, Funerals	
	Community based electronic media	
	Public Education Campaigns	
Safety Officers (RSOs)		Provides guidelines for commercial passenger operations.
Road Signs	Know your signs and markings	
Vehicle Safety		Vehicle tyres and road safety in Ghana
Driver	Guardian angel	
	Avoid swerving potholes	
	Avoid traffic jams on railways	
	A responsible driver is a defensive driver	
	There is no substitute for safety, "Making roads safer always starts with you,"	
	"Observe Safety and Save a Life,"	
Speed Control	Kill that speed (driver)	Minimize their speeds – Max. Speed Limit of 80kph on Highways, 50kph in Towns and Villages along Highways, 30kph in School Areas, 100kph on Motorway
Control of Wrongful Overtaking	Stop wrongful overtaking	Can overtake only when it is safe, i.e. Not in Curves, Not on Hills, ensure that no vehicle is approaching from the opposite direction
Fatigue Driving	"Don't Drive Tired,"	Stop driving and rest for 15 – 30 minutes after driving continuously for 4 hours
Mobile phones	Park off the road and listen to your call	Be attentive whilst on the road, e.g. Not to use mobile phones while driving
Alcohol Control	Drivers, avoid alcoholic beverages	Not to drive under the influence of Alcohol or Drugs
	Don't Drink and Drive,	
	Don't Drive and Drink	
Seatbelt	Seatbelts save lives	
	Why wear seatbelt?	
	Fasten your seatbelt, save your life	

C. Suggested Mitigating Factors for Driver Performance Improvement

i. Promotion of employer (Car Owner Safety Initiatives): Public transport vehicle owners must be engaged to have good understanding of the importance of safety and to assist with driver assessment eligibility such as conduct of Background checks, license validation, confirmation of the driver's safety record, health status etc. using a criteria for driver selection by consistent standards.

ii. Counselling of Newly Hired Drivers: Newly hired drivers must be oriented on the safety requirements of the new job, demands of the job, familiarity of the vehicles, rules and regulations on alcohol use, overloading, overtaking etc. There must also be a probation phase to monitor driver performance for corrections.

iii. Driver Motivation: There should measures for continuous driver upgrade through training, rewards, and disciplinary measures.

iv. Conduct of Post-Incident Coaching: There should post RTC training to address the type of collision that the driver was in with the level of the intervention equal to the seriousness of the incident.

v. Recognition for Effects of Corrective Measures: Recognition of effects of driver corrections must be well noted for further corrections if the need be.

vi. Provision of Field Station Manager Support: There should station managers for journey start and end points.

vii. Sample Guidelines for Driver Safety Management for Commercial Transport services: Examples of best practice driver safety management from literature is listed in Table 6.13.

Table 6.13: Summary of Best Practice Risk Management

1. Driver appraisal / assessment: Development of a method to evaluate driver candidates to determine if they are acceptable drivers by
i. verification that driver's license is valid.
a. Documentation of a photocopy of both sides of the license on a drivers file
b. Noting of any driving restrictions eg. corrective lenses, no night time driving, etc.
ii. Hiring of drivers with a minimum of 5 years of driving experience
iii. Hiring of drivers of 25 years and above
iv. Disqualification of drivers with the following
   -three (3) or more violations in 3 years involvement with a fatal crash;
   -involvement in hit and run driving;
   -driving under a suspended, revoked, or expired license;
   -committed felony with a vehicle,
   -record of false report to police department;
   -records of reckless, negligent or careless driving
   -engagement in Two (2) or more preventable RTCs in 3 years;
   -Failure of alcohol testing or convicted of any alcohol or drug related offenses including, but not limited to, driving while under the influence of alcohol or drugs within the past five years
   -poor knowledge on rules,
   -establishment of procedures in place to maintain "acceptable" driver behaviour

2. Demonstration of management support: Elements that demonstrate an organization's commitment to the driver safety programme includes:
a. Establishment of a safety policy statement with driver education on it
b. Engagement of experts to oversee driver safety
c. Establishment of writhe safety standards for operating procedures for drivers
d. Conduct of consistent enforcement with driver accountability for any RTCs sustained
e. Use of incentives for good performance
f. Placement of emphasis on recurring topic in driver meetings
g. Revision and update pf safety rules accordingly

4. Orientation and training programmes: This includes:
a. Conduct of refresher formal and informal training programmes to communicate important safety information;
b. Use of checklist to assure all topics are consistently covered
c. Assigning a driver Mentor as part of the driver safety training programme and ensuring driver accountability to RTCs

5. Incident reporting process:
a. Establishment of procedures and training of drivers in what to do in RTC situations eg important phone numbers to call
b. Engagement of legal advice for response to RTCs

76. Inspections and maintenance:
a. Training of drivers on how to do a thorough vehicle inspection;

Source: Components of Commercial Driver Safety Programme: Markelinsurance.com

6.4 MOTORCYCLE SAFETY

Motorcycle crashes constitute about 40 per cent of the road accidents in 2021

6.4.1 Introduction

According to Yousif (2020), motorcycles are associated with inherent instability that exposes users to much more danger than automobiles but with not so advanced safety research knowledge compared to that of automobiles. This is because the riding of motorcycle requires different riding skills, handling and safety responsiveness than automobiles though both are powered units which share the same road space and are required to meet common traffic standards. Radin U., (2006) intimates that motor rider vulnerability is based on the fact that exposed human body of a rider comes into direct contact with outdoor elements such as a hard road surface.

Motorcycles also have much, higher power-to-weight ratios than cars and are capable of high speeds (ec.europa-July 2020) and this takes the danger up to another level (Andijanto A, et al. 2016). Thus, in the Global Mobility Report, (2017), the WHO and World Bank advised for care to be taken to avoid the adoption of policies which could encourage the growth of motorized two-wheeler traffic by giving advantages to motorized two-wheeler users.

However, though an illegal operation in, Ghana, under the Traffic Act LI 2180 of 2012 there is growing trend of the use of motorcycles for commercial transport with escalating fatality and injury rates. This section of the chapter therefore highlights some of the critical issues associated with motorcycle safety in Ghana.

6.4.2 Conventions and Regulations on Motorcyclesafety

A. Global Conventions on Motorcycle:

i. Motorcycle Safety Regulations by Convention 68: The provisions of the Convention on Road Traffic, 1968, (article 33, paragraph 1) on bicycles which also applies to motor-cycles recommends the following guidelines as summarised in Table 6.14.

Table 6.14: UN Convention 68 on Motorcycles

6.1 Bicycles	6.1.2.1 Regulations concerning the use of bicycles	Applicability in Ghana
6.1.2.1.1	Visibility at night	It is mandatory for riders to wear reflective clothing at night LI 2180 84. (1)
6.1.2.1.2 Marking of trailers coupled to cycles	If a trailer is coupled to a cycle, it must be equipped with a red reflecting device if the rear lamp of the cycle is hidden by the trailer.	Motorcycle trailer must have two un-obscured and efficient red reflectors LI 2180 78. (1)
6.1.2.1.3 Special rules	(a) Wearing of helmets	It is mandatory for motor riders and pillion riders to wear helmets LI 2180 84.(1)
	Bicycle equipment and helmets should be the object of information or awareness campaigns	Road safety campaigns on helmet use are conducted in Ghana
6.1.2.3 Infrastructure for bicycles	Specific types of infrastructure, must be provided to protect two and three wheelers.	Limited provisions have been made.
6.2.2.1 Rider permits and licensing for mopeds and motorcycles	Initial rider training (pre-licence training) is very important. It should be affordable and accessible.	Motor riders are required to be licensed before being riding but some people fail to comply.
6.2.2.2 Rider training		Formal motor rider training requirements are yet to be established in Ghana only adhoc training programmes have been held. 84.(1)
66.2.2.5 Safety campaigns	Public information campaigns provide an opportunity to educate motorcycle and moped riders, as well as other motorists and road users.	There has been motorcycle educational campaigns
6.2.2.5 Law enforcement	Law enforcement personnel must play an important role in motorcycle and moped safety.	Failure of a motor rider to stop at Police signal is an offence LI 2180 169. (1)
article 36, paragraph 2 of the Convention on Road Traffic of 1968 6.2.2.6 Trailers	Trailers must ensure safe performance for operation (speed, visibility, braking) with uncovered number plate	This is in force under LI 2180 78.(1)
6.2.2.7 Infrastructure	Traffic engineering is a critical element of any crash reduction programme. The authorities responsible for road infrastructure should be aware of the needs of riders.	185. (1)
6.2.4.2 Riding motorcycles	(a) Aptitudes required for motor riders To obtain a motorcycle driving permit, (b) motor riders should drive with the passing lamps or daytime running lamps switched on	Motor Riders are licensed but without aptitude tests but are required to ride with daylight running light.

ii. DOA (2011-2020) Standards on Motorcycle Safety: A summary of the DOA standards for motorcycle safety is as presented below in Table 6.15.

Table 6.15: DOA Standards on Motorcycle Safety

Section	Details	Applicability in Ghana
Pillar 4:	Pillar 4: There must be public awareness/education to increase seat-belt and helmet wearing rates, and to reduce drink-driving, speed and other risk factors	This is applied in Ghana under LI2180 84 (1)
Activity 3	Set and seek compliance with drink–driving laws	This is applied in Ghana

B. Motorcycle Policy in Ghana: *Ghana's road safety policy as with the convention 68 does not have a stand- alone section on motorcycle safety but dovetails it into a broad Intermediate Means of Transport (IMT) section. The policy statement states that the design* *and construction of all road facilities and IMTs will take into account the safety needs of their users. Government will seek to promote the use of IMTs and also disseminate best practices to stakeholders such as town planners, architects, and highway and traffic engineers. Scheme swill also be introduced for the safe operation of IMTs. The summary of key challenges associated with motorcycle safety in Ghana and the related policy objectives are presented in Table 6.16.*

Table 6.16: Motorcycle Policy in Ghana

Policy Issue	Policy Objective/Strategy	Status of Application
Key Challenges	Strategies	
Inadequate dedicated bicycle tracks for the safe movement of cyclists forcing them to share the roadway with motorized transport.	Provide and maintain dedicated tracks for the use of IMTs to prevent IMTs from sharing the road with motorized traffic.	Some dedicated cycle lanes have been provided on some roads but are not adequate
Encroachment of the few bicycle tracks predominantly by traders further pushing cyclists into the roadway.	Create awareness for drivers of motorized and non-motorised vehicles on the safe use of the road.	This remains a challenge for the MMDA's to resolve
Disregard of cyclists by drivers of vehicles.	Enact appropriate legislation for the acquisition, licensing and operation of IMTs.	Some road safety educational campaigns have been conducted
Insufficient awareness, bad practices and inappropriate behaviour on the part of drivers of IMTs in traffic and inappropriate legislation for IMT operations.	Enforce laws and regulations on the use of motorcycles for commercial transport operations.	Some provisions have made in the LI 2180 of 2012 but has not been evaluated for extent of achievement of set objectives

6.4.3 Statistical Profile of Motor Riders in Ghana

Motorcycle ridership in Ghana is of three main categories, those used for private purposes, those used for corporate errands including courier services and those used for commercial transport activities. However, motorcycle crash records are not segregated by the type of ridership. This has resulted in limited availability of information per each category except for a study conducted in 2010 on commercial motorcycle operations in the country by the NRSA.

However, available statistics on RTCs involving motor riders in general show that the annual proportion of motorcycle fatalities has been increasing over the years as detailed in the immediate sub sections. Between 2009 and 2017, the number of registered motorcycles increased in Ghana by 81.2% whilst the related fatality rates increased by 135.9% (See Figures 6.34).

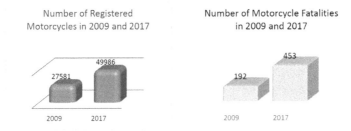

Figure 6.34: (a) Number of registered motorcycles and (b) Number of motorcycles fatalities in 2009 and 2017

A. Motorcycle RTC Statistics by Demography in Ghana

i. Distribution of Motor Cycle RTC Fatalities by Age of Victims in Ghana: Though others are of the view that age does not always translate to experience or ability, for RTCs with motorcycles, the highest risk was found in the age group of 20 to 29 years, (Barsi et al. 2002).

In Ghana, young people of up to age 35 constitute the highest (68%) of those involved in motorcycle fatalities and 86% are up to age 45 and this is consistent with global records, (See Figure 6.35). The same trend is observed for pillion riders with 72% of the fatality of pillion rider victims being involving those up to age 35 with 91% up to age 45. It is not uncommon to see underage children (those below or equal to 15years) riding motorcycles without any safety precautions and thus putting themselves and other road users at risk.

Also, more pillion riders of the same age die from motorcycle RTCs at 6% of pillion compared to the riders at 0.6%. Also 32% of pillion riders within age 16-25 die compared to 22% riders, (See Figure 6.33). This is because most pillion riders do not use helmets compared to the riders themselves. Mannering and Grodsky (1995) and Rutter and Quine (1996) also, identified particular patterns of youth behaviours, such as a willingness to break the law and to violate the rules of safe riding as having a much greater role in motorcycle RTC involvement. It is therefore said that targeting specific at-risk groups for edu¬cation, whether it be by age, experience, type of motorcycle, or a combination of these and other factors, may improve awareness of risks, (See Figure 6.35)

Figure 6.35: Age distribution of RTC fatalities for (a) riders and (b) pillion riders in Ghana

ii. Distribution of Motorcycle RTC Fatalities by Sex: Authors like Chang and Yeh (2007) explains that male motorcycle riders are more associated with risky behaviours such as disregard for traffic regulations, alcohol consumption and or drug abuse. The author adds that female riders with the least experience stand a high risk of being involved in RTCs due to requirements for particular control and balanced skills.

A study by the NRSA in Ghana in 2019 indicated that there were more male victims of motorcycle fatalities at 98.7% compared to 1.3% for females. The same trend is observed for pillion riders at 84% male fatalities compared 16% females.

ii. Educational Status of Motorcycle RTC Victims: Almost 92% and 74% of pillion rider of the motorcycle casualty victims had some form of education (NRSA, 2019). Whilst none of the motorcycle rider victims was illiterate, 27% of the pillion rider victims were illiterates. The same proportion had education up to JHS level with 31% riders and 25% pillion rider victims having had education up to SHS level. 19% of the rider victims had education up to tertiary level whilst only 8% of the pillion rider victims had education up to the same level (See Figure 6.36). This implies that the number of pillion riders reduces with higher education levels. This implies that most of the riders are in position to understand traffic regulation for better performance though not reflected in reality.

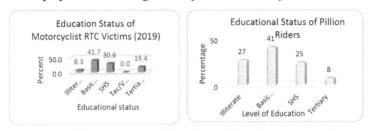

Figure 6.36: Education status of (a) riders and (b) pillion riders in Ghana

iv. Distribution of Motorcycle RTC Victims by Income: Most were relatively low-income earners who made up to GHC500 monthly at an average of 77.8%, though almost 43.3% had higher income than the national minimum wage of GHC319 as of 2019 (See Figure 6.37) while all pillion rider RTC victims interviewed earn up to GHC500 (NRSA, 2019). This implies that motorcycle users are of low-income bracket with higher possibility of being involved in an RTC compared with higher income earners with higher financial capacity for other options such as taxi hailing services or may even own private vehicles.

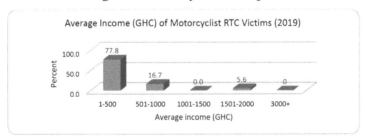

Figure 6.37: Average income (GHC) of motorcyclist RTC victims (2019)

B. Motor Rider Eligibility

i. Training for Motorcycle Riding: It is said motor riders do not fully appreciate the inherent operating characteristics and limitations of motorcycles due to limited training.

The same applies to Ghana since there is limited formal training establishments for motor rider training compared to automobile training. There is also a lack of mandated syllabi for the training of motor rider and riders of three wheelers with no examples of supervised on-road motor riding test by testing officers as with automobiles. Thus, most motorcycle riders are either self-taught or were taught how to ride by friends and family including corporate motorcycle who are only employed on the basis of ability to ride.

Only a few private driver training schools have expressed the willingness to train but are not effectively patronised because the charges are same as automobiles. Also, the motor bikers, tricycles and riders' association in Ghana (MOTRA) conducted training for some bikers in 2020 in joint association with police, the DVLA, the NRSA and some MMDAs however, this is not a scheduled sustainable programme but rather a one-off intervention with no provision for refresher training. Though, the DVLA has long indicated the intention to streamline motorcycle rider training in the country this has not commenced and so there are no rider testing mechanism, no training manuals and certification aided by instructors.

C. Motorcycle Rider Testing and Licensing: *The process of motorcycle rider licensing in Ghana requires training Regulation 26 of LI 2180. This is not done and most motorcycle riders in Ghana are not licensed. An assessment of the licensing status of sampled motor riders from a study by NRSA in 2019, showed that generally, 45.1% had a valid license while 54.9% did not. Also, 2% more commercial than private riders had valid rider's license but not for commercial operation (see Figure 6.37). This shows that some of those engaged in commercial operation are not even licensed to ride motorcycles in the first place which is a matter of safety concern.*

Figure 6.38: Motor rider licensing status by status by service type (2019)

i. Reasons for Non-Acquisition of Rider's License by Motor Riders: The key reason for the non-acquisition of licenses was limited affordability at 31%. Those with the intention to acquire their licenses but were yet to do so stood at 28% with 17% indicating that license acquisition was unnecessary. 16% also perceived the license acquisition process to be cum-bersome, (see Figure 6.39). This implies a serious lack of appreciation of the importance of licensing for some motorcycle riders because it is a small unit vehicle and this poses a serious safety threat.

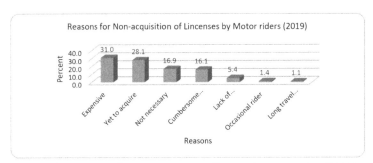

Figure 6.39: Reasons for non-acquisition of licenses by motor riders (2019)

ii. Insurance Coverage for Motorcycles: All motorcycles are required to be insured before being used on the road but, there is a significant violation of insurance coverage amongst motorcycle riders in Ghana at more than 85%. This implies most riders and pillion riders are not covered by any insurance and the problem is aggravated by the fact that insurance companies cannot insure motorcycles for commercial transport service because since it is an illegal operation. Thus, pillion riders who patronise such services must be educated for informed decision.

D. Motorcycle Rider Skills, Capability and Experience in Ghana: *A self-reported survey with motorcycle riders, showed that about 63% of motor riders claimed to have good knowledge on road traffic regulations (NRSA, 2019). However, this is yet to be validated through authentic research. This, may be the reason for the excessive level of motorcycle rider indiscipline and unsafe driving behaviour causing rising motorcycle RTCs in the country.*

6.4.4 Commercial Motorcycle Transport Operation in Ghana

Commercial motorcycle operation for the carriage of passengers and goods at a fee is popularly referred to as 'Okada' in Ghana, a name adapted from Nigeria for similar operations. Currently the service competitively plays a key role in connecting people to various destinations for diverse socio-economic purposes both in cities and in rural communities. This is mostly due to the advantage of provision of door-to-door services, ability to use narrow alleys, walkways and medians, ability to circumvent traffic congestion, availability and its efficient use for courier services of including catering services.

A. Reasons for Okada Operation: *In the rural areas they are used for diverse travel purposes, such as travel to farms, markets, health services including the carriage of pregnant women in labour and dead bodies as well as to school. Motorcycle taxis thus, provides* *essential transport gaps while generating employment and income, particularly for young men but with a consequent negative impact of increased RTC.*

All Okada operators are in the trade for economic gain and a study has revealed that 57% got into the business as a means of employment and 31% as means for supplementing the income from their major economic activities. About 7% found it lucrative and specifically left their previous occupation to operate Okada whilst about 3% were engaged in the trade on temporary basis to further finance their education and 2% were using the trade to raise capital for other business. Figure 6.40 provides a graphic representation.

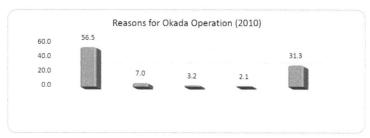

Figure 6.40: Reasons for Okada operation (2010)

The business is deemed so lucrative that only about an average of 11% of the Okada operators studied had no previous means of employment. All of the others left their previous jobs to operate Okada because of the benefits from the business. These include 36% who were traders; 26% who were self-employed artisan/skilled craftsman; 25% who were salaried employees with only 1.6% being farmers. Currently, there are even migrant Okada operators from other neighbouring countries who have come into the country to do the business in Ghana. The business is deemed to be so lucrative by them that even in situations of language barrier in some case, such operators use hand signs to seek directions from their customers. This conflicts with the current ban on the service and the issue would have to be revisited for the right thing to be done.

B. Reasons for Okada Patronage: *A comparative rating of okada service with other modes by users indicated that irrespective of its ban, there is a clear violation by the Okada operators and it is still thriving and growing by day with passengers willing to pay for their services though much more expensive. It was also rated highest in terms of speed and lowest in terms of safety, (See Table 6.17). Therefore, policy analysis for options and strategies on the mobility and safety of motorcycles for a radical reorientation to manage the commercial aspect is ongoing.*

Table 6.17: Comparison of Okada Services with other modes of Public Transport in Ghana

Service Condition	Ranking	Type of Vehicle		
		Motor Cycle %	Trotro %	Taxi %
Reliability	Poor	0	15	0
	Fair	5	10	10
	Good	65	70	85
	Very Good	30	5	5
	Excellent	0	0	0
	Total	100	100	100
Cost	Poor	0	0	0
	Fair	80	65	85
	Good	20	20	15
	Very Good	0	10	0
	Excellent	0	0	0
	Total	100	100	100
Speed	Poor	0	15	10
	Fair	25	60	40
	Good	25	25	50
	Very Good	50	0	0
	Excellent	0	0	0
	Total	100	100	100
Safety	Poor	25	15	0
	Fair	45	25	35
	Good	30	45	55
	Very Good	0	5	0
	Excellent	0	10	10
	Total	100	100	100

C. Reasons for Its Success: *Its success and continuous operation is attributed to; (i) poor enforcement due to limited commitment since it is not uncommon to see law enforcers patronising the operations in both rural and urban communities. There are also difficulties in the enforcement of the ban because speed and the inability of a law enforcer without a similar unit to chase them. Thus, most of the jump red light and create safety risks for fear of being arrested. Also, it is more or less an "invisible" operation and it cannot be easily differentiated from private motor cycle use. Finally, there is high demand for its services especially in rural communities due to limited reliability and availability of other alternative transport modes and its ability to circumvent traffic congestions in the cities.*

D. Sex / Age Distribution of Okada Operators in Ghana: *As at 2010, most if not all Okada operators were males though the current statistics is not known. None of them was above 50 years of age and majority were below 40 years of age with those of 20-29 years being the highest number of operators at 54% followed by 36% within ages 30-39 and a minority of 3% were 20 years and below. (See Figure 6.41).*

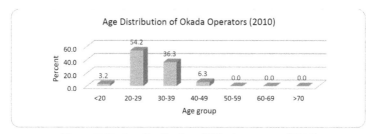

Figure 6.41: Age distribution of Okada operators (2010)

E. Educational Status of Okada Operators: *The majority (95.2%) of the Okada operators were educated and majority had education up to Junior High School (JHS)/Middle school level at 68%. Only about 5% are illiterate (see Figure 6.42), so most of the operators with the ability to appreciate and understand the illegality of their operations but this is disregarded.*

Figure 6.42: Educational status of Okada operators (2010)

E. Okada Market Entry: *There is easy entry into the Okada business with a prospective operator only requiring a little capital to buy a motorcycle, register it, acquire a riding license and operate. This is proven by the fact that almost 60% of operators own their motorcycle units used for the trade, out of which about 87% were bought with self-raised capital compared to other commercial transport operations where vehicle ownership is mostly by third parties. It is currently estimated that the average number of motor cycles per owner can be as high as about 3 motorcycle units with about 95% bought in brand new state as compared with automobiles.*

Since the level of affordability of the motorcycle investment threshold is about a quarter of a saloon car taxi but with the same level of returns in terms of revenue and low fuel consumption, most regular taxi owners are even selling their vehicles to operate Okada. Due to this the potential for Okada to grow beyond the current numbers cannot be underestimated and there is urgent need for perquisite policy interventions especially with regards to safety.

i. Operational Regulations: Officially, there are no statutory service regulations on the Okada operation because it is an illegal business. Operators have formed unions at self-designated parking turfs with leadership and payment of dues and a requirement to conform to set regulations at that turf. Some of the regulations binding on the members in the turfs include registration with the turf, payment of registration fees and ownership of a license and without a criminal record. However, since these are not legally binding some operators do not conform to the rules and they operate to their advantage without operational controls with safety implications, (See Figure 6.43). There is need therefore for responsible authorities to take the necessary action either to ensure effective enforcement or to effect the necessary training and controls and lift the ban.

Figure 6.43: Publication of Regulation of Okada Activities in Ghana

6.4.5 Motor Rider Safety Errors

A. Causes of Motor Rider Errors: *Some of the causes of motorcycle crashes from the results of a study conducted with motorcycle RTC patients on hospital admission by the NRSA in 2019 identified motor rider recklessness as the key reason for the occurrence of motorcycle RTCs at an average of 69.7%. This was followed by alcohol and substance abuse at 21.2% and mechanical failure and wrongful parking at 4.5% each (see Figure 6.44).*

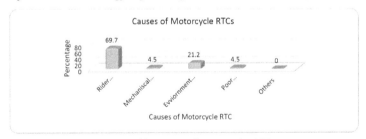

Figure 6.44: Causes of motorcycle RTCs

B. Types of Motorcycle Rider Errors: *A motorcycle RTC victim patient survey conducted by the NRSA in 2019, is as presented in Figure 6.45 and expounded in the subsequent sections.*

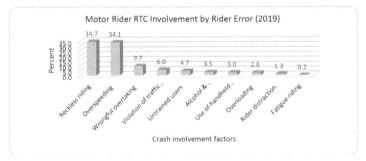

Figure 6.45: Motor rider RTC involvement by rider error (2019)

i. Reckless Motorcycle Riding: Rider recklessness was rated the highest cause of motorcycle RTCs at 35%. This included actions such as left turn and right of way issues, disregard for traffic regulations challenges with safe lane positioning causing lane splitting by riding between two without checking for blind spot or signal when changing lanes. This calls for mandatory formal training including both theoretical and practical lessons for both the existing cadre of motor riders already operating in the traffic system as well as new entrants with continuous re-fresher training.

Emphasis must also be on improving rider knowledge of traffic rules and regulations, skills development, how to maintain stability, concentration and focus on the road environment. Others are being gentle with e brakes, throttle, and steering to avoid sliding; safe management of unexpected sliding from sand, wet leaves, or pebbles and ascertaining the working condition of lights, horn, directional signals before take-off and rightful inflation of tyre must be emphasized. To achieve this, relevant training manuals for basic and advanced motorcycle training programmes must be developed. There should also be expanded training for prosecuting offenders as well as motorcycle rider escort/safety programme. This must be complemented with intensive enforcement of rider licensing and motorcycle insurance validity.

ii. Over speeding: The WHO, (2004) established a direct relationship between motor rider speeding and injury severity that arise from such speeds with increased crash impact. It is estimated that an increase in average speed of 1km/h typically results in a 3% higher risk of a crash involving injury and 4–5% increase in fatalities. This is because motorcycle as a mode of transport is of smaller size, shape, narrowness and high acceleration rate that enables it to filter past other vehicle of larger sizes in traffic. Also, the higher the speed, the less the reaction time to prevent a crash.

In Ghana, over speeding by motorcycle riders was responsible for 35% of the RTCs experienced by the motorcycle RTC patient survey by NRSA in 2019. The reason is that riders deem it as the most significant advantage of the use of motorcycles over automobiles especially in congested traffic situation. This is done by carelessly meandering through traffic jams at high-speed levels in order to serve more customers for more profit. It is not uncommon for Okada riders to jam into automobiles in traffic, destroying driving mirrors and speeding off without being caught.

a). Improper Overtaking: Motor riders indulge in risky overtaking by manoeuvring through narrow space in traffic even on the blind side of automobiles. In Ghana, a patient study involving motorcycle RTC patients caused by overtaking was estimated at 9.7% (NRSA, 2019

b). Overloading: It is said that overloaded motorcycles have a higher propensity for self-crashes without the involvement of other modes of road transport due to stability issues. In Ghana, the practice is very common especially in rural communities and on festive occasions. This is mostly done for profit making or when families travel together. The 2019 motorcycle RTC patient surveys revealed that overloading was the cause of 2.8% of the RTCs, (See Figure 6.46).

Figure 6.46: Examples of Overloaded Motorcycle in Ghana (Source NRSA)

iii. Motorcycle Rider Distraction: The European Commission, (2018), categorises the sources of this distraction into four; visual, auditory, manual and cognitive that engages a rider's attention from the road. Visual distraction includes activities that take the rider's eyes off the road e.g. interaction with other road users; auditory distraction include listening to the radio with earphones; manual distraction includes adjusting helmet and checking time; and cognitive distraction is when the rider is lost in thought.

In Ghana, 3.5% of motorcycle RTC is caused by rider inattentiveness. Thus, training in sharing the road with other road users and being alert by keeping a close eye on other motorists, avoidance of tailgating etc. should be ensured.

iv. Impaired Motorcycle Riding: Riding under influence of alcohol and drugs, impairs a rider's sense and ability to respond and avoid a dangerous situation.

In Ghana, a self-reported survey by the NRSA, (2019) revealed that about 3.5% of the motor riders engage in alcohol and drug use at 33%. Out of 21% are addicted to the use of alcohol, 22% do so occasionally at social events; 4% do so to manage stress and the remaining 41% do so for various other reasons.

v. Lack of Occupancy Compliance for Protective Clothing:

a). Motor Rider Knowledge on Crash Helmet Use: The use of crash helmets is essential for head protection which is the main cause of death in motorcycle RTCs because they create an additional protective layer for the head to reduce the risk of serious head and brain injuries from the impact of a force or collision to the head (WHO, 2006). Helmets are said to work three ways to prevent and/or minimise injuries to the head by absorbing some crash impact; spreading the forces of the crash impact over a greater surface and preventing direct contact between the skull and the impacting object as a mechanical barrier. It is also estimated that wearing a helmet lowers a motor rider's risk of fatalities by 29% and reduces the risk of traumatic brain injury by 67% (NHTSA, 2020).

In Ghana, a study by the NRSA in 2019, had 85% of motorcycle riders claiming to be knowledgeable about the importance of the use of crash helmets through self-reports.

b). Compliance of Crash Helmet Use by Motor Riders: A study by (BRRI, 2016) involving the observation of 26,222 motorcycle riders and 8,519 pillion riders showed that about 42% of all riders and 17% of pillion riders used crash helmets. Out of those who used crash helmets, it was also observed that just 37.3% of the riders and 13.7% of the pillion riders were properly wearing them. The key reason for not wearing helmets was attributed to limited affordability coupled with the requirement by law for two helmets to be provided for one motorcycle as provision for a pillion rider.

In some instances, also, available helmets were not used out of the fear of contracting some communicable disease. Some women also refuse to wear helmets in order not to destroy their hair style. Discomfort from high temperatures was cited by 53% of riders, weak enforcement was at 39% and ability to bribe to escape punishment was at 20% from a study by (Bishop et al. 2019). Another challenge is with the use of unstandardized helmet types and the influx of second-hand sub-standard helmets into the country.

Also, some riders use n open-faced helmet without a visor or goggle to protect their eyes from the wind, rain, insects and road dirt. Some attempt to address the issues includes mandatory sale of helmets as part of motorcycle sales and recommendations for helmets standardisation. It is proposed for intensive education of safety over comfort and the possibility of subsidization to be considered especially since the cost of a helmet is almost the same as the motorcycle itself.

c). Leg and Arm Protection: Various studies have determined legs to be the most common injury type, followed by the head and arms. This can cause permanent disability.

In Ghana, various medical documentaries on Television have affirmed the seriousness of leg injuries amongst motor riders in Ghana with treatment often characterized by leg amputations leaving the victims to be both physically and economically disabled. Thus, it alleged that there are instances where injured riders have refused to visit particular medical facilities with the notion and fear that such centres deliberately amputate the legs of riders as a punishment to deter them from engaging in the Okada business though discounted to be baseless by health experts (See Figure 6.47 for a sampled publication).

Figure 6.47: Examples of Casualties Resulting from Motor Rider RTC's in Ghana

d). Use of High Visibility Clothing: Literature indicates that protective clothing that contains fluorescent and reflective material increases the conspicuity of motor riders which in turn helps to reduce the likelihood of an RTC occurring in the first place.

In Ghana, others are the use of leather or other reinforced jacket, gloves, trouser, knee caps, boots and over-the-ankle footwear. However, very few motor riders conform to this code of dressing making it risky for them to safely use the road. Existing Also appropriate education must back the enforcement on the wearing of appropriate clothing since currently the focus is mainly on the wearing of helmets.

C. Motorcycle Rider Errors by Automobile Drivers: *In Ghana, some of the motorcycle RTC caused by other road user is presented in includes the following. (See also Figure 6.48).*

i.   *Failure of automobile drivers to yield to motor rider.*

ii.   *Automobile drivers failing to judge the speed of a motor rider.*

iii. *Large vehicles changing or merging lanes.*

iv.   *Easy miss of oncoming motorcycles from poor visibility.*

v.   *Driving closely at a rear end of a vehicle with sudden stops.*

vi.   *Sudden opening of car doors with disregard for an oncoming motorcycle.*

Figure 6.48: Examples of Motorcycle RTC's caused by Collision with Vehicles

D. vii. Motor Rider Fatalities by Pillion Rider Action: Since motorcycles are built without any enclosure nor physical restraints, it is common for pillion riders to be easily thrown off or ejected when there is a collision or even when riders lose control of their motorcycles. These includes lack rider good hold of the steering handle bar, a pillion rider wrongly getting aboard or alighting and a pillion not gaining a stable ground before a rider takes off or when the motorcycle stops suddenly without a firm grip by the pillion rider.

In Ghana, the distribution of fatalities by the action of pillion riders showed that almost 17% was attributable to their fall off motorcycles while in motion. About 1.5% and 0.5% occurred when they were boarding and alighting from motorcycles respectively and 81% were due to unspecified factors.

E. Other Motorcycle RTC Causative Factors: *In Ghana, an average of 25.8% of motor rider error causing fatalities are unknown (NRSA, 2019). These mostly include diverse forms of rule breaking behaviours that are habitual and often contribute to motorcycle RTCs. There is therefore a need for appropriate research into the issue for the right solutions to be effected.*

6.4.5. Motorcycle Casualties

A. Self-Reported Motorcycle Rider Involvement in RTCs: *Self reports by motorcycle operators from a study by the NRSA in 2019 showed that about 42% of motorcycle operators had been involved in RTCs. Out of this about 57% had been involved in RTC situations once and 47% had been involved more than once. About 39% of those who had experienced RTCs more than once had had it twice, 2.4% had been involved in RTC on three occasions and 2.4% had been involved for more than three times. This shows that even subjective reports from the motor riders themselves confirm the fact that motor rider safety must be given more attention.*

B. Trends in Motorcycle Casualties: *Between 1991 to 2018, an average of 150 persons are estimated to have been killed through motorcycle RTCs in Ghana annually and these were made up of about 43% of motorcycle riders and about 50% of pillion riders. Also, between 1991 and 2018 there was a total of 3393.8% increase in motorcycle fatalities as presented in Figure 6.50, (See also Figure 6.51 for examples of publications on motorcycle fatalities in Ghana).*

Figure 6.50: Trends in motorcycle fatalities

Figure 6.51: Other Publications on Motor Rider Fatalities in Ghana

Out of those who got involved in RTCs 51% pillion riders compared to 43% motor riders were hospitalized whilst almost 40% motorcycle riders and 34% pillion riders got injured but were not hospitalized. This means that 7% more pillion riders were hospitalized because of motorcycle injuries, (see Figure 6.49). Thus, pillion rider must also be educated on the dangers on motorcycle use.

Figure 6.49: Summary of motor rider casualties (a) and (b) pillion rider casualties

6.4.6 Motor Rider Errors by Road Infrastructure Features

Motor riders face higher dangers from road related conditions than automobiles especially with regards to road conditions such as potholes, uneven pavement, loose gravel, slippery pavement, sudden change in road surface, uneven heights between lanes and other irregularities. Others are the nature of the horizontal alignment of a road, shared road space with other road users especially automobiles, roadside hazards, presence of unexpected objects as well as lack of necessary signals and signs. Automobiles violating the motorcycle's right-of-way also pose a serious safety threat to motorcycles.

A. Motor Rider Fatalities by Prevailing Road Geometry: *In Ghana, motor rider casualties involving both riders and pillion riders mostly occur at straight road sections at 89.5% and 85.4% respectively. This is followed by casualties at curved road sections at 5.6%and 7.7% for riders and pillion riders respectively. The remaining is attributable to casualties on curves and inclines, bridges, and crests as depicted in Figure 6.52.*

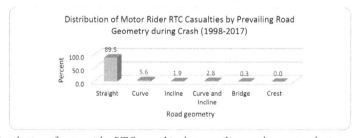

Figure 6.52: Distribution of motor rider RTC casualties by prevailing road geometry during crash (1998-2017)

B. Motor Rider Fatalities by Location Type: *In Ghana, an average of 80% of recorded motorcycle fatalities occur at non-junction road locations. This is followed by fatalities at T-junctions at an average of 14%, with the remaining occurring across other location types as depicted in Figure 6.53. This may occur w at an intersection, particularly when a rider moves in a cross-sectional direction into the opposite lane of the road.*

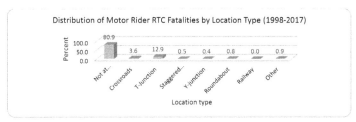

Figure 6.53: Distribution of motor rider RTC fatalities by location type (1998-2017)

C. Road Surface Condition Causing Motorcycle RTC: *From Figure 6.54, in Ghana, an average of 63% of motor rider crashes occur on paved road sections (without potholes); followed by RTCs on paved road section with potholes at 33% and unpaved road sections with potholes at 4%. The observed distribution is largely accounted for by the smooth ride quality on paved road sections which induces excessive speeding by riders, leading to their involvement in motorcycle RTCs.*

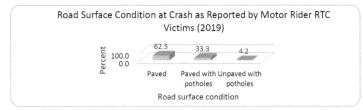

Figure 6.54: Road surface condition at crash as reported by motor rider RTC victims (2019)

D. Motor Rider Errors by Road Class: *In Ghana, motor riders travelling on trunk roads have the highest exposure to RTC at 49.3% and 53.8% respectively for riders and pillions riders (BRRI, 2018). This is followed by urban roads at 41%and 37.8% for riders and pillions riders respectively and 9.7% and 8.5% for motorcycle riders and pillions riders respectively on feeder roads (see Figure 6.55). This implies that almost every1in 2 motor riders exposed to RTCs is likely to be on a trunk road.*

This is mainly due to higher speeds on such roads. On urban roads, motor riders are mostly exposed to RTCs when they disregard traffic regulations such as jumping red lights and turning at junctions without observing the movement of other traffic. Motorcycle RTCs on feeder roads are mostly attributed to poor road condition, limited road furniture such as good lighting on such roads and failure to effectively negotiate bends with riders losing control without the involvement of other road users.

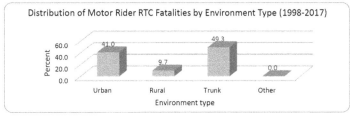

Figure 6.55: Distribution of motor rider RTC fatalities by environment type (1998-2017)

E. Motor Rider RTC Fatalities by Collision Type: When motor riders get into head on collisions with automobiles, they often result in fatalities due to motorcycles higher power-to-weight ratios than automobiles.

In Ghana the most significant motorcycle RTC fatality by collision type is head-on collision with other vehicle types at 37.8%. This is followed by rear end hits at18.3%, side wipe at11.2%, right angle hits at 10.7% and runoff roads at 10.6%, (see, Figure 6.56). The remaining (11.4%) is attributed to other collision types such as hitting pedestrians and parked vehicles. These could be attributed to over speeding, sudden stops, unsafe lane change, lack of conspicuity, dangerous road conditions as well as motorcycle defects. Others are close proximity of motorcycle to automobiles due to limited space for manoeuvring, jumping of red light and sudden stops by vehicles from behind.

In order to address the infrastructure challenges for safety needs of motorcycle riders there is need for the development of country wide based road network safety plans to guide the provision of such facilities, on the concept of the safe system approach to road design. There should also be construction of increased number of dedicated lanes for motorcycles.

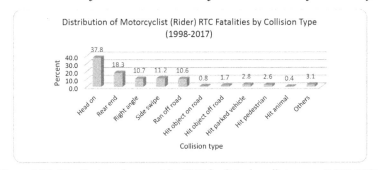

Figure 6.56: Distribution of motor rider RTC fatalities by collision type (1998-2017)

6.4.7 Motor Rider Error by Vehicle Safety

Several categories of motorcycle may be associated with different types of RTC situations and levels of risk. This together with variables like rider age, motivation and level of exposure implies that the motorcycle safety problem is much more heterogeneous than the car safety problem and that subsets of the problem may have to be addressed separately (Elliott et al., 2003). Since, a motorcycle is a single-track vehicle it can easily become unstable and capsize when braking, accelerating or when on a slippery road surface which causes the wheel to lose adhesion when the motor rider is taking a bend. Other factors relating to the safety of motorcycle include the following:

A. Motorcycle Defects Causing RTCs: Poorly maintained motorcycles reflect in worn out tyres, poorly lubricated chains, braking issues, handling problems and vibration among others. Braking can also cause a motorcycle to change its line on a bend when it is done in a fast manner and they are not able to stop in a distance from where they can see clearly. Locked up brakes also causes motorcycle to be involved in RTCs. Also, according to (Elliott et al., 2003), the need to avoid wheel locks means that riders may find it difficult to use the brakes in an emergency situation.

Studies in Ghana, indicated that motor riders on feeder roads experience the highest (41%) exposure to RTCs as a result of poor motorcycle condition due to general economic deprivation in rural areas and limited access to parts and maintenance services. This is followed by trunk roads at 34%and urban roads at 25%.

6.4.7 Motor Rider Fatalities by Environmental Factors

The effects of environmental factors create unfavourable riding conditions for the motor rider including the following:

A. Motor Rider Casualties by Day and Night Conditions: *In Ghana, majority of both rider and pillion rider crash casualties are recorded during the daytime at 70% and 67% respectively. The remaining proportions are attributable to night time (with no streetlights) for rider and pillion riders at 17% and 19% respectively as depicted in Figure 6.57. The significant share of motor rider casualties that occur during the day implies that though good day lighting enhances visibility, it also induces rider over confidence.*

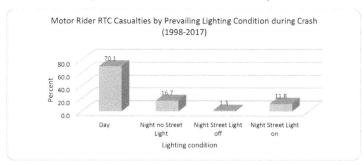

Figure 6.57: Motor rider RTC casualties by prevailing lighting condition during crash (1998-2017)

B. Motor Rider Fatalities by Weather Conditions: The impacts of adverse weather condition including rain, fog, high winds and high temperatures causes motorcycle rider visibility impairments (Andrey et al., 2001). This is because rain causes wet road surfaces through the process of aquaplaning to reduce the friction of the road surface in contact with a motorcycle's tyres causing reduction in friction and greater stopping distances It also causes spray from other vehicles to throw up surface water and dirt which can cause a motor rider to lose control of the motorcycle. (Brodsky and Hakkert, 1988).

In windy conditions, flying objects like loose plastic bags, papers and other light weight objects obstruct riders' visibility and concentration which can expose them to RTCs. Fog and (Edwards, 1999) and high day temperature (caused by the sun's heat) also causes motorcycle RTCs (Commission of Occupational Health and Safety, 2004). It can be deduced that rider ability to manage different weather conditions is critical to ensure safety.

In Ghana, approximately 83% of both motor rider and pillion rider crashes and related fatalities occur in clear weather conditions with good visibility, normally considered not to be hazardous in terms of crash risk. Only 17% are associated with adverse weather conditions including rainy, foggy and windy, with foggy weather accounting for an average of 1.3% of rider and pillion rider fatalities, rain accounting for an average of 0.4% and others at 15.3% as depicted in Figure 6.58.

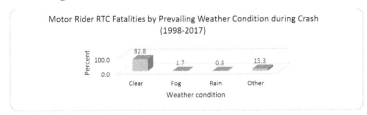

Figure 6.58: Motor rider RTC fatalities by prevailing weather condition during crash (1998-2017)

C. Timing of Motorcycle RTC Occurrence in Ghana: *In Ghana, motorcycle casualties increase steadily from the beginning of the year and peaks in the last quarter of the year with December recording the highest and February recording the least (see Figure 6.59). The high incidence of casualties in the last quarter of the year is as a result of high traffic volumes in the build-up to the Christmas festivities due to alcohol impairment and anti-social riding behaviours such as racing and sensation-seeking acts from excitement. Also, casualties are recorded when there is high patronage for commercial motorcycle services to evade the high vehicular traffic congestions on the roads during such periods.*

Figure 6.59: Publication on Motorcycle RTC during a Festive Season

6.4.8 Motor Rider Fatalities by Landuse Factors

Most motorcycle RTC fatalities occur in commercial zones for both riders and pillion riders at 50%, followed by school zone at 27.5% with undeveloped lands along major highways and residential zones taking12.5% and 10% respectively. There is also a split of 50% each of motorcycle fatalities for riders and pillion riders in commercial zones. This can be attributed to mixed traffic as well as high traffic activities around commercial zones with related issues of difficult manoeuvring through congested environments. The 30% RTC rider fatalities involvement around school zones is next and it requires serious attention.

6.4.9 Motor Rider Exposure to RTC by Weak Enforcement

According to existing data by the NRSA, motor riders experience the highest exposure to RTCs as a result of weak enforcement on feeder roads at 46%. This is followed by urban and trunk roads at 27% each. The relatively good enforcement on urban and trunks roads is due to the high physical presence of the MTTD and allied enforcement agencies in towns and cities.

6.5 PASSENGER SAFETY PROFILE

A passenger can be defined as a person in conveyance in an automobile who is not the driver (www.dictionary.com May 2020) and it is said that just the very presence of a passenger in a vehicle is enough of a risk factor. Because according to McEvoy, (2006) carrying passengers in the car has a number of potentially distracting effects with almost 60% likelihood for the occurrence of an RTC especially where there is more than one passenger. Thus, the higher a passenger vehicle kilometre of travel, the higher the risk of involvement in a crash. This section of the book examines the functioning of passenger RTC factors in Ghana.

6.5.1 Road Safety in the Context of the Passenger

Passenger safety issues are aligned with both the driver and the passenger as follows:

a. The safety risk of young drivers and young passengers in the vehicle Orsi C. et al. (2001)

b. The high safety risk of a young male driver accompanied by a male passenger and at the low risk of when a young male driver is carrying a female passenger Chen, et al. (2017).

c. The view by Geyer and Ragland (2005), that there is lower RTC risk for passengers driven by males aged 45 and above.

d. The view of Hing et al. (2003), that the opposite is the case with the presence of two or more passengers in the vehicle driven by a driver over the age of 75 years.

e. *The perception in Ghana by some drivers that the presence of female in the front seat of the vehicles are a distraction to safe driving especially with regards to their overreaction in near traffic crash situations*

However, Engström et al., (2008) insists that such assertions are inconclusive and Lee and Abdel-Aty, (2008) and Reiß, (1998) are also of the view that the extent to which the passenger presence can be of a safety RTC risk remains unclear.

In Ghana, authors like Abu Azabre (2013), attributed daily upsurge in RTCs as a clear manifestation of sheer failure in the protection of passenger rights rather than passenger influence on driver performance. A typical example of passenger safety law from the perspective of a consumer right is the Bangladesh situation where the country looks at passenger safety from the legal perspective as a consumer right within the purview of the countries Consumers' Rights Protection laws. This is due to limited provision for passengers in the country's traffic safety laws.

This perspective aim at fighting many irregularities with passenger's knowledge on their consumer right being a basis to collectively minimise the effects of road hazards on them. A is as presented in Box 6.4.

Box 6.4...Consumer Right Law for Passenger Protection in Bangladesh

The general negative instructions that are directly connected to the safety of passenger's are-no drunken or on-phone-call driver, no driving by conductors, no wrong-sided plying and no rooftop passenger accommodation etc. The passengers while on the roads can check these measures as consumers even before happening of any real accidents. The convenience is that the passengers can lodge real-time complaints with the Directorate of National Consumers' Right Protection and the Director General is bound by law to entertain the complaints especially connected to the safety of passengers' lives on roads and highways.

Section 21(2)(m) of the Consumers' Rights Protection Act 2009 very clearly posited that the Director General has a legal duty to monitor whether the life of passengers is being put into risk by illegally running general public transport such as minibus, bus, launch, steamer and train by unskilled or unlicensed drivers and also to take necessary actions. The law has empowered the Director General or his officer to suspend or shut down business operations of any enterprise for anti-consumer right practices [Sections 27(4), 27(5)]. So, everything that endangers the safety of passengers on roads is essentially an anti-consumer right practice as the consumers generally have a right to safety regarding the goods or services they pay for. The aware and activist passengers can play timely roles by checking any irregularities on the part of the service providers and lodge immediate complaints with the Directorate if any issue is detected. This way, the passengers can, as a collective, stop an unlicensed driver and even an unfit bus from plying. The business organisations can be challenged for every illegal action in running general public transport that can possibly put the passengers' lives into risk and the first challenge should come from the passengers' side.

Source: https://www.thedailystar.net/author/selimul-quader 21/04/20

6.5.2 Global Safety Regulations for Road Passengers

A. Passenger Safety by Convention 68: Globally, there are very few direct regulatory requirements on road passenger safety.

B. DOA Conventions on Passenger Road Safety: Passenger safety issues in the DOA, concerns requirement for the use of occupant restraints such as seat-belts and child restraints for automobile occupants a well as the use of helmets and protective clothing by pillion riders.

C. Safe Road Passenger Policy in Ghana: *Currently, the NRSP makes little provision for passenger safety. A study by (Abu Azabre2013), based on observations and interviews revealed that most passengers are not aware of any specific laws protecting their rights. Thus, the author concluded that passengers in Ghana are left to the mercy of their faith during travel rather than regulatory protection.*

D. Passenger Road Safety Regulations in Ghana: *The key passenger road safety regulations in Ghana are on seatbelt use with a few clauses on child restraints which totally not enforced. A 'summary of UN conventions on passenger safety, the DOA and Ghana's regulations on passenger safety is as presented in Table 6.18.*

Table 6.18: A Comparison of Passenger Regulations

Convention '68	DOA	LI 2180
Article 30 The number of passengers carried on a vehicle should not interfere with driving or obstruct the driver's view	Develop comprehensive programmes to improve road user behaviour. Sustained or increased enforcement of laws and standards, combined with public awareness/education to increase seat-belt and helmet wearing rates, and to reduce drink-driving, speed and other risk factors.	100. Prohibited passengers 115. Molesting or obstructing a driver Prohibition of nuisance 116. Prohibition of nuisance on commercial vehicle 117. Trading on the road 140. Offences in passenger carrying vehicle Reg. 155. Boarding and alighting from motor vehicle Reg. 156. Person being an excess passenger on motor vehicle

Source: LI 2180 Section 119

6.5.3 Passenger RTC Victim Profile and Characteristics in Ghana

A. Summary of Passenger Casualties Statistics in Ghana: *Passenger crash statistics in Ghana from 2001-2017, indicated that for every 12 casualties recorded, 1 is fatal. Casualties with serious injuries who are hospitalised constitute 36.5%, indicating the hospitalisation of 1 out of every 3 RTC casualties. The majority of passengers involved in RTCs also sustained minor injuries at 54.9%, representing 1 out of every 2 casualties being injured.*

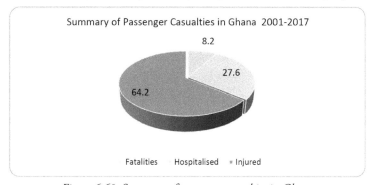

Figure 6.60: Summary of passenger casualties in Ghana

B. Socio-Demographic Attributes of RTC Passenger Victims: *The demographic profile of the passenger RTC victims interviewed from a study by the NRSA in 2019 are as discussed in the immediate sub-sections.*

i. Sex Distribution of Passenger Crash Victims: *The sex distribution of the RTC victims indicated that there were more male RTC passenger victims at 69% compared to 31% females.*

ii. Age Distribution of Passenger RTC Victims in Ghana: *The age distribution of passenger RTC victims in Ghana from the study indicated that those within the age cohort of 16 to 45 years constituted about 64.4%. Out of this, those within the 26-35 age cohort was at 27.3% followed by those between the ages 16-25 at 19.4% with those in 36-45 being at 17.7%.*

This is attributed to the fact that those in these age groups have active mobility regimes because they are either teenagers in school going age who are able to travel independently or those in the economically active group who work to support their families. The detail is as presented in Figure 6.61. Also of high concern are children within the age of 0-5 who constitute almost 18% of passenger RTC victims. This is attributed to the fact that these normally accompany adults on their trips.

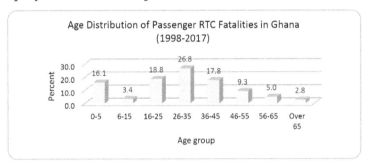

Figure 6.61: Passenger RTC fatalities by age

iii. *Educational Status of Passenger Crash Victims by Sex in Ghana: The educational distribution of passenger RTC victims indicated that majority (45.8%) were JHS graduates, followed by 25% of those who completed basic school, then 17% illiterates as well as 12.2% tertiary graduates (see Figure 6.62). This implies that both the educated and the uneducated are at risk of being involved in RTC fatalities but the majority are within lower to middle level educational status at 83%. Thus, it can be inferred that the lower the educational status, the higher possibility of a passenger being involved in an RTC because those categories of passengers mostly use commercial transport facilities.*

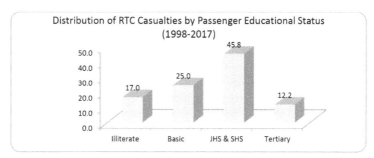

Figure 6.62: Educational status of passenger RTC Victims by sex

iv. Occupational Distribution of Passenger Crash Victims in Ghana: Majority (42.9%) of the RTC victims were traders followed by farmers at 28.6% with corporate workers and artisans being at 14.3% each (see Figure 6.63.) This can be attributed to the fact that traders travel at higher frequencies to the source of purchase of their goods as well as to the sales points.

Figure 6.63: Occupation of passenger RTC victims

v. Frequency of Travel by Passengers: From the study those who travelled on daily basis were those with the highest risk of being involved in RTCs at about 59% followed by those who travelled 4-6 times a week at 32% with the remaining 9% being those who travelled less than 4 times a week.

vi. Distribution of Income of Passenger Crash Victims: Form the same study, RTC fatalities cut across all income groups but the majority fall within those whose income are either below or equal to the national minimum wage of GHC500 at 33.3%.

6.5.4 Passenger Safety Practices by Transport Operators

A. Passenger Safety Concerns on Public Transport Operations: *In Ghana, there are no statutory guidelines on passenger safety welfare binding on transport operators in both formal and informal commercial transport operations as practiced elsewhere. However, the major safety challenge bothering passengers who use commercial transport services has to do with the lack of seatbelts in most of such vehicles at 25%. This is followed by driver disregard* *for passenger concern at 21% with careless driving rated in a third position at 20.8%). Other concerns relate to overloading, limited passenger knowledge of their rights and poor vehicle quality.*

6.5.5 Passenger Errors Contributing to RTC

A. Types of Positive and Negative Safety Behaviours: *Passengers can play both positive and negative roles to either contribute or avert the occurrence of RTC situations during journey times as summarised in Box 6.5.*

> **Box 6.5: Positive and Negative Passenger Behaviours**
>
> (i) Examples of Positive Passenger Behaviour
>
> - Passengers can help keep a journey safe by controlling radio and other dials.
> - Alerting the driver to the speed at which they are travelling.
> - Passenger observing risky driver behaviour and drawing attention to authorities on it;
> - Passenger not engaging the driver in anti-social behaviour;
> - Passenger spotting and drawing a driver's attention to impending hazard;
> - Passenger engaging a driver in conversation to keep them awake and alerting driver on over speeding
>
> (ii) Examples of Negative Passenger Behaviour
>
> - Passenger engaging in anti-social behaviour
> - Passenger not maintaining a calm environment by talking loudly on phone and enticing the driver to listen causing lack of driver concentration
> - Passenger distracting the driver when they are trying to keep their eyes on the road- Passenger not helping the driver when help is needed

B. Passenger Knowledge on Safety Laws in Ghana: *A survey conducted in 2019 by the NRSA indicated that about 54% of sampled passengers acknowledged some knowledge of Passenger Rights. These included knowledge on complaint about bad driver behaviour at 66% and laws on in-vehicle comfort at 34% including seating capacity. Other laws known to passengers include driver requirements, wrongful driver and vehicle safety laws as detailed in Table 6.19.*

Table 6.19: Passenger knowledge on safety laws in Ghana

Passenger Knowledge on Driver and vehicle safety laws	Average	Knowledge about wrongful driver behaviour	Average
Regular car maintenance	8.6%	Over speeding	18.3
Availability of first aid kit in vehicle	3.8%	Over loading	14.3
Avoidance of Fatigue Driving	11.8%	Lack of observation of road signs	15.3
Wearing of seat belts	18.6%	Poor Enforcement	2.8
Availability of fire extinguisher	6.8%	Drunk driving	14.2
Knowledge of road signs	8.3%	Non use of seat belt	11.9
Avoidance of drink driving	28.2%	Wrongful overtaking	11.0
Valid driver qualification	13.9%	Use of phones while driving	1.3
Total	100.0%	Impatient with passengers	2.6
		Wrongful Parking	0.9
		Indulging in conversation	0.6
		Lack of helmet Use	6.8
		Total	100.0

Source: NRSA Road User Safety, 2019

C. Causes of Passenger Safety Errors by Driver Perception: *In an article published in (General News of Thursday, 28 March 2019; www.ghanaweb.com), under the theme "Passengers mostly to blame for road accidents" drivers in Ghana laid the blame squarely on passengers due to the incessant pressure they give to them whilst driving and the detail is as presented in Box 6.6.*

Box 6.6: General News of Thursday, 28 March 2019: www.ghanaweb.com

According to the drivers, passengers often bombard them with insults when they fail to speed to their satisfaction. In doing the bid of the passengers, the drivers over speed to avoid all sorts of insults and name-calling. Recalling some of the names and insults given to them, one driver said "One time, I drove from here to Kintampo. A woman told me to stop driving as a profession and work on something else because I'm a slow driver. She told me bluntly to my face that I should work on the farm because driving isn't meant for me". "Most of the causes are from passengers, they hate it when a different car bypasses them and they will be putting pressure on you, the car is too slow, can't you speed, we've sat in the car for too long, why haven't we reached our destination yet. So they put too much pressure on us," another revealed. The drivers further indicated that sometimes the passengers also talk to them in harsh tones, which angers them; reason they often ignore the cries of passengers when they complain on a bus.

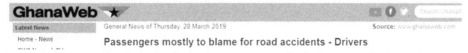

D. Passenger Actions Causing RTC Fatality: *In Ghana a study revealed that there are other diverse causes of passenger RTC but most (97%) of the causative factors cannot be easily accounted for (NRSA, 2019). However, some obvious passenger behaviours of high safety risks include a passenger sitting on the door of moving a vehicle with part of the body outside especially during funerals and other festive occasions; a passenger standing in a pick-up or sitting at its edge or passengers lying or even sleeping on top of overloaded trucks etc.*

Statistically, passenger RTC fatalities from 1998 to 2017 indicated that falling from a vehicle was about 2%, boarding was at about 1.1% and alighting or jumping from a vehicle was at 0.4% (see Figure 6.64).

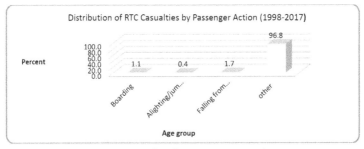

Figure 6.64: RTC casualties by passenger action (1998-2017)

E. RTC Caused by Occupant Restraints: Globally, it is estimated that up to 80% reduction in deaths of drivers and passengers can be achieved through the use of safety belts alone and mandatory laws by internal conventions such as the DOA are expected to be enforced by member countries.

i. Passenger Knowledge of Use of Seatbelts by Vehicle Type: In Ghana, private car and large bus users are the most knowledgeable passengers on the use of seatbelts at an average of 97% each followed by taxi and mini bus users at 93% each (see Figure 6.65). This is mostly due to the availability of seatbelts in those vehicles compared to the other vehicle types.

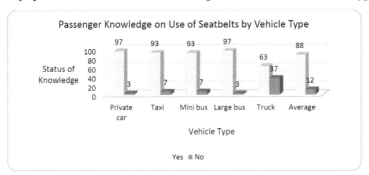

Figure 6.65: Passenger knowledge on use of seatbelts by vehicle type

ii. Seatbelt Use in Ghana: A study on the non-use of seatbelts by the by the BRRI for the NRSA in 2016, showed that less than (22%) of vehicle occupants use seatbelts. Also, comparatively, about 26% of females use seatbelts compared to 20% males. The limited use of seatbelts is mostly amongst users of commercial transport is mostly as a result of the unavailability of seatbelts in these vehicles and seatbelts not in good working condition. Other factors relate to dusty seatbelts especially in taxis which discourages passengers from wearing them.

iii. Child Restraint Compliance: Choosing and installing the appropriate child restraint system is also considered to be important since the child is placed at increased risk of both fatal and non-fatal injuries when restraints are frequently used inappropriately, (Zaza S, et al. 2001); (Anund A, et al, 2003).

However, the use of child restraint is hardly enforced in Ghana even though it is required by law and this needs to be further researched for informed decisions.

'Keep children in seat belts when driving'

Figure 6.66: A Publication on Child Restraints

6.5.5 Infrastructural Factors Affecting Passenger Safety

Infrastructural factors that affect passenger safety include the absence of appropriate facilities that provide security and comfort to passengers as summarised in Table 6.20.

Table 6.20: Required infrastructure for passenger safety

Facility Type	Service Required to be Provided
Terminals/stations	Waiting area with convenience shops, restaurants, washrooms, toilet facilities, potable water
Parking space	Safe and secure parking spaces
Road side Stops	boarding and dis-embankment points within safe walking space eg Footways, Side walking, guardrails etc.
Lighting	Adequate Lighting

6.5.6 Vehicle Factors Affecting Passenger Safety

A. RTC by Seating Position in a Vehicle: *From RTC statistics in (2018) by the NRSA, sitting at the back seat of a vehicle exposes passengers to higher levels of fatalities at 63% compared to the front seat at 20% in Ghana. This is because of the lack of seatbelts and airbags, "crumple zones" etc. to absorb the force of impacts during a crash as with front seats.*

Another reason is also due to the fact that there are more rear passenger seats with higher numbers of passenger carriage than the front seat for almost all buses in the country used for commercial transport. Those occupying the middle position on the rear seat have the most limited exposure to fatalities at (3%). (See Figures 6.67 and 6.68 for examples).

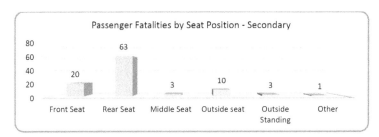

Figure 6.67: Passenger fatalities by seat position

Figure 6.68: Passengers in the bucket of vehicles

6.5.7 Passenger Safety Interventions

A. Recommended Best Practices for Passenger Safety: Although, there are limited international conventions and regulations for passenger safety, there are some 'good practice' reference material that offer guidance and recommendations on passenger safety. These are mostly based on what is expected from passengers. Typical examples are as presented in the extractions in Table 6.21 from diverse literature sources.

Table 6.21: Passenger Welfare; Challenging Behaviour and Safeguarding Procedures

Passenger	Safe Action
Planning a Trip	-Ask about safety records of service types and safety practices
	-Check for vehicle road worthiness
	-Identify situations that may be unsafe when travelling as a passenger
	-Enquire about the policy with regards to driving time
	-Ask about customer experiences.
	-Union record of regulatory violations
	-Notification procedures for roadside emergencies and breakdowns
	-Driver equipment with a wireless communications device
Rules for the Car	-Wear seatbelts if possible.
	-Never share seatbelts.
	-Children under 13 years old should always ride in the back seat to protect them from possible injury when a passenger-side air bag deploys to avoid serious hurt because they are designed to protect a person with a much bigger body.
	-Follow the rules in every car

Passenger	Safe Action
Passenger Action that can prevent RTCs	**Passenger Rules- Focus area 3:** -Good 'co-pilot', eg. acting responsibly by helping to navigate radio volume at a reasonable level -Keeping all interactions to a reasonable level from conversations, music, use of mobile phones -Paying attention to the road to see when a driver may need to concentrate more and could help the driver's focus by, for example, pausing a conversation or turning down the radio -Alerting the driver on emerging danger -Not shouting or trying to grab the steering wheel or hand brake -Not turning interior lights on at night while the car is moving as this can affect the driver's night vision -Avoid being a 'back-seat driver' - you can give the driver helpful information but refrain from being negative or giving a critical or 'witty' commentary on how they are driving, particularly if they are inexperienced -Speak out if you feel worried about mode of driving, waiting for a turn and knowing when to respond eg Speed - you are concerned about this, you might try something like: "I'm sorry but I'm not a good passenger. Could I ask you to slow down a bit"? This should cause no offence to the driver. Alternatively, you could say that you are feeling unwell. Few drivers are prepared to have their car interior spoilt! However, if the driver still refuses to slow down then you must be direct, after all you might save his or her life as well as your own. Drink or drugs - Never ever get into a car with a driver who has been drinking or taking drugs or who you suspect has been doing so. Do your best to persuade them not to drive. -Use verbal and non-verbal communication skills such as listening when others are talking **Federal Motor Carrier Safety Administration (FMSA)-** -Know Your Passenger Rights under the existing regulations -Take Action in an Emergency -If you believe you are in danger while aboard a bus, call emergency number Emergencies could include: -A bus driver who seems incapacitated, fatigued, intoxicated, or otherwise impaired (including by medical conditions). -Erratic or reckless driving (including speeding or texting) by a driver who won't comply with requests to stop. -A driver who refuses to stop despite an urgent safety problem (heavy smoke, skidding, etc.). **QFleet driver safety fact sheet** -locating and identifying landmarks and destination -not encouraging the driver to partake in risky or anti-social behaviour -not talking to the driver during times of high driver workload -detecting imminent hazards and warning the driver -helping young passengers to wear and adjust seat belts -supervising children in the rear seats -monitoring the driver's state of alertness -not placing feet on the dash of a vehicle, especially if the vehicle is equipped with a front passenger airbag -not leaning against or sleeping in contact with the door or side pillar of the vehicle, especially if the vehicle is equipped with passenger side airbags or side curtain airbags -keeping all parts of the body inside the vehicle -entering and exiting the vehicle via the kerbside -storing luggage in the boot and not in the vehicle cabin, and especially not on the rear parcel shelf
Child Safety	Children should be taught to understand that they can contribute to safer journeys by behaving responsibly and minimizing distracting behaviour. If young passengers are in the vehicle Discourage behaviours such as removing restraints, fighting, playing loud music or throwing objects around. -If there is a problem with a child while you are driving - stop the car in a safe place before resolving the problem. Avoid trying to resolve the problem while driving. -Allow additional time when embarking on longer trips with children to include time for rests breaks, eating and play activities. Baby capsules should only be fitted to the rear seating positions; utilities are an Exception If the vehicle has one row of seats only e.g., A child of any age can sit in the front seat if the vehicle has only one row of seats provided, they are properly restrained. If the vehicle has a passenger airbag fitted, a rear facing child restraint should not be used.

In Ghana, pre-departure inspections by the NRSA and some station masters, are undertaken in some instances to educate passengers on what to do (See Figure 6.69).

Figure 6.69: Pre vehicle Departure Checks in Ghana

B. Passenger Safety Interventions by Campaigns: *Passenger safety interventions by campaign by the NRSA have mostly been aimed to impress the need for passengers to take control of their own safety by demanding for quality safety requirements in vehicle and driver behaviour. The focus is on "Passenger Empowerment" through Pre-Departure Safety Campaigns aimed for the passenger to demand safety whilst on board a commercial vehicle, (See Figure 6.70). It encourages the passenger to speak against bad driver behaviour without engaging in an argument with the driver.*

Figure 6.70: Pre- vehicle Departure Education at Lorry Stations in Ghana, Source: NRSA

Special passenger focused campaign messages are based on passenger rights and responsibilities by the need for passengers to speak up against driver errors. A good example of passenger advocacy content published in the Daily Graphic Dec 18, 2014 is as summarised in Box 6.7.

Box 6.7: Daily Graphic; Dec 18, 2014, Category: Editorial

Yesterday, the Daily Graphic expressed some thoughts on the role of drivers, especially commercial drivers, in ensuring an accident-free Christmas, but we believe that that quest should involve a comprehensive role by all stakeholders. In that regard, passengers and other road users, who are often the victims of the road accidents, also have roles to play in averting accidents during the yuletide.

-Passengers must not, in the bid to get to their destinations on time, exert pressure on drivers to speed unnecessarily. They must know that wherever they are going, they need to get there alive. For it is better to arrive at their destinations late rather than to make drivers rush and get involved in accidents in which case they would never get to their destinations but rather cause pain to their loved ones. They must always bear in mind the dictum, "Better be late than the late passenger".

-Passengers must be resolute in protesting any negative action on the part of drivers. They should refuse to board a vehicle when they suspect that the driver has taken in alcohol. Also, they should all protest when a driver is speeding and call him to order. Quite often, only one person would do so while the others remain quiet, thereby giving the driver the opportunity to accuse that concerned person of being "too know". That should not be the norm during this year's Yuletide. The strong voice of all aboard a vehicle, protesting the wrongful acts of a driver and his mate, would go a long way to prevent mayhem.

-Some drivers have shown that they are stubborn; they do not listen to the pleas of passengers but rather continue their 'killer missions. When that happens, passengers, for their own safety, should alight from the vehicle at the nearest police checkpoint and report the conduct of the driver to the policemen.

-Citizens' action works through collective voices and it behoves all to ensure that their voices are part of decisions that affect their lives. It would be better if we take proactive steps to prevent accidents, rather than apportion blame when the unfortunate happens.

-Ensuring an accident-free Christmas cannot be the preserve or responsibility of any single entity. It is a collective responsibility and passengers must play their role to ensure that it succeeds. Ghana needs all its people alive to build a prosperous nation. When that happens, passengers, for their own safety, should alight from the vehicle at the nearest police checkpoint and report the conduct of the driver to the policemen.

https://www.graphic.com.gh/daily-graphic-editorials/the-role-of-passengers-in-ensuring-accident-free-xmas.html

C. Passenger Safety Challenge: *A critical assessment of the safety quality of commercial transport service by passenger expectations and satisfaction should be undertaken so that key interventions on journey time measures including expected behaviour before take-off; supervision during transit to ensure comfort and compliance to expected behaviour can be appropriately addressed.*

6.6 CHARACTERISTICS OF PEDESTRIAN SAFETY

Police officer under investigation for killing pedestrian

by Emmanuel Kwame Amoh · January 14, 2022

Walking is the commonest and most affordable mode of transportation and its safety is of prime concern because it involves unprotected vulnerable road users interacting with other modes of travel such as vehicles, motorcycles, bicycles and even inanimate objects in traffic. A pedestrian crash happens when a person hits the ground after colliding with a vehicle or solid object and bodily harm in the form of an injury or death occurs. Pedestrian crash can result from traffic errors committed by the driver, the pedestrian or both. It can happen when a pedestrian is crossing a road, playing in the right of way, standing by the road side, working by the road side, lying on the road, walking along the road, standing on the median etc.

According to the UNECE, (2015), walking is 2.5times more dangerous than travelling in a vehicle and in Ghana, pedestrian RTC fatalities is the second highest amongst road casualties and this section of the book reviews is on the essence of pedestrians as key component of road safety.

6.6.1 Pedestrian Safety Concepts

Pedestrian interaction in traffic is within a mixture of environmental conditions in situations of short time duration with restricted opportunities to communicate creating safety threats. It is within such situations that authors like Green, (2013), turn to blame pedestrians more for the occurrence of RTC compared to drivers. This assertion was validated with police records which proved that on the average pedestrians committed over 3.5 times more road violations than drivers.

The explanation was that drivers have to control their vehicles, look out for other vehicles as well as other road users which consumes much of their attention whilst pedestrians do not have any concurrent task. This makes them able to have greater control on whether a collision will occur. Other factors also attributed to pedestrian responsibility for RTCs compared to drivers are:

- The fact that vehicles are far more visible to pedestrians than to drivers, especially at night.
- The fact that vehicles travel highly on constrained paths but pedestrians know where to look for possible hazards and can make predictions.
- The fact that pedestrians have the choice of waiting for as long time as possible to cross the road whilst a driver may have only a few seconds to respond a pedestrian's sudden act of crossing the road.
- The fact that pedestrians can react, stop and turn faster and in a shorter distance than a moving vehicle.

However, authors like Preusser et al. (2002), counteract these assertions by insisting that both drivers and pedestrians should be equally held responsible for RTCs it is their mutual communication (formal and informal) which determines the outcome of their encounters.

In Ghana there has not been any concerted effort to validate or dispute any of these assertions.

6.6.2 Global Conventions and Regulations on Pedstrian Safety

A. Pedestrian Safety Regulations by UN Convention 68: The key aspect of pedestrian safety concern is focused on protective equality of road use and application of pedestrian protection regulations such as listed below and detailed in Table 6.22.

i. Setting rules for overtaking just before and on level-crossings

ii. Pedestrian awareness of the dangers of level-crossings;

iii. Provision for the needs of vulnerable pedestrians such as the disabled pedestrian, the elderly pedestrian and the child pedestrian especially for safe walk to school and back;

iv. Supervision and training for pedestrian safety;

v. Enforcement patrols for pedestrian safety checks; and

vi. The use of brightly coloured clothing especially for children who may use cycles or mopeds

Table 6.22: UN Convention 68 on Pedestrian Safety

UN Convention on Pedestrian Safety	Application in Ghana
i. Pedestrian Campaigns: (a) should project them as road users in their own right;(b) should inform all road users about the physical and psychological capabilities and limits of human beings in traffic, c) should also be used to inform pedestrians of road traffic rules, (d) should begin with young children; (e) should be on non-aggressive conduct towards pedestrians and stress their vulnerability	Pedestrian safety campaigns are consistently held by the NRSA as a key function but the extent of incorporation of the physical and psychological capabilities of human limits is not known.
ii. Disabled Pedestrians: (a)adoption of the international symbols and its incorporation in documents, road traffic signs, to facilitate the movement of persons with reduced mobility;	There is limited consideration for the needs of the vulnerable pedestrian in Ghana
Elderly Pedestrian: should be on dissemination of information regarding the needs of the elderly related to transport systems and facilities should be supported at all decision-making	Ditto
Child Pedestrians: (a)cover safety on the way to and from school in road safety instruction for children; (Patrols of specially trained persons eg. police, teachers, parents and possibly older pupil should be organized to protect children at dangerous places; Parents and school authorities should be made aware of the importance of making children more visible by having them wear brightly coloured clothing in particular in conditions of poor visibility; on the basic traffic rules;	Some safe walk to school interventions are in place but aspects on the safety of school transport, monitoring during school journey and wearing of brightly coloured cloths are not effectively applied
Vehicles: (i) on the importance of correct equipment of their vehicle (lighting, retro reflectors, brakes, etc.); on the use of protective devices (helmets, etc.); and on the particular dangers to be encountered in road traffic for their category of vehicle, especially in relation to heavy vehicles.	Recently, the NRSA has issued a statement on the poor quality of school bus service in the country but very little has been done about it.
Safe Walk to School: (a) If the children are allowed to use cycles at an early age, parents should be encouraged to accompany them; The transport of standing children should not be allowed; (b) The presence of a monitor is highly recommended.	Research into safe walk to school has been conducted in Ghana and various interventions including the installation of lollipop stands have been done. However, aspects on training of drivers on the needs of the child pedestrian have not been effectively done
Article 20- Infrastructure: (a) Pavements shall be used where available at the side of the carriageway; (b) Pedestrians walking on the carriageway shall; where possible, keep to the side opposite to that appropriate to the direction of traffic.	These are not effectively controlled
Article 26: Procession: (a) Road users are prohibited to cut across files of school children accompanied by a person in charge, and other processions; (b) Handicapped persons using invalid chairs propelled by themselves or moving at a walking pace may use pavements	Though there is some level of awareness by the NRSA it has not been emphasised as a key issue in pedestrian safety
Article 33: Groups of pedestrians led by a person in charge or forming a procession, must display, at least one white or selective yellow light to the front and a red light to the rear, or an amber light in both directions	Ditto

C. Pedestrian Safety Policy in Ghana: *Ghana's policy statement on pedestrian safety is that the design and construction of road infrastructure will incorporate facilities for safe pedestrian and vulnerable road user movements. Government will also promote awareness of safe behaviour in traffic by road users to minimize pedestrian-vehicular conflicts. The defined challenges associated with pedestrian safety and the related strategies for addressing them are as presented in Table 6.23.*

Table 6.23: Pedestrian Safety Policy in Ghana

Key Challenges	Strategies	Status of Application
Improper land-use planning resulting in excessive vehicular-pedestrian conflict.	Incorporate pedestrian safety facilities in road planning, design, construction and operation of roads and to provide for their special needs and requirements.	This is being done to some extent but there is room for more

Key Challenges	Strategies	Status of Application
Inadequacy in road safety education	Institute measures to ensure a sustainable road safety education programme for pedestrians and VRUs.	Pedestrian road safety campaigns are held
Poor road user awareness and behaviour in traffic.	Ditto	Ditto
Inadequate pedestrian safety facilities in communities and at relevant locations.	Provide and maintain walkways, lay-bys, safe pedestrian crossing points and traffic calming measures on all roads and highways.	This is being done to some extent but there is room for more
Non-compliance with appropriate legislation that govern pedestrian behaviour.	Enact and enforce effective pedestrian safety regulations.	LI 2160 of 2012 and the amendment of 2022 makes provision for this
Improper location of pedestrian facilities.	Plan, design, construct and upgrade roadways in accordance with set specifications in order to minimize the potential for conflict in the traffic environment.	This is yet to be evaluated and validated
Encroachment of pedestrian walkways by hawkers.	Keep pedestrian walkways free of hawkers, immobilized vehicles and other danger posing obstacles.	This has been difficult to be achieved by the Assemblies
Poor and inadequate street lighting and poor pedestrian conspicuity.		Some provisions are made on some urban roads but the same cannot be said for highways and feeder roads
Lack of facilities to segregate pedestrians from vehicles, and the on-adherence by drivers even in situations where they are available.		This has been achieved to some extent
Competition between road users for road space.		This has to be well studied and addressed
Lack of effective pedestrian safety programmes.		Some pedestrian safety campaigns are held
Lack of pedestrian safety facilities to cater for the physically challenged.	Update existing standards and develop new standards, guidelines and recommended practices in line with accepted international practices to facilitate safe accommodation of VRUs. Recognise VRUs as being equally important as the motorized vehicle in the planning, design, construction and operation of roads and to provide for their special needs and requirements.	This has not been given maximum attention
Poor traffic management (e.g. traffic lights, pelican crossings).		There are limited provisions on these

Source: NRSP 2008

6.6.3 Profile of Pedestrian Crash Victims in Ghana

A. Summary of Pedestrian Casualties in Ghana: *From 1998 to 2017 pedestrian RTC had 42.7% of them being hospitalized, 34.5 % were injured without hospitalization and 22% fatal (see Figure 6.71).*

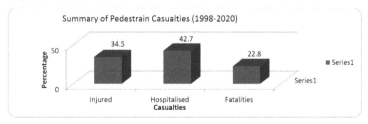

Figure 6.71: Summary of pedestrian casualties, Source (BRRI, 2020)

B. Socio-Demographic Attributes of RTC Pedestrian Victims in Ghana:

i. Pedestrian Involvement in Crash Fatalities by Age in Ghana: From 1998 to 2017 the age group with the highest incidence of pedestrian RTC fatalities was 6-15 years at an average of 21.3% (see Figure 6.72). These were identified mostly as children of basic school going age and those of early teenage years at the JHS school level who normally travel to school on daily basis either by walking or by commercial transport. They are mostly characterised with limited perception of danger with a poor sense of judgement of reaction time resulting in their frequent involvement in pedestrian RTCs.

Those in the age group of 16-25 constituted the second highest at19.3% followed by those in the age group of 26-35 at 18.8%. These are those who travel mostly for economic reasons. The fourth are children between 0-5 at 12% who are either left unattended or stray out of adult care by negligence. For example, it is not uncommon in Ghana to see two or three very young children strolling to school unattended and being randomly assisted by concerned adults. It also includes babies who are hit together with their parents especially mothers carrying babies and toddlers either in hand or at the back (see Figure 6.73).

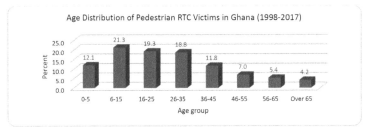

Figure 6.72: Distribution of pedestrian RTC fatalities by age – secondary

Figure 6.73: Mothers carrying babies at their back

ii. Pedestrian Involvement in Crash Fatalities by Sex in Ghana: Gender is another impact category for pedestrian safety. It is believed that male and female pedestrians have different perceptions, needs, interests, intuition etc. as with their societal roles. According to Di Zhu (2012) males relatively cross roads at higher speeds of 50mph with little caution and so are mostly hit by vehicles with higher speeds indicating a greater chance of death than females. In addition, there is a greater possibility of males crossing the road intoxicated or distracted by cell phone use etc. which may have similar effects.

In Ghana, males also get involved in pedestrian RTCs more than females at about 68% and 32% of pedestrian respectively. (NRSA 2019). This may be associated with the fact that male pedestrians engage in riskier behaviour that leads them to suffer greater risk of fatality compared to females in RTC situations. On the other hand, more female pedestrians carry more load than their male counterparts when crossing the road and this affects the speed of walking. A female pedestrian might also be carrying a child for which an RTC might have a more serious consequence than a male counterpart, (See Figure 6.74).

Figure 6.74: Examples of Pedestrian Mothers with Baby's

iii. Educational Status of Pedestrian Crash Victims: Pedestrians with education up to basic school level recorded the highest in pedestrian RTCs at 48.2% followed by those at SHS level at 22.7%. Those without formal education were at 14% and those with tertiary education at 10% with the least being those with technical and vocational education at 4.5% (see Figure 6.75). Thus, it can be inferred that educational status may in turn have some impact on social status with regards to distance of travel by walking which in turn reflects in the rate of RTC occurrence amongst such groups. The high proportion of pedestrian crashes among victims with up to basic school education also gives an indication of the vulnerability of children as pedestrian victims on Ghanaian roads.

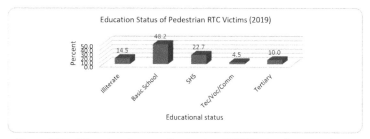

Figure 6.75: Educational status of pedestrian RTC Victims by sex - primary

iv. Educational Status of Pedestrian Crash Victims by Sex: A further breakdown by gender reveals that 80% of the female pedestrian crash victims are uneducated or have only had education up to basic school level. The remaining (20%) are educated to various levels up

to tertiary level. For the male victims, 45.4% have attained education up to the SHS and
technical level education with the remaining 54.6% being illiterates or educated up to
basic school level. It can thus be inferred that the higher the educational attainment of an
individual, the less likely s/he is to be involved in a pedestrian crash.

v. Occupation of Pedestrian Crash Victims: Records from studies in Ghana show that most
pedestrian RTC victims are traders, students and artisans at 25% each. This is because
is because these categories of pedestrians are characterised with higher travel frequencies
(Figure 6.76).

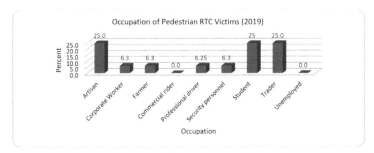

Figure 6.76: Occupation of pedestrian RTC Victims –primary

vi. Distribution of Pedestrian Crash Victims by Income: Though involvement in pedestrian
RTCs cuts across all income groups, it is evident from the survey that those in low-income
brackets are more prone to pedestrian fatalities than those in the higher income bracket
in Ghana (see Figure 6.77). This could be attributed to higher vehicle ownership and
transport affordability by those in higher income brackets. For example, children from
low-income group are more likely to walk unaccompanied to school compared to those
from higher income groups who may dropped in school in private cars or by paid transport
service.

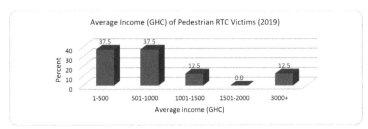

Figure 6.77: Average monthly income (GHC) of pedestrian RTC Victims - primary

6.6.4 Causes of Pedestrian Traffic Crashes

A. Pedestrian RTCS Caused by Bad Pedestrian Behaviour: *In Ghana a study by the*
NRSA in 2019 on pedestrian exposure to RTC fatalities by level of knowledge on road safety
issues had most (62%) of pedestrians indicating that they are knowledgeable in pedestrian

safety issues. However, the extent to which this is reflected in pedestrian behaviour in traffic situations could not be validated.

i. Pedestrian RTCs caused by Poor Pedestrian Decision Making: Poor pedestrian decision making due to misunderstanding and misinterpretation of the safety issues is the major causes of pedestrian. This is because of the pedestrian lack of self-judgement on what they do wrong. Others are:

a.   Lack of pedestrian compliance to regulations.

b.   Distracted walking by the use of mobile phones.

c.   Inattentiveness to the traffic environment by the use of earphones.

d.   Non-compliance to designated crossing areas out of comfort or convenience rather than safety e.g., cutting through or jumping over barricaded crossing points.

e.   Impatience from pedestrian delay at crossing points leading to carelessness.

f.   Crossing a road without waiting for the right signal.

g.   Pedestrian inability to balance judgement on speed and their pace of walking.

h.   Pedestrian under the influence of alcohol.

i.   Pedestrian Running across the road without looking out properly for an oncoming vehicle.

j.   Pedestrian over familiarity with the road environment resulting in carelessness.

k.   Pedestrian crossing at an unsignalised intersection and near roundabouts:

In Ghana the highest exposure to pedestrian fatality happened when they were crossing the road at 61% (NRSA, 2019). Other undefined pedestrian actions follow in exposing them to RTC fatalities at 18.9%. Walking along the road and on the edge of the road was the cause of 9.1% and 8.6% of pedestrian RTC fatality records respectively. The use of footpaths and playing on the road also recorded 1.1% and 0.5% respectively. (See Figure 6.78).

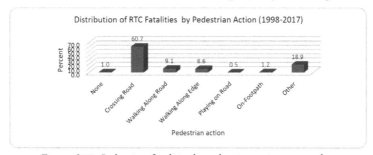

Figure 6.78: Pedestrian fatalities by pedestrian action – secondary

Bad pedestrian road crossing habits causing RTC's in Ghana are as summarised in Table 6.27 and exhibited in Figure 6.79.

Table 6.27: Distribution of Pedestrian Wrongful Road Crossing Behaviour in Ghana

Wrongful Pedestrian Behaviour	Average
Failure to use safe crossing facilities	46.4
Crossing the road from between parked vehicles.	10.0
Crossing the road between vehicles that are queued up along the road waiting for traffic signals to change.	11.0
Forcing to cross the road in a group.	11.8
Crossing a multi-lane highway where there is no pedestrian crossing and sitting on the concrete barrier	10.7
One person standing in the middle of the road, waiting for a clear gap for other to complete crossing	10.0
Total	100.0

Figure 6.79: Wrong and Right Pedestrian Crossing Modes in Ghana (Source: NRSA)

ii. Pedestrian Exposure to RTC Fatalities by Physical impairment: Currently this phenomenon has not been well studied in the country and there is limited knowledge of the magnitude of this challenge and what needs to be done for correction. Some recommended actions to positively influence safe pedestrian decision making include:

a. Pedestrians being prompted to wait by traffic signals or wardens.

b. Pedestrians waiting for a large enough gap between the pedestrian and vehicle before crossing.

c. Pedestrians walking to the middle of the road (Island or median) and waiting for safe crossing.

d. Pedestrians making eye contact with driver.

e. Pedestrians viewing conditions before decision making.

B. Pedestrian RTC caused by Bad Driver Behaviour: According to Zaidel, (1992), every individual driver is influenced by other road users, general social norms as well as formal traffic rules as follows:

i. Reckless Driving: This is when drivers do not drive with the consciousness of pedestrian presence on the road in mind let alone give way to them. An example is excessive speeding with an estimation collision speed of 50 km/h having the risk of fatal injury for a pedestrian at almost 8 times higher compared to a speed of 30km/h. Also, a reduction of 10 km/h in travel speed is said to prevent 50% of all pedestrian fatalities. Finally, 21% of all collisions with slower speeds is said to decrease total stopping distance and also create a larger reduction in impact speed (Pasanen, 1992),

In Ghana, speeding is also of high risk to the occurrence of pedestrian fatalities, especially in hit and run situations when a driver accidentally hits a pedestrian but fails to follow up on proper post-crash protocols for the victim (See Figure 6.80).

Figure 6.80: Examples of Publications on RTC caused by Speeding

Another example involves driver inability to manage pedestrian hazard such as pedestrian panic situations and vehicles proceeding straight to strike a pedestrian. This is mostly attributed to the fact that drivers faced with pedestrian hazard respond with excessive emergency braking, locking the wheels and putting the vehicle into a skid without steering control. Others are driver inattentiveness, impairment from alcohol or substance intake, inexperience, poor vehicular control etc. Statistically it is recorded that about a third (33%) of driver errors causing pedestrian RTC fatalities are not well defined. However, driver inattentiveness follows at 27%; followed by speeding at 22% and loss of vehicular control at 15% (NRSA 2019. (See Figure 6.81)

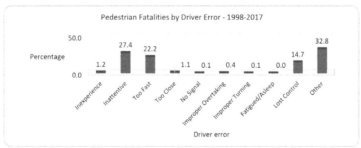

Figure 6.81: Pedestrian fatalities by driver error-secondary

B. RTC's caused by what Pedestrians consider to be Bad Driver Behaviour: According to Ross, (1977) the limited duration of road user interaction makes it difficult to be able to communicate with each other whilst still using the road. Rumar, (1990) adds that a lapse of cognitive expectation, illustrated by a failure to look for a specific type of road user, or a failure to look in the direction of the road user in question can also cause pedestrian hits. Typical, examples of what pedestrians consider to be bad driver behaviour that exposes them to RTC's includes the following:

i.   Driver disregard for pedestrian presence in traffic.

ii.   Driver disregard for green pedestrian signal.

iii.   Driver perception of having more right to use the road than a pedestrian.

iv.   Motorcyclists meandering in–between vehicles and hitting pedestrians crossing the road.

v.   Driver not yielding at pedestrian crossing.

vi.   Motor rider disregard for pedestrian at zebra crossings.

vii.   2nd or 3rd vehicle not yielding to crossing pedestrians on multi-lane roads.

viii. Driver distraction.

ix.   Driver irritation and aggressive acts towards pedestrians.

x.   Limited driver Knowledge of pedestrian safety laws.

In Ghana, a study by the NRSA (2019) revealed that only 33% of drivers are willing to give way to pedestrians at zebra crossings. High vehicular traffic volumes with little crossing gaps for the pedestrian was at 7% and the presence of parked vehicles from on street parking with limited pedestrian visibility for crossing was at 3%.

The study also revealed that 40% of drivers had knowledge on pedestrian safety requirements and 60% did not. Out of those who indicated that they had knowledge of pedestrian safety needs, 40% were aware of the need to yield to pedestrians at crossing points; 20% had knowledge on not stopping on the zebra crossings marking; 13% mentioned observance of traffic signals to allow for pedestrians to pass and 3% mentioned watching out for the movement of other vehicles in relation to pedestrian safety especially on multi-lane roads. See box 9 for a summary of pedestrian safety regulations in Ghana.

Box 9: Pedestrian Regulations in Ghana

LI2108 Reg. 101 (iii) item (e-f) which stipulates that

(e) at a pedestrian crossing of the type shown in the Third Schedule, give precedence to a person on foot on the pedestrian crossing if that person is in the roadway on the crossing while the vehicle is approaching the crossing;

(f) give preference to children, the elderly and the physically challenged who wish to cross the road at designated crossing points;

(g) give preference to a visually impaired pedestrian who carries a white stick or any sight aid and wishes to cross the road;

(e) at a pedestrian crossing of the type shown in the Third Schedule, give precedence to a person on foot on the pedestrian crossing if that person is in the roadway on the crossing while the vehicle is approaching the crossing;

(f) give preference to children, the elderly and the physically challenged who wish to cross the road at designated crossing points;

(g) give preference to a visually impaired pedestrian who carries a white stick or any sight aid and wishes to cross the road.

Source: LI2180, 2012

C. RTCs caused by what Drivers consider to be risky Pedestrians Behaviour:
Drivers also attribute pedestrian errors that cause RTCs to the following factors:

i.   A pedestrian running to catch a vehicle by disregarding an oncoming vehicle e.g. street hawkers who whilst engaging in their trade tend to disregard the traffic environment.

ii.   Pedestrian jaywalking and crossing at un-demarcated road sections.

iii. Pedestrian disregard for red traffic signals.

iv.   Pedestrian making unexpected or sudden movements by stopping or going when they should not.

v.   Pedestrian not paying attention to vehicles in traffic.

vi.   Pedestrian pretending not see a car approaching.

vii. Pedestrians not valuing their lives.

viii. Pedestrian starting to cross the road when they should rather be waiting.

ix.   Pedestrian moving slowly while crossing a road or engaging in other activities such as using a cell phone.

x.   Pedestrians who try to force drivers to lower their speed by stepping into the middle of the road whilst a vehicle is still in motion and approaching them.

xi.   Pedestrians who step in front of vehicles by mistake or without being aware of an approaching vehicle.

xii. Pedestrians who cross the road in groups with little caution.

xiii. Pedestrian who walks by the road in file rather than in line.

xiv. Pedestrians who do not face oncoming traffic.

xv.   Pedestrian who does not wear reflective clothing at night.

Pedestrian Behaviour causing RTCs identified by drivers includes slow moving pedestrians crossing at zebra crossings when granted access by them to cross a road at 48%; pedestrians crossing the road without looking out for oncoming vehicles at 19%; pedestrians who talk on phone whilst crossing the road at 13%; pedestrians who cross the road when the traffic signal has not given the green signal at 10% and pedestrians crossing the road at wrong places even when pedestrians crossing facilities are available at 8%, (See Figure 6.89).

Dahlstedt, (1994), intimated that what drivers claim to do is one thing and what they actually do is another. Drivers are also said to be subject to attribution biases when judging the behaviour of other road users especially pedestrians. Ross et al. (1977), explains this on the premise that there is a tendency of persons "to see their own behaviour choices and judgements as relatively common and appropriate to existing circumstances while viewing alternative responses as uncommon, deviant, or inappropriate". This is specifically so because most drivers focus their attention on other vehicles and tend to forget about pedestrians and it is argued that since the driver has more to do on the road it is the pedestrian who should take more precaution.

A study by the NRSA in 2019, revealed that in Ghana, 33% of drivers claimed that they seek equitable interaction with pedestrians to ensure that neither party is over delayed at locations with pedestrian presence. About 30% also insisted that pedestrians owe it to themselves to protect themselves and not the driver. 14% explained that their decision to stop for pedestrians at crossing points is determined by the prevailing situations at specific locations and 23% could not attribute it to any specific factor. Whichever way it is looked at both drivers and pedestrians must be made to understand that every traffic situation involving the two present unique challenges but what is of utmost importance is for every road user to look out for the safety of the other.

D. Pedestrian RTCs caused by both Driver and Pedestrian Actions: Pedestrian RTCs can happen by errors caused by both drivers and pedestrians when they act according to discrepant formal or informal traffic rules. This is because the ability of either the driver or the pedestrian to correctly predict the others behaviour is reduced if the other complies with a different rule system, (Wilde, 1976). This also happens when formal traffic rules do not correspond with the road design, informal traffic rules, wrongful behaviour etc. (Helmers and Aberg 1970), Examples of these are as follows:

i.   Where there is a relatively a long distance between the vehicle and the pedestrian's point of entry into the road, very little caution is taken by both the driver and the pedestrian.

ii.   When drivers fail to reduce speed with the miscalculation that the pedestrian will be able to cross in time or the pedestrian is obligated to cross in time irrespective of their speed.

iii.   When pedestrians assumes that the speed of their legs are faster than the speed of the vehicle

iv.   When the approaching vehicle is forced to apply a brakes a pedestrian's sudden move with little regard of the speed of the vehicle on assumption that no matter the situation, the driver must control speed.

v.   When there is a competitive behaviour and both the driver and the pedestrian decide to have their own way

vi.   Where the presence of pedestrians at a zebra crossing has little or no speed-reducing influence on the driver.

Based on the argument by Lurie (1968) that traffic rules are formal and informal and do not tell what is morally right or wrong, but merely tell on whether what is to be done some of these issues do not lend to easy solution.

In Ghana, joint driver-pedestrian educational sessions should be conducted to improve diver pedestrian relations in for better understanding of pedestrian driver safety issues.

6.6.6 Pedestrian Exposure to RTC by Infrastructural Factors

A. Road Infrastructure Factors that Influence Pedestrian RTCs: Infrastructure design and maintenance for pedestrian safety is identified as a significant factor in pedestrian fatality situations and the key aspects include the following:

i. Pedestrian ignorance of the importance and use of Road Safety Installations.

In Ghana, oftentimes road safety sensitisation is dovetailed into major road projects for affected communities and road users. Also, a study by the NRSA in 2019 indicated that pedestrian safety knowledge on the use of safety installation was at an average of 60% from self-reported surveys without any scientific proofs. Thus, it is difficult to posit the level of pedestrian understanding of their own traffic safety especially in regard of pedestrian refusal to make use of safety installations.

ii. Poor Utilisation of Pedestrian Safety Installations: According to (Helmers & Aberg, 1978), the provision of pedestrian safety installations is not congruent with adherence to safety rules and adjustment to human requirements or natural be-haviour patterns since other factors also expose pedestrians to RTC by their own actions.

This is very true of the Ghanaian situation where pedestrians who protested against the delayed completion of footbridges for safe crossing have to be whipped by law enforcers to use the same facilities they fought for. Others are the vandalisation of protective measures for unsafe road use such as barbwires and guardrails by the same pedestrians intended to be protected for purposes of convenience with little regard for their own safety. A list of assigned reasons for pedestrian failure to utilise available road furniture are as presented in Table 6.28.

Table 6.28: Reasons for the use of Pedestrian Crossing Facilities

Reasons for not using pedestrian safety facilities	Average
Not easily accessible	30.9%
Laziness	20.7%
Far from destination	29.0%
Fear of height (overpass)	1.2%
Ignorance	0.6%
Hawkers encroaching facility	4.0%
Inadequate Facilities	2.6%
Waste of time	5.4%
No idea	5.6%

C. Pedestrian RTC Exposure by Road Class: The frequency of the occurrence of pedestrian fatalities also varies by road type. This is mostly due to variations in the level of safety installations provided by road types. This includes the level of clearance from the on-coming vehicle, the number of lanes, width of the carriageway and the type and number of speed calming measures provided. For example, it is estimated that multi-lane roads with high traffic volumes above12,000vehicles per day and high-speed flow, having a marked crossing alone (without the substantial improvements) is associated with a higher pedestrian crash rate (after controlling for other site factors) compared to an unmarked crossing (TRB,2000).

Records in Ghana also indicate that the risk of exposure to RTC fatalities by pedestrians along trunk roads is the highest at 42%, followed by that of the urban roads at 41% with feeder roads recording the least at 8%. This mostly happens on high-speed trunk roads traversing linear human settlement patterns with utility facilities located at both sides of the road whereby residents have to cross the road to access such facilities. An example is crossing the road to fetch water at a very slow walking pace. Others are the absence of pedestrian safety installations on such road sections e.g. the absence of street lights and road crossing facilities.

The lack of provision of education in such communities on safe walking such as walking on the right side of the road to face oncoming vehicles, wearing of reflective clothing at night etc. also contributes to high pedestrian casualties on trunk roads.

Pedestrian challenges on urban roads are mostly attributed to jay walking, speeding and driver negligence though urban dwellers relatively have higher access to enforcement and education. Others are limited pedestrian crossing facilities, limited refugee islands, short pedestrian green phase of traffic signals, limited walkways obstructed by trading activities etc.

The low exposure of pedestrians to RTC fatalities on feeder roads can be attributed to the relatively low traffic volumes. Figure 6.82 present the details.

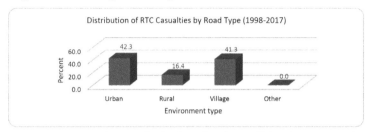

Figure 6.82: Distribution of RTC Casualties by Road Type (1998 – 2017).

E. Pedestrian Fatality by Road Surface Type: *In Ghana, pedestrian crashes mostly occur on paved road sections without potholes at 87.5%. This is largely accounted for by excessive speeding by motorised road users to the smooth ride quality.*

F. Pedestrian Fatalities by Road Geometry: *In Ghana, pedestrian casualties occur at straight road sections at 90% with those on curved road sections following at 9.05% with casualties at crests being the least recorded at (0.05%). This is also mostly attributed to over speeding.*

G. Pedestrian Fatalities by Road Location: *Pedestrian RTCs by road location is mostly at unsignalised midblock road segments at 79%. The potential factors influencing this include crossing difficulty due to limited availability of pedestrian refuge and median width.*

6.6.7 Pedestrian Exposure to RTC by Vehicular Factors

Some of the key vehicle factors often associated with pedestrian crashes includes the following:

- High vehicle volumes with potential for increased crash frequency.
- High vehicle mass which impacts on pedestrian crash severity especially from HGVs.
- The level of automation of a vehicle since automatic vehicles are said to high possibility for causing pedestrian deaths.
- Vehicles with bumpers or bull-bars have a higher possibility for causing pedestrian fatality.

In Ghana, saloon cars record the highest pedestrian crashes at 47% because cars constitute the highest composition in the total traffic stream in the country. This is followed by buses at 26% with pedestrian RTCs involving motorcycles constituting the third highest causing pedestrian crash rate at 10%. Light and heavy goods vehicles also follow at 9% with Pick-ups, bicycles/tricycles as well as others taking 5%; 1% and 2% respectively. However, heavy goods vehicles contribute to over 50% of pedestrian RTC fatalities though of low crash rate and this normally happens on highways.

6.6.8 Pedestrian Exposure to RTCs by Environmental Factors

A. Pedestrian Fatalities by Weather Condition: From literature, pedestrian crash records are highest at night time or dusk compared to day light globally due to poor visibility at the night time. Others are rainy and foggy weather conditions also due to poor visibility as well as inadequate response to the needs of victims in such situations.

However, in Ghana, pedestrian fatality situations in clear weather conditions are rather high at (90%), followed by other weather conditions such as dusty conditions at 7.5% with foggy and rainy conditions being at 2% and 0.5% respectively, (see Figure 6.83). The situation is first attributed more to bad driver and pedestrian behaviour rather than weather related factors. It is also attributed to reduced human activities at night hours and in rainy weather conditions since most people would be asleep in those hours of the days or would be taking cover from the rain.

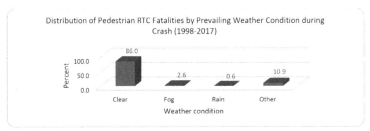

Figure 6.83: Pedestrian Fatalities by Prevailing Weather Condition

6.6.9 Pedestrian Crashinvolvement by Land Use Factors

The built environment influences pedestrian-vehicle collision. Studies in Ghana have confirmed that pedestrian crash fatalities are high in commercial zones at 48% compared to other land use areas. This is due to conflicts from a mix of different social and economic activities and related interaction within the traffic system. Past incidences in Ghana with a vehicle running through busy commercial areas such as at the Kaneshie market on 15th January 2008 after a Benz bus had a brake failure which resulted in several people dying and the Ashaiman market incident on 26th July 2018 when a cement truck run through traders. Also at risk are street hawkers with a typical example involving the killing and injuring of street hawkers and beggars on the 37 Hospital Road when two drivers raced each other and one veered of the road, running into them.

Pedestrian fatality crashes in residential zones are next at 19%, (see Figure 6.84). This mostly occurs where urban right of way limits is contravened on major arterials where a limit of not less 10meter gap is required and other road types where a limit of 5meters is required. This is followed by pedestrian crash fatalities that occur in school zones at 17% and these are mostly attributed to pupils/students walking along the road or crossing the road to school in areas with no provision for facilities such as guardrails and pedestrian crossing facilities.

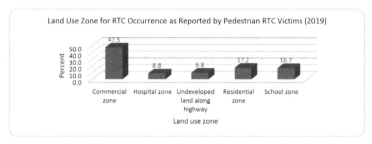

Figure 6.84: Landuse factors causing pedestrian injury severity/fatalities

6.6.10 Pedestrian Safety Enforcement Activities

In Ghana, enforcement activities for pedestrian safety includes control of pedestrian jay walking and compelling pedestrians to use pedestrian installations such as zebra crossing, walkways, footbridges etc. (See Figure 6.85). However, pedestrian safety enforcement can be said to be grossly inadequate. Currently, there are no records of pedestrian arrests from jay walking, failure to use designated crossing points etc.

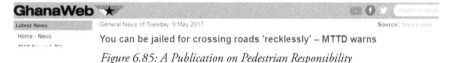

Figure 6.85: A Publication on Pedestrian Responsibility

6.6.11 Pedestrian Safety for the Vulnerable

A. Child Pedestrian Safety: According to the OECD, C1998) child pedestrians (below 10 years) are highly high and fast traffic situations due to since children's ability to cope with traffic remains severely limited in the first nine or ten years of their life. They cannot be relied on for better behavior on so it is the responsibility of decision-makers to allow them freedom of movement in appropriate surroundings and to promote more careful behavior of the drivers. It is also the responsibility of parents to protect them. (See Figure 6.86).

In Ghana, statistics indicates that about 21% of all fatalities involve children below the age of 16 years which is significant and must be addressed.

Figure 6.86: A Publication on Child Pedestrian Casualty in Ghana

i. Adequacy of Road Infrastructure for child Pedestrians: Another study by the NRSA on child pedestrian characteristics in 2019 indicated that an average of 66% of sampled children from three regions within the ages of 6 to 9 years were of the view that road safety infrastructure is good and safe to use. Due to interventions such as the promotion of safe walk to school concept involving the provision of safety infrastructure for school clusters. Example include the DUR's safe walk to school initiatives for school clusters and Amend's construction of zebra crossing and walkways for some basic schools in Ghana on 15th April 2020.

About 16% of the children however stated that road infrastructure is inadequate and the ones available are not easily accessible. 14% problems with the poor maintenance of such facilities by respective authorities and it is required for responsive agencies to act accordingly.

ii. Child Pedestrian Access to Road Safety Education: The study also revealed that an average of 58% of the child respondents had been educated in road safety whilst 42% had not had any education in road safety which is a very significant representation of the child pedestrian in the traffic system in Ghana. The two main sources of road safety education for the children were from school and at home at 76% and 24% respectively. This can be attributed to NRSA's child safety campaigns in schools and the introduction of the lollipop concept for the child pedestrian, (See Figure 6.87).

Figure 6.87: Examples of Good Child Pedestrian Education in Ghana

iii. Child Pedestrian Knowledge on Road Safety: An average of 34% each of the children from a study by the NRSA in 2019 indicated that they had knowledge on the use of traffic lights and zebra crossing for safe crossing of roads which is considered the basic safety precaution measure for the child. An average of 56% representing more than half of the responding children cross the road by first looking left, right and left again and an average of 28% of them cross the road only when they were sure the road is clear and 13% solicit help from adults or signal for drivers to stop for them. However, 4% had no idea at all about traffic safety because they are always dropped by parents.

iv. Child Pedestrians Challenges in Ghana: About 57% of the child pedestrians interviewed complained about impatient drivers who ignore their needs by not stopping for them as their major challenge and about43% complained of general lawlessness on roads. 45% of the children recommended for driver education on the dangers of reckless driving and 21% wanted more of the posting of traffic wardens especially in rural settlements to assist them in crossing the road.

B. The Aged Pedestrian: From literature, aged or elderly people show a gradual decrease of their abilities to cope with difficult traffic situations and therefore are at greater risk of being involved in RTCs and with potential for more severe consequences. Therefore, aged people who are aware of their own difficulties tend to disengage from traffic by reducing their mobility and the scope of their social life.

A study by the NRSA in 2019 on aged pedestrians in Ghana indicated that an average of 48% of the aged pedestrians had knowledge about road safety and.16% said safety infrastructure facilities are inadequate especially since they are not able to easily access facilities such as footbridges.

Some of the recommended safety interventions by the aged pedestrians include the need to specifically address the concerns of the aged pedestrians in the country at 36% and the need to construct more safety infrastructure for the aged at 42%. Others are the need for drivers to yield to traffic signals and other road safety regulations at 11%, better enforcement of the use of safety infrastructure at 15% and suggestions for recklessly driving to attract fine at 17%.

C. The Disabled Pedestrian: It is important for disabled pedestrians to have barrier free access to traffic with regards to the needs of wheelchair users, the sightless, those with impaired hearing etc. by the integration of the needs of such persons in transport design and vehicle standards etc.

In Ghana, the only traffic regulation concerning disabled pedestrians is the LI 2180 Regulation 26 7(b) which states that "a person with a physical disability who has to drive a motor vehicle adapted for a person with physical disability, or a motor vehicle adapted specially for that physically disabled applicant". However, a study in Ghana by the study by the NRSA in 2019 revealed that majority (78%) of them were not aware of any such law. This challenge is very significant because lack of knowledge of their right makes them highly vulnerable (See Figure 6.99).

Figure 6.88: A publication on Vulnerable Pedestrian Needs in Ghana

i. Traffic Challenges of Disabled Pedestrians: *Some of the challenges expressed by the disabled pedestrians are as summarised in Table 6.29.*

Table 6.29: Disabled challenges faced as a pedestrian

Disabled Challenges Faced as a Pedestrian	Average
Uneven surface that hinders or cause difficult movement	30.8%
Devices that are hard to reach, such as doors or push buttons for walk signals	22.4%
Narrow sidewalks that impede the ability of users to turn or to cross paths with others	22.0%
steep slopes that can cause slow and difficult movement or loss of control	24.8%
Total	100.0%

Some suggestions for addressing disabled pedestrian needs include:

a. *Provision of infrastructure to suit the needs of the disabled eg improvement of rough surfaces on walkways and cross slopes and improvement of sidewalks by the widening of narrow ones and enforcement of encroaching hawkers for ease of movement of wheel chair and white cane users.*

b. *Installation of additional road safety infrastructure at vantage points with special features for accommodating the use of wheel chairs, and special walking lanes for the blind such as push button for traffic walk signals within the reach of them.*

c. Placement of increased number of traffic wardens to help the disabled.

d. Provision of a separate transport system for the disabled

e. Focused campaign and education on disabled road safety needs.

D. Pedestrian Safety Interventions in Ghana: *Some pedestrian safety interventions implemented in Ghana includes the following:*

i. Pedestrian Safety Campaign: One of the major activities of the NRSC on pedestrian safety is nationwide education. These activities are conducted through periodic education and campaigns through outreach and the media. Some implemented programmes are as presented in Table 6.30.

Table 6.30: Summary of Elements of Pedestrian Road Safety Campaign

Description	Campaigns	Safety Issues of Focus	Types of Road Safety Campaign Strategy
Crossing points	Children and cyclists Safe crossing points Crossing the road	Crossing aids 'lollipop Stands' for schools along roads and volunteers to assist pedestrians in crossing.	Communication Road designs
Safety officers	Crossing the road	District Security officers to enforce Road Traffic Regulations focusing on pedestrian related/jay walking	Enforcement
Pedestrian safety skills	Crossing the road Pedestrian road safety slogans	Use of Pelican crossing Use of Zebra crossing Wearing reflective clothing at night Use of pedestrian walkways	Communication Road design
Road Safety in Schools	Development of road safety education as part of school curriculum, Training of teachers Formation of school clubs for road safety	This is to equip teachers with the necessary skills to effectively teach school children road regulations and to reduce accidents in future.	Communication

6.6.12 Integrated Factors for Pedestrian Crash Involvement

It is said that though there is currently much focus on education and enforcement for pedestrian fatality control; improved economy, engineering patterns and vehicle afford-ability should be given due attention in addressing pedestrian traffic challenges since these factors also determines the level of pedestrian vulnerability to RTC's. Effective pedestrian safety depends on good interaction between the driver/rider and the eventual effectiveness of any pedestrian safety initiatives must involve the two in tandem. There is therefore a critical need to engage in pedestrian driver issues in a joint fora. This is because of the difference in the level of appreciation of the concerns of each road user group.

CHAPTER 7

————————

POST CRASH CARE IN ROAD SAFETY

"I was in coma for 3 weeks, left crippled after road accident" – A Young man narrates his ordeal in an interview with Zionfelix. According to the victim, he has been abandoned by his family and loved ones. He said he could not afford to pay the money needed for a surgery. He is unable to walk and in constant pain." Narrating his story, the former car sprayer said living conditions have become very unbearable for him over the past few months adding that life in Accra became very difficult as his upkeep was becoming a major issue for him.

As a result of the predicament, Joshua said he relocated to Aburi for 10 months but later realised that he had become a burden to the people he was staying with so he decided to return to Accra. The paraplegic furthered that his girlfriend jilted him after returning to Accra because of his condition. "After returning to Accra, my girlfriend also left me," he said. Currently, Joshua is unable to go for check-ups because he is financially unstable to foot his medical bills.

7.1 INTRODUCTION

Post-crash care is the chain of care provided after an RTC has occurred in order to reduce the severity of a sustained injury or even prevent the death of an RTC victim. This is because prompt provision of emergency care and rapid movement of the injured from the crash scene to a fixed health-care facility increases the chance for a victim's survival as well as reduce the possibility of the victim suffering from a long-term disability outcome, (Sasser S., et al 2005). Thus, the WHO's WHA 72 resolution 12.9, (2019), likens post-crash care to an integrated emergency care system for delivering accessible, quality, time sensitive health care services for acute illness and injury across the life course.

The approach to post-crash care is either formal, informal or a combination of the two. The formal system involves the situation where there are established systems for the (i) notification of relevant authorities when a crash has occurred; followed by the (ii) dispatch of appropriate paramedics and resources to the scene to manage the crash situation; (iii) the provision of rapid intermediary medical care at the crash scene; and (iv) the transport of the injured RTC victim safely to a facility; that has the appropriate level of personnel and equipment necessary to provide substantive medical care to the injured victim in a timely fashion be it by care and discharge or referral to a higher.

An informal post-crash care system involves the handling of RTC situations by lay persons who are untrained and also use unconventional equipment and methods to attend to crash victims. It is also characterized by failure to apply intermediary medical care at the crash scene and the use of non-medically equipped means of transport to send the victim to a facility based medical centre.

In Ghana, though a combination of both formal and informal post-crash systems is applied, the informal approach is predominant because the formal approach is characterized by poor state of preparedness and uncoordinated response approach leaving lay untrained respondents who often act as good "Samaritans" to mostly assist RTC victims. This is with consequent negative effects on RTC victims though the actual impacts including the survival rate of RTC victims attended to by lay respondents and trained paramedics is not officially determined. This section of the book discusses the state of post-crash care in Ghana in an attempt to define what is done right, what is not done right and the aspects that needs to be improved.

7.2 THEORIES CONTEXTS AND PRNCIPLES IN POST CRASH CARE

7.2.1 Theories in Post-Crash Care

Theories in post-crash care are dovetailed in the theories of emergency care management. These are based on both normative and substantive factors that provide important and useful insights about the behavior of victims of emergency situations and what emergency managers must expect and deal with in the course of their work.

A. Normative Theories in Emergency Care: These are based on prescriptive ideas used for multi-year planning for integrated emergency management with specified actions on emergency preparedness, response, recovery and organization (McLoughlin 1985).

B. Substantive Theories in Emergency Care: These are based on community responses to emergency situations with respect to social vulnerability to emergency needs, (Enarson E., et al. 2003).

However, other authors are of the view that, whilst theory building is clearly necessary for the continued growth of emergency management, there is no consensus on what constitutes theory in the discipline, neither have standards been set for the development of theories on the subject matter and the typologies directly related to it. Theories are also not incorporated into the curriculum of emergency management in higher education programmes, (Public Entity Risk Institute, 2010). Thus, these theories are not often used in research beyond the work of the scholars who created them. However, what is important is that regardless of a nation's social, cultural or religious traditions, emergency care must be based on certain universal principles.

7.2.2 Prnciples of Post Crash Care

Brunacini, (2002), recommends for a conventional emergency management system to structurally provide links for emergency management activities delivered by different classes of emergency care agencies guided by the following principles:

A. Country Level of Post-Crash Care Policies: Effective post-crash care must be guide by good policies which are regularly updated to suit specific needs.

Ghana has both a post-crash care policy component within the National Road Safety Policy (NRSP) Framework and an Emergency Medical Care Policy Guideline which directs hospital-based accident and emergency services in the country. This policy specifically enjoins all medical facilities to provide Accidents and Emergency (A&E) Services in order to reduce disability, morbidity and mortality from emergency cases though this directive is not fully complied with in practical terms.

B. Legal support and legislation: All components of a post-crash response system must be backed by adequate legislation and regulations.

In Ghana, the work of all the affiliated emergency care agencies including NADMO, MTTD, GNFS and NAS etc. are backed by ACTs of Parliament.

C. Development of National Disaster Preparedness and Response Systems: this must be characterised by the following:

i.   Be based on the core values of simplicity; sustainability; practicality; efficiency and flexibility, (WHO, 2005).

   In Ghana, all the emergency response agencies are guided by some core values, but there is no single framework to guide post-crash activities in Ghana.

ii. Have good leadership to coordinate all the activities of the agencies involved in emergency response.

   In Ghana, NADMO is the designated lead mandated by law for emergency care in the country.

iii. Have a structure with a chain of events and standardized work processes including the prioritization of activities, conduct of simultaneous activities and risk reduction in pre-hospital care at the RTC scene, hospital and community level for a full range of continuity care.

There is no functionally integrated emergency response work structure in Ghana.

iv. Have a good access to quality care after an RTC has occurred in a timely and cost-effective manner to eliminate the risk of death or permanent injury.

Though there is an established policy on this, the system does not function efficiently in Ghana as it should.

v. Must be well coordinated with good cooperation amongst all the emergency response agencies through integrated planning and cross agency strategies. Such a framework must be well managed through inter-agency relationships coordination to guide and streamline required operations

There is no integrated framework and cross agency strategy well-coordinated for post-crash care in Ghana. Though NADMO by legal mandate has the overarching role for disaster management in the country, it operates more as an independent disaster management entity from all the emergency response agencies rather than a coordinating body. It also has a limited focus on post-crash emergency care response and management.

vi. Must have adequate supply of resources backed by well managed advance resource mobilization and stocking systems with efficient resource allocation mechanisms, effective records keeping and monitoring.

Post-crash care in Ghana is challenged with limited resource availability, inefficient resource distribution and a lack of cost effectiveness in resource utilization.

7.2.3 Types of Post Crash Systems

A. Types of Post-Crash Emergency Response System: According to the WHO, 2005), a variety of approaches have been used to develop, organize and regulate pre-hospital systems. These are classified as follows:

i. National systems: These systems may be designed, developed and controlled by a country's central governmental authority (for example, the ministry of health).

In Ghana, there are different agencies involved in emergency response each of which operates under substantive ministry, and a national head-office e.g. the NAS is under the Ministry of Health whilst the GNFS and MTTD are under the Ministry of Interior.

ii. Local or regional systems: Post-crash care at the local level may involve, provincial or regional and district or county level administration set up.

There are regional and district offices with operations for all the emergency response agencies in Ghana.

iii. Hospital-based systems: This set up has the hospital and its staff governing all aspects of both post-crash care and are described as the simplest to be established and maintained because they utilize the personnel, resources and infrastructure of a central or referral hospital.

This system is not practiced in Ghana though there is a policy for hospital staff to also be trained in pre-hospital care.

iv. Paramedic Based Pre-Hospital Care Delivery Systems: This system depends on pre-hospital care providers be it formal or informal.

Ghana reflects this model but the system is not purely developed and managed by paramedics.

v. Private systems: Private emergency medical service companies, operating either as non-profit or for-profit organizations, may contract with authorities to provide pre-hospital services throughout a specific neighbourhood, city or region.

In Ghana some ambulance and health care services are the privatised ambulance system but since the services involves cost payment but the current system does not lend to easy recompense them for such services.

vi. Volunteer systems: These systems depend on pre-hospital providers who donate their time and services to their community.

This model is the commonest in Ghana but it is operated by both trained and untrained lay respondents with no legal mandate.

vii. Hybrid systems: A country can also have a combination of the two models running concurrently based on local specific situations, financial and administrative concerns.

The situation in Ghana can be said to be based on this model with a combination some of the different models at different administrative levels.

7.2.4 Regulations and Guidelines on Post Crash Care

A. Global Standards and Guidelines on Post-Crash Care: Examples of global standards on post-crash care and related applicability in Ghana is as presented in Table 7.1

Table 7.1: Applicability of Global Conventions on Post-Crash Care in Ghana

Source	Details	Application in Ghana
World Health Assembly (WHA) 72 resolution 12.9 of May 2019	-Emergency care systems for universal health coverage ensuring timely care for the acutely ill and injured.	*Ghana has a universal emergency care system for all victims but it is challenged with ineffective operational activities.*
The UN Global Plan DOA - Pillar 5: Post-Crash Response Increase responsiveness to post-crash emergencies and improve the ability of health and other systems to provide appropriate emergency treatment and longer-term rehabilitation for crash victims	<u>Pillar 5:</u> Promotes the improvement of health care and other systems to provide the key elements of post-crash support: emergency care and rehabilitation for injury, mental health care, legal support, and data on crashes and injuries. <u>1.2:</u> It concerns emergency response to avoid preventable death and disability, to limit the severity of the injury and the suffering caused by it, and to ensure the crash survivors' best possible recovery and reintegration into society <u>Activity 3:</u> Provide early rehabilitation and support to injured patients and those bereaved by road traffic crashes, to minimize both physical and psychological trauma. <u>Activity 4:</u> Encourage the establishment of appropriate road user insurance schemes to finance rehabilitation services for crash victims through: introduction of mandatory third- party liability; and international mutual recognition of insurance, e.g. green card system. <u>Activity 6:</u> Provide encouragement and incentives for employers to hire and retain people with disabilities. <u>6.1</u> Support countries to develop Community-Based Rehabilitation (CBR) programmes and policies using CBR guidelines	*Emergency response and care is available in Ghana but rehabilitation services are diffused within the post-crash chain of care though mandatory third-party insurance system exist.*
Article 26, Habilitation and Rehabilitation, of the United Nations Convention on the Rights of Persons with Disabilities (CRPD)	This calls for: "… appropriate measures, including peer support, to enable persons with disabilities to attain and maintain their maximum independence, full physical, mental, social and vocational ability and full inclusion and participation in all aspects of life". with comprehensive rehabilitation services	*Issues of disability care do not fall directly under post -crash care systems in Ghana but rather in other jurisdictions such as social support systems*

B. Post-Crash Care Policy in Ghana: *In Ghana the Policy statement on post-crash care is that Government will strive to ensure that all persons involved in RTC's benefit from speedy and effective trauma care and health management. Such services would include the provision of rescue operation and administration of first aid at the scene of road traffic crashes, transportation of the victim from the road traffic crash scene to an appropriate nearby hospital and initial attention at the hospital, (NRSP, 2008). The challenges and related strategies for meeting the policy objective are as summarized in Table 7.2.*

Table 7.2: Polices Challenges and Strategies on Post-Crash Care in Ghana

Challenges	Strategies	Status of Application
Injury-related deaths prior to hospital care are increasing due to inadequate post road traffic crash services	Establish a National Trauma Management System for pre-hospital and hospital-based care to provide quick and effective treatment to road traffic crash victims.	A substantive national disaster management operational system specifically for post-crash response and care does not exist though some activities are in place for the purpose.
The current medical and rescue system in Ghana is woefully inadequate due to poor organisation and scarce budgetary resources.	Train targeted groups in pre-hospital injury care interventions.	An emergency medical training centre has been established at the Komfo Anokye Teaching Hospital in Kumasi but with limited capacity to meet the magnitude of need
There is limited first aid handling and specialized transportation for the injured from road traffic crash scenes to hospitals in the country so most injured people who make it to hospitals are transported by any means of transport available, mainly taxis and mini-buses.	Upgrade and equip strategic hospitals along the major highways to handle road traffic victims	Every health facility in the country is expected to be equipped with emergency care facilities by policy but very few are up to the required standard. Also, some health posts have been established on some high risk crash prone road corridors.
There are few well-equipped hospitals to treat road traffic crash victims along main roads.	Improve and encourage co-ordination and co-operation between Health Care Centres, National Ambulance Service (NAS), MTTU, Ghana Red Cross, Non-Governmental Organisations (NGOs) and other Emergency Service Organisations for quick response to road traffic crash situations.	A well set up integrated post-crash incident management system with defined roles and responsibilities, set protocols, procedures and coordination modalities for emergency response and care for RTC victims is yet to be defined in Ghana
Drivers and the first people who arrive at road traffic crash scenes are not trained to either handle the victims or provide any first aid.	Incorporate basic principles in First Aid in the syllabi of driving schools, Police Training. Courses and basic schools	This is currently in operation in the country but its effectiveness is yet to be established
There is limited co-ordination and co-operation between the Police, hospitals and first aid and fire service providers to handle road traffic crash victims.	No strategy was proposed	Discussions on the issue is ongoing but modalities are yet to be set
Lack of specialized equipment and trained personnel to handle road traffic crash victims when they arrive at the hospitals.	No strategy was proposed	Some specialised accident centres in some hospitals have been equipped but there is limited knowledge on capacity to deliver
Lack of facilities and promptness in informing the Police, National Ambulance and the Fire Service in case of road traffic crashes.	No strategy was proposed	Emergency response control rooms for receiving RTC notifications are available for all the emergency response agencies in Ghana with the exception of the Ghana Red cross Society (GRSC)
Lack of commitment by hospitals and staff in taking prompt action on road traffic crash victims under the present Health Care System.	No strategy was proposed	This can only be established through a careful study which is yet to be carried out
Uncleared obstacles and debris after road traffic crashes.	No strategy was proposed	The designated entity with responsibility for such has not been established

7.2.5 Components of Post Crash Emergency Management

A. Components of Post-Crash Care Management System: The chain of activities involved in Post-crash care is as presented in Figure 7.1, (Safety Net, 2009) and the effectiveness is dependent upon the strength of each link.

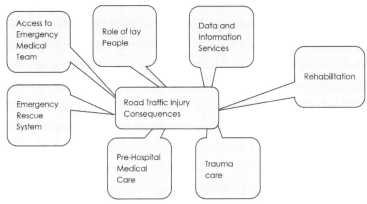

Figure 7.1: Post Impact Care – The Chain of Help: Source: Safety Net: Post Impact Care, Web Text (2009)

B. Roles and Responsibilities for a Post-Crash Management System: Conventional roles and responsibilities for post-crash care operations is as presented in Table 7.3.

Table 7.3: Framework of Post-Crash Management by Components and by Stage of Impact Care

	Emergency Preparedness Phase	Emergency Response Phase	Pre-Hospital care	Emergency Health Care Delivery Phase	Normalisation Phase
Leadership	Prepares Emergency response plans, compiles data and conducts monitoring activities	Defines and coordinates activities of emergency response activities	Ensures adequate resource availability for pre-hospital care eg. training	Liaises with health sector for effective and efficient health care	Facilitates provision of victim rehabilitation
Role of Lay people		Provides informal response to emergency crash needs and calls for help	Extricates victims and transports them to health care facility	Hands over victims to health care facilities	May assist with crash scene clearance
Emergency Rescue Team		Responds to emergency notifications	Provides scene management, extrication, pre-hospital care eg. patient stabilization and transportation	Hands over victims to medical facilities	Maybe involved in scene clearance such as cleaning of hazardous materials and removal of crash vehicles
Fixed hospital care givers but				Provides emergency care at health facilities as well as Data Information Services	
Other agencies involved in Rehabilitation					Provides different support systems for victim rehabilitation

7.3 EMERGENCY MANAGEMENT FRAMEWORK

7.3.1 Emergency Preparedness Components

The emergency management framework includes all actions taken in preparation ahead of the occurrence of an emergency situation. It sets out all the elements, protocols, methods and products for managing emergency care under a structured framework. Its key components are as follows:

A. Definition of Emergency Hazards: The emergency management framework must specify the types of disasters that occur for which emergency response and care is required using a set criterion defined from a range of hazards related to emergency situations by backed by relevant data. The process must by an evaluation of existing hazard response systems; revision of adequacy of policy and regulatory provisions on it; revision of effectiveness of codes of practice; determination of resource capability; and identification of constraints etc. to establish the true state of performance on emergency care management before selecting the types of hazards to be managed.

B. Definition of a Code of Practice: The emergency management framework what is needed to be done and common standards to follow. It also includes policy guidelines, rules and regulations, implementation strategies and operational modalities.

C. Establishment of an Emergency Response Planning Team: These must be a team of experts from all the related disciplines associated with emergency care who must be backed with a legal instrument on working relationships. This is important to ensure commitment and to avert situations of individual emergency response organizations seeking to preserve their autonomy, security, and prestige by resisting collaborative activities which threaten their operational autonomy, (Haas & Drabek, 1973). It is also critical to the allocation of power and resources (especially personnel and budget) commensurate with the role of each agency.

D. Establishment of a Governance System for an Emergency Management System (EMS): There should be a well-defined governance structure to manage complex intra and inter agency collaborative emergency care operations at all levels including national, regional to local government level interactions and interagency collaborations.

E. Identification of a Lead Agency: A lead agency must be identified with the legal mandate to manage emergency care. It can be an independent entity or can alternatively be selected from amongst existing emergency response entities.

F. Assignment of Roles and Responsibilities: Roles and responsibilities for the emergency response agencies during emergency management must be well specified with regards to the different techniques to be employed at different stages of work by the different organizations and the protocols on work collaborations.

G. Definition of work procedures and Division of Work Components: This involves the definition of work components and modalities which must direct multi-jurisdictional and multi-organizational emergency response activities since the types of work vary. It must guidelines for operational workflow amongst the emergency response agencies who play different roles with incident management work protocols, modalities for activity prioritisation, the steps of work implementation, resource mobilization supply/distribution, resource utilization as well as control and administrative processes.

H. Mobilization of resources: The framework must specify modalities for the mobilization of human, equipment and financial resources needed for the threshold of disaster management anticipated with modalities for effective resource utilization, capacity development etc.

I. Monitoring: A monitoring arrangement for ensuring quality control of emergency response and care delivering should be well defined.

In Ghana, the NADMO, is mandated by Act 517 of 1996 to lead in the management of all disaster related incidence including post-crash emergency care from preparedness to response and recovery. They are also required to work towards the prevention of disasters, create awareness, prepare disaster management plans, provide disaster management facilities and resources, train emergency response personnel, conduct disaster response operations, bring relief to disaster victims as well as monitor and evaluate disaster management in the country. The core components of NADMO's disaster management cycle are as graphically presented in Figure 7.2 and described in the immediate sub sections. However, currently in Ghana there is no guiding code so emergency response preparedness and operation does not function as a system.

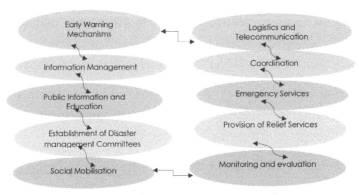

Figure 7.2: The Disaster Management Cycle

i. Early Warning Mechanisms: This involves the dissemination of early warning information to forge a common understanding of potential risks and their impact ahead of the occurrence of the disaster.

ii. Information Management: This is by the compilation and sharing of relevant information in disaster management

iii. Public Information and Education: It involves the provision of public information on what to do during disasters

iv. Logistics and Telecommunication: It includes the mobilization of appropriate and adequate facilities for provision of relief, rehabilitation and reconstruction after any emergencies.

v. Disaster Management Committees: It involves the establishment of disaster management committees at national, regional and district levels to ensure effective planning and coordination of disaster risk reduction and emergency response activities

vi. Social mobilization: This is by the mobilization of community level support programmes by various Government and Non-Governmental entities for the management of disasters at such levels.

vii. Coordination: It involves the coordination of the activities of various bodies (including international agencies) in the management of disasters.

viii. Emergency Services: It involves the conduct of adequate first-line emergency services using set disaster management plans and standard operating procedures.

ix. Relief Assistance: It involves organizing and coordinating the distribution of relief items during disasters by government agencies such as the MMDA's, NGOs religious organizations etc.

x. Monitoring and Evaluation: This involves progress monitoring and reporting on progress of work for accountability and auditing.

Though NADMO's legal mandate and functions in principle fits all the requirements of a lead agency for an EMS in Ghana, it functions in practice are mostly focused on the management of Fires and Lightning, Pest and Insect Infestation, Disease Epidemics, Hydrometeorological, Geological, Man-Made disasters, Nuclear and Radiological disasters, floods, coastal erosion, epidemics and droughts as well as Relief and Reconstruction activities with little focus on post-crash emergency response.

Currently, it is only affiliation with post-crash care its representation on the road safety stakeholder committee. It also collaborates with the GRCS at the community level for the training of community disaster volunteers in First Aid care. It is does not duly recognised as an overarching emergency management lead organization for post-crash care. There, there is need for re-organisation for the purpose.

7.3.2 The Emergency Preparedness Plans Care Plan

A. Definition of Emergency preparedness Plans: Emergency response and care plans/ provide guidelines for purposes of readiness ahead of the occurrence of a disaster. The (WHO, 2007) defines it as a state of readiness to respond to emergency situations so as to protect and meet the needs of injured individuals. It requires a broad spectrum of innovative thinking, planning, and adaptation particularly in areas with fewer resources and must have sub activity components at sub administrative levels.

According to Lindell and Perry, (1992), emergency planning is most likely to be successful when it is viewed, either explicitly or implicitly, from a systems perspective. Thus, post-crash crash response plans must integrate emergency care activities for the agencies involved care in the form of multi comprehensive emergency preparedness and response framework.

The framework must entail emergency response and care goals, the activities required for achieving the goals, the resources needed for implementing the activities with regards to personnel capability and capacity, the equipment types and the materials needed in terms of quantity and quality. It must also set out clear roles and responsibilities for all the post-crash emergency organizations for effective participation and commitment.

B. Development of an Emergency Response Plan: The specific steps proposed in literature for the development of a post-crash care system include:

Step 1: Definition of the content of the emergency response plan with the list of potential and appropriate emergency care products, services and operations categorized by the before, during and after emergency care activities needed for each situation.

In Ghana, the NADMO developed a National Disaster Management Strategy and an Emergency Preparedness/Response plan covering the period 2011-2012 as a national disaster management strategy with legal backing. The plan contains a hazard map and a national contingency plan for disaster management and is regularly updated.

Step 2: Development of Sub Emergency Response and Care Plans by stakeholder entities in the form of sub activities drawn from national plans for subcomponent/local level emergency management. This is to ensure effective implementation and accountability at all levels of administration. A summary of content of a post-crash emergency response plan is as provided in Table 7.4.

Table 7.4: Summary of Content of Emergency Management Plans

Planning Components	Examples of Content
Emergency situation before establishment of EMS	Background information to the establishment of the EMS Before incident; During Incident
Emergency system Goals	Ability to meet the needs of emergency patients
Emergency system Objectives	Multi-casualty capabilities
	Utilisation of qualified human resources
	Timely delivery of services
	Efficient Inter facility transfer
	Set Standards and protocols
Emergency Care Strategies and coverage	These include areas of coverage, specific activities to be conducted that is routine and specific specialty care systems such as mass casualty management needs, unique patient needs and alternative contingency approaches
Emergency Response and care resource base	
Financial Planning	Costing of set targets, identification of funding sources; Work prioritisation,
Personnel Planning	Human resource mobilisation; Education and training;
Transportation Planning	Emergency system Transportation and operational plans
Materials Planning	Protective clothing, first aid items, torches, raincoats,
Equipment Planning	Communications resources and systems; Hardware and equipment, software, emergency vehicles, extrication equipment, fire tenders, Technology and situational awareness
Roles and Responsibilities	Assignment of roles and responsibilities to emergency agencies by category of contribution to Emergency system
Monitoring and Evaluation Planning	Incident record system; Incident management record systems Patient information systems; Post incident review
Public notification and involvement in EMS planning	Public education and sensitization on the operations of EMS

In Ghana, since disasters and hazards vary, NADMO also has core plans on preparedness for different hazard care types such as flooding, fire etc. with the exception of a core plan for post-crash response and care. NADMO is therefore working towards mapping out a full scope of post-crash response and care framework. Currently the different post-crash response and care agencies including the MTTD, GNFS, NAS, GRSC, SJA as well as the NADMO itself have stand-alone plans dovetailed within the NRSS.

However, these are presented as stand-alone agency specific activities independent of each other which does not facilitate collaborative service delivery. The situation is further aggravated by the absence of a substantive legal obligation on the part of the agencies to practice joint service operations within a common framework. The following is therefore recommended for consideration in the Ghanaian situation, on the way forward:

- *Re-conceptualization of emergency response planning from a stand-alone operational planning activity into an integrated strategic problem-solving process conducted within an overall inter-agency framework by NADMO.*

- *Re-affirmation and consolidation of the commitment to support and be accountable for emergency preparedness, including contingency planning, as and when appropriate by legal requirement.*

Step 3. The testing of emergency plans: This is another key aspect for gaining real value and effectiveness of the plans often done through drills to determine the critical bridge between what is on paper and actual response for required upgrades from the documentation of lessons. Such exercises also provide the opportunity to anticipate operational difficulties and the remedies needed to solve them.

In Ghana this is hardly done. This is mainly attributed to the absence of a joint plan with well-defined roles for the emergency response entities.

C. Operation of Emergency Response Systems: Some of the key components for the operation of an emergency management systems includes the following:

i. Record Keeping: To operate emergency response as a system, there must also be good cataloguing and record keeping system at joint operation centres supported with an efficient distribution network to enable effective delivery mechanisms when and where such facilities are needed. This is because emergency care needs are often instant and must be responded to accordingly. Therefore, there is need to establish a consistent and efficient resource mobilization and stocking system for continuity of supply and distribution of resources backed by replenishment regimes to ensure efficiency.

In Ghana, limited resource availability is identified as key constraint to emergency care especially with regards to the availability of well-functioning communication facilities, extrication equipment, fire control equipment and ambulances with required medical accessories amongst others for post- crash care. Others are limited availability of essential life-saving medical equipment, materials, medications and poorly resourced maintenance systems for effective equipment utilization.

Thus, the generation and sustainability of resource inputs for post-crash care especially must be addressed. A typical example is how the cost of medical care for individual victims in emergency situations should be met. Currently in the country, aspects on emergency care system funded by Government includes, the provision of facilities, equipment, personnel, training and funding for operational costs whilst the users of the care system (RTC victims) pay for their care either through the 17% provision within the Ghana National health Insurance Scheme (NHIS) or out of their own pocket.

However, due to limited funding from all government sources for pre-hospital emergency care, practical challenges such as the cost of transporting RTC victims by informal entities to medical facilities and payment for treatment at the medical facility level remains a huge constraint to effective post-crash care. The situation is made worse by the limited mechanisms for offsetting the cost of care for RTC victims at the medical facility level especially due to ineffective implementation of the provision made in the NHIS.

Thus, often times good Samaritans or even trained respondents such as the police, ambulance red-cross etc. who transport RTC victims to fixed medical facilities for care are asked to pay for the medical bills of RTC injured victims out of their own pockets before the victims can be attended to.

This sometimes leads to delayed treatment and related consequences though, currently the lack of authentic statistics and research has not enabled the magnitude of the problem to be well understood and appreciated so it can be effectively addressed. There is need therefore to effectively assess the state of the financial operations of the emergency response and care system and its effects for appropriate interventions.

Some good funding options for emergency medical care that could be considered include direct and indirect taxes; compulsory insurances contributions, voluntary insurance premiums with medical savings components, universal care for victims stabilization before demanding out of pocket payments by health facilities, acquisition of loans and grants from external sources to support internal funds, technical and equipment capacity as well as institutionalization of modalities for soliciting for donations from relevant entities.

ii. Resource Management: Resource management for emergency care is complex and extensive since it involves the development of a comprehensive national resource need inventory based on set standards and certification of both equipment and personnel. Continuous supply of resources in required quantities through effective monitoring and updates to ensure efficient stocking, utilization, distribution good reporting is also critical.

In Ghana, the extent to these standards and protocols are applied is not known, well-studied or understood. Shared resource management through effective collaboration and coordination does not also exist. Also, though NADMO has established Emergency Operation Centres (EOCs) at the national and regional levels equipped with office space and tools to adequately perform some of these functions, they do not facilitate the operational coordination of the activities of all the key emergency management agencies including post–crash care.

Coordination is done on ad-hoc basis with no permanent structural arrangement or system to follow or comply with. This has caused lay responders to dominate emergency response operations.

Therefore, an efficient facility-based resource management system well-coordinated to deal with the wide spectrum of activities and joint services needed in emergency care must be researched. Critical aspects should include data and information share, shared equipment utilization systems as well as joint training and education for operational management. This is important to avoid duplication of efforts, gaps in service delivery, inefficient resource utilization, overlaps in service delivery, lack of accountability and poor service outcomes.

Specifically, NADMO's EOC's could be restructured to effectively also function as emergency post-crash operations centers with systematized/ integrated plans and other supporting resources such as generic relief items. This will facilitate the operation of well-coordinated emergency preparedness and response systems at all levels of administrative guided by legally agreed arrangements between the respective emergency response and care agencies.

iii. Emergency care information management: This must be based on mandatory and systematic data collection to support the operations is required for the identification of trends, challenges and new interventions needed. Such information management systems must entail well documented and stored data within a conventional information management system linked to other the databases of other emergency response entities at national, regional and local levels backed by efficient database management.

In Ghana there is no information exchanges between the agencies. A process for post-crash care using an automated system that simplifies the process and combines a manual system to feed into an aggregated national healthcare data management system with interoperability at all levels has been piloted but it is yet to be expanded for wider application at all levels.

iv: Application of supporting technologies and innovative operational methods: These are required to be encouraged and explored for the further advancement of emergency care operations. Examples include utilization of mobile trauma units, e-medicine, telemedicine and e-information for remote settings.

In Ghana, some current technological advancement in the emergency care service includes the use of drones for dispensing emergency medication and blood and discussions on e-medicine is also underway.

v. Research Development: It is important for consistent research to be conducted in order to determine the effectiveness of current policies, guidelines, practices resource allocations and system capabilities for emergency care response. Key aspects include research into innovative emergency response options such as treatment options e.g., establishment of mobile emergency units.

In Ghana, diverse research studies have been conducted on the topic but the information is scattered and not well collated for effective application. It is recommended for research repositories to be developed for ease of information access and utilization.

vi. Education and advocacy: This is necessary for the general populace to be well informed in all aspects of emergency response and care to stimulate appropriate actions and positive public response. This can be achieved through the incorporation of emergency preparedness education into school curriculums extra-curricular activities.

In Ghana, the administration of First Aid is taught in some schools. Drivers are also required to be taught in the application of first aid as a part of their initial training before being licensed and some community volunteers are also trained in the administration of emergency response care activities. However, its effectiveness is not well established.

vii. Emergency response management and supervision: Emergency response is required to have a team lead at both the management preparedness level and at the incidence scene. They are managers who provide oversight responsibility for compliance with due procedures, quality control and proper documentations for accountability.

In Ghana, all the affiliated agencies work as different entities so it is not easy to identify who should be held accountable for poor performance of post- crash care at the RTC scene.

7.6 THE PRE-HOSPITAL CARE FOR POST-CRASH VICTIMS

7.6.1 Steps in Pre-Hospital Care

Pre-hospital emergency or trauma care is the incident management phase of post-crash care when an RTC has occurred before the RTC victim is taken to a facility based medical centre. See Figure 7.3 for the key response steps after the occurrence of an RTC.

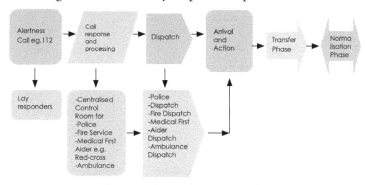

Figure 7.3: Steps in Pre-Hospital Care

A. Call or Alertness Phase: Prompt communication to call for help and immediate response after an RTC has occurred is the first critical step referred to as the alertness first phase of the pre-hospital care chain. Those who are present or who arrive first at the scene of a crash notifies the relevant authorities through a communication mechanism such as a telephone network, a radio communication system, running calls etc.

In Ghana, RTC a study by the NRSA in (2012) revealed that 72% of emergency calls about RTC's are made through telephone communication and 28% by running calls. Out of those who made telephone calls 31% called directly to emergency control rooms, 31% called to media houses and 1% called individual emergency service providers as presented in Figure 7.4.

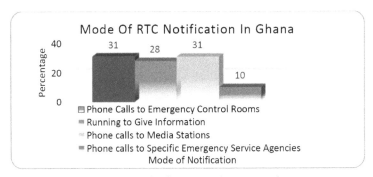

Figure 7.4: Mode of RTC Notification in Ghana

i. Requirements for Effective RTC Alertness: A good RTC alertness is required to be characterized by the following attributes:

a) Availability of a universal emergency telephone number: The DOA of 2011-2020 recommends for a single universal toll-free emergency number serviced from every telephone device (landline or mobile) with only up to 3- or 4-digit numbers for ease of remembrance.

Ghana has advanced through the years from the use of multiple toll-free emergency contact numbers for different emergency service providers as listed below to the establishment of a common toll-free hotline number which is 112 for reporting emergencies though all the other numbers can still be used.

- *(191-or (18555) for Ghana Police Service (GPS);*
- *(192 for the Ghana National Fire Service (GNFS),*
- *(193 for the Ghana Ambulance Service (GAS)*
- *(194) NRSA) (yet to be launched)*

b). Interoperability of the Emergency Communication System: It is required for the emergency communication system to be interoperable between all emergency responder organizations guided by procedures for message routing and recording to guarantee that all relevant emergency agencies are informed simultaneously about an RTC situation.

In Ghana the universal emergency number (112) is interoperable between NADMO, MTTD, NAS and GNFS and notification calls are received through their individual call centres. However, the key challenge has to do with the lead command for the control of the response process.

c) Notification Call Information: The RTC notification call is required to provide adequate information to enable efficient preparedness and prompt attention to be given by the emergency service providers and the standard protocol for achieving is as defined in the acronym "METHANE" by Cory J. (2002) defined as follows:

M   Major Incident Declared
E   Exact location
T   Type of Incident (Road, rail, factory RTC, fire etc.)
H   Hazards if any (Power lines down, fuel spilt, chemicals etc.)
A   Access (Best way in)
N   Numbers of Casualties
E   Emergency services required.

In Ghana, the extent to which standard protocols on notification information delivery are applied is not known or researched and neither is the issue accorded the relevant premium so the needed awareness must be created.

d). Public Education on Emergency Notification Numbers: It is also required for the public to be adequately informed on the use of emergency call numbers to allow for its effective use.

Currently in Ghana billboards displaying the emergency numbers have been installed at vantage points for easy reference and some of the emergency response teams displays their emergency call numbers whilst the NAS specifically displays the universal number as exhibited in Figures 7.5. However, an impact evaluation study would have to be conducted to determine whether the use of a common hotline is more effective than before.

Figure 7.5: Emergency Response Facilities in Ghana (Source: nas.gov.gh)

e). Sustainability of Emergency Call Processes: It is required for active communication to be always maintained within the service lines by the service providers for sustainable notifications. This is critical because if the communication lines fail to function the notification process will be handicapped.

A study by the NRSA in (2012) on effectiveness of the RTC notification system based on caller satisfaction with notification response rate before the introduction of the universal

telephone number indicated that almost 66% of callers believed it was very effective and only
6% said it was not effective as detailed in Figure 7.6.

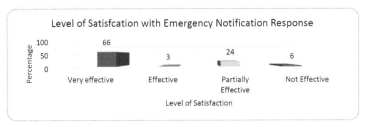

Figure 7.6: Caller Satisfaction with Response to RTC Notification in Ghana

f) Application of advanced technology in Notifications: Currently, advanced technologies in the form of Automatic Crash Notification (ACN) e-Call systems which provides information on the severity of the crash and the nature of injuries sustained as an in-vehicle emergency call service are in use in some advanced countries. This performs some of the tasks of the notification process with accurate information delivery. According to Comm P. et al. (2020), when an RTC occurs, the terminal dials the emergency response centre and sends the information on vehicle position and type of RTC to the control room. It also opens a voice connection between the vehicle occupants and the operator of the emergency response centre.

Currently in Ghana, these are not used but the possible use of such systems could be
explored to eliminate human limitations to emergency notifications and response in the
country.

g). Responsibility for RTC Notification: RTC notification is normally done by bystanders who though do might not play any role by way of assisting RTC victims at the crash scene and remain as mere spectators out of curiosity at the RTC scene, (Hansen C. M et al, 2015). It can also be done by lay persons who not only notify the relevant entities about the occurrence of an RTC but also further assist the RTC victims though they may be trained or untrained persons in post-crash care at the RTC scene. Being the first link in the chain of help for RTC victims, they are described as the foundations of an effective pre-hospital system and their attributes as described by, Callese T.E., (2014) is as summarized in Table 7.5.

In Ghana first respondents of all categories who assist victims have and continue to contribute
significantly to pre-hospital care in the country. These maybe trained or untrained to respond
to emergency care needs. It is estimated that such services apply to over 95% of RTC victims
in all parts of the country since they are the most available category of RTC care teams though
not properly documented, (NRSC 2012). The key challenge is that some of such people may
worsened and injured person's health situation by wrongful handling, some engage in theft

of valuables from the injured victims whilst most of them also obstruct security persons such as the Police in the operation of their functions at the RTC scene.

Table: 7.5 Lay Persons who assist RTC victims

Categories	Description	Roles Played	Disadvantages
Laypeople, layman, layperson, lay public, lay bystander etc.	They are members from public who attend at the crash scene with no knowledge and awareness about relief, rescue and first aid to the victims	-Calling emergency services for help Taking photographs or video recording the scene and posting on social media for assistance -Helping to extricate RTC Victims from damaged vehicles -Taking care of the security at RTC scenes to prevent further crashes such as directing traffic -Transporting the RTC victim to a health facility	They obstruct the activities of paramedics They can cause a new crash or hinder the timely arrival of relief organisations to the crash site, (Haghparast-Bidgoli H. et al, 2010).
"First responder"	They are trained people in basic level trauma care procedures to be able to provide primary medical care and relief to the injured at the time of a crash	-Calling emergency services for help for RTC victims -Helping to extricate RTC Victims from damaged vehicles -Taking care of the security at RTC scenes to prevent further crashes such as directing traffic -Providing first aid services; and -Transporting the RTC victim to a health facility.	-They are poorly resourced for the task -They use local resources
Lay first responder"	They are first responders without enough first aid skills to appropriately aid and transfer of injured. They include aid organisations workers that have no skill regarding life support for trauma victims.	-Calling emergency services for help for RTC victims -Helping to extricate RTC Victims from damaged vehicles -Taking care of the security at RTC scenes to prevent further crashes such as directing traffic -Providing first aid services; and -Transporting the RTC victim to a health facility	They can cause unintentional injuries from lack of technical expertise to handle injured victims -They are not able to stabilize victims before hospital transfer -They are unable to give medical details of the victim's condition ahead of victim's arrival at a medical facility

Source: (Mohan D., 2006).

B. The Dispatch Phase: Another aspect of the RTC emergency alertness phase involves receiving and processing the call information by a call taker in a control room for follow up actions and the key aspects are as follows:

i). Management of Notification Control Rooms: A control room is where the RTC notification information is received and processed for the dispatch of paramedics and response teams to the RTC scene. Such facilities are equipped with integrated and routed communication networks to facilitate effective decision making on what to do and who to do what in response to the RTC call.

Currently in Ghana the GPS, NAS and GNFS individual control rooms are integrated into each other with interoperability and well linked systems where notifications are received for processing. The key challenge is that it lacks a national coordination system and the modalities by which notifications are processed for joint response and incidence management at the RTC scene.

Aside this, some other problems reported so far by some of the responsive agencies include hoax calls and inaccurate information provision by callers making it difficult for appropriate response to be provided, (See Figure 7.7). A centralized communication centre linked to the control rooms of the mentioned agencies could be established by the use of NADMO JIC for the coordination of the dispatch process in the country with clearly defined protocols. Scam calls could be tracked for the necessary application of penalties backed by effective public education to control such behaviors.

Figure 7.7: An Illustration on Scam Calls in Ghana

ii). The Dispatching Process: This involves processing of a call information about an RTC situation from a caller in the control room by a call recipient tor dispatcher. The types of information processed by the dispatcher areas in the control room are as summarized in Table 7.6.

Table 7.6: Summary of Emergency Call Information

Type of Information	Description
Location	Where the RTC has occurred
	The quickest and safest route to get there
Vehicle	-Type and number of vehicles
	-Cargo or passenger vehicles
	-Whether vehicles are movable or not
	-Position of vehicles
Casualties	-Whether there is a pile of casualties
	-Whether there are any injured and the type of injuries
	-Whether there any trapped in the vehicles
	-Whether the RTC was of high or low impact
Risk Factors	What risk factors to consider eg. Fire, hazardous substances etc.

This information so obtained determines what must be done, who should go, where to go, how to get there, the kind of vehicle, the situation to be managed at the RTC scene and the preparations needed to manage them as well as who the lead command will be in that specific situation. It is required for the information provided by a dispatcher to be accurate and adequate because, failure to do so could distort and render the pre-hospital service ineffective.

The dispatcher is also expected to maintain enroute communication with the incident commander in case secondary responding information and other actions are also needed. Currently in advance countries, there are computerized aided dispatch (CAD) system which prompts the call taker, records responses, supports decision-making and provides information for all aspects considered to be essential, (Tech Note 2011).

In Ghana, the dispatching process is individualistic and contingent on which agency decides to respond to what and how the agency decides to respond to the situation. This is because there are no set protocols or standards on joint preparations and planned arrangements with regards to human, equipment and other resources mobilization needed to suit the requirements of the crash type reported on. Therefore, in some instances some of the response agencies do not act at all. This is due to the absence of a lead command in the process and the fact that the legal implication for failed response is not clear. The situation becomes more critical where specialized services are needed for specific situations.

A study conducted by the NRSA in 2012, revealed that the effective performance of the dispatching process is hampered by wrongful caller direction and incomplete information to RTC scenes at (36%). Others are prank and abusive calls at (22%), interrupted calls at 19% with system breakdowns at about (18%). Figure 7.8 provides the details. Therefore, further studies must be conducted to advance dispatching work in the country.

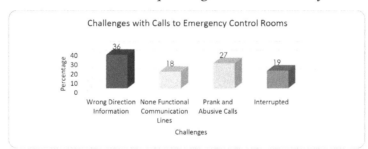

Figure 7.8: Challenges to Emergency Calls to control rooms

C. The Arrival Phase: After the dispatch phase, the next phase of the post-crash response chain is the arrival phase to the RTC scene. This refers to incidence management by multi-disciplinary response teams at the RTC scene in preparation of sending an RTC victim to a medical facility and includes the following:

i. RTC Scene Assessment: Upon arrival at the RTC scene by the respective emergency response agencies the state of casualties and how they are to be managed must be established. It involves an assessment of the RTC scene to determine what to do, how best to do it, when to do what and who to do what in accordance with laid protocols under a lead team command. Factors such as the state of the injured, kind of vehicle involved in the crash, need for vehicle stabilization, options for ease of entry to the RTC scene, extrication of RTC victims from damaged vehicles if required and determination of the direction in which the victim is to be removed so as to proceed accordingly are carefully assessed for necessary action.

In Ghana, efficient administration of this process at the RTC scene remains a critical challenge. Normally, the procedure must be undertaken by first responders who are either trained or not trained but often try their best to manage RTC scenes by best judgments on what to do. Oftentimes this is done with little or no resources such as protective clothing. In some situations, representatives of the designated emergency response entities may be present at the RTC scene or not.

Where the emergency response agencies are represented at RTC scenes, it is normally the Police who are regular with the other emergency response agencies not usually represented. The GNFS normally responds to RTCs involving fire outbreaks and the spill of hazardous materials and in recent times the presence of the NAS at RTC scenes is also increasing. Irrespective of these scenarios joint emergency response operations involving all the relevant emergency response agencies hardly happens in Ghana, (See Figure 7.9).

Figure 7.9: Publications on RTC Scene Assessments. (Source: Yen.com.gh)

ii. Securing the Accident Scene: On arrival at the RTC scene there is need to secure and protect the scene to make way for the operations of the emergency response service agencies.

In Ghana, the police is legally responsible for securing an accident scene to pave way for the work of paramedics at the RTC site. The process involves:

a. *Cordoning the RTC scene and posting a warning sign to alert other motorist about the situation to avoid further dangers,*

b. *Control of access to the scene by blocking lanes if necessary, instituting speed limits, providing detour routes and declaring road safe for use after operation. It also involves clearing of access route and guiding responding safety vehicles to the RTC scene, (See*

Figure 7.10.) Others are the removal of obstructive objects such as accident vehicles and electrical poles in case of power downs by involving the electricity company.

Figure 7.10: Access control at an accident scene (Source: Occypygh.com)

c. *Removal of damaged vehicles (See (See Figure 7.11).*

Figure 7.11: Removal of damaged vehicles (Source: GhanaWeb)

d. *Crowd control at the RTC scene to facilitate work processes, (See Figure 7.12).*

Figure 7.12: Crowd at RCT Scenes,

e. *Protection of property (See Figure 7.13).*

Figure 7.13: Protection of Property at an RTC Scene, (Source Sdda.or.gh)

The summary of duties of the police in Emergency Road Traffic Crash Situation is defined in the (Police Handbook, May 2010) and it is as summarized in Table 7.7.

Table 7.7: Role of the Ghana Police Service in Pre-Hospital Care Compared to Best Practices

Best Practice	Role of the Ghana Police Service
Stopping or re-routing other vehicle traffic	Stopping or re-routing other vehicle traffic by posting officers to stand at reasonable distances from the RTC scene on both sides of the road and at both ends of the RTC scene to caution other motorist by flagging them to slow down and directing traffic as safely as possible to prevent obstruction as well as the possibility of the occurrence of another RTC.
Crowd control	Crowd control to prevent obstructions
Scene security	Scene security to preserve life and property
Interference removal	Arresting & removing uncooperative persons who interfere with the rescue effort
Preserving scene evidence	Preserving scene evidence for investigation
Ordering obstructing vehicles to be moved	Ordering obstructing vehicles to be moved
Aiding injured persons if any	Aiding injured persons if any
Identify & protect dead bodies	Identify & protect dead bodies to mortuaries Conveying of dead bodies to mortuary
Recover & safeguard property	Preserving evidence at the scene; and Ensuring that drivers and witnesses will be available or can be traced for later investigation
Aiding injured persons if any	Aiding injured persons if any
Transport of Victims	Calling for an ambulance/ Looking for suitable means of transport to safely move injured patients to hospital, to a doctor or to his home by any suitable means of transport
Write damage & accident cause reports/ Photograph & document scene	Write damage & accident cause reports
Stopping or re-routing other vehicle traffic	Re-opening the road to normal traffic
Search and Rescue	Search and Rescue of displaced RTC victims
Control of Smoking	Warning about risks at the RTC scene such as smoking

However, a study by the NRSA in 2012 revealed that practically, the police often engaged in extrication at 100% though it is more of the responsibility of GNFS, they also called for ambulance at 100%, conveyed the dead to mortuary at 33% and the injured to hospital at 22% though this is more of the responsibility of the NAS (See Figure 7.15: Examples of additional police activities at the RTC is also as presented in and Figure 7.14.

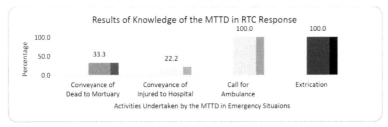

Figure 7.14: Results of Knowledge of the MTTD on RTC Response

Figure 7.15: Publications on Police Management of an RTC Scene, (Source: ghaniantimes.com)

A test of the knowledge of police MTTD personnel on their responsibilities at RTC scenes through the same study indicated that most of them had knowledge on clearance and traffic management, protection of life and property, transportation of RTC victims to hospital and investigations into RTC cases. The major challenge to the work of the police at RTC scene is the fact that none of their personnel have had formal/practical training in the additional activities that they perform at the RTC scene. Other challenges included lack of equipment and poor logistics for responding and handling RTC crash situations. (See Figure 7.16).

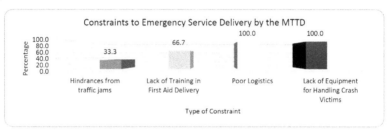

Figure 7.16: Constraints to Emergency Service Delivery in Ghana

Another issue is on how much premium the police service in general and the MTTD in particular accords to resource allocation for post-crash care activities in comparison with other policing activities. This is because effective response time of the police to RTC scenes is often hampered by logistical constraints such as readily available vehicles, fuel and adequate personnel to undertake activities with such impromptu demands.

The limited number of personnel particularly becomes serious when they have to conduct the other activities outside their domain in addition to their main function at the RTC scene which is to control traffic and the crowd. This is especially with regards to those who go to RTC scenes to steal from the victims. Currently NADMO has been conducting education in such communities against such acts.

iii. Extrication of Casualties from RTC Situations: Some crash scene management procedures may require prompt removal of injured vehicle occupants trapped in wrecked vehicles. This could involve cutting of vehicle glass, stopping fire and smoke, moving a vehicle from an obstructive position to give way etc. using appropriate equipment and skill and acting within the shortest time of a maximum of 10 minutes.

In Ghana, the GNFS is legally mandated to conduct extrication at RTC scenes though in their absence, the MTTD, NADMO or even lay community respondents may conduct the activity. In some instances, these may work together to attend to the needs on hand, (See Figure 7.17).

Figure 7.17: The GNFS Conducting Extrication at an RTC Scene (Source: Citinewsroom)

In addition to this, fire officers may also administer first aid procedures to RTC victims where needed because in Ghana, they are also trained to do so. Some of the standard operating standards of fire officers generally at RTC scenes compared to what pertains in Ghana is as summarized in Table 7.8

Table 7.8: Role of the Ghana National Fire Service in Pre-Hospital Car Compared to Best Practices

Recommended Best Practice	Role of the Ghana National Fire Service
-Extinguishing vehicle fires	-Extrication operation with requisite equip-
-Hosing down spilled fuels	ment and thereby rescuing and saving lives of
-Encasing spilled hazardous materials	entrapped victims in RTC situations,
-Directly rescuing patients from smoke areas	-Provision of power tools
-Stabilizing tilted vehicles	Control of burning vehicles
-Protection of other personnel and patients from downed electrical lines	-Conduct of resuscitation to victims in order
-Major vehicle disassembly to get access to patient or to free patient from entrapment	to preserve the lives of RTC victims.
-Extracting patient and / or rescuers up or down a steep slope	
-Turning, rolling, or moving a wrecked vehicle	
-Removal of physical hazards from the scene	
-Providing lighting or electrical power to scene for rescue	
-Prevention of pollution by encasing spilled hazardous materials	
-Warning about risks at the RTC scene eg. smoking	
-Search and rescue at the RTC scene	

A study by the NRSA to assess the knowledge of the fire service by the NRSA in 2012 in responding to RTC emergencies indicated that, over 80% of the GNFS personnel were knowledgeable on their responsibilities to RTC response and were able to apply this knowledge at RTC scenes. However, only 33% had adequate knowledge on the proper handling of the specialized equipment needed at RTC scenes (See Figure 7.18). What was not established from the study is whether the limited knowledge could be attributed to the lack of equipment availability or lack of training).

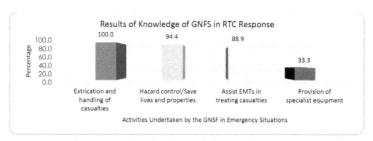

Figure 7.18: Results of Knowledge in RTC Response

The type of equipment used for conducting extrication by holding by the GNFS is as indicated Table 7.9.

Table 7.9: Recommended Tools for the Management of RTC Scene by the Fire Service

Recommended Tools	Recommended Tools
Scissors	Hydraulic Rescue Equipment
Splint	Four Stroke Power Unit
Suction device	our stroke united diesel power
Ram	generator
Manual Pump	Dedicated Cutter
Motor pump	Spreader
Hoses	Zip Gun
Cutters	Genger Saw
Compressed air tools	Vehicle Winch
Stabilization Equipment	Lifting Bags
Cutters	Zip Gun
Blocks	Fire Extinguisher
Wedges	

The major challenge faced by the GNFS for conducting extrication as expressed in the mentioned study was limited availability of the required equipment for post-crash delivery at 83%, inadequate vehicles to facilitate emergency response at 36%, public obstructions at crash scenes at 64%, lack of trained personnel at 42% and traffic congestions which hinders speed during response time at 36% as presented in Figure 7.19. Some of the mitigation measures recommended include continuous training of personnel, institution of coordination systems with other emergency service delivery agencies and provision of appropriate equipment.

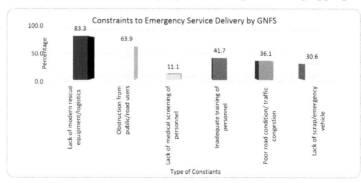

Figure 7.19: Constraints to Emergency Service Delivery by the GNFS

Though by legal mandate, extrication is the responsibility of the GNFS in Ghana, practically, this activity is usually performed by lay respondents with the assistance of the police where they happen to be present, (See Figure 7.20).

Source: NRSA   Source: dreamstime.com

[Video] Rescuers struggle to save 2 men trapped under caterpillar truck

Figure 7.20: Rescue Activities at RTC Scenes in Ghana

Of significant concern is the predominant use of unconventional extrication equipment/tools such as machetes, crowbar, planks etc. without the professional skills needed for not endangering the life of injured persons through unsafe handling. This has the potential for causing more injuries and even death of the RTC victim in some cases. The main reason is that lay respondents simply aim to remove the victims from damaged vehicles for transportation to the hospital. Therefore, the role of the fire service for RTC extrication should be well enhanced for effective post-crash response and if possible other emergency response personnel should be trained in the use of simple and available tools to safely extricate RTC victims where necessary.

iv. Conduct of Triage at RTC Scene: Triage is the term applied to the process of classifying patients at the RTC scene according to the severity of their injuries and how quickly they need care so care will be exacted in appropriate sequence to ensure that resources available are properly matched to each victim's needs. Failure to develop triage protocols may lead to over-triage or under triage which means neglecting the needs of those who critically need treatment and paying attention to those who do not need it most which may lead to death or worsened injury.

In Ghana, there is limited documentation on the extent of application of triaging at RTC scenes by trained professionals. Besides, since RTC response is dominated by lay respondents who lack knowledge on triaging, it can safely be said that the process is often not done at all. The common practice is to scoop RTC victims to the nearest medical centre for treatment. In some instances, patients assumed to be dead may be totally neglected because such people are not trained to determine who is dead and who is not. Therefore, there is need to ensure adequate preparedness for trained emergency teams to facilitate their increased presence in RTC situations or some level of triaging should be introduced in the training of lay respondents in the application of First Aid to RTC victims.

v. Application of First Aid at RTC Scenes: The application of first aid is sometimes required for injured RTC victims at RTC scenes in order to mitigate a more serious consequence of an injury which could even lead to a fatal outcome until full professional medical treatment is available. The key elements of this process are as follows:

a). Types of Injuries requiring First Aid: Examples of the types of injuries for which first aid is administered are airway compromise, respiratory failure and uncontrolled haemorrhage or bleeding.

b). Equipment and Supplies for Administering First Aid: It is essential for the following facilities to be available for effective administration of First Aid to RTC victims:

• Protective wear, especially gloves and aprons.

• A stretcher or the equivalent.

• Pressure dressings (bandages-elastic, if possible-and cotton or gauze dressings), splints-various sizes, made from local materials.

• Radio, telephone, or other mode of rapid communication for use when needed.

In Ghana, it is mandatory for every commercial vehicle to keep a first aid kit for emergencies and a survey conducted by the NRSA in 2012 established about 80% compliance level from commercial drivers with good contents as presented in Figure 7.21. Irrespective of this, most drivers fail to administer first aid to RTC victims. The key reasons attributed to this were fear of blood and lack of confidence to attend to an injured person. This requires appropriate psychological training to accompany driver training in first aid administrations.

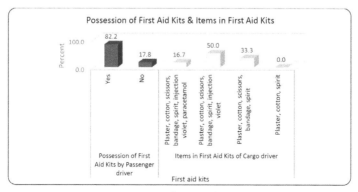

Figure 7.21: Possession of First Aids Kits and Contents

c). First Aid Posts: These provide intermediary facility based medical care for RTC victims in the form of advanced care for stabilization before an injured RTC victim is transported to substantive facility based medical care.

Currently, the number of first aid posts and their locations in Ghana are as indicated in Table 7.10. They are sited based on the level of traffic crash risk potential associated with a road from records of crash statistics and the availability of trained volunteers to man such posts. The structures are ultra-modern buildings constructed with American Technology.

They have enough space to keep all the emergency response first aiders deployed as well as the first aid equipment which includes stretchers, blankets, first aid kits etc. There is also enough room to provide first aid services as well as adequate space to accommodate and position emergency response vehicles and bikes to facilitate immediate rush to the RTC scene upon receiving signals. The types of supporting facilities include:

- *Pre-fabricated Post.*
- *Ambulance (vehicle) (Apam Jn.).*
- *Space for Keeping the Ambulance.*
- *Emergency Response Vehicle.*
- *Motorbikes.*
- *First Aid kit and equipment (Medicaments, Stretchers, Blankets etc.).*
- *Trained volunteers.*
- *Communication equipment (mobile phones).*

Though, the process of using an intermediary medical facility is deemed by some experts to be a weak link in the trauma care system because they may cause a delay process that can cause more harm to an injured RTC victim, given the current limitation in Ghana's post-crash emergency response the provision of first aid posts are deemed to be very relevant.

Table 7.10: Number of First Aid Posts in Ghana

Road Corridor	RTC Location	Nearest Referral Health Facility	
Accra–Aflao Highway	Tema motorway	37 Military Hosp & Tema General Hospital	
	Nokpokpo Jn	Aflao Jn	
	Ada Jn	Ada East Hospital	
Accra–Kumasi Highway	Asuboi,	-Juaso Hospital	
	Bunso Jn	Nsawam Hospital	
	Asankare	Suhum Hospital	
	Juaso Jn	Tafo Hospital	
		Osino Hospital	
Accra–Takoradi (2)	Okyereko Jn	Apam Hospital	
	and Apam Jn	Winneba Trauma Centre	

d). Principles of First Aid Training: The principles for the application of First Aid includes:

• Checking of the RTC scene for the number of casualties.

• Acting fast on anything that can endanger the life of the injured victim especially those who are with massive bleeding and lack of breath as well as those with life-threatening situations that might be difficult to notice such as those who are unconsciousness.

• Caring if a person is conscious and not bleeding.

• Monitoring the situation to ensure that all the important things are done.

e) Content of a First Aid Training: The content of First Aid training includes courses in the following:

• Lifesaving first aid skills such as the conduct of rapid assessment,

• performance of basic life support skills such as cardiopulmonary resuscitation (CPR) and Automated External Defibrillator (AED), Airway obstruction, assisted ventilation etc.

f). Roles and Responsibility for First Aid Administration at RTC Scene: These include trained paramedics legally mandated to administer First Aid and lay volunteers at the community levels also trained for the purpose. The paramedics are usually trained for advanced life support and community volunteers are only trained for basic first aid application.

In Ghana, the paramedics who are legally mandated to provide First Aid include GRCS, NAS, GNFS, NADMO and the Saint John Ambulance (SJA) however, predominantly, the GRCS and the SJA are the most active agencies in the provision of first aid care in the country. The GRCS specifically also engages in victim rehabilitation through psychological support to traumatized RTC victims.

The NAS are also trained in the administration of first aid and do apply the knowledge when required to do so. However, the level service delivery in this respect and its effectiveness is yet to be established. The key elements binding on effective performance by GRSC is in regard of victim stabilization since it is critical for the survival of an RTC victim. The role of the GRCS in Ghana compared to international practice is as summarized in Table 7.11

Table 7.11: Role of the Red-cross Society of Ghana Compared Best Practices

Core Functions of International Red-cross Society	Role of Ghana Red-Cross Society
Training in how to respond to emergency situations	
Engagement in Community Education and outreach in First Aid Care	Road safety Sensitization through School Link Programmes and Youth Programmes; Supporting of children to safely use roads especially at busy intersections by their Mothers Clubs -Establishment of emergency response teams in the communities along RTC prone roads -Training of community volunteers in first aid.
Disaster Management	Provision of other emergency services for support and participating in carrying victims to health facilities;
Provision of loans for borrowing practical aids and equipment at a nominal fee	
Operation of First Aid stations	Operation of First Aid stations
Provision of First Aid care at functions and events	Provision of First Aid care at functions and events
Provision of Home-based Care Training	
Welfare and feeding schemes	
Funding of projects	

Some of the challenges and constraints faced by the GRCS include:

- *Poor communication in reporting RTC cases which affects their response rate at the lower level of the governance system in Ghana. It is recommended for the activities of the centralized control room at national levels to be decentralized to the local level.*

- *Poor Corporation by medical centres where RTC victims are transported to for further care. Consideration should be given to the introduction and implementation of a mobile Emergency Medical Service (EMS) as with some developed countries.*

- *Limited logistic support for effective functioning of the first aid post administered by GRCS due to lack of consistent funding for covering overhead costs such as fuel costs, cost of consumables, utility costs and lack of resident ambulances amongst others remains a challenge. Since the GRCS is a charitable organization, some long standing corporate arrangements for sustainable support could be explored.*

- *Poor delivery by community-based emergency respondents trained for the purpose: It should be encouraged for the formation of Community Emergency Response Teams to ensure effective training impacts and cost reduction. There should also be increased campaign to solicit for funding from corporate and other goodwill sources to support the work of volunteers at the community level.*

g). First Aid Administration by Non-Paramedics: The WHO, (2012), intimates that many lives may be saved and disabilities prevented by teaching motivated people what to do at RTC scenes.

In Ghana, aside trained paramedics mandated to administer First Aid to RTC victims in Ghana, first respondents and drivers are also trained to administer First Aid though the legal status of their operations remains unclear. A study by the NRSA in 2012 on the level of first aid training provided by sampling, indicated that community first aid respondents and personnel from the GNFS are the groups with the highest number of personnel trained in the administration of first aid in Ghana followed by drivers. Indeed, the GRSC recommends for the entire populace to be trained in the administration of First Aid procedures, (See Figure 7.22.).

Figure 7.22: A call for First Training for the Public

i) A Comparison of Level of Application of First Aid Knowledge by Paramedics and Non-Paramedics: An assessment of the extent of application of knowledge gained from First Aid training including the GNFS, EMTs and drivers from a study by the NRSC in 2012 indicated that aside the trained personnel form GNFS, some trained EMTs (20%) are also able to apply First Aid to RTC victims. However, no driver had ever applied the knowledge at any RTC scene as indicated in Figure 7.23.

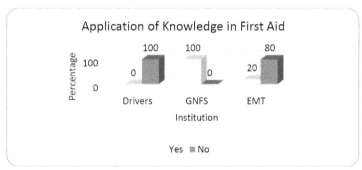

Figure 7.23: Level of Application of First Aid Knowledge by Trained Personnel

j). Training and Application of First Aid Knowledge by Lay Persons: A study by the NRSA, in Ghana, in 2012, revealed that training for first respondents have existed for over decades. See Figure 7.24 for trends of post-crash training for first respondents between 1991 and 2012.

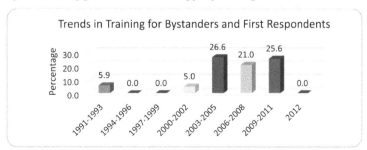

Figure 7.24: Trends in Training for Bystanders and First Respondents

An assessment of the knowledge and quality of First Aid measures administered by trained community respondents by the NRSA in 2012 revealed that most (56%) of them could recall how to move a patient; 15% could only recall the theoretical universal protocol of first Aid which is Danger, Response, Air and Breathing, Circulation (DRABC); 66% of the respondents could only recall the first step of acknowledging the danger associated with RTC situations and about 30% could recall step 3 that is the procedure on airways. 17% could recall step 2 and 12% could recall step 4 on breathing and circulation recording, (See Figure 7.25). This indicates a need for the conduct of continuous re-fresher courses for those already trained.

Figure 7.25: Respondent Ability to Recall Steps in First Aid Application

k). Activities Engaged by Trained Drivers in First Aid Application: The trained drivers and community first respondents who failed to apply their knowledge in First Aid mostly assisted with the extrication and transportation of RTC victims to a medical facility as presented in Figure 7.26.

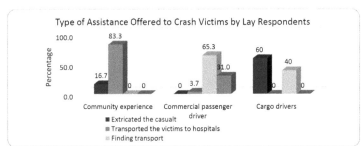

Figure 7.26: Types of Assistance to RTC victims offered by Lay Respondents

On the issue of non-performance by some trained drivers and some community members, it is debated for high attention not be given to such due to the lack of strong evidence that such training would decrease pre-hospital mortality in the first place. Another opinion is that, such a practice could adversely impact on outcomes as it consumes valuable resources that can be better spent on professional pre-hospital services that have demonstrated benefits.

These perceptions are not typical to the Ghanaian situation irrespective of the fact that some trained personnel do not apply the knowledge gained. This is because whether trained or untrained, the role of lay respondents is very significant in post-crash response in the country especially considering the fact that such people endanger their life to attend to such emergencies without protective clothing such as gloves etc. which puts them at risk for possible contraction of disease such as HIV, Hepatitis-B etc.

Also, whilst the paramedics in the formal sector maybe protected by social security, insurance systems, compensation schemes and risk allowances etc., the lay emergency respondents are not covered by any such schemes. Thus, there is need for substantive policies to address such concerns if the services of lay respondents are to be improved. The activities of such emergency teams should have legal backing with social protection frameworks supported with donations both in kind and cash to sustain such initiatives. It should also include considerations for the provision of protective wear, provision of some form of compensation and protection to motivate them into committed action rather than only their goodwill.

The approach can be based on a well-documented zonal community based first respondents team approach especially in remote parts of highways where serious RTC's often occurs but accessibility to post-crash care is very limited.

l). Role of Untrained First Respondents: The untrained first respondent is the last of the chain of post-crash care givers at RTC scenes. These are mostly first respondents from communities located along high risk RTC prone roads. Most of such people do acquire some unconventional knowledge and skill from the regular practice of engaging in rescue services to RTC victims.

In Ghana it is estimated that these constitute about 80% of those who attend to RTC victims. Such people are selfless people who apply any means available to assist RTC victims as and when there is need to carry out such procedures. In most instances they even assist the paramedics in the execution of their duties at the RTC scene, (See Figures 7.27). Thus, though untrained, their good intentions fill a critical gap in the provision of post-crash care in the country.

Figure 7.27: Lay Respondents Attending to RTC Victims at RTC Scenes

Some of the key challenges faced by them relates to the compulsion to use improvised methods such as attending to RTC victims at night with lanterns, packing of fatal and injured RTC victims in available vehicles e.g., pickup and truck buckets to be transported to health facilities. Box 7.1 gives a summary but vivid account of the findings of a study by Sam F. et al. (2018) on the experiences of untrained lay respondents.

Box 7.1: Feedback from Untrained Lay responders

-Generally, we noted that the majority of the participants have no practical training in pre-hospital care for RTA victims. For those who have received some training (n = 16 or 20%), the claimed it was just talk-based with a little demonstration. The rest acquired appreciable knowledge through years of rescue care for RTA victims.

-Yes. I remember one day; a group of people came here to talk to us about how we should handle accident victims. They said whenever we hear of a road accident, we should rush to the accident scene to help and try our best to call the Ambulance service and the Police. But it was mainly a talk show with little demonstration (Male, 32 years, Apam-junction).

-Regarding victim recovery position(s) in the event of suspected fracture (broken bone), 20% of the participants (those with some training) rightly revealed that victim recovery position(s) depends on the nature of the injury sustained. They emphasized placing the victim on the ground as it is difficult to determine the nature of the injury sustained.

-Not all victims who are involved in road accidents sustain serious or severe injuries. So those victims who are not hurt or injured, some of them could stand and others sit on the ground. But the severely injured victims should be placed on the floor with their backs to the ground (Male, 34 years, Apam-junction).

-If the victim has a broken leg or hand, let the victim lie with the back to the ground. Usually, the position of the victim depends on the form of injury I suspect might have occurred (Male, 32 years, Apam-junction).

I think the casualty should be made to lie down at the back to get enough air because the casualty may be suffering from a spinal problem or a dislocated waist or leg and so allowing such a victim to sit or squat may result in other injuries (Male, 30 years, Potsin).

Yet, others, like this respondent, revealed

-In case the victim is bleeding, most respondents (86%) demonstrated adequate knowledge of pre-hospital care including applying pressure to the affected area by pressing hard with the hands and subsequently applying local herbs or leaves and bandage to the bleeding part in order to stop or reduce bleeding (external compression for haemorrhage control).

-I tear the victim's shirt and use it to bandage the affected part. This helps to reduce the bleeding to prevent loss of blood, even if there is a delay in transporting them to the hospital (Male, 34 years, Apam-junction).

I am a driver, so I usually use dusters from my car or the shirts of (male) victims to tie the bleeding part before I transport them to the hospital (Male, 37 years, Apam-junction).

-It is evident from the interviews that bandaging or tying the bleeding area (haemorrhage control) is the common first aid most residents know of. However, others revealed different indigenous methods to stop bleeding.

For me, what I normally do is to look for leaves like "Acheampong" (a local herb) and I grind it on the road and apply it on the bleeding part to reduce the bleeding, or even at times I use plantain leaves, grind it and after that, I squeeze the water content on the bleeding part. Even though it hurts when the leaves are applied to injuries, but they help to reduce bleeding as soon as possible (Male, 35 years, Gomoa Mprumem).

-About 27% of the respondents rightly suggested checking the victim's pulse and body movements to determine the chances of survival and shouting into the victim's ear to determine if the victim responds or not. Other participants also think because most unresponsive victims become short of breath, the best way to assist them is by placing them on the ground with the head tilted backwards to open the airway in the throat to enable the victim to take in more air (basic airway control in unconscious persons).

-If the victim still breaths or the heart still beats, I put the victims in an open space to get more air. But if I cannot feel the heartbeat, I conclude that the victim is dead yet still we transport them to the hospital (Male, 35 years, Gomoa Mprumem).In sum, we realized that the study respondents were more adequate in their knowledge of pre-hospital care for bleeding accident victim(s) than in the case of the recovery position for the victim(s) who suffer fractured (broken bones) or are unresponsive.

Source: Sam F. E et al 2018

From literature, authors like Debenham S. et al. (2017), have expressed the view that although lay providers have long been recognized as the front lines of informal trauma care in countries without adequate formal EMS, few efforts have been made to capitalize on these networks. They therefore suggest that lay providers can become a strong foundation for emergency care through a four-fold approach as; (i) strengthening and expanding existing lay provider training programmes; (ii) incentivizing lay providers; (iii) strengthening locally available first aid supply chains; and (iv) using technology to link lay provider networks.

In Ghana, calls such as indicated in the publication below cannot be easily adhered to given the dominance of the role played by such people play in the post-crash care Figure 7.28. Thus, the role and impact of procedures by lay responders on victim survival rate should be well researched as basis for introducing formal structures into their operations for better performance due to the importance of the role they play in the post-crash response chain.

Figure 7.28: A Call by the NRSA Restraining the Handling of RTC Victims by Untrained Lay Persons

D. Transport of RTC Victims: This involves the quick and safe transport of severely injured RTC victims to facility based medical centre for the necessary treatment to be effected. It is the last step in the pre-hospital care phase of the post-crash care chain before facility based medical care takes over. It is an important activity because the mode of transportation can prevent a victim from dying or sustaining more serious injuries on the way to the medical based facility. The means of transport maybe by a medically based transportation vehicle such as air and road ambulance and non-medically based transportation vehicle where there is no ambulance, (See figure 7.29).

Figure 7.29: Scenes of NAS Personnel Demonstrating Application of First Aid (Source nas.gov.com)

i. Role of an Ambulance in Pre-Hospital Care: Ambulances provide both emergency response and patient transfer operations in a disciplined and organized way. It is medically based and enables the provision of both basic and advanced pre-hospital care services at the RTC scene as well as enroute to the medical facility. The process maybe of primary transfer or scene transfer when it involves the movement of the patient from the RTC scene to a hospital and of secondary transfer or inter-facility transfer when it involves the movement of a patient from one health facility to another for referral purposes.

ii. Categories of Ambulance Service: Ambulances are of two categories involving air and road ambulance:

a). Air ambulance rescue: Air ambulances are medically equipped aircrafts used for transporting RTC victims to medical facilities with the advantage of reduced travel time. Though deemed to be faster with about 16% higher survival rate from a study by Haider A. (2012) and Andruszkow H. et al (2013) have concluded that the impact of the use of air ambulance have remained evasive whilst others are also of the view that the use of helicopters to transport patients does not greatly influence their probability of survival though of higher cost to set up and operate compared to road ambulance. It is also deemed to be of higher risk due to the possibility of a tragic consequent of an air flight crash. However, these conclusions have been drawn on the basis of specific factors considered in different research case scenario.

In Ghana, Currently, the Tema- Port Hospital is the only facility with an air ambulance. Aside this, military helicopters are often also drawn on and used as substitutes in situations involving very critical emergency situations. On the way forward, Government could consider providing the service for only major teaching hospitals in the country to manage very serious emergency situations including. Also private investment opportunities based on private insurance schemes for the operation of the services of air ambulance in the country could be encouraged together with that of road ambulance as it is done in other advanced countries.

b). Road Ambulance: Road ambulances are of specified categories and standards by increasing order of the level of treatment required.

Established in 2004 the role of the NAS in emergency care in comparison with international best practice is as summarized in Table 7.12.

Table 7.12: Role of the National Ambulance Service of Ghana Best Practices

Role of Ambulance Service	Role of National Ambulance Service of Ghana
-Ambulance care assistance	-Training in basic life support,
-Patient Transport Services by drivers	-Standby duties at public events
-Call Handlers and control assistants	-inter hospital transfer:
-Emergency medical technicians	Patient Transport Services by drivers
-Experienced paramedic	-Call Handlers and control assistants
	-Emergency medical technicians
	-Experienced paramedic

As of 2020 the NAS operated within 296 stations in all the 276 political constituencies of the country. It has a total of 300 ambulances and staff capacity of 2175 emergency medical technicians (EMTs). However, the ambulance to population ratio approximately estimated at 1:250,000 patients is 5–10 times below recommended standards for lower-income countries. In addition to the number of ambulances operated by the NAS, there are a number of private ambulances owned by different health facilities at different levels and private corporate agencies though not officially documented and well quantified. These usually provide clinical assistance to their individual jurisdictions and may be drawn for assistance when a serious crisis occurs.

iii. Medical Facilities Required for an Ambulance: Since ambulances are mobile medical services they are required to be equipped with staff and life-saving medical facilities such as monitoring devices, a wide range of medicines and one or more modes of wireless communication used for a time sensitive and safe transport of patients. The list of standard equipment's for an ambulance operation is as provided in Table 7.13.

Ghana has the Mercedes Benz Sprinter 315 CDI equipped with life support equipment.

Table 7.13: Standard Ambulance Equipment Required and Available in Ghana

Standard Ambulance Equipment	Suction aspiration 12 VDC/220 VAC
FRP Stand Control Set (for Emergency warning light, siren and amplifier)	First aid kit (18 items)
Aluminum trolley stretcher (High-Low adjustable)	Foldaway Stretcher 4 Folds
Oxygen cylinder 20 litres	Stainless steel hand grip
Oxygen regulator with flow meter (for 20 litre oxygen cylinder)	Fire extinguisher
Oxygen cylinder 4 litres	Stainless steel rear step (small)
Blood pressure monitor (wall type)	Traffic pylon /
Digital clock (wall type)	Heavy duty air conditioner blower (without compressor)
Cervical collar	Fiberglass canopy ABL-1100-EXN
Stair stretcher	Suction aspiration 12 VDC/220 VAC
Spine board	Head immobilizer holder
Source: arryboyambulance.com/abl-1100-exn/?gclid	

iv. Application of preferential treatment method to emergency vehicles: For fast and effective transport, a preferential treatment method for emergency vehicles is required by law for other road users to give way to a moving ambulance, police vehicles, fire vehicles, officially escorted vehicles etc. to avoid delays from traffic congestions whilst enroute to or from a trauma scene. These vehicles use visible and audible signals by flashing lights and sirens to draw attention to indicate danger for other road users to comply with the law and to take extra care. In some countries, there may even be dedicated road lanes for such purposes.

The same conditions prevail in Ghana except for the use of dedicated lanes though in some instances delays maybe caused due to congested traffic situations in areas without alternative routes. Sometimes such vehicles are also compelled to use freeway opposite lanes for the necessary access to avoid delays. On the way forward preferential treatment method for emergency vehicles is one of the subjects that traffic management should address in the country.

a). Arrival Time: The mean response time, victim stabilization time and travel time to a health facility are critical performance measures of an ambulance system.

In Ghana, the average minimum response time to an RTC scene by the NAS from a self-reported study by the NRSA was estimated to be between 18 to 22 minutes though in practice unsubstantiated eye witness accounts have reported response time of beyond an hour, (See Figure 7.30).

Figure 7.30: A publication on delayed Arrival of an Ambulance

b). Handing over a patient to a medical care facility for treatment: This requires that relevant information about the condition of the patient is provided to the next care provider.

This process does not work effectively in Ghana. Some of the challenges includes lack of prior information about the state of a victim at the medical facility results in their inability to prepare in advance for the arrival of a patient with some rejections in some instances. The incidence of one medical facility or the other refusing treatment for RTC victims due to unpreparedness is common. There are reported extreme cases of ambulances leaving patients at the doorstep of some medical facilities or leaving their stretchers due to lack of available beds. The situation is aggravated when mass casualty cases are involved.

c) Responsibility for the Payment for Ambulance Services: In Ghana, the NAS is a public service financed through Government treasury under the Ghana Health Service (GHS). It provides a free service from the RTC scene to the medical facility, but further treatment referrals are paid for by the victims themselves. A study published in the BMC Emergency Medicine 18, Article 33 (2018) established the survival rate in 14 ambulance stations for the Greater Accra Region involving 652 pre-hospital care to be at an 87% survival rate from January to December 2014 for all trauma types including RTC's, however the exact proportion of RTC cases involved was not isolated from the study.

Another study by the NRSA in 2012 from self-reports with NAS also indicated that about 70% of all NAS stations have been involved in the transportation of RTC casualties to medical facilities but records of the exact number of RTC victims transported were not available and the survival rate was not also known. Some specific challenges confronting the NAS include:

a). Limited Number and Limited utilisation of Ambulances: In Ghana, RTC victims not transported by ambulance are still more than those transported by ambulance. This is mostly attributed to a number of factors including limited availability of ambulances and the fact that an ambulance is able to pick one injured victim at a time but often times very few ambulances arrive at the RTC scene etc.

Arrangements should be put in place for the mobilization of additional ambulances from other stations to support the transfer of mass RTC injury victims in times of such need within the shortest possible time. Also training of a core of informal commercial transport operators to provide ambulance services with non-conventional vehicles to complement conventional ambulance services for some minor cases under specialized arrangements to complement the work of the NAS in isolated areas and in extreme situations could be explored.

Currently in Ghana private initiatives such as Medicab – Emergency Medical Transport which can be reached on telephone numbers 0208664403/02088664404 or booked online on www.medicabgh.com) should be well streamlined with adequate training for enhanced performance. In the long term the possibility for the operation of private ambulance services on competitive basis for payment refunds through the NHIS should be explored as it is done in the advanced countries to ensure prompt and timely service since through effective competition on service quality.

b). Limited utilisation of Ambulance Services: Ironically, a study by Mould-Millman et al (2015), also asserted that there was generally low public utilization of the services of the NAS. The current norm in the country is to use any available vehicle to transport an injured person to the hospital, even when the NAS has an active presence in the community without waiting for an ambulance to arrive due to mistrust and lack of guarantee that an ambulance will arrive in a timely manner by majority of the populace. Another reason is attributed to poor knowledge about the consequences of RTC victims being transported with unconventional vehicles especially with regards to the health consequences of injured RTC victims being piled in cramped vehicles and the importance of patient care during transit. Thus, it is recommended for the populace to be educated on the importance of ambulance use.

c). Obstructions by other Road Users: Poor accessibility from public obstruction at RTC crash scenes, traffic congestion, poor road condition, none observance of sirens by other road users and difficulty in locating crash scenes causes delays in reaching and leaving RTC scenes. Innovative solutions that utilize location services could be explored and emergency routes could also be set for post-crash response.

Traffic congestion may also occur at an RTC scene until it has been cleared and this might cause delays and even disturb patient transport. Motorists are often alerted about the crash situation to drivers through media platforms and by the provision of detour information to discourage drivers from getting into the RTC site and practice must be commended and encouraged to for sustenance.

d). Funding Constraints: Poor funding and other resource constraints including poor office infrastructure, poor housing for the offices of the NAS, lack of access to basic safety equipment; inadequate staff capacity and limited first aid knowledge etc. mitigates against the effective operation of NAS. Arrangements should be made for cost recovery mechanisms such as private health insurance schemes could be explored to sustain the work of NAS.

f) Responsibility for Payment of Initial Patient Care at Medical Facilities: Resource availability for initial free emergency medical care is not well streamlined under the NHIS. This causes challenges for the NAS personnel at medical centres with patient rejection and delays in patient attendance in some cases resulting in the risk of possible death. Though by law 7% of the NHIS is supposed to be dedicated to the care of emergencies cases, the related protocols are not well defined so the applicability of this requirement remains a challenge. On the way forward, modalities for effective application of this policy requirement should be well defined for all medical centres since they are mandated by law to provide emergency health care by the Accident and Emergency (A&E).

E. The Normalisation Phase: After a crash a roadway can be littered with debris from stationary crash vehicles and other objects involved with the crash such as leaves, branches, pieces of a building, oil from fuel spillage and other hazardous materials, shredded vehicles parts e.g. pieces of glass and metals, obstructing elements and spilled cargo. In extreme cases, there could also be blood and other bodily parts or fluids considered to be bio-hazardous waste at the scene.

Quick clearance practices to tidy and clear the carriageway is necessary because such elements can cause further damages. While the cleaning of spilt hazardous material is necessary to prevent chemical accidents and even deaths, the cleaning of bio-hazardous substances from the roadway is also necessary to prevent infections and slip offs which can cause further injuries. Effective clearance of an RTC site is however contingent on the following factors:

ii. Regulations for Clearance and Cleaning of RTC Scenes: The cleaning procedure at an RTC scene must be determined by set legislation with regards to the types of elements to be cleared. This is because the cleaning of hazardous substances, bio-hazardous substances and oil and fluid spills require specialized clean-up processes such as the following:

a). Cleaning of Spilt Hazardous Materials: The clearance of such substances involves containing such substances and preventing them from spreading and applying any available absorbents-even dirt from the roadside. Others are applying mechanisms to reduce leaking vehicle fluids at the source or disinfecting bio-hazardous substances before cleaning, (See Figures 7.31).

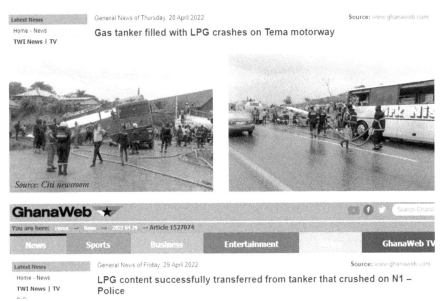

Figure 7.31: Clearance of Spilled substances at RTC Scene, (Source: Peacefmonline.com)

b). Clearance of Debris: Clearance by removing debris involves the creation of a road-block to the approach of the debris and removing the debris completely from the road-way system if possible. Where it cannot be removed, it must be placed well off the travel lanes and shoulder of the road to be picked up at a later time, (See Figure 7.32).

Figure 7.32 Pictures on Clearance of Debris from an RTC Scene, (Source – Assasefm)

c). Clearance of Crush Vehicles: Clearance of stationary crash vehicles requires the identification of vehicle classes involved in an RTC so that tow companies can respond to the required need within the shortest possible time with the right towing equipment be it with heavy-duty tow trucks, dump trucks, front-end loaders etc., (See Figure 7.33). Effective towing services must have efficient dispatch protocols with monetary incentives to promote safe and fast services to avoid congestion and secondary incidents. Operators must be certified by equipment type backed by inspections equipment and training for efficient services.

Figure 7.33: Crashed and broken-down vehicles being towed, (Source NRSA)

In Ghana, towing and recovery companies are normally provided by the private sector and paid for by owners of crashed vehicles. In instances of extreme need, towing services may be provided for free of charge by the GNFS. That of the Police is almost non-existent and is some extreme cases vehicles are left at the RTC scene with potential for the occurrence of another crash (See Figure 7.34). In some special instances the police collaborate with well-established private service entities such as the Road Safety Management Services (RSMS) to provide emergency services at a fee. Past efforts to streamline towing services by the institution of a generic fee charged to all motorists could not be passed into law.

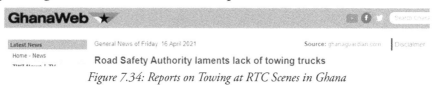

Figure 7.34: Reports on Towing at RTC Scenes in Ghana

iii. Responsibility for Clearance of RTC Scenes: In most countries the clearing and cleaning of vehicle crash scenes is normally undertaken by the fire brigade, the police, private cleaning entities and vehicle owners.

In Ghana, the GNFS is mostly responsible for the clearance of hazardous materials and sometimes blood and the Police is responsible for clearing human parts. However, it is not uncommon for scattered debris and vehicle parts to be left lying on roadsides long after crashes have occurred. This is because there are no clear regulations on the responsibility of clearance and cleaning of RTC scenes and this must be corrected.

7.6.2 Critical Components of Pre-Hospital Care

A. Time Management in Pre-Hospital Care: Generally, timing is considered to be the very critical factor to the delivery of pre-hospital care because of the survival of a critically injured RTC victim is contingent on it. The key aspects include:

i. The Golden Hour Rule Philosophy: Introduced by A. Cowley, (1961), it stipulates that casualties will have a much poorer chance of survival if they are not delivered to definitive care within one hour from the time of the RTC till definitive care is delivered at the hospital. The recommended time budget within the Golden Hour Philosophy is presented in Table 7.14.

Table 7.14: Time Budget within the Golden Hour

Time Budget	Description
RTC notification time	The time between the occurrence of RTC and the time the notification call is made
Response time	The taken by emergency response team to arrive at the RTC scene
Scene time	The time taken by pre-hospital care providers from arrival at the RTC scene until departure from the scene. The first 10 minutes of 'On Scene Time' are called the 'Platinum ten' because they are critical in determining patient outcome by actively managing the airway, controlling severe bleeding, and stabilizing multiple fractures. This time-scale does not allow for a lengthy extrication time at the RTC scene if lives are to be saved and healthy recoveries promoted.
Transport time	The time from leaving the RTC scene until arrival at the hospital or other treatment facility

Source: (Kobusingye et al., 2006.)

A proposed standard time budget for the different activities involved in pre-hospital care which is to serve as a guide for good timing in pre-hospital care for emergency services is also as presented in Table 7.15.

Table 7.15: Time Standards for the Golden Hour Philosophy

Cumulative Time	Action	Time Taken
0 Minute	RTC Occurs	0 Minutes
5 Minutes	Call to Emergency Services	5 Minutes
15 Minutes	Turn out and Travel to Scene	10 Minutes
30 Minutes	Extrication	15 Minutes
35 Minutes	Package and Transfer	5 minutes
60 Minutes	Transport to Hospital	25 Minutes

In Ghana, the statutory regulation on arrival time for all emergency response teams to an RTC scene is 5 to 10 minutes after notification. However, almost 90% of the time, the police is able to arrive at the RTC scene within 25 to 30 minutes whilst the ambulance is able to do so within 25 minutes from self-reported studies conducted by the NRSA in 2012. However, surveys from eyewitnesses account normally puts the response time to about an hour for most of the emergency response teams except for the police. A substantive study of the factors causing such delays should be conducted for mitigations. Also intensified training on this amongst the emergency response teams in preparation of RTC situations must be integrated into joint drill programmes.

B. Incident Documentation: Documentation of all significant incident scene information at arrival, during the clearance period, and at departure from incident scene is very important for planning and evaluation and performance upgrades of the whole post-crash system.

In Ghana, this is mostly done for internal purposes by the individual emergency response agencies but the extent of the use of such records for policy guidance is not very vivid.

C. Constraints to Effective Pre-Hospital Care Delivery: *Some of the relatable challenges with pre-hospital care systems are as follows:*

i. Unclear Guide on Activation and Implementation of Pre-hospital Care: In Ghana, the formal pre-hospital care system is characterized by fragmentation of activities inefficiencies,

disjointed and inconsistent mode of operations not well understood by both the service pro-
viders and users. Characteristically, in Ghana different jurisdictions feature intermittently
at RTC scenes whilst others do not feature at all. There is therefore a need to streamline
Ghana's pre-hospital care system for consistency and improved quality of performance at
national, regional, and local levels. The framework must be guided by defined protocols,
resourcing mechanisms and operational procedures and well set out legal obligations and
liabilities for all the entities involved.

ii. Dominant Role of Informal RTC Emergency Response in Pre-Hospital Care: Informal
pre-hospital care practices coupled with inefficient formal care systems is virtually the norm
in Ghana due partly to the lack of public awareness and demand for quality care. The lack
of statistics on the survival rate of the proportion of RTC's managed by paramedics and
those managed by untrained lay respondents does not motivate the need to improve formal
emergency service delivery systems.

There must be a study in emergency rooms to differentiate between the survival rate of RTC
emergency situations handled by paramedics and those handled by lay persons. The study
must also assess the causes of death for those who died at the crash scene and those who died
on the way to a medical facility by means of formal and informal handling at the pre-hos-
pital care stage to inform policy direction on the issue. Another study should be in relation
to the arrival time of injured RTC victims to medical facilities by the formal and informal
system based on the means of transport used to determine the adequacy of the informal means
of transport for the management of post-crash response in Ghana.

iii. Limited Technical Capacity for Pre-Hospital Care: According to the (WHO, 2004),
organized trauma teams have been shown to improve the process and outcome of
trauma care.

In Ghana, the capacity of emergency response teams is not well defined in content and in
quantity. A capacity needs assessment must be undertaken at the national, regional, and
local levels establish the level of available and skills for emergency care at all levels. A stra-
tegic approach for training to match the level of pre-hospital needs must be well ascertained.
The possibility of an integrated training system should also be considered where possible for
consistency and efficiency.

Past practices, whereby NAS personnel were trained by the fire service should be revived.
Standard training materials for similar activities should also be used. Courses to boost the
technical capability of relevant team members should be undertaken through refresher cours-
es. KPIs for pre-hospital care delivery must be constantly updated to validate performance
levels.

iv. Limited Funding and Logistics: Currently, all the emergency response entities are funded from government treasury with the exception of the GRCS which is an NGO supported by charitable donations. Therefore, common funding challenges are faced by all of them especially regarding funding shortfalls for planned activities. The problem becomes very aggravated in situations of mass casualties where there is need for adequate pre-planning for efficient logistic supply.

There is need to build sufficient evidence that pre-hospital emergency care actually has critical outcomes to make a case for the creation of a robust state-funding support. Funding constraints relating to victim care at the medical facilities for the emergency care should also be adequately addressed to avoid the current situation whereby lay respondents and the police and NAS personnel have to pay for patient registration etc. from out of their own pockets.

v. Limited Equipment Availability: Availability of specialized equipment is a perquisite need for the pre-hospital care agencies.

In Ghana, not only are more ambulances needed with complementary logistics, others such as extrication equipment and First Aid facilities for trained community first respondents must also be provided. The quantity of the needed equipment must be complemented with quality backed by a sustainable method of acquiring and replenishing them.

vi. Limitations of RTC Communication Processes: In Ghana, though there is a toll-free number, its effectiveness in all parts of the country is not known especially with regards to areas with poor communications services where running calls are mostly done with related consequences on delayed emergency service delivery. Since studies indicates that most of the citizenry are comfortable calling press houses to report RTCs a special programme should be instituted to improve the process by training.

vii. Poor Coordination of Interrelated Components: Timely and effective attendance to RTC victims requires effective coordination and team collaboration by all the agencies involved in such operations even before they arrive at the RTC scene. This is must be done through a clear understanding of the expected roles and responsibilities at the RTC scene guided by RTC scene management guidelines especially for agreed priorities for allocating scarce resources in joint operations. This is important for avoiding gaps, overlaps, repetitive bias and disjointed actions to ensure balanced operations. This is particularly critical for responding to multiple casualty crash scenarios.

A study by the NRSA in 2012 reported a cordial relationship between the emergency service providers. Some of the areas of cooperation include coordinated response action whereby anytime there is an RTC, any of the emergency services who receives the message can call the other. Other examples are as summarized in Box 7.2.

Box 7.2: levels of Collaboration amongst Emergency Service Personnel in Ghana

MTTD's Collaboration with Other Emergency Service Teams: The MTTD had had working experience with the fire service in some emergency response situation

GRCS's Collaboration with Other Emergency Service Teams: The GRSC had collaborated with NAS for determining the state of injured victim's condition, administration of first aid administration and handing injured victims over stage to a health facility.

NAS's Collaboration with Other Emergency Service Teams: All the ambulance stations had collaborated with the MTTD and GRSC joint first aid, collaboration at RTC scenes and information sharing.

Lay Respondent's Collaboration with Other Emergency Service Teams: Lay respondents had collaborated with other emergency team members through the placement of call to the MTTD and other paramedic agencies.

Irrespective of these self-reports by the emergency response agencies, the study established that in reality, the level of actual practice of good collaboration at RTC scenes is not known since there is limited evidence of clear modalities for guided and interrelated collaborative RTC response by the individual emergency agencies. Also, procedures for good work delivery and optimization of the use of limited resources e.g. shared logistics is also not well defined. This is reflected in failure to ensure adequate logistic stocking in advance for emergency responses and failure to track resource distribution to ensure continuous supply to relevant places when needed coupled with poor deployment mechanisms.

The result is that the full complement of emergency service operation by the emergency response teams to an RTC scene rarely happens in Ghana. Often times only one or two of the agencies especially the police is seen in attendance with the assistance of lay respondents. A governing committee of representatives from all emergency service providers should be set up within the JIC's of NADMO, to ensure that coordination can function better. Such a committee should be represented at the national, regional and district levels and must also coordinate joint RTC preparatory actions through the following interventions:

- *The conduct of Joint drills and simulation sessions on dispatching, scene control, conduct of triage, ambulance function and handover process etc.*

- *Development of guidelines for the arrangement of personnel, facilities and equipment for well- coordinated pre-hospital care delivery in emergency situations backed by effective control and monitoring.*

- *Development of strategies for appropriate substitution, conservation, adaptation, reuse and reallocation of scarce equipment and supplies system.*

- *Development of a system to enable the well-resourced agency at any point to provide the bulk of the resource needed to manage a specific RTC situation.*

- *Development of a clear guide on who is to do what at the RTC scene within a hierarchically structure for instructing, controlling and coordinating of activities.*

viii. Poor Incident Management at RTC Scenes: Joint incident management by the respective emergency teams at the RTC scene is a problem in Ghana. This is attributed to lack of guidelines for work processes at the RTC scene and lack of a clear team command during such situations. This should be corrected with a well laid work protocols, procedures, and reporting formats for RTC scene management in the country. Since currently NADMO is legally mandated to be the team lead for emergency management it must be supported through training and other resource provision to enable it deliver on its mandate.

In the interim also, the process of interfacing formal and informal systems of pre-hospital care approaches should be explored to maximize the available opportunities offered by the informal systems. This is because it will take some time for formal pre-hospital care to meet optimal performance standards in the country and such a blended system can fill in the current gap.

ix. Lack of Advance Calls to Medical Facilities: This includes failure to provide information about the condition of individual victims and the expected care on arrival at the medical facility

In Ghana, the situation is worsened by the predominance of lay responder input in post-crash management in the country. Due to their lack of technical knowledge, they are unable to provide such critical information with the related consequences of delayed treatment especially when victims are just dumped at the nearest health facility with little concern for the aftermath.

x. Importance of Professionalism in the Application of Pre-hospital care: All emergency service providers have an ethical and legal obligation to act and respect the limits of their training by not attempting procedures they are unqualified to perform.

In Ghana, the performance of the technical personnel is also yet to be validated with regards to the level of professionalism exhibited. Again, in Ghana, the predominance of the role of lay respondents defeats the purpose for any such requirement effect. Not only is there wide spread lack of knowledge on standards to apply by the lay rescuers who attempt to give aid to

RTC victims, they could also stand the risk of being held morally and even legally responsible if a patient dies or is left with a permanent disability.

Fortunately, in Ghana those who rush to the aid of RTC victims are usually upheld as good 'Samaritans' and the situation has been embraced as an accepted norm. However, this cannot be taken for granted and the situation cannot be allowed to remain forever. Attention must be given to the legal implications of their operations so that mechanisms could be put in place to streamline and protect those who volunteer to offer assistance in such situations.

7.7 POST CRASH CARE AT THE FIXED MEDICAL FACILITY LEVEL

After pre-hospital care, an RTC injury victim is transported to a fixed medical facility for follow-up medical treatment depending on the type of injury, the level of and closeness of the emergency medical to the RTC scene.

7.7.1. Types of Emergency Injuries and Hospital Based Care

A. Types of Injuries Reported: Injuries during RTCs are sustained through direct collision of the body with the vehicle and other road users. It could also happen through, ejection from the vehicle or motorcycle onto the road, entrapment within a mangled vehicle resulting in crushed body parts, burns and inhalational injury from vehicles on fire, (Chapman P. 2010). The common parts of the body susceptible to RTC injuries are the (i) central nervous system (head and spine injury), (ii) the cardiovascular system (injury to the heart arteries and veins resulting in haemorrhage), (iii) the respiratory system (rib cage and lung injury), (iv) the gastrointestinal system (abdominal injury), (v) the genitourinary system (abdominal and pelvic injury) and the (vi) musculoskeletal system (limb injuries and fractures), (WHO 2004).

B. Mortality from RTCs: This has been found to be trimodal in its occurrence, that is (i) about 50% of casualties are known to die at the RTC scene from their injuries such as severe head injuries and massive Haemorrhage. (i) about 30% survive but die in the following 4 hours (the golden hour) and these deaths are potentially preventable with Haemorrhage and cardio respiratory injuries falling in this category; (iii), the remaining 20% succumb to severe sepsis and multiple organ failure and die within 6 weeks from time of injury, (Demetriades et al D 2005).

In Ghana, a cross-sectional study of all RTC casualties in 37 Military Hospital from March 2018 to March 2019 by Aggrey Orleans J. (2019), indicated that there were 44.67% of lower limb injuries, 23.74% upper limb injury and 13.48% head injury with 20% having multiple injuries.

C. Emergency Procedure at Medical Centres: The medical treatment for such emergency cases normally involves the conduct of triage, running of tests, taking of x-rays, computed tomography scan (CAT scans) etc. to determine the extent of injuries suffered by the victim so that appropriate treatment can be effected. This therefore implies that medical facilities that offer care to injured RTC victims must be equipped with the necessary medical equipment and expertise to enable the right treatment to be effected. The facilities and the staff are also to be in well prepared state for good diagnosis, services and effective clinical care.

7.7.2. Policy and Planning for Hospital Based Emergency Care

A. Policy for Hospital Based Emergency Care: *Emergency care at the medical facility stage is required to be guided by laid policies, strategies and procedures for the attainment of required outcomes and expectations. This is particularly important due to the high-risk nature of emergency medical needs and the associated possibility of losing precious life if the right thing is not done.*

In Ghana, the GHS has accordingly developed an Accident and Emergency (A&E) Policy Guideline to support such a purpose in the country with the directive for all medical facilities to provide uninterrupted 24-hour accident and emergency service to patients in need of such care. The objective is for every health facility in Ghana to be able to provide at least a minimum treatment to stabilize the patient before the patient is referred to a higher order medical facility if the need be. However, in reality not all medical facilities are able to provide this service even with regards to the least care for emergency cases and the impact of this on RTC victim survival rate is also not known.

B. Hospital Based Emergency Medical Care Plans: By standard requirement, each emergency medical facility is required to have a plan compatible with national standards guided by the following essential elements:

a.   Regulations and laid down procedures for receiving emergency RTC cases at respective health facilities.

b.   Procedures to follow for arranging for additional facilities such as beds to wards and rooms and setting up cots in open spaces.

c.   Modalities for discharging less acutely affected persons.

d.   Pre-established procedures for calling back staff for extra shifts.

e. Modalities for maintaining or increasing stocks of equipment, supplies, and pharmaceuticals where necessary.

f. Agreements on how the various health care facilities will share staff and equipment based on formal Memoranda of Understanding.

g. Procedures to call up volunteers who have been identified as willing and able to provide assistance (e.g. retired health care providers).

h. Logistical systems to coordinate receipt and distribution of equipment, supplies, and Pharmaceuticals from other health facilities.

i. Procedures for referring serious emergency cases to higher order services Steps to follow for transporting a victim to and from medical facilities

C. Classification of Emergency Care System: According to the Australian collage for emergency medicine, (2015), the emergency medical system is classified under three main factors as Clinical, Professional and Administrative profiles.

i. Clinical Profile: This refers to the types of health facilities for treating emergency cases, the procedures followed in responding to and treating patients, the types of treatment involved and the types of equipment used for care administration.

a). Types of Emergency Health Care Facilities: Medical facilities are classified in a hierarchical order such that minor injuries are managed at the lowest level such that those who can return home are made to do whilst those needing to be transferred to the next highest medical facility are transferred for appropriate care at that level.

In Ghana, facility based medical centres are categorized into five (5) levels based on personnel and equipment threshold which determines the types of service rendered. (See Table 7.16 for a comparison of Ghana's level of Health facilities with international standards.

Table 7.16: Levels of Health Facilities from Diverse Literature

Levels of Health Facilities – Standard International Best Practice	Levels of Health Facilities in Ghana
Level 1: A Level I Trauma Center is a comprehensive care facility capable of providing total care for every aspect of injury from prevention through rehabilitation including: -24-hour in-house coverage by general surgeons and prompt availability of care in specialties such as orthopaedic surgery, neurosurgery, anaesthesiology, emergency medicine, radiology, internal medicine, plastic surgery, oral and maxillofacial, paediatric and critical care. -Referral resource for communities in nearby regions. -Provision of continuing education of the trauma team members. -Operates an organized teaching and research effort to help direct new innovations in trauma care. -Programme for substance abuse screening and patient intervention. -Meets minimum requirement for annual volume of severely injured patients.	Level 1: Teaching Hospitals are the first level service that provides the best quality of care possible in the country. -They have the best available and affordable equipment's -They are also sufficiently developed and supported by the establishment of proper referral system interlinked with other specialized and general hospitals within the country. -There are more health personnel in the Teaching hospitals than in the other health facilities. -There are four tertiary care hospitals in Ghana (one of which doubles as a regional hospital); all are affiliated with a medical school or residency programme and offer more specialized care.

Levels of Health Facilities – Standard International Best Practice	Levels of Health Facilities in Ghana
Level II: A Level II Trauma Center is able to initiate definitive care for all injured patient including: -24-hour immediate coverage by general surgeons, as well as coverage by the specialties of orthopaedic surgery, neurosurgery, anaesthesiology, emergency medicine, radiology and critical care. -Tertiary care needs such as cardiac surgery, haemodialysis and micro vascular surgery may be referred to a Level I Trauma Centre. -Provision of trauma prevention and continuing education programmes for staff.	Level II: Regional Hospitals: They provide general specialist care and skills with the following -Resuscitation equipment basic and advanced airway equipment, oxygen supply; pulse oximetry; blood transfusion capabilities; -Diagnostic services including, determination of blood electrolytes and stationary radiography, skin grafting or basic orthopaedic or neurosurgical operative. -Specialists such as general surgeons and orthopaedic and general medical physicians who provides general surgery and anaesthesia, RTC and emergency services -Contains between 100 and 400 beds. -More complex care are referred to one of the four teaching hospitals in the country
Level III: A Level III Trauma Center has an ability to provide prompt assessment, resuscitation, surgery, intensive care and stabilization of injured patients and emergency operations. The level of service include: 24-hour immediate coverage by emergency medicine physicians and the prompt availability of general surgeons and anaesthesiologists. -Offers continued education of the nursing and allied health personnel or the trauma team. -Involves prevention efforts and must have an active outreach program for its referring communities	Level III: District Hospitals: They are distributed by about 50km interval across the country and are the first point for referrals hospital before further recommendations to higher order medical facilities. -Available equipment include: Pulse oximetry, mechanical ventilation, and electronic cardiac monitoring, skin grafting and internal fixation for fractures. Others are intracranial pressure monitoring, neurosurgical operative capacity, and spinal fixation. -Provide clinical care and diagnosis services including surgery and anaesthesia. -Are staffed by medical officers and nurse anaesthetists, and usually offer surgical services and have between 50 and 100 beds. -Refers cases that are beyond its capability and skills to the regional or nearest hospital that can safely perform the required service.
Level IV: A Level IV Trauma Center has an ability to provide advanced trauma life support (ATLS) prior to transfer of patients to a higher-level trauma center. It provides evaluation, stabilization, and diagnostic capabilities for injured patients. The level of service include: -Basic emergency department with facilities to implement ATLS protocols and 24-hour laboratory coverage. -Available trauma nurse(s) and physicians available upon patient arrival. -May provide surgery and critical-care services if available. -Has developed transfer agreements for patients requiring more comprehensive care at a Level I or Level II Trauma Centre. -Involves prevention efforts and must have an active outreach programme for its referring communities.	Level 1V: Primary health Care Services such as CHPs Compound, Health Centres/Posts and private Hospitals located in most communities and distributed by a 25km geographical interval across the country -Has developed transfer agreements for patients requiring more comprehensive care at a Level I or Level II Trauma Centre. -Incorporates a comprehensive quality assessment programme. -Involves prevention efforts and must have an active outreach programme for its referring communities.
Level V: A Level V Trauma Center provides initial evaluation, stabilization and diagnostic capabilities and prepare patients for transfer to higher levels of care. The level of service include: -Basic emergency department facilities to implement ATLS protocols. -Available trauma nurse(s) and physicians available upon patient arrival. -May provide surgery and critical-care services if available. -Has developed transfer agreements for patients requiring more comprehensive care at a Level I though III Trauma Centres. Source: Diverse Literature Sources	Level V: These are the first pre-hospital medical contact after an RTC and it mainly involves the administration of initial first aid to an RTC victim either at the RTC scene or at a first aid post before the patient is transported to a substantive medical facility. It also includes First Aid Posts: recommended to be located at every 25km interval on high risk RTC prone roads

The key challenge in Ghana is that the services expected to be provided by the respective levels sometimes do not match actual service provision with most of them under-resourced. In some special cases, the inability of a particular medical facility to provide the required service may influence a decision to take a victim directly to a known facilities with good service using sound discretion. This may involve transporting an emergency victim over long travel distances with high risk to survival.

It also puts great pressure on higher order medical facilities who have to manage both primary and secondary level medical cases at the same time creating over-crowding, increased workload, delayed diagnosis, delayed care, poor quality care and inefficient utilization of limited resources described as the "perfect storm", by Campbell, et al., (2007). Such situations have also been known to be the cause of preventable deaths of some victims of RTC in some instances.

There is need therefore to ensure that the population is well informed about where to go first with emergency cases through the use of a well-publicised information platform where paramedics and even lay responders would be guided on where to take an emergency victim. This will also address the challenge of injured RTC cases being rejected on the basis of the "no bed syndrome".

There should also be training in emergency care for the staff of all medical facilities at facility based medical centres at least up to the conduct of triaging and procedures for victim stabilization before referrals if the need be. Since, there are also profound differences between emergency medical service provision in the rural and urban areas of Ghana with most well stocked medical facilities including private clinics concentrated in urban areas compared to rural with regards to the pool of resources such as staff expertise and numbers, equipment types, treatment types, access to training, telecommunication systems etc. RTC victims in rural areas may also be transported over long distances to higher order facilities with related risks.

Therefore, medical facilities at all levels should be well equipped with basic resources for the provision of basic treatment to RTC emergency victims as well as for the safe transport of such victims to higher order health care after the initial treatment and referrals are needed.

b) Equipment Supply for Emergency Care at Medical Facilities: (WHO published Guidelines for Essential Trauma Care (GETC) that defines minimum standards for human and physical resources necessary for managing injury.

Also, in Ghana the A&E guideline gives recommendations on the types of equipment needed for emergency care at the medical centres. However, according to Hesse & Ofosu (2014), the ideal situation where a health facility has all the needed equipment and consumables is uncommon in low- and middle-income countries (LIMCs) with Ghana falling into the same category and Razzak, et al., (2002) attributes this to the poor state of most emergency medical units.

In Ghana, a study comparing the status of equipment availability for emergency medical care in the country by Mock et al (2014) is as provided in Table 7.17. It indicated that most of the facility based medical facilities had limited equipment as compared to those recommended in the A&E guideline by type and in quantity. The current level of equipment inventory is not known so as to inform paramedics and other affiliates on which facility to best used in such circumstances.

Table 7.17: Comparison of Availability of Equipment for Trauma Care Services in 2004 and 2014 in Ghana

Item	District Level Hospitals		Regional Level Hospitals	
	2004	2014	2004	2014
Hospitals assessed, No	8	26	2	6
Airway				
Basic Equipment	1	2	2	2
Advanced Equipment	1	3	1	3
Oxygen Supply	1	3	1	3
Chest tubes	1	0	1	0
Pulse Oximetry	0	3	0	2
Big valve mask	1	3	2	1
Mechanical Ventilator	0	2	0	1
Urinary catheter	3	3	3	3
Blood transfusion capabilities	1	2	2	2
Electronic cardiac monitoring	0	0	0	1
Laboratory diagnostics				
Hemoglobin determination	3	3	3	3
Electrolyte determination	0	0	0	1
Arterial blood gas, lactate	0	0	0	0
Stationary radiography	1	2	2	2
Portable radiography	1	0	2	0
Computed tomography	NA	NA	0	0
Angiography	NA	NA	0	0

c). Equipment Maintenance: Aside the shortages in the types and quantity of equipment needed, the study also identified poor equipment quality, high stock of equipment break-down with poor maintenance as a constraint. Others are inoperative technological items as a result of non-durable technical consumables and technology breakage from overuse as well as equipment maladapted to cope with the dust, heat, and fluctuating power system in the country. Others are lack of in-service training for new equipment use, (with donated items being the most problematic) also mitigates against emergency care in the country.

d). Equipment Stocking: In-stock management and procurement policies in the entire trauma chain is necessary to ensure efficient supply of equipment and logistics for trauma care.

In Ghana, this remains a key challenge alongside others such as poor manual procurement processes and stores management and informal bedside inventory management with a low-level alert mechanism for items needing reordering. Reliance on hospital purchases on the basis of wholesale supplies on credit with frequent and unpredictably deficiencies in essential items causing inefficient service delivery at the medical facilities and frequent stock-outs is also common. Irregular service contracts from limited affordability resulting in lengthy breakage times and the practice of obtaining authorization to purchase supplies in the open with laborious processes causes excessive delays resulting in poor service delivery.

External challenges beyond the control of the medical centres such as frequent power outages coupled with the lack of affordability of generator fuel results in the inability of the medical centres to use some equipment operated by electricity such as ventilators and cardiac monitors. (Aggrey Orleans J. (2019). There is therefore a critical need for change.

e). Types of Services offered at Medical Centres: The emergency care for RTC casualties especially within the first forty-eight (48) hours has been shown to have a huge impact on reducing morbidity, mortality and economic losses to the individual and the state, (Liberman & Roudsari, 2010). The conventional order by which facility based medical care is administered to RTC victims is as summarized in Table 7.18.

Table 7.18: Order by which Conventional Medical Care is administered to RTC Victims

1.0 Pre-Arrival	
Pre-arrival notification	System for receiving information about the patient prior to arrival
Conduct of Triage	Assessment priority
Registration	Correct identification and to facilitate subsequent communication and follow up with the patient as well as relevant healthcare providers
2. Diagnostic and Investigation	
Physical examination	physical examination related to their presenting problem by a suitably qualified and experienced medical personnel
3. Intervention Procedures	
Resuscitation	Adequate resuscitation
Laboratory Assessment	Advanced Laboratory tests eg. ultrasonography, CT or MRI scanning
4. Recognition and Management of the critically Health Condition	
Treatment eg.	Advance Cardiac Life support
Basic Life Support and surgery, or reperfusion	Advance Trauma Life Support
	Pediatric Advance Life Support
	Definitive surgical management
Admissions procedures	Referral to the inpatient unit
	Bed management
Discharge procedures	Patient's suitability and safety for discharge;
Referral	Discharge to another health facility

In Ghana, the level of compliance with such procedures at all levels of medical care and management of emergency operations in the country at large is not known. Poor internal organisation to manage mass RTC casualties at some health facilities is a well-known challenge. It is estimated that in some cases, the problem can be serious to the extent that even five (5) severely injured patients arriving simultaneously would be sufficient to paralyse the activities of the entire hospital due to staff diversion. Though a study by (Mock, 2002) estimated that persons with life-threatening, but salvage able injuries were six times more likely to die in

Ghana than in the USA (6%), the current situation is yet to be ascertained and these needs to be researched.

B. Professional Profile: Well-trained multi specialist medical team is critical to facility-based emergency medical care. Thus, it is recommended for an emergency department to have a minimum threshold of dedicated staff with basic professional clinical capabilities for both out-of-hospital and in-hospital scenarios with expertise in one or more of the following for intensive care procedures; physicians, anaesthesiology, emergency surgery, traumatology, cardiology, general internal medicine, nursing and support staff etc.

In Ghana, the A&E guidelines recommends for competent and committed emergency health care professionals to include Doctors, Anaesthetist, Surgeons, Trauma/Orthopaedic Surgeon, Neurosurgeons, Radiologist, Emergency Physicians, Physician Assistants, Triage Personnel, Pharmacist, Nurses, Critical Care Nurse with a standby Consultant within 30 minutes of patient admission to a higher order health facility. A study at the 37 Military Hospital by Aggrey Orleans J. (2019), revealed that orthopaedic surgeons managed 56.34% of the casualties and Neurosurgeons 21%. However, it is generally of the view that there are normally shortages of these categories of health experts in most medical facilities.

i. Training of Medical Emergency Team Members: Aside the categories of medical personnel expected to constitute the emergency care team at facility based medical centres, all the professionals are recommended to be trained in basic life support measures by accredited trainers for uniformity and standardization. Other aspects are continuous professional development through training for emergency medical teams.

In Ghana, a novel Emergency Medicine (EM) training programme was established at the Okomfo Anokye Teaching Hospital in conjunction with the Ghana College of Physicians and Surgeons (GCPS), the University of Michigan, the Ghana Health Service, and the Ministry of Health in2015. The training includes training programmes for emergency physicians and other health professionals in emergency care including nurses, junior doctors and medical students, (Oduro G, D 2015). The programme was further upgraded to include Advance Trauma Life Support (ATLS) course in conjunction with GCPS in April/May 2015, (Osei-Ampofo et al, 2013).

A system has also been established for continuous professional development of the core staff working at the A&E unit based on set standards by the Ghana College of Physicians and Surgeons. It is also mandatory for each professional within the team to be re-certified every 3 years by accredited training teams and institutions and all emergency health care institutions are to ensure strict adherence to this provision.

Also, the Ministry of Health (MoH) has developed staffing standards including emergency care for Regional and District hospitals. However, informal reports indicate that low human resource capacity is still a challenge irrespective of the establishment of the emergency training centre at the Okomfo Anokye Teaching Hospital in Kumasi. This is attributed to the lack of consistent and dedicated human resource development programme to guide the process. Thus, the skills to manage emergency surgical cases are still inadequate for all cadres of staff needed.

Currently, emergency medicine has not yet been formed as a separate subspecialty within most medical facilities in Ghana. Therefore, the workers are from different background specialization which makes it difficult for them to function as specialized emergency medical care experts. The programme on staffing standards by the MoH is not effectively implemented because of limited training for emergency care staff and the difficulty in moving staff from urban and more endowed areas to the rural areas as well difficulties in staff retention. A study by the NRSC in 2012 indicated that none of the health facilities could form the minimum of three teams required to handle fifteen (15) emergency cases simultaneously but the current situation is not known.

Therefore, there should be more focus on the intensification of training in the application of simple and effective strategies for all emergency medical staff in Ghana. There should be an institution of designated emergency centres with dedicated team and theatre for only emergencies within every medical facility in Ghana as proposed by the A&E guideline. Additional training outside the hospital could also be designed based on best practice examples and integrated into the curricula of the Institute of Public Health for specialist training.

Aside the formal training of emergency care teams, other medical personnel must be encouraged to take advantage of the nature of their work to acquire and retain important skills, know-how and experience in the management of emergency cases. This may in turn prove useful in times of crisis where conventionally trained emergency team members may not be available. Support in this respect could be provided through in-service training and regular drills by establishing trauma teams within existing medical facilities. This can go a long way to improve the emergency staffing capacity and capability needs for managing the RTC cases in the country.

Writing in the World Journal of Surgery in July 2014 Yeboah, Mock, Karikari, and others reported that a high proportion of trauma fatalities could have been prevented by decreasing pre-hospital delays, adequate resuscitation in hospital, and earlier initiation of care, including definitive surgical management in Ghana. It was suggested for, hospitals to look for causes both within and outside A & E departments in order to reduce delays in the patient journey.

The OECD (2017), also intimates that poor emergency quality care can be attributed to the absence of widespread periodical public reporting based on a standard set of quality indicators.

Widespread periodical public reporting based on a standard set of quality indicators should also be considered as a part of the emergency care system in Ghana.

ii. Leadership for Facility Based Emergency care: Medical facility-based emergency care must be under good leadership preferably a trained specialist e.g. emergency physician, a surgeon (orthopedic surgeon, neurosurgeon, and general surgeon), an anesthesiologists or specialists in intensive care. Such a leader is expected to be available on a 24-hour basis.

In Ghana, according to the A&E guidelines emergency departments are to be headed by an Emergency Physician (EP) in whose absence a Medical Practitioner with requisite skills in A&E shall replace. However, ineffective management structures and capacity to manage hospitals efficiently remains a challenge.

C. The administrative Profile: This is about best practice emergency care protocols required for medical based facilities. The concept is focused on comprehensive trauma management protocols described as follows:

i. Notification and Preparedness: It is required for medical facility-based emergency care departments to be equipped with communication systems for the receipt of advance notification about impending emergency cases to enable adequate time for preparations ahead of the arrival of emergency cases especially for situations of mass casualties.

In Ghana, this is often not done and such impromptu emergency victim arrivals at even higher order medical facilities with related challenges.

ii. Triage: Triaging is also required at the facility based medical centres based on the injured person's ability to walk, breathe and maintain a pulse, followed by a scored physiological assessment placing the victim in different categories with four (4) main categories being: (a) The Emergency Group (red); (b) the Urgent Group (yellow); (c) the Minor Injury Group (green) and (d) the Dead Group (black). The colour scheme used in identification may differ from one geographical region to the other. *The extent to which this is done in Ghana is yet to be ascertained from an authentic study.*

iii. Patient Registration: Demographic information of a patient is collected as a part of jurisdictional requirement through patient registration to provide records of unique identifiers of a patient whose identity is unknown before clinical assessment. This is to help support correct identification and to facilitate subsequent communication and follow up with the patient as well as relevant healthcare providers.

This is also done in Ghana however; the issue of payment often results in rejections and in some cases, patients get stacked in ambulances causing life- threatening conditions due to treatment refusals. This is because irrespective of the existence of the NHIS a registered emergency victim might not have proof of registration at the time of need and the practice of cash and carry is applied at the medical facility. This is often of high risk to the helpless RTC victim caught in the moments of the occurrence of RTC's. Thus, even a well- resourced person might not be in a position to fund an urgent medical care need when caught in a helpless situation of being in an emergency victim.

iv. Patient Assessment and Investigations: It involves prioritising and determining the nature of the injuries and preparing the patient for definitive care, be it within or outside the hospital. The protocol can be grouped into three (3) main stages as primary survey, secondary survey and definitive care. Each stage can also be grouped into Resuscitation and Investigations. The performance of resuscitation is done in a standard way for all patients regardless of their ability to pay. The activity of resuscitation ensures the immediate stabilization of the patient and does not focus on making a diagnosis. The investigations ensure that a diagnosis is made and the diagnosis made would guide further care.

v. Emergency Patient Referrals: Emergency patient referrals is about referring cases that are beyond a medical facility's capability and skills to a higher order medical care facility that can safely perform the required treatment through a set referral system.

Ghana has an emergency referral policy and it states that the district hospital should be the first referral hospital providing good clinical care and diagnosis services including surgery/ anaesthesia and other emergency care services. Where this is inadequate it should follow up to regional and teaching hospitals accordingly. However, in reality strict adherence is not ensured and patients are referred to the most available health facility for purposes of convenience when a referral is made. Poor information flow regarding inter-hospital transfer procedures also sometimes possesses a great challenge to emergency care givers at the receiving medical facilities.

vi. Patient Discharge: Patients not requiring hospital admission are screened, treated and discharged with written and verbal instructions regarding follow-up care through laid discharge processes on when to seek further assistance. Where appropriate, community option for follow up treatment is encouraged. The pre-discharge process includes consultation and authorization by an emergency physician or a delegated doctor in charge of the emergency department.

vii. Emergency Admissions: After conducting a triage at the emergency department, patients whose condition are deemed to require hospital treatment under observation are admitted for in-patient treatment based on the decision by an emergency physician or their delegate. Admission procedures are required to be done in accurate and timely manner from the outpatient department. This could be by direct admission from an outpatient unit or transfer from another hospital based on clinical criteria such as availability of a bed, equipment and medical experts. The admitting unit is responsible for the timely development a treatment plan and associated medication administration with consistent monitoring.

Ghana's emergency medical response policy also outlines a criterion for which an emergency medical case can be referred, admitted or discharged.

viii. Key Elements for Effective Clinical Care

a) Time Factor: It is required for facility-based emergency care to be characterized by minimized delays with recommended guidelines such as; (i) Availability of the attendance of a consultant within 30 minutes; (ii) Emergency theatre available within 30 minutes; (iii) CT scan available 24/7; (iv) Pathology service available 24/7 and agreed transfer protocols.

In Ghana, a study at the 37 Hospital by Aggrey Orleans J. (2019), revealed that majority (87.01%) had x-rays and laboratory investigations done in the first 48 hrs. at the A&E, however, the findings of some studies into the quality of emergency care system have found that, most of the health facilities are not well prepared to cope with the demands of emergency care and this impact on the quality of emergency care delivery.

b). Teamwork: Workers across the whole emergency care system are required to collaborate effectively, follow internal arrangements, respond to each other's needs, jointly follow laid treatment procedures, iron out problems, and complement each other during work operations with a common objective of saving the life of an injured victim in the emergency department. This is to be achieved through effective planning and organization of trained staff for effective work delivery (Burdett-Smith P, 1995).

In Ghana, there is also a lack of clarity in the definition of essential services by levels and types of emergency needs. This has resulted in limited and inequitable distribution of personnel in emergency centres coupled with knowledge and skill deficiencies among hospital staff. A study at the 37 Military Hospital in 2019 by Aggrey Orleans J. (2019) on emergency care revealed that a lack of trained personnel commonly resulted non-availability of in-service opportunities at night and during weekends. Aside this, essential items were also often not used when indicated despite being in stock due to the fact that they may not have been requested for or procured. Also, technicians often refused to move mobile technology from their home departments (e.g., portable X-ray, radiology; ultrasound) to the resuscitation area due to fear of 'wear and tear.'

Medical audit/assessment is one important tool that has been found to improve quality of care in many health institutions and very useful in changing health personnel's behavior, especially when linked to individualized feedback, (Piterman I, et al., 1997).

In the advanced countries, it is required for the conduct of care audits based on the presence and composition of trauma teams and their mobilization in case of emergency but this is yet to be done in Ghana.

c). Funding for Unplanned Medical Emergencies: Funding constraints remains a key issue in emergency health care at all levels of such care due to several factors.

In Ghana, a study by (Mock, 2014), revealed that every hospital was strained financially due to the following factors:

a. *Budgetary cuts and frequent fluctuations from Government funding putting a lot of pressure on limited available funds.*

b. *Poor cost recovery arrangements from the NHIS scheme since those who are insured with the NHIS are not totally covered for all hospital charges in relation to trauma care and untimely NHIS reimbursement rates.*

c. *The fundamental issues on estimating financing need for emergency care to be funded by the NHIS based on uniformed classification of the levels of treatment required.*

d. *Lack of modalities for cost sharing amongst levels of medical facilities including private hospitals who provide emergency care under the NHIS is not also well defined.*

e. *Poor financial management modalities to ensure maximum utilization of limited resources.*

According to Mock, due to these challenges medical facilities were unable to keep up with the demands on non-drug consumables neither were they able to repair broken equipment or conduct in-service trainings. Some recommendations for improving emergency care funding are:

• *Lobbying the health ministry and the ministry of finance for increased emergency health care funding.*

• *Practice of patient population-based funding allocation by matching sources of emergency care funding to expenditure so that the amount of money allocated at a level of use will be commensurate with the magnitude of need and the designated activities to be funded.*

• *Raising additional domestic funding by strengthening and encouraging firms and corporate entities to establish funding pools for the health care of their employees and encouraging individuals and households who are able to afford private health insurance to do so to ease pressure on central government funding sources.*

• *Recovery and recycling of initial corporate sponsored free emergency care schemes.*

- *Expansion of current arrangements for instant loan facilities for conscious RTC victims.*

- *Encouragement of private health insurance schemes aside the NHIS for those who are able to afford.*

f). Emergency Care Data: It is required for accurate and reliable emergency patient data to be collected and stored in a safe and secure manner for effective planning, equitable resource allocation, monitoring, quality assurance and auditing. A well-maintained hospital Information Technology (IT) service is recommended to ensure efficient information management systems.

In Ghana the situation varies with different health facilities but majority still operates manual data record keeping with related challenges.

g) Research Profile: It is required for a good emergency medical system to have consistent research support in order to improve service delivery.

In Ghana, various research studies in respect of emergency medical operations have been undertaken but the extent of application to upgrade emergency care services is not known.

7.8 POST-CRASH REHABILITATION AND INTEGRATION

According to Mayou R, et al (2002), RTC incidents can cause both physical injuries and also have psychological effects which in some cases might lead to permanent psychological disabilities such as post trauma stress disorder, major depressive disorder and anxiety disorders. It is estimated that about 90% of trauma victims who are temporarily or permanently rendered disabled are associated with RTCs, (Cartwright, 2017 and Rissanen et al 2017). The WHO (2013) also ranked injuries from RTC's as the 9th leading cause of disabilities worldwide and even projected it to become the 7th by 2030 for all age groups.

It is estimated that globally about 20 million are disabled each year from RTCs and also in LMICs where for every RTC related death, three (3) victims suffer permanent disability and many more dependents of these victims are affected socio economically, (Adogu, Llika, & Asuzu, 2011). These arise from loss of jobs, high cost of treatment and the potential harmful effect on the family's functioning. The rehabilitation of an RTC victim to enable them function normally and integrate well into society therefore identified as the final and an important stage of post-crash care.

7.8.1 Elements of the Rehabilitation Process:

A. Relevance of the RTC Victim Rehabilitation Process: Rehabilitation care helps a person to be as independent as possible in everyday activities and enables participation in education, work, recreation and meaningful life roles such as taking care of family rather than becoming a burden.

B. The Rehabilitation Process: Rehabilitation involves identifying an RTC victim's need for integration into society and the provision of the necessary support and assistance to enable them lead a normal life as much as possible. The process involves establishment of rehabilitation goals, planning and implementation of measures and assessment of its effects. This includes the identification of the type of service needed, its availability and where they are located.

C. Global Guidelines on Post-Crash Rehabilitation: In 2011, the first-ever World Report on Disabilities issued by WHO and the World Bank indicated that globally, an estimated 2.4 billion people are currently living with a health condition that benefits from rehabilitation. It outlined the scope of rehabilitation services available worldwide. In 2017, WHO also launched the Rehabilitation initiative for up to 2030 as follows:

i.   Improvement of leadership and governance for rehabilitation.

ii.   Establishment of a strong multidisciplinary rehabilitation workforce.

iii. Expansion of financing for rehabilitation.

iv.   Improvement of data collection and research on rehabilitation.

v.   Provision of technical support and building capacity at country level.

vi.   Prioritization and resource mobilization.

vii. Development of norms, standards and technical guidance.

viii. Shaping the research agenda and monitoring progress.

In Ghana, the rehabilitation workforce is made up of different health workers, including but not limited to physiotherapists, occupational therapists, speech and language therapists and audiologists, orthotics and prosthetics, clinical psychologists, physical medicine and rehabilitation doctors and rehabilitation nurses. However, there is very little knowledge of the degree of utilization of the knowledge for improved rehabilitation of RTC victims.

7.8.2 Principles of Rehabilitation

Some recommended principles for post-crash rehabilitation in literature such as Gopinath et al (2017) include the following:

• Survivors of RTC with a disability should be empowered to re-integrate into society.

• Rehabilitation must be voluntary for the victim though some may need support for choices.

- Those with impairments after RTC must have early treatment
- Demographic factors in terms of the type and degree of injury and pre health status of an RTC victim must inform how long injury recovery may take since younger people heal faster.
- Simple therapeutic strategies must be delivered through rehabilitation workers or taught to individuals with disabilities or a family member.
- Specific rehabilitation programmes must be tailored to an individual patient's need.
- Rehabilitation can include one or more types of therapy due to the type of physical and psychological barriers and how a person deals with such barriers.
- Information to guide good practice is essential for building capacity, strengthening rehabilitation systems and producing cost-effective services and better outcomes.

7.8.3 Forms of Rehabilitation and Integration Activities

The types of disabilities affecting crash survivors determine the forms of rehabilitation which are classified as physical, psychological and economic rehabilitation or social protection measures.

A. Physical Rehabilitation: Physical rehabilitation facilitates increased physical movement and enhance the strength and endurance of the body.

i. Types of Physical Rehabilitation: The types of physical rehabilitation measures include improving the body functioning through diagnosis and treatment of health conditions.

a). Convalescence that is the situation where an RTC victim may need physical assistance to move about as a part of the recovery process

b). Therapy involving the restoration of a deteriorating area of a person's body part through training, exercising and compensatory strategies such as education and counselling support.

c). Seeing a specialist with expertise in specific area of medicine required for special injury care.

d).Taking of Medication through prescription and complementary or herbal treatments.

e). Provision of financial assistance for the payment of the medical bills of patients experiencing financial difficulties.

f). Provision of assistive technologies for supportive of self-care including equipment used to increase, maintain, or improve the functional capabilities of individuals with disabilities to help them gain more independence. Examples are crutches, walking frames and braces prostheses, orthoses, wheel-chairs and tricycles for people with mobility impairments. Others are hearing aids and cochlear implants for those with hearing impairments; white canes, magnifiers, ocular devices, talking books, and software for screen magnification and reading for people with visual impairments. It also includes devices to support communication such as communication boards and speech synthesizers for people with speech impairments; as well as day calendars with symbol pictures for people with cognitive impairment.

g). Pain management for those with acute persistent pain through supportive services eg. home modification, organisation of caregivers, assistive products, medical supplies and support groups.

ii. Types of Care Managers for Physical Rehabilitation: These are as listed in Table 7.19.

Table 7.19: Types of Care Managers of Physical Rehabilitation

Case Manager	The role of case manager was introduced when managed care sought to save costs by streamlining care. Managed care initiated the use of external case managers—that is, clinicians, who do not provide direct care but who review and manage catastrophic cases with high costs to insurance companies and are employed or contracted by the insurer.17
Rehabilitation Nurse	Rehabilitation Nurses, is to assist individuals with disability and/or chronic illness to attain and maintain maximum function.16 The rehabilitation nurse, in addition to providing hands-on nursing care, is responsible for coordinating the educational activities. The rehabilitation nurse is teacher, caregiver, collaborator, and client advocate.
Physiotherapist	Treats patients who problem with pain or movement using physical techniques to improve movement, reduce pain and stiffness, speed up the healing process and increase quality of life.
Allied Health practitioners	Allied health practitioners are trained health professionals who may work as part of the rehabilitation team by bringing many different skills to the care team and they include prosthetics and orthotics, psychology, neuropsychology, Chiropractors, osteopaths, medical radiation practitioners
Social workers	Social workers provide assistance to those in crisis and in need of support through counselling, information and referrals to other services

In Ghana, physiotherapy by Prostheses and Orthoses (P&O) services are provided even at small or intermediary health facility. Detail and routine training and care for persons with disability, illness, postoperative and post illness to evolve, maintain, and enhance development potential and functional ability throughout the lifespan is provided. Examples of external facilities providing. P&O services in Ghana includes the Orthopaedic Training Center (OTC) in Nsawam – Adoagyiri Municipality of the Eastern Region of Ghana and the National Prosthetic and Orthotics Center (NPOC). These cover transtibial prostheses, transfemoral prosthesis, chopart, splints, clutches, callipers among others.

According to a study by Aduayom A. (2018) independent access by disabled persons is yet to be attained in the country due to challenges with prosthetic and orthotic education in Ghana with the services characterized by lack of trained professionals, lack of infrastructure, lack of materials, and machines including motions analysis devices for outcome measurements etc.

Also, physical accessibility remains a challenge for most disabled person in the effort to integrate into society due to lack of provision for accessible environment due to infrastructure barriers in, public buildings, existence of open gutters and drainage systems etc. Others are difficulties in the payment of medical bills by affected persons. Some interventions include the benevolence of well-wishers bearing part of the cost and occasional government intervention as presented in Figure 7.35).

Government Settles Bills of Dompoase accident victims

Figure 7.35: Government Intervention on Settlement of RTC Victim's Medical Bills

B. Psychological rehabilitation: This is to prevent psychological distress and the risk of victims developing psychological disability.

i. Types of Psychological Impacts and Rehabilitation Support Services Required: RTC injury victims may have to manage emotional and mental health difficulties years after the initial injury (Nasirian et al, 2018). These includes major depressive disorder; adjustment disorder; post-traumatic stress disorder; acute stress disorder (which is another form of anxiety disorder associated with stress) and depression (Vincent et al, 2015). However, Cuijpers et al, (2018) observed a worrying situation in the fact that a vast number of individuals with mental health disorders in LMICs do not get suitable treatment.

ii. Treatment options for Psychological Rehabilitation: These include:

a). Application of counselling for emotional support.

b). Provision of psychological support for families to enable cope better with a victim's situation.

c). Provision of emotional care support systems such as creation of supporter network of social workers and psychologists.

iii. Types of Care Managers for Psychological rehabilitation: These are as listed in Table 7.20.

Table 7.20: Types of Care Managers for Psychological rehabilitation

Case Manager	The role of case manager was introduced when managed care sought to save costs by streamlining care. Managed care initiated the use of external case managers—that is, clinicians, who do not provide direct care but who review and manage catastrophic cases with high costs to insurance companies and are employed or contracted by the insurer.17
Psychologists	Experts in human behavior who have studied how the mind works and how people think, react and behave
Social workers	Social workers provide assistance to those in crisis and in need of support through counselling, information and referrals to other services

Ghana has a mental Health Act 2012 (Act 846) and all teaching hospitals provide physiotherapy and psychological counselling services as part of medical care. There are also specialist service centre's that facilitates such processes. In Ghana, a study by Assah Yaw Augustine (2020), observed that the psychosocial problems resulting from physical trauma sustained in RTCs in the country is not well established and goes further to make the following recommendations:

- *Clinicians should routinely assess all trauma victims for possible development and symptoms of psychological problems, whilst managing their physical problems.*

- *Clinicians working on trauma victims should liaise with other care providers such as mental health nurses and clinical psychologists to conduct intermittent comprehensive checks.*

- *Psychosocial assessment must be done on patients with RTC injuries, especially those that result in major disabilities and/or may require prolonged hospitalization.*

- *General practitioners at emergency and orthopaedic wards should work hand in hand with the family members and other significant people of the injured victim to promote good psychosocial wellbeing.*

- *Nurses who work on outpatient should also assess for psychosocial problems during visit of injured patients since some OPD patients may also be at risk for psychosocial problems.*

- *Since personnel responding to a crash provide a sense of order and security at the scene, they can also be trained to identify individuals at greatest risk for acute psychological stress.*

- *Psychologists rehabilitation must be integrated with the public health system since the quiet physical environment in hospitals can facilitate the recovery process, (See Figure 7.36).*

Figure 7.36: Publication on Psychological Care for RTC Victims

C. Economic or Social Protection Measures: According to the (WHO, 2016), survivors and families affected by RTC's have a wide range of economic needs which they must be compensated for in order to achieve security in the face of vulnerabilities. Also lack of appropriate education and training makes it impossible for persons with disabilities to take advantage of policies and programmes meant to increase their participation in the labour market, (Curtis j. & Brading j. 2001) and occupational, compensation, financial and other support services are proposed.

The policy context for Economic and Social Protection Measure is critical and in Ghana, the process is supported by a wide range of policy provisions including the following:

i.   *The Social Security Act 1965 which provides a provident fund scheme, lump sum payment for old age as well as invalidity and survivor's benefits for those on the scheme.*

ii. *The amended section of the above into the Social Security Law 1991 which converts the Provident Fund Scheme to a Pension Scheme (SSNIT).*

iii. *The National Health Insurance Scheme (NHIS) 2003 which introduced a contribution scheme for Health Insurance purposes.*

iv. *The Ghana School Feeding Programme (GSFP) 2005 which provides one hot meal a day for every schoolchild in Government school.*

v.   *The National Social Protection Strategy (NSPS) 2007 with several social Protection programmes such as the Livelihood Empowerment Against Poverty (LEAP) 2008 involving Social Cash Transfers and free health insurance membership for the vulnerable people*

vi. *The Youth Employment Agency (YEA) Act 887 and the Council for Technical and Vocational Education and Training (COTVET) Act 718.*

vii. *Persons with Disability Act, 2006 (Act 715) in ratification of the United Nation's Standard Rules on the Equalization of Opportunities for Disabled, (United Nations, 1993 and The Ghana Legal Aid Scheme Act 1997 (Act 542)*

i. Occupational Rehabilitation: Both minor and major injuries can cause an RTC victim to lose or forgo their regular employment or cause them to take time from work with some unable to return to former line of work. Those who lack the necessary knowledge, skills, and abilities, needed for the available jobs in the competitive marketplace are mostly also found wanting (Atkins D. & Guisti C. 2001). Occupational rehabilitation for RTC victims may require training/retraining in necessary skills for jobs or change of jobs to provide for their financial needs and ensure their economic independence and it includes the following:

a). Vocational Training: vocational rehabilitation is provided to assist in the learning of new job skills that can help a person to get a new job or start a business. This is because most employers entertain prejudices and misconceptions about disability among employees and tries to avoid the cost of providing reasonable accommodation, inaccessible infrastructure and information on job vacancies to such, (The Disability Act, Act 715. 2006). Dankwa A. L. (2013), recommends for it to be seen as urgent and should be made to complement general education.

In Ghana, special education/rehabilitation facilities on vocational training and vocational rehabilitation are available in different parts of the country. They provide free courses in various trades such as carpentry, tailoring, masonry, blacksmithing, mechanical, electronics, printing and spraying, shoemaking, chalk making, home crafts production (dress-making, kente cloth weaving and dyeing, farming, poultry production, shoe-making and tailoring etc. These are available in both urban and rural centres.

Examples are the Industrial Rehabilitation Center in Accra which offers training in skills such as rug- and bag making, copy-typing, carpentry, metal work and other trades and The Vocational Training Rehabilitation Center in Biriwa in the central region which offers skill training in construction, metal work and wood carving, with emphasis on rural and self-employment for urban and rural scenarios respectively. In addition, there are also programmes such as the National Youth Employment Programme; Integrated Agricultural Support Programme. However, a study by Botchie, Ahadzie, (2004) revealed the following key challenges:

- *There is duplication of training activities for the same target groups with so many trained in certain crafts with limited market opportunities at the expense of others.*

- *There is no underlying curriculum with rigid start and end dates for practical skills.*

- *The training is also not integrated into other support measures so is of limited impact.*

- *It reaches only a limited number of beneficiaries due to poor training facilities, limited and untrained staff and significant geographic distance from clients.*

- *In some respect, there is a degree of disconnect and lack of responsiveness to such programmes due to indigenous culture*

Some recommendations to address these challenges include:

- *There is a need to increase socio-economic prospects and labour market access for disabled trainees.*

- *There is a need to refurbish, retool and upgrade most of the existing formal vocational and technical training institutions with staff capacity development.*

b) Categories of occupational care managers: The categories of care givers and their roles in occupational rehabilitation are as listed in Table 7.21.

Table 7.21: Occupational Care Managers

Case Managers	The role of case manager was introduced when managed care sought to save costs by streamlining care. Managed care initiated the use of external case managers-that is, clinicians, who do not provide direct care but who review and manage catastrophic cases with high costs to insurance companies and are employed or contracted by the insurer.
Occupational therapists:	They provide support to people whose health or disability makes it hard for them to do the things they would like to do by identifying their strengths and difficulties and helping with solutions that enables them to take part in everyday life.
Social workers	Social workers provide assistance to those in crisis and in need of support through counselling, information and referrals to other services

In Ghana, these include government institutions, public sector vocational training institutes for the disabled, integrated community centres for employable skills, local NGOs, church agencies, private institutions using the apprenticeship system on the job training and skills training. Specifically, the key Government Institutions include the following:

- *The Ministry of Health, the Ministry of Labour (Social Welfare, Community Development and Cooperatives), and the Ministry of Education and Culture have primary responsibility for servicing and educating disabled persons in Ghana.*

- *The Ministry of Labour maintains overall responsibility for the vocational rehabilitation of disabled persons while working with other ministries, Ghana's Employers Association and the Trade Union Congress.*

- *The council for Technical and Vocational Education and Training (COTVET) collaborates with other stakeholders to give skills to Persons with Disabilities (PWDs).*

ii. Rehabilitation by Compensation: After an RTC situation, there can be a legal sequel that can impair reintegration of a crash victim into work and family life, (WHO, 2016). These include the following:

a). Payment of Insurance, Compensation, claims and finances: It involves financial compensation after an RTC e.g., insurance for medical services and compensation for pain and suffering which makes up a good portion of any personal injury claim. This helps to relieve the stress over a loss of earnings brought about by injury and the effect on the family. It might include legal assistance for the payment of insurance premiums, replacement of vehicle and damaged property.

In Ghana, an example is the National Disability Insurance Scheme (NDIS) which supports people with disability access funds to enable them achieve their goals and participate fully in community life (See Figure 7.37).

Follow up to make insurance claims upon accidents – Insurance expert

Figure 7.37: A Publication on Insurance Claims after RTCs

b). Compensation for Loss of Physical Abilities: This maybe done through the introduction to the use of aids or wheelchairs,

These are also applied in Ghana, (See Figure 7.38).

Mps demand financial support for Kintampo accident survivors

Figure 7.38: A publication on Demand for Compensation for RTC Victims

c). Financial Assistance: In Ghana, persons with disabilities are being assisted economically by the Municipal Assembly through the allocation of three percent (3%) from the District Assembly Common Fund (DACF). The fund is generated from government subventions which the government transfers to all Metropolitan, Municipal, and District Assemblies (MMDAs) every quarter. These are normally provided to persons with disabilities as start-up capital to help them start businesses to earn income and MMDAs make provisions for the activities of persons with disabilities through their internally generated funds.

iii. Support from Programmes on Social Protection: In Ghana, in addition to the above there are also formal and informal social protection systems as follows.

a). Formal Support Structures: Examples are

- *Supplementary Feeding Programme.*
- *Capitation Grant for free education.*
- *Microfinance Schemes.*
- *Emergency Management Schemes.*
- *Livelihood Empowerment against Poverty (LEAP) Social Grant Scheme.*
- *National Health Insurance Scheme (NHIS).*

b). Access to healthcare: The right to healthcare is fundamental to all persons including persons.

In Ghana under the Disability Act (Act 75) the provision of free healthcare (general and specialist care) for persons with disabilities should be free. However, this is challenging for them to access since the NHIS is not clear on the procedure in identifying eligibility.

c). Assistance with Formal Education: These services are provided to both children and adults with disabilities who are not able to enrol in basic schools due to rigid curriculum, architectural barriers such as inaccessible rigid school buildings, inaccessible transportation, long distance to school, inadequate special educators and many more which need the assistance of others.

In Ghana, the special education division of the GES has been piloting inclusive education in schools for those with disabilities to enable them get access to formal education. However, the extent to which this has benefit disabled people is not known but rather such activities are mostly undertaken by religious bodies and NGOs.

d). Institutional Structures for Managing Social Protection Schemes: In Ghana, it includes the following:

- *MMDA's have some responsibility for the welfare of persons with disabilities through the management of the disability common fund that is taken from the District Assemblies' Common Fund (DACF) to assist persons with disabilities to improve on their wellbeing.*

The DACF is a pool of resources created under Article 252 of the 1992 Constitution of Ghana. It is a minimum of 5.0% of the national revenue set aside to be shared among all MMDAs.

• *Department of Social Welfare and Community Development (DSWC): The Social Welfare and Community Development Department exist to facilitate the mobilization and use of available human and material resources to improve the living standards of individuals, groups, families and communities within an effectively decentralized system of administration. It also prevents and responds to social exclusion and maladjustment needs at all levels.*

e). Challenges with Formal Social Support Systems: These include the following in Ghana:

• *There is poor data on persons with disabilities and it is suggested for the MMDAs send information to all their constituents to bring their wards with disabilities for a census.*

• *Though some rehabilitation services are available it is characterized by fragmented uncoordinated systems which makes it difficult for victims to know where to go for what kind of support, (See Figure 7.39).*

Figure 7.39: Publication on a Call for the Welfare of RTC Victim's by the National Insurance Commission (NIC)

• *Inadequate information flow and excessive bureaucracy from service providers to the disability causes, stressful, and frustrating situations which restricts accessibility to the services and programmes so there is therefore a need to reduce excessive bureaucracy.*

• *Delays in Accessing Support from the NHIA for the medical services remain a challenge since victims have to wait for three months after their registration to receive their insurance card and to benefit from the scheme. The premium is also being deemed to be high.*

• *It is also of the view that what is given to the persons with disabilities is not enough to sustain them and prevent them from continued dependence on family and government support. It is also irregular. There is also a lack of an alignment of the different measures and there is a need for harmonizing various support arrangements to include persons with disabilities.*

• *A stronger disability movement is deemed necessary for the integration of persons with disabilities into mainstream society and it should engage actively with government, CSOs and society as a whole to advocate for themselves.*

iv. Informal Support Structures: These are based on traditional social protection systems such as the following:

a) Support from family members and Friends: These include family members, friends and community members who assist with material support, food, clothing, cash remittances and cash donations as well as some physical assistance when the need be. This is because they are the first contact for persons with disabilities with regards to everyday assistance. However, even though the family is supposed to give the highest support irrespective of the difficulty in coping with a disabled person in the house the structure is being weakened due to urbanization and migration.

b). Nongovernmental Organisations (NGOs): These include various groups of persons who work together to create awareness about the capabilities of persons with disabilities and also to promote equal opportunities for them through advocacy, lobbying, and collaborating with other relevant stakeholders to improve on their wellbeing).

c). Religious/Faith-based Organizations: Religious organisations, from churches and mosques provide support from churches in the form of clothing, food, to mention but a few to disabled people. These could also be in the form of NGOs.

d). Community Based Rehabilitation Services (CBRs): CBRs are used to promote positive attitudes towards people with disabilities at the community level. In Ghana the Ministry of Employment and Social Welfare initiated a national CBR programme in 1992 for persons with disabilities in Ghana. It was a collaborative effort between the ministries of Employment and Social Welfare, Health and Education. The major goals of the programme were:

- *To promote the human rights of persons with disabilities by raising awareness and mobilizing resources in the districts and communities.*
- *To establish links between service providers in health, education, community development and social welfare.*
- *To strengthen associations of disabled persons.*
- *To develop a National Policy on Disability and appoint a National Advisory Committee on Disability*

Its key activities included awareness-raising through social counselling to families and individual persons with disabilities, provision of rehabilitation and support services, provision of income maintenance and social security through apprenticeships facilitation using a revolving loan fund amongst others.

v. Combination of the Formal and Informal Social Protection Systems: The two systems often coexist in most communities in Ghana due to the need for multidisciplinary rehabilitation services. Social work is multi-sectoral and requires participation from a range of govern-ment and nongovernmental stakeholders. This is done through collaborative efforts between various ministries, Departments, and agencies; and a guideline for vertical and horizontal collaboration has been developed by the Inter-Service and Sectoral Collaboration and Co-Operation System (ISCCS). A draft guideline on collaboration that extends beyond MMDAs to include other institutions is being validated.

vi. Also of high importance is the need to protect the economically vulnerable in society who are forced by circumstances to beg for alms for their upkeep in traffic. This is especially with regards to children and disabled persons who mingle with traffic on the road for alms at the risk of their life. Deliberate attention should be given to such people to enable then benefit from the social protection systems.

7.9 CONCLUSION

In Ghana, efficient and effective post-crash care remains a challenge and not much is known about the psycho-social and economic burden of post the RTC period for victims. This is because multidisciplinary services available to meet the different aspects of post-crash reha-bilitation needs are very fragmented and not well understood. Therefore, the management of post-crash to optimize survival rate requires, systematic re-organisation of existing systems and structures both formal and informal to meet the extent of need. There should therefore be intensive research into all aspects to achieve this purpose. Also, on the way forward an in-depth rehabilitation research and the effectiveness of care interventions currently available must be conducted to inform on the measures that should be put in place to ensure effective post-crash rehabilitation care in the country so as to avoid incidence of the narrative below

Woman disfigured in tragic accident begs for financial aid to undergo surgery: "Madam Peace Negble Adzaho left her home in Teshie on August 29, 2015 to Teacher Mantey, a small town lying between Nsawam and Suhum. As a businesswoman who traded in corn, she goes on this trip on regular basis. What was meant to be one of such fruitful business trips turned out tragic. She became a victim of a horrific accident when the vehicle in which she was travelling knocked down a pedestrian. The commercial car flipped over leaving occupants severely wounded, some beyond recognition. The accident on that day has maimed Madam Peace and rendered her disabled. Her face is disfigured and part of the lower side of her body, arms and shoulder, badly scarred. Five years after this tragic accident, she is seeking financial assistance to correct her deformity.

The 59-year-old tells freelance journalist and blogger, Selorm Helen that she has difficulty eating and thus, has to swallow every food, including fish. According to her, the pain becomes unbearable whenever she tries to open her mouth to eat or talk. She said, "I fear to eat and I don't eat in public because I have to raise my head before I put food in my mouth. It hurts and makes me shy in the midst of others," To help Madam Peace Negble Adzaho, please get in touch with the writer via email: selormhelen25@gmail.com, +233240791289, General News of Friday, 4 September 2020, Source: Selorm, Helen-Contributor.

CHAPTER 8

ROAD SAFETY EDUCATION (RSE)

"My people perish for lack of knowledge (Hosea 4:6) but the excellency of knowledge is, that wisdom giveth life to them that have it. (Ecclesiastes 7 12)"

8.1 INTRODUCTION

Road safety education (RSE) entails awareness creation to promote knowledge and understanding to address road user ignorance and functional limitations to avert traffic safety risks. According to Rose (2005), it is also about the development of the technical know-how of experts for the scientific application of road safety skills and abilities necessary to address human error in the road traffic system.

Integrated into all the road safety pillars, it is deemed as the single road safety intervention factor which affords a common channel by which all aspects of road safety can be addressed. Under pillar 1- Road Safety Management an example of RSE is education in traffic regulations under pillar 2- Safe Mobility an example is education in the conduct of road safety audit; under pillar 3 - Safe vehicles an example is training in vehicle inspections; under pillar 4- Safer Road Users examples are education in effects of impaired driving; speeding control etc. and under pillar 5- Post-Crash Care an example is training in First Aid application.

Thus, RSE is progressively engaged by all countries to promote knowledge and understanding of road traffic safety. In Ghana, RSE is also an important road safety activity mostly engaged by the NRSA itself but sustained road safety cultural change is yet to be attained. This section of the book discusses the components of RSE, the level of its development, the extent of its influence and requirements for strengthening RSE efforts for enhanced road safety progression in the country.

8.1.1 Theories and Principles of RSE

Human behaviour in traffic is complex due to wide variations in mobility objectives, perceptions, risk taking, attitudes to road traffic task, cultural differences, confronted pressures etc. These factors influence what road users actually do in traffic and the related safety consequence. Due to this, wrongful road user behavior is considered as the main risk factor in road traffic crash (RTC) causation making it the core target of RSE. It is within this context that some theories on how people choose to cope with the demands of the traffic system have been propounded as basis for determining the modes of social control necessary for shaping good road safety behavior through RSE. A brief overview of these theories in the context of road user practices in Ghana and the corresponding RSE needs are provided as follows:

A. The Theory of Reasoned Action and Theory of Planned Behaviour: The Theory by Fishbein and Ajzen, (1975) stipulates that road user behaviour is determined by peoples' intention irrespective of their knowledge level of road safety. They are those who know traffic rules but disobey them when they are in a hurry or the circumstances do not favour them.

Examples in Ghana, are trotro drivers who load and off load passengers in traffic rather than park off the road in order to maintain their position in the traffic queue by disregarding the safety of the passenger who embarks or disembarks in traffic at some safety risk. RSE in such situations must focus on the need for drivers to be responsible road users at all times.

B. The Theory of Interpersonal Behaviour by Triandis, (1977): It states that road user behaviour may be influenced by the fact that some bad habits that may have been formed have become automatic processes rather than intentional acts.

In Ghana, examples are drivers who try to circumvent traffic during congestions by driving on the road shoulder in order to be ahead of other drivers with little care for pedestrians using the shoulders as walkway.

C. The Health Belief Models (HBM) Theory by Rosenstock 1966): The theory describes road users who try to avoid a negative health outcome in traffic based on perceived threats.

In Ghana, examples are drivers who stop on impulse for pedestrians especially children at undesignated road sections with little consideration for the action of other drivers especially on multi-lane roads where the unaware other driver may fail to stop and cause an RTC.

D. Theories explaining social persuasion views: These are focused on the use of persuasion as a means of forming or changing attitudes. The first is (a) the

Elaboration-Likelihood Model by (Petty & Cacioppo, 1986); identifies two routes of persuasion by which attitudinal change may occur as central and peripheral routes based on the extent of motivation as determined by an individual's sense of importance of given information. Others are the level of personal responsibility, ability to comprehend and process campaign messages by judging, evaluating and linking the content to information already stored in their memory.

The second is the Associative-Propositional Evaluation Model (APE) by (Gawronski B. S & Bodenhausen, G. V. 2009) which is a dual attitude model evaluated to be implicit or explicit whereby implicit attitudes require incremental changes and the explicit attitude requires changes to new beliefs/knowledge or by additional consideration of existing beliefs/knowledge.

In Ghana, an example includes drivers who believe that alcohol and substance use are positive boosters for better driving ability rather than an impairment to safe driving. Popularly referred to as "For the Road" it is not uncommon for a driver to go for a drink just before take-off especially for long distance travel. It is also common to see kiosks in which alcoholic beverages are sold at lorry stations and transport terminals, though the NRSA has called for a ban of such situations.

E. Road user behaviour theories that explain the process of behaviour change:
These theories provide insight into why a desired behaviour has not occurred. The first is the Theory of Self-Regulation which describes the way in which individuals change their behaviour based on the concept of negative feedback by comparing their current situation with a goal (attainment or avoidance) or reference situation, (Carver & Scheier, 1981). The second is the Trans theoretical Model of Change which considers the readiness of the individual to change their behaviour and outlines six stages of change before a new behaviour can be established as pre-contemplation, contemplation, preparation, action and maintenance. (Prochaska and DiClemente, 1983). The approach to RSE includes the use of feedback of context analysis of driver behaviour as basis for influencing bad behaviours positively.

In Ghana, this includes drivers/riders who disregard and undermine the importance of the use of vehicle restraints such as seatbelts and helmets with the thought that nothing will happen to them.

F. Theories based on social norms: The theories suggest that behavior is influenced by (often inaccurate) perceptions of how other members of their social group think and behave by Yanovitzky (2004).

In Ghana, these include drivers who race each other by indulging in excessive speeding in order to be ahead of the other for more passengers. Others are those with the habit of jumping red lights with the consequent impact of hitting complying drivers in front of them on assumption that they were going to do the same.

(a) Situations where individuals are motivated to process a message if it is viewed as personally relevant or if they feel a high level of personal or social responsibility regarding the behavior are described as the Elaboration-Likelihood Model by Wundersitz et al. (2010);

In Ghana, examples are those who believe that RTC's are spiritually motivated rather than human, road and vehicles errors so fail to value any form of RSE.

(b) Fear-based campaigns which capitalizes on human fears using the negative consequences of risky behaviours by SWOV (2009). This includes the posting of gory RTC scenes on hazardous road sections in order to serve as a deterrent to motorist in order to avoid RTC's. However, research into fear appeals have revealed that they strategies do not have an effect on risky driving attitudes.

In Ghana, there are no examples of the use of gory pictures except for the skeleton sign and the signs post indicating records of fatalities at particular road sections. Others are campaign messages such as 'over speeding kills', 'kill your speed before your speed kills you' and 'better to reach home in peace than in pieces' etc. However, its impact is not well researched.

(c) Visual, Auditory, Kinesthetic (VAK) model: This states that certain individuals are better able to learn new information depending on how it is disseminated i.e., seeing it, hearing it or touching it by Fleming, N. (1987). This theory has greatly influenced the use of modern systems such as simulations to upgrade driver training methods.

In Ghana, some post campaign road safety evaluations by the NRSA have often rated seeing and hearing as the most impacting modes of RSE.

Commenting on the theories, Delhomme et al. (2009) expressed the view that there are no fundamental differences between the theories and neither are they mutually exclusive from practical applications. Thus, RSE is not done on the basis of behavioral science but rather it is done with the assumption that once people are informed on the right thing to do, they will conform and change from negative behaviors. As such, they concluded that there is no complete model of how people behave so effective RSE must be guided by data and situational dynamics.

In Ghana though a study has been conducted into road user behavioral patterns and related impacts on RTC's, the findings have not been well disseminated and the extent of its applied influence on RSE is not known. (See Figure 8.1).

Ghana News Agency Home Social Business Education Entertainment Science Health

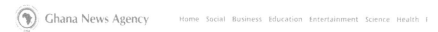

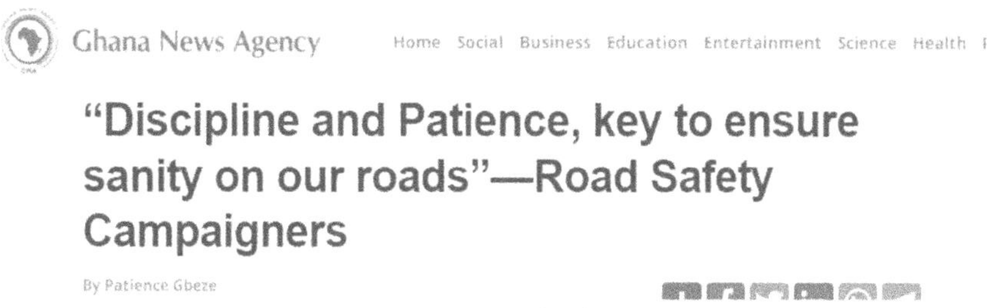

"Discipline and Patience, key to ensure sanity on our roads"—Road Safety Campaigners

By Patience Gbeze

Figure 8.1: Perception on Key Road Safety Campaign Focus

8.1.2 Principles of Road Safety Education

Some key underlying principles which must be considered for RSE interventions include the following:

A. Social Norms: Since social norms have significant effect on the way people behave, insights into human behaviour are essential for behaviour modification through RSE.

For example, in Ghana, consideration must be given to the acceptance of use of tree branches and leaves as indicators of broken-down vehicles as a standard norm alongside the use of a reflector triangle since leaves are very available and most drivers do not have triangles). The arguments for and against such a move on the basis of lack of reflection from the leaves can be justified on the ground that a line of leaves in the night can be seen from the vehicle headlights.

B. RSE Implementation: RSE must provide the road user with the necessary knowledge and skills to integrate into the traffic system in a safe way by being able to react appropriately and timely manner to avoid casualties in risky traffic situations.

For example, in Ghana, it should be a requirement for every commercial driver to be trained in defensive driving.

C. Integration of RSE into all Road Safety Components: Effective RSE must be combined with other road safety measures in a holistic approach.

In Ghana, traffic enforcement could be combined with road user education in addition to being penalised as it is sometimes done to enlighten the road user on the right thing to do.

D. Education and Training of RSE staff: There is need for adequate expert capacity of the trainers in the field of road safety who will in turn train others to facilitate RSE processes.

In Ghana, there are examples such as training of trainers in different jurisdictions e.g. training of driver's instructors who in turn train drivers. However, situations such as the

challenge of informally trained drivers training others by passing on wrongful behaviour must be avoided.

F. RSE Outputs and Outcomes: RSE must be well targeted and should provide the road user with the knowledge that will help them with lifetime traffic safety practice. However, it should not lead the road user to become overconfident about their ability to cope with hazardous traffic.

In Ghana, high records of RTC casualties in clear weather and on straight road sections with good ride quality indicates some level of driver over confidence which must be addressed.

G. Life Time Learning: RSE must be a continuous activity since RTC is a recurring phenomenon in any society.

In Ghana, though, this is well acknowledged, there are challenges with resource availability for achieving this purpose.

8.1.3 Key Elements of Road Safety Education

Road safety education can be classified into different categories as follows:

A. Formal and Informal Learning: The approach to RSE can be formal that is within a classroom setting and informal such as fun educational activities.

In Ghana, both approaches are applied in the form of classroom training for school pupils as well as informal public education on the streets, (See Figure 8.2).

Figure 8.2: Road Safety Sessions in Ghana

B. Group or Individual Road Safety Educational Practices: It is perceived that group training in RSE is superior to individual training because it allows for interactions amongst peers and also facilitates positive influence of one participant over another. *In Ghana, both individual and group RSE sessions are applied (See Figure 8.3).*

Figure 8.3: Examples of Group and Individual Road Safety Education Sessions

C. Technology based and non-Technology based RSE Programmes: Hoekstra and Wegman (2011), suggests for RSE campaigns to test technology-assisted versus non-technology methods because it is increasingly becoming clear that technological applications have better advantages over non technology assisted methods.

Ghana is gradually advancing towards the use of technology assisted methods in RSE such as the use of simulators and driving instructors in driver training but these are yet to be evaluated to determine its comparative advantages.

D. Primary and secondary objectives of RSE Programmes: RSE educational programmes are distinguished by primary objectives which are directly related to the ultimate goal of RSE and secondary objectives which facilitates the process of achieving the ultimate goal.

In Ghana, core RSE activities are undertaken on their own merit whilst it is also sometimes used to complement other activities such as training in the use of road safety installations on roads.

E. Theoretical and Practical Road Safety Education: In RSE both theoretical and practical training (in real traffic situations), are provided in order to develop knowledge and skill. However, according to Schagen & Rothengater (1997) practical RSE training is most effective, so RSE training should be more practically focused.

In Ghana, both practical and theoretical RSE approaches are applied depending on specific factors, (See Figure 8.4).

Figure 8.4: Theoretical and practical road safety education for students and pupils

F. Sufficient and Insufficient Training: Since it cannot be concluded that a person has received sufficient training, road safety education must be a continuous process. *For example, in Ghana refresher training for drivers can be institutionalised to achieve such a goal.*

G. Combination of RSE with other Road Safety Measures: RSE is more effective if it is embedded in a wider strategy to continuously engage with road users. A meta-analysis by Elvik et al. (2009) on this showed that the effects of mass media campaigns alone are small, especially when compared to the effects of campaigns combined with other measures.

In Ghana, combined road safety methods such as the use of mass media education and the conduct of drills are sometimes applied. (See Figure 8.5).

Figure 8.5: Combinations of Road Safety Education and Enforcement Sessions

8.2 POLICIES AND REGULATIONS ON RSE

8.2.1 Global Standards, Regulations and Guidelines on RSE

Some global policy guidelines on RSE and the level of applicability in Ghana are as summarised in Table 8.1.

Table 8.1: Summary of Global Guidelines on Road Safety Education

Global Standards	Description	Applicability in Ghana
Convention 1968	Article 3: Obligations of the Contracting Parties 5 bis. -Contracting Parties will take the necessary measures to ensure that road safety education be provided on a systematic and continuous basis, particularly in schools at all levels.	Applied in Ghana
DOA	Pillar 4: Safer road users -Safer road users: Turn road safety training, education and behavior into knowledge management -Develop comprehensive programmes to improve road user behavior. -Ensure sustained or increased enforcement of laws and standards, combined with public awareness/education to increase seat-belt and helmet wearing rates, and to reduce drink-driving, speed and other risk factors	Applied in Ghana with the exception of aspect of knowledge management

Global Standards	Description	Applicability in Ghana
	Pillar: Safer Roads: Activity 5-Encourage capacity building and knowledge transfer in safe infrastructure by: -creating partnerships with development banks, national authorities, civil society, education providers and the private sector to ensure safe infrastructure design principles are well understood and applied; -promoting road safety training and education in low-cost safety engineering, safety auditing and road assessment; and -developing and promoting standards for safe road design and operation that recognize and integrate with human factors and vehicle design.	Applied in Ghana with the exception of aspect on integration into road design which is done on a limited scale and that of vehicle design which is not done at all
SafetyNet African Decade of Action	-Raise awareness through education and campaigns -Educate the General Public (Road Users) -Establish/strengthen school clubs -Undertake & intensify safety awareness campaign -Develop national communication framework -Include Road Safety in school curricula; -Produce and distribute standardized road safety educational and awareness materials for schools -Support the implementation of road safety education in all primary schools -Harmonize Road Safety in school curricula at the Sub-regional level;	Applied in Ghana Applied in Ghana

8.2.2 RSE Policy in Ghana

Ghana's policy on RSE is that the Government will make increased efforts to promote awareness through education, about the seriousness of the road traffic crash problems, its social and economic implications and the necessity to curb the rising menace of road traffic crashes. This will encourage various stakeholders to play their rightful role in promoting road safety. The key road safety policy challenges, the strategies to address them and the status of application in Ghana are as summarised in Table. 8.2.

Table 8.2: Road Safety Education Policy in Ghana

Theme	Challenge	Strategy	Status of Application
Road Safety Campaigns	-Little or no safety awareness exist among most communities. -Poor response and commitment to current road safety programmes and activities. -So far, messages of road safety programmes and activities have been concentrating on moral appeals rather than strong socio-economic impact	-Raise awareness of the socio-economic implications of road traffic crashes to all levels of society. -Create a sense of shared responsibility and accountability from liable agencies among the populace. -Enlighten various road user groups with respect to their roles and responsibilities for minimizing road traffic crashes. -Raise awareness among key decision and policy makers. -Incorporate road safety education at all levels of the educational system	-Socio economic implications of RTC not well disseminated to the public
Professional Training	-Transport Industry- -Lack of organized training to facilitate continuous professional education for operators	-No concrete strategies were defined in the policy framework	-Idea of refresher courses for commercial started on a limited scale

Theme	Challenge	Strategy	Status of Application
Training	-The Driver- Professional education to upgrade the levels of expertise and competence of drivers is virtually non-existence and where available most drivers do not attend any periodic re- training or refresher courses to upgrade their driving skills.	-Institute and legalise appropriate requirements for upgrading the knowledge, skills and capability of drivers through continuous education and refresher courses	-The process is yet to be backed by a legal instrument
	-Pedestrian Safety and Vulnerable Road Users - Inadequacy in road safety education	-Institute measures to ensure a sustainable road safety education programme for pedestrians and VRUs.	-Sustainable education is subject to funding availability
Capacity development	-Human Resource Development for Road Safety- -There are no specialized courses that have been structured to provide training for road safety -There is no structured road safety education for teachers from the basic level through to the tertiary level. -Inability of the road safety sub-sector to retain the few professionals who are trained for road safety work.	-Ensure adequate road safety capacity development at all levels of society for effective promotion and implementation of road safety activities -Train enough personnel in safety issues for targeted stakeholders	-The level of capacity development for road safety education is not assessed, established and certified
Medical Training	-There is limited first aid handling and specialized transportation for the injured from road traffic crash scenes to hospitals in the country so most injured people who make it to hospitals are transported by any means of transport available, mainly taxis and mini-buses	-Establish education and training programmes including the use of applied technology, for law enforcement agencies to improve their capacity at enforcement. -Incorporate basic principles in First Aid in the syllabi of driving schools, Police Training Courses and basic schools.	-Process is functional except for limited use of technology
Research	-Database	-Educate the general public and the responsible agencies on the need to report and document road traffic crashes.	-Except for eye witness account RRTC is recorded by the Police
Research Uptake	-Research- Inability to disseminate research results	-Develop mechanisms for consolidating and disseminating road safety research findings	Diverse research is undertaken continuously

Source; NRSP 2018

8.3 ROAD SAFETY EDUCATION PROCESS

According to the WHO (2019), the approach to RSE involves a four (4) stage structure including research and design, production, dissemi¬nation and evaluation as presented in Figure 8.6 and discussed in the immediate sub sections.

Figure 8.6: The Road Safety Educational Process

8.3.1 RSE Design

This phase development of RSE plans and strategic actions to guide the implementation of RSE activities in an orderly manner and it involves the following steps:

Step 1: Conduct of an RSE Needs Assessment: It involves an assessment to identify the types of RSE needs, the intervention and methods required to address such needs.

Step 2: Development of RES Plans: Based on the good understanding of road user knowledge needs, RSE plans are prepared with defined goals and objectives, strategies and actions to be implemented. Others are timelines, budgets, work plans, implementation processes, role and responsibilities for activity implementation. It must also define corresponding synergies and combinations for departmental/sectoral integrations as well as national and local plans.

In Ghana, RSE plans are of different categories including those defined in the NRSS by the NRSA and those defined by other road safety stakeholder agencies including both formal education and conduct of campaigns. Some RSE training interventions in Ghana are as summarised in Table 8.3.

Table 8.3: Sample RSE Interventions for Specific Needs

Road User Challenge	Reasons for RSE Intervention	Examples in Ghana
Advisory Support	-Information provision and risk mapping -Motivation underlying offensive behavior and rightful behavior	-Policy formulation -Development of legal instruments
RSE for different disciplines	-Professional development in Road safety	-Education sector -Road transport sector -Road Engineering -Traffic enforcers -Health agencies -Judiciary -Media -Landuse planning and development
Unsafe road traffic environment for school children	-To ensure adequate knowledge impartation for safe traffic environment for school children, teachers and family	-Safe walk to school
High risk RTC situations within communities and its environments	-Detection and management of Risk in real traffic situations -Development of abilities -Impartation of reliable information on safe road user Attitudes	-To Raise hazard perception, awareness, by observational behavior and anticipation skills -Community sensitization on road safety
Driver Training	-Development of basic driver training standards -Driver training and education,	-Driver training -Driver certification -Driver upgrades -Driver refresher training
Traffic Offenders Programmes	-Rehabilitation sessions	-Driver rehabilitation
Increasing abilities to act for Emergency response	-Training of emergency response agencies	-Drill demonstration for emergency workers

8.3.2 RSE Production Phase

This phase involves the preparations that are made towards the conduct of RSE through the following processes:

A. Categorisation of RSE target audience/groups: RSE must be targeted to a specific audience with common needs e.g. groups in particular geographic location etc.

In Ghana, RSE in all categories are applied both formal such as professional development and informal through educational campaigns.

B. Definition of RSE Methods: Following the identification of RSE target audience, implementation methods must then be identified to match respective activities.

8.3.3 RSE Dissemination/Implememtation Phase

This phase involves the actual implementation of RSE activities within set timeframe using the content of the RSE plan and allocated resources for set targets.

Examples of agencies involved in RSE in Ghana and types of education offered are as listed in Table 8.4.

Table 8.4: Summary of Roles and Responsibilities for RSE Implementation in Ghana

Category of Institution	Roles and Responsibilities
Government and the Public Sector	-Provides, leadership, Resources, regulations, standards, -Funds and ensures effective policies for the control and enforcement of laws. -A large proportion of funding for RSE is provided from Government treasury
Local and Regional/ County Governments	NRSA in collaboration with MMDAS, DVLA, MTTD etc.; -ensures the planning and implementation of RSE at the local level -Where possible, fund and implement road safety programmes and initiatives at that level -coordinates effort to educate community groups within their particular administrative area. -RSE is conducted by NRSA regional offices but funding is provided from Headoffice. -some MMDA's also engage in RSE within their jurisdiction but on a limited scale
Communities and Cultural or Ethnic Organisations	-Provide support and leadership for road safety campaigns and initiatives. -Demonstrate a concern for the number of road deaths occurring and a commitment to foster improvements. -Persuade various communities to accept a greater participatory role in road safety improvements. -Work with other organisations in providing road safety education/publicity and other road safety programmes. -This is normally activated by the NRSA representative regional offices, NGO's and other corporate bodies
Education Sector	-Ensure formal commitment to promote effective road safety education in schools and pre-schools so that appropriate behaviour is fostered from early age. -Develop links between schools and other agencies, such as the Ministry of Transport, Ministry of Health and police, in relation to road safety. -Assist in the life-long education of road users. -collaborates with some NGO's and corporate entities for road safety education in schools

Media	-The media in Ghana enhances community road safety awareness and understanding of the causal factors and real costs of road crashes, in order to influence societal changes which, lead to a reduction in unacceptable driver behaviour and poor attitudes through various educational programmes in diverse local dialects including eg.
	    Adult Education on GTV,
	    One Front Kantanka TV road safety show,
	    e. TV Road Safety Tips on Happy FMS- Facebook
	 -They also support road safety initiatives through responsible and objective reporting.
	 -NRSA engages with the media at different levels to promote RSE e.g. media education, media coverage of RSE events by the NRSC, advertisements e.t.c.

Police and Enforcement Agencies	-In Ghana, the Police contributes to RSE education at all the mentioned levels. Specifically, the MTTD improve road user behavior and vehicle standards through a balance of education, encouragement and effective enforcement strategies.
Health Agencies and Professionals	-The Ministry of Health is a key road safety stakeholder entity and it provides health promotion road safety programmes by providing training in diverse aspects of health delivery for emergency victims
Transport and Land-Use Planners	-They collaborate with MMDA's to ensure safe traffic management measures in planning transport and land-use developments. However, in Ghana this activity lacks prominence in road safety interventions because of limited local level inputs

Category of Institution	Roles and Responsibilities
Road Engineers and Highway Authorities	-They improve the safety performance of the road network by ensuring that planning, design, construction and maintenance places a high priority on safety outcomes. -They train in the application of crash reduction and crash prevention techniques to create safer road networks for the future. They conduct road safety training. -They train personnel for the conduct of road safety audits -They provide education in the safe use of road safety installations and device -They pay particular attention to the safety requirements of people with disabilities, older people, children, pedestrians, bicycle riders and other non -motorised road users in the planning task
Insurance Industry	-They sensitise road users on insurance premiums and claims
Alcohol and Hospitality Entertainment Industry	-They promote and sensitise on alcohol responsibility in road use though of limited collaboration in this respect
Vehicle Manufacturers and Importers	-They promote the safety features and safety performance of vehicles and their responsible use.
Heavy Vehicle Transport Industry	-They train in the prevention of the abuse of alcohol and drug stimulants and promote healthy lifestyle habits amongst drivers. -They train in high standards of vehicle, mechanical safety, and load stability and security. -They train in industry professionalism and safety through improved fleet management
Driver Training Providers	-They equip learner and novice drivers with the necessary skills, attitudes and behavior needed to drive safely on our roads. -They maintain and foster a high standard of driver training, instruction and professionalism. -They promote and foster the upgrading of driving skills amongst drivers, particularly drivers of heavy and public service vehicles. -They have established an Association and enhance industry professionalism by developing a Code of Providers teaching materials, Driving Instructors training programmes, etc., for their members -The DVLA engages with them in all aspects
Motoring Associations	-They promote road safety amongst their memberships by providing up-to-date and relevant information on traffic laws, safe driver behavior and techniques, road conditions, maintenance procedures and vehicle safety. -They provide support, promote and sponsor effective road safety initiatives and campaigns. -They provide membership feedback to government and industry on road safety policy and new initiatives. -Transport unions collaborate with NRSA for diverse RSE interventions except for the use of their own resources
Advertisers	-Conducts advertisements which promote knowledge on unsafe road safety practices and products to actively encourage safer practices and products.
Researchers/ Universities	Promote the conduct of research and research dissemination on basic and applied topics. -Ensure that road safety research is of high quality, timely and that its implications are identified and promoted. -Ensures the development of high-quality databases. -Provide reliable research results and knowledge against which policy decisions can be made.
All Organisations	-In future it is anticipated for all organizations to develop internal safety policies for their staff including host responsibility. -Promote safe practices in fleet operation especially larger fleet operators eg. training in defensive driving at own premises.
Individual Road Users	-Mass and targeted RSE are continuously provided to all road users at different forums to enable them attain a greater understanding, awareness, and practice of safe behavior and skills

8.3.4. Monitoring and Evaluation (M&E) of RSE

During the implementation and completion of RSE plans, monitoring and evaluation (M&E) is done to assess performance and impacts for further adjustment or development of set objectives through the collation and analysis of both primary and secondary data obtained from surveys and desk reviews. Process monitoring is done by comparing planned and actual outputs using performance indicators whilst the RSE process is on-going. Evaluation of impacts is done to ascertain extent of achievement of set objectives and changes gained from the RSE programme.

RSE evaluation however is often challenged with the inability to isolate the specific factors contributing to the achieved results due to its complexity. Aside this, it can also be difficult to identify comparable or representative control groups (i.e., similar populations who are not exposed to the RSE programme) whose behaviours can be compared to those who are exposed in order to measure behaviour change across groups.

In Ghana, various evaluation studies by the NRSA including evaluation of speed control programmes, alcohol control programmes and seatbelt and helmet education programmes etc. have established the fact that road user knowledge on safe traffic practices do not match what happens in the traffic system. Also, the overall consequence effect of the gains and failures in the approach to the implementation of road safety campaigns in Ghana is not well established due to the fact that different RSE content with different timetables and implementation durations are effected.

There is need therefore for further research into this area of RSE to ensure that appropriate interventions are implemented for good outcomes. Specifically, the psychological theories on how people choose to cope with risks as basis for predicting behaviour change and for inform-ing the approach to effective RSE must be applied. Such studies should also consider social norms, values and perceptions of traffic hazards that confront individual road users as well as the environmental conditions which also affect how they think, behave and act within the traffic necessary to inform an appropriate RSE approach in the country. This is important setting psychological and physiological limits verified as contributing to operational mistakes in traffic in Ghana.

8.4 RSE BY PROFESSIONAL DEVELOPMENT AND SKILLS TRAINING
8.4.1 Elements of RSE for Professional Development
Adequate expertise for road safety work is identified as one of the key aspects hindering the progress of road safety management. RSE by professional development and training involves both knowledge acquisition in scientific fields of academic qualifications and skill development by vocational training and the transmission of "life-skills" e.g. train-ing to become a driving instructor or a paramedic. This is often done through formal education on the basis of standardized conventions within formally set structures.

A. Description of RSE for Professional Development: According to Catchpole & DiPietro (2003), there have always been considerable expectation for the value of formal education and training in road safety in almost every country in the world. This is because the scale and complexity of the road safety problem generates a need for highly skilled, analytical and multidisciplinary safety experts who will guide wider and continued delivery of effective road safety knowledge with scientific knowledge to promote authentic RSE and training.

Since road safety is of diverse disciplines and complex, it is not as yet developed as a distinct profession so there is a lack of a single constituent for road safety professional development with no standard definition of a discipline for road safety expertise. To this effect, road safety courses are offered ne mostly as core courses within formal academic settings for different fields of specialisation in relation to the five road safety pillars. Expertise is often based on the mastering of the road safety demands of that particular discipline.

Currently, the various fields related to design and use of traffic systems, which are of economic importance is being recommended to be unified into a common discipline. This common discipline is recommended to have a balance of expertise in subject areas such as Administration, Engineering, Transportation, Planning, Education, Health, Law Enforcement, Social scientists, Economics and Disaster Management.

Dragutinovic N. et al (2006) also recommends for the learning approach to be made flexible for those willing to learn for the formation of communication of ideas, even if there is no general agreement about what content or form it should take. The ultimate goal is to bridge the gap between current and desired performance by empowering people to become active contributors to the process for positive road safety outcomes.

Examples of countries which have taken such an initiative includes Australia which is in a process of developing an academic discipline in road safety and Nigeria which has gone ahead to establish an academic based training and certification for professional and career development in road safety.

A similar training programme in Ghana or utilization of such opportunities will go a long way to improve road safety management in the country. Examples of Target Groups for professional road safety educational development are as presented in Table 8.5.

Table 8.5: Target Groups for Road Safety in Formal Educational System – Professionals

Target Group	Description	Justification
Professionals		
Related Disciplines	Training of professionals ensures the development of high-quality safety experts and these include Urban planners, Road engineers, Road Safety Managers, Psychologists, Social scientists, Statisticians, Lawyers, Media consultants, Traffic Educators etc.	
	-It promotes high quality road safety research by ensuring a balance between research on basic and applied topics	
	-This provides reliable knowledge against which policy decisions can be made.	
	-This provides dedication to road safety that may not necessarily be evident in one profession but can imply a long-time commitment	
Managers at different levels and policymakers	-Often times it is undertaken to develop the internal capacity of organizations engaged in road safety through further-training for professionals already involved in road safety.	
	-Higher sensitivity to traffic safety problem is required to make it a priority in all policymaking.	

In Ghana, whatever formal road safety professional development and training represents and the related requirements and the outcome effects of road safety knowledge development cannot be easily assimilated. Thus, since a complete science on road safety is yet to be established, it is difficult to determine who a road safety expert is and what qualifies an individual to be one and typical examples are as follows:

"I call myself a road safety practitioner/expert, however, I have not received any certified formal education to describe myself as such. I do so because I have worked on diverse road safety research studies over a 20-year duration and is very well versed in cross sectional road safety issues and does describes myself as such

Victor is a civil engineer and has been involved in safety related infrastructure development supported with diverse safety related short courses and so describes himself as a safety expert but without a substantive certification for such.

Nana is a road safety advocate and a passionate one at that. He has taken it upon himself to educate himself on road safety issues and has been appointed as an advocate to educate road users on media platform and yet without any formal certification to recognize him as such"

B. Development of Road Traffic Safety as Distinct Career Path: There is also no definitive career development path for road safety practitioners. Basic road safety knowledge is often obtained on the job for full time workers in lead road safety agencies with limited progression to advanced levels. Professionals in different disciplines which have road safety integrated as sub components can also progress on their career development in road safety in their area of work through individual formal education and training agenda.

The development of traffic safety as a profession in its own right requires consideration from two different perspectives. The first is the availability of suitable continuing education opportunities up to post graduate level and the second relates to the integration of traffic safety for the development of career paths for traffic safety workers (TRB, 2007). This is because, until substantive educational opportunities are developed for road safety to become a distinct discipline there can be no desirable career path.

Therefore, educational opportunities for career development in road safety must be developed to consciously build a pool of safety professionals across all disciplines. This can provide expertise for the institutions and agencies with road safety responsibilities since safety gains are not random occurrences but a consequence of well-informed and well-implemented decisions.

In Ghana, the threshold of employment opportunities in the field of road safety is not known or well researched. It is only the NRSA that has developed some sort of road safety workforce by the recruitment of professionals of diverse disciplines backed by training in some instances. On the way forward career development in road safety must be duly recognised to enable future students embark from the onset on a career path as managers, practitioners and researchers. Such an initiative will ensure specialization and the development of a standard of excellence in the field of road safety.

C. Levels in RSE for Professional Development: The learning objectives for formal RSE are categorized into two levels. Level - 1 involves basic or elementary road safety courses and level - 2 involves advanced road safety levels. The basic course includes generic road safety themes mainly with a practical focus for specific problem solution.

Advanced level formal road safety course involves intensive and comprehensive theoretical teaching for persons with previous road safety knowledge or experience mostly in a post-graduation format. It is also required to respond to demands of changing circumstances as well as to introduce new approaches and technology. An overview of some of the existing courses in formal road safety learning is as listed in Table 8.6.

Table 8.6: Classification of Levels of Road Safety Training Programmes

Level of Formal RSE and Training	Level 1- Basic /Training Programmes	Level 2- Advanced/ Academic Courses
Objective	-To give a general introduction on traffic safety issues	-To give a more specialized education/training on specific issues
Detailed Description	-It involves a broad range of people who are interested in road safety issues and wants to have a more general overview of the field. -They specifically include people who are already active in road safety domains such as engineering, policy, education, enforcement, amongst others.	-This is for those who have a good background knowledge in traffic safety sciences with proof of certification from an existing academic or related institution.
Access	-There is no strict criteria except for certification in basic education	-Criteria: have already a basic education in traffic safety that is bachelor or master in related studies,
Structure	-One basic course, with 5 or 6 sessions is deemed adequate.	-Must involve several independent courses grouped in one of the 5 pillars with each consisting of minimum 2 sessions

Level of Formal RSE and Training	Level 1- Basic /Training Programmes	Level 2- Advanced/ Academic Courses
Content	- The content serves as an introduction course for high level students (bachelor and master) in, for example: engineering, transport, economy, political studies, etc. Introduction on traffic safety covering the 5 pillars	-For each pillar several independent courses are developed
Road safety management	-Road Safety and the media training -Road safety legislature -Fundamentals of Road Traffic Injury Prevention -Concepts in Injury Prevention -Risk Factors and Choosing Interventions for Road Traffic Injuries -Injury Surveillance Systems -Evaluation of Road Safety Interventions-Influencing Policy for Road Traffic Injury Prevention -Safety impact assessment	-Road Safety Management & policy -Basic concepts of RS / conceptual framework -Public transport safety -Data collecting and analyzing -Safety benefits / cost effectiveness -Transport and sustainable development -Implementation & innovation processes -Politics, the law and sociology of transportation -Road Safety as an individual, economic, social and health Problem -Cost of accidents -Road safety education psychology -Safe system approach
Infrastructure	-Road Safety audits -Studies in hazardous road sections -Road restraint systems -Introduction of various traffic control devices -How road users interpret infrastructure	-Highway & Transportation Engineering -Traffic Engineering, -Transport modelling, -Road design -Safe Traffic Systems -Design & Analysis and Transportation -Engineering -Road infrastructure management
Vehicle	Control on vehicle charge -Technical maintenance inspection -Expertise in inspection and evaluation of automobiles -Vehicle regulation harmonization -Vehicle inspection and identification of chassis and engine adulteration -Vehicle modifications	-Automotive Engineering -Vehicle dynamics -Automotive engineering projects -Vehicle and traffic safety -Speed impact / vehicle crashworthiness -Modern Vehicle Technology Issues -Standards for technical inspection of vehicles, -Active safety of vehicles
Landuse planning		-Urban planning and transport -Secure urban development
Transportation	-Specific elements or truck and truck drivers -Strategies on a company level -Work related road safety -Professional drivers and their health -Professional drivers and workload	-Mobility management -Management and Operation of Transport -Technology and intelligent transport systems -Road and Transport Safety Planning and Management -Road safety economics -Transport and Road Safety -Management in Freight transport
Road user behavior	-Increased positive behaviors -Driver training eg. Drunk Driving course -Road User Education Programmes -Traffic education for pedestrians, the vulnerable etc. -Road safety education for schools -Training of drivers' instructors -Warning and guidance needed for the operation of the traffic stream -Mobility for handicapped people'	-Road user behavior effectiveness of education -Behavioral influences -Modification of the behavior of road users and exploring human factors -Research on behavior measures -Traffic and travel behavior -Commuting and professional drivers eg. risk profiling, Licensing systems', and 'Raising awareness and campaigning
Enforcement	-Training in traffic regulations -RTC investigation and reporting procedures -Road safety inspections -Training in enforcement	-Effective enforcement -Accident investigation -Frequency and nature of injuries

Level of Formal RSE and Training	Level 1- Basic /Training Programmes	Level 2- Advanced/ Academic Courses
Post-Crash	-RTC scene management -Post-accident care / optimization -Pre-hospital care eg. first aid training for lay persons -Emergency vehicle operations and rehabilitation	-Trauma Sciences -Epidemiology & statistics applied to RS -Special research in emergency situations -Injury severity scaling and care -Organization of emergency care -Incident management in an urban environment
Outcome	-A general certificate on 'introduction course for traffic safety'	-A specific certificate covering the content of the course with access to a discussion forum about the pillar in which the course is classified.

D. Learning Units for Formal RSE: *The units for formal RSE learning includes various tertiary and none tertiary institutions and examples are as listed in Table 8. 7. However, there are no specialised institutions solely dedicated for road safety studies.*

Table 8.7: Learning Units for Formal RSE Learning and Training

Categories Available	Those Applicable or Applied in Ghana	Qualification/ Academic certification	Course Description
School Conclave	-Early childhood education settings, such as child care centres -Teachers Training	-Changed behavioral practice/ -Certificate of participation	-Trainer of Trainer courses
University/College/ Tertiary Institution	-Takoradi Technical -University	-Higher National Diploma -(HND) Civil Engineering -BTech. Civil Engineering	-Highway & Transportation Engineering
	-Kwame Nkrumah University of Science & Technology	-BSc. Civil Engineering -MSc. Road & Transportation -Engineering	-Highway & Transportation Engineering -Road Safety.
	-Kumasi Technical University	-HND Civil Engineering -BTech. Civil Engineering	-Highway & Transportation Engineering
	-Koforidua Technical University	-HND Civil Engineering -BTech. Civil Engineering	-Highway & Transportation Engineering
	-University of Cape Coast	-Diploma in	-Transport and Road Safety Management
National specialist institute	-Workplaces eg. Ministries of transport or health; - -Local secretariats or departments for health or traffic; -School of Traffic enforcement - police; -Centre for Road Safety Education and Media -Development -School of Public Health Disaster Management	-On the job training/ -Certificate of participation	
Research Institutions - Local	-Centre for Analysis & Research in Road Safety eg. Building and Road Research Institute	-Certificate of participation	-E.g. Road Safety Audit
Independent private training set ups	-Advocacy groups. -Driver Training schools	-Certificate of participation	
NGO's	-Training by Nongovernmental organizations	-Certificate of participation	

In Ghana, comprehensive road safety curriculum and modules must be developed by relevant academic institutions in identified road safety areas of specialisation using the existing academic institutions offering core courses and programmes in road safety studies. A criterion should be set on the level of certification by course type by first surveying existing road safety affiliated educational programmes compared to the competencies needed to guide the development of the right training courses.

The NRSA could also form road safety education partnerships with relevant academic and industry affiliates to further develop and expedite the training of road safety professionals to meet the demand for road safety expertise in all sectors. Centres of excellence in road safety education could also be developed in association with both local and external academic and relevant institutions to strengthen the process though there should be inclusion of local content in such programmes.

E. Institutions for Road Safety Research Development: Road safety professionals must be exposed to science-based safety research.

In Ghana, capacity for the type and level of road safety research is not well defined. With the exception of BRRI which has a long record for road safety research and the newly established the Transport Research and Education Centre (TRECK) at the School of Engineering at the Kwame Nkrumah University of Science and Technology (KNUST), there cannot be said to be a substantive research entity for road safety work in the country. However, these two institutions could be developed in the interim to support road safety research. However, there should first be research into the types of road safety professionals likely to be needed in the future.

G. Development of Lifelong Road Safety Education (RSE) in Schools: Lifelong learning throughout the entire school career of children (4 to 16 years) such as the examples in the Netherland which involves the option of achievement of certificates by schools that participate in road safety programmes and that of Denmark which involves the nomination of road safety contact teacher responsible for RSE in schools is recommended to be emulated.

In Ghana, an RSE Resource entitled 'Safe Ways' along with accompanying Teacher Training materials developed by Sayer I A, et al (1997 - TRL Report 265), provides a guide to the approach for teaching road safety in basic schools. The resource contains five lessons which cover the following teaching points: walking safely; observing the road environment; using protected crossings; crossing where there are no protected crossings and; choosing safe routes. The resource is tailored to Ghana's educational context within which it is to be used, (See Figure 8.7).

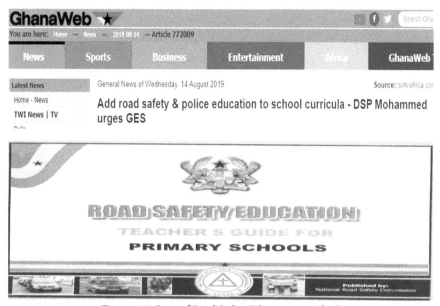

Figure 8.7: State of Road Safety Education in Schools

The major limitation has to do with the fact that road safety is yet to be upgraded to the level of a school curriculum. Thus, the road safety school educational materials are yet to be adopted as a full-fledged text book by the Ghana Education Service (GES). Also, the educational materials are in limited quantities because the entity responsible for the cost of production for the supply of the road safety educational materials in required quantities for all schools in Ghana is not yet defined. Thus, with the exception of the few copies produced for initial distribution to some schools by the NRSA, there is not enough to go round all schools. There is therefore a need to ensure its adoption as an official text book in Ghana's basic school educational system to be supplied by Government and other relevant institutions followed by an assessment of its use and related impacts.

8.4.2 RSE for Skills Training

"My cousin Nana Yaw, learnt how to drive through a friend and drove on the roads of the country for over 10 years before his wife Christie learnt how to drive. Due to work absenteeism, he paid for Christie to learn driving at a driving school. Sooner or later Christie was teaching him one or two things on the road which he did not learn from his training background."

"Kwame is a professional driver (at least by self-report), he claims to have driven for over 35 years without any RTC involvement and yet he learnt how to drive by apprenticeship by observing he master".

From these accounts, it can be concluded that formal RSE programmes are of diverse aspects and opportunities but are not well documented for effective appreciation of what is available, the gaps and what could be done for improvement purposes.

A compendium of target groups for formal road safety learning by Bakhtari Aghdam et al (2020) is as summarised in Table 8.8.

Table 8.8: Target Groups for Road Safety in Formal Educational System – Non Professionals

Target Group - Non Professionals	Description
Preschoolers	-It includes traffic safety courses at the kindergarten level, this is because early childhood education is considered important for teaching the children at that age because it is believed that behavior originates from childhood, becomes institutionalized and grows
Children	-According to the WHO's definition, those below 18 falls into the category of children. These are often trained in safe walk to school, safe road crossing in order to ensure to increased pupils/students' knowledge and basic skills in road safety practice
Youth	-This includes those at the age of getting a driver's license who are considered to be of high-risk road use behavior and for whom adequate education is required to mitigate the risk factors: -Made aware of the extremely high levels of crash involvement risk factors -Trained in strategies to reduce these risks when driving with peers e.g. adherence to the zero blood alcohol requirement; driving solo - especially driving at night; the influence of peers travelling in their vehicle; over-confidence while driving or taking overt risks such as speeding
Teachers	-Teachers are those who are responsible for traffic safety education and they must receive specific training because they have a special impact on pupils/student in role modelling and safe road use practices. -The Teacher is also a role model for children and adolescents; therefore, they should learn proper traffic behavior and transfer it to those who make the future. -The training must inform and advice teachers in how to guide the child in knowledge of traffic legislation, teach them safety skills eg safe road crossing behaviors and provide supervised opportunities for them to apply these skills in real traffic environments
Parents	-Due to the interaction between parents and children the involvement of parents is to provide information and advice on how to guide their child, create awareness of the 'development stage' of their child in traffic safety. This is because parents are the primary role model for children." They determine when children are safe to walk unsupervised; and help children determine safe routes to school and other destinations therefore it must be ensured that parents have received appropriate information and advice about child restraints e.g. safe bicycle use and helmet wearing as well as good riding skills -It involves mothers and fathers being trained about safe traffic behaviors and observance of safe traffic practice by their wards on daily basis. E.g. how to hold their wards hand when crossing roads; ensuring that helmets are worn when on wheeled toys, bicycles or tricycles; and providing close supervision when children are near traffic and safe practices when crossing roads. -They should also be trained in becoming good road safety role models for their wards.
Elderly	-The WHO classifies the elderly as vulnerable groups who are at a greater risk due to the reduced motor and cognitive skills and they must be assisted with skills for safe road use eg. provision of information for older people about how to use other forms of transport, if they need to stop driving as well as awareness of the risks they face as pedestrians -Training the aged in traffic safety is essential because they turn to lose cognitive abilities for safe road use
Special groups (disabled, blind, etc.)	-The WHO classifies people with disabilities as vulnerable groups who require specific training. This is because the use aids such as crossing the road in a wheelchair requires special safety training -It raises awareness of good safe self-regulation and of safe driving practices for them

Target Group - Non Professionals	Description
-Drivers	-It encourages safe road practice by the driver through training and compliance to road traffic regulations -It involves the establishment of code of teaching materials, Certification of Driving Instructors and training programmes, etc., for their members -It also promotes and encourages and 'share the road' culture, supported by good road rules compliance, provision of forgiving, safe infrastructure and speed limits; -Initial basic training for drivers including, Regulations cover standards of instruction, driving tests and penalties for essential driver training, professional driver training, driver refresher and periodic training of Young Drivers, Novice Drivers and others in immediate post-crash training -Others are safe driver behavior and techniques, road condition, maintenance procedures and vehicle safety etc. -It provides up-to-date and relevant information on traffic laws and skills in co-creating engaging communication with drivers and passengers -Given the high rate of accidents, deaths, and injuries caused by driving in the country, the drivers need to receive special training programmes.
Instructors of Driving Schools Driving license applicants, instructors and managers of driving schools	-Drivers must be trained about introduction to driving skills, for correct behaviors and rules related to traffic. This is because a 'Driver's license is not a right for everyone, it doesn't mean that everybody is supposed to have it, it is competence gained through training. -Driver's license centers give an identity of driver to the applicants, given that driving is not just done but involves establishment of code of teaching materials, certification of driving instructors and training programmes, etc., for their members -Instructors and managers of driving schools must receive special training to transfer it to students.
Driver Unions	-There is need to provide membership with training for feedback to government and industry on road safety policy and new initiatives as well as develop internal safety policies for their staff including host responsibility. It is to promote road safety amongst their memberships -There is need to encourage staff to participate in defensive driving courses, and where feasible, sponsor or buy in defensive driving courses for own staff at own premises -There is need to promote safe practices in fleet operation for larger fleet operators can.
Motorcyclists/ Cyclists	-Motorcyclists are the major group at risk of injury and experience the most severe damage in traffic accidents so it is essential that all motorcyclists receive the required trainings to reduce accidents as well as injuries during an accident. Such Knowledge is about-traffic rules and behavior as cyclist -Handling and vehicle command -Training of motor skills in protected area (if possible initial training with scooters rather than on bicycle) -Training in traffic rules/signs and behavior of cyclist, use of helmets and safe bikes -Communication and interaction with other road users, observance of Blind spot -Risk awareness and risk seeking, speed, peer pressure, overestimation of own skills etc. -Motorcyclist must be trained in safe ride and in traffic regulations but "There are a small number of cycling training and schools."
Pedestrians	There is need for the pedestrian to understand the legislative (or regulations on pedestrians); basis traffic rules (e.g. right of way, traffic signs) and skills (e.g. crossing streets) because training informs pedestrians about their responsibilities when using shared paths and explain and promote key road rules for pedestrians -Others are communication and interaction with other road users -Transfer of specific life skills, such as estimation of distances and speed -Hazard and risk awareness related to their own behavior, and the behavior of other traffic participants -Being watchful despite friends and other distractions such as the use of headphones/mobile phones -Others are the use of visible clothing, Traffic fears and mobility patterns and safe routes
Managers of Car Manufacturing Plants/Mechanics	-This includes the training of those in the motor industry and members of Motorists' associations, Managers of Car Manufacturing Plants etc. because they set vehicle safety standards for use on the roads as well as service defective vehicles
Media	-It involves training to support, promote and sponsor the media for effective road safety initiatives and campaigns. This is necessary to support road safety initiatives for responsible and objective information delivery -The training is also to ensure discouragement of advertising which glamorises and/or promotes unsafe practices and products. -It also promotes active safer practices and development of good products

Target Group - Non Professionals	Description
Post-trauma support groups;	-It involves, the training of paramedics, medical facility-based care givers, Insurance companies and rehabilitation centres. -It requires all those who apply a depth of knowledge and experience to the road trauma problem must be a part of the process.
First Respondents	It sensitises on how to call for help for any person in a road accident situation using emergency numbers, victim handling, First aid provision and transport of the injured to the nearest medical facility or to the nearest trauma care centre -It facilitates the creation of a location-based platform for volunteer trauma care corps
Family of Victims	Training creates a post RTC direct communication campaign for customers by providing immediate Information on access to relief for accident victims and family -It provides support to accident victims and the family of Victims
Law enforcers	It involves the education for the Police and Judiciary because they apprehend and determine punitive and non-punitive measures to determine the level of user compliance or non-compliance
Politicians	It involves the training of relevant government officials such as ministers and parliamentary standing committees on transport etc. This is because, they control policy approvals and funding threshold for effective road safety implementation
A wide range of commercial and community-based organisations'	This is because, these are back up commercial entities who when well are trained contributes to effective road safety practices -This includes establishments of rehabilitation units; private consulting and research organisations; heavy vehicle operator groups; education of vehicle fleet operators; medical organisations; insurance companies; etc.
Communities	-It involves training in greater understanding, awareness, and practice of safe behavior and skills. Such as adoption of more courteous and considerate road behavior and demonstration of care for the safety of others such as -Road Reminder Communication -Post Accident -Making road safety a collective responsibility for whole families -It creates community awareness and understanding of the causal factors of road crashes as well as community responsibilities and practices for keeping safe

Source: Adapted from Bakhtari Aghdam et al. program in Iran, BMC Public Health (2020)

8.4.3 Design RSE for Professional Development and Skills Training

A. Development of Training Programme Content: Formal RSE for the above is based on empirically developed curriculum which demonstrates experiences and values in road safety practices. Its content is developed from seminar papers, collaborative reports from traffic safety research institutes and books from experts and typical examples are as sampled in Table 8.9.

Table 8.9: Professional Road Safety Education Materials

Course Aspects	Traffic Documents from International Sources	Traffic Documents in Ghana
-General education on the principles of road safety for a broad spectrum of professionals -Multidisciplinary courses on road safety provided by universities or other institutions, eg Specific road safety courses in the educational curriculum at basic, secondary and tertiary levels -Specialized courses for road safety professional development -Short courses on road safety management -Road Safety Engineering -Safety in Transport Management -Post crash emergency care as part of public health education	-Training manuals of all Categories e.g. -Traffic Engineering manuals -Traffic control devices -Case Studies -Accident Analysis -Road Safety Audit -Signage studies -Protective devices studies -Training materials for emergency medical response and care	-Ghana Highway code -Driver Training manuals -Low Volume Road Safety Design standards -Teacher Training materials developed by (Sayer I A, et al, 1997 - TRL Report 265),

B. Methods for RSE for Professional Development and Skills Training: The methods for formal RSE and skills training are within both academic and non-academic institutions and they can be short-term or long-term processes. They can be done through single or multiple learning regimes. For purposes of greater impact, it is often recommended for classroom teaching to be backed by practical training to provide hands on practice of what is expected. A compendium of methods for RSE and the associated advantages and disadvantages are as presented in Table 8.10.

Table 8.10: Road Safety Education Methods:

RSE method	Description	Advantages	Disadvantages
Lectures	-Lectures by regular full course programmes for One/Two/Three- and Four-Year classroom formal educational programmes eg. -Classroom Lectures (large group activity) -Individualized Classroom Activities (small groups or individually)	-Mastery of classroom instruction -Capacity development for continuous life-long safety practice and knowledge share	-Participants for a formal road safety education programme maybe from different background but the lecture might not recognize individual differences
Workshops and Discussions,	-It gets people talking about issues. -Maximum exposure in the road safety field. -Workshops for management courses for managers at different levels to increase the empowerment and literacy of managers	-It keeps people involved and engaged with the content of the training	-It needs proper preparation and the facilitator must give a clear and concise briefing to participants
Case studies,	-Case studies give people a chance to apply their understanding to a real case and to learn from discussing it. This method uses a specific detailed problem, usually in written form. Participants will read it and will then suggest the best possible solutions based on the given facts	-They must be prepared to discuss not only their proposals for solutions, but also how and why they reached their decision.	-Case based methods may pose challenges where the participants are not familiar with the case since road safety education is very diversifies
Role playing,	-Modeling behaviors	-Different target groups have specific models and references that can be used as training practices, including movie stars, artists, teachers, parents, friends, and other important people can affect the behavior of users as role models.	-Not all participants may have the opportunity to play a role
Group exercise,	-Social networks	-Participation in group discussions creates a commitment to behavior	-Method is used depending on the target group and educational content
Brainstorming	-To get participation from the floor during a plenary session. The facilitator puts a question on newsprint/overhead and asks participants to say what they think about the issue	-It is a good way to generate lists	-Some people get confused, go off the point or simply talk about their own favorite topic, regardless of the question

RSE method	Description	Advantages	Disadvantages
-Practical training/ -Simulation -Modeling -Demonstration -Drama -Job training, -Mentorship, -Coaching, -Mentorship, -On-site training, -Counterpart training, -Observational training etc. -Apprenticeship Internships	-Real and practical training of behaviors in real-world environments of society, such as traffic parks, streets, etc. that stabilizes behavior. For children and license applicants, the practical traffic safety training will be more effective	-real tasks as part of skills practice -Valuable knowledge and skills are imparted -Parental/Mentor involvement	-The situation might be unrealistic and impractical to real life situations
E-learning	This is by online correspondence	-Theoretical Training -Virtual and real networks in the community increase the communication between individuals. This increases the social support of individuals within the network. The use of social networks on training of traffic behaviors increases social support for individuals within the network and safe traffic behaviors	-It focuses on more theory and lacks requisite interactions
Seminars, Practical, Research etc.,	-Discussions or meetings by conference	-Specialized seminars and meetings for experts on professional issues.	-In a more limited state such as seminar."

8.4.4 Production of Formal RSE and Skills Training

The production and implementation of professional RSE and skills training involves the determination of the learning processes, development of the training content, determination of methods and approaches to the implementation of training programmes and resource mobilisation as discussed below:

A. Determination of the Learning Process: Learning is largely believed to be the process of acquiring, understanding, and absorbing of new information and attitudes, (Pfeffer and Sutton 2000). Since people learn in different ways, there are variations in learning styles. Due to this, understanding the process of learning and the various ways in which people retain information in relation to the following factors amongst others:

i.   Visual stimuli

ii. Verbal interactions,

iii. Learning by doing

However, experts are of the view that most people respond best to a combination of approaches and specific skill deficiencies must be addressed through diverse communication platforms so that target groups can be effectively reached and influenced.

In Ghana, the basis for determining the learning processes applied in RSE and the extent to which specific audience needs are used as basis for the selection of learning methods is not known.

B. Resources Mobilisation for Formal Learning System: Aside the determination of the learning process, adequate resource mobilization is the critical need for RSE for professional development and skills training and these include the following:

i. Mobilisation of Resource Persons: Academic and professional road safety experts with teaching skills such as school and university teachers; instructors of driver's license, NGOs and charities, practicing road safety project managers; instructional designers; content experts; writers and editors, driver training instructors amongst others must be available.

ii. Mobilisation of Funding Resources: According to Bok D. (2008), "if you think that investment in field of education is expensive, you must calculate the costs of ignorance." Therefore, sufficient budget allocation and financial administrative support is contingent to the production of formal road safety learning. Funding sources such as University, Industry, Private organizations and Donor organisations in addition to Government are recommended.

In Ghana, all formal entities with RSE components are required to make budgetary provisions for the purpose of their educational and training contribution to road safety. Some of the funds are generated from cost recovery measures and internally generated funds such as training fees. Entities without cost recovery measures are often characterized by budgetary shortfalls though some maybe supported by donor contributions etc., (See Figure 8.8).

Figure 8.8: Publication on Road Safety Funding Constraints in Ghana

iii. Mobilisation of Training Equipment: Proper technology is also required for providing good educational content for road safety. These includes, electronic content for virtual education, physical space for training with appropriate technological installations such as testing grounds, equipment for cycling, motorcycling and driving schools, simulators, traffic laboratories, software and hardware technology for training data bases, registry of accidents etc.

In Ghana, currently technological initiatives for driver training such as the use of double gear and breaks vehicles is mandatory for driving schools. In addition, the GTTC and some driving schools have acquired simulators to support advance driver training activities. Others are the use of drivers on line meetings applications such as zoom services to facilitate virtual meetings.

C. Implementation of RSE for Professional Development and Skills Training: The implementation of formal road safety learning includes the scheduling of training activities, launching/promotion and conduct of educational/training sessions.

D. M&E of RSE Professional Development and Skills Training

It is usually recommended for formal RSE Education and training to be well monitored for quality control with required evaluations to determine performance levels. Typically, most course sessions end with an opportunity for participants to say what they thought of the session as basis for reinforcing additional skills by reviewing training materials.

In Ghana, the extent to which formal RSE training is monitored or supervised and the responsibility for it such as the driving schools is not clear. There are also no known publicised records of evaluated outcomes for formal RSE sessions.

8.5 ROAD SAFETY EDUCATIONAL CAMPAIGNS

8.5.1 Road Safety Campaigns Design

A. Definition Road Safety Campaign: Road safety communication campaigns can be defined as purposeful attempts to inform, persuade, or motivate people for changed behaviour but which cannot be assessed as a single measure. Delhomme et al. (2009), also describes it as a means for decreasing the frequency and severity of RTCs by; providing information about new or modified laws; improving knowledge on risk factors especially priortised risk factors and the creation of awareness of new technological systems.

As a widely-used tools to promote and improve road safety through the dissemination of information in order to increase public awareness and knowledge about safe road use, it is typically conducted within a given time period by means of organised communication activities involving specific media channels (Elliott, 1993). The aim is to address the driving force behind problematic traffic behaviours by road users.

In Ghana road safety campaigns are also a very relevant for correcting wrongful road user perceptions, attitudes and conducts in a wide range of traffic situations and the target groups are as listed below.

i.   *Vehicle Drivers*

ii.   *Motorcyclists*

iii. *Rickshaw users*

iv.   *Bicycle riders*

v.   *Pedestrians*

vi.   *Vehicle Passengers*

vii. *Pillion Riders/Co Pilots in Mopeds*

viii. *Driver Unions*

ix.   *Driver's wives' association*

x.   *School pupils, students' parents and teachers*

B. Principles for Road Safety Campaigns: Road safety campaigns are guided by the following principles

i. Application of the A B C Curricula: A publication by Brake.org stipulates that road safety campaigns must be based on a coherent curriculum dubbed as "A, B, C" by whereby:

'A' is for awareness - traffic is dangerous and can hurt people.
'B' is for behaviour - things you should do to stay safer.
'C' is for choice and campaigning - how to make safer choices and to help others make these choices too.

In Ghana, awareness creation through safety campaigns aim to help citizens to understand their responsibilities when using the road but coherent campaign systems are not applied due to resource constraints.

ii. Advocated behaviour: Since it is difficult to determine the market benefits of road safety, consideration is given to the possibility of a recipient regarding advocated behaviour as non-beneficial.

iii. Impact Expectations: It is said that road safety through educational campaigns should only expect small changes since it goes against the tide of existing behaviour or opinion and is sometimes negative and often highly ego-involving.

In Ghana, the level of expectation from road safety campaigns is not weighed against any standard. Information is just released with expectation of some positive impacts.

iv. Non-Passive Receivers: Targeted road safety campaign audience are not passive receivers in but are selective in their demand considerations because their motivation is not just through the campaign since giving information does not automatically result in desired behavior change. This is because human error is complex and difficult to change and as such requires a large effort (Twisk, 2004).

In Ghana, the extent to which road user concern is considered in the design and implementation of road safety campaigns is not known.

C. Effects of Campaigns on Road Safety: According to Delhomme et al. (2009), for effective road safety campaigns, must be characterised by the following:

i. Provision of information about new or modified laws.

ii. Improvement of knowledge and/or awareness of new in-vehicle systems, risks, etc., and the appropriate preventive behaviours.

iii. Change of underlying factors known to influence road-user behaviour.

iv. Be able to modify problem behaviours or maintain safety-conscious behaviours.

v. Decrease the frequency and severity of accidents."

However, since RTC occurrence is multi-causal and highly influenced by chance there is rarely a direct link from a campaign to RTC reduction but campaigns can also be used to establish favourable preconditions in the public for new legislation.

D. Steps in the Design of Road Safety Campaigns: The recommend steps for designing a road safety campaign it is crucial to follow:

Step 1: Define specific road safety problem and plan: This must be done so as not to deviate from actual needs. It must specify the campaign goal and contents for implementation with set targets, timelines, roles and responsibilities in the form of a campaign brief or campaign brand. This serves as an identifier and the guiding framework for the conduct of after project assessment and it normally covers the aspects summarised in Table 8.11.

Table 8.11: Road Safety campaign Stages

Actions Before Campaign	Actions During Campaign
The problem area.	-content area of the messages
-ultimate objective and sub-objectives.	-Suggestions for audience activation.
-strategies to be adopted that is the total mix of campaign activities.	-expected main and secondary media.
-non-media activities including what activities will be on-going when the advertising ceases.	-campaign timing, duration and budget.
-target audiences, the rationale and suggested approaches for motivating them	

Actions After Campaign	Cross cutting actions
-behavioural changes expected to be achieved by each activity. -expectations regarding assessment; who, when, how and what.	-additional expectations (e.& preparation of reports by consultants or agency on what was done, why and what change would be recommended). -constraints, if any, by authority on talent, codes, themes, images. -contractual arrangements -role of further formative communication research and who should carry it out.

Step 2: Definition of Target Audience: This is about the identification of who the campaign must be targeted at as informed by research on behavioural insights to match specific needs with specific actions. They can also be identified from known problems from past experiences with road safety campaigns. The target groups must be segmented into meaningful subgroups by important characteristics such as age, gender, socio-economic status, risk levels, personality traits, social groups, occupational groups etc. in order to have positive commitment.

Step 3: Definition of Campaign Message: Road safety campaign messages must highlight aspects of campaign challenges that need to be addressed by the campaign

C. Development of Road Safety Campaign Messages: Road safety campaign messages utilize recognized psycho-social and theoretical foundations of education to direct and increase good understanding of the factors that contribute to RTC's and how to avoid or prevent them. They can also draw on social marketing strategies to create awareness on traffic laws and also provide guidance for safe road user behaviour and changed attitudes. The development of road safety campaign messaging is characterized by various factors including the following:

i. Determination of a Road Safety Campaign Theme: Every road safety campaign message should be based on a topic of focus which must be distinct and able to convey the objective to be achieved. It must also promote social and ethical values that aim to overcome psychological resistance to the acceptance of change.

In Ghana, examples include run-up to festivities road safety campaigns by the NRSA e.g. "Easter Stay Alive"; the launching of the "Save a Life" Road Safety Campaign; "Stop Road Accidents" campaign; "Road Safety in Ghana Preserving lives, Sustaining our Nation" etc., (See Figure 8.9).

Figure 8.9: The Launching of the Stay Alive Road Safety Campaign

ii. Style of Road Safety Campaign Message: Road safety campaign themes must define what the targeted audience must feel with respect to both rational and emotional appeals such as threat, fear and positive emotional messages. Specifically, such messages must be characterized by the following factors:

a. Be of relevance, coherent, cohesive and logical to the removal of the barriers to rightful conduct by the road user.

b. Be guided by appropriate and well researched psychological theories of behaviour change that can enable the achievement of desired outcomes.

c. Be based on social norms, motivations, perceptions, attitudes, behaviours, habits, cultural barriers etc. that causes road users to behave in the way they do in order to motivate the recipient to listen, process and engage with the message as well as desire change through the campaign message.

d. Be based on one risk factor at a time with a realistic or hard-hitting approach phrased to empower in simple language.

e. Should identify and address both intrinsic (innate factors) by relating road safety issues to real life situations that affect people individually and extrinsic (external factors) so that both the internal state that guides and sustains behaviour and intentions and the effects on desire or willingness to learn will be addressed.

f. Must be able to establish progressive engagement with the day-to-day operational practices of a wide range of road users such that their natural abilities or the ease with which they can do things will be kindled.

g. Must highlight the consequences of failing to make the proposed change.

In Ghana, the extent to which these principles are applied in the development of road safety campaign messaging is not well studied. Examples are as summarised in Table 8.12.

Table 8.12: Road Safety Campaign Focus

Targeted Components	Thematic Components	Key Messages
Road Infrastructure	-Promotion of knowledge in use of safe road features such as signs and markings	-Observe your road signs
Traffic	Promotion of knowledge in Traffic rules	
Drivers	-Development of safe and positive attitudes	-Over speeding kills
	-Increase perceptions of dangerous road user behavior	-Don't Drink and Drive
	-Development of respect for other road users	-Don't Drive tired
	-Safety for all	
Passengers	-Promotion of use of occupant Restraints	-Buckle up
Pedestrians	-Encouragement of Precaution	-Look left, right and left again before crossing the road
Motorcyclist	-Promotion of use of occupant Restraints	-Wear your helmet

iii. Creativity of Road Safety Campaign Message: The campaign message must be credible, trustworthy, honest, achievable, consistent and clear with ability to evoke the emotional response that will lead to rightful road user be¬haviours. This is because an individual's ability to process a campaign message is based on their cognitive ability and their level of understanding. Specifically, the campaign message must;

a). be creative enough in order to engage the road user with the necessary attention and influence them. E.g. the Metwa Mentwe slogan on avoidance of drunk driving literally translated that 'when I drink I will not drive', (See Figures 8.10 and 8.11).

Figure 8.10: Launching of the Metwa Mentwe Road Safety Campaign

b). use of elements such as images, adverts, film clips, info graphics and media coverage, writing issuance up to selling in media releases are often used.

c). use the types of communication mechanisms or tools which the target audience are able to effectively relate to in order to strengthen campaign penetration and reach must be applied. An example is as presented in Figure 8.11.

Figure 8.11: Examples of Road Safety Campaign Communication Messages

v. Framing of Road Safety Campaign Message: The campaign message framing may be one or two sided. The one-sided enables the target audience evaluate risk as a gain. The two-sided argument targets audience to evaluate risk as either a gain or a loss. According to O'Keefe & Jensen, (2006) framed messages are more important when the goal is one sided and is on prevention, (See Figure 8.12) for examples.

Figure 8.12: Examples of Frame of Road Safety campaign Messages (Road safety images from across the web).

According to Bradbury and Quimby (2008), road safety campaign messaging is frequently based on dominant but ineffective educational models imported from other contexts especially in LMICs. This is normally done without any background into psycho-social behavioural patterns and how they should be tackled.

However, transferring road safety education practices from developed to developing countries is arguably unfeasible because of variations in education systems, teaching methods, traffic regulations and exposure to risk. Thus, the design of road safety campaigns in such countries lack local content and is often locally inappropriate and impractical.

Currently in Ghana, the SSATP guideline for Road Safety campaign has been the key reference to the development of road safety campaign messages in the country with slight adjustments by set committees. The approach is not based on what informs road user behavior and what may influence them and the extent to which targeted audiences engage with such messages are not known.

It is therefore suggested for underlying beliefs and motivations influencing typical wrongful road user behaviours and attitudes to be carefully researched in order to inform the development of relevant road safety campaign messages. Specifically, the following road user behaviours typical to the Ghanaian traffic system must be researched to inform road safety campaign messaging:

a. *The reasons for the choice of road user convenience over safety such as the risky behavior of jumping over of fenced walls unto a high-speed road rather than the utilization available overhead footbridges by pedestrians.*

b. *The reasons for higher driver rating of economics over safety resulting in delayed vehicle maintenance, overloading of vehicles for higher profits, over speeding to overtake the driver ahead for more passengers at the risk of the lives of the passengers etc.*

c. *The reasons for egocentric driver behaviour causing confusion at junctions without signals or police presence so as to beat the other driver to it with a sense of achievement and the practice of one driver racing another driver to be ahead on a highway for no justifiable reason etc.*

d. *The impact of religious beliefs relating to the fact that every death is ordained by God and nothing can be done and the belief that RTCs are caused by spiritual forces so God can protect road users if they pray irrespective of their mistakes. Others are the, beliefs that people can be protected from RTC's by their talisman, charms etc. with the following as typical examples.*

Example 1: In Ghana asked why pedestrian had refused to use a footbridge she responded that "Every day when I pass by, I see vehicles hitting other pedestrians but I am protected by God so it cannot happen to me"

Example 2: Another example is in Nigeria, when a driver near hit of a pedestrian who complained was told by the driver that he had a talisman so could not be involved in a traffic crash.

e. *Negligent and Irresponsible Behaviour that are of high Risk but are disregarded such as:*

   • *Parental neglect of very young children by allowing them to use the road unaccompanied by adults.*

   • *Driving of motorcycle without license and helmets with no sense of wrong doing.*

   • *Motorcyclist sharing the road even with provision of segregated lanes.*

   • *Cyclist pitching on moving vehicles to avoid paddling.*

   • *Pillion rider disregard for the use of an unlicensed, uninsured motorcycle without the use of a helmet.*

   • *Keeping of gallons of fuel in vehicles over long distances travel with little regard for the dangers involved.*

   • *Contractor stockpiling materials on the road as if it is a bonafide right to do so.*

   • *Blatant neglect of broken-down vehicles in wrongful positions unattended to on the road.*

   • *The psychological sense that it can happen to others and not me*

f. *Research into commercial driver's knowledge of written road safety campaign messaging. This is because often times the messages are in English and only those with some level of literacy can relate to such messages. This is against the backdrop that the results of some random surveys on the knowledge base of road signs among some drivers have displayed some level of ignorance irrespective of the fact that literacy level up to JHS is a mandatory requirement in driver training such as the following which gives room for concern;*

   • *Reference to road safety signage on bumpy roads as breasts*

- *Reference to road safety sign with a cattle image as a location for a chop bar*
- *Reference to an H road sign indicating the presence of a hospital as a high-speed zone*

It is expected that the outcome of such research initiatives should guide the formulation of road safety campaign messages by adopting appropriate measures using local dialects for effective results.

8.5.2 Road Safety Campaign Production and Dissemination

A. Road Safety Campaign Methods: Road safety campaign method refers to the type of communication channels adopted to transmit the campaign message to attain the required results. It involves the use of different communication tools for information dissemination and outreach.

i. Classification of Road Safety Campaign Methods: These can be classified as mass media and Inter-personal media communications as well as indoor and outdoor.

a). Mass Media Campaigns: These are organised to gain national coverage for increased awareness about a topic or issue. It employs the use of diverse array of media technologies such as television, radio, newspaper etc. with a wide reach making them cost efficient. However, it is with a one-way communication.

b). Targeted or Inter-personal Media Campaign is media targeted for specialized groups through public meetings, lectures, group discussions, home visits and demonstrations.

c). Indoor media include communication mediums conducted in enclosed environments with specific characteristics long hours of exposure and a strong local market presence. The approach is deemed to be cost efficient.

d) Outdoor media communication mediums involve those seen outside the home such as billboards, posters, stickers which can also be in transit or static such as adverts on transit vehicles etc.

e) The mode of communication can also be broadcasted, written and spoken.

ii. Selection of Road Safety Campaign Methods: This is determined by the context in which the traffic behaviour occurs, the characteristics of the target audience and availability of the appropriate communication tools. Table 8.13 provides the array of media community channels and their advantages and disadvantages.

These communication tools can be engaged and combined in different ways for effective results especially with regards to how and where the target audience will have easy access.

Table 8.13: Examples of Road Safety Campaign Methods

RSE method	Advantages	Disadvantages	Applicability in Ghana
Audiovisual Media			
Workshops Seminars Discussions Events Forums Lectures Exhibitions Public Meetings	-Participatory -Wide Reach target group. -Stimulates discussions -Enhances group consciousness -Enhances exchange of opinion -Experts in the field provides valuable insights -Discussions are based on all aspects of road safety	-Speakers must be encouraged to participate to achieve effectiveness -There is need for visual aids for more effectiveness -There is need trained moderator.	-All modes are applicable in Ghana
Television	It combines sight, sound & motion. -Has very large reach -Is accessible to everyone -It allows for more complex messages -It is cost efficient	-It has short lived duration of messages -Involves high cost of production -It provides less efficient delivery against narrowly defined targets	-Production of Television documentary -Television airing of campaign messages -Conduct of television discussions -Airing of television commercials are all available in Ghana
Radio	-It creates visual impressions of the mind -It is of high reach -It is good for reaching local audience -It is dynamic and allows for on spot presence -It stimulates imagination and has possibility of eliciting emotions in target audience -It has low production cost -It can reach mobile population remote audiences.	-It has low attention -It is of short lifespan -There is fleeting duration of message -It is not for complicated messages	-Radio commercial is produced and aired on local FM radio stations -Holding of radio discussions -Radio discussions combined with phone-in programmes
Cinema	-It allows for more complex messages -It has possibility for eliciting emotion in target audience	-High cost of production	They include features and stories presented as feature films and documentaries
Printed Media			
Newspaper	-Newspapers have immediacy and announcement value -It has a better scope for providing detailed information. -There is a geographic flexibility It has special interest targeting -There are vehicles for Coupon delivery.	However, newspapers have two major short-comings, First, the lower literacy levels are barriers in growth and secondly, Newspapers have a very short life span	-Newspaper publications are made eg Crushed by JoyNews documentary -16th August 2021 -Bloody roads of Bolgatanga -Ghanaweb.com 3rd Dec 2020 -How do we curb accidents on our roads, dailymotion.com - 15th March 2022
Magazines	-Magazines have specific audience selectivity, as they are specialized. -It is excellent at reaching mass media -It has large reach -It allows for geographical selectivity	-It has poor demography selectivity It has poor re-production quality -It is of short lifespan -It has long lead time -It is of slow production cycle -It is not flexible -It is of low frequency	NRSA has a periodic Magazine Bulletin
Flyers, Leaflets, Brochures Stickers Posters Billboards Banners Notice Boards	-High Selectiveness -High exposure -Able to reach a wide audience -Allows for complex messages -Long lifespan -Low cost	-Low attention -Low Information capacity	-Bill Boards -Leaflets/ Pamphlets -Stickers handed out to tro-tro and bus drivers by the police and other stakeholders -Banners -Posters put up at trotro stations and other relevant places
Direct Mailings	Selective Communication	Junk mail	Not Applied

RSE method	Advantages	Disadvantages	Applicability in Ghana
Community Based Programmes			
Campaign Talking Drums Information Services Outreach programmes Role Play Folk songs Testimonies Open forum Drama Quiz Floats with music and banners	-Possibility of reaching people more than once -Use of innovations, like use of drama or role playing, achieved enhanced effectiveness -They help in through a real like experience -Provides wider public participation and awareness, as well as making necessary changes in behavior and environment	High cost per contact	-Use of Public Address System -Information services (P A system) -Outreach Programmes in churches, mosques, lorry parks and market place, festivals and durbars, drivers' wives' associations, lorry –stations, Drama, Testimonies from local accident victims -Folk songs / drumming and dancing, -Floats with music and banners, Role Play, -debates
E-Facilities			
Internet Websites Social Media Local websites, forums, blogs and social media pages	-Can be used to maintain the campaign momentum for a longer period. -It utilises existing communication -It is of high selectivity, Interactive, Flexible -It allows for complex messages -It is low Cost	-It is of Low impact -It has audience controls and exposure -There is need to simplify information	E-facilities are not widely explored in Ghana

Source: Delhomme et al. (2009)

In Ghana, the Ghana News Agency (GNA), MTTD, NRSA, DVLA and some corporate bodies collaborates on various platforms to create consistent and systematic awareness for road users (See Figure 8.13).

Figure 8.13: Publications by the GNA NRSA Associations

Examples of road safety campaign programmes by the NRSA are as summarised in Table 8.14.

Table 8.14: Examples of Road Safety Campaign Programmes in Ghana

NRSA sensitises children, drivers on road safety in Kasoa – By Calvis Tetteh, June 11, 2021,
The National Road Safefy Authority in the Central Region has begun a sensitization exercise on road safety tips in some schools in the Awutu Senya East Municipality. School children were sensitized on the need to stay focused and behave appropriately when using the road.

Ghana embarked on a safety awareness campaign to promote safety during Easter - GNA News by Patience Gbeze on March 29 2022 - Discipline and Patience key to ensure sanity on our roads – road safety campaigners by Pernod Ricard Ghana – A spirit and Wine Company in collaboration with Street Sense Organisation (SSO)

NRSA launches road safety sensitisation campaigns in three regions- Wednesday, December 2, 2020, NRSA launches road safety sensitisation campaigns in three regions The Bono, Bono East and Ahafo Regional Offices of the National Road Safety Authority (NRSA) have launched the Christmas road safety campaign to sensitize road users on traffic regulations and road safety precautions. Dubbed "Arrive Alive", the campaign also sought to prioritize and intensify road safety education to control crashes and fatalities on the highway in the Christmas festivities, and the Election 2020 season as well.

Metwi a Mentwa road safety campaign launched in Accra: Ghanaian Times by Anita Nyarko-Yirenkyi - As part of efforts to prevent drink-driving and promoting road safety in the country, a campaign dubbed "Metwi a Mentwa" (literally meaning If I drink, I won't drive), has been launched in Accra.
The programme seeks to sensitise drivers on the dangers of drink-driving. The campaign is under the auspices of Pernod Ricard (PRG) Ghana, producers of wines and alcoholic drinks in collaboration with the Ghana Police Service, Street Sense Organisationm(SSO) and the National Road Safety Authority(NRSA).

Kpeshie MTTD steps up sensitisation of road users Graphic Online: Date: Dec - 26 - 2020, 23:07 by: Edward Acquah - The Kpeshie Divisional Motor Traffic and Transport Department (MTTD) at Nungua in Accra has stepped up efforts to sensitise and educate motorists and pedestrians on road traffic regulations to ensure an accident-free festive season at Teshie, Nungua and surrounding communities.
The MTTD command has also increased police visibility on the main Teshie-Nungua-Tema beach road and other busy routes within the area to enforce the law and forestall vehicular congestion.

Precise Driving School launches road safety awareness programme to educate motorcycle riders - B&FT Online December 9, 2021 - Precise Driving School has launched a road safety awareness and sensitisation campaign to reawaken motorcycle riders' consciousness to the hazards their activities pose to themselves and other road users, and the need for them to comply strictly with road traffic
rules. The programme is under the theme 'Stop the Motorcycle Crashes Now', and advocates for the right riding behaviour to prevent motorcycle crashes, serious injuries and fatalities in Ghana through road safety awareness and education campaigns.

Haulage truck drivers and owners receive sensitisation on road safety and traffic regulations in Takoradi Ghana Shippers' Authority (GSA): 23rd October, 2019: The Ghana Shippers' Authority (GSA) has organised a sensitisation workshop on road safety regulations for haulage truck drivers and owners in Takoradi on 23rd October, 2019. The workshop, the first of its kind to be held in the oil city, comes after the GSA organised a similar one earlier this year in Tema for transit truck drivers who ply Ghana's transit corridors to destinations in Burkina Faso, Niger and Mali.

Prudential Life launches Safe Steps Road Safety campaign, December 1, 2021 -…with Didier Drogba as Ambassador Prudential Life Insurance, one of the leading life insurers in the country, has partnered with Prudence Foundation, the National Road Safety Authority (NRSA) and the Didier Drogba Foundation to launch the Safe Steps National Road Safety campaign in Accra. Core to the campaign is a series of 60-second public service announcement videos and educational posters featuring Safe Steps Road Safety Africa Ambassador Didier Drogba, who advises on key road safety topics: namely drunk-driving, distracted driving, seat-belts, speed limits, motorcycles and pedestrians.

The Pediatric Society of Ghana (PSG) has launched a National Child Road Safety Campaign with the slogan: "Stop! Think Child Safety," to intensify public awareness about the dangers that children faced as pedestrians or road users. Dr John Adabie Appiah, a Senior Specialist for Paediatric Critical Care at the Komfo Anokye Teaching Hospital (KATH), Kumasi, in his opening remarks at the virtual meeting for the launch, said road accidents were becoming a major global public health threat and required a multi-sectorial approach to address it.

Obour launches Go Come' road safety campaign - Myjoyonline December 26, 2021 National Road Safety Campaign Ambassador Bice Osei Kuffour aka Obour has launched the Go Come Campaign in response to the rising and rampant road carnage on Ghana's roads. The campaign is aimed at helping educate road users, especially drivers to tread cautiously. The National Road Safety Ambassador, who was recently appointed Managing Director of the Ghana Post, intimated that his long-standing passion and desire to see Ghana's roads safe has driven him to embark on this National Campaign.

B. Engagement of Communication Services for Road Safety Campaign: This includes the following:

i. Road Safety Campaign Branding: Every campaign must be uniquely defined with concepts that purposely focuses on the main determinants of behaviour for the particular audience, provides ease of engagement with such audience, incorporate the use of local resources and determine the scale of application be it of a national or local coverage. There are three (3) key branding concepts proposed by Lutzke J. and Henggeler M. F. (2009) on this as:

a. Logos: when logical arguments are pursued to appeal to people's common sense and rational position.

b. Ethos: when the focus is on the image of the organisation or company e.g. NRSA and the feelings that the recipient (the target group) has towards it as a sender because the more ethos the organisation has the higher their credibility is among the recipients.

c. Pathos: when the recipients' emotional engagement is aimed to be activated by drawing the attention to dramatical issues such as the use of powerful photos and moving background music.

ii. Campaign Identifiers: These are described as elements that give identity to a campaign and also bring consistency. They constitute visual or audio elements strong enough to get people's attention such as the use of logos, mascots, brands, photos, film clips, adverts, banners and graphics, posters on notice boards and adverts on billboards or on bus backs. In addition, infographics can also be an effective way to convey facts and figures in the campaign.

iii. The Media Plan: The media plan incorporates the media coverage, advertising rates of each media tool and supportive activities for the launching of the campaign within available budgets.

iv. Selection of Media Services: Professional communication services are engaged by the choice of a media option in order to deliver road safety campaigns. These are determined by the number of media choices available, ability to reach certain target, geographical coverage and flexibility.

v. Recruitment of Advertising Agency: Advertising agencies are employed to facilitate the implementation of the media plan.

Examples of common road safety media campaign types in Ghana are as presented in Table 8.15 and Figure 8.14.

Table 8.15: Example of Road Safety Campaign Focus by Theme

Targeted Theme	Description
Drivers	Drinking and driving campaigns -Distraction campaigns eg. use of handheld devices -Seat belt campaigns -Helmet use, -Speeding and aggressive driving campaigns -Fatigue campaigns -In Ghana the NRSC organizes data-led mass campaign programmes on speeding, fatigue driving, drink driving, helmet use.
Vulnerable road users	-Campaigns on passenger empowerment, pedestrian safety, among other. Such campaigns are used to conduct a passionate appeal to passengers and pedestrians not to allow reckless drivers to kill and endanger their lives and those of other road users in the country eg. -Corporate support entities and NGOs such as the Corporate supported entities and NGO's such as the Vision for Alternative Development (VALD), in collaboration with National Road Safety Commission (NRSC), AMEND and Puma Energy Foundation, has launched a road safety programme, with a charge on pedestrians and passengers to speak up against reckless driving by motorists. -Teams made up of VALD, AMEND and NRSC will be deployed to lorry terminals and strategic locations on the roads to educate motorists, pedestrians and passengers during the period.
School Campaigns	- This is about child pedestrian safety on the roads in the country who face grave risks as they walk to and from school. E.g. -NRSA embarks on media, public and school outreach educational programmes on road safety. Resource persons from the, Ghana Police Service (MTTD), Child Road Safety". -Safe walk to school interventions including infrastructure provisions on speed calming measures for school zones and sensitization on road crossing are also conducted with corporate road safety support entities and the Department of Urban roads. -Introduction of a number of road crossing aids known as lollipop stands, to help children, cross the road at some road points,
Seasonal Campaigns	Christmas and Easter road safety campaigns to sensitize road users on traffic regulations and road safety precautions. These seek to prioritize and intensify road safety education to control crashes and fatalities on the highway during festivities. Road users and the public are sensitised safety ahead, before, during and after the season as part of efforts to reduce fatalities on the road. Others are election season campaigns

Figure 8.14: Graphical Presentation of Road Safety Campaign Focus by Theme, Source: NRSA

C. Use of Non-Media Campaign Activities: Mass media campaigns are known to be of high profile rather than efficacy with little effect on human behaviour change because extended reach of a wider population does not necessarily translate into compliance. Though highly visible they also turn to be expensive.

Thus, non-media activities such as the application of standards for legislation, land use planning, engineering design enforcement, adjudication, rehabilitation of defaulting road user etc. are recommended to complement the process. An overview of combined road safety campaign methods and modes of communications are as summarised in Table 8.16.

In Ghana, the means of communication used for road safety campaigns are varied and the extent of consideration for the advantages and disadvantages of the media tools used in which circumstance is often informed by outcome evaluation of previous campaigns. However, increased use on non-media activities especially the provision of lorry stations off the roadway to prevent the use of laybys as lorry stations could go a long way to help.

Table 8.16: A Matrix of RSE Method by User Group compiled from Literature

Road user Target	Road Safety Campaign Programmes	Methods and Procedures
Drivers	-Encourage the separation of drinking from driving -Travelling at unsafe speeds; -Exposure to alcohol and other drugs; -Driving/riding while fatigued or distracted; -Driving a car with a low crash protection rating -Promotion of 'share the road' culture	-Publicity and promotional campaigns -Public education through mass media campaigns -Advice in combination with leaflet, brochure etc. Workshops Seminars Discussions Events Forums Public Meetings
Passengers General safety in car	-Encourage use of seatbelts and helmets -Consequences of non-use, incorrect and inconsequential use -Promote the risks of detection and the sanctions for illegal behaviors; -Encourage the development of best practice; -Encourage the use of protective clothing by motorcyclists;	-Public education through mass media campaigns Public Meetings
Pedestrians	-inform pedestrians and cyclists about their responsibilities when using shared paths; and -explain and promote key road rules for pedestrians and cyclists -Communication and interaction with other road users -Hazard and risk awareness related to their own behavior, and the behavior of other traffic participants -Being watchful despite friends and other distractions, like during the use of headphones/mobile phones -Visible clothing -Traffic fears -Mobility patterns and safe routes	-Publicity and promotional campaigns -Public education through mass media campaigns -Field Demonstrations -Public Meetings

Road user Target	Road Safety Campaign Programmes	Methods and Procedures
Cyclists	-use of helmets and safe bikes -Communication and interaction with other road users -Blind spot -Visibility (lights/reflectors on the bike, clothes, flag, etc.) -Risk awareness and risk seeking, speed, peer pressure, overestimation of own skills -The use of motorcycle protective clothing	Ditto
Communities- Co-Creating Engaging Communication with Drivers and passengers	-Community awareness and understanding of the causal factors of road crashes. -Greater understanding, awareness, and practice of safe behavior and skills. -Adoption of more courteous and considerate road behavior and demonstrating care for the safety of others Road Reminder Communication Post-crash Making road safety a collective responsibility for whole families	-Lecture, discussion and media Discussion, reflections, group work Campaign Talking Drums Information Services Outreach programmes Role Play Folk songs Testimonies Open forum Drama Quiz
Peer Road Users- being aware of the extremely high levels of crash involvement	-Strategies to reduce these risks when driving with peers -Importance of separating drinking and driving, and adhering to the zero-blood alcohol requirement; and -Driving solo, especially driving at night; -The influence of peers travelling in their vehicle; -Exposure to alcohol and other drugs and arrangements to avoid driving after drinking (alternate transport); -Over-confidence while driving or taking overt risks such as speeding; and -Driving a car with a low crash protection -Engaging in speeding behavior or driving at unsafe speeds	-Formation of traffic clubs -Lecture, discussion and media -Discussion, reflections -Group work
Driver Unions- Promote road safety amongst their memberships	Provide up-to-date and relevant information on traffic laws, Safe driver behavior and techniques, road conditions, Maintenance procedures and vehicle safety -Provide membership feedback to government and industry on road safety policy and new initiatives Develop internal safety policies for their staff including host responsibility. -Promote safe practices in fleet operation. -Larger fleet operators can encourage staff to participate in defensive driving courses, and where feasible, sponsor or buy in defensive driving courses for own staff at own premises.	-Group Discussions -Field Events
Vulnerable Road Users- Older Road Users/Disabled	-Raise awareness of good safe self-regulation of driving practices -Inform older people about how to use other forms of transport if they need to stop driving are not aware of the risks they face as pedestrians	-Information Services Outreach
Children	-Teach their children important road safety behaviors. use the correct child restraint for their child's age/size; -Ensuring children always travel in an appropriate restraint that is correctly installed is a key way of protecting children as vehicle occupants School based education and learn to ride centres can be helpful in increasing students' knowledge and basic skills,	-Mass media campaigns -School Road Safety clubs -Field Demonstration
Teachers	-Information and advice for teachers how to guide their child, legislation -Teach them safe road crossing behaviors and provide supervised opportunities for them to apply these skills in real traffic environments	Role modelling safe road use practices

Road user Target	Road Safety Campaign Programmes	Methods and Procedures
Families and Parents of Children	-Determine when children are safe to walk unsupervised; and help children determine safe routes to school and other destinations -Ensuring parents have received appropriate information and advice about child restraints -Hold their hand when crossing roads; Ensure helmets are worn when on wheeled toys, bicycles or tricycles; and -Being a good road safety role model. Close supervision when children are near traffic and safe practices when crossing roads, specifically always holding hands with an adult (Muir et al, 2010). -Good riding skills (such as being confident and predictable) as well as safe bicycle use and helmet wearing -Involvement of parents: information and advice how to guide their child, awareness of the 'development stage' of their child	Role modelling safe road use practices
Media	-Support road safety initiatives through responsible and objective reporting -Support, promote and sponsor effective road safety initiatives and campaigns -Discourage advertising which glamorises and/or promotes unsafe practices and products. -Actively encourage safer practices and products	-Workshops -Seminars -Discussions -Events -Forums -Lectures -Exhibitions -Public Meetings
Family of Victims	Create a post-crash direct communication campaign for customers Provide Immediate Information and Access to Relief, For Accident Victims and Family Passengers Drivers/ Riders Vehicle Owners	-Outreach programme -Open forum Role Modelling

D. Road Safety Campaign Dissemination: Road safety campaign dissemination is about the campaign delivery itself by the launching of the campaign after relevant preparations as follows:

i. Pilot testing of Media Concepts: This is done on target audience before wider application to identify weaknesses to be corrected and adjustments to be made.

In Ghana, some technical reviews are conducted on media concepts for road safety campaigns but the level of its efficacy is not known.

ii. Road Safety Campaigns Exposure: Proper timing in terms of the season, duration and frequency of advertisements are essential for reaching the target audience because these determine effectiveness. Particularly, continuous campaign reinforcements as to maintain consistent campaign momentum is very important. Thus essentially, if resources were available in required thresholds, there should be no end to the process. Examples of best practice road safety campaign message characteristics from literature sources is a summarised in Table 8.17.

Table 8.17: Distillation of road safety campaign Message and Dissemination

Best Practice	Details
Linklatefs' Five Essential Ingredients	-The campaign should be addressed to a particular target audience who have been identified to be at a high risk of road trauma.
	-It should include a specific, clear message (rather than just the non-specific "drive safely" type of communication).
	-The message should be seen as coming from a highly credible source and must also present more than just a one-sided biased argument.
	-The campaign should definitely not use fear, shock, honor or threat tactics.
	-The campaign should be based on motivational research by finding out why people behave the way they do before attempting to change their behavior.
	-Success is dependent upon the existing behaviors and beliefs of the audience.
	-Guidelines should not be seen as inviolable principles since knowledge or wisdom changes with the passage of time.
Freimuth's Guidelines for Effective Public Service Announcements	-"Use of humor, entertainment, and drama to attract the audience's attention;
	-Use of high-quality production;
	-Use of redundancy to improvise retention;
	Use of credible sources.
	-The provision of communicate specific mode should apply but limited information;
	-There should be inclusion of concrete art recommendations and visual enactments of the recommended behavior;
	-Use of more positive appeals as they appear to be more effective than negative ones.
	-Use of two-sided arguments if the audience is likely to be exposed to other communication-arguments;
	-Use of appeals carefully and only when adequate information is available to predict audience reactions.
	-Use of appropriate channel for the target audience.
	-Segmentation of the audience based on all available audience data."
	-"Use of only a few actors, not a large crowd scene.
	-Repetition of the subject in the audio four or more times.
	-Use of an audio slogan.
	-Use of a presenter, demonstration, or slice of life rather than vignettes.
	-Use of live action.
	-Statement of the social benefits from admiring the hateful behavior.
	-Use of a straight forward presentation of information.
	-Use of a high or moderate emotional appeal. "
Twelve Guiding Principles Suggested by (Elliott & Shanahan)	-Respect for audience and a look out for clues about "class" values.
	-The message and execution must not provide an excuse to dismiss the message;
	-General admonitions must not only be avoided but suggestions must be made (show) for desirable alternative behaviors;
	-Show of any undesirable behaviors must be avoided.
	-Modeling or social imitation must be built in so that the viewer will want to do the right thing because of the modeling (i.e. use positive images and desirable models).
	-Motivation by irrelevant appeals must be avoided;
	-Since RTC's are not relevant to most people behavioral modeling or advocacy must be ensured to be relevant and practical (achievable).
	-There should be provision of an excuse for people to change their minds. Eg. Signpost is a real change in the environment which can act as an excuse.
	-Some sense of urgency must be built by choosing media which reaches people before or in close proximity to the behavior being advocated.
	-Campaign must not aim for too big a change. A relative change is preferred to no change. To ask for a big change is likely to result in rejection of any change since the key to change is not the advertising but what the advertising is supporting and what other environmental supports are needed, especially personal and social.
	-A range of possible strategies must be considered and experimented with through creative development research.
	-Information must be built into the campaign to allow for people's bad memories and it must be capable of irritation?
	-The interpretation by the audience, the personal relevance and consequences of the interpreted messages, what is perceived to be of likelihood of compliance and what factors are perceived to hinder and assist such compliance must be determined.
	-Research must be integrated into the creative development process.

ii. Roles and Responsibilities for Road Safety Campaigns: Road safety campaigns must be managed by a lead agency in consultation with other stakeholders and the campaign development must be best done by qualified professionals involved in such promotional activities.

In Ghana, the NRSA sometimes collaborates with media institutions like the Ghana Journalist Association (GJA), the Ghana Independent Broadcasters Association (GIBA) for the process.

8.5.3 Road Safety Campaign Monitoring and Evaluation

A. Campaign Monitoring: Continuous monitoring to determine the level of campaign coverage at national, regional and local levels is useful for of quality control of the timing, maintenance of standards, efficiency in work implementation, budget control and problem mitigations.

B. Road Safety Campaign Evaluation: This is used to determine campaign effects on road user knowledge, attitudes and behaviour change guided by the following:

i. Timing of Evaluation: Since sustainable behavioural changes take time to be achieved this should be done long after a campaign has been launched. Also, it is of the view that the actual impacts of road safety on behavioural change is difficult to determine accurately because comparable or representative control groups control group who may o be exposed to other factors or campaigns that could influence behaviour in similar ways to the experimental group are not easily identified. Chaudhary et al. (2014).

In Ghana road safety campaign evaluations have been conducted in the past but the extent of consideration of time durations is not known. Also, evaluations have not been benchmarked against control groups because similar activities are often carried out country wide.

ii. Determination of Effectiveness of Campaign Methods: Since many factors affect road safety and even campaigns consist of multiple strategies it becomes difficult for researchers to discern which campaign components contributed most to the effectiveness, or lack thereof.

iii. Determination of Road Safety Campaign Impacts: Road safety campaigns often go against the tide of existing behaviour or opinion and it is vital not to provide the audience with any excuses to ignore the message by modelling any undesirable behaviours.

In Ghana, the findings from road safety campaign evaluations rarely show any measurable effects beyond mere awareness with limited impact on behaviour change even in product advertising. (See Figure 8.15). Also, there are no set regimes on campaign frequencies due to limited funding. Therefore, campaign dissemination should be coordinated and reinforced by increased and targeted local law enforcement actions and initiatives.

Figure 8.15: Publications on Road Safety Campaign Impact

8.6 CONCLUSION

Without knowledge, there can be no rightful road safety action and good knowledge must be acquired for expected results. So, in order to address the myriad of road traffic indiscipline on Ghanaian roads the level of education provided must be stepped up with appropriate procedures by the road safety authorities in the country.

CHAPTER 9

ROAD TRAFFIC LAW ENFORCEMENT

"Enforcement is based upon the assumption that not all road users will adhere to the specified traffic rules and regulations, and may need to be encouraged, educated and persuaded to do so, (Zaal, 1994)".

9.1 INTRODUCTION

Road transport systems provide ample opportunities to make both intentional and unintentional errors for which enforcement of set road traffic regulations is required to ensure compliance by road users, (WHO, 2015b). Also, what is planned, designed and promised on road safety can only become a reality through enforcement (UNECE, 2015). This is by the application of sanctions or threat of sanctions to road users who break the law, (Division of Transportation Safety, DoT Maryland). Further to this, Wegman F.C.M, (1992) intimates that, everyday reality shows that a law alone is not enough to change the behaviour of road users and enforcement must be applied.

Ghana has road traffic laws and regulations enforced by designated agencies, mostly the MTTD to reduce RTC fatalities and injuries. However, an evaluation report by ADB, (2013) on road safety performance in the African region, identified effective road safety enforcement as a key challenge in Ghana's road safety work mostly due to inadequate resources. This section of the book discusses state of Ghana's road traffic safety enforcement and the opportunities for improvement to achieve intended purposes.

9.1.1 Key Elements of Road Traffic Enforcement

A. Definition of Road Traffic Enforcement: This is about the detection, sanctioning and application of relevant penalties in to encourage responsible road user behaviour in traffic. Some wrongful road user behaviour usually enforced by traffic law enforcers includes the following:

i.   Driving with high levels of blood alcohol concentration.

ii.   Driving above speed limits.

iii. Disobeying traffic signals or signs.

iv. Not using seatbelt, helmets and child restraints.

v.   Driving without a valid license.

vi. Use of a vehicle without roadworthiness.

vii. Loading a vehicle above legal limit.

viii. Use of defective vehicles on the road.

In Ghana, road safety enforcement is normally on speeding, seatbelt and helmet use, drunk driving, unlicensed driving, and other aberrant driving behaviours, (Boateng, 2021).

B. Road Traffic Crash Enforcement Process: According to ESCAPE, (2002), enforcement is done on a basis of continuum of essential steps involving the

i.   Formulation of legislation;

ii.   Conduct of education;

iii. Surveillance of traffic systems;

iv. Detection of traffic offences;

v.   Apprehension of violators of traffic laws for non-compliance and

vi. Application of legal proceedings and related or may not be applied with the type of measure depending on the seriousness of the offence by law.

C. Effects of Road Traffic Enforcement: According to the Maryland Police Training Commission, enforcement is characterized by three major types of resultant effects as follows:

i. Direct Effects: This is based on direct effect of changed attitude and sustained compliance from prompt apprehension and appropriation of punishment through.

In Ghana, though enforcement by direct apprehension is a common practice in the country, direct effects of road traffic law enforcement in Ghana is of mixed outcomes. This is because whilst some people will avoid causing any traffic violations after apprehension and punishment some are not in the least motivated to change their ways because to them the law is ineffective. Typical examples include those who will blatantly disregard an order to report to the police station or those who will ignore the signal to stop.

Others are those who create an impression of stopping but will zoom off before records of vehicle details are made. In such an instance only MTTD officers with means of mobility are able to chase them. In situations where their details are recorded an order maybe issued for apprehension by officers ahead of the location of incidence.

ii. Observational /Symbolic Effect: This is based on the perception that an individual can be deterred from violating a traffic offence from the observation or knowledge about the punishment imposed on another violator.

In Ghana, there is a lot of ignorance about traffic regulations and the corresponding penalties. Also, the apprehension of traffic offenders, the related punishment effected and its resultant effect on the offender is not very vivid. It is not common to see law enforcers engaging with traffic offenders on individual merit so lessons are not known and shared. Thus, the level of appropriation of punishment and its effect on changed attitudes of individuals is not known.

iii. Reputational Effect: This is based on a community wide general perception about the status of a person in society which can influence good traffic behaviour.

The reputational effect of enforcement is also difficult to analyse in the Ghanaian situation since very important persons (VIPs) are afforded the privileges to violate traffic on the basis of preferential treatment and though in some cases it is for security reasons. Others are law enforcers letting off VIP violators of traffic laws because of an intervention from superiors.

Indeed, the opposite is even possible, whereby the offending VIP can even threaten the law enforcer about having the power to deal with them. The outcomes of a few cases publicised cases of VIP traffic violations regarding wrongful use of sirens were never known and as of now even some non-VIP personnel with installed sirens continue to use them to circumvent traffic congestions.

9.1.2 Theories, and Principles on Traffic Law Enforcement

A. Theories on Traffic Law Enforcement: The traffic law enforcement system is underpinned by some theoretical perspectives with regards to factors influencing compliance and violations of traffic laws with respect to factors such as ignorance, fear of being sanctioned and complete disregard for traffic rules as follows:

i. The Deterrence Theory: The theory purports that individuals will avoid offending traffic behaviours(s) if they fear the perceived consequences of a violating act, (Maneepakorn, 2010). In such instances the creation of such deterrence factors will make it unnecessary for the police to catch and punish any offender in the first place. Stafford and Warr, (1993) categorises this into as general and specific deterrence,

General deterrence is on road user's compliance with traffic road rules influenced by the risk of being detected and punished (Rothengatter, 1990) and specific deterrence relates to a situation where an experience with a specific enforcement violation deters a road user from future offending behavior as a result. However, Sally Leivesley & Associates, (1987), disagrees with the fact that there is a relationship between enforcement and safe (or unsafe) road user behaviour due to the complexity of the interplay between factors.

In Ghana, this is difficult to establish since consistent records on same person violations are not available nor researched.

ii. Theories on Crime Control and Due Process: The theory stipulates that from a policing perspective, law enforcement can be divided between the notions of crime control and due process. The crime control notion is on the importance of an efficient justice system and the due process is in relation to the occurrence of justice and the protection of personal rights (Packer H. 1964). In practice law enforcement officers tends to primarily apply the due process theory with crime control as supplementary.

In Ghana, both approaches are effected but the margin by which one is applied over the other and the related benefits is not studied or researched though, due process may seem to be more applied.

iii. Social Learning Theory: The theory is based on the perception that deviant behaviour can be learned through social relationships and through imitation of the behaviour of others (Agnew 1991).

This is very common in Ghana and relates to diverse traffic violations such as wrongful driver behaviour by commercial drivers who are always in are rush and commits diverse traffic violations in a similar manner with the notion that it is a right. Thus, it is not uncommon for them to shout "Myself" at a private driver who fails to commit such as offence.

It is also not uncommon to see a driver joining a convoy of VIP vehicles to beat traffic congestion. It has also become a norm for funeral processions and celebrants of diverse occasions to circumvent traffic congestions by their own authority as a form of right without any apprehension.

B. Principles of Traffic Law Enforcement

In addition to the theories on traffic enforcement some underlying principles for effective enforcement are recommended in literature as follows:

i. Effectiveness of Enforcement by Educational Campaigns: Papadimitriou E. et al, (2016) recommends for traffic enforcement programmes not to be implemented as standalone activity but be combined with widespread publicity at national and local levels.

ii. Effectiveness of Enforcement by Social Values: A model based on the application of psychology to explain actual behaviour on the road by the by OECD (2017), established that enforcement can only be upheld if the following are achieved.

a) A society is of the opinion that certain hazardous behaviour should be prevented.

In Ghana, it is not well established as to what road users actually considers to be hazardous due to the blatant disregard for some road safety interventions aimed to protect road users themselves.

b) A good understanding of the real reasons why violations occur since a traffic violator may be responsible for violating the law but might not always be necessarily liable for the violation.

In Ghana, the acceptance of other modes of driver training and the limited knowledge and understanding of traffic regulations coupled with enforcement challenges remains critical might have to be re-examined.

c) Specific high risk road user behaviour and traffic accident locations must be targeted by the use of selective enforcement strategies designed as a cost-effective alternative.

This is applied in Ghana to some extent with good examples of police locating check points at high-risk road sections but the margin of cost effectiveness of such practices are yet to be established.

d) High-risk non-compliant operators are targeted with supporting compliance activities.

In Ghana, the targeting of alcohol impairment for enforcement is a typical example but specific enforcement actions targeted at individual transport operators who violate the law does not happen. It becomes even complex when the law enforcers establish cordial relationship with some drivers. Also, some road users are of the opinion that they can easily bribe the police out of their violating acts in traffic

e) Enforcement is visible enough to enhance the probability for detecting offenders based on the ability to create highly perceived apprehension by surveillance.

In Ghana, the MTTD has introduced the "Visible Eye Operation" based on preventive actions with a visible presence of MTTD personnel at strategic locations. The concept is working since the level of apprehension of traffic violators has increased and the service is sometimes extended to solving other traffic problems such as sudden traffic management requirements for example helping to push a defective vehicle from the roadway.

The key recommendation is that there should be a before and after evaluations to determine impacts. Also, the services should be extended to major highways.

f) The use of automated enforcement devices is adopted as a matter of priority.

This is an emerging enforcement strategy in Ghana but at a low pace of expansion due to funding constraints.

g) Short-term intensive enforcement operation which is more cost effective are applied. The state of application of this strategy in Ghana is yet to be attained.

9.1.3 Key Global Standards for Road Traffic Law Enforcement

Some key global standards and guidelines on effective enforcement are as summarised in Table 9.1.

Table 9.1: Examples of key global standards and guidelines for Enforcement

Source	Enforcement Guidelines	Applicability in Ghana
General Assembly - Approved resolution 66/260 (6), In April 2012	• Encourages Member States to adopt and implement national road safety legislation and regulations and improve implementation through social marketing campaigns with consistent and sustained enforcement activities.	There are statutory traffic rules and regulations in Ghana to guide effective enforcement but wilt limited publicity on such is limited
UNECE ITC	• Emphasizing on the role of social norms in enforcement based on cultural influences, religion, socioeconomic level, violent conflict, experience and the related influence on driving behaviours.	The margin of influence of social norms in traffic enforcement Ghana is not well studied in Ghana.
DOA	Pillar 3: -Sustained or increased enforcement of laws and standards, combined with public awareness/education -Implement or strengthen enforcement in accordance with good practices -Educate the general public (Road Users): Pillar 4 -Law enforcement must enhance ensure adherence to basic safety standards. -There must be full engagement and commitment from participating traffic enforcement agencies. -There should be twinning arrangements among Road safety agencies, e.g. International Road Policing Organisation (RoadPOL), -Partnership with the private sector should be pursued, including users, providers, financiers and insurers of transport services	-Most of these aspects apply in Ghana with the exception of twinning arrangements with International Road Policing Organisation (RoadPOL) -Some partnership with the private sector has been initiated with regards to the introduction of spot fines and enforcement technologies but these are yet to be fully implemented
(WHO, 2017c), Save LIVES: a road safety technical package"	-Key evidence-based measures and interventions, and standards, for enforcement of traffic laws and post-crash Survival are outlined with emphasis on evidence-based measures	Most of the aspects are applied in Ghana
United Nations Road Safety Trust Fund 2018 (UNRSTF, 2018)	-Carry out road side checks on compliance of traffic rules -Use of enforcement technology e.g. speed cameras -Cary out other checks on driving-rest times of professional drivers) -Prevent public spaces – sidewalks and cycle lanes from being appropriated from vehicles or commercial activities -Apply penalties effectively and use anti-corruption mechanism -Enable multiple offence enforcement mechanism (e.g. speed – technical inspection -Institute liability insurance) by interlinking and providing access of enforcement authorities to databases on vehicles -Support development and use of more sophisticated technology -Assess effectiveness of user enforcement activities by use of appropriate indicators. -Ensure sufficient budget for enforcement activities.	Most aspects are applied in Ghana with the exception of weak enforcement of encroachment on pedestrian walkways. -Evaluation of enforcement impacts with set indicators are not done. -There is limited application of technology due to limited capacity, funding and equipment

9.1.4 Road Traffic Enforcement Policy in Ghana

The policy statement on enforcement is that Government will take appropriate measures to assist relevant agencies to improve the quality of their services to ensure best road safety practices. The contents of Ghana's road safety policy framework on enforcement can be said to correspond to some aspects of international regulations as listed in Table 9.2. However, detail aspects, processes and the effectiveness of it impacts on reduced RTC will be discussed in the subsequent section of this chapter.

Table 9.2: Traffic Safety Enforcement in Ghana

Key Enforcement Challenges	Enforcement Strategies	Status of Application
-Current enforcement unit is considered a normal part of the operations of the Ghana Police Service with regular rotation of staff. -High attrition rate of trained traffic enforcement personnel unit.	-Set up traffic enforcement unit for effective enforcement of road traffic regulations under the NRSC.	-A dedicated Motor Traffic and Transport Department (MTTD) has since been established to replace the Motor Traffic and Transport Unit (MTTU) of the Ghana Police. However, level of trained capacity is not known
-Poorly equipped and under-staffed existing enforcement -Lack of motivation (pay structure)	-Provide equipment usage and video guidelines and training to law enforcement agencies. -Apply modern technology to facilitate the processes for road safety enforcement.	-This has been addressed by a small margin
-The apparent lack of a structured enforcement programme that often leads to inconsistencies in traffic law enforcement practices and tactics.	-Establish "free call" lines for citizens' to use in reporting offences such as aggressive, unsafe and impaired driving to the law enforcement agency -Encourage law enforcement agencies to collaborate with other affiliated stakeholders to work together to ensure safety on the road.	Ghana has established free call lines as detailed in other sections in this report -The police administration has placed issues of traffic management and road safety management high on its agenda. -The 5-year strategic National Policing plan has adequate and elaborate strategies towards halting the ever-increasing carnage on our roads. -The MTTD collaborates with DVLA and NRSA for enforcement
-Lack of specialist training available for MTTU officers because the Police administration does not consider traffic enforcement as a specialized activity.	-Establish education and training programmes including the use of applied technology, for law enforcement agencies to improve their capacity at enforcement	-Some MTTD personnel have benefited from external training programmes

Source: NRSP 2008

9.2 ROAD TRAFFIC LAWS AND TRAFFIC OFFENCES

9.2.1 Road Traffic Laws

Traffic laws set out legal requirements on unlawful behaviours by road users which may attract punishment and lawful laws to be complied with. These laws are required to be easy to understand, not to be contradictory and without conflict so they can be easily identified and complied with. Of critical importance is the equipment of both law enforcers and road user with such knowledge to enforce and prevent violations.

A. Categories of Traffic Laws: Traffic rules may be in different categories such as rules for vehicles, for the roadway, for the driver and for road users, (Britanica.com/technology/road) and it is recommended for traffic rules to be reasonably uniform throughout the world.

In Ghana traffic rules include laws that regulate vehicles, drivers, passengers, pedestrians, and other conveyances and they are categorized as listed below and detailed in Appendix 9.1.

i. Rules for Vehicles: These rules apply vehicle registration, road worthiness and insurance. Others are, truck weights, vehicle license, related traffic lights and signs, vehicle alterations, vehicle safety equipment etc.

ii. Rules for Drivers and other Road users: These are on driver training and re-training, testing and re-testing, driver licensing and movement rules, motor rider and pedestrians' rules, rules on prohibition on use of communication device while driving, issuance of commercial road transport operating permit, use of protective devices, passing and stopped vehicle at pedestrian crossing amongst others.

iii. Road Use Factors: These dictate which side of the road to use, maximum speeds limits, right of way and turning requirements, axle load limit to protect pavements and bridges from damage, one-way operations and turning controls, parking etc.

9.2.2 Elements of Traffic Offences

A traffic offence is a violation of a section of the traffic law by way of a failure to perform a required procedure or commitment of a forbidden act classified. (NTHSA, 1973). Others are:

A. Traffic offences by Human and Mechanical Factors: Traffic offences by human factors are those which include wrongful road user behaviour by omission or commission on the road whilst traffic offences relating to mechanical factors include vehicular and equipment safety defects.

In Ghana, common traffic offences by human factors include illegal, dangerous and careless behaviour on the road such as over speeding and rash driving, drink driving, fatigue driving, distracted driving, disregard to road signs or regulations, limited road user competence, failure to yield, failure to use restraints, overloading, driving on the shoulders of the road etc.

Others are the use of fake driving licenses and noncompliance to requirements on road worthy and insurance, failing to keep safe distance and rear end collisions, failing to check when reversing, unsafe overtaking, dangerous driving by racing, incapable of having proper control of a vehicle, noncompliance with vehicle restraints, use of mobile devices whilst driving, wrongful parking, not signalizing, no proper vehicle registration, passing other vehicles in no passing zone, not stopping for pedestrians etc.

Pedestrian rules include jay walking, distractions by the use of mobile phones, pedestrian use of unmarked road sections etc. That of mechanical failures includes driver behaviour by vehicle types, safety devices, defective vehicle condition such as the use of vehicles with worn out tyres, defective braking systems and poor vehicle lighting systems etc. (See Figure 9.1).

Figure 9.1: Examples of Checks by the MTTD for overloading and Vehicle defects

B. Traffic offences by 'Shall do' and 'Shall not do basis': Traffic offences labelled as 'shall do' applies to those offenses characterized by a person's failure to perform required acts under the conditions specified by the motor vehicle laws (for example: Stop, Yield, or Keep Right) and the 'Shall not do', offences are characterized by the commission of an act that is prohibited by the motor vehicle law (for example: No Passing, No U Turn, exceeding the speed limit etc.) etc. *all of which apply in Ghana.*

C. Traffic Offences by Momentary versus Continuous Acts: Momentary hazard offences are acts committed over a short period of time whilst continuous acts are habitual.

In Ghana these include failure to stop at a stop sign and failure to yield right-of-way; and continuous hazard offences includes impaired driving from substance use which is habitual and ritualistic to some drivers in Ghana but are often difficult to detect and control.

D. Traffic offences by Judgment of the seriousness of the violation: The seriousness of these offences is often belittled by drivers as not being serious.

Some examples in Ghana includes lack of knowledge of traffic rules, driving for long time durations without a license, overloading, speeding on wet asphaltic road surfaces with worn out tyres, driving with poor vehicle lighting systems in the night. Others passengers sleeping on top of overloaded vehicles, and drivers driving without a spare tyre etc. Table 9.3 provides a summary of examples of traffic offences.

Table 9.3: Summary of Typical Traffic Offences for Which Enforcement is done

Type of Offence	Details	Situation in Ghana
Speed:	• Globally excessive speed is deemed to be the leading cause of traffic crashes which have effective enforcement focus	• In Ghana urban speed limit is 30-50kPH • Rural Speed is 80KPH • Motorway Speed is 100KPH
Drink driving:	• A drink driving related crash is defined as a crash caused by a road user with a BAC over the limit. • The maximum authorised blood alcohol content (BAC) is 0.5 g/l for all drivers.	• In Ghana (BAC) is 0.08 g/l for all drivers
Drugs and driving	• Impaired driving from the use of substances	• Ghana is challenged with the use of diverse intoxicating drug formulas including the use of bitters, "asra", wee toffee etc.
Distraction	• The new land traffic law bans hand-held mobile phones while driving. Hands-free phones can be used	• There is a ban on the use of hand-held phones but higher penalties are given for RTC's caused by hands free phone use
Seat belts and helmets	• Seat belt wearing has been compulsory on front seats since 2007. Seat belt wearing is not compulsory for rear-seat passengers. Enforcement is weak and the rate of use is low	• Though prohibited by law it is the least enforced
Violation of Licensing Conditions		• Driving without license • Driving without valid license • Driving without insurance • Driving unauthorised vehicle
Interpersonal violations		• These are of diverse dimensions and difficult to apprehend in most instances

9.2.3 Features of Traffic Violators

A "traffic violator" may either be a motor vehicle operator, a motor rider, a cyclist, a passenger or a pedestrian with the acts of violations often based on the following elements (NTHSA (1973):

A. Personality Characteristics of Traffic Violators: This is in reference to the effects of personality differences in individuals on traffic violations and they include the following:

i. Malfunctioning in the Human Senses: The human senses including sight that is the ability to see well, auditory that is the ability to hear and feeling that is the ability move the body is critical for effective performance in traffic. When any aspect of the human sense is not functioning well especially due to illness and age a traffic crash may occur.

In Ghana, with the exception of the conduct of an eye test, other health impairment issues are not given serious attention. Even with the eye test drivers who use fake license or who drive without valid licenses remain a threat to other road users because they fail to subject themselves to such tests. Thus, other health issues such as allergies to drug effects, diabetes, joint pains, heart problems, headaches, negative emotions etc. are not given much attention especially with some drivers disregarding their state of health before or when driving.

There are instances of apprehension of some disabled drivers with leg and limb problems also driving without appropriate vehicles or health certificates which must be well investigated.

The mental state of a road user can also impair an individual's performance in traffic but in Ghana this is yet to be given the necessary attention

Also, a study by the NRSA in 2012, revealed that almost all commercial drivers abuse different types of pain killers especially for the treatment of bodily pains at the end of each day's work. Since as of now it is not mandatory for the commercial driving industry to use spare drivers, this poses a serious challenge. It is critical for study of the effects of medical conditions on driving performance to be undertaken to inform necessary mitigations in the future.

ii. Poor Road User Attitude to Authority: This refers to road user attitude the rights of others in traffic which can be positive, negative or neutral in challenging situations. Whilst an impatient road user may take high risk in traffic to serve their purpose an overly cautious road user may lack the confidence to do the right thing in the right situation and cause a crash.

Typical examples in Ghana includes driver impatience with being stuck in one lane from an obstruction such as contractor stockpiled material, sudden vehicle break down, traffic in one lane moving faster than the other, sharing of one lane with motorists from opposite direction or same direction etc.

In such situations, whilst those in the right of way are reluctant to give way to the motorists from the blocked lane those who are trying to join the lane do so with a lot of aggression by just jumping ahead of the moving vehicle with showing and indicator with associated risk of a possible crash.

Similar situations occur when slow moving vehicles such as learner driver vehicles and slowing moving units like tricycles cause's delays in traffic movement forcing other motorists to undertake risky overtaking with little caution. Wrongful practices such as, not using the rightful lanes even where provision has been made for segregated road use by motorcyclists and cyclist are also common occurrences.

It is suggested for studies to be conducted in road user understanding of their own attitudes and that of other road users for better appreciation of RTC causative factors to for better understanding of interpersonal attitudes in traffic.

iii. Poor Traffic Judgment in Decision Making: This is about road user capacity to size up a traffic situation and determine an appropriate course of action based on acquired knowledge and past experience (Horrey W. J. et al, 2015).

In Ghana, examples are when an overly conscious driver causes unnecessary delay in joining a main road from a side road at an intersection out of fear. In such instances not only are wrongful decisions made from bad timing after excessive honking from the other waiting drivers behind such a vehicle. Such a situation can also instigate an impatient driver to try to bypass the delaying driver from behind with little caution which can cause the front driver to panic with the possibility of an RTC occurring.

Also, a driver who lacks confidence may be unable to overtake a slow-moving vehicle causing an impatient driver to overtake more than one vehicle at a time at a risk of a crash. The situation is made worse when the overly cautious driver suddenly jumps ahead of the overtaking driver at a very slow pace and an on-coming vehicle suddenly appears.

Such drivers often try to revert back to their former position in traffic or try to fix themselves into available limited space posing a potential threat of a head-on collision or causing the driver in the rightful lane to embark on a sudden break with dangerous consequence.

iv. Lack of Attention/Awareness on the Road: This is based on the importance on the ability of the individual to focus and concentrate on the task being performed on the road. According to Rogers R et al. (1990), a man can direct his attention to one thing at a time and does not have the capacity to rapidly shift his attention among several things so it is important for drivers on the road to fully concentrate on the task So it is important that road users do not become preoccupied or distracted with feelings of strong emotions such as excitement, anxiety, worry, rage, etc., which diverts their attention from the traffic situation causing a risk of an RTC.

In Ghana, it is not uncommon to see some drivers honking and driving recklessly during funeral possessions due to excitement from grief or honking and driving recklessly due to excitement from the success from national football team etc. Others are sleeping behind the wheel at an intersection or engaging in a conversation not noticing when there is a change over at a signalized junction.

Road rage causing feuding drivers to park anyhow in the middle of the road with little care for other motorists are of RTC risks. Nursing mothers trying to control or give attention to their young children whilst driving, breast feeding and eating whilst driving, adjusting a radio whilst driving and bad weather conditions which may limit a driver's peripheral vision all fall under this category of road user violation characteristic.

v. Motives and Emotions: Motives driven by factors such as fear, need for love, need for power, prestige, etc. are also identified as the conditions that initiate and control road user behavior These can also cause anxiety, anger, worry, aggression, hostility, elation, exuberance and grief which can preoccupy the road user and distract attention for safe traffic performance.

In Ghana, people hardly relate to the demands of driving to such emotional elements. An example is the dangerous practice of asking a driver who has just knocked down a pedestrian to drive the victim to a medical facility in a confused state of mind.

Another example is mob action against a driver involved in pedestrian hits in some communities causing such communities to disregard road user caution and putting themselves in danger amidst the confusion. With the exception of sensitization of the spouses of commercial drivers not to engage in arguments with their partners before they go on the road very little has been done in Ghana about such issues.

vi. Bad Road Use Habits: These are the consistent and automatic reactions of people to reoccurring traffic situations through good and bad traffic habits.

Typical examples in Ghana include motorists buying from roadside vendors in moving traffic rather than properly stopping their vehicles for such transactions etc. Others include the occupation of pedestrian walkways by hawkers causing them to share the road with moving vehicles.

vii. Poor Traffic Knowledge: This relates to poor knowledge and understanding of traffic laws/ traffic operations determined by road user mental and physical capabilities for good performance.

In Ghana, the level of road user knowledge of traffic safety laws in not known or well understood and most road users are also ignorant about the consequences of the law. Example of driver failure to identify the meaning of road signs and markings at random surveys have implications on road safety outcomes. Typical examples include;

a.   *'reference to warnings on bumps as 'female breasts'.*

b.   *'reference to warning signs on cattle crossing presence of a chop bar or local restaurant'*

c.   *'reference to the 'H' symbol for the presence of a medical facility indication for 'high speed' etc.*

Others are inability to use fire extinguishers even where available when there is need to due to lack of knowledge of its use.

viii. Poor Motor skill: This is the ability to control bodily movement in a smooth and coordinated manner based on an individual's inherent capacity to quickly and efficiently respond to external events or stimuli within reasonable reaction time.

Examples in Ghana are the inability of some manual vehicle drivers to apply the half clutch technology when they stop in traffic situations especially on slopes and the lack of knowledge about not applying immediate breaks in certain hazardous situations such as tyre bursts.

Also, common factors such as giving way to traffic on the right at an intersection, stopping at the amber sign at a signalized intersection or moving on when the last stop marking has already been crossed at a signalized intervention are not well interpreted by most motorists. Others are the ability to engage in defensive driving and the use of high-speed expressways to train new drivers.

This is because people do not consciously relate their habits and motivations to what they do on the road and how this is likely to be a safety threat. Most road users use the road more as a matter of course with little care about what could be influencing their actions in traffic. This generates a need for a wide scope of enforcement capability and capacity to adequately manage them.

Also, the difficulty in addressing these issues in Ghana is due to the level of diversity and the challenge of application of common corrective measures. This is because, the science of most of these factors is not well understood and the necessary attention has also not been given to them.

Most importantly, the margin to which these issues affect RTC situations has not been given much premium to match the level of enforcement required. A conscious effort should therefore be made to give such issues the due attention. The factors influencing road user violations and related impacts must be well analysed and understood so that appropriate corrective measures and support systems can be well channelled for effective results.

Road users must also be made aware that road traffic laws must be understood, respected and complied whilst the police apply sufficient effort to enforce the laws and the judiciary also administer rightful penal systems.

B. Reasons for Road User Violation of Traffic Laws: Some of the reasons why people violate traffic laws compiled from different sources include the following:

i. Lack of Understanding of the Importance of Traffic Laws: Where road users fail to place much premium on the traffic laws meant to protect them they violate the laws.

For example, in Ghana, some road users perceive traffic laws as distractions rather than helpful elements for their safety and that of others. That is why some drivers give other drivers a head start about the presence of the police on the road and others are easily willing to bribe their way out of an offence rather than succumb to the requirements of the law. Others are those who seek redress through higher official to get away with a traffic offence. This can be addressed where traffic offences are made visible to road users with clarity of the regulations and related road user benefits.

ii. Risk of Neglected Traffic Safety Challenges: Road users violate traffic laws when inherent safety risks in the traffic system are not given the rightful attention.

A typical example in Ghana is the persistent neglect of formal training for motorcycle riders leaving them to self-train themselves with the consequent result of poor traffic knowledge and bad riding practices with safety risks. Though this is causing increasing crashes with severe injuries and fatalities the situation has been overlooked except for the arrest of commercial motor riders by the police. Another example is the wrongful demand for occupant compliance for the use of seatbelts though most commercial vehicles lack them.

Others are lack of standards for passenger handling by commercial drivers and poor and inconsistent regulation of the commercial transport industry though the NRSA has been currently assigned for the purpose. Such situations do not make sufficient means by which police and legislature can take action against the traffic offender and the threat of punishment as a means of correction is not realistic in such cases.

It is also important that once a new law becomes operational, road users are adequately educated about the content and intent of that law so road user knowledge will be well aligned with the objectives of the legislator for higher level of compliance.

Therefore, road traffic law enforcement should be logical and understandable to the road user backed by the necessary complementary measures such as intensive education of the traffic laws even if it must be done in local dialects so road users will be well informed about what is expected of them

iii. Disrespect of Road Traffic Laws: Where road users disrespect traffic laws, they willfully disregard them:

In Ghana, this situation occurs when some motorists develop the mindset that the police can easily be bribed so disregard the law with impunity. For example a study by Sam E. F., (2022) revealed that most private drivers deem traffic enforcement to be of benefit as it helps deter wrongdoing on the road; but on the other hand commercial drivers had the negative opinion that the police are on the road to extort monies from motorists. Others are vandalisation of traffic signs for selfish economic gains without fear of the consequences from the law due to lack of effective control.

9.3 FUNCTIONS OF TRAFFIC ENFORCEMENT AGENCIES

There are various entities involved in the traffic enforcement process such as the detection of traffic violations, application of enforcement methods and tools as well as legal handling of the violators. This includes the police who are responsible for the detection and handling of road traffic offences and the judiciary who renders the required penalties for corrective measures.

In Ghana, the responsibility for basic Traffic Law Enforcement is mostly undertaken by the MTTD with the legal aspects being handled by the judiciary service. Other subsidiaries such as the DVLA and the Customs Division of the Ghana Revenue Authority (GRA) also ensure compliance with vehicle standards. Others are the use of traffic wardens and city guards by MMDAs and the traffic police assistants commissioned by the NRSA. Figure 9.2 provides an overview of the entities affiliated with traffic law enforcement in Ghana.

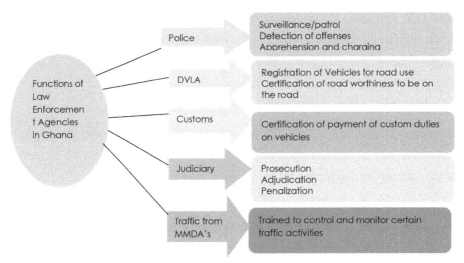

Figure 9.2: Functions of Law Enforcement Agencies in Ghana

9.3.1 Road Traffic Law Enforcement by Policing

Traffic law enforcement by policing is done through the establishment of a traffic police force provided with the highest responsibility for ensuring compliance by road users. Some of the critical aspects of effective traffic policing include the following:

A. Establishment of a Dedicated Police for Traffic Enforcement: The establishment of a dedicated traffic enforcement unit through the provision of specialized training enforcement practices, principles, skills and techniques for the detection of road user errors as a best practice in road safety.

In Ghana, the MTTD was established on March 2013 to replace (MTTU) in 1952 with dedicated jurisdiction over traffic issues over their service time following the enactment of the Police Service Regulation 2012 (C.I 76) with the head reporting to the Inspector General of Police (IGP).

i. Objectives of the MTTD: The objectives of the MTTD are:

a. To prevent and detect motor crimes and offences.

b. To prevent loss of lives and damage to property on Ghana`s roads.

c. To ensure free flow of motor traffic.

d. To arrest and prosecute motor traffic offenders

ii. Mandate of the MTTD: The mandate of the MTTD is to formulate policies in line with general service goals and conduct research into emerging challenges in traffic enforcement by:

a. Formulating major policies and operational steps for implementing them.

b. Providing appropriate training in enforcement practices.

c. *Developing and implementing public education and sensitization programmes on enforcement.*

d. *Providing periodic information to the Director General/Services and Director General/ Technical on procurement of relevant logistics for the (DVLA).*

e. *Conducting research into emerging challenges in traffic enforcement and road safety.*

iii. Departments and Divisional Units within the MTTD: The MTTD is organised into 11 units as listed below with one in each of the eleven (11) Police regions of Ghana.

- *Motorized Highway Patrol Teams.*
- *Towing Services Teams.*
- *Town Patrol Teams.*
- *Investigations and Processing Teams.*
- *Traffic Management Teams.*
- *Accident Investigations Squads.*
- *Presidential Route Team.*
- *The Research and Education Team.*
- *The traffic offences Management systems Team.*
- *Dispatch Riders team.*
- *Red light team*

There are also divisional and district MTTD accidents squads headed by a Director General who is also a Police Management Board Member (POMAB) stationed at the police head-quarters. The regional, division's districts and accidents squads are administratively under the command of the Regional Divisional and Districts Commanders.

B. Duties of the Police in Traffic Enforcement: *By law some of the functions of the MTTD are as follows:*

i. *Authority to exercise given powers in uniform with an official badge.*

ii. *Authority to demand information from a road user as and when required.*

iii. *Authority to inspect, test or examine a vehicle, driver's license and other official documents displayed or carried on the vehicle.*

iv. *Authority to enter and move a vehicle to a place where it will not obstruct traffic or cause traffic hazard or order a driver to move a vehicle to a safe place as well as order a vehicle to be towed if it is of safety risk or inconvenient to the public.*

v. *Authority to arrest a traffic offender.*

vi.   *Authority to forbid a driver with no valid driver's license from driving and authority to stop a driver from driving on the road if certain traffic regulations are not being complied with.*

vii. *Authority to pursue and effect arrest a violating road user.*

viii. *Authority to arrest a traffic offender without a warrant if there is good reason to suspect driving under the influence of alcohol and if there is failure of an impairment test. Arrest can also be effected if a driver refuses to oblige to instructions such as the conduct of a blood alcohol content test and when an officer is assaulted.*

ix.   *Authority to apprehend and prosecute a violator for court proceeding.*

It is also required that no person shall fail or refuse to comply with or perform any act forbidden by any lawful order, signal or direction of a traffic or police officer with regards to the above an example is as reflected in Figure 9.

Figure 9.3: A Publication on Police Enforcement on Driver's License

C. Functions of the Police in Traffic Law Enforcement: *In addition to the above, personnel of the MTTD control and manage traffic as well as enforce all traffic regulations. The members of the MTTD are also to spot, warn and arrest offending motorists. They also record all RTCs and publish statistics on RTC on quarterly basis in the print and electronic media. The department is also in-charge of investigating RTCs. The functions of the police in traffic law enforcement are as summarised in Table 9.4.*

Table 9.4: Functions of the Police in Road Safety Enforcement

1. ENFORCEMENT PLANNING -Violation and Enforcement Record Keeping: Data Collection by recording all RTCs and publishes the statistics -Research into Traffic Violations -Development of Strategic and operational plans -Development of Monitoring and Evaluation Indicators
2. ENFORCEMENT IMPLEMENTATION -Conduct of Traffic Management -Traffic management for general and special events); -Traffic directing/Control including -Traffic surveillance/patrol/Detection/Apprehension and Charging (in general and special events) to control drink driving; speeding; child restraints; non-use/incorrect use of helmets; seatbelts; distracted driving. Others are reckless driving, wrongful overtaking, overloading; traffic surveillance on vehicle defects, road worthiness, insurance, driver eligibility -Traffic escort of VIPs -Processing and prosecution of traffic offenders -Investigation of road traffic crashes -Provision of VIP escort -Violation handling -Prosecution of traffic offences/ procedural justice practices eg. Fine administration -Adjudication -Penalization -Improvement of Laws

3. MONITORING AND EVALUATION

4. RTC HANDLING
-Protection of RTC site
-Maintenance of traffic flow at RTC site for safe traffic flow and emergency vehicle access
-Documentation of facts on the RTC and the contributory factors
-Initiation of warranted law enforcement acts
-Clearance of RTC scene
-Conduct of Education and Sensitization
-Traffic education/ publicity for road users on accident-free road practices by training motorists and pedestrians.
-Driver Refresher Training

Irrespective of this there are some constitutional laws that restrict law enforcers from also violating the rights of traffic offenders. Some of the constitutional violations by traffic law enforcers include;

i.   *alleged excessive use of their powers,*

ii.   *misrepresentation of charges,*

iii. *false arrests, thefts,*

iv.   *deliberate indifference to urgent situations etc.*

Thus, law enforcers are liable to prosecution by constitution in instances of obstruction of justice. (See Box 9.1).

Box 9.1: The right of the road user in Ghana. Ref: Road Traffic Act, 2004 (Act 684), Criminal and Other Offences (Procedure) Act, 1960 (Act 30) and Road Traffic Regulations 2013 (L.I. 2180).

• *No traffic officer is allowed to get and keep your license, they are only allowed to get your details off it. You are not required to have a category (professional driving permit) if you are driving a vehicle for private use.* This is false. A police officer in uniform and not below the rank of an Inspector, may where necessary, retain your driver's license for the period that that license is required and is mandated to issue an official receipt for the retention of the license. Thus, a holder of a particular class of license can only possess another class after passing the relevant and appropriate test conducted by the DVLA. For example, if you possess a Class B license, you cannot drive a bus.

• *If you do not have your license on you, no police officer is allowed to charge you on the spot. You should be given time to produce it (according to the law its 21 days).* This is false. A person can only drive a vehicle if the person has a Learners License or Drivers License. A driver is required to carry the original license whilst driving. On the request by a police officer in uniform or an authorised officer of the DVLA, the driver is required to produce the driver's license that authorises that person to drive the motor vehicle for inspection. If you do not have the license on you, the police officer may request that you produce it within twenty-four hours at a police station or to another police officer as may be directed by the officer.

- *When stopped for speeding, there is an allowance of up to 8kms above the speed limit. You should not be charged for over speeding.* This false. Unless otherwise indicated by the GHA, a person driving a motor vehicle must not exceed the maximum permissible of speed limit. 50km/hr. There is no allowance. The law imposes another responsibility on drivers to drive a motor vehicle at speed lower than what is indicated on the road "if the actual and potential hazards relating to the environmental conditions exists then it is required for the motor vehicle to be driven at a lesser speed". For example, you are required to slow down at zebra crossings and traffic intersections. It is an offence to breach the speed limits.

- *You are within your rights to ask for the calibration certificate of the radar gun used to capture your speed.* This is false. Traffic offences are usually strict liability offences. For a crime to be committed, there must be two elements present: i.e. the prohibited mental state of the act and a prohibited act or omission i.e. the physical element. However, in strict liability offences, you do not need the requisite mental state to prove the occurrence of a crime. That is strict liability. Thus, if you exceed the maximum speed limits, you are liable. The police have a duty to inform you of the nature of the offence you have committed, the charges they will prefer against you. In addition, they are to provide before trial, all documents (which will include the calibration certificate) they intend to rely on at trial. If you have any dispute regarding the calibration of the radar gun, you can do so in court as part of your defence.

- *You are within your rights to ask for a police officer's man number, which should be worn on the uniform. This true.* It is an offence for a police officer when on "duty to anytime disguise or conceal his or her identification number, name or rank". Consequently, it will be within reasonable limits for a road user to request the name and identification number of the police officer if the number has been disguised, concealed or is not being worn.

- *If you feel a check point has illegally been mounted, drive to the nearest police station and handle your issues from there. This is true.* This is because it is only an offence to interfere directly or indirectly with a barrier if that person does not have reasonable excuse and it is obvious to a reasonable person that such interference is not dangerous. For instance, once your safety is concerned and you drive to the nearest police station you would have to satisfy the requirements of the law.

- *They have no right to jump in your car.* This true to the extent that your car is not being used for the commission of a crime or is harbouring any proceed of crime, the car as a property is protected from any form of interference as it is reasonably necessary for public safety, the protection of health or morals, the prevention of disorder or crime or for the protection of the rights or freedoms of others.

- *Every traffic officer is required to greet you politely; they are a service not a force. This is true.* To the extent that the police is a service and not a force, one would expect that they would exercise some decorum when dealing with the motorist. Police officers are required to be of "good conduct", with a good "attitude towards work and a sense of responsibility". These criteria are taken into account during the promotion of a police officer. Hence, being polite and courteous to the public may go a long way to advance the career of a police officer.

- *No traffic officer is allowed to cause undue delay to a motorist. This is true.* The police cannot hold you beyond a period of time necessary for them to conduct their checks and examinations.

- *It is within the law to record a video or capture photos of your encounter with a traffic police officer. This is true.* However, such recording must be done taking into account the rules on privacy which every individual is guaranteed under the 1992 constitution. The overriding point is that any secret recording can only be justified in law if it is for the protection of health or morals; for the prevention of disorder or crime; or for the protection of the rights or freedoms of others.

- *You have up to 48 hours to report to the Anti-Corruption Bureau of any misconduct (eg receiving or demanding a bribe) by a traffic officer. Be sure you have evidence such as a video or photos. This is false.* There is no limitation on reporting crime in Ghana. Every citizen has duty to co-operate with lawful enforcement agencies in the maintenance of law and order in Ghana. The Police Intelligence and Professional Standards remains an important institution in fighting the bad nuts within the police service.

Police activate hotlines to report officer misconduct on roads

Source: What Does the Law Say – "Traffic Police: Things to Remember" Samuel Nartey February 4, 2019

9.4 POLICE ENFORCEMENT PLANNING

This involves the development of enforcement plans to address identified enforcement needs in order to direct activity implementation and the approach includes the following:

9.4.1 Identification of Enforcement Needs

A. Violation and Enforcement Record Keeping: This is determined from recorded data and research. This is important because according to the NHTSA, (2009) and

WHO, (2010 data led enforcement is crucial to the understanding of the enforcement activities to be targeted and to increase its influence on road safety, especially due to the need to introduce more effective measures, (ESRA 2016). Some recommended aspects to be targeted in enforcement planning are:

i.   The types of road traffic offences committed persistently and why.

ii.   Target road users and behaviours needing special attention.

iii. Legal and administrative aspects of the enforcement system.

iv.   Enforcement tools and resources especially needed.

v.   New approaches, methods and solution in road traffic enforcement management.

In Ghana, the MTTD compiles information on public offences without the details of those one traffic violations specifically in a consistent manner. This makes it difficult to understand the underlying causes of pervasive violations so that enforcement activities can be prioritised to address such. It is therefore of critical importance for enforcement records to give details on the causes of the types of traffic violations for the necessary focus to conserve limited resource. There must be research to establish the effectiveness of methods and related impacts in order to establish the modes the most effective.

9.4.2 Development of Road Traffic Enforcement Plans

Enforcement plans should set goals, objectives, list the enforcement activities and the frequencies required to address violation challenges with estimated resource inputs and a monitoring strategy based on defined performance indicators on set targets. This is necessary for assessing progress on work achievement and ensuring necessary adjustments where necessary. *In Ghana, this done at two (2) administrative levels as follows:*

A. National Level Enforcement Plans: *Road traffic enforcement plans are dovetailed into the (NRSS). The trend has continued since 2000. Within each of these strategies, specific enforcement activities are outlined for implementation by the police as summarised in Appendix 3.5.*

B. Local Level Enforcement Plans: *Following the development of national plans local specific enforcement action plans are also drawn from the national plans to guide effective road traffic law enforcement activities across different administrative jurisdiction in the country. The key challenge is the difficulty in ascertaining what enforcement activity and by what frequency is able to achieve the level of expected outcome and related impacts.*

Also, joint enforcement activities with other stakeholder entities such as the DVLA and NRSA are done on adhoc basis with unmeasured effects.

On the way forward detailed aspects on activity implementation frequencies needed should be researched and matched with resource provisions for better enforcement outcomes. Also, contributions from other stakeholder entities must be well structured through set identification processes at the enforcement planning stage by the MTTD.

9.5 ROAD SAFETY ENFORCEMENT IMPLEMENTATION METHODS

Porter (2011) identified two types of traffic enforcement: manual and automated traffic enforcement involving evident police presence on the roadways and the use of technology to locate and apprehend traffic offenders respectively, to ensure traffic compliance.

9.5.1 Manual Traffic Enforcement Methods

Manual road traffic enforcement involves the physical presence of a law enforcement officer who conducts traffic surveillance and control.

A. Manual Traffic Control: It mainly involves guiding road users on where, how and when they may or may not move in traffic especially during periods of congestion eg. peak traffic hours or in emergencies with the use of voice, hand gestures or other signals to ensure compliance.

Ghana mainly employs the manual traffic enforcement approach with police officers deployed on targeted roadways to control traffic. This is done either on daily basis in the cities and intermittently on highways. The first is mostly aimed at decongesting areas prone to traffic jams, particularly intersections and roundabouts in urban centres during the morning and evening rush hours and the second is often done to check for traffic offences on selected roads mostly highways. (See Figure 9.4).

MTTD personnel are also deployed to control unusual traffic situation which calls for special attention. In some instances, they are used to complement automated traffic control system such as signalised intersections to enhance operations. This is particularly necessary for intersections where traffic congestion creates overlaps with one lane unable to move at the green signal due to a blockade.

This is done at both controlled and uncontrolled junctions especially when there is a power cut or a when a traffic signal at a controlled junction is not working. It is however, not uncommon to see ordinary citizens, mostly street vendors at traffic intersections assuming the role of traffic control officers in critical situations to direct traffic. Much as such acts laudable, the legal implications could be of high consequence should there be a traffic crash involving such persons.

This is because in some instances some motorists do not feel obliged to abide by the instructions of such people and so disregards their directives whilst others comply. This is very risky since such good Samaritans are not formally trained to manage traffic so could put their lives in danger. This is also of significant importance given the fact even in some instances some MTTD personnel who are trained for the job do suffer casualties.

Therefore, road users must be educated to alert law enforcing authorities about such situations as soon as they are detected so that appropriate response can be effected. The performance of other duties by the traffic police in traffic enforcement such as undertaking of traffic management responsibilities implies that the police are made to deal with more responsibilities than they are supposed to. There are even situations where law enforcers have to coerce and pay out of pocket for responsible technicians to restore defective traffic signals due to recurring RTC situations.

It is therefore important for responsible road agencies to be more proactive in undertaking their duties to ease the pressure on the police. Such measures will enable them give full attention to core enforcement activities with regards to traffic offences.

Figure 9.4: Examples of Manual Police Enforcement Activities on the Road

B. Manual Traffic Surveillance: This involves traffic observation by routine and random surveillance through special and selective operations as discussed below:

i. Routine Traffic Surveillance: This is done on continuous basis to detect and apprehend violators at fixed or different road locations at different or regular times with visible police officers to instigate compliance. Traffic violators are apprehended when caught in the act of violation such as a defaulting in producing valid vehicle and driver documentations.

Effective routine traffic surveillance must be at road sections with high crash records with available refuge area for observing violators and for adequate spacing for vehicle pull over as well as be informed by relevant hours suitable for such operations. Since this activity is continuous it is also resource intensive and adequate resource provisions must be made for the purpose.

In Ghana, this approach to police enforcement of traffic regulations is common. It is often done in the urban areas to check for the apprehension of drivers jumping red lights, drivers engaging in improper 'U' turns, detection of vehicles with defective parts or without valid documentations Figure 9.5 provide examples and the types of fixed police check points and the technical considerations are also summarised in Table 9.5. However, their effectiveness is not proven by research.

Figure 9.5: Sample Graphical Presentation on Routine Surveillance by the Police

Table 9.5: Types of Police Enforcement Checkpoints in Ghana

Police Checkpoints At authorised checkpoints the police may check any of the following documents: -International Driving License -International Driving Permit -National ID Card/Passport -International Green Card -ECOWAS Brown Card	Roadworthiness Certificate Local driver license Legitimacy of vehicle registration and licensing Vehicle Insurance Unsafe Driving e, careless and reckless driving Drink driving Seatbelt compliance Helmet use compliance Overloading Carriage of Dangerous goods
Customs Checkpoints On duty customs officers patrol transit corridors checking for -relevant customs certification and documentation such as: -Letter of Guarantee (for imported vehicles) -Inter-State Road Transit Logbook (ECOWAS ISRT Logbook) for transit cargo -Inter-State Waybill for transit cargo -Customs Declaration for transit cargo -prohibited or restricted goods. In case these documents are not available Customs have the right to impound the vehicle until proper documentation is provided	
Axle Load Check Points -Weighbridges are operated by private companies under the supervision of Ghana Highway Authority (GHA) officials with police officers to enforce laws on overweight axles in order to control overloading and the related dangers. Trucks are required to stop at all weighbridge stations and drivers who refuse to stop face a 300 GH¢ fine and/or 8 months' imprisonment. -Upon entering a weighbridge, a police officer signals a truck to stop. A GHA official will weigh the truck and provide a printout showing the recorded weight. If a truck is overweight. The official will collect the original logbook and waybill, copy them and return them to the driver. -Overloaded trucks can be detained until fines are paid and, in some instances, the truck driver will be required at his own expense to shed any excess weight to meet axle load restrictions before continuing. Ghana also implements regional axle load restrictions with two tiers of axle load tolerances exist above ECOWAS'/UEMOA's original regulation.	

 Ghana News Agency   Home Social Business Education Entertainment Science Health

Enforce Axle load control regulations-
Antobam

By Justina Paaga

ii. Traffic Patrol: This is the movement of traffic law enforcers by driving, riding or walking within on selected roadways within designated geographical areas to deter would be traffic violators with their presence. This may be on several roads or selected road sections. During the operation, traffic road users are assisted with challenges and where necessary also apprehended for traffic violations.

(For example, enforcement officers are required to assist motorists to remove broken down vehicles on the road when present at the occurrence of such incidence in Ghana).

The patrol team may adopt the visible and conspicuous surveillance approach by attracting attention and remaining in the full view of motorists with marked patrol vehicles or may adopt a concealed surveillance approach where the patrol team may not be visible to motorist.

This approach is also applied by the MTTD in Ghana for diverse reasons such as night patrol to apprehend criminals aside traffic control but its effectiveness is yet to be studied. (See Figure 9.6).

Figure 9.6: Police Patrol Unit of Ghana

iii. Operation of random check points: This is by spontaneous police patrol without a fixed schedule on a particular road or on different roads with or without fixed time schedules on irregular basis. These maybe complemented with temporary road barriers to apprehended offending drivers especially in RTC prone areas.

This is a resource conservation approach since traffic law enforcers do not have the manpower and resources to patrol at all times and in all places. The effectiveness is contingent on the following:

a. Need for long duration of surveillance in order to produce consistency and long-lasting effects.

b. Need for repetition of surveillance to allow for ample time to re-observe suspicious situations for possibly apprehension of traffic violators.

c. Need to deploy several surveillance units to control locations known to have a history of violations.

d. Need to apply varying visibility of surveillance to prevent would-be violators from taking risk and taking evasive actions but without apprehension.

e. Need for continuous patrolling in traffic on selected roads to monitor traffic behaviour.

In Ghana, this is especially common on highways for the conduct of random checks on blood alcohol limit and over speeding. In case of apprehension of a violating road user, the police officer records the number plate of the vehicle and its model, the type and time of offence, the location, particulars of the offender and the type of offence etc. for processing to court. (See Figure 9.7).

Figure 9.7: Examples of Police Random Check Activities

Some challenges with the use of police check points are as follows:

a) The approach is resource intensive and difficult to sustain.

In Ghana, inadequate personnel, limited transport/communication facilities and other lo-gistics remains a key challenge to this approach. As of 2020, the MTTD had about 1,500 personnel trained by the various Ghana Police Service training academies and posted to all the district police stations to work hand in hand with the general police force to ensure road safety in an area.

Coupled with this, most of the MTTD personnel were on temporary attachment with exper-tise and experience gained being taken away when an officer leaves divisional, district and unit points. They may also be withdrawn for other important assignments causing on-going training programmes for such officers to be abandoned.

To address this Boateng G, (2021) recommended for road safety enforcement should to shift from enforcing greater punishment against drivers and focusing on broader safety systems such as:

• *Ensuring efficiency in secondary controls measures by the issuance of valid vehicle/driving licenses from source with alertness on road worthy and insurance renewal.*

- *Introducing speed calming measures on roads and installation of weigh bridges at loading points.*

- *Ensuing effective communication of road safety benefits and results of enforcement.*

- *Targeting specific violations strongly associated with RTC's either by vehicle types, drivers, locations and time periods*

b) Ineffective police checks resulting from driver familiarity with locations and time periods where police enforcement takes place with awareness and expectancy among motorists about the possible presence of the police, (Leggett, 1990). This may cause motorist to comply with expected rules when approaching such locations only to revert to the violating conduct after passing such locations and thus defeating the purpose of the enforcement activity. Figure 9.8 presents a word cloud of the typical driver responses to police road presence.

Figure 9.8: Illustration of Typical driver response to police road presence -
Word cloud showing driver communication to signal police presence,
(Source: Humanities and Social Sciences Communications, ISSN 2662-9992).

This is also typical to the Ghanaian situation whereby drivers tend to reduce speed on approaching known police check points or are warned by other oncoming drivers with familiar gestures such as the flashing of their vehicle headlights (in quick succession) and the pointing of their index fingers (hand gestures) toward the ground as an indication that there is a police checkpoint ahead to help their colleagues avoid arrest as an unwritten code of driver solidarity.

Once the driver passes the checkpoint, they revert to the wrongful behaviour. This needs to be addressed with intensive publicity on the safety benefits of enforcement rather than as a punitive measure in order to instigate public support for compliance on issues that affect their safety and that of others.

Also, self-anticipation arising from the driver's past encounters with the police at some road section(s), informs drivers on the possible presence of the police. The results of a study by Enoch F. Sam (2021), suggested there are widespread driver tactics used to outwit the police and to avoid police extortion. Such behaviours undermine and negate the seriousness and expected general deterrent effect of the police road. Additional studies are, however, needed to explore this phenomenon further.

iv. Selective Traffic Enforcement: This has to do with the targeting of traffic enforcement of specific traffic violations deemed to be of high risk to the occurrence of RTCs (O'Brien, 1980). The approach must be data led for the establishment of specific locations, day and time for such operations (Leggett, 1990) but the approach is of narrow enforcement scope.

In Ghana, though this is done by some margin, through targeted operations to control commercial motorcycle operations, axle load control etc. there are no evaluated outcome comparisons of before enforcement and after enforcement interventions to validate its benefits.

v. Integrated Traffic Enforcement Operations: Combination of traffic enforcement activities with other road safety measures such as education is recommended to be best practice for effective police traffic enforcement operations.

vi. Management of Traffic at Special Events: This involves traffic control at special events impacting on locational traffic dynamic be it permanent or temporary. It may involve the creation of detour routes for non through fare situations, placement of signs to inform and direct motorists, ensuring safe parking and control of intersections with increased conflicts form high volume traffic.

In some instances, the demand for such services can be of short time for occasions such as national parades, festivals, sporting activities etc. They could also be of medium-term duration such as high-profile conferences, sporting tournaments, fairs, road repair works, etc. Under such circumstance adequate safety measures are put in place ahead of the event.

In Ghana, others are traffic management by road closures for occasional events such as funerals, weddings etc. effected by private entities without valid permits though illegal. In some instances, such road closures frustrate some drivers who are forced to divert their routes. Irrespective of the fact that some offenders are sometimes prosecuted, such violations continue unabated because the attention of law enforcers are often not drawn to such situations.

Also, in addition to these special safety operational programmes are sometimes conducted to check driver indiscipline over some defined time period. An example in Ghana is the War Against Indiscipline (WAI)" driving launched by the Motor Traffic and Transport Department (MTTD) of the Ghana Police Service and Citi TV/FM (a media house in

Ghana) since July 2019 to crack down on road traffic violations and other acts of indiscipline on the country cited by Boateng, (2021).

The operation involved traffic police officers and reporters from Citi TV monitor motorists' traffic behaviour working together to arrest and prosecute drivers for various road traffic violations in Accra. It generated financial benefits to the state to a tune of about US $5000 within the first two days of the operation from the prosecution of about 500 drivers for various traffic violations (Boateng, 2021), (See Figure 9.9).

Figure 9.9: Police Conducting WAI Activities

Also on July 2020, the GPS introduced the Police Action against Rider Indiscipline (OPERATION PAARI) to deal with motor rider indiscipline on the road including riding through traffic lights, failure to wear crash helmets and general disregard for road traffic regulations, (myjoyonline.com – April 2022). The later could also cause motorists who are not trained in defensive driving in congested traffic situations to engage in high speed with the possibility of an RTC occurring.

9.5.2 Automated Traffic Enforcement

Due to human limitations to effectively meet all the demands of traffic enforcement, the use of automated technologies in traffic safety enforcement work to complement manual methods are also adopted. These are mostly commonly used in advanced countries.

A. Examples of Types of Automated Traffic Enforcement Devices: Some automated traffic enforcement systems are mentioned as follows but with no detailed description by the author:

i.   Red Light Evasion Detection (RLC

ii.   Automated Speed Enforcement (ASE).

iii. Combined Systems involving the use of both the RLC and ASE.

B. Automated Traffic Enforcement Chain: The application of automated enforcement systems is bound by set protocols described as a chain with various separate and inter-dependent links as elaborated in Box 9.2.

Box 9.2: The Automated Traffic Enforcement Chain

Stage 1 - Detection: It is done with types of equipment with a high detection rate. Identifying all passing vehicles is mandatory because this is the primary requirement to catch all potentially violating vehicles. Reliable and durable detection methods like inductive loops or modern tracking radars can be used to maintain a consistent high detection rate.

Stage 2 - Measure: After the detection of a vehicle, its speed needs to be measured correctly with a legally pre-defined accuracy. The most common average speed enforcement systems, section control, calculate speed based on errorless time measurement over a pre-defined distance and not by measuring the speed at a particular spot

A decision on the violation: When a vehicle is measured exceeding a legally set speed limit, this must be determined as a violation. The decision-making algorithm simply compares the speed values measured by the enforcement cameras with two-speed values; the local speed limit and the registered speed. Concurrent violations can be handled with the latest radar technology and the efficient data processing capacity of the advanced enforcement cameras.

Stage 3 - Register: Once a positive decision has been taken on a violation, the photographic or video data for the violation need to be registered instantly in a secure, correct and unchangeable way. The use of cryptography is vital while registering the evidence properly

Stage 4 - Transfer: After registering, the evidence data need to be transferred from the enforcement camera to a central server which can be located with the municipality, central or regional government organization or might be with a private entity depending on the contract. Such data can be transferred by means of Wi-Fi, data line or 3G or 4G mobile broadband connection

Stage 5 - Storage: Violation information is transferred to a secure data house or data storage location to issue citation from the back office and is kept for longer-term storage and future reference for the police, violators, police, public prosecutor or judge. These data should be properly backed up and mirrored in reliable robust data centres.

Stage 6 - Process evidence, issue and send a ticket: The captured pieces of evidence require further processing in the back office so that the notices can be issued and sent to the owner of the violating vehicle. The operations and functionalities in there completely depend on the legal framework and process architecture

The error rate of the manual procedure is considerably higher than the ANPR processing. After justifying the evidence, the authority accesses the vehicle registration database to match license plates with the owner's addresses and process the penalties Countries like France and Netherlands are able to annually process millions of violations from automated enforcement systems without human intervention with the help of a combination of administrative law, clear license plates, high-definition enforcement cameras, effective ANPR software and owner liability etc.

Stage 7 - Receipt of ticket: After sending out just a citation by means of the post is an excellent opportunity for the violators to ignore the penalty by refusing acceptance of registered mail. Therefore, the authorities include email addresses and mobile phone numbers in the vehicle registration database. If the violator doesn't pay within the due time, the detection should be implemented in toll points and traffic points to block that particular vehicle above the road

Stage 8 - Provide evidence upon violator's request: While providing violation evidence to the owners, other relevant information can also be shown. A key aspect that should be presented to a violator is targeted publicity on why enforcement takes place on that specific location

Stage 9 - Court: If all the above fails, the violator must know that a judge will ultimately cast a final verdict at the end of this traffic enforcement chain. The authority should support the public prosecutor and the judge by typed approval, verification and calibration certificates in their judgment.

Source: making-traffic-safer.com/automated-enforcement-chain/

C. Advantages and Disadvantage of Automated Enforcement Systems:

i. Advantages: Southgate & Mirrlees-Black, (1991), observed that driver awareness of automated enforcement measures serves as a deterrent to violators and the payment of on-the-spot fines is also a strong disincentive. However, administratively, it is observed that fine collection can be a laborious process if the violator has no intention to pay. Therefore, it is required for authorities to have accurate and adequate evidence that the violation took place. There must also be an alternative to the payment of the fine as well as penalty to the fine if the payment is delayed.

ii. Disadvantages: Disadvantages include invasion of privacy and public perceptions and acceptance regarding the use of such devices is highly recommended.

Following various calls on the automation of traffic enforcement activities in Ghana, (See Figure 9.10), the Ghana Police Service has rolled out an automated traffic policing system known as TRAFFITECH to integrate all sit alone enforcement technologies such as OPERATION PAARI (Police Action against Rider Indiscipline) and Police Invisible Eye (PIE).

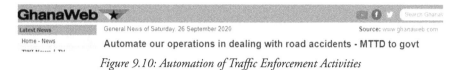

Figure 9.10: Automation of Traffic Enforcement Activities

The PIE is a police vehicle mounted with secret cameras to record any reckless and dangerous motorist activity/indiscipline with an authorised outrider (police rider) to arrest culprits. Additionally, the intention is to collaborate with the National Intelligence Bureau (NIB) towards an integration of their street CCTV cameras with the Police's TRAFFITECH.

Surveillance cameras have also been mounted at selected signalised traffic intersections involving about 3000 intelligent surveillances nationwide at significant traffic intersections to monitor and apprehend traffic offences for possible prosecution (Myjoyonline.com, 2021). It is reported that the monitoring and surveillance system captured over 2000 cases of traffic violations in barely two months of its installation.

The Traffic Monitoring and Surveillance Centre is housed at the Police Headquarters in Accra, the capital city (3News, 2021). The centre collaborates with the DVLA to retrieve details of vehicles captured by the system and identify the vehicle owners for prosecution (Myjoyonline.com, 2021).

In addition to this, Ghana is in the process of developing a cooperative system whereby an integrated communication and database system between road side equipment, the road infrastructure, the vehicle, the offence committed and the necessary penalty will be well coordinated. This will involve the linking of vehicle data base with the driver apprehension process whereby data on the vehicle involved in a violation and the driver will be retrieved at the scene of the incidence via a computerized system installed in the police vehicle or on mobile devices used by the police. This is to identify the vehicle type and owner from the registered vehicles database by accurate alignment of the offence with the vehicle and its registered owner for ease of tracking in case of default etc.

However, the introduction of automated enforcement system is fairly new in the country and its operation is currently not very visible to the driving population. Aside this, its effectiveness is not well known. This is because the process of transition to automated system has not been well disseminated.

The mode of apprehension of violators and the punitive process are also visible and motorists are not well informed on the whole concept, how it works and how they should relate to its processes. It would have been more beneficial if the baseline conditions before the introduction of such automated systems had been well documented for comparison after operating the automated systems over a period to allow for effective monitoring and online impact assessment. It is suggested therefore that, the weak links in the newly introduced automated enforcement chain be studied and addressed accordingly.

Some recommended best practices in literature for a well-functioning automated traffic enforcement system include the following:

a. Expedition of the process of integrating the vehicle and driver registration databases into enforcement databases.

b. Establishment of a quick violation notification system through a paperless process such as settlement on digital platforms.

c. Inclusion of enforcement reason in violation notification with evidence to avoid conflicts.

d. Fine assignment to be revised after payment with issuance of valid receipts

9.5.3 Non-Police Organisations in Enforcement

Currently in several countries enforcement is no longer the exclusive right of the police but it is complemented with activities of other sectors either than the police referred as "non police based" enforcement and they are of various forms as follows:

A. Provision of Safe Infrastructure to support Enforcement Activities: Road infrastructure deficiencies hamper enforcement operations whereby the police might not be wholly able to hold a defaulting driver accountable for an offence influenced by poor road furniture.

In Ghana, typical examples include lack of adequate parking space in central business centre causing congestions, delays and related safety challenges and the absence of traffic control devices such as traffic signals at critical intersections, etc. to regulate traffic flow etc. This is made worse by the lack of monitoring of roadway performance by road engineers with the consequent effect of delayed response to identified defects.

Others are poor response to the vandalisation of traffic signs such as signage poles and crash barriers for scrap causing safety defects due to limited funding availability. Also, the practice of collaborations with research institutions and contribution of enforcement inputs in road engineering design etc. is not.

Therefore, there is need for effective attention to be paid to the management of road infrastructure systems by the provision and maintenance of safety installations before road user compliance with traffic regulations is enforced. This must be effectively complemented with continuous upgrade and maintenance of such facilities through adequate commitment of funding. The process could be greatly effective by the involvement of the police through consultations to provide enforcement inputs into road engineering schemes.

B. Promotion of Road User Education on Traffic Enforcement: A sufficiently well-informed road user community facilitates effective enforcement. This is because compliance with what is not known is not feasible besides poor knowledge of traffic rules and regulations by road users also causes most of them to perceive traffic offences as insignificant since it is not easy relate high risk road safety acts to the occurrence of RTC.

Therefore, within the UN's next steps for road safety from 2021-2030, it is proposed to focus on undertakings that offer many opportunities for the public to actively support the work of road safety enforcement through the encouragement of sound public attitudes.

In Ghana, the real state of road user understanding of road traffic laws and related enforcement measures especially the traffic regulations and the Highway Code is not well established since records on road traffic offences by violation type are not well defined and this must be researched to inform a better approach to traffic law enforcement. Traffic law enforcement agencies themselves should first be trained in traffic regulations, before being allowed to conduct enforcement, (See Figure 9.11).

In addition, there should be focus on the tracking of the prevalence of key behavioral risk factors to guide the development of educational resources suited to the achievement of intended behavioral changes.

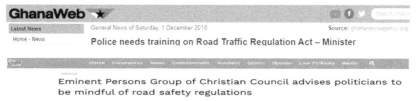

Figure 9.11: A Publication on the need for Law Enforcers to be trained

Also, road traffic laws, policies and administrative activities interpreted into local must be explained over and over again to gain to enhance public insight with simple and summarised traffic safety guidelines developed for targeted road users. Specific emphasis and arrangements should be made for those with special needs such as the less educated, the less-skilled, beginner/novice drivers, young and vulnerable road users etc.

C. Interagency Collaborations for Traffic Enforcement: This involves collaboration between the police and other stakeholder road safety entities such as local authorities, vehicle and driver licensing authorities, engineers and transport planners, emergency response teams and other relevant entities such as communication specialists, psychologists, NGOs, transport unions etc. to ensure effective enforcement of traffic laws.

This helps to pool resources together, build relationships, share expertise and provide ways for agencies to work together. These must be based on well-defined channels of law enforcement cooperation, direct contact, information sharing and cooperation. Others are building of public trust, better sharing of information, conduct of joint training exercises and establishment of two-way communication.

In Ghana, aside the MTTD's collaboration with the NRSA and DVLA for joint enforcement patrol and public education others such as the GNFS and NAS for emergency response measures. There is also room for improvement with regards to the institutionalisation of such processes with legal mandates. This, must be supported with set guidelines to ensure that enforcement collaboration activities are not implemented as ad hoc actions.

It should be a part of a comprehensive strategy linked with integrated communication systems and well monitored for effective results. It must also be supported by higher level technical and administrative authority within the police force to ensure good commitment.

D. Public Support for Road Safety Enforcement: It is said that there is generally poor public support for with some road users very indifferent to traffic enforcement measures. This is because some public members deem enforcement to be confrontational. Therefore, social support for road safety enforcement based on public understanding and acceptance is essential for controlling road user indiscipline and might perhaps even instigate self-initiated enforcement activities.

To achieve this, it is recommended to ensure that legislation and enforcement are suited to the particular cultural climate and other (economic) realities of a country. Thus, it must be structured so as to pose a meaningful and immediate deterrence threat to would be traffic offenders backed by appropriate penalties y the courts as discussed in the immediate subsection.

Figure 9.12 provides examples on the call for stakeholder support in traffic regulation in Ghana

Figure 9.12: Publications on Stakeholder Support for Traffic Enforcement in Ghana

9.5.4 Violation Handling

The apprehension of road traffic regulation violators is often backed by measures for correcting them. This could be by punitive or non-punitive measures as discussed as follows:

A. Violation Handling by Non-Punitive Measures: They are described as alternative prosecution measures that do not use the court system to correct a violating road user but rather may resort to other methods such as persuasion. However, the rational for considerations on the application of non-punitive enforcement measures is subjective, variable and inconsistent and examples are:

i. Enforcement by Preventive Measures: These are measures put in place to possibly prevent traffic violations from being committed in the first place.

In Ghana, this includes the conduct of educational campaigns at transport terminals and in commercial transport vehicles (See Figure 9.13).

Figure 9.13: Police Engagement in Traffic Regulation Educational Activities

ii. Enforcement by Warning Measures: They include the issuance of written warning and verbal warning to caution a violating road user. It may be recorded or unrecorded and also be of formal or informal approach.

In Ghana, the MTTD also sometimes correct traffic violators with words of caution or the use of hand gestures to warn a traffic offender from repeating an offence especially in regard of first-time offenders. However, the use of written warnings and community service is usually not done.

iii. Enforcement by Corrective Measures: This mode of enforcement is done by emphasizing on corrective measures when traffic violations are committed.

In Ghana, emphasis on rightful road user conducts is done to help the road user do the right thing rather than focusing on punitive measures. Typical examples are as presented in, (See Figure 9.14). However, its effectiveness as an enforcement measure is yet to be assessed and validated. This is because there are no effective mechanisms in place to track, monitor and record the performance to determine the benefits of the interventions made.

Figure 9.14: Examples of Enforcement by Corrective Measures by the NRSA

B. Violation Handling by Legal Punitive Measures: Law enforcement actions taken with punitive measures against a traffic violator may involve legal prosecution by the court system. This is because the court has original jurisdiction for the trial of offences. The objective is to deter road users from breaking the law and the approach involves the following aspects:

i. Legal Proceedings for Traffic Offences: The legal system for handling traffic violations has to do with the detection of violations against existing traffic laws, prosecution and sanctioning.

ii. Key Players in Legal Proceedings for Traffic Offences: The key players of legal proceedings include the following:

a). The Police: The role of the police in the prosecution process involves the introduction of competent, relevant and material evidence in support of the State's/People's case against the accused. An offender is often summoned by notification of intention to prosecute with the stated offence for court proceeding to commence after the offender has been apprehended by the police or caught on camera for committing a traffic offence. The notification specifies the court, date and the time to take plea, statements etc.

An example of a notification of arrest for court prosecution in Ghana is as presented in Figure 9.15.

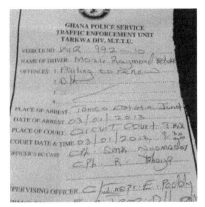

Figure 9.15: A sample of Police Notification to a Traffic Offender

b). The Judiciary: After a suspected traffic offender has been issued with a court summons/ notification of intended prosecution by the police for court attendance with the charges, the court process by both the prosecutor and defendant with evidence of the committed offence is held before the type of penalty is imposed if found guilty. The court then processes the payment of the traffic fines which the offender must remit to court if the need be.

In Ghana, most motorists are ignorant of the judiciary processes for handling traffic cases so most of them would normally negotiate for out of court settlement. Therefore, it is recommended for judicial guidelines to be developed for commercial drivers with intensive education to create awareness. Perhaps increased knowledge will encourage motorists not to resort to bribing the police to avoid court proceedings.

iii. The Concept of Traffic Courts: It is encouraged by best practice for countries to established dedicated traffic courts to support effective traffic enforcement. This is because violators of traffic laws are not strictly considered as criminals in the usual sense of the word so it is recommended to separate such cases by the creation of fulltime traffic courts. These are to be complemented with revenue generation components which could be plugged back to support effective enforcement activities.

In Ghana, motor courts have been established as specialised district courts mandated to handle motor traffic cases. This was to isolate the prosecution of motor traffic cases from other criminal cases in the court of law so as to ensure speedy and efficient adjudication of such cases. It was accompanied with other administrative reforms to make the judicial system more responsive to traffic law enforcement needs.

Judiciary training in the administration of traffic regulations have also been provided for personnel on the bench in the prosecution of traffic cases. However, the efficiency with which the justice system is applied through the traffic courts and its contribution to reduced RTCs is not well studied or understood and its benefits are also not yet known.

C. Legal Prosecution by Minor and Major Offences: The legal prosecution for traffic offences is classified as minor and major traffic offences:

i. Legal Prosecution for Minor Traffic Offences: Minor offences are the types of traffic offenses that are not considered serious enough to attract a jail sentence. Penalties for such offences usually involve the imposition of fines and imposition of community service on the offender amongst others. The amount paid for the fines depends on the type and degree of seriousness of the offence. However, failure to redeem a fine may attract imprisonment.

The payment of a fine could also be on the spot. Since the process is entirely manual, a key challenge associated with the application of spot fines is revenue leakage through the existence of parallel receipting. Others are bribery by the payment of reduced amounts to a law enforcement officer rather than a higher amount to the state. It is therefore required for such a system to be backed by automated payment systems rather than manual systems. Should manual systems be used, there should be intensive integrity training among police officers and motorist to address this challenge.

In Ghana, legal proceedings for minor traffic offences include the imposition of fines of which failure to pay attract a jail term. The process of introducing a spot fine into the traffic enforcement system has effected under regulation 157 of the LI 2180 of 2012 whereby by violators of minor offences will have spot fines imposed on them ranging from five to fifty units or equivalent of an average of an average of ¢600 per offense. However, the passing of the regulation is fairly new and there should be evaluation after its implementation over a certain time duration to assess its impacts. Some of the common offences and related fines as presented in Table 9.6.

Table 9.6: Spot Fines for Minor Driving Offences

Road Traffic Regulation 2180 - 2012	Fines
Non-Conformity with restrictions on Horns and Sirens	GH¢300
Driving a motor vehicle without reflectors (Back and front)	GH¢60
Failures to carry advance warning devices	GH¢300 - GH¢600
Failure to wear reflective clothing and protective helmets	GH¢300 - GH¢600
Non-compliance with regulations on the carriage of persons and goods	GH¢600
Driving on the shoulder of a road	GH¢120 - GH¢600
Prohibition on the use of Communication Device	GH¢600
Non-Compliance with maximum driving periods	GH¢300
Failure to use seatbelts	GH¢120 - GH¢600
Operating a commercial vehicle without a commercial vehicle driving permit	GH¢300
Prohibition of use of motorbikes and tricycles for commercial passenger services	GH¢300
Non-compliance with regulations on speed limiters, logbooks and tachographs	GH¢300
Exceeding the prescribed number of persons to be carried	GH¢120 - GH¢600
Particulars to be written on commercial vehicles	GH¢60
Failure to comply with regulations on visitors permit	GH¢240 - GH¢300
Use of Foreign driver's license	GH¢240 - GH¢300
A person being an excess passenger on a vehicle	GH¢60
Non-compliance on regulations on speed limits	GH¢60
Obedience to police and fire service officials	GH¢120
Obstructing intersections and pedestrian crossings	GH¢240 - GH¢300
Disregarding signs and barricades	GH¢60
Stopping and parking if buses and taxis regulated	GH¢120 - GH¢300
Parking in Highway and town roads	GH¢120 - GH¢300

ii. Prosecution for Major Traffic Offences: Serious driving offences might attract a longer jail sentence from a court system. The process commences with the issuance of an order for the offender to appear in court with submission to trial adjudication in order to determine a violator's guilt or innocence. This may involve or not involve taking the suspect in physical custody before a court appearance and a suspect may also leave custody after posting a bail. This is normally done in situations of continuous violation or where there is a chance that the suspect may not appear in court.

See Table 9.7 and Figure 9.16 for penalty levels for traffic offences in Ghana.

Table 9.7: Common Offences and Penalties for Major Violations in Ghana

Offence	Maximum Penalty- Fines	Equivalence in Jail Term
Dangerous driving	GH¢600	7 years' imprisonment
Careless driving	GH¢2,400	Up to 3.3 years' imprisonment
Driving under the influence of alcohol or drugs	GH¢2,400	Up to 3.3 years' imprisonment
Holding on, getting into, or alighting from a vehicle in motion	GH¢120	Up to 4 months' imprisonment
Contravening prohibitory road signs	GH¢120	Up to 4 months' imprisonment
Failing to stop at the signal of a police or other authorized personnel	GH¢300	Up to 8 months' imprisonment
Wrongful parking (e.g. parking within 50 feet of a no parking sign, within 30 feet of a junction, or on a pedestrian or rail crossing)	GH¢300	Up to 8 months' imprisonment
Leaving vehicles or trailers in dangerous positions	GH¢300	Up to 8 months' imprisonment
Driving with defective brakes, tyres and steering gear	GH¢300	Up to 1.5 months' imprisonment
Driving with an invalid Ghanaian or international driver's license for the class of vehicle being driven	GH¢300	3-8 months' imprisonment
Using an unregistered vehicle or trailer	GH¢300	8 months' imprisonment
Not fixing a registration number on vehicle or trailer, or obscured registration numbers	GH¢120	4 months' imprisonment
Providing false information to a traffic officer	GH¢ 3,000	1 year imprisonment
Overloading	GH¢ 500	
Driving without a License	GH¢1,500	
Over speeding	GH¢1,000- 2,500	1 year imprisonment
Use of unlicensed HGV in public	GH¢5,000	5 years
Driving with an expired license	GH¢300 - 1,500	
Failure to wear a seatbelt	GH¢2, 500	1 year imprisonment
Hitchhiking while driving	GH¢3,000	1 year imprisonment
Driving a Vehicle without insurance	GH¢1,000	

Sources: Act 683, Act 761, LI 952, LI 953

In some extreme case scenarios such as indicated in Figure 9.16 a driver maybe banned for life for an RTC involving the loss of many lives.

Figure 9.16: A publication on Penalty for Traffic Offence

However, the margin to which the use of a fine is deterrent to traffic violation is yet to be studied or proven though drivers complain a lot about the court charges. Writing for example under the theme "Why fines and jail time won't change the behaviour of Ghana's minibus drivers", Oberg –Odoom F. (2009) indicated that a range of structural factors including exploitative labour relations between car owners and drivers and police corruption compel and solicit dangerous driving behaviour.

He argued that fines and prison sentences are not suited for inducing safer driving behaviour among "tro-tro" drivers in Ghana because such interventions don't tackle the range of polit-ical-economic causes, motivations and constraints that result in dangerous driving. Besides, it could generate general social disturbance with regards to affordability. Therefore, the effectiveness of these measures as a penal system will have to be well studied, (See Box 9.3).

Box 9.3: Why Africa cannot prosecute

Authorities in Ghana frequently blame drivers for the country's road transport problems and poor safety record. For instance, in parliament recently, the country's Roads and Highways Minister cited driver indiscipline as the cause of RTCs. His predecessor made similar claims, as have presidential committees, parliamentarians; former presidents and the National Roads Safety Authority. These claims often end up forming the basis of public policy. For instance, based on a presidential committee report claiming that: "Indiscipline is the main contributory factor to the increasing incidents of road traffic crashes" in Ghana, the government approved a colossal 1 billion Ghana Cedis ($175 million) to tackle driving behavior through road surveillance, sensitization and public education.

The Ghanaian authorities have good cause to be concerned. Today, road trauma is among the top 10 causes of deaths in Ghana. One report suggests that about $230 million is spent annually on emergency and trauma care from motor accidents alone. And it's true that driver factors such as recklessness, unruliness, indiscretion, inattentiveness and poor judgment are important for understanding road transport problems. But there is more to it. A deeper understanding of Ghanaian drivers' roles in road transport miseries lies in the policy choices that shaped the country's transport sector into its present form.

My study of measures to deal with road accidents in Ghana suggests that blaming drivers deflects attention from inappropriate policies. Identifying the wrong cause of the problem means that it can't be fixed comprehensively

It has been shown that tro-tro drivers in Ghana operate within a precarious work climate marked by cut-throat competition; low wages; job insecurity; non-negotiable daily fees by car owners and harassment from corrupt police officers. These numerous financial and other demands are what push the drivers to undertake the dangerous driving behavior that earn them public opprobrium. Thus, contrary to popular opinion, tro-tro divers in Ghana drive dangerously not because they are inherently bad or morally bankrupt people, but because their work systems and conditions compel or incentivize them to do so. This analysis is not intended to shield any drivers from personal responsibility or accountability. The point, simply, is that much of their dangerous behaviour is driven by systems and structures beyond their control.

Boateng, F.G. Why Africa cannot prosecute (or even educate) its way out of road accidents: insights from Ghana. Humanity Soc Sci Commun 8, 13 (2021). https://doi.org/10.1057/s41599-020-00695-5

D. Factors Undermining Traffic Prosecutions: *In Ghana, the major factor undermining traffic prosecutions by the judiciary has to do with the following:*

i. Delays and costs involved in court procedures: This creates inconvenience to offenders so most of them prefer to resolve matters outside the court system through quick fix solutions such as the payment of bribes to the police to avoid court processes. Therefore, delays in court proceedings should also be well addressed.

ii. Stigmatization: Another factor has to do with the public stigma and public embarrassment attached to a court appearance for even a minor offence. The public must be educated to accept the court system as a corrective measure.

iii. Development of Informal Relationships with Law Enforcers: The development of informal relationships between the police and offenders resulting in the offering of bribes as a matter of course for offences committed. A Study in Ghana by Sam F. E (2022), revealed that most drivers bribe the police (willingly or are coerced) by giving them monies (usually between GHS 2 and GHS 5) concealed in leaflet or license cover.

This practice has become the norm, the failure of which often results in unnecessary delays and the threat of prosecution for traffic offences (albeit minor). It is also usually the case that "at-fault drivers" resort to bribing the police to avoid scrutiny and the associated delays (e.g., driving license and vehicle and roadworthy inspections) and the threat of prosecution for road traffic offences. It is recommended for a staged enforcement of a law over time, to allow the public to integrate the law into their daily lives and foster community integration.

iv. Perception of Possible Police Frame ups: In Ghana, another factor has to do with the perception of possible police frame ups and distortion of evidence through additional charges which did not happen to make the case more serious than it is. This must be counteracted with the instant digitisation of traffic offences to minimise this challenge.

v. Ownership of Commercial Vehicles by Law Enforcers: In Ghana, this creates a situation where law enforcers are not able to arrest offending commercial drivers of vehicles owned by colleague law enforcers for purposes of solidarity. Technology based enforcement should be encouraged to reduce human interactions.

vi. Vehicle Vandalisation at Police Stations: Also in Ghana, the fear of an impounded vehicle by the police being vandalised that is the possibility of theft of vehicle parts at the police station without police liability discourages offending motorists from obliging with due process of the law. Special depots with adequate security should be made available for keeping impounded vehicles from traffic offences for safe keeping.

vii. Factors not Amendable to Law Enforcement: Some of the charges on traffic offences in Ghana are also not amendable to law enforcement especially in cases that the motorist cannot be solely held responsible. Other obligations to road safety should be ensured to support effective traffic regulatory compliance by road users. In situations where the law enforcers themselves lack good understanding of the circumstances surrounding the commitment of and offence, this may also apply.

viii. Interferences from Higher Authorities: Undue interference in traffic offence investigations and prosecution from higher authorities which may mitigate against effective prosecution. This is because, such requests in many instances lead to the discharge of the accused or failure of court to award stiffer punishments. It is proposed for such situations to be counter addressed through the development of a suitable legal framework with minimised court processing backed by effective education and digitisation of the process to minimise human interferences.

ix. Difficulties in Tracing Traffic Violators: In some instances, there may be difficulties in tracing the whereabouts of witnesses to testify in pending cases therefore effective mechanisms should be put in place to ensure legal data integrity, avoidance of backlogs with processing and delays in judicial proceedings. There should also be application of decentralised legal systems and the application of registered vehicle owner liability enforcement under administrative law to facilitate the tracking of offending drivers.

x. Lack of Systematic Approach: Since the forms of misconduct in traffic behaviour are numerous, systematically focusing on all of them is not easily achieved. Therefore, efforts should be made to focus on highly prioritised road traffic offences with serious consequences on RTCs.

xi. Limited Application of Technology: The limited availability of modern technology to support enforcement activities such as video recordings of offending drivers, display of pictures etc. makes it difficult to achieve efficiency. There should be gradual transition from over dependence on manual enforcement measures to automated systems which Ghana is on its way to achieving.

xi. Poor records on non-compliance: Records on the extent and frequencies of non-compliance with traffic regulations provides knowledge of the true incidence and nature of non-compliance which is critical for the planning and evaluation of enforcement activities.

Currently in Ghana valid records on non-compliant traffic behaviour continuously and systematically compiled does not exist. This is largely attributed to the prevalence of outside the court settlement of such cases. Public education for awareness creation as well as the process of linking enforcement with other databases by the application of digital system should be expedited.

E. Alternative Prosecution Measures: Other alternative options for punishing traffic violators include the use of non-cash transactions such as driving license suspension for a period of time, the re-licensing system and the demerit system. The demerit points systems involve the record of points against a driving license on the basis of the level of offence leading to an eventual loss of the license should the points received reach a certain threshold. The commitment of further traffic offences by the same driver might have a driver's license being evoked or a driver being totally disqualified from driving.

Currently, the demerit system is not applied in Ghana due to the absence of modalities for effective implementation. Factors such as lack of easy access to driver registration data by patrol police, inability to track activities of culprits to ensure compliance or sanctions are the major reasons why the demerit system is not applied in Ghana.

Also currently, the fact that drivers are able to disregard their ceased license and continue to drive even after having their licenses revoked due the lack of effective management remains a key challenge. The piles of drivers license currently sitting in various MTTD offices is a good indication of a possible failure of such system. This is due to lapses in the enforcement system whereby same drivers cannot be easily monitored and tracked for licensing defaults. A suggested solution is as captioned below:

"I wish to also call on the DVLA to design the driving license in such a way that it will attract severe penalty points for reckless driving with the maximum penalty points leading to suspension or revoking of the license in extreme cases," Rev. Antwi-Tumfuor said in his 31st Watch Night sermon at the Kekeli Congregation in Tema Community 11. He said it was strange that drivers who caused fatal accidents found their way to drive other cars as if nothing had happened at all or had done nothing wrong because they still had access to their license". Currently the DVLA has embraced the concept but are yet to operate the system, (See Figure 9.17).

DVLA to revoke and suspend license of reckless drivers

Figure 9.17: Publication on DVLA's Efforts on Driving License Control

9.6 POLICE ENFORCEMENT TOOLS

9.6.1 Tarffic Police Equipment

Traffic policing must be equipped with the necessary facilities for effective conduct of their tasks and responsibilities. Some of the mentioned tools required for police enforcement are as presented below

A. Patrol Equipment: *In Ghana, these include (i) stationary and patrol vehicles for tracking recalcitrant traffic offenders; (See Figure 9.18); (ii) communication and tracking gadgets such as Walkie Talkies needed to alert enforcement patrol teams at different locations ahead of reported cases of emergencies; (iii) personal protective equipment etc.*

Figure 9.18: Examples of Police Enforcement Vehicles in Ghana

B. Equipment for Speed Control: *These in Ghana include road traffic radar measuring instruments eg. radar speed gun, speedometers, hand-operated laser measuring instruments, laser scanner, video traffic control systems, (See Figure 9.19).*

It is also suggested for the NRSA to design special stickers that will indicate when a vehicle sets off, so that when it arrives at its destination, one can check at the final destination if there was speeding, because there is a standard time for which one should cover a certain distance. It can also help deal with floating drivers as they will be compelled to load from designated points in order to get such stickers, which the police can use to check their speed in addition to the use of the speed gun by the police.

Figure 9.19: Speed Enforcement by the Ghana Police,
Source: (ptb.de/cms/en/ptb/fachateilungen/abt1/fb-131/instruments-for-speed-control.html).

C. Equipment for Alcohol Control: *Driver alcohol detection system using Breathalyzers or alcometers for breath test is used in Ghana, (See Figure 9.20). It is also recommended that Driver Alcohol Detection System for Safety (DADSS) – a technology that measures blood alcohol levels under the skin's surface by shining an infrared light through the finger tip of the driver should be explored in the future. Other recommended options include acquisition of equipment for urine test on drug use.*

Figure 9.20: Police Enforcement on Blood Alcohol Levels

D. Traffic Surveillance by Cameras: This involves the use of digital video cameras by the placement of closed-circuit television cameras in the road environment.

Examples in Ghana are presented in Figure 9.21. However, in Ghana, these are certified not to be in appropriate quantities for effective support to the manual enforcement efforts used by the police. There should be an assessment of the state of available enforcement-related equipment matched with the magnitude of enforcement demands to establish the current gap in equipment holding by the MTTD.

Figure 9.21: A. Surveillance Camera and a Control Room in Ghana

E. Equipment for Accident Handling: *In Ghana, these include road signs, cones, flares, communication gadgets, torch lights, towing equipment etc. (See Figure 9.22).*

Figure 9.22: Examples of Police Enforcement Tools

Alternative funding sources for targeted traffic law initiatives could be explored. Some of these could include the promotion of increased support from other affiliated entities such as the following:

i. *Increased support from revenue generated from road safety stakeholder entities engaged in enforcement such as the DVLA through the provision of complementary resources such as vehicles and associated logistics such as fuel in joint operations.*

ii. *Supply of Alco-meters by manufacturers of alcoholic beverages to support responsible drinking initiatives as part of their corporate responsibility to road safety*

Aside the issue of availability, the quality of equipment is also an issue. In the past some challenges that have been experienced in association with this by the MTTD include wrongful calibration of speed guns resulting in erroneous detection of violations with potential legal consequences. It is therefore recommended for such equipment to be standardised and approved by the GSA and other related agencies before being used.

9.6.2 Benefits and Challenges of Traffic Law Enforcement

A. Benefits of Traffic Law Enforcement: The effectiveness of traffic law enforcement can be measured by the amount of officer time spent on certain activities etc. From literature, it is recommended for traffic law enforcement to be recognized as one of the top priorities in road safety interventions through the promotion of positive road policing due to the following factors:

i. Facilitation of Achievements of Other Road Safety Targets: Road traffic law enforcement identifies the causes of crashes so that other road safety activities can be targeted appropriately.

ii. Deterrence of Road traffic law Offences: Enforcement can deter illegal, dangerous and careless behaviour on the road since the very presence of the police on the road has a positive effect on driver behaviour.

iii. Contribution to Behaviour Change: Road traffic law enforcement contributes to the modification of road user behaviour with a subsequent reduction in deaths and injuries from accidents through education on traffic laws and on corrective behaviours.

iv. Promotion of Sustained Compliance: Road traffic law enforcement promotes sustained compliance with traffic laws through its contribution to road user deterrence from violating traffic laws and avoidance of hazardous traffic situations which in turn preventions the prevalence of risky road user behaviour.

v. Identification of Road Traffic Law Offenders: Road traffic law enforcement enables serial and dangerous road traffic offenders to be identified and prosecuted.

vi. Definition of Appropriate Sanctions: Road traffic law enforcement contributes to the definition of appropriate convictions and sanctions for motoring offences.

vii. Education of Road Users: Road traffic law enforcement also plays an important role in educating the road user to help change social attitudes since the Police are often directly involved in training schemes.

viii. Removal of Dangerous Vehicles: Road traffic law enforcement results in the identification and removal of dangerous vehicles from the road.

In Ghana, there is hardly any research finding to validate most of the mentioned benefits of traffic law enforcement though some of them do apply. Therefore, it is recommended for research studies about the effectiveness of enforcement to be undertaken to validate these benefits in Ghana.

B. Key Challenges Associated with Road Safety Enforcement: Road Traffic enforcement may also be inadequate because of a variety of social, economic, technical capacity, political and other factors some of which are discussed below with recommended proposals for mitigating them.

i. Technical Challenges: Adequate technical capacity and capability is therefore essential for effective traffic law enforcement practices. According to Rottengather, (1990), one of the fundamental problems hindering the road traffic law enforcement process is the inability of the relevant authorities to maintain high levels of enforcement standards. This is in respect of both the size of the police traffic law enforcers and the technical knowledge for effectively performing their duties.

In Ghana, there have been repeated discussions on the issue of insufficient traffic police officers to handle both incident management and traffic control with the MTTD having to work with fewer officers to meet the demands of the job. This challenge must be a pre-cursor to the training and development programmes for additional traffic police officers to fill the current gap. Some of the key interventions that could help address the situations include the following:

a). Conduct of a an MTTD Capacity Needs Assessment: A dedicated study to establish the threshold of MTTD capacity and capability needs should be conducted to determine the exact state of the MTTD's capacity and capability needs for effective traffic enforcement in the country.

b). Development of Training Plans and Strategies: Following the capacity and capability needs analysis, a strategic plan to fill the shortfalls together with succession plans should be developed for the MTTD. In addition, a strategic plan for continuous human resource development for the MTTD must be developed to meet the technical demands of traffic safety enforcement in the country for capacity sustainability. This must entail aspects on technical training, coaching and mentoring on a wide range of topics to enable the delivery of diverse courses. This should be based on the establishment of internal police trainers who can conduct continuous, refresher and upgrade training programmes.

Professional standards development in police enforcement must be given a high premium for increased efficiency and effectiveness in the country. The standard of traffic enforcement in the country must be upgraded at all levels of the MTTD's administration. This is of critical importance because there are cases where MTTD officers' default in their judgement of a traffic violation.

An example is a situation where the driver passes the stop line with the signal immediately changing from green to amber. In such situations the Highway Code allows the driver to pass. Besides it becomes unsafe for a driver to stop in the middle of the road especially at a cross junction with divers from the moving traffic trying to bypass vehicle at the back and at the front. It even becomes more critical when the driver tries to reverse when this is going on.

According to the (Global Road Safety Partnership, 2008) enforcement training programmes should also focus on leadership of the police and frontline operational officers to ensure that knowledge and capacity are retained and transferred in the local policing agencies. The training must also be as practical as possible through participatory and observational learning.

It is also equally essential to expose the MTTD to international good practice especially with the application of scientific methods. Partnerships should also be developed with institutions of higher education for the running of specialized courses up to post graduate level for professional traffic law enforcement with a well-developed curriculum to incentivize higher performance.

c). Improvement of Working Methods: Enforcement operations must explore innovative simple but cost-effective methods for new but effective procedures and upgraded performance.

d). Coordination: Fragmented enforcement training activities must also be well coordinated for effective results.

ii. Limited Funding for Effective Traffic Law Enforcement: This is very important and maximization of limited resources must be ensured.

In Ghana, traffic enforcement needs are not matched with required funding thresholds. Besides the budget for the work of the MTTD is not solely dedicated for the purposes but rather integrated into the budget of the entire police force. Thus, the task of traffic law enforcement has to compete with other law enforcement activities.

Some best practices for addressing this challenge includes prioritising enforcement activities with direct impact on RTCs (SafetyNet, 2009), as well as increased adoption of other measures which will dissuade drivers for committing higher traffic violations so as to minimise the work of the law enforcers. Typical examples include imposition of stringent penalties, driver retraining, introduction of drink driver rehabilitation programmes etc.

Increased funding options should also be sought from measures such as the allocation of portions of traffic fines for enforcement backed by sufficient fine levels. Others factors such as early payment incentive and late payment penalty impositions should be introduced to further enhance the process.

A study to identify third party collaboration in enforcement activities such as equipment supply backed by payment from fines to allow the private party recover from its investment over time should be conducted.

f). Corruption: Corruption by both the police and motorists does not make traffic law enforcement credible enough to support effective road safety work. This is because law enforcers are made to compromise on their responsibilities, abuse the power given to them, breed mistrust, lowers community standards as well as damage the reputation of all honest traffic officers and supervisors.

The outcome is continuity of bad driver behaviours since it does not encourage them to modify their wrongful behaviours resulting in the creation of serial traffic offenders who continue to violate traffic rules and regulation with impunity.

In Ghana, the findings by the study by Sam F. on the subject are as summarised in Box 9.4.

Box 9.4: Traffic Enforcement and Bribery in Ghana- Driver Opinion

Most drivers revealed bribing the police (willingly or coerced) by giving them monies (usually between GHS 2 and GHS 5) concealed in leaflet or license cover. Commercial drivers indicated that this practice had become the norm, the failure of which often resulted in unnecessary delays and the threat of Prosecution for traffic offences (albeit minor). It is also usually the case that "at-fault drivers" resort to bribing the police to avoid scrutiny and the associated delays (e.g., driving license and vehicle and roadworthy inspections) and the threat of prosecution for road traffic offences as presented below.

Sometimes it depends on the MTTD team on the road; if the team is not strong, I will just put money in my license cover and hand it over to them. However, if the unit is strong and I am at fault, I can hand over my passengers to another car and stand by until the police leave the road, and then I continue my journey (34 years old, Male, Commercial driver). Often, these delays are believed to constitute a financial loss to commercial drivers (i.e., loss of sales), so they do anything possible to avoid the same (Dotse et al., 2019). In essence, commercial drivers have learnt, and try as much as possible, to avoid punishment (Porter, 2011) by engaging in road tactics and bribery. Dotse et al. (2019) and Tankebe et al. (2020), corroborate the study finding that motorists in Ghana (mainly commercial drivers), in most cases, attempt to bribe traffic police officers to escape/avoid punishment.

Anecdotal evidence suggests that this "bribe-giving behaviour" (bribery) is typical among commercial drivers as they are often the most likely of all motorists to be stopped by traffic police officers for various traffic offences (violations and lapses), including overloading, over speeding and driving without proper documentation (Dotse et al., 2019)

This situation is worrying given the body of evidence that suggests that punishment avoidance (i.e., not being punished for committing an offence) means that drivers will continue to engage in illegal behaviours (Stafford and Warr, 1993; Armstrong et al., 2018; Bates and Anderson, 2021).

Some best practice strategies to mitigate corruption includes the following:

a. *There should be extensive research to understand the compulsive factors exposing both road users and the MTTD officials to acts of corruption.*

b. *There should be a multi-faceted approach to road safety law enforcement including the following.*

   • *Better remuneration / Increasing salaries for the traffic officers.*

   • *Introduction of merit-based bonus system.*

- *Public sensitisation on zero tolerance on corruption acts.*
- *Conduct of regular reshuffling of MTTD officers.*
- *Institution of anonymous corruption reporting measures.*
- *Establishment of a disciplinary committee to deal with corrupt practices promptly.*
- *Conduct of joint all party in corruption sensitization sessions.*
- *Promotion of internal principles of transparency and accountability for MTTD officers.*

c. *Proactive promotion of public trust by positive non punitive measures to give police departments an opportunity to constructively engage and dialogue with road users and to enhance their image.*

d. *Introduction of on-the-spot roadside police fines with video coverage and issuance of receipts with counter foils for fines.*

e. *Institution of traffic safety rights to guide civil and human rights protections.*

f. *Introduction of officer wellness with rightful protective gears and resources.*

iii. Social Challenges to Effective Road Traffic Safety Enforcement

a). Lack of Compliance Motivation: It is said that motivations for driver compliance must be with fairness, consistency and well-publicized actions, (Homel, 1988, 1990) sine there are variations in what is possible with regards to deficiencies to be rectified within existing legislative parameters.

In Ghana, it is necessary for law enforcers to consistently engage with road users for good understanding and support.

b). Poor knowledge of Traffic Laws: Not only do road users lack knowledge on the traffic laws and related legal obligations, some are also of the opinion that there are too many regulations for easy comprehension.

In Ghana, a simple code of conduct that dictates road user behavior could be developed to guide motorists.

c). Unintended consequences of enforcement: Unintended consequences of road traffic law enforcement can impede well-meaning enforcement efforts.

In Ghana, this includes incidence of drivers and the mates beating traffic officials for doing their world. This demoralizes enforcement from according seriousness to their work. Others are manipulation by pleadings for mercy. Also, since vehicle use is a symbol of economic status in the country, those who drive the big ones are deemed to be "big men and untouchable". Due to this, some of those who drive V8 SUVs take advantage of the situation and misbehave on the road by way of speeding, engaging in wrongful overtaking on the road and illegally using sirens reserved for VIP to indicate give way to the other with impunity.

d). Abuse of Power by the Police: The abuse of power by police officers is a great impediment to effective road traffic law enforcement.

In Ghana, examples include the allegations that a police officer could implicate a victim by depositing false evidence e.g. narcotic drugs in their vehicle to be used against them. This must be addressed through the promotion of police integrity and ethics training backed by training in accountability.

9. 7 ROAD TRAFFIC CRASH HANDLING BY THE POLICE

This is about the ability of law enforcers to respond adequately to RTC situations with regards to the management of operations at the RTC scene and the key aspects are as follows:

9.7.1 Protection of Road Traffic Crash Scene

This is done to ensure the safety of road users and other vehicles from further crashes, by increasing road capacity for road users who may be passing by the crash scene or for reducing demand on the available space at the crash scene. Other activities are protection of property and ensuring sanity and order at the crash scene.

In Ghana, this done by the police through actions like traffic management etc. summarised in Table 9.8.

Table: 9.8: Controlling the RTC Scene

Proper handling	Based on circumstances at the RTC scene
Determination of need for additional assistance	Summons for additional assistance eg additional police personnel, ambulance service, fire service, towing machines, utility services and special equipment, volunteer and bystander assistance
Identification of potential hazards	Factors which might make the situation worse or endanger life's eg fire, dangerous cargo, explosives,
Procedures for protecting the scene	Keeping of spectators away from the scene Protecting the injured Traffic crowed control Placement of warning devices Maintaining traffic flow Facilitate movement of emergency vehicles
Preserving physical evidence	Preserving RTC evidence, such as debris and skid marks,
Moving Damaged Vehicles in Emergencies	Arrange to have the vehicle moved or impounded by driving the vehicle, shoving or pushing it off the roadway
Theft Prevention Measures	In situations where large crowds of spectators may have formed and there is a great deal of confusion and keeping them away

9.7.2 Conduct of Crash Investigations

Investigating individual RTC situations enables the cause of a crash to be identified. Thoroughly reported information is used to draw conclusions and form opinions about how and why the RTC happened. RTC investigations are of two types. The first involves routine investigation conducted on every reported crash and the second is the constitution of a special committee for detailed investigations into some specific RTC cases.

A. Routine RTC Investigations: This type of investigation informs on what could be done in future to avoid a similar occurrence. It is also normally used as evidence for prosecution in court for RTC involving deaths, injuries and those that do not involve any of such. The Police is solely responsible for the conduct of this type of RTC investigations and the information is also used to support several activities including the following:

i.   Identification of those who have behaved illegally for possible prosecution, damage claims etc.

ii. Identification of priortised issues for targeted enforcement by police with respect to time devotion, place of operation and frequency of application of intervention.

iii. Application of lessons for the conduct of traffic engineering re-structuring for effective outcomes.

iv. Use of the information to inform the content of traffic education, driver education, public safety education, safety research and traffic legislation.

v.   Use of the information as evidence to support court proceedings and for insurance claims.

This is conducted by the reconstruction of the chain of events that constituted the traffic crash in a sequential order with analysed information from drivers and witnesses. It also includes photographs, measurements and diagrams/sketches of the RTC scene to identify operational factors that contributed to the RTC.

Where there are surveillance cameras and video records of the incidence, they are also used to inform the investigation process supported by conclusionary findings and judgments of the causes or causal factors of the RTC. A summary of the primary tasks undertaken by the police in RTC investigations are as summarised in Table 9.9.

Table 9.9: Summary of Primary tasks undertaken by the Police in RTC Investigations

Element	Description	Details
Proceeding to the Scene	Learning of an accident	Information about the occurrence of the RTC from control room or by radio call; dispatcher, passing motorists, coming across or witnessing the RTC
	Obtaining the information about the accident	A clear understanding of
		When the accident occurred, location, severity, extent of injury and damage, emergency services informed
	Anticipating the situation at the scene	Likely nature and extent of associated traffic problems, extent of hazard and what might be required
	Planning the route to the scene	Determination of the shortest route to the RTC scene
	Proceeding to the route	Aiming for prompt arrival at the scene
	Observation of enroute situations and conditions	Notification of the conditions in the immediate vicinity of the RTC scene, which may have been contributing circumstances
	Arrival at the scene	Parking considerations
Obtaining Information	Compulsion to obtain information	Interviewing drivers, passengers, and witnesses
		Written Statements
	Obtaining Information from Vehicles	Circumstances of the RTC suggesting certain defective vehicular conditions
	Specific parts contributors	Tyre blowouts
		Side marks proving inadequate braking
		Steering gear, wheels and springs breakage
		Wipers not functioning properly or not working at all
		Poor lighting
		Trailer decoupling
		Broken doors
		Accelerator throttle leakage
		Engine transmission
	Vehicle Condition	RTC versus pre RTC condition
		Collapsed vehicle i.e. nature and extent
		Overlapping vehicles with each other or fixed objects
		Thrust i.e. nature contact damage
		Speed estimate
		Imprints i.e. dents
		Rub –off of surface material eg paint
		Road contact damage
		Interior damage
	Pedestrian RTC	Signs of vehicle contact with the pedestrian
	Roadway	Deficiencies eg view obstruction
		Reduced visibility
		Surface conditions
		Curbs and low shoulders
		Road Alignment
		Traffic control devices in proper use
	Physical Evidence	Debris
		Marks on roadway by hard objects
		Tyre. Imprints
		Tyre skid marks
		Tyre scuffmarks
		Damage to roadside objects
		Miscellaneous road marks
		Vehicular fluids
		Cargo
		Blood

Element	Description	Details
RTC Crash Scene Measurements	Diagrams	Accurate location of significant objects and events at the RTC scene
		Skid mark measurements
		Field sketch
		Scale diagram
	Speed estimation	Statements of drivers and witnesses
		Vehicular damage
		Road marks
		Movement of vehicles after the key point or point of maximum engagement
		Incurred damage
		Side marks
Photographing the Accident Scene	Location of the scene or objects photographed	When and what to photograph
		Photographing vehicular damage
		Road marks/Tire marks
		Final position of objects
		Roadway environment
Taking Law Enforcement Action	On-view versus Investigative" enforcement	Traffic Accident Law Enforcement Policy and Procedures
		Public attitude and support for taking law enforcement action
		Violations at the RTC scene
		making traffic arrests, issuing citations and warnings
	Terminal Accident Management Activities	Verification of the fact that all requisite forms have been completed and distributed,

In Ghana, the key challenge with recorded road traffic crash statistics by the police is the omission of the causes of RTC in the database. This makes it difficult to ensure targeted road safety interventions for effective outcomes.

B. Detailed RTC Investigation by a Special Committee: These are RTC investigations by the police, by special committees for detailed RTC investigations for special purposes.

In Ghana, the NRSA is mandated by law to systematically investigate every crash that claims five (5) or more deaths with the view to determine the factors (immediate/proximate, remote/ indirect and root causes) to the crash with recommendations for policy reforms as defined in NRSC Act 567 and NRSA Act 993 as summarised in Table 9.10.

Table 9.10: NRSA Acts on Crash Investigations

	Act 567	Act 993
Mandate	The NRSC Act defined a broad mandate to; *'Conduct investigations into road safety issues and advise the Minister on them'*	The NRSA in exercise of its investigative mandate is empowered to; -*'receive complaint and investigate violation of road safety standards, Regulations and best practices and advise the Minister on the measures required to minimize the road safety risks*
	Further the Board was empowered to; *'investigate or authorize a person to investigate and make report on a matter in respect of its functions'*	Specifically, the Authority is empowered to collaborate with other agencies to; *'investigate road traffic crashes that the Authority considers necessary to establish the contributory cause or lapse in road safety operational standards'*

	Act 567	Act 993
Regulations	-Minister may on the recommendations of the Board make Regulations for the conduct of Investigations. This was not done	-Minister may on the recommendations of the Board make Regulations for the conduct of Investigations. -A Revised Draft is ready for laying at Parliament
General Comment	-The scope of investigations was not very clear. However, the Commission developed administrative guidelines to cure the gaps. -These administrative guidelines were exercised to investigate crashes involving 5 or more deaths as the Commission deemed necessary.	-The scope is well defined in the Act with laid down procedures almost ready.

i.   *Objective: The Investigation is conducted to establish the underlying contributory factors to the crash event. It is required to probe deep into all the reasons and factors contributing to the fatal crash in order to make appropriate recommendations.*

ii. *Approach: The NRSA is required to set up an 8-member multi-disciplinary committee to carry out the crash investigation into the particular fatal crash, (See Figure 9.23).*

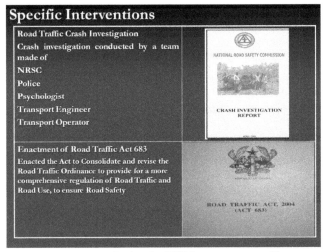

Figure 9.23: Membership for RTC Investigations in Ghana

The Committee of inquiry adopts a scientific approach for the crash investigations by a combination of on-the-scene and post-scene fact-finding procedures to undertake the investigation. The sole aim is to establish direct and indirect causes of the crash such as weather conditions, the time of the RTC, road environment and design factors e.g. recoverable zones, vehicle factors such as availability of emergency exit doors, availability of safety facilities on the road etc.

This includes other factors that specifically contributed to the increase of the number and severity of fatalities and injuries associated such as the availability of post-crash response facilities around the crash spot, delays in the crash response time and administration of first-aid to victims among others. This is complemented with

a.   *Visits and inspection of the crash spot.*

b.   *Inspection of vehicles involved.*

c.   *Consultations with the Police Command in the Region for crash investigation reports by the police.*

c). Output and Outcome of RTC Investigations: Following the investigations the committee produces a report with recommendations to prevent such crashes in the future. If a investigations pointed out that the driver was the cause of someone's death, he or she could either spend up to 10 years imprisonment or be fined, or both. If the driver was the reason for someone attaining a serious injury, then he or she could either spend up to five years imprisonment, be fined or both. The results also serve as basis for insurance claims.

The key challenge is that often times the outcome of such reports are not well disseminated or used as lessons points for road user education. The extent of application for policy reforms is also not publicised.

9.8 CONCLUSION

It is important to have strong road traffic safety laws but the presence of just the law is not sufficient. There must be effective traffic enforcement to influence safe road user behaviour. This requires sustained well-resourced law enforcement with education on the prevention of traffic violations. Acts of enforcement must also be backed by good credibility on the part of the law enforcers because little acts of compromise with small handovers not only undermines a significant proportion of road safety works in the country, it could also result in the loss of many lives which could have been prevented. Enforcement must also be by evidence based policing operation, facilitated by new technologies for improved performance to minimise human errors.

Appendix 9.1 Categories of Traffic Laws in Ghana

Vehicle	Driver	Road use Factors
1. Register	25. Driver's License	83. Advance warning device
2. Application to register	26. Learner's License	91. Failure to comply with axle load conditions
3. Verification of weights	27. Application for Driver's License	93. Imposition of penalty for overloaded vehicle
4. Registration of vehicle and trailer	28. Conditions for grant of Driver's License	94. Fees and permit for an abnormal and super dimension loads
5. Tests of condition of motor vehicle	29. Eye test	95. Liability of owner
6. Person to conduct examination of motor vehicle	30. Driving with uncorrected defective eyesight	96. Axle load control and enforcement
7. Road use certificate	31. Upgrading of class	97. Powers of authorized officer
8. Issue of road use certificate	32. Issuance of driver's license	98. Exemptions from payment of fees
9. Exemption from requirement for road use certificate	33. Renewal of driver's license	99. Appeal
10. Vehicle registration number plate	34. L - Plate	105. Registration and operation of commercial towing services
11. Refusal to fix registration number plate	35. P - Plate	106. Rules of the road
12. Renewal of registration number	36. Revocation, suspension endorsement or cancellation of license	110. Noise
13. Withdrawal of registration number	37. Persons disqualified from holding a driver's license	112. Placing injurious substances on the road
14. Registration of number plate manufacturer and embosser	38. Disqualification on revocation of license	113. Placing of construction materials and equipment on the road
15. Vehicle Lay-Off Certificate	39.Revoked or suspended license	114. Damage to roads
16. Re-registration of existing registered motor vehicle	40. Driving while license is suspended or revoked	116. Prohibition of nuisance on commercial vehicle
17. Change of ownership	41. Unlawful use of license	117. Trading on the road
18. Procedure where motor vehicle is destroyed	42. Prohibition of unlicensed person to operate motor vehicle	128. Prohibition of use of motor cycle or tricycle for commercial purpose
19. Change of use and physical conversion	43. Driver re-training and re-testing	129. Issuance of hiring r rental vehicle identification number plate
20. Update of Register	44. Replacement of driver's license	130. Use of taxi
21. Copy of entry	45. Change of name	131. Use of passenger carrying vehicle
22. Register of Licenses	46. Armed Forces and Police driving permit	132. Private use of passenger carrying vehicles
23. Trade License	47. Production of Driver's License	133. Route and bus lanes for passenger carrying vehicles
24. Trade License Log book	84. Compulsory wearing of protective clothing in respect of motorcycle	137. Maximum number of passengers
48. Vehicle not conforming to Regulations	85. Use of agricultural tractor on road	139. Property left in passenger carrying vehicle'
49. Mobility	100. Prohibited passengers	140. Offences in passenger carrying vehicle
50. Width and length requirements	101. Driving of motor vehicle	141. Other offences relating to passenger carrying vehicle
51. Height	107. Prohibition on use of communication device while driving	149. Definition
52. Carriage of loads	108. Turning right on red	150. Other rules of the road
53. Carriage of hazardous goods	109. Hand signals	151. Bicycles, hand carts, animal drawn carts; roller skates
54. Safety requirements for carriage of hazardous goods	115. Molesting or obstructing a driver	152. Animals on road at night
55. Registration of liquefied petroleum gas or compressed natural gas fitted motor vehicle	118. Maximum driving periods	153. Transportation of animal
56. Numbering of liquefied petroleum gas or compressed natural gas cylinder and issuance of sticker	119. Use of seatbelt	154. Use of road by pedestrians
57. Use of motor vehicle run on liquefied petroleum gas or compressed natural gas	121. Registration of commercial vehicle operator	155. Boarding and alighting from motor vehicle
58. Licence for installation of liquefied petroleum gas or compressed natural gas cylinder in a motor vehicle	122. Issuance of commercial road transport operating permit	156. Person being an excess passenger on motor vehicle
59. Non-transfer of liquefied petroleum gas or compressed natural gas cylinder	123. Issuance of commercial vehicle driving permit	157. Spot fine
60. Offences and penalties for liquefied petroleum gas or compressed natural gas fitted motor vehicle	124. Registration of foreign commercial vehicle operator	158. Power to inspect, impound and prohibit the use of motor vehicle
61. Transitional provisions for the use of liquefied petroleum gas or compressed natural gas by motor vehicles	125. Continuing education of commercial vehicle drivers	159. Traffic warden
62. Tyres	143. Documents for a person driving a vehicle outside Ghana	160. Prohibition of use of certain roads
63. Brakes	147. Visitor's driving permit	
64. Engines	148. Use of Foreign Driver's License	
	163. General speed limits	

Vehicle	Driver	Road use Factors
65. Lamps	164. Speed limits for particular class of vehicles	161. Application for Police Report on an accident
66. Mirror, windscreen and glass	165. Reasonable and prudent speed for conditions to be observed	172. Exceeding weight limits on certain roads
67. Materials for windscreen, windows and partitions	166. Exemption from speed limit	184. Provision for facilities for persons with disability on public transport
68. Windows and windscreen of a commercial vehicle	168. Obedience to Police and Fire Service Officials	185. Causing danger to road user
69. Fire extinguisher and first aid kit	169. Fleeing or attempting to elude Police Officer or authorized person	186. Provision of rest stop and lay-bys
70. Wheels and axles	170. Obstructing intersection or pedestrian crossing	188. Outdoor advertising sign
71. Steering		191. Highway Code
72. Suspension	171. Disregarding signs and barricades	192. Transportation of perishable goods and livestock
73. Wings, fenders, mud guards, wheel or mud flaps	173. Racing on streets or roads	194. Revocation and saving
74. Horns and Sirens	174. Obedience to stop light, stop sign and yield right-of-way sign	195. Interpretation
75. Trailer	175. Obedience to signals indicating approach of train	
76. Direction indicator		
77. Position of indicator	176. Passing stopped vehicle at pedestrian crossing	
78. Red reflector	177. Passing of school buses	
79. Fitting of retro-reflectors at the front and rear corners of a motor vehicle	178. Obedience to traffic control officers and devices	
80. Fitting of retro-reflectors on the body of certain motor vehicles	179. Restricted use of bus stop and taxi stand	
81. General requirements for retro-reflector	180. Parking in places reserved for persons with disability	
82. Warning chevron sign on rear of certain motor vehicles	181. Driving in a procession	
86. Maximum permissible axle load	182. Driving through a procession	
87. Devices for detection of overloaded motor vehicle	183. Stopping and parking of buses and taxis regulated	
88. Checking of weights	187. Parking on highway and town road	
89. Grant of special permit	189.Use of television monitor on the dash board of motor vehicle	
90. Special permit form	190. Counterpart Driving License	
92. Application of motor vehicle weight control regulations	193. Penalties	
102. Regulations on broken down motor vehicle and trailer		
103. Requirements for towing of motor vehicle		
104. Specifications of towing truck and other requirements		
111. Discharge of oil and other substances on the road		
120. Manner of fitting of seatbelt		
126. Standards and specifications for taxis and buses		
127. Issuance of commercial vehicle license		
134. Construction of passenger carrying vehicle		
135. Speed limiter, log book and tachygraphy		
136. Passenger vehicle carrying freight and persons		
138. Particulars to be written on passenger carrying vehicle		
142. Documents for vehicle being taken out of Ghana		
144. Visitor's vehicle		
145. Exemption of visitor's vehicle		
146. Registration plate and nationality sign		
162. Exemption from registration and licensing of motor vehicles and trailers		
167. Authorised emergency vehicles		

CHAPTER 10

THE FUTURE OF ROAD SAFETY DEVELOPMENT

10.1 INTRODUCTION

Global and local efforts to identify the significant factors causing RTCs and the appropriate remedies for addressing them has been ongoing in the past decades. However, the WHO's global report (2018) on the achievements of the DOA 2011-2020 stated that no country had been able to attain the set targets for reducing road safety fatalities as at that time with countries at different stages of progress in managing their road safety issues.

Also, according to the GRSF (2021), the scale of the current response to the continuing crisis of RTCs does not match the size of the problem in any country and Ghana is no exception. This is because some high-risk RTC factors may be particularly resistant to countermeasures than others even in the same country context.

Moreover, even when a countermeasure is technically effective, it may be incompatible with social, political, or legal requirements or may be prohibitively expensive. This makes the future of road safety to be very uncertain and the search for solutions must be with intensive commitment.

This book has expounded on the state of Ghana's road safety work in comparison with recommended global best practices and targeted actions. The object has been to draw on available knowledge, ideas and good practices for sustaining the achievements made in road safety work so far. It has highlighted on good outcomes to build on, challenges to address and good innovations to be explored on the way forward for better outcomes.

This final chapter concludes the book with an overview of the prioritised aspects recommended for the NEXT STEPS of the extended DOA – (2021-2030) as it applies to Ghana in the context of prioritised country specific needs. It is hoped that the critical insights provided on road safety in the book will instigate and facilitate the necessary actions to enhance road safety work in the country.

10.1.1 Evolution of Road Safety Implementation Approaches

Globally, there have been varied approaches to road safety management by set priorities (See Table 10.1) and with the completion of the DOA (2011-2020), the Next Steps to road safety management (2021 – 2030) is focused on a Zero Vision approach. This is aimed at preventing traffic deaths and injuries by the extended use of the DOA (2011-2020) road safety pillars of intervention with expanded partnerships and increased use of technology to mitigate human errors as proven in the HICs from the implementation of the DOA (2011-2020). (See Table 10.1 for an overview of the evolution of road safety approaches.

Table 10.1: Overview of the Stages of Road Safety Approaches

Themes	Description	State of Application in Ghana
Traditional approach		
Road-user approach	1. Considered human errors as the major cause of road traffic crashes (RTCs). 2. Road-user has almost total legal responsibility for safety. 3. Major attention to RTC prevention. 4. Countermeasures are basically determined to change the behavior to adapt the road-user to the system. 6. 3Es: engineering, enforcement, and education.	Focus was on the enforcement of safety practices by road users
Causal approach	1. Road traffic crash can be prevented only by a precise knowledge of the real crash factors. 2. Two main trends: deterministic (sequence of events) and probabilistic (set of factors). 3. Enhancing human behaviour (speed, alcohol, seat belts, and helmets) by legislation, enforcement, and campaigns. 4. Planning and designing to make safer infrastructure. 5. Safer vehicles through better crashworthiness, active vehicle safety, and vehicle inspections.	Policy guidelines, rules and legislation to guide road safety work were established
Systemic approach		
Sustainable safety	1. Functionality of roads. 2. Homogeneity of mass and/or speed and direction. 3. Predictability of road course and road user behaviour by a recognizable road design. 4. Forgivingness of the environment and of road users. 5. State awareness by the road user.	Development of strategic frameworks

Themes	Description	State of Application in Ghana
Safe system	1. People make mistakes. 2. Human physical frailty. 3. A 'forgiving' road transport system. 4. Building a national road safety culture. 5. Data driven targets. 6. Corporate responsibility. 7. International collaboration. 8. 7Es: engineering, enforcement, education, economics, emergency response, enablement, and ergonomics (safe interaction of people and safety).	Establishment of c commission to coordinate road safety actions
The UN plan for decade of action	1. Road safety management. 2. Infrastructure. 3. Safe vehicles. 4. Road user behaviour. 5. Post-crash response.	Adoption of the tenets of the DOA for road safety work
Vision zero	1. Three dimensions: ethics, responsibility, solutions. 2. Traffic deaths and serious injuries are acknowledged to be preventable. 3. Human life and health are prioritized within all aspects of transportation systems. 4. Acknowledgement that human errors are inevitable, and transportation systems should be forgiving. 5. Safety work should focus on systems-level changes above influencing individual behavior. 6. Speed is recognized and prioritized as the fundamental factor in road traffic crash severity.	Alignment with the next steps for road safety agenda for up to 2030

Source: The common road safety approaches

10.2. SUMMARY REVIEW OF DOA (2021-2020)

10.2.1 Summary of Achievements of DOA (2021-2020)

The DOA (2011-2020) aimed to commit all UN member states to a single road safety vision, agreed objectives and guideline to motivate positive road safety actions by rectifying major causes of traffic safety challenges with a package of polices defined as pillars for road safety actions. The key achievements included the following:

A. Systemization of the Approach to Road Safety Implementation: The DOA provided a structured framework of road safety actions to streamline the implementation of substantive road safety tasks in a given timeframe as better alternative unstructured approaches to road safety work.

Ghana had a road safety plan ahead of the DOA 2011-2020 with the launching of the DOA providing additional benefits to what was already being done.

B. Improvement in Road Safety Management: Road safety management as a key component of road safety work was first identified by the DOA (2011-2020) for effective and efficient coordination of the multi sectoral components of road safety work.

Ghana recognised the importance of road safety management way ahead of the DOA (2011-2020) with the establishment of a dedicated institutional leadership for road safety and the introduction of the DOA (2011-2020) mainly enhanced it significance to road safety work in the country.

C. Policy Direction for Road Safety Work: The DOA emphasised the importance of policy guidelines to provide relevant content and consistency in the approach to road safety work.

Ghana's, NRSP of 2008 prepared ahead of the DOA (2011-2020) requires an upgrade to match with current needs and emerging changes in road traffic safety dynamics especially with the call for road safety to be made a public health issue.

D. Creation of Societal Awareness of the Road Safety Problem: According to Salmon P.M et al. (2016), of all road safety interventions, it is road user behaviour that affects the magnitude of the effectiveness of road safety work. This is because it is the society that carries the weight of the road traffic injury and fatality burden much as they do not make final road safety decisions (Fahlquist, J.N, 2006), The DOA (2001-2020), therefore promoted increased margin of social responsibility with user accountability and compliance to road traffic laws and regulations.

Awareness creation has always been a key road safety measure in Ghana though the country is yet to attain the level of social cultural recognition for personal safety. (See Figure 10.1.).

Figure 10.1: A Perception on Public Attitude to Road Safety

E. Adequacy of Road Safety Budgets: The DOA (2011-202) promoted the introduction of dedicated funding for sustainable road safety work through increased political support.

Ghana has gained some political support for road safety work but is yet to achieve the dearth of importance that will influence politicians to commit adequate funds to the required levels.

F. Impact of the DOA: Globally, the impact of the DOA 2011-2020 has been difficult to be established. It has not been same for all regions and countries of the world with diverse outcomes in different regions and countries of the world. However, the WHO (2018) reported that HICs achieved significant progress compared to LIMCs. The progress made by the HICs was attributed to the use of matured and proactive road safety approaches and innovative measures such as the safe system approach and advanced technologies. Whilst there was over reliance on traditional approaches to road safety management in the LMICs.

On the way for, the recommendation by Hakkert V. (2007), for successful cost-effective interventions to be implemented in the LIMCs must be advanced towards the bridging of the technological gap between the HIC's and LMIC's, with the support and assistance of the international community by the deployment of accessible and harmonized technologies to LIMCs.

Likewise, though Ghana can continue using the traditional methods it must also gradually transition into the use of the modern methods as the necessary resources become available.

10.2.2 Summary of Challenges to the DOA (2011-2020) Implementation

Some of the key constraints to the effective implementation the DOA (2011-2020) are as follows:

A. Over Ambitious Targets: It was predicted before the implementation of the DOA 2011-2020 that it is not possible to determine around the decade or in advance what level of intervention would be economically efficient or necessary to meet a given target as specified. (Department for Transport-Strategic Framework for Road Safety 2011).

The 2018 Global Status Report by the WHO on road safety also stated that, data on injuries were insufficient to measure progress on road safety due variations in demography, geographic conditions, economic factors, technical applications, the quality of medical services etc.

At the end of the DOA 2011-2020, Ghana's aim to reach global road safety performance targets could also not be attained, even though some progress was made in some of the outlined measures on the DOA agenda. However, the lack of a more precise knowledge of the contributions of the various interventions made makes it difficult to determine how much effort should have been focused on particular road safety actions.

This has generated a mixed perception about the impact of the DOA 2011-2020 (See Figure 10.2) for a publication on an extreme perception of Ghana's road safety situation after the DOA 2011-2020).

Figure 10.2: publication after DOA Implementation in Ghana

B. Poor Data Management and Research: The DOA recommended for accurate RTC records for appropriate interventions.

In Ghana, measures have been made for improved road safety data management by the adoption of an automated RTC data recording and management system however data integration is yet to be attained.

C. Limited Coordination of Road Safety Work: The EU Policy Framework for 2020-2030, prepared in 2019 observed that international support has not effectively fostered actions to complement one another in assisting countries to build comprehensive road safety management systems.

Ghana must foster increased international collaborations for technological solutions in road safety management on the way forward.

D. Poor Delivery of Road Safety Interventions: Poor delivery of interventions resulted in the build-up of road safety challenges and difficulties. It is recommended for this to be addressed in a prioritised order in terms of what is likely to work and what is not likely to work and the level of required impacts from start to end with emphasis on quality over quantity to maximize the value of benefits.

The same must apply to Ghana's situation. (See the Figure 10. 3).

Figure 10.3: A Lesson to Take Road Safety to the Next Step in Ghana

10.2.3 Key Lessons from the DOA (2011-2020)

The lessons from the implementation of the DOA (2011-2020) for future consideration on the way forward on road safety includes the following:

A. Changing Scenario's in the Transport System: It is projected that population and vehicular growth will continue into the future and both passenger and freight traffic will grow alongside. This will require for road safety policies to be of broader perspectives with integrated approaches into various sectoral policies for holistic solutions. Ghana, must work towards this.

B. Importance of the Road Pillars for the Future: It is proposed for an extended use of the road safety pillars:

Ghana has aligned with this objective as reflected in the NRSSIV for 2021 – 2030.

C. Economic Justification of Counter Measures: Investment returns on road safety work needs to be proven through socioeconomic analysis to justify the returns on monies used for road safety work so as to convince decision makers on benefits. This is yet to be applied in Ghana.

D. Shared Responsibility for Road Safety Work: Since road safety is multi-sectoral all elements of society must share in the responsibility to improve road safety and there is need to identify mechanisms by which this can be done stakeholder entities can be identified to effectively enhance their contribution to road safety work.

In Ghana, a widened scope for shared road safety responsibilities by society at large must be researched.

E. Importance of Research: Good research outcomes still remain a very crucial need in road safety because the most significant crash factors cannot be said to have been identified.

In Ghana, good research has been an integral part of the functions of the NRSA but the procedures for the selection of research themes, coordination of research studies by other institutions, dissemination and utilization of research outcomes with feedback mechanisms must be worked on.

F. Promotion of the Benefits of the SDGs: The SDGs are expected to offer an opportunity to achieve set road safety objectives to accelerate achievement of its multiple components.

In Ghana, good understanding of the role of road safety in sustainable mobility and as a facilitator of multiple SDGs has not been well projected and there is need to develop a framework to exhibit road safety connectivity with other aspects of the SDG's and the related demands for achievement.

10.3 THE NEXT STEPS TO ROAD SAFETY IN GHANA

Whilst the principles of successful strategies in the Next Steps could be used, the proposals are rather universal and suitability to local need and capacity cannot be guaranteed. This is because, local circumstances differ and the approach should be by the reflection of local priorities, circumstances and conditions.

Thus, the final recommendations on the approach to road safety in Ghana on the way forward considers both the new aspects of road safety interventions proposed in the Next Steps and value addition to ongoing practices based on cost effective measures especially in regard to preventive rather than reactive measures for better outcomes.

10.3.1 Background to the Next Steps

According to the experts who participated in the 3rd Global Ministerial Conference on Road Safety in 2019 and the UN Next Steps for 2020-2030, the following are the key aspects for consideration.

A. Key Road Safety Challenge for the Next Steps: Increased vehicles volumes from increasing population and economic growth, the related RTC challenges and its demand on road safety management.

In Ghana, aside this potential, there are a backlog of numerous road safety problems from the implementation of the (DOA 2011-2020) which must be tackled on the way forward.

B. The objective for the Next Steps: The objective of the next steps in road safety management for the projected period of 2021 to 2030 is to provide access to safe, affordable, accessible and sustainable transport systems for all.

In addition, Ghana must also focus on how to effectively integrate road safety to the changing dynamics in road traffic situations.

C. Content of Road Safety Management for the Next Steps: The operational targets for the next steps in road safety management is by the strengthening of the road safety pillars with evidence-based solutions. (Saving Lives beyond the Next Steps, (2019).

Ghana's approach to road safety on the way forward must be by an all-inclusive good understanding of the causes of RTC's. (See Figure 10.4).

Figure 10.4: Importance of Knowing the Causes of RTCs for the Future

D. Approach to Implementing Road Safety Interventions in the Next Steps: Road safety must be an ongoing process because all potential solutions cannot be met at a go with key focus on three components as enhancement of existing interventions activities; introduction of new interventions and adoption of innovative measures.

i. Improvement of Existing Measures: As much as possible good road safety measures must continue by the completion of partially completed activities, filling of implementation gaps as well as a determination of how things could be done differently to achieve better results.

In Ghana, existing processes must be modified where necessary to optimize outcomes.

ii. Introduction of New Road Safety Measures: Due to changing population and traffic dynamics new road safety demands must be addressed accordingly so should always be means of looking out for the development of new programmes and adoption of new products.

In Ghana, this must be based on knowledge search for new and successful road safety interventions internally and externally especially for proactive and preventive measures.

iii. Introduction of Innovative Measures: This is about the approach to the implementation of road safety measures by new processes to improve efficiency of delivery.

In Ghana, innovative road safety ideas should be established by a back analysis of existing research outcomes together with the conduct of new research for improved methods and ideas on road safety management by embracing advanced methods and discarding obsolete ones.

10.3.2 Summary for Next Steps in RSM for Ghana

Ghana's RSM on the way forward must align with that of the next steps by accepting it to be a crosscutting bridging pillar for all other pillars rather than a standalone pillar of intervention as presented in See Figure 10.5.

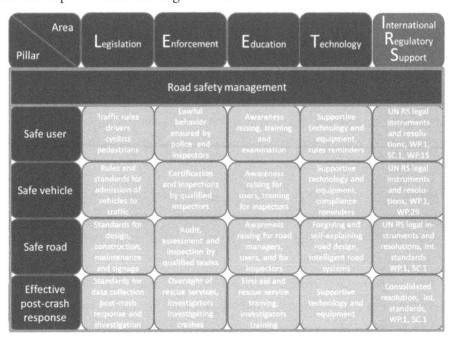

Figure 10.5: New Global Framework Plan of Action for Road Safety

A. Road Safety Vision for the Next Decade: The next steps engender all road safety visions to by the Vision Zero (VZ) philosophy with the idea that death and injury from RTC is not acceptable.

Considering the state of Ghana's RSM, the possibility for achieving the (VZ) may be over ambitious so the following must be prioritised:

i. *Ensuring, a good comprehension and understanding of the nuances of the state of the road safety problem in the country and the critical causes of RTCs.*

ii. *Critical examination of what is working and what is not working with current for necessary changes and improvement.*

iii. *Establishment of basic but solid systems and structures for ensuing consistent processes at all administrative levels.*

iv. *Prioritisation of persistent difficulties with serious RTC effect for elimination*

B. Road Safety Policy Guidelines: The next steps require for road safety policy guideline to be based on effective marketing through the collation of public information and support for road safety delivery on best behavioural practices/ actions that will reduce deaths and injuries on the roads with high value for money.

The following are recommended for Ghana:

i. *There must be a new policy approach to road safety to match up with changing needs the upgrade of the NRSP 2008 to match up to this requirement.*

ii. *The policy direction must be by a collective approach with shared ownership of challenges and solutions.*

iii. *Consideration should specifically be given to the Public Health approach to road safety management.*

C. Road Safety Legislation: The next steps require legislation must be based on ability to ensure reasonable compliance levels, consistent, updates according to need and adequate education for both law enforcers and road users.

i. *In Ghana, the need for law enforcer and road user education in traffic regulations must not be underestimated. Rather it being a road user responsibility, a deliberate effort must be undertaken on this so both the police and road users cannot enforce or comply with what they do not know.*

ii. *The level of ignorance of the traffic environment especially how humans, vehicles, and the environment interact and the related potential for RTC's must be enhanced for greater understanding, awareness, and practice of safe behaviour and skills.*

iii. Road users must be encouraged to respect road safety laws to motivate them to act within rules as well as avoid creating hazards for themselves and other road users.

iv. Compliance of traffic regulations must also be continuously monitored for necessary amendments in traffic regulations.

v. Consideration should be given to translation and education in road safety regulations using local languages.

D. Road Safety Strategies and Action Plans: The next steps require road safety strategies to focus on the multiple causes of RTC and the corresponding multiple ways for prevention. Ground-breaking ideas on what people care about and what actually works and not on commonly accepted standards are also encouraged.

In this regard it is proposed that the following be considered in Ghana:

i. The link between selected activities and empirical evidence must be clearly established. Every road safety measure must target an identified problem backed by factual evidence.

ii. Selected interventions must also tackle new and emerging trends in the traffic system e.g. increased motorcycle use.

iii. The assignment of quantities to activities must be of scientific basis and not on ad hoc or haphazard basis.

iv. Target setting must be balanced with resource availability to avoid inconsistent deliverables from limited resources and the creation of gaps in achieving the end benefits.

- *Specific emphasis must be placed on the development of scientific facts to counteract faith-based perception of road traffic crashes.*

- *People's characters in traffic and the acts of expression of what road users deem to be right and wrong with regards to the severity of different traffic offences must also guide the selection of interventions*

- *Selected activities must complement each other in order to ensure that all aspects of a particular road safety challenge have been fully addressed. For example, driver training and certification must be complemented with performance monitoring and refresher training.*

F. Roles and Responsibilities for Road Safety Work: Road safety must have shared responsibility ownership and accountability with road safety partnerships integrated into the entire value chain of the daily operations by government agencies, private businesses enterprises, social groups etc.

In Ghana, road safety partnerships must draw on varied backgrounds including those in the formal and informal sectors as follows:

i. Engagement with Formal Sector Entities

a). By policy, all formal institutions and sectors must mainstream road safety as recommended for HIV education, gender and environmental issues.

b). Road safety by law should become a human rights issue or as a consumer right to ensure demand for accountability from political authorities under the universal right to health by civil rights groups and consumer rights associations.

c). Ghana must ensure adequate professional knowledge t for road safety work through professional training by earmarked academic institutions including the building of innovative capacity to meet peculiar needs.

d). Transport and non-transport related industries and businesses must be encouraged to implement effective internal road safety policies with codes of safety practices to guide their operations.

f) Automotive companies must drive the road safety process by complying with approved vehicle safety standards in the industry.

g) Statutory road safety agencies must work with common purpose for change guided by relevant professional knowledge and skills to meet safe road demands to achieve required outputs.

e). The media must continue to play an important role in broadcasting and covering road safety initiatives both for commercial gains and as social responsibility.

ii. Informal Entities: This must include engagements with the following entities:

a) Informal Transport Related Industrial Operations: Road safety practices must be promoted within the operations of informal transport unions, local vehicle servicing garages, vulcanizers, business dealers in vehicle spare parts, towing companies and goodwill ambassadors for road transport passenger safety through institutionalized engagement systems.

b). Local level: Individual responsibility for self-safety must be achieved by intensified engagement on the effects of people's choice and skills in traffic safety with an interactive map and set guidelines to guide the process on continuous basis

Figure 10.6: A Publication on Importance of Stakeholder Collaboration in Road Safety Work

E. Road Safety Financing: The next steps also recommend for a dedicated fund for road safety work with options for accessing additional fund to be established to support effective road safety work.

In Ghana, there should be a dedicated funding with increased utilization of opportunities for funding the following to ensure that all aspects of the road safety system are reached.

i. Allocation of Road Safety Revenue by Type of Expenditure: Real cost components of different road safety activities must be adequately provided for. For example, the;

a. *safety component of the road fund could be used for the safe aspects of road maintenance,*

b. *insurance premiums committed to road safety could be used for the development, sponsorship and funding of crash prevention programmes;*

c. *proportion of the revenue from the DVLA could be committed to effective licensing, vehicle inspections, enforcement activities and road user education;*

d. *revenue from fines could be committed to road traffic enforcement work;*

e. *the proportion of the NHIS for emergency response to the treatment of RTC victims could be well appropriated;*

f. *other sources of funding from the consolidated fund, donor funds etc. could then be used for data collection, education, research, coordination of general RSM activities etc.*

ii. Alignment of Road Safety Activities with other Policy Agenda: This could be done to reduce pressure on the main budget as follows:

a. *Integration of road safety into mass transit programmes aimed at air pollution reduction to reduce the number of low occupancy vehicles on the road and related RTC consequences.*

b. *Use of proportions of internally generated funds by stakeholder entities for road safety work.*

c. *Integration of traffic enforcement activities with other police road check objectives e.g. checks for illegal mining and logging, customs control etc.*

d. *Integration of road safety into other health sector programmes such exercising by cycling and alcoholic disease control programmes.*

e. *Linkage of road safety to human rights drive to reduce violent deaths to increase advocacy on consumer rights on road safety.*

f. *Encouragement of insurance companies to sponsor good road user conduct schemes to encourage good road user behaviour.*

g. *Sponsorship of advocacy on responsible drinking by producers of alcoholic beverages and the hospitality industries.*

- *Collaborative research with common goals and methods involving the NRSA and the academia with respect to student thesis must be encouraged to reduce cost.*

iii. Timelines for Road Safety funding Releases: There should be timely approvals and release of funds.

iv. Emergency Road Safety Fund: This should be in place for emergency requirements on road safety activities such as the correction of hazardous road sections rather than waiting for complex bureaucratic procedures to avoid further RTCs.

F. Professional Capacity Development: Development road safety as a professional discipline.

In Ghana, professional networking amongst road safety experts for effective collaborations must be established whilst modalities for continuous professional development are assessed.

G. Application of Technologies in Road Safety Management: The application of technology-driven solutions especially with regards to how to manage human weaknesses in the road traffic system must be encouraged.

i. *In the interim Ghana should focus on the application of available and affordable low-tech solutions whilst exploring more opportunities for increased technological applications in the future.*

ii. *In the long term, there should be global support for making existing safety devices more available and affordable for LMIC like Ghana. This must be done to enable the country to keep up with technological progress backed by legal framework (See Figure 10.7).*

Figure 10.7: Enhancement of Technological applications in road safety.

H. Road Safety Data Management: There should be effective road safety database management to enable good judgment of the road safety situations across all relevant sectors.

In Ghana, the following must be ensured.

i. Data Quality: Ghana must not wait for a perfect data but focus on basic investments in good enough data that will enable effective prioritisation of activities with relevant causative factors.

ii. Data Collection Regimes: In the long-term automated data collection should be established to facilitate data collection frequencies and updates.

iii. Database Management: Data collection indicators must be continuously reviewed to suit the needs of the time. A clear system for the storage and transfer of research knowledge between sectors should be established.

iv Data Ownership: NRSA must develop capacity for the ownership and control of its data management systems currently hosted by the BRRI for possible revenue generation for entities needing such data.

I. Road Safety Research: According to the next steps, the relationships between RTC types, road user behaviour, vehicle types and injuries types as well as how road crash risk factors evolve through different life stages and modifications in social environments should be scientifically established.

In Ghana, basic research topics must precede complex ones. Efforts should be made to coordinate road safety research by different entities in order to harness its benefits.

J. Monitoring and Evaluation of Road Safety Strategies: There should be continuous monitoring of project activities and working for quality control

The following must be considered in Ghana:

i.   *There must be deeper understanding of how road safety work can be measured in its totality and the responsibility by different stakeholder entities for achieving this must be well defined.*

ii.   *There should be component specific monitoring frameworks with defined indicators guided by set targets for each problem area with adequate resources for continuity and necessary corrections.*

iii. *Regular monitoring of outcomes on key aspects such as speed management, alcohol impairment, fatigue driving should be instituted.*

10.3.3 Summary of Safe Infrastructure in the Next Steps for Ghana

In the next steps implementing safe infrastructure means changing infrastructure in order to increase road safety.

Specifically, in Ghana the importance of safety standards in road infrastructure development, maintenance and operation must be given due prominence and aside safe geometric design, installation of safety measures, safe traffic management etc. the following must also be addressed.

A. Safe Road Priortisation by the IRAP: *This should be done for roads with high traffic volumes and of high risk.*

B. Establishment of Model Roads: *A model stretch of a Safe Highway should first be developed for research with all the required elements as pilot for expanded replication on other prioritised roads.*

C. Application of the Zero Speed Concept: *Issues on speed standards for multi-lane highways traversing built up communities should be addressed.*

D. Safety Standards in Road Design: *The next steps recommend for impact assessment of the safety of engineering interventions in LMICs to be undertaken for effective upgrades.*

In Ghana, this is critical for determining outcomes and impacts of applied speed levels on safety.

F. New Road Construction: The Next Steps recommends for this to be driven by the concept of self-explaining and forgiving roads in order to achieve good outcomes.

In Ghana, these concepts must be developed as a part of the technological advancement process.

G. Safe Traffic Management: The next steps propose for traffic management measures to incorporate road safety in the planning of transport and land-use developments.

In Ghana, the diverse urban transport and land use development projects being implemented must be safety audited to determine the extent of safety considerations for appropriate amendments if the need be. On the way forward same must also be applied for new projects.

H. Modal Shift: The Next Steps proposes for road users to be encouraged to move from personal motor vehicles toward safer and more active forms of mobility.

The ongoing operations of rapid transit bus services in Accra must be safety audited to guide intended expansions to other parts of Ghana.

I. Safe Rood Infrastructure Sustainability: There should be a road safety data analysis, performance tracking, monitoring and evaluation in place.

In Ghana there should be inventorisation of road safety installations on high-risk roads with evaluation of performance for corrective purposes and to inform the design of new roads.

J. Capacity Development for safe Road Infrastructure: There should be capacity development of engineers involved in planning, design, construction and operation of highways as well as consultants, contractors and concessionaires in safe road engineering.

In Ghana, collaborations could be made between the NRSA and academic institutions such as the TREK for the development of training courses suitable to country specific needs.

K. Establishment of Infrastructure Safety Units for the Road Agencies: *In Ghana existing road safety units within the road agencies must be adequately resourced to oversee safe infrastructure planning, design, construction, operation and maintenance.*

G. Control of Vandalisation of Traffic Installation: *There must be widespread education on this in Ghana backed by research to identify alternative of no commercial value.*

10.3.4 Summary of Safe Vehicles Factors in the Next Steps for Ghana

The Next Steps requires for countries to promote progressive purchase, operation and maintenance of vehicles that offer advanced safety technologies with improved crash worthiness features. Others are promotion of the use of vehicles with high occupancy and other road-user protection measures compatible with local traffic conditions to reduce negative consequences. Specifically, it is required for the following to be considered.

A. Vehicle Safety Policy: The next steps recommend for vehicle manufacturing and assembling to be compliant with international safety regulations.

In Ghana, vehicle assembly plants of local origins must be tested for safety compliance to suit international marketability.

B. Safety Standards by the use of Technology: In the next steps, safe vehicle technologies are recommended to be facilitated and expanded for use.

In Ghana this must include:

i. *Definition of a clear policy direction on the large fleet of old vehicles with little or no compliance on essential vehicle safety systems such as the lack of seatbelts in most commercial buses.*

ii. *Progressive introduction of in-vehicle crash avoidance technology into the country backed by legal instruments.*

iii. *Definition of a clear policy on the importation of crashed with the lack of capacity for local repairs/restoring especially with regards to the safety systems. Arrangements should be made for these to be serviced in the originating country before being imported into the country.*

iv. *There should be training in for the use of advanced in- vehicle safety features for vehicle operators before being put on the road.*

v. *Local artisans must be sensitized on the importance of vehicle safety features with training for knowledge and skill development.*

C. Vehicle Testing Procedures: This is especially considered to be important for vehicles with high safety technologies by the next steps.

i.   In Ghana, PVTs should be continuously upgraded through training to keep them updated with emerging vehicle safety technologies on continuous basis.

ii. They must also have their company names embossed on the on roadworthy certificates for tracking and possible sanctions if rickety vehicles are approved for use on the road by them. There should also be road worthy alertness approach as with the insurance companies with feedback response rate to the DVLA via vehicle ownership records for necessary sanctions.

iii. Periodic auditing of Vehicle Inspection Centres should be done to sustain vehicle safety quality in the country.

D. Promotion of the Use of Alternative Modes of Road Transport: The promotion of walking and cycling as ready substitute to the large share of trips which cover less than 5km is recommended in the next steps with the promotion of mass transit by high occupancy vehicles.

i.   In Ghana, the promotion of walking and cycling as alternative safe modes of transport must be encouraged by disabusing the mind-set that it is for low class people who are not able to afford motorized transport especially with regards to the health benefits of such modes.

ii. Provision of safe infrastructure and education of motorist on how to safely share the road infrastructure with pedestrians and cyclists.

iii. Expansion of the BRT system for nationwide coverage towards the progressive replacement of low occupancy bus transport operation in the country.

iv. Enforcement of guidelines on vehicle withdrawal with the issuance of a signed certificate based on number plates and chassis number of the vehicle in question for effective control.

v.   Research into the potentials and necessary preparations for emerging technologies such as the use of automatic cars, electric vehicles and drones for the distribution of courier goods which aimed for the future.

E. Safe Fleet Management: Safe fleet management for both formal and non -formal commercial transport operators is recommended in the next steps.

i.   A safe commercial transport fleet management guideline should be developed for enhanced safe operations.

ii. Fleet owners in commercial operations must be encouraged to buy vehicles with safety features as well as also ensure safe performance of their vehicles at all times.

F. Research into Mechanical Failures of Vehicles: The next steps require for the actual contribution of mechanical failures to RTC's to be well researched. Consequently, measures are far advanced towards the development of a black box device in vehicles to facilitate research into RTC situations caused by vehicle factors.

i.   *In Ghana, due to the challenge of the use of diversified models of second-hand vehicles at different age levels with varied safety installations including those with little or no safety technologies, there must be effective research to determine how best to effectively manage the safety requirements of such a fleet in the country.*

ii. *Long term financial arrangements for capitalization of new vehicle fleet especially for commercial operations should be revisited with private sector involvement and negotiated collateral arrangements involving the vehicle assembling plants now operating in the country.*

10.3.5 Summary of User Safety Factors in the Next Steps for Ghana

It is said that human factors are more complicated to deal with in road safety because it is much more difficult to change human behaviour than to change vehicle or roadway design.

In the next steps the following aspects are recommended for consideration in Ghana.

A. Road User Research: *There must intensive engagement with road users for better understanding of behaviour and attitudes that influence RTC for consistent prediction of road user behaviour and for better interventions.*

i. Personal risk perception in road traffic: The next steps recommend for a well-informed and educated road user community who acts within rules backed by punitive measures for those who violate traffic laws. It is to be done by the determination of the psychological, social, institutional and cultural influences on people's traffic safety risk ratings, the differences in attitudes towards mobility and the differences in road safety performance.

In Ghana, complex road user attitudes and expectations must be shaped in a sustainable manner with continuous education of road users to constantly adapt to changing challenges on the roads.

ii. Focus on Safe Road Use and Practice: There should be a keen focus on the transformation of road user culture by the development of best traffic safety behavioral science for the road user.

Road user responsibility for their personal safe must be upgraded to the point where people question the attitude of themselves as well as of others while using the road.

iii. Tackling Entrenched Behaviours: Entrenched wrongful behaviours of road users must be well targeted researched and tackled.

Effective road user diagnoses through consistent tracking on the road over an acceptable duration inform education in safe traffic behaviour and skills.

B. Methods for Road User Safety: A combination of measures including enforcement, incentives, training, campaigning, etc., must be applied in tandem to influence road user behaviour guided by conscious interactions between road users and decision makers. Good examples of the methods for ensuring this include the following:

i. Road User Interventions for Increased Responsibility: People's safety decision-making skills must be guided by the following measures:

a) Targeting of road users by identified groups:

Road user education for commercial transport operators must target specific issues peculiar to their conduct on the road especially for motorcycle riders.

b). Assessment of Changed Road User Behaviour: In Ghana, this must be done by the use of attitude-scales.

c) Promotion of the Consumer Rights Approach: A 'road safety consumer rights' organization should be created in Ghana.

d) Promotion of Adoption of Courteous and Considerate Road User Behaviour:

The importance of courteous and considerate road user behaviour in traffic and the need for caution and respect for other road users and related impacts on safety must be integral to education.

ii. Road User Skills Development by Group: There should be mechanisms to develop safety skills, competences and knowledge for different categories of road users such as vulnerable road users.

In Ghana, aside the education of drivers and school children, other road user groups such as cyclists, pedestrians, riders of two and three wheelers, disabled road users, hawkers on road pavements, heavy goods carriers must also be educated. Where necessary, they must be equipped with appropriate survival skills necessary for the safe use of the road environment.

iii. Promotion of Safe Driving: The next steps require drivers to have a greater sense of responsibility at the wheel, be able to manage crash survivability, to be tolerant of other road users and be able to apply defensive driving skills.

In Ghana, there is need to consider all these. See Figure 10.8 for an example by the GRTU for this to be achieved.

Figure 10.8: Examples on Publications on Safe Driving in Ghana

a. *To promote safe driving, Ghana must first get the driver training and certification system right.*

b. *Driver training must be constantly adapted to changing traffic dynamics on the road with a multi-phase approach and reforming regimes for re-testing with wider trials/test levels.*

c. *There must be third party audit of driving schools with annual ratings to promote good performance.*

d. *Professional driver training and certification with post-test vocational qualification backed by graduated licensing for commercial operations by distance of travel must be promoted.*

e. *Special skills for long distance professional driver training must be provided to include defensive driving skills, overtaking skills, consistent driving at stipulated speed limits and fatigue management.*

f. *There should be mechanisms for tracking known serial offenders on specific routes for targeted training to correct repetitive errors.*

g. *Impaired driving from alcohol and drug intake should be made a shameful offense with stiffer punishment.*

h. *Driver unions must establish safety codes to qualify drivers for membership with effective supervision by station masters.*

iv. *Promotion of Driver Welfare: In Ghana, the following must be considered:*

a. *Driver Health Management: Driver's should be sensitized to take their health conditions and fitness to drive seriously including the effects of prescribed drugs and medication on their performance on the road.*

b.   *Driver Payments: The practice of driver payment by commission should be reviewed to ensure that vehicle owners pay for spare drivers for long distance travel.*

c.   *Social Security: Drivers must be encouraged to contribute towards the social security scheme in addition to insurance for any eventualities as well as for ensuring secured livelihood when they go on pension or are disabled through RTCs.*

d.   *Development of Driver Welfare Packages: Consideration should be made to identify a driver friendly insurance and banking schemes which will encourage dedicated savings and contributions in exchange for specific facilities and package for driver welfare needs.*

e.   *Fatigue Driving: From Literature, it is said that though fatigue driving affects cognitive abilities past studies have been unable to validate the actual impacts of fatigue driving since it is not easily observable and drivers must be well convinced on this.*

In Ghana, this must be tackled with tangible interventions such as the following:

• *The application of the logging of odometer measurements and speed levels through a record of the start time, break time and end of journey time matched with the distance of travel to establish the incidence of fatigue driving or otherwise must be well enforced.*

• *There should be adequate rest stops on all high safety risk highways through PPP arrangements with the district assemblies contributing landed space especially for long distance drivers to recuperate.*

iv. Promotion of Road User Compliance: In Ghana, the following must be promoted:

a). Seatbelt Use:

• *Compliance must be by a mix of safety awareness creation, attitudinal change and enforcement.*

• *Overtime, the number of persons in a vehicle must correspond to the number of functioning seat belts.*

• *Commercial vehicles fitted with seatbelts for both drivers and passengers must be targeted.*

• *There should be adequate education to discount reasons for the non-use of seatbelt including discomfort, short distance trips, dirty seatbelts etc.*

• *Commercial vehicles without seatbelts musts be retrofitted with seatbelts where feasible in the short term to save some lives in the interim.*

• *Policy discussions on the operation of vehicles that cannot be retrofitted with seatbelts in the country must be initiated not ignored for solutions even if it is for the long term.*

b). Use of Crash Helmets

- *There should be intensified education on the benefits of helmet use including affordability by subsidisation, sanitisation for public health concerns, sensitisation to dissuade thoughts on not using helmets for short distance trips and the ignorance of ladies' concern for their hair rather than safety.*

- *Specifications must be set to standardize the type of helmets to be used in the country.*

- *Disregard for helmet use must be treated as a more serious offense to save lives.*

c) Child Restraints: This is a neglected need in Ghana requiring serious attention especially with regards to children standing in vehicles, parents carrying babies on their laps and breast feeding of babies by driving mothers, failure to use child locks etc. Others are the limited or lack of use of child safety restraining systems and the lack of its enforcement with seriousness.

v. Driver Performance: In Ghana safe driver performance must focus on the following aspects:

a). Over Speeding:

- *Over speeding must be an immoral action due to the need to place human life above any other motivation for engaging in it.*

- *Reported impacts on exceeding speed limits must form the basis of education on speed limits.*

- *Motorcycle riders with the mindset that the utility value of motorcycle usage is reduced travel time causing them to over speed must be well educated on the dangers of speeding.*

b). Use of Handheld Devices: Road users must be made to appreciate the impacts of not hearing sounds from the environment while using hands free devices for both drivers and pedestrians.

c). Drunk Driving:

- *There should be scientific evidence to disprove the 'energy boosting' effect of alcohol to the drivers who engage in such acts.*

- *Offending drivers must be made to bear the cost of alcohol and drug use tests in addition to stipulated penalties required by the law. Unions could sponsor such tests at lorry terminals from their membership contributions*

- *Consideration for drug testing through the application of urine test at established test stations along major highway should be undertaken before driver take off and at arrivals.*

- *Passengers must be sensitised to object to be driven by a drunk driver.*

- *The practice of a sober driver amongst a group of people to driver a group after a drinking session must be introduced in Ghana.*

d) Wrongful Overtaking: Critical knowledge of the factors which should inform a decision to overtake other vehicles such as the surrounding traffic, road line markings, road signs, the speed of oncoming vehicles, visibility, the speed of vehicle in use, the speed of the vehicle ahead etc. must be imparted to drivers.

e). Overloading: This affects the stability of a vehicle can also potentially increase traffic congestion due to slow movements which instigates impatience by other drivers leading to reckless overtaking.

In Ghana, reasons for overloading, includes the desire to increase income, passenger influence to avoid delays in the loading of the next vehicle, to avoid multiple trips with related costs for carting large quantities of goods, ignorance about the safety impacts of overloading etc. This must be addressed through the following measures.

- *Drivers must be educated on the safety consequences of overloading with regards to vehicle stability control and the related RTC challenges especially for goods on worn out tyres.*

- *Vehicle owners must be educated on what they stand to lose in RTC situations from overloading such as the cost of damaged vehicle, the value of the goods destroyed, the cost of lives lost, cost of damage to the road structure etc. when an RTC occurs which offsets any financial gains made from the overloading.*

f). Adherence to Traffic Signals: Road users must be impressed with the utility value of compliance to traffic signals for their safety to discount the thought that it is better to gain time advantage than the risk of jumping the red light.

g). Driver Yield at Pedestrian Crossings: The safety implications of rightful conduct at road crossings must be well emphasized for both motorists and pedestrians especially with the following.

- *Drivers must be sensitized on how limited braking time and poor anticipation of pedestrian speed can result in RTC and pedestrian must be educated on how the tyres are faster than the legs.*

- *Pedestrians who place convenience above safety by crossing the road anyhow must be sensitised on their ability to control their own actions compared to the driver's ability to control a motorised system.*

- *There should be installation of devices that will help alert/calm the speed of motorists as they approach designated crossings could be useful to their response to pedestrian traffic.*

h). Query of Unsafe Driver Behaviour.

- *Passenger empowerment to boldly report to enforcement entities at the next stop without arguing with the driver and to station masters on driver conduct without feeling intimidated or yielding to ignorant condemnation by fellow passengers must be promoted.*

- *Passengers should be made aware that speaking against poor driver conduct does not imply a bad omen for an RTC to occur.*

- *Legal provisions for querying unsafe driver behaviour must be clearly defined, so drivers who are reported will not take out on the passenger for the remaining part of journeys.*

- *Records of offending drivers could be tied to the level of insurance premium paid and the qualification for the issuance of a road worthy certificate in the commercial transport industry.*

i). Carriage of Dangerous Goods: It must be ensured that vehicles used for transporting dangerous goods meet, to the extent possible, the requirements of set standards concerning the international regulations on the Carriage of Dangerous Goods by Road (ADR), taking account of national mandatory requirements that may have to be applied in the country of use. The practice of some commercial drivers carrying extra gallons of fuel for long distance trips must be addressed.

j). Transport Unions: These can sponsor the services of technical experts to upgrade e membership performance by providing up-to-date and relevant information on traffic laws, safe driver behaviour and techniques, road conditions, maintenance procedures and vehicle safety from membership dues to protect their own and to conserve their resources.

vi. Pedestrian Safety Performance

a). Use of Walkways: There should be conduct of studies into the social and ethical norms and cultural elements affecting pedestrian behaviour at crossing points before rigorous enforcement is applied e.g. the feasibility of enforcing the use of footbridges by female porters ('kayayoo's) carrying heavy loads.

There must also be a study to establish the impact of encroachment, jaywalking, hawking in traffic and disabled persons/children scuttling through traffic with little safety concern form motorist perspectives.

This must inform necessary actions on pedestrian safety such as relocating encroachers, provision of financial support for alternative economic activities to meet the financial needs of street beggars and hawkers who put their lives at risk for engaging in such ventures.

b). Pedestrian Education: There should be intensive education to address pedestrian igno-rance and unsafe pedestrian behaviours including exposing themselves willingly to danger but not using safety installations.

c). Enforcement of pedestrian laws: Due attention must be given to the enforcement of pedestri-an regulations in addition to education which is a neglected aspect of enforcement in the country by not only physically preventing them from jaywalking but also by prosecution as a deterrence.

d). Validity of Engineering Standards for Locational Spacing of Pedestrian Crossing Facilities: This must be carefully and safely aligned with pedestrian crossing behaviour in order not to inconvenience or cause pedestrian distress in using such facilities e.g. avoidance of longer travel distances by pedestrians to access crossing facilities.

10.3.6 Summary Post-Crash Care for the Next Steps in Ghana

In the Next Steps, it is recommended for the effectiveness of post-crash emergency services to be promoted for optimized trauma management. This is because reduction in road fatalities cannot be achieved without a well-developed rescue system since if injured people are not provided with a fast medical treatment, the number of fatalities can increase substantially.

The development of a coherent emergency response system is also an important step towards more road safety work in Ghana. Specifically, the following measures could also be consid-ered alongside the recommendations in the Next Step for post-crash care:

A. Policy for Joint Post-Crash Care:

i.   *A clear policy set on responsibility for the handling of RTC victims at the RTC scene with regards to the role of lay respondents in terms of survival risks and related legal implications must be set.*

ii.   *Provisions in the NHIS for emergency care must be activated for at all medical facilities in the country.*

B. Pre-Hospital Care: According to the Next Steps, the best medical care must be guaranteed at the early stage of the victim's care need. That is at the RTC site with much focus on training in First Aid for everyone and everywhere.

In Ghana, the following must be considered:

i. *Establishment of a Model of a Formal Emergency Response Systems:*

a.   *To begin with a model of an emergency response system with the full complement of all the emergency response elements required at the RTC scene by all agencies should be set on a high risk RTC prone road e.g. Accra- Kumasi Road, Tema- Aflao road and the Accra – Takoradi road as pilot for expansion to other relevant roads in the country after evaluation.*

This can be backed with the conduct of joint drills, allocation of responsibility for over-lapping activities, geographical zoning for common resource sharing and joint evalua-tion of work interventions for correction of errors and upgrade of service efficiency must be instituted.

ii. Enhancement of First Aid Care:

a. *In the short term before formal emergency response services become fully efficient and effective, informal systems for first aid care must be expanded and improved across the country e.g. first aid training must be introduced at all stages of a person's life - at home, in school and at the workplace.*

b. *It can also be popularized through vivid demonstrations on relevant media platforms such as the television on continuous basis across the country.*

iii. Enhancement of Informal Emergency Response Activities

a. *The training of lay persons in emergency response of RTC victims must place emphasis on cautious extrication of RTC victims, safe handling of injured victims, triaging, bleeding control and cautious transport of the victim to a medical facility to avoid further damage.*

b. *The use of innovate tools in situations where there are no conventional first aid tools to work with must be explored and disseminated whilst the concept of first aid posts is expanded.*

c. *There should be open knowledge on options for closest health facility in an RTC vicinity.*

iv. Facility based Care for RTC Victims:

a. *Existing healthcare facilities along the Highways must be assessed for possible upgrade. Those found deficient of minimum facilities and resources must be provided with ade-quate facilities where there is a deficit.*

b. *As much as possible the policy of ensuring the availability of one emergency care facility at every 50km along the national highway should be applied.*

c. *There should also be a plan for seamless networking amongst health facilities, rescue services, existing fleet of ambulances etc.*

C. Funding Provisions for Emergency Health Care: The Next Steps recommends for a dedicated health grant from the insurance industry for the funding of crash manage-ment programmes.

i. *In Ghana, passenger records at the lorry stations with telephone contacts of the next of king should be established to enable emergency call to relatives by union members to engender the necessary financial support to victims be their families within the shortest possible time.*

ii. *Passengers should be encouraged to provide travel details to family members e.g. vehicle model, registration number, take-off time, arrival time etc. to facilitate emergency needs.*

D. RTC Victim Rehabilitation: The next steps indicates that psychological implications of crashes (on victims, their family, those responsible for the crash, and the relevant consequences of road crashes for victims must be addressed with long-term tracking of the recovery process.

In Ghana, knowledge on the available of such service should be well disseminated to create awareness for those in need of such services.

10.3.7 Summary of RSE for the Next Steps in Ghana

The next steps require RSE to be actively encouraged safer practices and products by the education of all road users to motivate them to act in a responsible way in traffic as follows:

A. Road Safety Educational Research: RSE must be well researched.

In Ghana, this is long overdue.

B. Duration of Road Safety Education: Road safety education must become a life-long process.

In Ghana, life-long education of road users through a formal commitment to promote effective road safety education must be the goal in addition, there should be a policy for RSE to begin in schools and pre-schools so that appropriate behaviour is fostered from early age.

C. Transport Unions: *In Ghana, the commercial transport unions can be encouraged to provide RSE feedback to government and industry for policy considerations especially on new initiatives.*

D. Approach to the Marketing of Road Safety: The next steps recommend for the following:

i. Road safety measures judged necessary should be marketed such that if the public is negative to a chosen road safety measure they can be convinced to change.

ii. It should also be marketed as a product using all the knowledge that commercial companies have collected over the years.

iii. There should also be targeted marketing influenced by many psychological, social, institutional and cultural factors.

iv. Advertisers must be discouraged from the use of advertising styles which glamorises and/or promotes unsafe practices and products but rather should actively encourage safer practices and products.

v. This must be complemented with the reverse chronology scenario whereby; for instance, road users are sensitised on the effects of not wearing seat belts, rather than simply focusing campaign messages on only the wearing of seatbelts.

In Ghana, in addition to the above there, RSE should more targeted on specific hazards and when deemed necessary for specific zones. Also, a post RTC direct communication campaign should be created for effective awareness creation to the relevant entities

E. Promotion of the Benefits of Road Safety: According to the next steps RSE must also achieve the following:

i. RSE must convince road users about the benefits of road safety measures by sharing information on RTC risks.

ii. The media must enhance community awareness and understanding of the causal factors and real costs of road crashes.

In Ghana, communities must be made aware of the causal factors and real costs of road crashes so as to influence societal changes which can lead to a reduction in unacceptable driver behaviour and poor attitudes.

F. Application of modern technology in RSE: The application of modern technologies must be used to strengthen and further improve RSE for different road users and groups.

i. In Ghana, the use of social media for road safety education must be well researched.

ii. Road safety slogans should be popularised to become household words through mobile SMS messages and caller tunes.

G. Use of Testimonials of Road RTC Victims: This must be focused on the repercussions of drunk driving, high speed driving, negligent and rush driving, non-use of vehicle restraints e.g. seatbelts/helmets, use of mobiles when driving, etc., use of defective vehicles, etc.

In Ghana, the work of the profile of the association of RTC surviving victims must be enhanced with the necessary funding support and expanded to enable effective contribution to evidence-based education on road safety.

10.3.8 Summary of Road Safety Enforcement Factors in the Next Steps for Ghana

According to the next steps, the enforcement agencies can improve road user behaviour and vehicle standards through a balance of education, encouragement and effective enforcement strategies and the following must be considered in road safety enforcement.

A. Road Safety Enforcement Research: Research into effective road safety enforcement.

Specifically, the following must be undertaken in Ghana:

i.   *The extent to which RTC punitive measures affect road safety behaviours must be researched together with the most suitable approaches for the rehabilitation of offenders.*

ii.   *The study should establish the conditions where "awarding enforcement" is better suited than punishing enforcement.*

iii. *The types of penalizations or alternative punishments most effective in particular circumstances and/or for particular target groups should be defined.*

iv.   *The study must investigate how law enforcers can differentiate between road user ignorance and indiscipline to guide road user education.*

B. Application of Counter Measures: *Effective enforcement should be maximized based on proven enforcement systems and technology including the following in Ghana:*

i.   *Application of Counter Measures without Public Acceptance: Creation of countermeasures by the full use of existing enforcement powers with tougher penalties.*

ii.   *Enforcement of High-Risk Behaviours: Enforcement with key focus on high-risk behaviours.*

iii. *Expanded Technology in Enforcement: Evaluation of the pilot phase of the use of surveillance cameras should be conducted for expanded application especially on major highways.*

iv.   *Enforcement Monitoring: Mechanisms to monitor enforcement compliance levels in the country should be in place to inform for policy directions.*

10.4 THE ESSENTIALS FOR ROAD SAFETY IN GHANA ON THE WAY FORWARD

In summary it is proposed that the quest for successful road safety management in Ghana in future must deliberately take the following principles into consideration.

i. Acknowledgement of the State of Ghana's road Safety Performance: There is need for road safety managers to acknowledge the fact that though the country has made good road safety efforts with significantly good achievements there is still need to improve and expand on road safety management in the country on the way forward into the Next Steps.

ii. Determination of what has worked and Not Worked: The fact that not all road safety interventions have been equally effective must be recognised to inform necessary changes.

iii. Completion of Prioritised Projects: All highly prioritised projects to meet high risk road safety needs still ongoing must be completed by rolling them over for continuity before new ones are implemented.

iv. Application of Solutions: Due to limited capacity and resource availability, sustainable road safety systems must focus first on simple and practical solutions with flexibility, innovation and maximised use of resources to attain maximum outcomes.

v. Problems with Difficult Solutions: Existing RTC problem areas with difficult understanding and solutions must further be researched for appropriate solutions.

vii. Maximum Utilisation of Existing Opportunities: All efforts must be made to maximize the utilization of existing opportunities including research outcomes, available data, institutional reforms, developed capacities, opportunities for collaboration with global agencies, possible exchange programmes for international exposure, regional networking and knowledge share options at all levels towards accelerated road safety results.

viii. Improvement of Existing Countermeasures: Existing Countermeasures should be more effectively and potentially developed and improved for maximized outcome.

ix. Enhanced Proactive Approach to Road Safety Management: The approach to road safety must be more preventive rather than reactive.

x. Consolidation of Road Safety Gains: The gains made so far in road safety management must be consolidated and sustained to avoid wastage.

xi. New Opportunities: New opportunities for sustainable road safety work should continuously be explored and pursued.

xii. Change of Wrongful Road Safety Mind-set: Emphasis must be placed on road user perception and understanding of the factors that cause RTCs and the role played by them so that appropriate mechanisms can be made towards changed mind sets with regards to behavioural problems.

xiii. Expansion of Road Safety into All Sectors of Development: In the long term: Ghana should work towards including road safety interventions across all sectors of development as prerequisites for change. This must be the ultimate goal in Ghana.

10.5 CONCLUSION

Ghana is committed to road safety but it might be prudent not to emphasis so much on the attainment of an end target of a vision zero at this stage of Ghana's road safety development. Rather, the focus should be on ensuring that the best systems for making consistent progress within available and affordable means are working efficiently. This should involve improving, adding value and innovation to existing measures whist seeking for new improvements in road safety activities. Road safety accelerators to combat and reduce RTCs must be given high premium especially preventive measures. Optimal investments must be made in highway safety to increase knowledge, improve infrastructure and vehicle systems as well the application of advanced technological solutions which is yet to be attained. With a focused consistency and adequate resourcing, though the target of a zero fatality in Ghana's road safety in the next steps might be too ambitious and unlikely to be met some gains will be made to reverse current trends in RTC records in the country. Of critical importance will be emphasising on the factors critical to the sustenance of the good results achieved and those that will direct further advancement in Ghana's road safety work.

ACRONYMS

A&E	Accident and Emergency
AADT	Average Annual Daily Traffic
AASHTO	American Association of State Highway and Transportation Officials
ABS	Anti-Lock Braking System
ACN	Automatic Crash Notification
ADAS	Advanced Driver Assistance Systems
ADT	Average Daily Traffic
AED	Automated External Defibrillator
AfCFTA	African Continental Free Trade Agreement
AfDB	African Development Bank Group
APE	Associative-Propositional Evaluation Model
ARSO	African Road Safety Observatory
ASIRT	Association for Safe International Road Travel
ATLS	Advance Trauma Life Support
AU	African Union
B&D	Births and Deaths
BECE	Basic Education Certificate Level
BRRI	Building and Road Research Institute
CAN	Automatic Crash Notification
CBOs	Community-Based Organisations
CCE	Cycling Expertise-Ghana
CCVR	Customs Classification and Valuation Report
CEPS	Customs Excise and Preventive Service
CEPS	Customs, Excise and Preventive Service
CI	Compression Ignition
CKD	Knocked Down Vehicles
CoP	Commissioner of Police
COTVET	Council for Technical and Vocational Education and Training
CPR	Cardiopulmonary Resuscitation
CSOs	Civil Society Groups
CVT	Continuous Variable Transmission

DAC	District Assemblies' Common Fund
DALY	Disability-Adjusted Life Years
DFR	Department of Feeder Roads
DPOs	Disabled People's Organizations
DRABC	Danger, Response, Air and Breathing, Circulation
DUR	Department of Urban Roads
ECOWAS	Economic Community of West African States
EM	Emergency Medicine
EOCs	Emergency Operation Centers
EP	Emergency Physician
ESC	Electronic Stability Control
ESP	Electronic Stability Program
ETSC	European Transport Safety Council
EVS	Electronic Vehicle Safety
FIA	Foundation for the Automobile and Society
GADP	Ghana Automotive Development Policy
GCPS	Ghana College of Physicians and Surgeons
GDP	Gross Domestic Product
GES	Ghana Education Service
GETC	Guidelines for Essential Trauma Care
GHA	Ghana Highway Authority
GHS	Ghana Health Service
GNA	Ghana News Agency
GNCAP	Global New Car Assessment Program
GNFS	The Ghana National Fire Service
GoG	Government of Ghana
GPRTU	Ghana Private Road Transport Union
GRCS	The Ghana Red Cross Society
GRoSS	Ghana Road Safety Support
GRPTU	Private Road Transport Union
GRSF	Global Road Safety Facility
GSA	Ghana Standards Authority
GSFP	Ghana School Feeding Program
GTC	Global Technical Committee
GTR's	Global Technical Regulations

GTTC	Ghana Technical Training Centre
HGV/LGV	Heavy Goods Vehicle/Light Goods Vehicle
ICT	Information and Communication Technology
IGF	Internally Generated Funds
IMT	Intermediate Means of Transport
iRAP	International Road Assessment Program
IRF	International Road Federation
ISCCS	Co-Operation System
ISIP's	Infrastructure Safety Invest Plans
ISO	International Organization for Standardization's
ITST	Intelligent Transport Safety Technology
JHS	Junior High School
KNUST	Kwame Nkrumah University of Science and Technology
KPIs	Key Road Safety Indicators
LCI	Law Compliance Indicator
LEAP	Livelihood Empowerment Against Poverty
LGSS	Local Government Service Secretariat
LICs	Low-income Countries
LOS	Level of Service
LPG	Liquefied Petroleum Gas
MAAP	Microcomputer Accidents Analysis Package
MICs	Middle-Income Countries
MMDA's	Metropolitan, Municipal and District Assemblies
MoH	Ministry of Health
MoT	Ministry of Transport
MoTC	Ministry of Transport and Communication
MOTRA	Motor bikers, Tricycles and Riders Association in Ghana
MRT	Ministry of Road and Transport
MSD	Meeting sight distance
MSLC	Middle School Leaving Certificate
MTNDPF	Medium-Term National Development Policy Framework
MTTD	Motor Traffic and Transport Department
MVR	Motor Vehicle Record
NAD	Norwegian Association of the Disabled
NADMO	The National Disaster Management Organization

NAS	The Ghana National Ambulance Service
NASS	National Accident Sampling System
NCAP	New Car Assessment Program
NDPC	National Development Planning Commission
NG	Natural Gas
NGOs	Non-Governmental organizations
NHIS	National Health Insurance Scheme
NIC	National Investment Corporation
NPOC	National Prosthetic and Orthotics Center
NRSA	National Road Safety Authority
NRSC	National Road Safety Commission
NRSP	National Road Safety Programme
NRSP	National Road Safety Policy
NRSS	National Road Safety Strategy
NSPS	National Social Protection Strategy
NTP	National Transport Policy
OBD	On Board Diagnostic
OCE	Off-Cycle Emissions
OECD	Organization for Economic Cooperation and Development
OEMs	Original Equipment Manufacturers
OIC	Occupant Injury Classification
OTC	Orthopedic Training Center
P&O	Prostheses and Orthoses
PAARI	Police Action Against Rider Indiscipline
PI	Positive Ignition
PIARC	Permanent International Association of Road Congresses
PIE	Police Invisible Eye
PPP	Public-Private Partnership
PROTOA	Progressive Transport Owners' Association
PSD	Passing or Overtaking Sight Distance
PSI	Presidential Special Initiative
PTI's	Periodical Technical Inspections
PTSD	Post-traumatic stress disorder
PVOC	Pre-Verification of Conformity
PVTS	Private Vehicle Testing Stations

QALY	The Quality Adjusted Life Years
RADMS	Road Accident and Data Management System
RAI	Road Accident Investigations
RCI	Road Crash Indicator
RISM	Road Infrastructure Safety Management
RSE	Road Safety Education
RSI	Road Safety Inspection
RSI	Road Safety Index
RSIs	Road Safety Indices
RSIS	Road Safety Information System
RSM	Road Safety Management
RSPI	Road Safety Performance Index
RTC	Road Traffic Crashes
RVAIS	Regional Vehicle Administration and Information System
SDGs	Sustainable Development Goals
SHIA	Swedish Organizations of Disabled Persons International Aid Association
SJA	Saint John Ambulance
SMSs	Safety Management Systems
SMTDF	Sector Medium Term Development Framework
SOE	State Owned Enterprise
SPIs	Safety Performance Indicators
SRIP	Safer Roads Investment Plans
SRS	Star Rating Scores
SSATP	Sub-Saharan Africa Transport Policy Program
SSD	Stopping Sight Distance
SSO	Street Sense Organization
SUVs	Sub-Urban Vehicles
TGC L	Toyota Ghana Company Limited
TMI	Traffic Management Indicator
ToT	Trainer of Trainer
TPI	Traffic Performance Index
TRECK	Transport Research and Education Centre
TRL	Transport Research Laboratory
TRP	Traffic Risk Perception
UNECA	United Nations Economic Commission for Africa

UNECE	United Nations Committee of Experts
UNECE	United Nations Economic Commission for Europe
UNRSC	United Nations Road Safety Collaboration
UNRSF	United Nations Road Safety Fund
UTP	Urban Transport Project
VAK	Visual, Auditory, Kinesthetic
VELD	Vehicle Examination and Licensing Division
VRC	Vehicle Registration Certificate
WARSO	West Africa Road Safety Organization
WHO	World Health Organization

REFERENCES

Introduction

Bliss, T., & Breen, J. (2011). Improving road safety performance. Lessons from international experiences, a resource prepared for the World Bank. Washington DC: World Bank.

BRRI (2020) Road Traffic Crashes in Ghana Statistics 2020

Carlsson, G. & Hedman, K. (1990). A systematic approach to road safety in developing countries. World Bank Technical paper.

CUTS (2014). Competition reforms in key markets for enhancing social and economic welfare in developing countries (CREW) project for bus transport in Ghana.

DVLA (2012). Diagnostic study of driver and vehicle licensing authority, FWC Beneficiaries 2009 - LOT 2: Transport and infrastructure.

Ferrell's Human Factors Theory | RLS HUM Ferrell's Human Factors Theory | RLS HUMAN CARE (rlsdhamal.com) AN CARE (rlsdhamal.com)

Firenze, R. J. (1978). The process of hazard control. New York, Kendal /Hunt.

Fu, G., Chen, P., Zhao, Z., & Li, R. (2019). Safety is about doing the right thing. *Process Safety Progress*, *38*(4)

Geller, E. S. (2001). Keys to Behavior-Based Theory

Gur-Ze'ev, I. (2003). The metaphysics of traffic accidents and education toward an alternative public sphere. *JSTOR, 141*, 318-345. http://doi:www.jstor.org/stable/42980024

Haddon, W. (1972). A logical framework for categorizing highway safety phenomena and activity. *Journal of Trauma*, 193-207. http://dx.doi.org/10.1097/00005373-197203000-00002

Haddon, W. (1970). Energy damage and the ten countermeasures strategies, insurance institute for highway safety. Washington, DC

Heinrich, H. W. (1950). Industrial accident prevention. New York McGraw Hill https://rlsdhamal.com/v-l-groses-multiple-causation-theory/

IBIS Transport Consultants Ltd. (2005). *Public Private Infrastructure Advisory Facility: Study of urban public transport conditions in Accra.* Accra, Ghana

Koornstra et al. (1992). Traffic safety principles and physical road infrastructure measures.

Kouabenann, D. R. Beliefs and the Perception of Risks and Accidents, Risk Analysis, 18,3

Leplat, J. (1983) Accident une Fatalite? Cahier de la Mutaulitedansl'Enterprise, Santeet Conditions de Travail 5.

Mavoori, A. K. (2020). An activity for Indian Road Safety, Avdelning Institution Division, Department

MRH, Presentation May (2021)

National Transport Policy (2008)

National Road Safety Strategy III 2011-2020

DVLA (2017). Vehicle Registration Records,

OECD (1984). Integrated road safety programmes. Organisation for Economic Co-operation and Development, Paris, France. ISBN 92-64-12620-1

OECD/ITF (2016). Road Safety Annual Report

OECD/ITF (2012). *Sharing Road Safety, Developing an International Framework for Crash Modification Factors.* Paris: OECD.

Omnibus Services Authority Decree (NLCD 337)

Rubin, Z. & Peplau, L. A. (1975). Who Believes in Just World? https://doi.org10.1111/j.1540-4560.1975.tb00997.x

Tradingeconomics.com/Ghana/gdp.

United Nations Convention, 1949

United Nations Convention, 1968

Vehicle Regulations (1958, 1997 and 1998)

WHO (2004). World Report on Road Traffic Injury Prevention

WHO (2018). Nine Common Road Safety Myths Factsheet

WHO (2009). Global Report on Road Safety

WHO (2017). Save LIVES Technical Package

WHO (2006). World Road Association

UNECE (2015a). Together with UNECE on the road to safety. Cutting road traffic deaths and injuries in half by 2020.

UNECE (2015b). Transport for Sustainable Development. The case of Inland Transport.

Background

Al Haji, G. (2005). Towards a Road Safety Development Index (RSDI): Ph.D. thesis. Norrköping, Sweden: Department of Science and Technology, Linköping University.

Al-Haji, G., &Asp, K. (2006a). New Tools for Assessing and Monitoring National Road Safety Development. The 2nd International Road Safety Conference, Dubai - United Arab Emirates, pp.31.

Al-Haji, G. (2007). Road Safety Development Index (RSDI): Theory, Philosophy and Practice. Department of Science and Technology, Campus Norrköping, Linköping University, Norrköping

Baluja, R. (2009). Road Safety Problems in Developing Countries. 10th meeting of the United Nations Road Safety Collaboration. Bangkok, Thailand.

Bhalla et al. (2011). Road Injuries in 18 Countries, Department of Global Health and Population, Harvard School of Public Health, Boston, MA, USA. Available from road injuries.globalburdenofinjuries.org

Bolorunduro, et al. (2011) Validating the Injury Severity Score (ISS) in Different Populations: ISS predicts mortality better amongst Hispanics and females. https://doi:10.1016/j.jss.2010.04.012

Botha, G. (2005). Measuring road traffic safety performance. Manager Information Management and Strategy, Department of Transport, Pretoria, South Africa

BRRI (2021). Consultancy services for a study on the level of discrepancies in road safety data in Ghana, Final Report

CIDA (1997). Results based management framework. The Logical Framework: Making it Results-Oriented

Davies J. et al. (2003). Safety Management: A Qualitative Systems Approach.Taylor and Francis, UK

Drucker, P. (2014). Innovation and entrepreneurship. Routledge - London, https://doi.10.4324/978131574753

ECMT (2002). Trends in Road Accidents and Policy Issues, CM (2002) 10, Paris France

Etika, A. et al. (2018). A developing safe system road safety indicator for the UK. London: Parliamentary Advisory Council for Transport Safety

ETSC (2001). Transport safety performance indicators. European Transport Safety Council.

Evans, L. (2003). Chronic posttraumatic stress disorder and family functioning of Vietnam veterans and their partners. Aust NZJ Psychiatry, 37(6)

Frederik, B. (2002). An overview and evaluation of composite indices of development. *Soc. Indic. Res.* 59, 115–151

Hakim, S., Shefer, D., Hakkert, A.S., & Hocherman, I. (1991). A critical review of macro models for road accidents. *Accident Analysis and Prevention, (23)*5, 379-400

Hermans, E., Brijs T., &Wets, G. (2008) Developing a Theoretical Framework for Road Safety Performance Indicators and a Methodology for Creating a Performance Index

Koornstra, M. J. (2007). Prediction of traffic fatalities and prospects for mobility becoming sustainable and safe, Sadhana.

Kopits, E. & Cropper, M. (2005). Traffic fatalities and economic growth. Accident Analysis and Prevention. 37(1)

LTSA (2000). Road safety strategy 2010; A consultation document. National Road Safety Committee, Land Transport Safety Authority LTSA, Wellington, New Zealand.

Mathers, C. D., & Loncar, D. (2005). Updated Projections of Global Mortality and Burden of Disease 2002-2030: Data Sources, Methods, and Results. Geneva: World Health Organization.

Mohan, D. (2002) Road safety in less-motorized environments: Future Concerns. International Journal of Epidemiology, 31, 527-532.

Morsink, P., Oppe, S., Reurings, M. & Wegman, F. (2005). Sunflower+6: Development and application of a footprint methodology for the sunflower+6 countries. Leidschendam, SWOV: 125

Nantulya, V. M., & Reich, M. R. (2002). The neglected epidemic: Road traffic injuries in developing countries. BMJ.324, pp. 1139–1141. https://doi.org/10.1136/bmj.324.7346.1139

OECD (2003). Intervention-related with reference to policies, strategies, and action interventions,

Phillips, R.O. & Fyhri, A. (2009). Road users' knowledge of and attitudes towards road safety —2008. TØI Report 1023/2009. Institute of Transport Economics (TØI), Oslo.

Ra–Mow (2008). Developing a theoretical framework for road safety performance indicators and methodology for creating a performance index

Rumar, K. (1985). The role of perceptual and cognitive filters in observed behaviour. In: L. Evansand R.C. Schwing, (Eds.), Human Behaviour and Traffic Safety, New York: Plenum Press.

Road Transport Research (1997a). Performance indicators for the road sector, Prepared by OECD Scientific Expert Group, Paris (IRRD No.: 887580).

Saisana, M., Saltelli, A. &Tarantola, S. (2005). Uncertainty and sensitivity analysis techniques as tools for the quality assessment of composite indicators. *Royal Statistical Society, 168*(2), 307-323

Sassi, F. (2006). Calculating QALYs, comparing QALY and DALY Calculations, PMID: 16877455 https://doi.org.10.1093/heapol/cz1018.

Schwaab, J. & Thielmann, S. (2002). ECMT- Economic Instruments for Sustainable Road Transport Sustainable Transport and Performance Indicators, Ministers of Transport, Paris

Stewart, D. E. (1998). A proposal for the development of exposure (to Risk) information for measuring and monitoring road accident risks: A Risk Analysis System for Improving Road Safety.

Stewart, D. (1998). A Risk Analysis and Evaluation System Model (RAESM) for estimating road travel risk performance measure indicators: Ideas, Concepts, and Methodologies for Measuring, Monitoring, Comparing and Evaluating the level (s) of Safety on Road and Highway Systems.

WHO (2009). Global Status Report on Motor Vehicle Safety: Time for Action. Geneva: WHO.

WHO (2010). Global Status Report on Road Safety Time for Action.

WHO. (2011) Saving millions of lives - Decade of action for road safety 2011-2020. Geneva: WHO.

Van den Berghe, W. & Martensen, H. (2017). Presentation for European Road Safety Charter (ERSC) Webinar on Road Safety Performance Indicators

WHO. (2018). Global status report on road safety 2018. Geneva: WHO.

Education

Ajzen, I. (1991). The theory of planned behaviour. *Organizational Behaviour and Human Decision Processes*

Baluja, R. (2009). Road Safety Problems in Developing Countries. *10th meeting of the United Nations Road Safety Collaboration.* Bangkok.

Benner, L. (1975). Accident theory and accident investigation. *Proceedings of the Society of Air Safety Investigators Annual Seminar.* Ottawa, Canada.

Böcher, W. (1995). Traffic Safety Campaigns and Traffic Safety Education. In Hilse, H.-G. & Schneider, W (Ed): Traffic Safety. Manual for Development of Concepts. Stuttgart: Boorberg.

Bok D. (2008). Our underachieving Collages: A Candid Look at How Much Students Learn and Why They Should Be. https//doi.org/10.2307/j.ctvcm4jco

Brake Factsheet (2014). Saving money through fleet risk management. European Transport Safety Council, PRASIE Work- Related Road Safety, The Business Case for Managing Road Risk at Work

Bradbury & Quimby (2008), Community Road Safety Education: An international perspective, ISSN 0965-0903 l E-ISSN 1751-7699 Volume 161 Issue 2

Carver, C. S. & Scheier, M.F. (1981). Attention and Self-Regulation: A Control Theory Approach to Human Behaviour. New York: Springer

Catchpole, J. & DiPietro, G. (2003). Road Safety Education in Schools: What to do, what not to do. In Proceedings conference "Road Safety research policing and education Conference: From research to action" Sydney, Australia, September 2003

Chaudhary, N.K. et al. (2014): Evaluation of NHTSA distracted driving demonstration projects in Connecticut and New York. Washington D.C. National Highway Traffic Safety Administration. DOT HS811 635.

Cismaru, M., Lavack, A. M., & Markewich, E. (2009). Social marketing campaigns aimed at preventing drunk driving: A review and recommendations. *International Marketing Review, 26*(3), 292-311. https://doi:10.1108/02651330910960799

Congiu, M., Whelan, M., Oxley, J., D'Elia, A., Charlton, J., & Fildes, B. (2007). Crossing roads safely: the effects of training on improving children's road crossing decisions. In: Paper presented at the Australasian Road Safety Research Policing Education. *Australasian Road Safety Research Policing Education Conference.* Melbourne, Victoria, Australia: The Meeting Planners.

Delhomme, P., De Debbeleer, W., Sonja, F., & Simoes, A. (2009). Manual for Designing, Implementing, and Evaluating Road Safety Communication Campaigns. Brussels: Belgian Road Safety Institute (BIVV - IBSR).

Dragutinovic, N., & Twisk, D. (2006). The effectiveness of road safety education, a literature review. Leidschendam: SWOV Institute for Road Safety Research.

Duperrex, O., Bunn, F., & Roberts, I. (2002). Safety education of pedestrians for injury prevention: A systematic review of randomised controlled trials. *BMJ, 324*(7346), 1129. http://doi.10.1136/bmj.324.7346.1129

Elvik, R., Vaa, T., Erke, A., & Sorensen, M. (2009). The handbook of road safety measures. Bingley: Emerald Group Publishing.

European Commission (2005). Good practice guide on road safety education: Inventory and compiling of a European good practice guide on road safety education targeted at young people. EU.

Fishbein, M. & Ajzen, I. (1975). Belief, Attitude, Intention and Behaviour: An Introduction to Theory and Research. Reading, MA. Addison-Wesley.

Fosser, S. (1992). An experimental evaluation of the effects of periodic motor vehicle inspection on accident rates. *Accident Analysis and Prevention, 24*(6), 599-612

Freimuth, V.S. (1985). Developing the public service advertisement for nonprofit marketing. In R. W. Belk (Ed.), Advancement in Nonprofit Marketing, Greenwich, JAI Press Inc.

Gawronski, B. & Bodenhausen, G.V,. Associative and Propositional Processes in Evaluation: An Integrative Review of Implicit and Explicit Attitude Change

Greenwood, M., & Woods, H. M. (1919). A report on the incidence of industrial accidents upon individuals with special reference to multiple accidents. London: British Industrial Fatigue Research Board.

Habyarimana, J., & Jack, W. (2011). Heckle and Chide: Results of a randomized road safety intervention in Kenya. *Journal of Public Economics, 95*(11-12),1438-1446. https://doi.org/10.1016/j.jpubeco.2011.06.008

Heinrich, H. W. (1936). Industrial Accident Prevention*: A Scientific Approach.* New York: McGraw-Hill.

Hoekstra & Wegman, (2011). Improving the effectiveness of road safety campaigns: Current and new practices.

Linklater, D. (1980) Road Safety Media Campaign to Protect the Young and Old; ISBN-13: 978-0-7240-4136-2

Lutzke, J. & Henggeler, M.F. (2009). Understanding and Using Logos, Ethos and Pathos, School of Liberal Arts, University Writing Centre

Mckenna (2011). Learning Theories Made Easy: Humanism. Nurs Stand.

Martinez, S., Scanchez, R., & Yanez-Pagans, P. (2019). Road Safety: Challenges and Opportunities in Latin America and the Caribbean. *Latin American Economic Review, 28*(17). https://doi.org/10.1186/s40503-019-0078-0

Muir, C., Devlin, A., Oxley, J., Kopinathan, C., Charlton, J., & Koppel, S. (2010). Parents as role models in road safety. MUARC Report No. 302.

National Safety Council. (1976). Accident Prevention Manual for Industrial Operations. Chicago: IL.

Pashley, C. R., Robertson, R. D., & Vanlaar, W. (2014). The Road Safety Monitor 2013: Drugs and Driving. Ottawa: Traffic Injury Research Foundation.

Petty, R. E. & Cacioppo, J. T. The Elaboration Likelihood Model Persuasion. In: Communication and Persuasion. Springer Series in Social Psychology, Springer, New York, NY.

Pfeffer, J. & Sutton, R. I. (2000). The knowing–doing gap: How smart companies turn knowledge into action.

Prochaska & DiClemente (1983). Stages and processes of self-change of smoking. Toward an integrative model of Change. Journal of Consulting Clinical Psychology. 51(3) http://dx.doi.org/ao.1037/0022-006x.51.3.390

Elliot, B. & Shanahan (1993). Road Safety, Mass Media Campaigns: A Meta-Analysis for the Federal Office of Road Safety CR 118

Rosenstock, I. M. (1996). Why do people use health services? Milbank Memorial Fund Quarterly, 44.

Sayer I. A., et al, (1997). Improving road safety in developing countries; Ghana. TRL Report 265, Crowthorne

Schagen & Rothengater (1997). The Effectiveness of Education a Literature Review

Schneider, F. W., Gruman, J. & Coutts, L.M. (2005). Applied Social Psychology: Understanding and Addressing Social and Practical Problems. Sage Publications, Inc.

Schwebel, D. C., Barton, B. K., Shen, J., Wells, H. L., Bogar, A., Heath, G., & McCullough, D. (2014). Systematic review and meta-analysis of behavioral interventions to improve child pedestrian safety. *J Pediatr Psychol., 39*(8), 826-845. http://doi.10.1093/jpepsy/jsu024

SWOV (2009). SWOV fact sheet: Fear-based information campaigns. Leidschendam, the Netherlands: Institute for Road Safety Research.

Trandis, H. C. (1997). Cross-cultural social and personality psychology. Personality and Social Psychology Bulletin, 3(2).

Tay, R., & Watson, B. (2002). Changing drivers' intentions and behaviours using fear-based driver fatigue advertisements. *Health Marketing Quarterly, 19*(4), 55-68.

Teye-Kwadjo, E. (2020). How fatalistic beliefs influence risky driving in Ghana. And what needs to be done. https://theconversation.com/how-fatalistic-beliefs-influence-risky-driving-in-ghana-and- what-needs-to-be-done-140576

The Boeing Company (1966). Fault Tree for Safety. Seattle, WA.

Thomson, J. A. (1997). Developing safe route planning strategies in young child pedestrians. *Journal of Applied Development Psychology,18*(2), 271-281. https://doi.org/10.1016/S0193-3973(97)90041-1

Transportation Research Board of The National Academies (2007). Building the Road Safety Profession in the Public Sector, Special Report 289.

US Army Materiel Command (1971). *Fault Tree Analysis as an Aid to Improved Performance.* AMC Safety Digest.

van Schagen, I., & Rothengatter, J. A. (1997). Classroom instruction versus roadside training in traffic safety education. *Journal of Applied Developmental Psychology, 18*(2), 1-10.

WHO (2019). Road Safety Mass Media Campaigns: A Toolkit. WHO.

Wunderitz, L. N., Hutchinson, T. P., & Woolley, J. E. (2010). Best practice in road safety mass media campaigns: A literature review. Adelaide, Australia: Centre for Automotive Safety Research.

Yanovitzky, I. (2004). Defensive processing of alcohol-related social norms messages by college students. Paper presented at The 132nd Annual Meeting of APHA. *The 132nd Annual Meeting of APHA.* Washington, D.C: American Public Health Administration.

Enforcement

Agnew (1991). Strain and Subcultural Crime Theory. *In J Sheley (Ed), Criminology: A contemporary,* 30-47-87

Boateng, F. G. (2020). Indiscipline in Context: A Political-economic Grounding for Dangerous Driving Behaviors among Tro-Tro Drivers in Ghana. *Humanit Soc Sci Commun, 7*(8). *https:// doi.org/10.1057/s41599-020-0502-8*

Boateng, F. G. (2021). Why Africa cannot Prosecute (or even Educate) its way out of Road Accidents: *Insights from Ghana. Humanities and Social Sciences Communications, 8(13), 1-9. https:// doi.org/10.1057/s41599-020-00695-5*

Department of Transportation (1973). National Highway Traffic Safety Administration Police Traffic Services Basic Training Program Student Study Guide U.S., 3(3)

Enoch, F. S. (2022). How Effective are police road presence and enforcement in a developing country context. *Humanities and Social Sciences Communications 9,55*

Enoch, F. S. (2022). How effective are police road presence and enforcement in a developing country context? *Humanities and Social Sciences Communication, 9(55), 1-9. https://doi.org/10.1057/ s41599-022-01071-1*

ESRA (2016). Enforcement and support for road safety policy measures, ESRA thematic report no. 6

Franklin, O. (2009). The Political Economy of Urban Transport in Ghana

Homel, R. (1988). Policing and Punishing the Drinking Driver: A Study of General and Specific Deterrence, New York

Homel R., (1990). Random Breath Testing in Australia, paper presented at the international conference on drinking and driving 28-30 March 1990, *Edmonton* Canada.

Leggett, L.M.W. (1990) Innovative quality control-based programme helps police combat road toll. *Highway Engineering in Australia, p12, 14*

Leivesley S. & Associates, (1987). Road Safety Enforcement: A Literature Review, Consultant Report 67.

Maneepakorn, P. (2010). Criminology theory, World Trade Thailand Limited Partnership, Bangkok.

Myjoyonline.com (2021). Police MTTD mounts 3000 intelligent surveillance cameras to capture negligent drivers. R*etrieved from* https://www.myjoyonline.com /police-mttd-mounts-3000-intelligent-surveillance-cameras-to-capture-negligent-drivers/

National Highway Traffic Safety Administration (2009). Data-Driven Approaches to Crime and Traffic Safety (DDACTS): *Operational Guidelines. DOT HS 811 185, Washington, DC.*

NHTSA (2009). Highway Safety Performance Plan

Obeng-Odoom, F. (2009). The Political Economy of Urban Transport in Ghana

Obrien, T. P. (1980). Concrete Deterioration and Repair. Proceedings of the Institution of Civil Engineers, *68(3), 399-408.*

OECD (1990). Behavioural adaptations to changes in the road transport system: report. Paris: *Organisation for Economic Co-Operation and Development.*

Packer, H. (1964). Two Models of the Criminal Process. *University of Pennsylvania Law Review*

Papadimitriou, E., Yannis, G., & Laiou, A. (2016). Best Practices for Efficient Traffic Safety Law Enforcement Programs. *3rd International Congress "Traffic Enforcement: Challenges & Perspectives" pp. 1-21*

Rogers, R. & Monsell, S. (1995). The costs of a predictable switch between simple cognitive tasks. *Journal of Experimental Psychology: General, 124,*

Rotherngatter, R. (1990). Automatic Policing and Information Systems. In Enforcement and Rewarding: *Strategies and Effects: Proceedings of the International Road Safety Symposium. Copenhagen, Denmark: SWOV Institute for Road Safety Research.*

SafetyNet (2009). Speeding (retrieved May 2016), http://goo.gl/x8c3s2

Southgate, P. & Mirrlees-Black, C. (1991). Traffic policing in changing times. *Home Office Research Study No. 124. HMSO, London, United Kingdom.*

Stafford, M. C. & Warr, M. (1993). A reconceptualization of general and specific deterrence. *A Journal of Research in Crime and Delinquency*

UNECE (2015). Together with UNECE on the road to safety. New York and Geneva: United Nations.

Wegman, F. (1992). Legislation, regulation, and enforcement to improve road safety in developing countries: *Contribution to the World Bank Seminar on Road Safety. Washington.*

Zaal, D. (1994). Traffic Law Enforcement: *A Review of the Literature, Report No 53. Melbourne: Monash University Accident Research Centre.*

Infrastructure

Afukaar, K.F. (2003) Speed control in developing countries: Issues, challenges and opportunities in reducing road traffic injuries. *Injury Control and Safety Promotion, http://dx.doi.org/10/1076/ icsp.10.1.77.14113*

Ali, A. (2010). Effective safety factors on horizontal curves of two-lane highways. *Journal of Applied Sciences: Volume 10 (22), 2814-2822, 2010*

Austroads (2019). Passing lanes: Safety and Performance.

Caliendo, C. & Lamberti, R. (2001). Relationships between accidents and geometric characteristics for four lanes median separated roads. In: Proceeding of Road Safety Three Continents, Moscow, Russia, September

DeoChimba (2004). Evaluation of geometric and traffic characteristics affecting the safety of six-lane divided roadways. The Florida State University College of Engineering.

Elvik, R. (1995). *A Handbook of Road Safety Measures*

FHWA (2016a). US Department of Transport Federal Highway Administration, Unit 1

Glennon, J. (1987). Effect of Sight Distance on Highway Safety

Glennon, J. (1985). Effect of Alignment on Highway Safety, Relationship between Safety and Key Highway Features. SAR6, TRB Ltd., Washington, D.C., P.P 48-63.

Hadi, et al. (1995). Estimating Safety Effects of Cross-section Design for Various Highway Types using Negative Binomial Regression.

Harkey et al. (1998). Development of the Bicycle Compatibility Index: A Level of Service Concept.

Hauer, E. (2004). Statistical Road Safety Modelling. Transport Research Record 1897

http://irap.org/about-irap-3/methodology

http://toolkit.irap.org/

http://vida.irap.org

Hydén C., & Várhelyi, A. (2000). The effects on safety, time consumption and environment of large-scale use of roundabouts in an urban area: a case study. Accident Analysis and Prevention 32, pp. 11–23

iRAP Star Rating and Investment Plan (2015). Implementation Support Guide, International Road Assessment Programme (iRAP)

Jerry, P., John, S., Wendel, R., & Dominique, L. (2009). Impact of Shoulder Width and Median Width on Safety. NCHRP Report 633. Transportation Research Board of the National Academies, Washington D. C.

Kapila, K., Prabhakar, A., & Bhattacharjee, S. (2013). Safe Road Infrastructure Design for Highways.

Karlarftis et al. (2000): Effect of Road Geometry and Traffic Volumes on Roadway Accident Rates. Accident Analysis and Prevention 34.

Koornstra et al. (1992). Traffic Safety Principles and Physical Road Infrastructure Measures, *19th ICT workshop Proceedings.*

Lamm, R. et al. (1984). Design Friction Factors of Different Countries Versus Actual Pavement Friction Inventories

McMahon, et al. (2002). Analysis of Factors Contributing to Walking Along Roadway Crashes: *Research Study and Guidelines for Sidewalks and Walkways, TRB Annual Meeting*

Mouskos et al. (1999). Impact of Access driveways on accident rates at multilane highways, National Centre for Transportation and Industrial Productivity, New Jersey Institute of Technology

Nikiforos et al. (2004). Safety Impacts of Design Element Trade-off for Multilane Rural Highways. *ASCE Journal of Transportation Engineering*

Pasanen, E., (1992). Driving Speeds and Pedestrian Safety: *A Mathematical Model. Helsinki University of Technology, Transportation Engineering, Publication 77.*

Persia, L. et al. (2016). *Management of road infrastructure safety, 6th Transport Research Arena April 18-21, 2016 Transport Research Agenda, Transportation Research Procedia 3436 – 3445*

Sawalha, Z., & Sayed, T. (2001). Evaluating Safety of Urban Arterial Roadways. *Journal of Transportation Engineering, 127* (2), 151-158.

UNESCAP (2017). Development of Road Infrastructure Safety Facility Standards for the Asian Highway Network

www. Dacota-project.eu

www.irap.net.

Zegeer C. V., Reinfurt W., Hummer, J., Herf, L. & Hunter, W. (1988). Effect of Lane and Shoulder Width on Accident Reduction on Rural, Two-Lane Roads. *Transportation Research Record. 806*

Zhang, Y. (2009). Analysis of the Relationship between highway horizontal curve and traffic safety. *International Conference on Measuring Technology and Mechatronics Automation, China*

Post-Crash

Adogu, Llika, & Asuzu, (2011). An Investigation of Injury Patterns and Emergency Care in Road Traffic Accidents

Aduayom-Ahego, A., & Ehara, Y. (2018). Prostheses Provision Approach in Sub-Saharan Africa Country. *Niigata Medical Welfare Society Journal, 18*(1), 21-21.

Aggrey Orleans J. (2019). Injury Patterns and Emergency Care in Road Traffic Accidents in Accra

Andruszkow, H. (2016). Impact of Helicopter Emergency Medical Service in Medical Service Traumatized Patients: Which Patients Benefits Most

Asbridge, M., Desapriya, E., Ogilvie, R., Cartwright, J., Mehrnoush, V., Ishikawa, T., & Weerasinghe, D. N. (2017). The Impact of Restricted Driver's Licenses on Crash Risk for Older Drivers: A Systematic Review. *Transportation Research Part A: Policy and Practice, 97*, 137-145.

Assah, Y.A. (2020). Psychosocial Effects of Trauma Injuries in Road Traffic Accident victims in the Kumasi Metropolis

Atkins, D. & Guisti, C. (2001). The Confluence of Poverty and Disability 2000.

Australian College for Emergency Medicine, (2015). Quality Standards for Emergency Departments and other Hospital-Based Emergency Care Services, 1st Edition

Australian College for Emergency Medicine, (2015). Quality Standards for Emergency Departments and other Hospital-Based Emergency Care Services

Barclay, T. S., Quansah, R., Gyedu, A., Boakye, G., Abantanga, F., Ankomah, J., Donkor, P., Mock, C. (2018). Assessment of Trauma Care Capacity in Ghana in 2004 and 2014. *BMC Emergency Medicine 18, Article 33*

Botchie, A. (2004). Poverty Reduction Efforts in Ghana - The Skill Development Option, *Accra University of Ghana Legon*

Brunacini (2002). Fire Command Workbook to Fire Command, National Fire Protection Association

Burdett-Smith, P., Airey, M., & Franks, A. (1995). Improvements in trauma survival in Leeds. 26, 455-458.

Callese, T. E. et al. (2014). Layperson Trauma Training in Low- and Middle-Income Countries: A Review

Cartwright, A. (2018). The psychological effects of road traffic accidents (RTAs): An exploration of a United Kingdom medico-legal examiner's career of RTA assessments. *Psychiatry, Psychology and Law, 25*(2), 303-324.

Chapman, M.W., Lane, R.A., Mann, R.A., Marder, R.F., McLain, G.T., Rab, A., & Vince, K.G. (2010). Chapman's Orthopedic Surgery, 3rd ed. Philadelphia, Pennsylvania: Lippincott Williams & Wilkins.

Clark, D.E. & Cowley, R.A. (2017). The Golden Hour, the Momentary Pause, and the Third Space. Am Surg. 83(12),1401-1406

College of Emergency Nursing in Australia (CENA), (2015). Quality Standards for Emergency Department and other Hospital-based Emergency Care. Web: www.acem.org.au

Comp, G.B., Silver B.V., Elliott, J., & Kalnow, A. (2020). Utilization of Simulation Techniques to Enhance Quality Improvement Processes in the Emergency Department. 16,12(2)

Cory, J. (2002). Major Incident Management (METHANE). Retrieved from First Aid Training Co-operative: https://firstaidtrainingcooperative.co.uk/about-us/

Cuijpers et al., (2018). Psychotherapies for depression in low- and middle-income countries: a meta-analysis. World Psychiatry off. J. World Psychiatry. Association WPA 17,90-101 https://doi.or/10.1002/wps.20493

Curtis, J. & Brading, J. (2001). Disability Directory for Museums and Galleries. Resource Publications 16, London: Queen Anne's Gate

Atkins, D. & Guisti, C. (2001). The Confluence of Poverty and Disability 2000

Dankwa, A. L. (2013). Vocational Training for Students with Hearing Impairment

Debenham, S., Fuller, M., Stewart, M., & Price, R. (2017). Where there is no EMS: Lay Providers in Emergency Medical Services Care as a Public Health Priority. *Prehospital and Disaster Medicine 32*(6), 593-595.

Demetriades et al. (2005). Trauma deaths in a mature urban trauma system is 'trimodal' distribution a valid concept?

Enarson, E., Cheryl, C., Betty, H. M., Deborah, T., & Wisner, B. (2003). A social vulnerability approach to disasters. Emmitsburg, Maryland: Emergency Management Institute, Federal Emergency Management Agency. http://www.training.fema.gov/emiweb/edu/complete Courses.asp

Gopinath et al. (2017). Overview of findings from a 2-year study of claimants who had sustained a mild to moderate injury in road traffic crash prospective study (BMC Research Notes)

Haas, J.E. & Drabek, E. Complex Organisations: A Sociological Perspective.

Haghparast-Bidgoli, H. et al. (2010). Barriers and facilitators to provide effective pre-hospital trauma care for road traffic injury victims in Iran: A Grounded Theory Approach.

Haider, A. (2012). Transport of Trauma Patients by Helicopter is Costly but Effective. Johns Hopkins Medicine

Hansen C. M., Kragholm K., Granger, C. B., Pearson, D. A., Tyson, C., Monk, L., et al. (2015). The role of bystanders, first responders, and emergency medical service providers in timely defibrillation and related outcomes after out-of-hospital cardiac arrest: *Results from a Statewide Registry.*

Hesse & Ofosu (2014). Epidemiology of Road Traffic Accidents in Ghana ESI, 10(9) ESI March Edition. https://doi.org/10.19044/esj.2014.v10n9%25p

https://carryboyambulance.com/half-body/abl-1100-f-ex/gclid

Kobusingye et al. (2006). Disease Control Priorities in Developing Countries 2nd edition. Washington (DC): The International Bank for Reconstruction and Development/The World Bank

Lindell & Perry (1992). Behavioural Foundations of Community Emergency Planning.

McLoughlin, D. (1985). Framework for Integrated Emergency Management. Public Administration Review 45:165-172.

Mental Health Act 2012 (Act 846).

Ministry of Health, Ghana (2011). Policy and guidelines for hospital accident and emergency services in Ghana

Mould-Millman, C., Oteng, R., Zakariah, A., Osei-Ampofo, M., Oduro, G., & Barsan, W. (2015). Assessment of emergency medical services in the Ashanti Region of Ghana. *Ghana Med J. 49*(3),125–135.

Nasirian et al. (2018). Patients experiences of their recovery process after minor physical trauma. *Journal of Trauma Nursing 25*(4) 233-241

National Ambulance Service (2012) Annual Report. Ministry of Health, Ghana.

NRSA (2012). Post-Crash Response Needs Assessment in Ghana

Oduro, G.D. (2015). Improving emergency care in Ghana. Teaching Hospital, Accident and Emergency Centre, Kumasi, Ghana Postgraduate Medical Journal of Ghana, 4, (1)

OECD (2017) European Observatory on Health Systems and Policies

Osei-Ampofo, M., Oduro, G., Oteng, R., Zakariah, A., Jacquet, G., Donkor, P. (2013). The Evolution and Current State of Emergency Care in Ghana. *Afr J Emergency Med 3*, 52- 58.

Piterman I, Yasin (1997). Medical Audit – Why Bother? Hong Kong Practitioner, 19(10)

Police Handbook, May 2010

Rissanen, R., Berg, H. Y., & Hasselberg, M. (2017). Quality of Life Following Road Traffic Injury: A Systematic Literature Review. *Accident Analysis & Prevention, 108*, 308-320.

Sasser, S., Varghese, M., Kellermann, A., et al. (2005). Prehospital Trauma Care Systems. Geneva, World Health Organization.

The Disability Act 715 of Ghana

WHO 2005 Prehospital Trauma Care Systems, www.who.int/violence_injury_prevention

WHO 2007 Post-crash plan

WHO 2016 Post Crash Response, supporting those affected by road traffic crashes.

WHO WHA 72 resolution 12.9, (2019)

Wilde, G. J. (2014). Target Risk. *Risk Homeostasis in Everyday Life. Digital Edition. Version, 20.*

Yeboah, D., Mock C, Karikari, P., Agyei-Baffour, P., Donkor, P., & Ebel, B. (2014). Minimizing Preventable Trauma Multidisciplinary Panel Review Approach at the Komfo Anokye Teaching Hospital in Ghana. World J Surg 38,1707-1712

Yiadom et al. (2018). Public Health Rationale for Investments in Emergency Medicine in Developing Countries – Ghana as a Case Study

Road User

Agbozo, E. (2017). An E-policing Model for the Ghana Police Service. *Policija isigurnost, 26*(4), 365-374.

Andrey, J. C., Mills, B. E., & Vandermolen, J. (2001). Weather information and road safety.

Andrijanto, A., & Pandgaribuan, A. G. (2016). Riding a Motorcycle Safety Issues in Term of Socio-Technical and Human Machine Interaction Perspective (Case Study: Road Traffic in Bandung).

Anna, A., Falkmer, T., Farsman, S., Matstoms, Y., Sorensen, G., Turbell, T., & Wenall, J. (2003). *Child safety in cars - Literature Review.* Stockholm: Swedish National Road and Transport Research Institute; VTI-rapport 489A.

Anund, A. et al. (2003). Driver Impairment at Night and its Related Physiological Sleepiness

Azabre, A. I. (2013). Government must Enact a Law to Protect Passenger Rights. Retrieved from Modern Ghana: https://www.modernghana.com/news/491294/government-must-enact-a-law-to-protect-passenger-rights.html

Barsi T. S, Faergemann, C. & Larsen L. B. (2002). Road Traffic Accidents with Two-Wheeled Motor Vehicles During a Five-Year Period in Odense, Denmark, Traffic Injury Prevention, 3, 283-287.

Brodsky, H., & Hakkert, A. S. (1988). Risk of a road accident in rainy weather. *Accident Analysis & Prevention, 20*(3), 161-176.

BRRI (2016). Building & Road Research Institute. Road Traffic Crashes in Ghana, Statistics 2015. Kumasi: National Road Safety Commission, Ministry of Transport

Chang, H.L., & Yeh, T.H. (2007). Motorcyclist Accidents involvement by Age, Gender, and Risky Behaviors in Taipei, Taiwan. Transportation Research Part F: Traffic Psychology and Behaviour 10, 109-122.

Chen, C.F. & Chen, C. W. (2011). Speeding for fun? Exploring the speeding behavior of riders of heavy motorcycles using the theory of planned behavior and psychological flow theory, Accident Analysis & Prevention, 43(3), 983-990

Dahlstedt, S. (1994). The satre table: Opinions about traffic and traffic safety of some European drivers.

Dapilah, F., Guba, B. Y., & Owusu-Sekyere, E. (2017). Motorcyclist characteristics and traffic behaviour in urban Northern Ghana: Implications for road traffic accidents. *Journal of Transport & Health, 4,* 237-245.

Di Zhu, Analysis of factors affecting motorcycle -motor vehicle crash characteristics. University of Dayton.

Dulisse, B. (1997). Methodological issues in testing the hypothesis of risk compensation. *Accid Anal Prev, 29*(3), 285-292.

ec.europa-July 2020: Powered Two Wheelers – Road Safety

Edwards, D. (1999). Emotion discourse. *Culture & psychology, 5*(3)

Elvik, R. (2004). To what extent can theory account for the findings of road safety evaluation studies? *Accid Anal Prev, 35*(5), 841-849.

Elvik, R., Vaa, T., Erke, A., & Sorensen, M. (2009). *The handbook of road safety measures.* Bingley: Emerald Group Publishing.

Engstro¨m, J. & Hollnagel E. (2007). A general conceptual framework for modeling behavioural effects of driver support functions. In: Cacciabue, P.C. (Ed.). Modelling Driver Behaviour in Automotive Environments. Springer-Verlag, London. Network (2005). 2005 environmental sustainability index. Yale University and Columbia University.

Farmer, E., & Chambers, E. G. (1940). A study of accident proneness among motor drivers. *Rev Stat Eons Books, 103*(2), 254-356.

Froggatt, P., & Smiley, J. A. (1964). The concept of accident proneness: a review. *Br J Ind Med, 21*(1), 1-12.

Fuller, R., & Santos, J. (2002). Psychology and the high engineer. *In: Fuller R, Santos J (eds) Human factors for highway engineers.* Pergamon, Amsterdam.

Geyer, J., Raford, N., Ragland, D., & Pham, T. (2006). The continuing debate about safety in numbers—Data from Oakland, CA. Safe Transportation Research ...

Global Mobility Report (2017). https://sdgs.un.org/publications/global-mobility-re-port-2017-30368lity Report 2017, Department of Economic and Social Affairs (un.org)

Green, D. (2006). A comparison of stopping distance performance for motorcycles equipped with ABS, CBS and conventional hydraulic brake systems. Proceeding of the 2006 International Motorcycle Safety Conference, Long Beach, CA.

Helmers & Aberg (1978). Driver Behaviour in Intersections as related to priority rules and road design. An exploratory study. Report Number 167

Hing, J. Y., Stamatiadis, N., & Aultman-Hall, L. (2003). Evaluating the impact of passengers on the safety of older drivers. *Journal of Safety Research, 34*, 342-351.

https://www.ghanaroadtransport.com/2019/0 1/11/classification-of-ghana-driving-license/

Kovacs, I., Kozma, P., Feher, A., & Benedek, G. (1999). Late maturation of visual spatial integration in humans. *Proceedings of the National Academy of Sciences of the United States of America, 96*(21), 12204-12209. doi:10.1073/pnas.96.21.12204

Lee, C., & Abdel-Aty, M. (2008). Presence of passengers: Does it increase or reduce driver's crash potential? *Accident Analysis and Prevention, 40*(5), 1703–1712. https://doi.org/10.1016/j.aap.2008.06.006

Elliott, M.A., Baughan, C.J., Broughton, J., Chinn, B., Grayson, G.B., Knowles, J., Smith, L.R. & Simpson, H. (2003). Motorcycle safety: a scoping study Prepared for Road Safety Division, Department for Transport

Mannering, F. L., & Grodsky, L. L. (1995). Statistical analysis of motorcyclists' perceived accident risk. Accident Analysis and Prevention, 27(1), 21–31. https://doi.org/10.1016/0001-4575(94)00041-J

McEvoy, S P, Stevenson M.R., & Woodward, M. (2006). The impact of driver distraction on road safety: results from a representative survey in two Australian states

Michon, J. (1989). Explanatory pitfalls and rule-based driver models. *Accid Anal Prev, 21*(4), 341-353.

modernghana.com/news/102068/publictransportoperations-inghana.html

Naatanen, R., & Summala, H. (1974). A model for the role of motivational factors in driver's decision-making. *Accid Anal Prev, 6*(3), 243-261.

NHTSA (2020). Motorcycle Safety. New Jersey, Washington D.C: U.S Department of Transportation.

OECD (1998). Keeping Children Safe in Traffic

Orsi, C., Marchetti, P., Montomoli, C., & Morandi, A. (2013). Car crashes: The effect of passenger presence and other factors on driver outcome. *Elsevier*, 35-43.

Pasanen, E. (1992). Driving Speeds and Pedestrian Safety: A Mathematical Model, Helsinki University of Technology, Finland 02150 Espoo 15, Finland

Peltzman, S. (1975). The effects of automobile safety regulation. *J Political Econ, 83*(4), 677-725.

Preusser, D.F., Williams, A.F., & Ulmer, R.G. (1995). Analysis of fatal motorcycle crashes: Crash typing. Accident Analysis and Prevention, 27, 845-851.

Radin, U. (2006). Motorcycle Safety Programmes in Malaysia: How Effective are they?

Reason, J. (1990). Human error. Cambridge: Cambridge University Press.

Regan, M. A., & Mitsopoulos, E. (2001). *Understanding passenger influence on driver behavior.* Monash University Accident Research Centre Report No. 180.

Reiß, M. (1998). Mythos Netzwerkorganisation. *Zeitschrift Fuhrung und Organisation, 67,* 224-229.

Ross D. Petty, Regulation vs. the Market: The case of bicycle safety - Endnotes

Ross et.al (1977). Regulation vs. the Market: The case of bicycle safety – Endnotes

RoSPA (2018). *Road Deaths in 2018*

Rothengatter, J. (1997). Psychological aspects of road user behaviour. *Applied Psychology: An International Review,* 223-234.

Rumar, K., Fleury, D., Kildebogaard, J., Lind, G., Mauro, V., Berry, J., Carsten, O., Heijer, T., Kulmala, R., Machata, K., &Zackor, I. (1999). Intelligent Transport Systems and Road Safety. Report prepared for the European Transport Council, Brussels.

Rutter, D. R., & Quine, L. (1996). Age and experience in motorcycling safety. *Accident Analysis & Prevention, 28*(1), 15-21.

Talukdar, A. (2011). Importance of a Driving License

Taylor, D. (1964). Drivers' galvanic skin response and the risk of accident. *Ergonomics, 7*(4), 439-451.

Tillmann, W. A., & Hobbs, G. E. (1949). The accident-prone automobile driver; a study of the psychiatric and social background. *Am J Psychiatry,* 321-331. doi:10.1176/ajp.106.5.321

TRB (2000). National Research Council, Washington D.C.

UNECE (2010). *Consolidated Resolution on Road Signs and Signals.* Geneva: UN.

UNECE (2015). *Together with UNCE on the road to safety: Cutting road traffic deaths and injuries in half by 2020.* New York and Geneva: UN.

Watson, B., Tunnicliff, D., White, K., Schonfeld, C., & Wishart, D. (2007). *Psychological and social factors influencing motorcycle rider intentions and behaviour.* Canberra: Australian Transport Safety Bureau.

Wilde, G. J. S. & S. L. Simonet (1996). Economic fluctuations and the traffic accident rates in Switzerland. Report R9615, Beratungsstelle furUnfallherhutung Bern

Wilson, T. (2006). *modernghana.com/news/102068/publictransportoperations-inghana.html*

WHO (2004). World Report on Road Traffic Injury Prevention,

World Health Organization (2006). *The world health report 2006: working together for health.* World Health Organization.

WHO (2018). *Global status report on road safety 2018.* Geneva: WHO.

Yousif (2020). A review of Behavioural Issues Contributing to Motorcycle Safety

Zaidel, D. M. (1992). A modeling perspective on the culture of driving. Accident Analysis & Prevention, 24, 585-597. doi: 10.1016/0001-4575(92)90011-7

Zaza, S. A. (2001). Reviews of evidence regarding interventions to increase the use of child safety seats. *Am J Prev Med,* 31-47. doi:10.1016/s0749-3797(01)00377-4

Road Safety Management

Bhalla, et al. (2009). Building national estimates of the burden of road traffic injuries in developing countries from all available data sources: Iran.

Bhalla et al. (2014). Involvement of Family Members in Caring of Patients an Acute Care Setting Vol. 60, Issue 4

Breen J, Howard E, & Bliss, T. (2008). Independent Review of Road Safety in Sweden, Swedish Roads Administration, Börlange.

Bliss, T. & Breen, J. (2009). Implementing the Recommendations of the World Report on Road Traffic Injury Prevention. Country guidelines for the Conduct of Road Safety Management Capacity Reviews and the Specification of Lead Agency Reforms, Investment Strategies and Safe System Projects, Global Road Safety Facility World Bank, Washington DC

DaCoTA 2013, Road Safety Data, Collection, Transfer and Analysis Developing a Road Safety Index

DVLA Act 1999, Act 569

Ghana Highway Authority ACT 540 of 1997

Ghana Highway Code of 1974

GRSP Global Road Safety Partnership. (2003). Road Crash and Injury Data Systems.

Heinrich and Mikulik, 2005: IRTAD – Reliable Past and Challenging Future

Hills, B.L. & Baguley, C.J. (1994). Accident Data Collection and Analysis: Progress in the use of the Microcomputer Package MAAP in the Asian Region. In Proceedings of the 8th REAAA Conference, 17-21 April 1994

Kazentet M.H. (2015). An Assessment of Internally generated Fund and Its Contribution for District Development Expenditure: A Case of Asutifi District, Ghana.

Muhlrad, N. (2015). Road Safety Management from the National to the Local Level, In G. Tiwari, and D. Mohan, Eds., *The Way Forward: Transportation Planning and Road Safety*. Kolkata: Macmillan India Ltd.

Navarro-Moreno J et al., (2020). Road Investment and Traffic Safety: An International Study, Sustainability 2020, 12(16), 6332, https://doi.org/10.3390/su1216632

NRSA (2018). Consultancy Services for Capacity Needs Assessment for the National Road Safety Commission by M/s Ablinconsult Engineers and Planners

OECD. (2002). Road Safety: What's the vision? Paris: 0rganisation for Economic Co-operation and Development.

Papadimitriou, E., & Yannis, G. (2013). Is road safety management linked to road safety performance? *Accid Anal Prev, 59,* 593-603

Small, M. & Breen, J. (2017). Start-up Guide to ISO 39001 Road Traffic Safety Management System

Small, M., & Runji, J. (2014). Managing Road Safety in Africa: A Framework for National Lead Agencies. Africa Transport Policy Program (SSATP). Retrieved from https://www.ssatp.org/sites/ssatp/files/publications/SSATPWP101-Road-Safety-Fra...

SSATP: Interventions to improve road safety: Community participation in traffic safety.

Transportation Research Board of The National Academies 2007: Building the Road Safety Profession in the Public Sector, Special Report 289.

Transport Research Laboratory (TRL) (1994). Microcomputer Accident Analysis

Package, Version 5 (MAAPfive), User Guide. Crowthorne, UK. Nationwide Implementation Report Document Ref No: 4 iMAAP/GH/NRSC/24/01/18/R/011

Varhelyi, A. (2016). Road Safety Management: The Need for Systematic Approach. Lund, Sweden: Department of Technology and Society, Lund University.

WHO (2010). The Work of WHO in the African Region 2008-2009. Brazzaville: WHO Regional Office for Africa.

WHO (2013). Global Status Report on Road Safety 2013: Supporting a Decade of Action. Geneva: WHO.

WHO (2013). Strengthening Road Safety Legislation: A practice and resource manual for countries. Geneva: WHO.

www.globesafe.org

Saving Lives Beyond 2020: The Next Steps, Recommendations of the Academic Expert Group for the 3rd Global Ministerial, Conference on Road Safety

Vehicle

Akayeti A. (2015). African Journal of Applied Research (AJAR) Development of Indigenous Automobile Design and Manufacturing in Ghana

Amedorme, S. K. (2013). Investigation of Vehicle Alterations and Modifications at Suame Magazine in Kumasi, Ghana. *International Journal of Mechanical Engineering Research & Application*, 48-53.

Bayly et al., (2007). Intelligent Transport System for Motorcycle Safety, Monash University Accident Research Centre Report 260. MUARC: Clayton, Australia

DaCoTa, (2012).

Dinye & Nyaba (2001). Trade Policy and Domestic Manufacturing in Ghana, *Accra Sapri Research Report*

Driver and Vehicle Licensing Authority Act. (1999). ACT 569.

DVLA Driver and Vehicle Licensing Agency Annual Report and Accounts 2015 to 2016.

Global NCAP (2015). Democratising Car Safety: Road Map for Safer Cars 2020.

Kwakye E.A. & Fouracre, P.R. (1998). Urban Transport Policy in Ghana, Transport Research Library, and DFID Department for International Development. *CODATU VIII Conference Cape Town.*

Padmanaban (2003). Influences of Vehicle Size and Mass and Selected Driver Factors on Odds of Driver Fatality, AnnuProcAssocAdvAutomot Med 47; 2003, PMC3217563

Queensland Transport (2008). Queensland Road Vehicle Modification Handbook

Ribbens H. et al., (1992). Understanding Automotive Electronics

www.Mongnabay.com

www.oica.net/category/safety

Next Steps

Bonnet, E., Lechat, L., & Ridde, V. (2018). What Interventions are Required to Reduce Road Traffic Injuries in Africa? A Scoping Review of the Literature. *PLoS ONE 13*, e0208195.

Department for Transport-Strategic Framework for Road Safety (2011). EU Road Safety Policy Framework 2021-2030, Next steps towards "Vision Zero"

Fahlquist, J.N. (2006). Responsibility ascriptions and Vision Zero. *Accid. Anal. Prev. 38*, 1113–1118.

GRSF (2021). Road Safety Management Capacity Reviews and Safety System Projects Guidelines

Hakkert, A. S., Gitelman, V., & Vis, M. A. (2007). Road Safety Performance Indicators: *Theory. Deliverable D3.6 of the EU FP6 project SafetyNet.* Loughborough: European Commission, Directorate-General Transport and Energy.

Salmon, P.M., Read, G.J.M., & Stevens, N.J. (2016). Who is in Control of Road Safety? A STAMP control structure analysis of the road transport system in Queensland, Australia. *Accid. Anal. Prev. 96*, 140–151.

Saving Lives Beyond 2020: The Next Steps - Recommendations of the Academic Expert Group for the 3rd Global Ministerial Conference on Road Safety, February 2020

Saving Lives Beyond 2020: The Next Steps: Recommendations of the Academic Expert Group

GRSF (2021). Guide for Road Safety Interventions: Evidence of what works and what does not work, 2021 could serve as the reference point for this.

Wegman, F. et al (2015). Evidence-Based Data Driven Road Safety Management, IATSS Res.39

WHO (2017). Road Safety Factsheet on Sustainable Development Goals: Health targets

ABOUT THE AUTHOR

Dr. Paulina Agyekum is very passionate about road safety and the need to save lives and avoid trauma. To her road safety is everyone's issue and there is need for the community at large to work towards the elimination of high-risk road use situations for the good of our beloved ones as well as for the good of Ghana's economic growth. Thus, the goal of the book has been an attempt to examine Ghana's road safety content in order to instigate the depth of attention to road safety management in the country and beyond.

With a span of education in development-oriented studies, transport distribution and road infrastructure development and management, she has extensive experience in the transport industry with respect to policy formulation, planning and strategy development, project implementation, monitoring and evaluation. Specifically, she has expansive experience in the conduct of research into transport issues to identify challenges and priorities in transportation systems, information analysis related to the development of potential solutions with regards to transport investments projects, coordination of improvements and assessment of project impacts.

Dr Agyekum has a Bachelor of Science in Development Planning from the University of Science and Technology Ghana, Master of Science in transportation from the Cranfield University UK and a Doctor of Philosophy in Road Management from the University of Birmingham, UK with intermediary courses in project management, road safety, research methods, technical and economic analysis for transport projects. Dr Agyekum is the Managing Consultant of M/s Ablin Engineers and Planning Ltd, a consultancy establishment which offers diverse consultancy services in transportation planning and engineering.

She is also a director of M/s Memphis Metropolitan Ltd, a construction company. She has headed the execution of several consultancy assignments spanning from project/programme preparation and planning including the conduct of feasibility studies of road, rail, air and water projects; assessment of infrastructure requirements of new and existing developments; preparation of the designs for road and transportation infrastructure projects; supervision of works; monitoring and evaluation of project impacts;

and review of project/programme performance in relation to project development objectives.

Specific to road safety, Dr Agyekum has supported partners in the development of evidence-based national and region policies and strategies that promote road safety through the development of the national road safety policy, the national road safety strategies (NRSS I, II, III and IV) and action plans as well as the ECOWAS road safety policy framework. She has also been involved in national and regional e.g. ECOWAS, road safety programme evaluations of diverse road safety interventions implemented. Dr Agyekum has also collaborated on several large-scale transport projects through international partnerships including holding the position of West Africa Regional Technical Manager for Africa Community Access Partnership (AfCAP) which was a research programme for the rural transport sectors of Africa, funded by UK aid.

Milton Keynes UK
Ingram Content Group UK Ltd.
UKHW051940310124
437007UK00008B/118

9 781735 885230